No ⩗	omit comma 11.9
⩘	semicolon 12.1
⩘⩗	colon 12.2
/--/	dash 13.1
(/)	parentheses 13.2
[/]	brackets 13.3
⸌⸍⩗	quotation marks 14.1
/ . . . /	ellipses 14.2
/-/	hyphen 15.2
⩗	apostrophe 15.3
Ref	reference of pronoun unclear 8.1
Rep	careless repetition 28.3
Rest	error in punctuation of restrictive or nonrestrictive modifier 11.4
Run-on	run-on or fused sentence 4.3
Shift	shift (inconsistency) in pronoun form 8.6 in verb tense 6.1
Sp	spelling error 17
Stilt	stilted language 30.1
Sub	faulty subordination 26.3
T	error in use of tense 6.1
Trans	needs better transition 25.4
Trite	trite expression 30.3
Var	ineffective or insufficient sentence variety 27.1
Vb	error in verb form 6
Wdy	wordy 28.1
WW	wrong word 17.3, 29.3
‖	elements should be parallel in form
◡	close up space
#	separate with a space
ℓ	omission
X	careless error
√	good

HANDBOOK
of CURRENT
ENGLISH

SEVENTH EDITION

HANDBOOK *of* CURRENT ENGLISH

Jim W. Corder
Texas Christian University

John J. Ruszkiewicz
University of Texas at Austin

Scott, Foresman and Company
Glenview, Illinois London, England

An Instructor's Annotated Edition of *Handbook of Current English*/7 is available through your local Scott, Foresman representative or by writing the English Editor, College Division, Scott, Foresman and Company, 1900 East Lake Avenue, Glenview, Illinois 60025.

Acknowledgments for photographs and literary selections appear on p. A-1, following the glossaries, which is an extension of the copyright page. Permission to reprint additional selections is acknowledged within the text.

Library of Congress Cataloging in Publication Data
Corder, Jim W. (Jimmie Wayne).
    Handbook of current English.

    Includes index.
    1. English language—Rhetoric.   2. English language—
Grammar—1950–   . I. Ruszkiewicz, John J.,
1950–   . II. Title.
PE1408.P4376   1984   808'.042   84-20219
ISBN 0-673-15968-X

This book was previously published under the title *The Perrin-Smith Handbook of Current English.* Copyright © 1962, 1955 by Scott, Foresman and Company.

Some of the material in this book was first published in *Contemporary Writing* by Jim W. Corder. Copyright © 1979 by Scott, Foresman and Company.

    2   3   4   5   6-KPF-89   88   87   86   85

PREFACE

Work on this seventh edition of *Handbook of Current English* began where it might well have ended: with a sixth edition generally admired for its sensitive and sophisticated view of language. But much has occurred in recent years to change the way writing is taught, the way writing is regarded, and the way writing is done. A new version of *Handbook of Current English* provided an opportunity to enhance an existing emphasis on teaching writing as a process, to acknowledge more explicitly that writing is now regularly taught across the disciplines, and to recognize the impact that computer technology is having on the way we write. The goal of this revision was to introduce these new directions while retaining the best features of the existing book. The result is an edition that represents a cover-to-cover and line-by-line rethinking of the *Handbook of Current English.*

This seventh edition of the handbook reaffirms, however, principles that have guided the book from its beginning: that a selective and thoughtful use of language is important in every part of everyone's life; that some forms of expression are more effective and appropriate in given situations than others; that a "good" language is a language decently suited to its writer, to a subject, and to an audience. The seventh edition retains all the features that have made the book popular over the years both as a reference tool in the study and a textbook in the classroom, including the review charts, the introductory essay on "Using the Language," and the convenient system of numbered tabs.

The numerous changes and additions to *Handbook of Current English* fall into four major categories: improvements in structure and format, enhancements of existing material, new sections and features, and a greatly expanded package of supporting materials.

Improvements in Structure and Format. A new arrangement of materials in this seventh edition clarifies the relationship among the major parts of the book and emphasizes the writing process and professional occasions for writing. The book now has three divisions:

I. A Writer's Resources. This section contains a systematic discussion of grammar, usage, and conventions of punctuation, abbreviation, spelling, and so forth. While it contains the fewest major revisions, each chapter in *A Writer's Resources* has been reworked and revised as necessary. The chapter on the dictionary now follows the discussion of spelling.

II. A Writer's Choices. This part is concerned with the options writers face in doing their work. It provides a comprehensive examination of issues such as audience, purpose, invention, structure, revision, style, and diction. Much of the material in this section is either new or heavily reworked to provide students with a consistent discussion of the writing process. Completely new is a chapter entitled "An Essay in Progress" tracing the development of a student paper from assignment sheet to rough draft. While the chapters in this part are written so that they may still be read or referred to individually, they now follow in a sequence that enhances their value as a full and up-to-date rhetoric text.

III. A Writer's Work. This new major division emphasizes the particular features of writing in the professional and academic worlds. Although the previous edition did treat aspects of professional writing and research, this new edition goes farther in examining the concerns of writers in many fields. "Writing for the Professional World" (Chapter 31) provides detailed suggestions about how to write business letters, resumés, and reports, and now includes a section on word processing. "Writing in the Academic World" (Chapter 32) gives more comprehensive advice about preparing abstracts, taking efficient lecture notes, and writing a literary paper than did the previous edition. A sample literary analysis (with annotations) is included, along with a thorough discussion of plagiarism and collusion. "Writing and Research" (Chapter 33) presents the traditional library paper as a serious vehicle for research and education in both the academic and professional worlds.

In addition to these overall structural changes, there have been many smaller-scale rearrangements throughout the handbook. For example, the chapter on "Common Sentence Errors" in the new edition follows (rather than precedes) the discussions of sentence structure on which it is conceptually dependent. The material on sentences has been increased, reorganized, and divided into three chapters instead of the previous two, with a full chapter given to sentence economy. Chapter 17, "Spelling," has been rearranged to move from principles to practical tips (rather than vice versa). The rhetoric section opens more logically now with the discussion of purpose and audience preceding the treatment of invention. Within chapters, new concepts or ideas are followed immediately and regularly by explanatory examples. The principles guiding these and the numerous other reorderings—both major and minor—are clarity, simplicity, and increased readability. The same principles motivate important changes in format and design in the seventh edition. Pages are cleaner, more open, and more inviting. Examples and exercises are easier to locate, and headings are more prominent.

Enhancements of Existing Material. Many of the popular features of previous editions of *Handbook of Current English* have been significantly improved in the seventh edition. For teachers, the most obvious enhancement may be the increased number of exercises. Exercise sets now follow most individual sections within the handbook, especially in the chapters on grammar, punctuation, and usage. Many of the exercises from the previous editions have been updated and designed to incorporate materials from many disciplines so that the students in the natural and social sciences, business, nursing, or other fields are apt to be as comfortable with the book as those in the humanities or arts. Many new exercises have been added—with a consistent emphasis on composing, revising, and thinking. The handbook offers various suggestions for writing and revising, almost all of them providing or asking students to provide a rhetorical context. A selection of intriguing casebook assignments appears at the end of Chapter 24, "An Essay in Progress." And for easier reference, each exercise now has its own number.

Other improvements in this edition include revised review sheets, an expanded glossary of usage, separate checklists for revision and editing, a more graphic presentation of titles (when to employ italics? when to underline?), a section on "Acronyms and Abbreviations," and an enlarged spelling/

vocabulary list featuring the kinds of terms students are likely to encounter—and misspell—in college courses *(renaissance, bourgeoisie, empirical, malfeasance, soliloquy)*. In many parts of the book, the examples have either been increased in number or changed to make a point more forcefully, simply, or memorably. And, as is true of the exercises, the examples draw their materials from across the disciplines.

As important as what has been added to *Handbook of Current English,* seventh edition, is what has come out. Many sections, especially the introduction and chapter openings, have been tailored to make their points more economically and directly. Handy lists are used in many places to summarize major concepts, and the book is tighter and more readable within individual sections. It maintains, however, the open and friendly tone that readers have long appreciated.

New Sections and Features. Three of the new sections in *Handbook of Current English,* seventh edition, merit special attention: Chapter 24, "An Essay in Progress"; a heavily revised concluding chapter entitled "Writing and Research"; and a new "Glossary of Grammatical, Rhetorical, and Literary Terms."

"An Essay in Progress" graphically summarizes the five chapters on rhetoric that precede it by showing how one student, Ken Duncan from the University of Texas at Austin, actually goes about using concepts such as purpose, audience, and structure in preparing a paper on Western Art. The chapter presents not an idealized process few students can relate to, but a realistic account of how writing gets done. It includes all the materials Ken Duncan produced, including rough notes and drafts, as well as his teacher's comments and photographs of the works of art he discusses in his paper.

The revised chapter on "Writing and Research" attempts to move the research paper assignment into a more realistic, practical, and professional context. While retaining all the information and apparatus needed to lead a student through a typical library research project, the chapter also shows how more sophisticated research is done by employing tools and techniques such as interviews, data bases, citation indexes, surveys, and so forth. The chapter includes a professional research article (in shortened form) to provide a model of the kind of writing real research produces. The goal is to assure students that research is a significant and complex process, not a mere academic exercise. The chapter now includes augmented reference lists, information on computer searches, and a model research essay (on geothermal energy) that features **process** annotations to explain how the piece was composed and **product** annotations to show what a completed research paper should look like. The revised MLA documentation style is used in the model research paper and throughout the book. The 1984 MLA revision eliminated the need for nearly all footnotes and endnotes through the use of brief parenthetical in-text citations that include only the author's name or the title of the work, and the page number. The bibliography contains any other necessary information. The minor punctuation changes in documentation style are also reflected throughout the book. Proper documentation style is provided for items such as video tapes, computer software, and government documents, as well as for more traditional bibliography entries.

Also new is the alphabetical listing of grammatical, rhetorical, and literary terms at the end of the handbook. While many of the definitions here appear elsewhere in the text or on review charts, this glossary makes reference easier by eliminating the need to turn to the index or table of contents to locate a definition. The glossary also defines some important terms (especially literary ones) not introduced in the handbook itself.

Other Features. Retained from previous editions is the system of marginal tabs; the numbers on the colored thumb tabs correspond to the major divisions in the text, and the revision symbols or abbreviations on the tabs indicate what material is discussed on those pages. Comments on papers can be enhanced by using these revision symbols to direct students to pertinent discussions in the handbook, whether they need to review the section on comma splices or to try some new techniques for developing a topic idea. In the text of the handbook itself, the symbols, printed in colors, appear with specific suggestions for revision. A complete list of the symbols is provided on the inside front cover.

Ancillary Program. The *Handbook of Current English* is supplemented by the most complete ancillary program available. The third edition of *Workbook of Current English* has been expanded to include more student writing and to build students' mastery of writing skills. Exercises have been carefully and thoroughly refreshed and updated. The continued emphasis on writing problems, as well as the number and variety of exercises, makes the third edition of *Workbook of Current English* more comprehensive than ever. The *Answer Key with Teaching Suggestions to accompany Workbook of Current English* provides suggested answers to nearly all the exercises in the *Workbook*. Scoring guides and charts enable the instructor to assess students' strengths and weaknesses and to determine a percentage score for each student based on the number of correct items in an exercise. The *Objective Tests of College-Level Competencies to accompany Handbook of Current English* provides two tests of 48 questions each. Originally developed to correspond to Florida's state-mandated college competency requirements, the tests are appropriate for any situation that gauges students' progress toward mastering writing skills. The tests are printed on freesheets for easy duplicating; an 8-page instructor's booklet supplies suggestions for administering the tests and an answer key. The *Diagnostic Tests to accompany Handbook of Current English* includes two 100-question tests covering the complete spectrum of basic grammar, punctuation, and mechanics; the tests are printed on freesheets for easy duplicating. The instructor's booklet has an answer key and a scoring chart to help identify students' weak areas. *500-Word Dash: A Handbook for Essay Exams* is a 16-page booklet that provides instruction in practical methods for dealing with the problems of writing under time constraints. A variety of timed writing assignments is included. *45 Ideas for Teaching Writing* supplies interesting and helpful in-class writing and discussion activities that correspond to sections of the *Handbook*. The perforated pages of the book make it possible to duplicate many of the professional writing examples and exercise activities for distribution to students. The *Instructor's Annotated Edition* provides instructors with handy marginal teaching suggestions and information related to the exercises. A special section in the back of the *Instructor's Annotated Edition* discusses methods of teaching freshman composition and provides several course outlines for using the *Handbook* in one and two semester courses. These new and expanded ancillaries make the *Handbook of Current English* program the most comprehensive available.

Acknowledgments. It is impossible to list all of the teachers, scholars, students, and friends who have contributed to this text. But some must be recognized, beginning with Porter Perrin, who first conceived this handbook.

The many users of the previous editions of the book and the reviewers of the current edition in manuscript form deserve special recognition. They include Gerald J. Alred, University of Wisconsin-Milwaukee; Elouise Bell, Brigham Young University; James Berlin, University of Cincinnati; Alma Bryant, University of South Florida; Barbara Carson, University of Georgia; Joseph Comprone, University of Louisville; Elizabeth Cooper, University of Houston; Alger Doane, University of Wisconsin-Madison; Michael C. Flanigan, University of Oklahoma; Anna Maria Gardini; Dorothy M. Guinn, Arizona State University; Rosemary Hake, California State University; John Harwood, Pennsylvania State University; Christine Hult, Texas Tech University; Michael Johnson, University of Kansas; Edward H. Jones, El Camino College; Julie Lepick Kling, Data General Corporation; Stanley Kozikowski, Bryant College; Wayne Losano, University of Florida; Frank McHugh, Eastern Michigan University; George Miller, University of Delaware; Mary Northcut, Richland College; Elizabeth Penfield, University of New Orleans; JoAnne M. Podis, Dyke College; Robert S. Rudolph, University of Toledo; Charles I. Schuster, University of Washington; LaVerne Summerlin, University of Cincinnati; Thomas Trzyna, Seattle Pacific University; Richard Verrill, Boston University; Charles J. Wagner, Sinclair Community College; Peter Zoller, Wichita State University.

Gratitude is owed to Mary Trachsel and Nancy Gore who contributed to the exercises, to Donald Weeda who assisted in manuscript preparation and copy editing, and to Carol Rhoades who provided moral support. Special thanks to two students who contributed major pieces to the handbook, Ken Duncan and Michael Gragg, and to Matt Houston, Jacki McCue, Rock McMahon, Craig Chapman, and other students whose sentences and paragraphs appear in examples and exercises.

Finally, the staff at Scott, Foresman deserve consideration for their vision, their attention to detail, and their commitment to the book's potential readers. Amanda Clark, the editor on the project, realized early on what a thorough revision would entail and faced the task with intelligence, commitment, humor, and one superb idea after another. Kathy Lorden guided the formidable manuscript through its difficult last stages—editing, proofing, design—with skill and endless patience. Harriett Prentiss made it possible to do the book with few compromises. And thanks must go to many others in Glenview for their assistance and support, including Constance Rajala, Pearl Lumpp, Ginny Guerrant, Juan Vargas, Barbara Schneider, Kathy Cunningham, and Paula Riggs.

Jim W. Corder
John J. Ruszkiewicz

CONTENTS

HANDBOOK
of CURRENT
ENGLISH

INTRODUCTION: USING THE LANGUAGE

In reading and writing, there are none of those helpful accompaniments we count on in the actual practice of conversing, such as vocal intonation, facial expression, gesture. One of the writer's principal problems is to compensate for these losses, for most people are more convincing in person than on paper. That is why writing has to be learned; that is why books like this one are offered as helps for writers. Somehow the writer has to evoke, out of mere ink marks on paper, a character whose language the reader will trust, enjoy, profit from.—Walker Gibson, PERSONA

English is both easy and difficult to study. Easy, because we already know the language. Difficult, because English is varied and changing. Native speakers of English grow up able to use the language in various ways, in unlimited combinations of words and phrases. Yet using a language well depends on more than an awareness of our abilities to speak and understand different varieties. It is also more than writing "complete" sentences, using correct verb forms, making verbs agree with their subjects and pronouns with their antecedents. Beyond these forms and conventions, using a language well is a matter of choosing from the broad range of our language the words and constructions that will best convey our ideas to an unspecified or a particular audience, that will best enable us to present ourselves fully and honestly to others. But no one can make choices unless choices are available. To make good choices in language, we must recognize different versions of English and know the various ways English is used in contemporary writing and speaking.

The Elements of Language

Basically a language consists of a system of sounds, a collection of words, some changes in word forms, and some patterns into which the words fit to convey meaning. A language may or may not have a system of writing and printing.

Sounds

English has between forty and fifty sounds (about twenty of them vowel sounds and the rest consonant) and variations in pause, pitch, and stress. Each sound is used with slight modifications in actual speech; for example, some people have a full *r* and others a very slight indication of the sound. The pronunciation of words varies considerably among the different regions in which English is used, so that we can easily identify some people as New Yorkers, others as Southerners, others as New Englanders.

Words

Counting everything from slang and local words to rarely used words and limited scientific terms, there are well over two million English words. Many of these are used in several different senses—one dictionary gives forty different meanings for the word *check*. An unabridged dictionary has about 500,000 entries; a college dictionary has about 150,000 entries; a college student probably uses or recognizes over 50,000 basic words, not counting forms made by changes in tense (*-ed*) or number (*-s*). English forms many derivatives by adding prefixes (*in-, anti-, re-, super-*) and suffixes (*-er, -ish, -ship, -teria*), and it makes compounds freely by putting two or more words together (*bookcase, streamlined*).

Word Forms

Some languages are *inflected;* that is, their words change form to express grammatical relations in case, number, gender, person, tense, and the like. Latin and German, for example, are highly inflected. English uses very few changes in word forms: only a few endings, like the -s or -es of nouns _(boys, churches)_, the -s, -ed, -ing of verbs _(asks, asked, asking)_, -er and -est for comparing adverbs and adjectives _(hotter, hottest; nearer, nearest)_, and a few internal changes, like the changes in vowels in _man–men, sing–sang_.

Constructions

There are two basic ways to combine English words into groups: with phrases centered on nouns or their equivalents _(in the morning; crossing the streeet)_ and with clauses centered on verbs _(he runs the forty yard dash; when she saw the results)_. We interpret the meaning of these familiar patterns according to the order in which the words stand, an order that we pick up naturally as children and follow almost instinctively. Out of these simple word groups we build sentences of varying length and complexity. The study of the relationships between words and word groups in sentences is _syntax_, a large part of what we call _grammar_.

Writing Practices

English, which like other languages first developed in speech, is represented in writing and printing by the twenty-six letters of the alphabet, a dozen or so punctuation marks, and devices like capitals and italics. Our accepted habits of spelling, punctuation, capitalization, and other practices were developed mostly by printers and serve chiefly to represent the spoken language.

These are the _materials_ of language. Both these materials and what we do with them are the concern of this handbook. Of the many varieties of _current_ English, _Handbook of Current English_ uses—and usually recommends—Edited American English, that is, the English you'd expect to hear from people who have spoken, heard, written, read, and examined English long enough to be familiar with its characteristics and the ways it is typically employed in many books, magazines, classrooms, and public forums. When you use Edited American English you are, in effect, acknowledging judgments on usage made by many people over many years.

Intro

There is good reason to do so. When you write, you usually want to be understood and appreciated by a diverse and often unpredictable audience of readers. You want a language whose characteristics will be familiar to all of them. For most readers, that will be Edited American English, a language which is widely used because it is flexible and serves many purposes, from summarizing the results of a scientific experiment to describing the events at a wedding. Because of its widespread use, Edited American English does not belong to any single person, group, or region. In a nation blessed with diversity, it is as close as we are likely to come to a common language.

Varieties of English Usage

Living languages such as English grow and change continually. Ordinarily the changes are slow and barely noticeable—slightly different pronunciations, new shadings in the meaning of words, and gradual shifts in grammatical constructions—but their cumulative effect can be dramatic. The works of Shakespeare, written four centuries ago, are difficult for many modern readers. Many of the words are unfamiliar and the grammar occasionally seems strange:

> BANQUO.   This guest of summer,
> The temple-haunting marlet, does approve,
> By his lov'd mansionry, that the heaven's breath
> Smells wooingly here; no jutty, frieze,
> Buttress, nor coign of vantage, but this bird
> Hath made his pendant bed and procreant cradle.
> Where they most breed and haunt, I have observ'd
> The air is delicate.
> *Macbeth*, I.vi.3–10

The works of Chaucer, written in the fourteenth century, are hard to read without a large glossary and a grammar guide:

> A Clerk ther was of Oxenford also,
> That unto logyk hadde longe ygo.
> . . . .
> Of studie took he moost cure and moost heede.
> Noght o word spak he moore than was neede,
> And that was seyd in forme and reverence,
> And short and quyk and ful of hy sentence;

Sownynge in moral vertu was his speche,
And gladly wolde he lerne and gladly teche.

The Canterbury Tales, I.285–86, 303–308

Still earlier works, like _Beowulf_ (ca. 750), can be understood only by specialists who have studied Old English much as you would study a foreign language:

Hwilum cyninges þegn,
guma gilphlaeden, gidda gemyndig,
se ðe ealfela ealdgesegena
worn gemunde, word oþ er fand
so ðe gebunden; secg eft ongan
si ð Beowulfes snyttrum styrian,
ond on sped wrecan spel gerade,
wordum wrixlan.

Beowulf, 11.867–74

Yet all these works are written in a language that can be called English, and all have been admired by many generations of readers.

The changes we observe over great periods of time are not the only variations that occur in a language. At any moment in its history, a language also shows many internal variations. English, both spoken and written, must accommodate all the needs and situations its many users find for it. It must be capable of dignity, clowning, precision, ambiguity, anger, effacement, explanation, and entertainment. It must be capable of serving every conceivable audience, from scientists gathered at a conference to teenagers hanging out at a video arcade. It must provide its users with the choices of vocabulary, tone, syntax, and structure they need to convey who they are, what they know, and how they wish to be perceived at any given time.

Until fairly recently, it was common for students of language to assume that "good" English was fixed by an inflexible set of rules, and that any variation from this norm was automatically "bad" English. This highly _prescriptive_ approach to language study reflected the belief that there was some ideal form of English, orderly and uniform. Students had merely to learn its laws and apply them, just as they would in studying physics or chemistry. Although the prescriptive approach often produced good results, both practical experience and modern linguistic scholarship—called _descriptive_ because it studies and describes the language as it *is*—have shown it to be less than satisfactory. No single system of conventions and rules can accurately describe all the complexities of a language. Whether we like it or not, our language is changing and varied, and because it is, it offers choices. When you write for academic or professional reasons, you will ordinarily employ Edited American English. But other legitimate varieties and versions of English—some mainly spoken, others both spoken and written—serve individuals and groups in special times and particular places. These idiolects and dialects are also "good" English.

Idiolects

Everyone has a personal language. It may be different from the language of someone who lives two hundred miles away or of the neighbor next door; it may be scarcely distinguishable from another person's language. This personal language can be called an *idiolect*. The word combines two terms, the first of which *(idio)* originally meant something like "personal," "separate," or "one's own"; the second comes from a word meaning "to converse." An idiolect grows out of your own life and may change as your life changes. Shakespeare's Bottom the Weaver, a comic character in *A Midsummer Night's Dream*, has an idiolect marked by a tendency to say only approximately what he means:

> . . . The eye of man hath not heard, the ear of man hath not seen, man's hand is not able to taste, his tongue to conceive, nor his heart to report, what my dream was.
>
> IV.i.211–14

Very different is the idiolect of a character in Stephen Crane's "The Bride Comes to Yellow Sky." His language tells us something about his age, his location, and the kind of life he has led:

> His enemy's face went livid. He stepped forward, and lashed his weapon to and fro before Potter's chest. "Don't you tell me you ain't got no gun on you, you whelp. Don't tell me no lie like that. There ain't a man in Texas ever seen you without no gun. Don't take me for no kid." His eyes blazed with light, and his throat worked like a pump.

Part of John F. Kennedy's idiolect was the phrase: "Let me just say this about that." And until the *idio*syncrasy was pointed out to him, President Reagan's replies to questions invariably began with a thoughtful "Well, ..."

An idiolect is not necessarily restrictive. People can usually understand other people's idiolects, and almost everyone regularly shifts from one idiolect into another and then another. The same harried householder may find suitable language for addressing his boss, his minister, his two-year-old daughter, and his schnauzer, all within a few minutes and all without much consideration. An idiolect, in essence, may be characterized as a person's verbal *style*.

Intro

Dialects

When a community of speakers and writers uses idiolects that have much in common in pronunciation, grammar, and vocabulary, the combined idiolects are referred to as a *dialect*. We usually think of a dialect only as the language of a particular geographical region, but the word can name any gathering of idiolects that share essential characteristics. A dialect is almost like a code: speakers and writers of a dialect can usually converse with and write to speakers of the general language, but they also know the special language of their group or region. Dialects can be classified as regional, temporal, occupational, public, and general.

Regional Dialects

There are many *regional dialects;* some of them are readily recognizable. Migration habits, work habits, geographical features, plant and animal life, and other characteristics of a particular region sometimes help create a language for the area that is distinguishable from other dialects. A regional dialect may be marked by special words. Depending upon what part of the country you're in, you will put your *pop, soda,* or *soda pop* in a *bag, sack,* or *poke.* If you are from Western Pennsylvania you might substitute *younse* for your friend from Missouri's *you-all*'s. People in the Southwest have more occasion to talk about *canyons, mesas,* and *arroyos* than people in Massachusetts do, both because of the southwestern topography and because of their exposure to Spanish languages.

A regional dialect may be identified at times by special pronunciations of ordinary words or phrases. Texans manage to compress "Did you eat?" into the single word, *Jeet?*, while some natives of Columbus, Ohio, pronounce their city in a single syllable: *Clumbs*. A regional dialect may be marked, too, by characteristic constructions, by pronunciations, and by words not commonly used elsewhere.

Temporal Dialects

Dialects can also be temporal. Language changes faster in some communities than in others; sometimes a group preserves usages or words while another group hurries into acceptance of new terms and constructions, discarding the old. Quite often these temporal dialects reflect social, cultural, or political movements that thrive for a while and then fade away, depositing a residue of words, constructions, and intonations that linger in the general dialects. The slang of the beatniks of the 1950's, the hippies of the 1960's, and the Valley Girls of the 1980's all represent temporal dialects that readily accepted changes in vocabulary and usage: *cool, man; daddy-o; right on; turn on; gag me with a spoon; fur shure.*

Occupational Dialects

Professional languages, craft languages, and shoptalk may be called *occupational dialects*. Such dialects occur most frequently in writing or speech connected to particular jobs or professions, but parts of some occupational dialects have entered our general language. We frequently borrow words from occupations and use them in our writing and conversation: *feedback, EKG, microchip, input, huddle, graphic equalizer, close-up,* or *program* (as used with computers).

Occupational dialects occur in many ways. We may expect to find such languages in professional journals and specialized books written for audiences that share a common technical expertise and vocabulary. But, more and more, occupational dialects are being employed to enhance the credibility of information and advertisements aimed at a more general readership:

> All other cordless phones (including other Freedom Phone models) use a 49 MHz signal for handset to base transmission, and a 1.7 MHz signal for base to handset reception.

This system is completely satisfactory for most situations. But if you're surrounded by steel construction, heavy concrete, abundant FM radio interference or other problems, the double 49 MHz system provides the ultimate solution.—advertisement for Freedom Phone 4000

Public Dialects

Words, phrases, and constructions that come from politics, television, magazines, motion pictures, and other kinds of public communications form special languages that might be called _public_ or _media dialects_. With amazing speed, the various media can put a new word, phrase, or slogan on every tongue or at the tip of every pen: _America Held Hostage!_, _runaway inflation_, _Star Wars weapons_, _generation gap_, _stagflation_, _"At this point in time,"_ _crisis in Lebanon_, _missile gap_, _gender gap_. Similarly, news commentators, sports reporters, film stars, and television characters can exert extraordinary influence on public discourse. How many people have borrowed the glib retorts of _M.A.S.H._, the malapropisms of Archie Bunker, the tag lines of Johnny Carson and Joan Rivers, or the clipped phrasings of David Brinkley? All of these become part of fluctuating, often short-lived, but consequential public dialects.

General Dialects

Although the _public dialects_ are extraordinarily pervasive, most of the language you ordinarily encounter doesn't belong to any of the particular classes of discourse we have examined so far—the personal idiolects and the regional, temporal, occupational, and public dialects. If you take into account all of the language you hear or read in a given week, from newspapers, magazines, radio, television, classrooms, friends, and elsewhere, you will find that most of it falls into that broad range of language so commonly used it attracts no attention to itself. The varieties of language within that range can be described as _general dialects_ or _general English_. General English varies in formality, complexity, tone, and specificity; the three passages which follow show some of that variety, but have in common the naturalness, simplicity, and closeness to speech typical of general dialects:

> Once there was a lot of sound in my grandmother's house, a lot of coming and going, feasting and talk. The summers there were full of excitement and reunion. The Kiowas are

a summer people; they abide the cold and keep to themselves, but when the season turns and the land becomes warm and vital they cannot hold still; an old love of going returns upon them.—N. Scott Momaday, *The Way to Rainy Mountain*

Yet if our agriculture-based life depends on the soil, it is equally true that soil depends on life, its very origins and the maintenance of its true nature being intimately related to living plants and animals. For soil is in part a creation of life, born of a marvelous interaction of life and nonlife long eons ago.—Rachel Carson, *Silent Spring*

How to complain
Your service representative is available to answer your questions and resolve your problems. If you're not satisfied, feel free to ask for a supervisor. If your problem can't be solved by the supervisor, ask for the manager or higher levels of management.—Southwestern Bell telephone directory

The most casual and informal varieties of general English tend to use words and phrases more characteristic of speaking than of writing: *cop, deadpan, iffy, chancy, phony, peeve, whodunit*. Such words are called *colloquial* by some dictionaries. When we are writing or speaking informally, we are also likely to use slang (*mug shot, flatfoot*), regional expressions (*coal oil, fried pie, bayou*), and words that, for one reason or another, enjoy a temporary fashion or popularity (*bottom line, anomaly, negative cash flow*).

"Nonstandard" English

The term *nonstandard* must be carefully qualified when applied to the varieties of language we have examined. Any language can be a nonstandard form. In a special sense, idiolects and dialects associated with particular groups, particular places, and particular times can be considered nonstandard only in that they are not languages for wide use. In a more general way, a language may be called nonstandard if its spelling is inconsistent, its punctuation idiosyncratic, and its usage not widely accepted. And while nonstandard English is most often defined by its vocabulary, its sounds, or its grammatical construction, we might also count as nonstandard any language that fails in its purpose to communicate as effectively as possible.

Edited American English

For use in writing, almost any language has to be edited. When you write, you ordinarily present your language in consistent and corrected form. *Edited American English* is a version of the language associated with schools, good newspapers, good books, and good public speakers. It is an idiolect or dialect that has been modified to produce a uniformity in sound, a consistency with the grammatical standards traditionally taught in English and American schools, and a vocabulary that can be shared by people in different places at different times. Edited American English results from a filtering process. What separates people linguistically is trapped and discarded, while what binds people linguistically is left for use. Few people speak edited American English; many write it. It is another variety of language available to you.

Intro

All the dialects and forms of English discussed in this introduction can become appropriate edited American English when edited for public presentation. The language of our casual conversations—of our idiolects and dialects—can be the basis of a kind of *informal* edited American English. General spoken English is the basis for a *general* edited American English. And, finally, we can describe a *formal* English, found chiefly in writing, that is a more consciously constructed and more complex development from general edited American English. This formal English, which is the appropriate language of much academic and professional writing, is heavily influenced by the conventions established by writers and editors in the past. It usually treats specialized topics and addresses relatively limited audiences. Its vocabulary is derived from the language of its subject matter as well as from general English and, when appropriate, from idiolects and dialects. It may also employ many abstract words. Its grammatical constructions tend to be fuller than those of general English, and ordinarily its sentences are longer and more complex. Formal writing tends to follow older practices in punctuation and to use more frequent and heavier punctuation than is typical in general English.

The formal English used in academic, scientific, technical, and scholarly writing is often impersonal. Good formal writing, however, is not stilted or dull. This account of the mapping of Switzerland shows the single-minded attention to the subject, the compact and orderly statement of ideas, and the moderate use of technical terms that characterize good impersonal formal English:

> The heroic task of making a topographic survey and map of Switzerland fell to the lot of General Guillaume Henri Dufour (1787–1875). Under his personal supervision the work was begun in 1830 and the first sheet was published in 1842. Thirty-four years later the entire survey, on a scale of 1:100,000 was finished and the last of the 25 sheets came from the press. Soon after, the map appeared in atlas form, published at Berne. Far from being a pioneering effort that would require immediate revision, the Dufour atlas proved to be a model of accuracy and artistic delineation, not only for future map makers of Switzerland, but for cartographers at large. The sheets of the atlas were used as a basis for later surveys on different scales, and on the sheets of Switzerland's new survey references were made to the corresponding sections and subsections of the original Dufour map. The art work and conventional signs on the new map were almost identical with those on the Dufour originals. The lettering and bench marks (figures denoting heights), prominent buildings, roads, boundaries and forests were printed in black. Small slopes and passes, ravines and narrow defiles that could not be shown by equally spaced contour lines were printed in brown hachures. Black hachures were used to indicate rocky prominences and precipices, the general effect being a pictorial representation by oblique lighting. Horizontal surveys were shown in bronze and water was indicated by shades of blue.—Lloyd A. Brown, *The Story of Maps*

A more personal type of formal English is shown in the following passage. Some of the words and phrases are formal— *inert knowledge, radical error,* and *delicate, receptive, responsive to stimulus.* The constructions are full: note the sentence beginning *Whoever was the originator* and the following sentence, beginning *But whatever its weight of authority.* But some constructions *(I appeal to you, as practical teachers. So far, so good.)* carry an unmistakable personal emphasis and keep us aware that the writer is expressing himself as an individual.

> I appeal to you, as practical teachers. With good discipline, it is always possible to pump into the minds of a class a certain quantity of inert knowledge. You take a textbook and make them learn it. So far, so good. The child then knows how to solve a quadratic equation. But what is the point of teaching a child to solve a quadratic equation? There is a traditional answer to this question. It runs thus: The mind is an instrument, you first sharpen it, and then use it; the acquisition of the power of solving a quadratic equation is part of the process of sharpening the mind. Now there is just enough truth in this answer to have made it live through the ages. But for all its half-truth, it embodies a radical error which bids fair to stifle the genius of the modern world. I do not know who was first responsible for this analogy of the mind to a dead instrument. For aught I know, it may have been one of the seven wise men of Greece, or a committee of the whole lot of them. Whoever was the originator, there can be no doubt of the authority which it has acquired by the continuous approval bestowed upon it by eminent persons. But whatever its weight of authority, whatever the high approval it can quote, I have no hesitation in denouncing it as one of the most fatal, erroneous, and dangerous concepts ever introduced into the theory of education. The mind is never passive; it is a perpetual activity, delicate, receptive, responsive to stimulus. You cannot postpone its life until you have sharpened it. Whatever interest attaches to your subject-matter must be evoked here and now; whatever powers you are strengthening in the pupil, must be exercised here and now; whatever possibilities of mental life your teaching should impart, must be exhibited here and now. That is the golden rule of education, and a very difficut rule to follow.—Alfred North Whitehead, *The Aims of Education*

These are some forms of our language: countless idiolects, many dialects, edited American English, formal language. Each can be used to move or to inform; each can be warm, generous, and powerful; each can be used with precision.

Some Qualities of Good Writing: A Checklist

The objective in writing is not to conform to some previously established system of grammar, but to use the language to speak fully, precisely, honestly, and appropriately. Good writing is not born of a system of rules and usages; systems of rules and usages are born of good writing.

Writing is a kind of contract between you and the reader. You take care with your work because you expect someone to invest time in reading it; the reader owes you a little curiosity, patience, and attentiveness. You usually aren't present when your words are read. They stand alone, conveying your meanings and intentions. You cannot respond immediately to the questions or doubts your sentences raise, or modify your statements, or add material where your coverage is incomplete, or shift emphasis when your reader begins to nod. Consequently, you must anticipate the needs of your readers—often people not much different from you—and you must write with care and vigor in appropriate language.

Language is appropriate when it is honest—for the writer, the subject, and the audience. It is appropriate when its user treats evidence fairly, without falsification or manipulation, and when it arises from open motives.

Language is appropriate when it rests upon a suitable history—that is to say, the writer or speaker has had the experience, acquired the evidence, and done the thinking implied in what he or she says. Language is appropriate when it works as nearly as possible without manipulation or coercion. Conversely, language is inappropriate when it is unnecessarily ambiguous or uninterpretable, when it denies hearers or readers access to information needed for a full interpretation, when it tries to coerce audiences, when it is empty noise, or when it somehow violates the possibilities of expression and communication. When you write, the choice of vocabulary, usage, and construction is, in a way, not yours alone. Your subject makes certain demands. Your audience, which has certain expectations, deserves good treatment. You cannot use language as your private toy or solely to please others. If you are to use a language well, you must be certain that it is appropriate to you as the writer, to your audience of readers, and to the situation you are addressing.

Appropriateness to the Writer

 Whatever your purpose in writing, express your ideas in language that seems natural to you.

Intro

This doesn't mean that you should necessarily rest content with the idiolect or dialect or language you already speak. It means, rather, that you ought to make any language you use your own so that you understand it and feel comfortable using it. Start with your present language. How well do you understand the way you already speak and write? What is your present language like? Does it have special traits that other people won't understand? Are you sure of yourself in spelling, punctuation, sentence structure? When you write a paper for a college course, do you choose the best part of your natural language, or do you assume an entirely different sort of English? If you return to a paper that you wrote some time ago and read it aloud, does it sound at all like something you would or could say? If it doesn't, can you tell what happened to your language in the paper?

The suggestions and the pressures of teachers or critics may have some brief effect on the way you use language, but in the long run you set your own standard. The language you use is your responsibility. Good English is not primarily a matter of rules, but of judgment. You are not struggling under a series of *don't*s but trying to discover among the wide resources of modern English the language that best suits your purpose, your audience, and yourself.

Appropriateness to the Reader

 Adjust your subject matter and your language to the expectations of your readers.

Your readers are as real as you are. If you want to influence them, reach them, or instruct them, meet them on their own ground. If the language you use is not one your readers can respond to, then your ideas won't reach them. It might make you feel good to know that you are right in what you say, but you shouldn't expect applause from readers who can't respond to your language. Meeting your readers on common ground, or on their ground, is often easy. You make some adjustments in your language almost automatically in letters,

writing in somewhat different ways to different people. You don't have to abandon your natural language, but you need to focus on the intelligibility of what you are saying or writing.

 Since your aim in writing is to communicate, use clear and exact words, straightforward sentences, and careful punctuation.

If the subject requires terms that may be unfamiliar, try to make them clear by the way you use them or add a tactful explanation. In some instances you may have to provide a formal definition. Clarity also calls for sentences that are not too long and that have a natural, direct movement—though you must remember the demands of your subject and situation as well. Experienced readers can grasp more elaborate sentences than those who read little or read hurriedly. But anyone will be pleased with direct, straightforward sentences.

Careful attention to punctuation is also necessary if you are to make your statements clear to your readers. The various marks—commas, semicolons, and periods—indicate the groups of words that are to be understood as units and often show the relationship between these units. Omissions or misused marks may force readers to go over a passage two or three times; superfluous marks may keep them from grouping words that belong together or may slow the speed of reading to the point of exasperation.

 Proofread your work carefully.

Part of a writer's concern for readers is meeting their expectations in language. This means avoiding careless and elementary errors. Elementary errors may indicate to some readers that you just can't be bothered, that you aren't doing as well as you easily could and should. When you finish writing a paper, take time to check it carefully for errors in spelling, punctuation, and other matters of usage.

 Be lively and specific. Use details.

All readers will appreciate some liveliness in what they read, in the writer's expression as well as the choice of material. Too many students seem to feel that serious writing requires a flat and lifeless or a pompous sort of language. In striving for liveliness, you needn't try for novelty or use words that are out of the ordinary; draw on the vocabulary you might use in an intelligent, reasonably animated conversation. Avoid dragging and monotonous sentences; vary their length and pattern so as to please active, alert minds. Attract your readers' interest by referring, when appropriate, to things people have said and done, and use details to demonstrate your ideas.

Intro

One warning: In gearing your writing to your readers' background and expectations, don't underestimate their intelligence, compromising yourself and insulting them. Visualize them at their best and write for them as they are then.

Appropriateness to Purpose and Situation

 Use edited American English when writing for school or at work.

The standards of written usage in a composition course are about the same standards that would be expected in similar published material. This means that papers about personal experiences, college activities, or your own private reflections might be in general American English. It also means that papers required in other college courses, where your writing will usually carry less of your own character and attitudes and will usually focus with greater concentration on an impersonal subject, may have to meet other expectations and be more nearly formal English.

This expectation for college writing is not the result of an arbitrary decision. By acquiring the ability to use a more formal variety of language, you have won a larger vocabulary for yourself and probably a wider variety of sentence structures. The vocabulary and structure of formal language are often necessary if you wish to say anything about many academic subjects. Consider a single instance. Suppose that you are in a philosophy course; one of your assignments is to write a critique of a book on philosophy that will include an examination of the author's premises, the mode of his argument, and the style of his presentation. To complete the assignment means, among other things, that you must know what a *critique* is, and that you must command a language that will let you talk about *premises, modes of argument,* and *styles of presentation.*

The rather formal language that will enable you to discuss these things may not, however, be useful in a meditative reminiscence about the time you sat on an Appalachian hilltop awaiting the sunrise. If you pay attention to purpose and situation, you should be able to treat most subjects in the language they deserve.

 Do not write too formally.

Inexperienced writers frequently use language that is too heavy to be appropriate for them or their subjects. For example, a student who wanted to say that he had rebelled against his parents despite having come from a happy home wrote:

> Although my domestic environment was permissive and munificent and my sibling relationships were good, I found it necessary to express my generation's mores in reaction to paternal supervision.

The student may seriously have believed that this kind of writing was better than a simple statement. He would almost certainly object to being told that his sentence was bad English—worse perhaps than if it contained some inaccurate or illogical expressions. Inaccuracies can be quite easily corrected, whereas inflated and pompous language must be completely rewritten to be effective. The artificial "formality" of such language is not found in good formal writing, and it should be avoided in student papers.

Maintain a consistent tone.

Once you find an appropriate tone for your situation, stay with it unless there is some special reason for changing. Although the lines between varieties of usage cannot be drawn precisely, you can usually detect when something has gone awry. In the following example, the shift in tone between the first and second sentence is probably too conspicuous:

> The committee labored for months to secure passage of the charter amendment to limit liquor sales on Sunday. But their work wasn't worth a plug nickel to voters who clobbered the proposal.

Superficial consistency is not so important as fundamental appropriateness, but ordinarily one variety of English should be used throughout a piece of writing.

 Know what you are writing about and whom you are writing for.

Reading the work of practiced writers is one way to increase your sensitivity to language and its various uses. Before attempting to write for an unfamiliar situation, read and study some example of good writing done for a similar purpose. Don't try to write an article for a magazine that you have never read, and don't try to write a technical report or reference paper without ever having seen one. Try to learn what is typically done and follow the accepted practices unless you have a good reason for some other usage.

The Design of the Book and Its Focus on Writing

The first part of this book, "A Writer's Resources," focuses on particular features of the English language—grammar, usage, punctuation, and other conventions. This portion, describing the way edited American English typically behaves as a system of language, concludes with a chapter on using the dictionary. The second part, "A Writer's Choices," is about the process of writing. It discusses how you go about using the language to say what you have to say. It describes the options you have as a writer and offers recommendations about how you can make your process of composing more inventive and more efficient. The final major section of *Handbook of Current English*, "A Writer's Work," explains some particular occasions for writing in the professional and academic worlds. It includes a full chapter on writing about research.

As the book is arranged, the first part can be used for study in its own right or can be treated as a reference for writing assignments. The parts entitled "A Writer's Choices" and "A Writer's Work" reflect the sequence of events that many of us go through when we write, from identifying our purpose and audience, through the first efforts at planning, drafting, and revising, to concern about particular features of the writing, and on to completed works.

Much that is said throughout the book applies to both speaking and writing, but the focus is on writing. Most of us will be doing more and more writing and reading in the future. New information and word-processing technologies will increase the control we have over a piece of writing, allowing us to reconsider and revise it simply and efficiently. New video technologies will bring the printed word into our homes and offices in ways that vastly increase our access to information. More than ever, we will find that our ability to read, think, and write well will shape our future as individual citizens on the job and as a people collectively charged with the responsibility of maintaining a humane, educated, and free republic. We can never separate the quality of our thinking from the quality of our expression. By its very nature, writing compels us to be human, to remember what we have been and to imagine what we can be.

Exercises

Most of us do not pay much attention to language differences unless we hear words or phrases that are new to us or startling in their context. One way to work toward using your language thoughtfully is to pay close attention to what you say and hear and to become more conscious of the languages around you. You may want to work with a group or your entire class in gathering information and examples for the exercises and writing assignments below.

1. What are the identifying marks of the language used by your family and the people you were closest to in your early years? List words, expressions, special ways of saying things that you have heard from family and friends, but do not commonly hear elsewhere.

2. List new expressions and ways of saying things that you have heard since starting school. Which of them have you started using yourself?

3. Which words and expressions that you use or hear appear to have been popularized by their use on some television program?

4. Which words and expressions are used to express approval by your family? Your friends and associates now? Which words and expressions are used to express disapproval by your family? By your current friends and associates?

5. Which words and expressions that you use or hear seem to be associated with a particular region?

6. If you have a large family with relatives scattered across the country or the world, write a short essay analyzing some of the differences you detect in the English your parents, grandparents, brothers, sisters, aunts, uncles, cousins, and others write and speak. You might want to account for differences by examining variations due to location, occupation, education, age, and ethnic background. Be sure to incorporate specific examples and features of their language into your essay.

7. Why do some dialects or ways of writing seem more prestigious than others? Write a short essay in which you explore what the terms *prestige* and *power* might mean when applied to language, and what possible abuses might arise from assumptions about the superiority of any one dialect.

8. What potential short- and long-term harm might result from sloppy, careless, and inappropriate language?

Write a short essay exploring this question from the point of view of individual professions (journalism, engineering, medicine) or disciplines (philosophy, economics, political science). If you are familiar with what Edwin Newman or John Simon have said about the condition of the English language in America, you may want to examine their observations in your essay.

9. Write a paragraph in formal edited American English explaining what factors led to your choice of a particular school, profession, or sport. Then rewrite the essay in an informal style, as if it were part of a letter to someone who knows you well. Finally, attempt to put this same information into dialogue that represents the way you typically speak. Compare your versions.

10. Examine a single edition of your local or college newspaper and identify some of the varieties of English in it. What style dominates the paper? Where do you find the most formal English? The least formal? Where do you find written forms of spoken English or examples of idiolect? Classify the forms you discover and write an essay reporting your results, using selections from the newspaper as support for your observations and conclusions.   ■

SOME VERSIONS OF AMERICAN ENGLISH—A SUMMARY

■ Spoken Language

Idiolect: An individual's personal language, influenced by environmental factors (geographical area, occupation) and personal characteristics (age, sex, personality).

Dialect: The combined idiolects of a *community of speakers*, classified as regional, temporal, occupational, public. Dialects can overlap.

General English: The dialect of the great majority of speakers of American English without the strong modification of other dialectical factors. General English includes the languages above.

Nonstandard English: Any variety of English that does not meet generally accepted measures of consistency in usage and grammar.

■ Written Language

Edited American English

Informal English: Characterized by short sentences, "breezy" style; includes personal and journalistic writing.

General English: Characterized by the constructions and vocabulary of general English, with more attention paid to grammatical conventions; includes most books, magazines, and other popular publications.

Formal English: Characterized by full constructions and specialized vocabulary; generally impersonal and found mostly in academic, scientific, technical, scholarly, and other specialized forms of writing.

Nonstandard English: See above.

GRAMMAR
AND USAGE

Part
ONE

A WRITER'S
RESOURCES

1

GRAMMAR OF
SENTENCES

. . . the right to utter a sentence is one of the very greatest liberties; and we are entitled to little wonder that freedom of utterance should be, in every society, one of the most contentious and ill-defined rights. The liberty to impose this formal unity is a liberty to handle the world, to remake it, if only a little, and to hand it to others in a shape which may influence their actions.—Richard Weaver, THE ETHICS OF RHETORIC

The sentence is the primary constructed unit in edited American English and in all other forms of English. Indeed, some kind of sentence form exists in most, if not all, languages. Because of their almost infinite variety, sentences are difficult to explain or define in ways that account for all the occasions of their use.

We may define a written sentence as one or more words, punctuated as an independent unit, that say something. A sentence is made complete either by its grammatical form and meaning or—in special circumstances—by the context in which it appears:

Noel Coward wrote *Blythe Spirit* in 1941. [complete grammatical form]

Snails and slugs are among the most familiar members of the class *Gastropoda*. [complete grammatical form]

Nuts! [complete in context]

It is helpful to understand the different kinds of sentences English offers, what each can do, and the way the parts of a sentence fit together. This section reviews the basic grammatical terms you'll need to analyze and describe sentences and to discuss the relationships between the words that form them.

1.1 Main Sentence Elements

Most English sentences are made with a subject and a verb, in that order. You may see this pattern referred to as the "major" or "favorite" sentence type in English:

> s | v
> Photocopiers | break.

The Subject

The subject (s) is the starting or focal point of a sentence, the noun or noun equivalent (pronoun, noun clause, gerund, infinitive) that states what the sentence is about:

> s
> Hurried **students** often make careless mistakes. [noun]

> s
> **She** runs faster than her brother does. [pronoun]

> s
> **What he doesn't know** is that he talks too much. [noun clause]

> s
> **Talking** is his only exercise. [gerund]

> s
> **To listen** is to suffer. [infinitive]

The _simple subject_ of a sentence is a single word, like _decision_ in the example below:

> s
> The Marbury v. Madison **decision** of 1803 established the power of the Supreme Court to declare an Act of Congress unconstitutional.

The _complete subject_ of a sentence consists of the simple subject plus any words that modify it. In the preceding example, the complete subject is _The Marbury v. Madison decision of 1803._

In many cases, you can identify the subject of a sentence by asking *who* or *what* is doing the action or *who* or *what* is the focus of attention in the sentence:

Isamu Noguchi has created numerous architecturally significant sculptures. [The doer of the action is *Isamu Noguchi*.]

Kepler's laws describe planetary movement. [*Kepler's laws* do the action here.]

Among those responsible for distorting the historical record of Richard III's reign was Sir Thomas More, the Lord Chancellor of England under Henry VIII. [The focus of attention—and the subject of the sentence—is not the *historical record* or *Richard III* but *Sir Thomas More*. In this case, a rearrangement of the sentence makes matters clearer: *Sir Thomas More* was among those responsible. . . .]

Exercise 1.A

Identify the simple and complete subjects in the sentences below. Place an s above the simple subject, and underline the complete subject.

Example   The first fighter to regain his title after retiring was Sugar Ray Robinson.

1.   A mole of NaCl weighs 58.5 grams.
2.   Knowing when to make a decision can be as crucial as the decision itself.
3.   The six thousand survivors of Spartacus' rebellion were crucified by Pompey along the road to Rome.
4.   According to Jean Piaget's theory of cognitive development, most children go through sequential stages of intellectual growth.
5.   Not until decades after the discovery of radioactivity in 1896 were scientists aware of the damage radiation could do.   ■

The Verb

A verb (v) is a word that signals an action, a condition, or a process (see 6.1). In a sentence, a verb agrees with the subject (see 5.1) and takes forms like *ask, asks, asked, asking* or *sing, sang, sung, singing*. In the typical sentence the verb follows

the subject and, like the subject, is often a nucleus for modifying words. The verb may consist of one or more words:

> S   V
> Hurried students often **make** careless mistakes.

> S   V
> Leslie Jones **has driven** for twenty years without getting a
> ticket.

>   V
> Perhaps the defendant **should be given** the benefit of the
> doubt.

The *predicate* is the verb and whatever words are related
to it, such as objects, complements, and modifiers. In the following sentences the complete predicate is in boldface type,
the verb itself marked with a V:

>   S   V
> Hurried students **often make careless mistakes.**

>   S   V
> The doorbell **rang.** [The verb is the complete predicate.]

>   S V
> After finishing his second year, George **spent two long ses-
> sions talking with his advisor about his major.**

Simple sentences are sometimes said to consist of a subject
and a predicate, that is, a subject with all its modifiers and
the verb with all the words related to it:

Subject +	*Predicate*
Solzhenitsyn	won.
Solzhenitsyn, the Russian novelist,	won a Nobel Prize.
Solzhenitsyn, the Russian novelist and critic of Soviet society,	won a Nobel Prize for literature in 1970.

Exercise **1.B**

Identify the verb and the complete predicate in the sentences
below. Place a v above the verb and underline the complete
predicate.

Example   V
San Francisco <u>rests precariously near the San
Andreas fault.</u>

1.   Movement in the San Andreas fault was responsible for
the great earthquake of 1906.

2. Reaching as deep as twenty miles into the crust of the earth, the fault causes numerous minor quakes annually.

3. Fires raged for three days following the calamitous San Francisco quake, virtually destroying the city.

4. Nothing can be done to prevent another quake along the fault line.

5. Only the construction of earthquake-proof buildings and careful disaster-relief planning will forestall another catastrophe.   ■

The Object

The *direct object* (DO) of a verb is a noun or noun equivalent that completes the statement. It answers the question asked by adding "what?" or "whom?" after the verb. (Hurried students often make *what?* Careless mistakes.)

>   S   V   DO
> Hurried students often make careless **mistakes.** [noun]
>   S   V   DO
> The Sherwoods have decided **to buy a house.** [infinitive phrase]
> S   V   DO
> He wondered **what he should do.** [noun clause]

The *indirect object* (IO) is used with verbs of telling, asking, giving, receiving, and so on. It names the receiver of the message, gift, or whatever, answering the questions "*to* whom or what?" or "*for* whom or what?" It comes *before* the direct object.

>   S   V   IO   DO
> He gave the **church** a memorial window.

The same meaning can usually be expressed in a prepositional phrase placed *after* the direct object:

>   S   V   DO
> He gave a memorial window **to the church.**

The Complement

A complement (C) is a noun or an adjective in the predicate that follows a linking verb (LV). Unlike an object, a complement is related to the subject rather than to the verb, because a linking verb expresses a condition or quality rather than a direct action. A noun used as a complement is called a *predicate noun*; an adjective used as a complement is called a *predicate adjective:*

>   S   LV   C
> Mary Enderby is a skilled **architect.** [predicate noun]
>
>   S   LV   C   C
> Tomatoes are actually **fruits,** not **vegetables.** [predicate nouns]
>
>   S   LV   C
> The tenor sounded a little **flat.** [predicate adjective]
>
>   S   LV   C   C
> The sky seemed **low** and **heavy.** [predicate adjectives]

A linking verb is sometimes called a *copula.* The most common linking verb is *be* in its various forms: *is, are, was, were, has been, might be.* Other linking verbs include *seem* and *appear* and, in some contexts, *feel, grow, act, look, smell, taste,* and *sound.*

     See also 9.2, Predicate Adjectives.

Exercise **1.C**

Identify any direct objects, indirect objects, or complements in the sentences below. Label direct objects with a DO, indirect objects with an IO, and complements with a C.

                                     IO   DO
Example   The librarian gave *me* the periodical *index.*

1.   T. H. Gallaudet introduced manual sign language to the United States.
2.   The restaurant failed to turn a profit.
3.   Buy me that book.
4.   The outlook for future grain sales is promising.
5.   Nuclear fission releases enormous quantities of energy.
6.   Marcus Aurelius was a stoic thinker and emperor of Rome.
7.   The senators sent their constituents conflicting messages by voting both to lower taxes and to increase spending.
8.   Drip irrigation uses water more efficiently than the free-flooding or furrow methods.
9.   All the teachers seemed content with the new contract.
10. Karl Marx believed that economic competition would lead only to monopolies.   ■

Word Order

In English we identify the main sentence elements chiefly by their position in the sentence—by word order. For example, it makes a great deal of difference whether you say "The ball hit the boy" or "The boy hit the ball."

Typical Word Order. The typical order of the main elements is subject–verb–object (or subject–linking verb–complement). We use this order to make most statements and to understand them.

In "The class congratulated Rachel" we know through experience that *class* is the subject of *congratulated* because it comes before the verb, and that *Rachel* is the object because it follows the verb. When the verb is in the *passive voice* (a past participle following some form of the verb *be*), the order of sentence elements remains subject–verb: *Rachel was congratulated by the class.*

Inverted Word Order. The typical order of sentence elements is reversed in questions and in some exclamations and emphatic statements:

Question	$\overset{V}{\text{Have}}$ $\overset{S}{\text{you}}$ a $\overset{O}{\text{minute}}$ to spare?
Exclamation	How $\overset{C}{\text{wasteful}}$ these $\overset{S}{\text{meetings}}$ $\overset{LV}{\text{are}}$!
Emphatic object	A better $\overset{O}{\text{job}}$ $\overset{S}{\text{I}}$ never $\overset{V}{\text{had}}$.

In sentences with *there* or *it* as an *expletive* (E) or *anticipating subject*, the real subject comes after the verb:

$\overset{E}{\text{It}}$ $\overset{V}{\text{is}}$ a difficult $\overset{S}{\text{choice}}$. [Compare with: *The choice is difficult.*]

$\overset{E}{\text{There}}$ $\overset{V}{\text{are}}$ several $\overset{S}{\text{reasons}}$ for the difficulty.

When the usual order of elements is reversed, you can find the subject of the sentence by locating the verb and then seeing what word answers the question formed by putting "who" or "what" before it. Thus in the expression "A lot he knows about it," *knows* is the verb, and since the answer to "*Who* knows?" is obviously *he, he* (rather than *lot*) is the subject.

MAIN SENTENCE ELEMENTS

Subject: A noun or noun equivalent that performs an action or is in a particular state of being; it usually appears before the verb and determines the number (singular or plural) of the verb.

Verb: A word that signifies the action or state of being of the subject. It is inflected to show tense, person, and number.

Predicate: The verb and all words related to it.

Linking verb: A verb that expresses a condition *(to be, to seem)* rather than a direct action. Also called a *copula*.

Direct object: Noun or noun equivalent that answers the question asked by adding "what?" or "whom?" to the verb.

Indirect object: Noun that answers the question asked by adding *"to whom or what?"* or *"for whom or what?"* to the verb. It comes before the direct object.

Expletive: *There* or *it* used with a form of *to be* to begin a sentence: *There were . . . ; It is. . . .* Also called an *anticipating subject*.

Complement: Noun or adjective in the predicate, following a *linking verb*; it refers to the subject rather than the verb because a linking verb expresses a condition rather than direct action.

Predicate noun: A noun used as a complement: She is the *president*.

Predicate adjective: An adjective used as a complement: I am *cold*.

These basic sentence elements can be combined into the five basic sentence patterns in English:

1. Subject + Verb: Rain falls.
   $$\overset{S}{\text{Rain}} \overset{V}{\text{falls}}.$$

2. Subject + Verb + Direct Object: The lawyer filed a brief.

3. Subject + Verb + Direct Object + Complement
   The people elected Cullingford mayor.

4. Subject + Verb + Indirect Object + Direct Object
   The assistant brought the manager a print-out.

5. Subject + Linking Verb + Complement
   Some drivers are careless.

Exercise 1.D

Identify the subjects (S), expletives (E), verbs (V), linking verbs (LV), direct objects (DO), indirect objects (IO), and complements (C) in the following sentences with inverted word order.

Example

There will be a time for questions following the lecture.
(E V S above "There will be a")

1. How did scientists measure the chemical makeup of Jupiter's swirling atmosphere?
2. There wasn't a coffee machine in the union.
3. How difficult it is to anticipate movements in the stock market.
4. A simpler and more ingenious stratagem Napoleon himself could not have devised.
5. Will you help me focus the slide projector?
6. What does the term *dumping* mean in international trade?
7. How should I know?
8. It was not merely a matter of opinion, we realized.
9. How complex is the transportation problem in Los Angeles?
10. There are some solutions. ∎

1.2 Secondary Sentence Elements

In addition to the main sentence elements (subject–verb–object or subject–linking verb–complement), most sentences also contain secondary elements. Secondary elements are typically used as modifiers (M)—they describe, limit, or make more exact the meaning of main elements. The table on page 40 shows the various ways in which modifiers—single words, phrases, and clauses—might be used to qualify or expand a simple statement.

Adjectives and Adverbs as Modifiers

Single words used as modifiers are ordinarily related to the element they modify by means of word order. *Adjectives* relate to nouns and usually stand before the words they modify, but sometimes they come immediately after; in both examples, the noun *climb* is the word modified:

> It was a **slow**, **dangerous** climb.

> The steepness of the slope made the climb **slow** and **dangerous**.

Adverbs are more varied in position because often they relate to the sentence as a whole. However, when they modify a particular word (verb, adjective, or adverb) they usually stand close to it:

> They **particularly** wanted to go. [modifies the verb *wanted*]

> He came home from the movies **quite** late. [modifies the adverb *late*]

> The plumbers worked **unusually** fast to repair the pipes. [*Unusually* modifies the adverb *fast*, which modifies the verb *worked*.]

> **Truthfully**, the matter was not settled. [*Truthfully* modifies the whole sentence, not the verb *was settled*.]

See 9, Adjectives and Adverbs.

Other Words and Word Groups as Modifiers

In English a noun often modifies another noun: *glass* jar, *ski* pants, *dance* hall. Nouns used in this way are usually called *modifiers* (not adjectives) or, more exactly, *nouns used attributively*. (See 7.4, Noun Modifiers.)

Prepositional phrases function as modifiers in many English sentences:

> An apartment-dweller **in a large city** [modifies *apartment-dweller*] can live **in the same place** [modifies *can live*] **for a year** [modifies *can live*] and never speak **to his next-door neighbor** [modifies *speak*].

Verbal phrases and subordinate clauses also can function as modifiers:

> M
> **Finding no one at home,** he scribbled a note and left it under the front door. [participle phrase modifying *he*]
>
> M
> He needed a way **to make money.** [infinitive phrase modifying *way*]
>
> M
> People **who live in glass houses** shouldn't throw stones. [subordinate clause modifying *People*]

See 2, Subordinate Clauses, and 3, Verbals.

Exercise **1.E**

Identify the underlined modifying words as adjective (ADJ), adverb (ADV), modifier (M—noun used attributively), prepositional phrase (PREP PH), verbal phrase (V PH), or subordinate clause (SUB CL). Use an arrow to indicate the words being modified.

Example   The sturdy van plowed through the snow relentlessly.

1. Ring Lardner wrote <u>tough</u> tales about <u>ordinary</u> people.
2. Blue <u>spruce</u> trees <u>are not cultivated</u> in <u>the South</u> <u>successfully.</u>
3. <u>Certainly,</u> we could use another <u>parking</u> lot.
4. <u>In a single bound,</u> Superman could leap <u>tall</u> buildings.
5. <u>Thick and gooey,</u> <u>Chicago-style</u> pizza has grown <u>very</u> popular these days.
6. Cyrus McCormick invented a device <u>to harvest crops</u> <u>mechanically.</u>
7. The <u>quickest</u> way <u>to find friends</u> is to win the state lottery.
8. <u>In the early nineteenth century,</u> <u>swift,</u> <u>narrow</u> frigates were <u>widely</u> employed by the navies <u>of Europe and America.</u>
9. <u>Excusing his tardiness,</u> the speaker stood at the podium <u>sheepishly.</u>

10. Japanese *kamikaze* pilots of World War II took their name from the "divine wind" that destroyed the fleet Kublai Khan had sent to invade Japan in 1281. ∎

Appositives

An appositive (A) is a noun or noun equivalent placed beside another noun to supplement or complement its meaning. It has the same grammatical function as the noun to which it relates. An appositive in mid-sentence is usually preceded and followed by a comma; an appositive at the end of a sentence is preceded by a comma:

* *1.2*

Gram

A
Your lawyer, **Mr. Jenkins,** is on the telephone.

A
The story takes place in Thebes, **a city in ancient Greece.**

See 11.4, Appositives.

Exercise 1.F

Add appositives at the points indicated by the brackets in the sentences below to modify the italicized nouns.

Example   *Smith* [1] tackled *Jones* [2].

            Smith, the immense lineman, tackled Jones, the quarterback.

1. The *car* [1] rolled driverless toward the wharf.
2. *Montreal* [1] hosted the Olympic games in 1976.
3. The meeting would be in *San Juan* [1].
4. *Alexis* [1] encountered *Krystal* [2] in the lobby.
5. *Orville Wright* [1] was born in Ohio, as were *John Glenn* [2] and *Neil Armstrong* [3]. ∎

Modifiers of Modifiers

Words, phrases, and clauses that modify the main sentence elements may themselves be modified. These expressions are called *modifiers of modifiers* (MM):

      MM   M   S   V   M   M
The **local** high-school orchestra played several difficult
      O   MM M
selections **very** well.

Exercise   1.G

Use modifiers to expand the following sentences to at least twelve words each.

Example   The orchestra played.

> *The orchestra on the Titanic played serenely as the stricken vessel slid into the icy waters of the North Atlantic.*

1. Dogs bark.
2. This typewriter works well.
3. The car runs.
4. The house is old.
5. The people elected a new mayor.
6. The windows trembled.
7. The gears were stripped.
8. The guillotine broke.
9. Senior citizens demand power.
10. Economies stagnate.

1.3   Phrases and Clauses

English sentences are constructed of single words, phrases, and clauses. Main (or independent) clauses form the principal grammatical units of sentences; they express completed statements and can stand alone. Phrases and subordinate clauses, on the other hand, are dependent on other sentence elements.

Phrases

Phrases are groups of related words connected to a sentence or to one of the elements in it by means of a preposition or a verbal. A phrase has no subject or predicate and cannot stand alone.

Prepositional Phrases. A prepositional phrase consists of a preposition (*at, from, by, in, of, under,* and so on) followed by a noun or noun equivalent, plus whatever modifiers it may have. It functions like an adjective or adverb, depending on what element it modifies:

> He came **from a small town** [modifies the verb *came*] **in northeastern Minnesota** [modifies the noun *town*].

Verbal Phrases. A verbal phrase consists of a participle, gerund, or infinitive (none of which has full verb function) plus its object or complement and modifiers. A participial phrase functions as an adjective; a gerund phrase as a noun; and an infinitive phrase as either a noun, an adjective, or an adverb. (See 3, Verbals.)

> Sentences **containing several unrelated ideas** [participle phrase modifying *Sentences*] are seldom effective.
>
> **Containing the enemy** [gerund phrase used as subject] was their first objective.
>
> The easiest way **to correct a problem** [infinitive phrase modifying *way*] is **to fix it yourself** [infinitive phrase used as a complement].

Clauses

Main Clauses. A main (or independent) clause contains a subject and predicate and is the grammatical core of a sentence. In the three sentences below, the main clauses are in boldface. Each is a complete expression and could stand alone as a sentence. The third example is a compound sentence with two main clauses:

> _S _V
> **I laughed** because I couldn't help myself.
>
> _S _V _O
> If I were you, **I would find a new job.**
>
> _S _V _O _S _V _O
> **She hated English,** but **she needed one more course to graduate.**

Subordinate Clauses. A subordinate (or dependent) clause also has a subject and a predicate, but it functions as *part* of a sentence. It is related to the main clause by a connecting word that shows its subordinate relationship, either a relative pronoun (*who, which, that*) or a subordinating conjunction (*because, although, since, after, if, when,* and so on):

> I laughed **because I couldn't help myself.**
> **Since it was late,** I left.
> The engineer **who created that circuit** earned a promotion.

MODIFIERS

■ **Modifiers of the Subject**

A word: The ^M*local* ^Sorchestra played a selection.

A phrase: The ^Sorchestra, consisting ^M*largely* of amateurs, played a selection.

A clause: The ^Sorchestra, *which had ^Mpracticed hard for several weeks*, played a selection.

■ **Modifiers of the Verb**

A word: The orchestra ^Vplayed the selection ^M*badly*.

A phrase: The orchestra ^Vplayed the selection ^M*with more enthusiasm than technique*.

A clause: The orchestra ^Vplayed the selection *as if ^Mthey had never rehearsed together before*.

■ **Modifiers of the Object**

A word: The orchestra played a ^M*difficult* ^Oselection.

A phrase: The orchestra played a ^Oselection *of old ^Mfolk tunes*.

A clause: The orchestra played a ^Oselection *which no ^Mone in the audience had ever heard before*.

■ **Modifiers of the Main Clause**

A word: ^M*Nevertheless*, the orchestra played the selection.

A phrase: *Considering their ^Mlack of experience*, the orchestra played the selection fairly well.

A clause: *Since there were ^Mno other requests*, the orchestra played the selection.

Subordinate clauses are used like nouns (as subjects, objects, or complements), like adjectives (modifying nouns or pronouns), or like adverbs (expressing relationships of time, cause, result, degree, contrast, and so forth). The subordinate clauses are emphasized in the following examples:

He confessed **that he liked quiche.** [noun clause, object of *confessed*]

Many of the criminals **whose cases crowded the docket each year** were third- or fourth-time offenders. [adjective clause modifying *criminals*]

After you have filed the new document, you should make a copy of the diskette. [adverb clause of time]

The athlete injured her knee **because she had not warmed up sufficiently.** [adverb clause of cause]

See 2, Subordinate Clauses and Connectives.

Exercise 1.H

Start with this sentence: *She walked.*

1. Add a *phrase* that tells where she walked.
2. Add a *phrase* that tells how she walked.
3. Add a *phrase* that tells when she walked.
4. Add a *phrase* that tells where she walked and a *clause* that tells why she walked there.
5. Add a *clause* that tells when she walked, a *phrase* that tells where she walked, and a *clause* that tells to what place she walked. ∎

Exercise 1.I

Start with this sentence: *The customers complained.*

1. Add a *clause* that explains why they complained.
2. Add a *phrase* that explains where the customers are.
3. Add a *phrase* that explains to whom they complained.
4. Add a *phrase* that describes the customers and a *clause* that explains when it was they were complaining.
5. Add a *phrase* that explains who the customers are and a *phrase* that explains how they went about complaining.

6.   Try combining the *phrases* and *clauses* from several of your versions into one long sentence.   ■

1.4   Sentences Classified by Clause Structure

Sentences may be classified according to the kind and number of clauses they contain as *simple, compound, complex,* or *compound-complex.*

Simple Sentences

A simple sentence contains one independent clause and no subordinate (dependent) clauses:

> The man went across the street.
>
> Something is wrong.
>
> Who wrote the letter?

Although simple sentences contain only one clause, they need not be limited to a small, simple idea. They may contain any number of modifiers, and either the subject or the predicate (or both) may be compound:

> To write a complete book on aerospace engineering requires a thorough knowledge of the field.
>
> For the first time in four billion years a living creature had contemplated himself and heard with a sudden, unaccountable loneliness the whisper of the wind in the night reeds. [compound predicate]—Loren Eiseley, *The Immense Journey*
>
> Journalism professors, books, editors and reporters often explain news in terms of characteristics or values. [compound subject]—Ivan and Carol Doig, *News: A Consumer's Guide*
>
> Colleges and universities do not exist to impose duties but to reveal choices. [compound subject, compound object]—Archibald MacLeish, "Why Do We Teach Poetry," *The Atlantic Monthly*

Compound Sentences

Compound sentences contain two or more main clauses and no subordinate clauses:

The phone rang [first main clause], and she answered it.

The nations of Asia and Africa are moving with jet-like speed toward gaining political independence [first main clause], but we still creep at horse-and-buggy pace toward gaining a cup of coffee at a lunch counter.—Martin Luther King, Jr., "Letter from Birmingham Jail"

Each clause in a compound sentence is independent and is *coordinate* (of equal rank) with the other clauses. The clauses may be joined (or separated) in one of three ways:

1. **With Coordinating Conjunctions.** Independent clauses are most frequently linked by the coordinating conjunctions *and, but, or, nor, for, yet* or the correlatives *either . . . or, neither . . . nor, both . . . and, not only . . . but (also):*

   It rained all morning, **but** it cleared up for the picnic.

   Either you play to win **or** you don't play at all.

2. **Without Connectives.** Independent clauses not joined by coordinating conjunctions are conventionally separated by semicolons:

   I didn't study; I failed the test.

   They are generous-minded; they hate shams and enjoy being indignant about them; they are valuable social reformers; they have no notion of confining books to a library shelf.—E. M. Forster, *Aspects of the Novel*

3. **With Conjunctive Adverbs.** The clauses in a compound sentence are sometimes linked by a conjunctive adverb such as *accordingly, also, consequently, however, nevertheless, therefore, then.* Because the connective function of these adverbs is weak, a semicolon should be used before them:

   Fuel prices declined; **consequently,** they bought a larger car.

   The urban renewal program has many outspoken opponents; **nevertheless,** some land has already been cleared.

Omitting the semicolon before the conjunctive adverb, and using a comma instead, produces a comma splice—a major sentence error (see 4.2, Comma Splice):

| Comma splice | The pay was dismal, **nonetheless,** he worked hard. |
| Corrected | The pay was dismal; **nonetheless,** he worked hard. |

When you link two sentences together with a conjunctive adverb, be sure to check your punctuation. See 12.1, Semicolons.

Complex Sentences

A complex sentence consists of one main clause and one or more subordinate clauses:

> Prairies are valuable [main clause] because they are fertile and flat [subordinate clause].

> As far as I could determine [subordinate clause], Paris hadn't changed at all [main clause] since I last visited it ten years before [second subordinate clause].

In published writing today, complex sentences appear far more often than the other types do. They offer more variety than simple sentences, and express relationships between ideas more precisely than compound sentences usually can.

Compound-Complex Sentences

A compound-complex sentence contains two or more main clauses and one or more subordinate clauses:

> When two men fight a duel [first subordinate clause], the matter is trivial [first main clause], but when 200 million people fight 200 million people [second subordinate clause], the matter is serious [second main clause].—Bertrand Russell, *The Impact of Science on Society*

Compound-complex sentences occur far less frequently than the other types do.

Exercise   1.J

Combine the short sentences in each group below into a single sentence by reducing some to phrases or subordinate clauses. Arrange the parts as necessary to create sentences.

1.   He left before sunrise.
     He reached his old country home by noon.
     He had time to look around a while.
     He went on to his aunt's house.

2.   The ball took a bad bounce.
     It hit the second base player in the eye.
     She picked it up anyway.
     She threw it to first base.
     The runner was out.
     The second base player fell to her knees.

3.   The wind died.
     It was sunset.
     The night was clear.
     There were stars.
     It was still.
     The crackling of the fire was the only sound.

4.   She opened the door of the woodstove.
     She put another log inside.
     The cat was lying in front of the woodstove.
     An ember fell out onto the cat.
     The cat kept sleeping.

5.   The truck hit a patch of ice.
     The truck slid into the ditch.
     The driver radioed for help.
     A landscaper received the signal.
     He relayed the information to the police.   ■

Exercise   **1.K**

Write one sentence on each model shown below. An example of each is given.

1.   compound: main clause + conjunction + main clause
     He read the calculus problem, but he didn't understand it.
2.   complex: subordinate clause + main clause
     When she had completed the design, she wrote up the estimate for the entire project.
3.   compound-complex: subordinate clause + main clause + conjunction + main clause
     After he subscribed to the service, he regretted his haste, but then it was too late.

4. complex: main clause + subordinate clause
   Tracy disliked the list-processing program because it was too complicated.
5. compound-complex: main clause + subordinate clause + conjunction + main clause + subordinate clause
   He went to the country whenever he could, and he was sorry that he couldn't stay longer. ∎

Exercise 1.L

Combine the following groups of short sentences into longer ones. Identify the type of sentence you have created (simple, compound, complex, compound-complex). Try to create more than one version of the combined sentences.

Example The sycamore was huge.
It was also cherished.
It had shaded the neighborhood for two generations.

The huge and cherished sycamore had shaded the neighborhood for two generations. [simple]

The huge sycamore was cherished because it had shaded the neighborhood for two generations. [complex]

1. Alfred Nobel was a chemist.
   His family manufactured armaments.
   He invented dynamite.
   He established the Nobel prizes.
   The prizes included an award for contributions toward peace.
2. The wound was infected.
   It had not been dressed properly.
   It had not been cleaned.
   The patient's finger might have to be amputated.
3. The jury was tired and angry.
   The jury came to a decision.
   It was not the verdict the judge expected.
4. First he tilled the soil.
   Then he dug the furrows.
   He planted the seeds.

He anticipated a bountiful crop.
The crows ate most of the seed.

5. The old Packard chugged and sputtered.
Steam hissed from its radiator.
Oil dripped from its undercarriage.
The driver was confident he would complete his journey.

6. An oxygen tank exploded on Apollo 13.
The explosion endangered its crew of three astronauts.
The explosion forced cancellation of its moon landing.
The spacecraft looped the moon.
It returned safely to earth.
Its safe return was a miracle of technological improvisation.

7. In the late 1970's inflation was in double digits.
Many experts predicted it would go higher.
They doubted it could ever be controlled again.
The experts were proved wrong.
The recession of the early 1980's reduced inflation significantly.

8. Lemmings are European rodents.
They resemble woodchucks.
They migrate annually.
They cross all obstacles.
They head for the sea and plunge in.
They commit mass suicide.

9. Vince Lombardi coached high school football.
He coached college ball at Fordham.
He is best known as the head coach of the Green Bay Packers.
He won five NFL championships with that team.

10. Robots are appearing on assembly lines.
They can weld.
They can assemble parts.
They can paint.
They can supervise other robots.
They are expensive to purchase.
They do not collect disability, demand overtime pay, or take vacations.   ■

1.5 Sentences Classified by Purpose

Sentences are conventionally classified by meaning or purpose as follows:

1. **Statements** (often called *declarative sentences*):

   Judy laughed.
   Most of the sentences we speak and write are declarative.

2. **Questions** (often called *interrogative sentences*):

   At what temperature does water boil?
   Why do you ask?

3. **Commands** (often called *imperative sentences;* includes requests and instructions):

   Write soon.
   When the liquid boils, remove it from the heat.

4. **Exclamations** (feelings, facts, or opinions expressed emphatically; also called *exclamatory sentences*):

   How lucky you are!
   He should be thrown out!

1.6 Unorthodox Sentences

While the great majority of written sentences contain both subjects and verbs, some do not. In speech, we may express ourselves by a single word *(Yes; Oh?)*, a phrase *(In a minute)*, or a clause *(If you say so)*. Similarly, we occasionally find single words, phrases, and subordinate clauses used as sentences in published material:

> And so on to Bangkok. Spit and hiss of water, the gramophone quiet. The lights out along the deck, nobody about.—Graham Greene, *The Shipwrecked*

We do not have to supply any "missing" words to get the author's meaning (such as "And so *the ship sailed* on to Bangkok"). Such statements are meaningful and complete as they stand. But they are minor types, exceptions to the typical English sentence pattern of subject and predicate. When they appear in print, they are used deliberately and for a special purpose—to imitate dialogue, for example, or to create emphasis, or to avoid colorless, repetitive verbs. Don't use such a construction unless it would make sense to your reader.

Subjectless Sentences

Commands and requests generally do not have expressed subjects:

> Please try. [*You* is the implied subject.]
>
> Help! [*You*—meaning "anyone"—is the implied subject.]

The subject is sometimes omitted in informal writing (seldom in serious writing) when it is easily carried over from the preceding sentence by the context:

> They took no interest in civilized ways. Hadn't heard of them, probably.—Clarence Day, *Life with Father*

Verbless Sentences

Several types of sentences without a main verb are used in all levels of speaking and writing. The verbs are not left out; they are not thought, spoken, or written. The statements are complete and independent without them.

Exclamations. *Ouch!*, *Oh!*, and similar words make complete exclamations, as do such phrases as *What luck!* and *How terrible!*

Answers to Questions. Short answers without a main verb (*Yes. No. Not if I can help it.*) are considered complete sentences. Occasionally a writer may use a verbless construction to answer a question he has raised himself:

> What is a hero? **The exceptional individual.** How is he recognized, whether in life or in books? **By the degree of interest he arouses in the spectator or the reader.**—W. H. Auden, *The Enchaféd Flood*

Exercise 1.M

Advertising makes heavy use of unorthodox sentences. Identify the unusual sentences in the following advertising copy. Then rewrite the ad, using more conventional sentence structures with fully expressed subjects and verbs. What are the differences between the two versions?

MOVE INTO MORE.

New Chevrolet Celebrity.

Four or five years ago, your smaller car seemed enough car. But now you're ready to move into more.

More room. More comfort. More engine. And more than just a little more prestige. For which we introduce our smooth, quiet, front-drive Chevrolet Celebrity.

Move into Celebrity comfort, Celebrity convenience. Comfort that begins with more passenger room than 91 out of 95 import cars. More passenger room, in fact, than Chrysler LeBaron. And more trunk space than Mercury Marquis.

More? Turn the key. Celebrity's standard electronically fuel-injected engine gives you more standard cubic inches than any front-drive Datsun, Toyota, Honda, Mazda, Ford, Mercury or Dodge.

More excitement. And front drive. Exemplified by our new Celebrity Eurosport shown here. All the virtues of Celebrity, wrapped in head-turning European styling, mounted atop a Special F41 Sport Suspension. All at a price that will make Europe's best blush with envy. And you with pride.

Isn't it time you moved into more car? Especially when it doesn't cost that much more. In fact, try to find any other front-drive car with more passenger room at a lower sticker price.

You'll see what we mean by Chevrolet—Taking Charge. ■

2

SUBORDINATE CLAUSES AND CONNECTIVES

Subordinate (or dependent) clauses, like independent clauses, have subjects and predicates. But unlike independent clauses, subordinate clauses are incomplete statements. They cannot stand alone:

Independent clause	He ran for reelection.
Dependent clause	when he ran for reelection
Independent clause	Light bends in a prism.
Dependent clause	why light bends in a prism
Independent clause	The Salmon River is in Idaho.
Dependent clause	that the Salmon River is in Idaho
Independent clause	It irritates me.
Dependent clause	what irritates me

Various connective words make subordinate clauses dependent on a main clause. In the examples above these connectives are *when, why, that,* and *what*. Such words enable subordinate clauses to operate as modifiers, subjects, objects, or complements in a sentence:

> **When he ran for reelection,** Jimmy Carter faced opposition in the primaries from Ted Kennedy. [The clause modifies the verb *faced*.]

Why light bends in a prism mystified the ten-year-olds. [Here the subordinate clause is the subject of the sentence.]

I know **that the Salmon River is in Idaho.** [The subordinate clause serves as the object of the verb *know.*]

Your insolence is **what irritates me.** [The subordinate clause is a complement in this sentence.]

Depending on the grammatical function they serve, subordinate clauses are classified as adjective clauses (2.1), adverb clauses (2.2), or noun clauses (2.3).

2.1 Adjective Clauses

A subordinate clause that modifies a noun or pronoun is an adjective clause. Adjective clauses are introduced most frequently by the relative pronouns *who, which,* and *that* (p. 170). These pronouns also serve as subjects or objects within the clause:

Some people **who buy modern paintings** are interested in them more as investments than as art. [*Who* is the subject of the clause, which modifies *people.*]

The goals **for which he had fought all his life** no longer seemed important to him. [*Which* is the object of the preposition *for;* the clause modifies *goals.*]

Many books **that are commercially successful** do not qualify as serious literature. [*That* is the subject of the clause, which modifies *books.*]

He received a letter from an uncle **whom he had not seen for twenty years.** [*Whom* is the object of the verb *had seen;* the clause modifies *uncle.*]

Adjective clauses may also be introduced by the relative adverbs *when, where,* and *why:*

It was a day **when everything went wrong.** [The clause modifies *day.*]

She returned to the town **where she had lived as a girl.** [The clause modifies *town.*]

The reason **why these early settlements disappeared** has never been explained satisfactorily. [The clause modifies *reason.*]

Clauses Without Relative Words

In some cases, you can omit the relative word in a subordinate clause:

> He is a person **[whom]** everyone trusts.

This is typically the case when an adjective clause functions
as a restrictive modifier, that is, as a modifier essential to the
meaning of a sentence (see 11.4):

> The only books **[that] Alice read in high school** were those
> **[that] her teacher assigned.**
>
> The patients **[whom] Dr. Jordan treated** survived.

Exercise   **2.A**

Combine the following short sentences to create longer ones
containing at least one adjective clause. Underline the relative
word or place in brackets [ ] a relative word you might omit.

Examples   Mr. Pearson lived in a Victorian house.
He had built it on a beach.

Mr. Pearson lived in a Victorian house
[which] he had built on a beach.

I entered the hangar.
Everyone in it was working.

I entered the hangar <u>where</u> everyone was working.

1. There are engineers.
    They design nuclear power plants.
    They believe such power plants are safe.

2. I spoke the language.
    No one else spoke it.

3. Her great cause was woman suffrage.
    She gave her life for it.

4. His automobile failed inspection.
    The reason was not clear to him.

5. The legislator returned to the chamber.
    She had won her greatest triumph there.

6. Some students seem unable to spell.
    They are dyslexic.

7. Children should not eat some cereals.
   These cereals have a high sugar content.

8. It was a rare performance.
   Everything went right.

9. The library card catalogue is outdated.
   It is clumsy and expensive to maintain.

10. Cable television is threatening the major networks.
    The major networks previously had no serious competition. ■

Incorrect Use of *and which, and who*

And is sometimes needlessly used between an adjective clause and the rest of a sentence. The relative pronoun *who, which,* or *that* is the only connective needed; the use of *and* or *but* is superfluous and defeats the subordination:

Careless	The sea anemone is a fascinating creature **and which** looks more like a plant than an animal.
Revised	The sea anemone is a fascinating creature which looks more like a plant than an animal.

The only correct use of *and which* or *and who* is in a compound parallel structure:

The sea anemone is a fascinating creature which looks more like a plant than an animal **and which** eats algae.

2.2 Adverb Clauses

A subordinate clause that modifies a verb, adjective, adverb, or main clause is an adverb clause. It expresses a relationship of time, place, direction, cause, effect, condition, manner, or concession, answering questions such as *when, where, why,* and *how:*

He lived abroad for three years but returned to the United States **when war broke out.** [The clause modifies the verb *returned.*]

During her husband's absence she managed the business better **than he had.** [The clause modifies the adverb *better.*]

He becomes very stubborn **when he meets opposition.** [The clause modifies the predicate adjective *stubborn.*]

Because she was a woman of principle, even her opponents respected her. [The clause modifies the main statement *even her opponents respected her.*]

English has many subordinating conjunctions for expressing
these adverb relationships. The following are among the most
common:

after	even though	since	when
although	except that	so	whenever
as	if	so that	where
as if	if only	than	whereas
as long as	in case	that	wherever
as though	in order that	though	while
because	now that	till	
before	once	unless	
even if	provided that	until	

Exercise **2.B**

Combine the following short sentences to create longer ones
containing at least one adverb clause.

Example Terry Fox ran a Marathon of Hope across Canada.
He succumbed to cancer.

*Before he succumbed to cancer, Terry Fox ran a Mar-
athon of Hope across Canada.*

1. We took a shortcut.
    We got lost.
2. Lon stirred the gravy.
    The lumps finally disappeared.
3. Bring me that lantern.
    I can read in the tent.
4. We trust you.
    We cannot leave the money here with you.
5. The tough anticrime legislation was in force.
    Violent crime continued to rise.
6. You must write eight essays and a research paper.
    You will pass the course.

7. He doesn't tolerate insubordination.
    He was dismissed from his administrative position.

8. The ceiling on the national debt was reached.
    Congress voted to raise the limit.
    It had done so in the past many times.

9. The sergeant-at-arms begged the delegates to clear the aisles.
    An elderly man needed medical attention.
    The delegates did not move.

10. Cars were a new-fangled invention.
    The World Wars had not yet been fought.
    The year was 1910.
    Halley's Comet made its first appearance of the twentieth century.   ■

2.3 Noun Clauses

Subordinate clauses used as subjects, objects, complements, and appositives are called noun clauses because they function as nouns. Most noun clauses are introduced by *that*. But *whatever, whoever, who, what, why, when, where,* and *whether* are also used to introduce noun clauses.

As Objects

Noun clauses are most frequently used as direct objects:

> The President said **that his meeting with the Pope had been fruitful.**

> No one knows **why the settlement at Roanoke disappeared.**

> They wondered **what would happen next.**

Noun clauses also serve as objects of prepositions:

> From **what you have told me,** I think the plan will succeed.

> There is a prize for **whoever gets there first.** [*Whoever* (rather than *whomever*) is the correct form in this sentence because the pronoun is the subject of the clause.]

As Appositives

Noun clauses are quite often used as appositives. Such clauses supplement or complement a noun:

> Most people still accept the myth **that progress is inevitable.**
> N AP

> The possibility **that she might lose** never occurred to her.
> N AP

Clauses of this kind are not set off with commas or other punctuation.

As Subjects

Noun clauses may function as subjects:

> **Whatever is worth doing at all** is worth doing well.
> S V

> **Whether D. B. Cooper survived** is a matter of conjecture.
> S V

Sometimes, however, sentences beginning with a subject clause introduced by *that* or *whether* seem rather stilted. This is especially true if the subject clause is long:

Stilted   **That he could raise his grade by studying harder** had never occurred to him.

Stilted   **Whether we should revise our foreign policy** was the principal topic of discussion.

Such sentences can usually be improved by moving the noun clause to a position after the verb:

Revised   It had never occurred to him **that he could raise his grade by studying harder.**

Revised   The principal topic of discussion was **whether we should revise our foreign policy.**

Exercise 2.C

Improve these sentences by revising noun clauses that seem stilted. Some passages may not need revision.

1. Whether I am right about the need to stop funding the sewage treatment plant in the southern suburbs is not the concern of this forum.

2.3
Sub

2.3
Sub

2. That the sun stood at the center of the universe and that the planets, including Earth, revolved around it was Copernicus' theory of planetary motion.

3. That which we call a rose by any other word would smell as sweet.

4. That the people shall be secure in their persons, houses, papers, and effects from unreasonable searches and seizures is guaranteed by the Fourth Amendment.

5. Whether you stay or not makes no difference to me. ■

As Complements

Noun clauses sometimes occur as complements, particularly in definitions and explanations. Such constructions are sometimes awkward, however, and it is often better to substitute a different wording:

Awkward	Usually the winner is **whoever has the most endurance.**
Better	The person with the most endurance usually wins.
	Whoever has the most endurance usually wins.
Awkward	Our materialism is **why some Europeans criticize us.**
Better	Some Europeans criticize us for our materialism.

One clumsy noun clause construction you should avoid is "The reason is because . . . ." The word *because* means "the reason that." Thus, when you write "The reason is because," in effect you are saying "The reason is the reason that." The preferred connective after "The reason is [*or* was]" in formal and general writing is *that*. The *best* connective may be *because*:

Awkward	**The reason** he lost the election **was because** he lacked the support of labor.
Revised	The reason he lost the election was **that** he lacked the support of labor.
	He lost the election **because** he lacked the support of labor.

Exercises **2.D**

Combine the following pairs of sentences by making one of the sentences into a subordinate clause.

Example   The golden, or Syrian, hamster is a rodent.
             It is virtually unknown in the wild.

             The golden, or Syrian, hamster is a rodent which is
             virtually unknown in the wild.

1.   He was a courageous executive.
     He was feared and admired.
2.   The rain has fallen for two days.
     It has washed the bridge away.
3.   Those delegates are not here yet.
     They attended a seminar on regional economics last
     night.
4.   He was fourteen years old.
     He began to shave.
5.   Enormous pressure had built up under the lava dome.
     It is the reason for the eruption.
6.   They parachuted from the plane.
     We do not know where.
7.   Those are the only bills that the President would sign.
     They are the ones that cut spending.
8.   She is a skilled negotiator.
     Everyone respects her.
9.   You have explained the rules to me.
     I think I can play now.
10. The danger never threatened the town before.
     It was the danger that the river would crest at thirty feet
     above flood stage.   ■

Exercise 2.E

Combine each group of sentences below into a single sentence with one main or independent clause and at least one
subordinate clause.

1.   Fort Phantom Hill is in ruins.
     It is twelve miles northeast of Abilene.
     I had never seen it before.
     I had erected the fort many times in my mind.
2.   Construction of the fort was authorized in November
     1851.
     Major General Smith gave the order.
     He commanded the 8th Military Department.
     The 8th Military Department included Texas.

3. Major General Smith wanted a fort.
   He wanted it to be on the Clear Fork of the Brazos River.
   It would protect settlers in the upper Brazos.

4. He had seen reports on the site.
   The reports were favorable.
   The site was "alive with deer, turkey, and bear."

5. The troopers arrived on the site.
   There was no timber for construction.
   Water had to be hauled from four miles away.

6. The fort took its name from a nervous sentry.
   He was on night duty.
   It was just after they had camped.

7. He fired at something.
   He testified later.
   It was "an Indian on the hill."

8. They could not find the marauder.
   It was a phantom on the hill.
   They called it Fort Phantom Hill.

9. The Olympics are burdened.
   They are burdened by political and military interests.
   These interests have haunted the games for years.

10. Individual countries use the Olympics.
    These countries may stage the games.
    These countries may participate in them.
    They use the Olympics to showcase their political doctrine.

11. Hitler attempted to use the 1936 Olympics.
    The 1936 games were held in Berlin.
    The games were to be used as a display of Nazi and Aryan superiority.

12. He might have succeeded.
    He was thwarted by Jesse Owens.
    Jesse Owens was a high school track star from Cleveland.
    Jesse Owens was black.
    Jesse Owens won four gold medals.

13. In 1972, terrorists raided the Olympics.
    These Olympics were held in Munich, Germany.
    The terrorists murdered Israeli athletes.
    The terrorists threatened the continuity of the games. ■

SUBORDINATE CONNECTIVES

■ Subordinate Clauses

1. May serve as adjective clauses, commonly introduced by:

   who   when
   which   where
   that   why

2. May serve as adverb clauses, often introduced by (among many others):

   after   so
   although   until
   as   when
   because   where
   if   wherever
   since   while

3. May serve as noun clauses, usually introduced by *that*, but also introduced by:

   whatever   why
   whoever   when
   who   where
   what   whether

3

VERBALS

Verbals are forms of verbs that act as nouns, adjectives, or adverbs. They are classified as:

1. **infinitives** *(to ask, to buy)*, which can serve either as nouns or as modifiers;

2. **participles** *(asking, asked, buying, bought)*, which modify nouns and pronouns; and

3. **gerunds** *(asking, buying)*, which are verbal nouns.

Although the present participle and gerund are identical in form, they differ in the way they are used in sentences:

Participle	a **dancing** figure [modifier]
Gerund	**dancing** takes skill [noun]

Verbals cannot serve as predicates to make full sentences; consequently, they are described as *nonfinite* (or "unfinished") verbs. *Finite* verbs are needed for full sentences:

Verbals	the man **watching** [participle]
(nonfinite forms)	**making** love, not war [gerund]
	to drive skillfully [infinitive]
Verbs	The man **watches.**
(finite forms)	**Make** love, not war.
	I **drive** skillfully.

3.1 Using Verbal Phrases

Verbals do have many of the qualities of verbs: aided by auxiliary verbs, they can show tense, for example, and they can
take objects. In many sentences, however, verbal phrases
function much like subordinate clauses in showing the relationship between main and subordinate ideas:

> **When she graduated from college,** she went to New York
> in search of a job. [subordinate clause]
>
> **Having graduated from college,** she went to New York in
> search of a job. [verbal phrase, modifying _she_]

The forms and principal uses of verbals are illustrated in the
table on page 76. See also 6, Verbs.

Subjects with Infinitives

An infinitive phrase often has an expressed subject:

> He wanted **the whole department** [subject of the infinitive]
> **to be reorganized.**

If the subject of an infinitive is a pronoun, it is in the object
form:

> They asked **her** [subject of the infinitive] **to run for senator.**
>
> Their mother told **them** [subject of the infinitive] **to behave.**

Subjects with Gerunds

When a noun or a pronoun precedes a gerund, serving as its
"subject" (the accountant _calculating,_ the tenor _singing_), some
questions of usage arise. Sometimes the possessive form of
the noun is used, sometimes the common form:

> the **accountant's** calculating [possessive form]
> the **accountant** calculating [common form]
>
> the **tenor's** singing [possessive form]
> the **tenor** singing [common form]

In choosing the right form, you must often depend on
what sounds natural. In formal situations, the possessive
form is preferred:

> The **tenor's** singing was the breathtaking climax of an as-
> tounding evening of music.

In less formal writing, the common form is used most often:

> The **tenor** singing drowned out the baby's cries.

A major exception to using the common form occurs when the subject of a gerund is a personal pronoun or a proper noun. In this case, the possessive form is generally used:

> The less said about **his** singing, the better. [rather than *him*]
>
> They insisted on **Bob's** playing the piano. [rather than *Bob*]

When the subject is modified by other words, the common form is used:

> There was something suspicious about **Celia,** the daughter of the sponsor, winning the $10,000 prize. [not *Celia's*]
>
> At the outbreak of the Civil War, no one in Washington foresaw the possibility of **Grant,** who had failed in so many undertakings, leading the Union forces. [not *Grant's*]

When the subject is a plural (or collective) noun, the common form is usually preferred:

> The manager disapproves of **people** smoking in meetings. [rather than *people's*]
>
> The staff will not tolerate **visitors** coming and going at will. [rather than *visitors'*]

If the subject is abstract, the common form is used:

> It was a case of **panic** getting the upper hand. [rather than *panic's*]
>
> There is a danger of the **temperature** dropping suddenly. [rather than *temperature's*]

When the subject is stressed, the common form is usually preferred with nouns and the object form with pronouns:

> Did you hear about the **mayor** being arrested for speeding? [rather than *mayor's*]
>
> I can't imagine **him** winning an award. [rather than *his*]

With other nouns forms, usage is divided. If you are writing a formal paper, it is usually best to use the possessive form, but the common form of the noun is widely used in general English:

Formal	The neighbors complained about the **dog's** barking at night.
General	The neighbors complained about the **dog** barking at night.
Formal	Dr. Jones worried about her **secretary's** taking another job.
General	Dr. Jones worried about her **secretary** taking another job.

Exercise   **3.A**

Create sentences that include the terms below. The noun or pronoun (the first term) should be the subject of the gerund (the second term).

Example   Ricardo/strumming on his old guitar

   The dog howled at the sound of **Ricardo's strumming on his old guitar.**

1. the cousin of the senator/getting the contract for the bridge
2. orchestra/talking during rehearsal
3. pronoun referring to Amelia/giving up
4. fear/overcoming his sense of responsibility
5. baseball fans/rioting in the stands
6. Nixon/visiting the People's Republic of China
7. anger/overwhelming the minister
8. Paul Newman, the perennial favorite/never winning an Oscar
9. the Chief Justice of the Supreme Court/writing a dissenting opinion
10. the semiconductor firm/offering a new product   ■

Exercise   **3.B**

Identify the underlined verbals as infinitives, participles, or gerunds. (See the chart on page 76 for a review of verbal forms.)

1. <u>Taking</u> charge is a new experience for her.
2. Carol especially enjoyed <u>sprinting</u>.
3. To be frank, <u>speaking</u> terrifies me.
4. The contestant <u>coming</u> closest to the actual price without <u>going</u> over wins.

5. The bonds were removed from a sealed envelope.
6. Duplicating copies of my sources prevented a charge of plagiarism.
7. After a while, her constant comings and goings began to wear our patience thin.
8. To be or not to be is the famous question posed by Hamlet.
9. The NASA crews worked to recover the jettisoned fuel tanks from the shuttle launch vehicle.
10. Having been nominated for the award was reward enough, the actor insisted, wiping away tears of joy, but winning was not to be imagined. ■

3.2   Idiomatic Use of Infinitives and Gerunds

Sometimes we say things in a particular way not because it is grammatically proper, but simply because it is customary or *idiomatic.* When we say that we *put up with* something, the expression makes little sense grammatically, but we know that it means "tolerate" because it is a familiar *idiom.*

Some expressions are regularly completed by infinitives (privileged *to attend*), others by gerunds (the privilege *of attending*). When one form is substituted for the other, the result is an unidiomatic construction: for example, "eager *to join*" is a standard idiom, but "eager *of joining*" is not. Here are typical expressions, some that call for a gerund, others for an infinitive. You will find others in your dictionary under the key (main) word in each construction.

Gerund	*Infinitive*
cannot help doing	compelled to do
capable of working	able to work
skilled in writing	the desire to write
the habit of giving	the tendency to give
successful in getting	manage to get
ignore saying	neglect to say
my object in paying	my obligation to pay
satisfaction of doing	satisfying to do

With many words, especially common ones, either a gerund or an infinitive may be idiomatic: a way *of doing* it, a way *to do* it.

Exercise 3.C

Insert idiomatic prepositions between the pairs of words below and, when necessary, complete the verbal. Then incorporate the resulting expression into a complete sentence.

Example   incapable _____ drive

incapable _of_ driving

Your great aunt is incapable of driving.

1. compel _____ flee
2. averse _____ speak
3. refrain _____ applaud
4. threaten _____ prosecute
5. insist _____ stay
6. succeed _____ build
7. capable _____ understand
8. prior _____ leave
9. agree _____ sign
10. object _____ stay

Gerund Phrases Using *the* and *of*

Gerunds are less wordy when they are not preceded by *the*
and followed by *of*. Both words can often be cut:

Wordy	By **the** singing **of** the national anthem, citi-zens acknowledge their love of home and country.
Revised	By singing the national anthem, citizens ac-knowledge their love of home and country.
Wordy	In **the** revising **of** the first draft, writers should check their spelling.
Revised	In revising the first draft, writers should check their spelling.

The and *of* are appropriate, however, in some formal expressions:

> **the** changing **of** the guard
> **the** making **of** the president
> **the** parting **of** the waters

Split Infinitives

Most infinitive constructions are introduced by *to*:

She needed time **to think.**

They hoped **to get** home before dark.

His efforts **to be promoted** failed.

If an adverb comes between *to* and an *infinitive,* the phrase is called a *split infinitive:*

to go	to **boldly** go
to see	to **ever** see

Avoid awkward split infinitives or those that call undue attention to themselves:

Awkward   I will not describe the circumstances of our meeting, or even attempt **to** physically **describe** her.

Better   I will not describe the circumstances of our meeting, or even attempt **to describe** her physically.

Some readers categorically object to split infinitives, but constructions of this sort are not always awkward. When the normal position of the adverb is after the word *to,* a split infinitive is standard usage:

The receptionist asked them **to please sit** down.

Moreover, in some statements, putting the adverb modifier immediately before or after the infinitive would be unnatural or misleading:

Unnatural   Autumn is the time **really to see** Europe.

Better   Autumn is the time **to really see** Europe.

Unnatural   **Fully to appreciate** a Porsche, you have **actually to drive** one.

Better   **To fully appreciate** a Porsche, you have **to actually drive** one.

Whether to retain a split infinitive in a sentence is often a judgment call.

Exercise   **3.D**

Revise the following sentences to eliminate unnecessary words or awkward expressions. Not all sentences will require changes.

1. Fully to understand calculus is to know the foundations of physics.
2. The audience protested the violent film by the leaving of their seats.
3. We expected the situation to not change much.
4. The middle of the service will include the laying on of hands.
5. A substantial increase in product quality will be required to successfully turn the company around.
6. The teaching of foreign languages in all high schools should be required.
7. You must have a frosted mug to savor beer truly.
8. A huge iceberg was responsible for the sinking of the *Titanic.*
9. The mission of the Starship *Enterprise* was to boldly go where no man had gone before.
10. To ruthlessly charge that the tax assessor solicited bribes is to more than endanger your position as county prosecutor; you are exposing yourself to grand jury indictment. ■

3.3 Misplaced Modifiers

Mod **Revise the sentence so that the modifier is clearly related to the word or statement it modifies.**

Like other modifiers, verbal modifiers should be clearly related to the words they modify. Verbals, either as single words or in phrases, most often modify individual words:

> I first noticed <u>him</u> **sitting alone in a corner.** [present participle, modifying <u>him</u>]

> He still had three <u>years</u> **to serve in the U.S. Senate** before he would face reelection. [infinitive, modifying <u>years</u>]

When a verbal construction seems to refer to a word it cannot sensibly modify, it is said to be *misplaced* or *misrelated.*

Misplaced	**Grazing peacefully like cattle,** we saw a herd of buffalo. [The phrase seems to refer to *we.*]
Revised	We saw a herd of cattle **grazing peacefully like buffalo.** [The phrase now clearly refers to *buffalo.*]

Misplaced	**Caught wearing nothing but a raincoat,** the police arrested the flasher. [The phrase seems to modify *police*.]
Revised	The police arrested the flasher caught wearing nothing but a raincoat. [The phrase now clearly modifies *flasher*.]

Because misplaced modifiers may be momentarily confusing (or unintentionally humorous), you should avoid them. Sometimes you can correct a misplaced modifier simply by putting it immediately before or after the word it is intended to modify, as in the examples above. But often it is better to rewrite the entire sentence:

Misplaced	One frontier-days senator is said to have passed out campaign cards to the voters **pinned together with five-dollar bills.** [The participle phrase seems to refer to *voters*.]
Revised	One frontier-days senator is said to have pinned five-dollar bills to the campaign cards he passed out to voters.
Misplaced	**Our hands locked and staring into each other's eyes,** we would talk about love.
Revised	Our hands locked, we stared into each other's eyes and talked about love.

Occasionally verbals or other kinds of modifiers are so placed that they can refer to either of two elements in a sentence. These confusing constructions are called *squinting modifiers*:

Squinting	The woman standing in the doorway **to attract attention** dropped her purse. [Did she attract attention by standing in the doorway or by dropping her purse?]
Squinting	She knew **intuitively** he would find a solution. [Does the adverb **intuitively** explain how she knew or how he would find a solution?]

You can solve such problems by:

1. moving the modifier to a less confusing position;
2. revising the sentence to clarify the modification.

Revised	The woman standing in the doorway dropped her purse **to attract attention.**
	or

The woman, who was standing in the door-way **to attraction attention,** dropped her purse.

Revised   She **intuitively** knew he would find a solution.

or

She knew he would use his **intuition** to find a solution.

Other types of misplaced or misrelated modifiers are discussed in 9.5, Position of Adverbs.

Exercise 3.E

Correct any misplaced or squinting modifiers in the following sentences. You may need to move words or phrases, or completely revise the passage.

1. Stranded on an island, native plants and animals provided Crusoe with food, shelter, and clothing.

2. Calling out in a single voice, the football team was cheered on by the spectators.

3. Weighing less than steel, engineers have turned to aluminum seeking greater fuel efficiency in cars and trucks.

4. Often avoiding me now, my political arguments have alienated many of my friends.

5. The student who was writing his autobiography to relax built houses.

6. She felt like a hunted animal pursued through life by a criminal record.

7. Costing less, the administration purchased manual rather than electric typewriters.

8. Playing your tuba terribly angers her.

9. Believing that he could create a more elegant unified field theory, quantum theory did not satisfy the restless mind of Albert Einstein.

10. Even when wrapped securely around the attendant's arm, the spectators would not approach the boa constrictor, laughing squeamishly.

3.4 Dangling Modifiers

DM   **Revise the sentence to include the word the dangling modifier actually refers to.**

3.4

DM   Dangling modifiers are verbals, prepositional phrases, or other constructions that try to modify a word or phrase that is not actually in a sentence:

Dangling	**Having moved away at fifteen,** his hometown no longer seemed familiar. [The main clause contains no word that could have *moved away at fifteen*. The word must be supplied in a revised version.]
Revised	**Having moved away at fifteen,** Joseph found his hometown unfamiliar. [Now the participle clearly modifies *Joseph*.]
Dangling	The dogs need to be fed **after washing your hands.** [Are the dogs going to wash your hands? The sentence needs to be revised to include the person who will wash his hands.]
Revised	**After you wash your hands,** feed the dogs. [The subordinate clause *after you wash your hands* solves the difficulty.]
Dangling	**Behind the curtain,** Hamlet's sword was fatal. [The sentence is vague because the prepositional phrase *behind the curtain* doesn't seem to modify *sword*.]
Revised	Hamlet's sword was fatal to Polonius **standing behind the curtain.** [Now we know who is behind the curtain. This version is much clearer.]

Dangling modifiers often occur when passive verbs are used:

Dangling	**In painting four of these pictures,** his wife was used as his model.
Revised	**In painting four of these pictures,** he used his wife as his model.
Dangling	**To find the needed information,** the whole book had to be read.
Revised	**To find the needed information,** I had to read the whole book.

As the examples above demonstrate, dangling modifiers can usually be corrected:

1. by naming the agent or "doer" of the action immediately after the modifying phrase;

2. by revising the sentence entirely to make the relationships between sentence elements clearer.

Dangling	**Having been delayed by a train accident,** the leading role was played by a local actress.
Revised by naming agent	**Having been delayed by a train accident, the leading lady** was replaced in her role by a local actress.
Revised by recasting the sentence	**Because the leading lady was delayed by a train accident,** her role was taken by a local actress.

Exercise 3.F

Correct any dangling modifiers in the following sentences. You may have to identify and name the "doer" of the action in some cases. In others you may want to revise the entire sentence.

1. Speaking for this company, our safety record is excellent.
2. It is evident that, before consulting the Department of Commerce, the contract should be cleared by our lawyers.
3. The surgery began, having anesthetized the accident victim.
4. Considered among the greatest of American novelists, we enjoyed reading F. Scott Fitzgerald's *The Great Gatsby*.
5. In buying a piece of real estate, delays in title transfers can occur.
6. To be satisfied with your new video recorder, instructions are to be followed carefully.
7. Helping her unload the van, the traffic grew snarled and congested.
8. After reading the letter, the secretary's fingers pounded out a snarling reply.

9.   Thought to be among the favorites in this year's competition, delays wilted Jane's confidence.
10. Called the "Father of Waters," we admired its muddy power.   ∎

3.5   Absolute Modifiers

A writer should distinguish clearly between verbal modifiers that obviously dangle, such as those cited above, and *absolute modifiers*—participle or infinitive phrases that modify the statement as a whole and thus do not need a specific reference word in the main clause. As the word *absolute* suggests, these modifiers are complete and independent; their form does not depend on anything else in the sentence.

A number of absolute constructions are common expressions:

Everything considered, this plan seems best.

To make a long story short, we bought the house.

Considering the cost of labor, the price is reasonable.

Absolute modifiers usually can (but need not) be converted easily into subordinate clauses:

When everything is considered, this plan seems best.

An absolute phrase with a subject is sometimes called a *nominative absolute*. This construction is often used in descriptive and narrative prose for adding details or parenthetical material:

He stalked like the specter of a soldier, **his eyes** [subject] **burning** [participle] with the power of a stare into the unknown.—Stephen Crane, *The Red Badge of Courage*

The Portuguese listened with his head cocked to one side, **his dark eyes** [subject] **ringed** [participle] with ash-gray circles, and now and then he wiped his damp veined dead-white hands on his stained apron.—Carson McCullers, *The Member of the Wedding*

Exercise 3.G

Some of the sentences below contain misrelated or dangling modifiers. Rewrite the sentences to make the relationships clear. The sentences with absolute modifiers need no revision. Notice that the sentences needing correction can be revised in more than one way.

Example   Having grown tired of them, their actions no longer concerned me.

Because I had grown tired of them, their actions no longer concerned me.
or
Having grown tired of them, I felt that their actions no longer concerned me.

1. Being thoroughly persuaded by them myself, the arguments I used seemed completely reasonable.
2. After having convinced the judge to free the accused rapist on bond, both the lawyer and the judge began to have second thoughts.
3. To be perfectly honest, it makes no sense for you to take that course.
4. Above and beyond the call of mere friendship, being more important, truth is what matters.
5. The engines roaring, the air filled with the aroma of ethanol and rubber, the greatest spectacle in racing was about to begin.
6. Having seen enough, the arrests followed swiftly.
7. To be honest, your cat speaks French about as intelligently as you do, and makes less fuss about it.
8. By citing authorities to prove your point, it does not really convince anyone.
9. Trying to convince the electorate to support the tax proposal, the outlook for passage seems dim.
10. Considering what we paid, it is a superb antique for the collection.

FORMS AND USES OF VERBALS

■ Infinitives

An infinitive is (1) the base form of a verb (with or without *to*) or (2) any verb phrase that can be used with *to* to function in a sentence as a noun, an adjective, or an adverb.

Forms:	Active	Passive
Present	(to) ask, (to) be asking	(to) be asked
Past	(to) have asked, (to) have been asking	(to) have been asked

Principal uses:
Subject: *To be called* by the IRS would make anyone nervous.
Object: He does not like *to express his opinion.*
Modifier (adjective): I have plenty of work *to do.* (Modifies *work*)
Modifier (adverbial): The students came *to learn Russian.* (Modifies *came*)
Absolute phrase modifying the main clause: *To tell the truth,* he is a bore.

■ Participles

A participle is a verb form, typically ending in *-ing* or *-ed*, used as a modifier.

Forms:	Active	Passive
Present	asking	being asked
Past	having asked	asked, having been asked

Principal uses:
Modifier of a noun: a *smiling* candidate; a *clogged* drain
Participial phrase modifying a noun: The candidate *getting a majority of the votes* will be nominated.
Absolute phrase modifying the main clause: *Everything considered,* a portable typewriter seems the most practical gift.

■ Gerunds

A gerund is a verb form, typically ending in *-ing* or *-ed*, used as a noun.

Forms:	Active	Passive
Present	asking	being asked
Past	having asked	having been asked

Principal uses:
Gerund as subject: *Having been asked* made him happy.
Gerund phrase as subject: *Taking anthropology* opened a whole new field.
Gerund as object: He taught *dancing.*
Gerund as complement: Seeing is *believing.* (*Seeing* is also a gerund.)
Gerund as a modifier of a noun: the *dining* room, a *fishing* boat
Gerund as appositive: She had only one hobby, *collecting* gold coins.

4

COMMON
SENTENCE
ERRORS

The three most conspicuous errors in sentence construction are sentence fragments, comma splices, and run-on sentences. If these errors occur frequently in your writing, they suggest either you are failing to distinguish between separate complete statements or you are not editing your writing carefully.

4.1 Sentence Fragments

Frag   **Revise a sentence fragment by joining it to another sentence, by making it into a complete sentence, or by rewriting the passage.**

A sentence fragment is an incomplete statement—a phrase or a subordinate clause—punctuated as a complete sentence:

Fragment	It's a new design. **Which hasn't been tested.**
Revised	It's a new design which hasn't been tested.
Fragment	I can't go. **Because I'm sick.**
Revised	I can't go. I'm sick.

A sentence fragment can be corrected in various ways:

1. by joining it to another sentence;
2. by supplying a subject and a predicate;
3. by rewriting the passage in which it occurs.

Each of these ways is illustrated below.

See 1.3 for a discussion of phrases and clauses.

Joining a Fragment to Another Sentence

A sentence fragment may actually belong to the preceding sentence. You should link the fragment to the preceding sentence, usually with a comma. Sometimes the fragment and the preceding sentence will need to be rephrased.

Fragment	Researchers have not demonstrated a link between consumption of caffeine and disease in humans. **Although many people believe that caffeine is a health hazard.**
Revised	Researchers have not demonstrated a link between consumption of caffeine and disease in humans, although many people believe that caffeine is a health hazard.
Fragment	The next afternoon we made our way through the harbor of Okinawa. **That island, which had made history during World War II.**
Revised	The next afternoon we made our way through the harbor of Okinawa, the island which had made history during World War II.

Phrases should not be punctuated as complete sentences because they are subordinate sentence elements:

Fragment	I cite these examples to show you how interesting accounting can be. **And to give you an idea of the kind of problems an accountant has to solve.** [The fragment has no main subject and verb. It is an infinitive phrase. In the revised form, *to give* is moved into the first sentence where it is parallel with *to show*.]
Revised	I cite these examples to show you how interesting accounting can be and to give you an

idea of the kind of problems an accountant has to solve.

Fragment   For the past five years I have been contributing annually to the March of Dimes. **Without ever suspecting that one day a member of my own family might benefit from this foundation.** [prepositional phrase]

Revised   For the past five years I have been contributing annually to the March of Dimes, without ever suspecting that one day a member of my own family might benefit from this foundation.

Fragment   Professor Brown suddenly glanced up from his notes. **His eyes twinkling with suppressed laughter.** [*Twinkling* is a participle, which is a verbal, not a true verb.]

Revised   Professor Brown suddenly glanced up from his notes, his eyes twinkling with suppressed laughter.

Explanatory phrases beginning with *such as, for example, that is, namely,* and similar expressions belong in the same sentence as the statement they explain:

Fragment   They had a wonderful time on the Chocolate Getaway Cruise because at each meal the dessert cart was bedecked with their favorites. **For example, chocolate-dipped strawberries, chocolate mousse, truffles, Black Forest cake, chocolate eclairs, and French Chocolate Genoise.**

Revised   They had a wonderful time on the Chocolate Getaway Cruise because at each meal the dessert cart was bedecked with their favorites, for example, chocolate-dipped strawberries, chocolate mousse, truffles, Black Forest cake, chocolate eclairs, and French Chocolate Genoise.

Subordinate clauses are only parts of sentences and should not stand alone without a definite reason. A relative pronoun *(who, which, that)* or a subordinating conjunction (such as *although, because, if, when, while*) indicates that what follows is a subordinate clause and that it should be combined with a main clause.

Fragment	At the time, my old rowboat with its three-horsepower motor seemed a high-speed job to me. **Although it attained a speed of only twelve miles an hour.** [adverb clause, beginning with *Although*]
Revised	At the time, my old rowboat with its three-horsepower motor seemed a high-speed job to me, although it attained a speed of only twelve miles an hour.
Fragment	The whole area is honeycombed by caves. **Many of which are still unexplored.** [adjective clause, introduced by *which*]
Revised	The whole area is honeycombed by caves, many of which are still unexplored.

Supplying a Subject and Predicate

If the fragment deserves special emphasis, it can be made into a sentence by inserting a subject and a predicate:

Fragment	She talked for fifty minutes without taking her eyes off her notes. **Apparently not noticing that half the class was asleep.** [*Noticing* is a participle, not a verb.]
Revised	She talked for fifty minutes without taking her eyes off her notes. Apparently she did not notice that half the class was asleep. [The subject is *she*; the predicate is the verb *did notice* plus the words related to it.]
Fragment	National elections and student elections may be compared as closely as an object and its photograph. **The only difference being in size.** [*Being* is a participle, which is a verbal, not a true verb.]
Revised	National elections and student elections may be compared as closely as an object and its photograph. The only difference is in size. [*Is* is a verb.]

Rewriting a Fragment

Sometimes hopelessly snarled sentence fragments have to be completely revised. The following long "sentence" has three phrases that seem to be subjects, but there is no *main* verb. A number of verbs appear, but each one is in a subordinate construction.

Fragment	Some artists who attended the opening at Gallery Five because it was being covered by the media, the others who gathered to gossip about anyone who was not within earshot, and the photographer whose works were among those being displayed and who seemed to be the only one interested in the exhibit.
Revised	Some artists attended the opening at Gallery Five because it was being covered by the media; others gathered to gossip about anyone who was not within earshot. Only the photographer whose works were among those being displayed seemed interested in the exhibit.

Acceptable Fragments

Sentence fragments are acceptable in some situations, especially as answers to questions, in exclamations, in dialogue, and in descriptive passages. Fragments may consist of single words, phrases, subordinate clauses, or other constructions punctuated as complete sentences:

Where did Ryan spend his Friday evenings? **In the library, of course.**

"Bitzer," said Thomas Gradgrind. **"Your definition of a horse."**
"Quadruped. Graminivorous. Forty teeth, namely twenty-four grinders, four eye-teeth, and twelve incisive. Sheds coat in the spring; in marshy countries, sheds hoofs, too. Hoofs hard, but requiring to be shod with iron. Age known by marks in mouth." Thus (and much more) **Bitzer.**—Charles Dickens, *Hard Times*

Around the front steps, assurance came back. There were my fellow "greats," the graduating class. **Hair brushed back, legs oiled, new dresses and pressed pleats, fresh pocket handkerchiefs and little handbag, all homesewn.** Oh, we were up to snuff, all right.—Maya Angelou, *I Know Why the Caged Bird Sings*

Fragments are usually avoided in formal and academic writing except where they serve a definite purpose. If you use a fragment, be sure your readers are not likely to mistake it for a sentence error. When in doubt, make the fragment a complete sentence.

Exercise   **4.A**

Advertisers make heavy use of sentence fragments and other unorthodox sentence structures (see 1.6, Unorthodox Sentences). In their ads, the name of a product may be punctuated as a complete sentence, followed by copy which is heavy with clauses and phrases. Short phrases punctuated as sentences apparently seem more direct and to the point and they can be moved around more easily for purposes of design and emphasis. Below is a passage from an advertisement that relies heavily on fragments. Rewrite the text with complete sentences. Find two other ads that similarly rely on fragments for their effect. Rewrite them. Be prepared to discuss which versions you think are more effective.

Introducing American's Rio Vacations.

Here's the vacation bonus of a lifetime. American Airlines and Vacation Travel Concepts can offer you 8 days and 7 nights in exotic Rio de Janeiro. For just $99 when you purchase a round-trip Economy ticket.

Your vacation includes accommodations at the Acapulco Copacabana Hotel. And all service charges and taxes. With many extras. Like round-trip airport transfers, baggage handling and a morning tour of Rio.   ·   ■

Exercise   **4.B**

Rewrite the following sentences so that they contain no fragments.

1. Statistics are not yet available to show the actual decrease in accidents. Since this program is still in the process of being completed and traffic has doubled in the past few months.
2. The area thrives on competition since the same kinds of shops are all grouped together. An example of this being the three supermarkets, which are within a mile of each other.

3. Public transportation will have to be subsidized by the government. Because it will be too expensive for people to ride otherwise.
4. A popular person usually has three good personality traits. A good sense of humor, consideration for others, and good grooming.
5. The director was obviously displeased with their performance. His eyes flashing with anger.
6. Watching the halftime show, awed by the brilliance of the uniforms, instruments, and flags. You long to be part of the marching band.
7. When a patient experiences cardiac arrest, he will take short, gasping breaths. If he is breathing at all.
8. In order to study properly. The student should arrange all study materials before her. To minimize distractions caused by getting up to find books, papers, pens, and notes.
9. To get to the creek, one had to traverse a dangerous winding path. A path bordered by a sheer cliff on one side and heavy foliage on the other.
10. Ray pedals slowly and steadily along his route. With his six-foot frame bent over the cycle. His grey hair blowing in his face.
11. Winning is important to the conscientious football fan. The strain of urging his team on tires him by the end of the game.
12. A time-share system. That's when several computer terminals use the same main computer.
13. *Oil and Gas Journal* is a weekly publication covering almost every aspect of the petroleum business. Including the technical aspects of drilling and production.
14. Most students on campus wear casual suedes. A few wear clogs. Others wear boots.
15. It seems that every time I walk across campus, I am handed a half dozen pamphlets. Which I immediately throw away. ■

4.2

CS

4.2 Comma Splice

CS Change a comma splice to a period or semicolon, or revise the passage to make an acceptable sentence or sentences.

A comma splice (also called a comma fault) occurs when only a comma is used to join two or more independent clauses. A stronger link between the clauses must be provided:

Comma splice	A football player must condition his muscles for **endurance, a** baseball player must tone his muscles for quickness.
Revised	A football player must condition his muscles for endurance. A baseball player must tone his muscles for quickness.
Comma splice	The card catalogue is the key to the books in the **library, many** libraries have separate author/title and subject catalogues.
Revised	The card catalogue is the key to the books in the library; many libraries have separate author/title and subject catalogues.
Comma splice	Canaletto's paintings of Venice are like **photographs, they** capture time, not feelings.
Revised	Canaletto's paintings of Venice—like photographs—capture time, not feelings.

A comma splice may be corrected in various ways:

1. by removing the comma and creating two separate sentences;
2. by substituting a semicolon (or more rarely, a colon) for the comma;
3. by revising the passage and (usually) adding a connective.

Each of these techniques is discussed on the following pages.

Making Two Sentences

A comma splice may be corrected by using a period instead of the comma, making two full sentences:

Comma splice	He took a couple of steps, stopped, reached out, and turned a **valve, as** he did so he told us the valves had to be checked daily.
Repunctuated	He took a couple of steps, stopped, reached out, and turned a valve. As he did so, he told us the valves had to be checked daily.

This solution to a comma splice usually works best when the ideas are clearly distinct or when there are many commas in either or both statements. Correcting a comma splice by putting a period between two very short, closely connected statements, however, may only result in two weak sentences:

Comma splice	I opened the door **noisily, she** didn't move.
Revised, but still weak	I opened the door noisily. She didn't move.
Revised	I opened the door noisily, but she didn't move. [*But* helps to explain the relationship between the two independent clauses.]

Using a Semicolon or Colon

Comma splices may sometimes be corrected by substituting a semicolon for the comma. This is appropriate when the ideas expressed in the two clauses are closely related:

Comma splice	Charley then crossed the room and threw a switch which started the **motor, returning**, he wiped the sweat from his forehead with the back of his hand.
Repunctuated	Charley then crossed the room and threw a switch which started the motor; returning, he wiped the sweat from his forehead with the back of his hand.

A great many comma splices in student papers occur with "conjunctive" adverbs such as *accordingly, consequently, however, therefore.* When such adverbs appear at the junction of two independent clauses, the conventional punctuation is a semicolon:

Comma splice	The person with a college education has training far beyond that which can be obtained solely from **books, therefore** his or her chances for success may be greater than are those of a person without this education.
Repunctuated	The person with a college education has training far beyond that which can be obtained solely from books; therefore, his or her chances for success may be greater than are those of a person without this education.

Other uses of adverbs like *however* and *therefore* are discussed on page 200.

A colon may be used to link independent clauses when the second clause serves to illustrate, amplify, or restate the initial one:

Comma splice	Fountain pens have one **disadvantage, they** leak.
Revised	Fountain pens have one disadvantage: they leak.
Comma splice	The evidence is in on processed cheese **products, even** rats won't eat them.
Revised	The evidence is in on processed cheese products: even rats won't eat them.

Revising the Passage

Often the best way to remove a comma splice is to revise the sentence, using a connective that will show the relationship between the statements. The connective may be a coordinating conjunction (such as *and* or *but*), subordinating conjunction (*although, because, if, since, when),* or a relative pronoun (*who, which, that*) referring to a noun in the first statement. Sometimes one statement can be revised as a phrase, as in the third example:

Comma splice	It is a personal **matter, everyone** has to cope with it sooner or later.
Revised	It is a personal matter that everyone has to cope with sooner or later.
Comma splice	I enjoy being in the midst of a **party, particularly** if I feel some responsibility for its success, conversation is a stimulant more powerful than drugs.
Revised	I enjoy being in the midst of a party, particularly if I feel some responsibility for its success, because conversation is a stimulant more powerful than drugs.
Comma splice	Many companies are looking for experts in pollution **control, this** is a rapidly expanding field.
Revised	Many companies are looking for experts in pollution control, a rapidly expanding field.

There are many ways of correcting comma splices. The method of revision you choose ought to depend as much as possible upon what you are trying to do in the passage where the splice occurs. Consider this comma splice:

> The war provided the setting for many **novels, three** of them were especially outstanding.

Suppose this occurs in the opening paragraph of a paper in which you intend to review a number of war novels very briefly and then focus at some length on three that you think are outstanding. You might revise the sentence as shown below, subordinating the first statement to show that the review of several novels is less significant in the paper than the close study of three (see 2 and 26.3):

> While the war provided the setting for many novels, three of them were especially outstanding.

If you intend in your paper to give equal time and attention to the review of several novels and to the close study of three, you might revise the splice in this way:

> The war provided the setting for many novels. Three of them were especially outstanding.

If the review of a number of novels is what is most important in your paper, and the three novels are simply being used as examples, then you might revise in this way:

> The war provided the setting for many novels, including three that were especially outstanding.

> If you tend to employ comma splices when you write, review 1.4, Sentences Classified by Clause Structure.

Exercise **4.C**

Comma splices can often be corrected in several different ways, as the example below suggests. Study the example, and then correct the sentences following it in the way you believe is most effective. Be prepared to discuss your revisions in class.

| _Comma splice_ | Aaron Burr challenged Alexander Hamilton to a duel, the outcome ruined both men. |
| _Revised as_ _compound_ | Aaron Burr challenged Alexander Hamilton to a duel; the outcome ruined both men. |

Revised as two	Aaron Burr challenged Alexander Hamilton
sentences	to a duel. The outcome ruined both men.
Revised by	Aaron Burr's challenging Alexander Hamilton
rewriting	to a duel ruined both men.

1. I'd like to have a bigger apartment, I don't think I could afford the rent.
2. Bricklayers were hired on a contingency basis, that is, they weren't paid until the building was finished.
3. Jim hit a single down the right-field line, Roberta scored from second base.
4. Julie is an excellent guitarist, she taught herself.
5. The electricity went off during the storm, we could not watch television or read.
6. Winning is something you want to share with your friends, they smile and are happy for you.
7. When there is a fight at a hockey game, the brawlers are given five minute penalties, this means each team plays a man short for five minutes.
8. In many states, the law discriminates against women and homosexuals, hence, the law is not providing equal protection.
9. To teach physical education today you need a college degree, practical experience with sports instruction is also needed.
10. As I looked down to be sure my foot was on the brake, I could hear the tires screeching, there was nothing I could do to stop the crash. Except maybe pray.
11. I remember everything in slow motion, yet, it all happened so fast.
12. I decided to read *Anna Karenina,* then I began thinking about *War and Peace* and *The Brothers Karamazov.*
13. Adults are forcing children to grow up faster today, children's literature is more realistic as a consequence. Because adults write the books children read.
14. During the 1960's, fraternities became a target of the new liberal establishment, they were criticized for being elitist.
15. More money is put into a commercial at times than into the show it sponsors, it may have a bigger cast, a more elaborate set, and better direction.   ■

Exercise   **4.D**

Decide whether a comma or a semicolon is required in the following sentences at the points indicated by brackets.

1. The issue [1] nevertheless [2] requires the mayor's immediate attention.
2. Close the door [1] then come here.
3. Close the door [1] and then come here.
4. Fuel prices rose [1] hence [2] he bought a diesel automobile.
5. Too much salt can cause health problems [1] however, most people use it regularly.
6. We were not consulted, and [1] consequently [2] we will not accept the decision.
7. If the door was, in fact, locked [1] then the burglar entered through the window.
8. Of course we were disappointed [1] however [2] we cannot stop the experiment now.
9. He failed the final examination [1] moreover [2] he did not turn in his term paper.
10. I am inclined [1] however [2] to be lenient. ■

4.3 Run-on Sentences

Run

on

Use a period or semicolon to separate the two statements or revise the passage to make an acceptable sentence or sentences.

A run-on sentence (also called a fused sentence) occurs when no punctuation is used between two or more independent clauses. The clauses are simply run together:

Run-on sentence	Two volumes of this work are now **completed the** first will be published next year.
Possible revisions	Two volumes of this work are now completed. The first will be published next year.
	Two volumes of this work are now completed, the first of which will be published next year.

Run-on sentences are corrected exactly like comma splices:

1. by making two sentences out of the run-on sentence;
2. by using a semicolon to separate the two main clauses;
3. by rewriting the passage to show relationships clearly, for example, by subordinating one clause.

Run-on sentence	Salt will sink in a glass of **water pepper** will float lazily on the surface.
Revised by making two sentences	Salt will sink in a glass of water. Pepper will float lazily on the surface.
Revised by using a semicolon	Salt will sink in a glass of water; pepper will float lazily on the surface.
Revised by rewriting	While salt sinks in a glass of water, pepper floats lazily on the surface.

Exercise   4.E

Revise the fused sentences below. Repair other sentence problems as well.

1. The steak was very expensive it was a prime cut.
2. "What is the purpose of this form?" he asked he did not like bureaucratic interference.
3. Nuclear protection was a major issue in 1961 "fallout protection for every American" was President Kennedy's civil defense goal.
4. In pro football, two defenses are commonly used they are the 3–4 and the 4–3.
5. Most people use the terms "punk rock" and "new wave" interchangeably contrary to popular belief these musical styles are opposites. Because of their different emphases and musical structures.
6. Punk rock uses simple progressions in major chords new wave employs more complex progressions and minor, seventh, and diminished chords.
7. The author of the play confuses the audience he introduces unreasonable and unexplainable incidents he builds expectations which he does not satisfy.
8. Genocide is the greatest crime against humanity it negates values.
9. I began at the top of the hill in front of the bike shop I gained the speed I needed to clear the steps I leaped the

steps and landed safely. But the frame of my cycle was bent.

10. Newborns aren't cute their skin is wrinkled they spit up and they cry constantly.

11. It is a depressing thought man's aggressiveness will soon extend to outer space. Inevitably.

12. Elizabeth Stanton's home was the meeting place of movers and shakers in the nineteenth century Frederick Douglass, the abolitionist, John Greenleaf Whittier, the poet, and Sojourner Truth, the black women's rights leader all visited her.

13. Elizabeth Stanton voted in the presidential election of 1872 despite the law that denied women the right to vote she wanted to challenge this injustice.

14. The blind seem to develop acute senses of touch, taste, hearing, and smell they are remarkably aware of their surroundings.

15. College athletic teams make more money when they win contributions from alumni increase. ■

4.4 Mixed Constructions

Mix Revise the mixed construction to make an acceptable sentence or sentences.

When several sentence faults are combined or when a construction is not one of the standard sentence types, the result is sometimes called a mixed construction:

Mixed construction	I had always admired his novels, and when I had a chance to meet him, a real delight. [independent and subordinate clauses improperly joined by *and*.]
Possible revision	I had always admired his novels and was delighted when I had a chance to meet him.

Repunctuating cannot correct errors of this kind; the whole passage must be rewritten into acceptable sentence units.

Mixed construction	Charles was a hard worker, but I wondered how he would get everything finished on time? [shift from statement to question]
Possible revision	Although Charles was a hard worker, I wondered how he would finish everything on time.

Since mixed constructions usually involve a combination of errors, their variety is almost infinite. The only sure way to avoid them is to be sure you understand the principles of sentence construction.

Exercise   4.F

Revise the mixed constructions in the following sentences.

1. An important factor in choosing a brand of deodorant is the possibility of allergic reactions and when skin irritations occur.
2. The passenger train no longer stops in Galena, and is that committee petitioning to restore the service?
3. Not long ago I had a letter from Lily, a good friend and who is considered a "kissing cousin."
4. In Denmark, dating starts around age twelve, this is unusual pressure for young adults.
5. Because there are no launching facilities and parking is limited, no trailers are allowed in the park, bringing private boats into the park by car top only for use on the Fox River and the northern lakes.
6. Local television stations, affiliated with the national networks, control a fixed number of television hours daily and are filled with local news shows and comedy reruns of *I Love Lucy* and *Gilligan's Island.*
7. So-called action news reporters featuring on-the-spot coverage give the impression of "real" news when actually the film used on the air often having been cut, spliced, and voiced over to the approval of the director and station manager.
8. When asked for or against capital punishment, 90 percent favoring capital punishment which shows the need for stronger court action and less legal delay.
9. Carbon dioxide (CO_2) is a heavy, odorless, colorless gas and which is released in large quantities by the industrial burning of coal, petroleum, and wood.
10. It was Galileo who proving that all bodies, regardless of their mass, fall toward the earth at the same rate of acceleration (980 cm/sec^2) by dropping a ball of feathers and a ball of lead from a tower and showed that they hit the ground at the same time.   ■

MAJOR SENTENCE ERRORS

■ **Sentence Fragment**

An incomplete statement punctuated as a complete sentence is a sentence fragment:

> The fuse blew. **Which darkened the house.**

A sentence fragment is corrected:

1. By joining it to another sentence;

2. By supplying a subject and a predicate;

3. By rewriting the passage in which it occurs.

■ **Comma Splice**

A comma splice occurs when only a comma is used to join two or more independent clauses:

> Gallup predicted Dewey would defeat Truman in **1948, his** poll was wrong.

A comma splice is corrected:

1. By removing the comma and creating two separate sentences;

2. By substituting a semicolon for the comma;

3. By revising the passage and adding a connective such as a coordinate or subordinate conjunction.

■ **Run-on Sentence**

A run-on sentence occurs when no punctuation is used between two or more independent clauses:

> I'll never forget Sea **Island it** is a wealthy community in Georgia.

A run-on sentence is corrected:

1. By making two sentences out of the run-on passage;

2. By using a semicolon to separate the two main clauses;

3. By rewriting the passage.

5

AGREEMENT
OF SUBJECT
AND VERB

Agr **Make the verb agree in form with its subject.**

Singular nouns and pronouns take singular verb forms; plural nouns and pronouns take plural verbs. This correspondence is called subject-verb agreement:

Singular	A tree falls.
Plural	Trees fall.
Singular	He sees it.
Plural	They see it.

Agreement between subject and verb is not ordinarily a problem because English verbs—with a notable exception—do not change form much. That exception is the verb *be,* which changes often—I *am,* you *are,* he *is,* if she *be,* and so on. Most other English verbs have only two forms in the present tense and only one form in the past tense:

present tense	I/you/we/they	}	swim
	he/she/it	}	swims
past tense	I/you/he/she	}	
	it/we/they	}	swam

present tense	I/you/we/they	}	laugh
	he/she/it	}	laughs
past tense	I/you/he/she	⎱	
	it/we/they	⎰	laughed

Ordinarily, adding *-s* or *-es* to a noun makes it a plural form, but adding *-s* or *-es* to a verb indicates a singular form:

S   V
Bees buzz.
A bee buzzes.

Questions about agreement of subject and verb are most likely to arise in the following circumstances:

1. when verbs seem to have compound subjects *(neither you nor I; the Prime Minister, along with her cabinet);*
2. when verbs have collective nouns as subjects *(the orchestra, the choir, the jury, the family);*
3. when the number of the subject, whether singular or plural, is blurred by other words that separate subject and verb (A politician *who appeals to laborers, senior citizens, and neighborhood organizations,* stands a good chance of being elected in Pittsburgh).

These problems are discussed in the following sections.

5.1 Verbs with Compound Subjects

A compound subject is made up of two or more words, phrases, or clauses joined by *and, or, nor.* The number of the verb depends on which conjunction is used and on the meaning of the subject.

Subjects Joined by *and*

The conjunction *and* is used to join coordinate items, to add them together. Thus subjects joined by *and* usually take a plural verb:

Bob, Ted, and **Sandra swim** with the varsity team.

The first **draft** of your essay and the final **version differ** significantly.

Exception: When the words of a compound subject refer to the same person or are considered together as a unit, the verb is usually singular:

His warmest **admirer** and severest **critic was** his wife.

Law and **order means** different things to people with different political opinions.

Gin and **tonic** is his favorite drink.

Subjects Joined by *or, nor*

Compound subjects joined by *or, nor, either . . . or, neither . . . nor* sometimes take singular verbs and sometimes plural. Here are some ways to tell the difference:

1. When both subjects are singular, the verb ordinarily is singular:

   One or the **other is** certainly to blame.

   Neither **IBM** nor **Xerox has been** intimidated by foreign competition.

Exception: In questions, where the verb precedes the subject, general usage favors employing a plural verb:

   Are [formal: **Is**] either **Kemp** or **Metzenbaum** supporting the bill?

2. When both subjects are plural, the verb is plural:

   No artificial **colorings** or **preservatives are used.**

3. When one subject is singular and the other plural, usage varies. In formal writing the verb usually agrees with the nearer subject:

   One major **accident** or several minor **ones seem** to occur at this corner every weekend.

   Several minor **accidents** or one major **one seems** to occur at this corner every weekend.

   Neither the **revolutionaries** nor their **leader was** blameless.

   Neither the **revolutionary** nor her **leaders were** blameless.

In general usage a plural verb is often used even if the nearer subject is singular:

   Neither the **revolutionaries** nor their **leader were** blameless.

4. When the subjects are pronouns in different persons (neither *I* nor *they*), formal usage requires that the verb

agree in person and number with the nearer subject. In general usage (and even in formal usage if the alternative is awkward) the verb is usually plural:

Formal	Either **you** or **she is** likely to be elected.
General	Either **you** or **she are** likely to be elected.
Formal and general	Neither **you** nor **I are** trained for that job. [*Am* would sound awkward.]

Such problems of agreement can usually be avoided by substituting a different, more natural construction:

> **One** of you **is** likely to be elected.

> **Neither** of us **is** trained for that job.

Subjects Followed by *as well as*

In formal usage a singular subject followed by a phrase introduced by *as well as, together with, along with, in addition to* ordinarily takes a singular verb:

> The **president as well as the treasurer** manages the stock fund.

> The **teacher, together with her students,** writes daily.

But a plural verb is often used in these situations when the added phrase is clearly intended as a compound subject:

> The **production** of small cars, **together with the supply** in the dealers' showrooms, **have been outstripped** by the demand.

A simple solution—and one that may make the statement more direct—is to use *and* wherever appropriate:

> The **production** of small cars **and** the **supply** in the dealers' showrooms **have been outstripped** by the demand.

Exercise 5.A

Compose sentences using the subjects given below, making sure that the verb agrees with the subject.

Example:	backaches, dizzy spells, and blinding headaches *Backaches, dizzy spells, and blinding headaches are signals that you should see a doctor.*

1. tape deck, turntable, and speakers
2. neither aspirin nor sinus tablets
3. both alligators and crocodiles
4. neither the horses nor the trainer
5. the teacher, together with the class

6. tea and sympathy
7. no friends or family
8. the coach as well as her players
9. paint, canvas, and inspiration
10. New York and New Orleans, in addition to other ports of call
11. either the shock absorbers or the brakes
12. no drinking and smoking
13. both friend and foe alike
14. her best friend and confidant
15. neither he nor we   ■

Exercise 5.B

In each of the following sentences, two verb forms are listed in parentheses. Underline the verb form most appropriate in formal English usage. Rewrite any sentences to enhance clarity. Discuss any sentences that might be acceptable with either verb choice.

1. Her conduct during the recent audit proved that the comptroller (be, is) a clever person.
2. (Do, Does) all who claim to have been immunized still require a booster injection?
3. The master of ceremonies, along with his staff members, (assume, assumes) responsibility for seeing that the proper level of pomp and ceremony (is, are) attained.
4. Members of the jury (sit, sits) in two rows of seats behind an oak partition.
5. (Does, Do) you, who support the zoning restriction, and she, who objects to it, expect to devise a compromise before the council meeting?
6. No one who has worked on these projects, seen their results, and watched their successes (object, objects) to their continued funding.
7. Blood, toil, tears, and sweat (is, are) what Winston Churchill had to offer the British nation in 1940 when he became prime minister.

8. Neither the United States nor the nations of the Third World (were, was) satisfied with world monetary policies.

9. Two short research essays or one longer one (is, are) a course requirement.

10. Either they or I (am, are) destined to choose whether she or you (is, are) to be selected for the scholarship.

11. The land-based missile force, together with the Trident submarines and the long-range bombers, (is, are) the elements of the defense triad.

12. Wheat prices, along with prices of sorghum and other grains, (is, are) remaining stable.

13. Neither the engineers nor the project manager (give, gives) any indication when the process will be perfected.

14. Workers on the line and each supervisor in the plant (have, has) the power to halt production if a defect in quality is found.

15. "Life and death (hang, hangs) in the balance; truth and falsehood (stand, stands) in conflict today in this court," the prosecutor declared. ■

5.2 Verbs with Collective Nouns as Subjects

Words that refer to a group of people or objects but are singular in form are called collective nouns or group nouns: *army, audience, choir, committee, crowd, faculty, gang, group, government, jury, mob, orchestra, public, team.* Verbs and pronouns used with such collective nouns are either singular or plural, depending on how the group word is used in context.

Nouns Referring to the Group as a Unit

Singular verbs and singular pronouns are used with collective nouns that refer to the group as a unit:

Class is dismissed.

The **committee has** already held **its** first meeting of the year.

The **audience is** requested to remain seated during intermission.

Nouns Referring to Individuals in a Group

When a collective noun refers to the members of the group, especially if it represents them as acting individually, a plural verb and plural reference words are used:

> The graduating **class have** all agreed to have **their** pictures taken.
>
> The **committee are** arguing among **themselves.**
>
> The **audience have** taken **their** seats.

Since sentences like these often sound rather awkward, it is better in most cases to substitute a clearly plural subject:

> The graduating **seniors have** all agreed to have their pictures taken.
>
> The committee **members are** arguing among themselves.
>
> The **members** of the audience **have** taken their seats.

Verbs with Measurements and Figures

Expressions indicating quantity or extent *(miles, liters, years, pounds)* take singular verbs when the amount is considered as a unit:

> **Five dollars is** too much to pay for a book in that condition.
>
> **Four quarts** of oil **is** all the crankcase holds.
>
> **Three months passes** in no time at all on a dude ranch.

When the amount is considered as a number of individual units, a plural verb is used:

> **Two more dollars are** missing from the till this morning.
>
> There **are three quarts** of milk in the refrigerator.
>
> The last **three months have been** the driest in California's history.

In expressions of addition and multiplication, either a singular or plural verb can be used:

> Five and seven **is** [or **are**] twelve.
>
> Five times seven **is** [or **are**] thirty-five.

A singular verb is used in expressions of subtraction and division:

Twenty-five from thirty-one **leaves** six.

Six divided by three **is** two.

Verbs with *data, number, public*

Data is a plural form and is generally so considered in formal, particularly scientific, writing; but since the singular *datum* is rarely used, *data* is often used for both singular and plural in general writing. Agreement often depends on context:

5.2

Agr

Singular idea	The **data** the president needs **has been analyzed** by his assistant. [*data* refers to a body of facts]
Plural idea	After the **data** [individual facts] **have been gathered** and **analyzed,** you can decide which elements are most essential to your study.

Number may be either singular or plural: preceded by *the,* it refers to the total sum and takes a singular verb; preceded by *a,* it refers to the individual units and takes a plural verb:

A number of pages **are** badly torn.

The number of pages assigned for daily reading **is** gradually being increased to twelve.

Physicians were disturbed to find that **an** alarming **number** of bacteria **were** developing a tolerance to penicillin.

Public takes a singular verb if the writer wishes to signify the whole group; it takes a plural verb if the writer is considering the individual members:

The **public is** invited to attend.

The **public are** invited to express their opinions.

Words Ending in *-ics*

Physics, mathematics, economics, civics, linguistics, and similar *-ics* words that refer to a science, art, or a body of knowledge are usually considered singular; other words ending in *-ics* that refer to physical activities or qualities (*athletics, acrobatics, tactics*) are generally treated as plurals.

Singular forms	**Physics was** my most difficult subject in high school.

Ballistics is the study of the motion of projectiles.

Plural forms   **Athletics have** been virtually abolished from some smaller schools.

New **calisthenics are** designed for older people.

Some words ending in *-ics* (*ethics, politics, acoustics*) may be used in either a singular or plural sense:

Singular idea   In almost every group, **politics is** a controversial subject.

Plural idea   Radical **politics were** offensive to the Federalists.

Singular idea   **Acoustics is** a branch of science that is growing fast.

Plural idea   The **acoustics** in this room **are** not all they might be.

When you are in doubt about the number of a word ending in *-ics*, consult a dictionary.

Exercise   5.C

For each of the following collective terms, create two sentences, one in which the group noun operates as a unit and one in which the focus is on individuals within the group.

Example   the crew

The crew changes tires and pumps gas. [as a unit]

The crew wear different emblems to identify their responsibilities. [as individuals]

1.   the choir
2.   the majority
3.   the army
4.   the committee
5.   the assembly   ∎

Exercise   5.D

Choose the appropriate singular or plural verb in the following sentences. If both forms might be acceptable, indicate both and discuss.

1. Ten liters (is, are) the capacity of the jug.
2. Aerobics (grow, grows) more popular every year.
3. The public (was, were) being asked to reply by signing individual pledge cards.
4. We will have to start over unless the data (prove, proves) to be more reliable.
5. *The High and the Mighty* (was, were) one of John Wayne's best-known films.
6. Two and three (is, are) five.
7. Dividing fifty-four by six (give, gives) you nine.
8. The jury (was, were) strongly voicing opinions, none of which seemed to be based on the same evidence.
9. His ethics in the property transfer (leave, leaves) a great deal to be desired.
10. The acoustics in the hall (was, were) so bad that the choir (was, were) unable to follow its director's tempo.

5.3 Blind Agreement

Sometimes writers incorrectly make a verb agree in number with a nearby expression rather than with its actual subject. This error is called blind agreement because the writer accepts a word or phrase that looks like a subject rather than identifying the real thing:

Blind agreement	I hope to discover why **one** of the **packages** always **arrive** opened. [The verb *arrive* incorrectly agrees in number with the plural noun *packages,* not the actual subject of the clause, *one.*]
Revised	I hope to discover why **one** of the packages always **arrives** opened.

Blind agreement problems usually occur in the following situations:

1. when plural nouns come between a subject and verb;

2. when a complement is mistaken for a subject;

3. when the word order of a sentence is inverted.

These problems are discussed below.

Plural Nouns Between Subject and Verb

A singular subject followed by a phrase or clause containing plural nouns remains singular:

> Time and again an **explorer** [subject] such as Columbus, Galileo, and others **has** [not *have*] ventured into the unknown physical and intellectual worlds.

> The **lumberman** [subject] who previously sold only to carpenters and builders now **finds** [not *find*] hundreds of amateurs eager to build their own homes.

> I decided to see exactly how **one** of those new racquets **is** [not *are*] constructed.

Clauses Beginning *one of those who*

In formal English, the verb in clauses that begin *one of those who* (or *that*) is plural:

> He is one of those men who never **care** how they look. [The verb is plural because its subject *who* refers to *men*, not to *one*.]

> "The Lottery" is one of those stories that **leave** you more puzzled when you finish than when you began. [*Stories* is the antecedent of *that*.]

Although a singular verb is common in spoken English (one of those girls who *plays* in the band) and in a good deal of published material, the plural verb is customarily used in formal English.

Exception: When *the only* precedes *one of those who* the verb is singular, since the pronoun *who* then refers to a single person or thing:

> She is the only one of those women who **plays** bridge well.

Sentences Beginning *there is, there are*

When a sentence begins with the introductory word *there*, the number of the verb is determined by the subject which follows:

> There **are** conflicting **opinions** [subject] about smoking in the classrooms.

> There **is** great narrative and dramatic **power** [subject] in the first part of this novel.

> At our camp there **were** at least a dozen **men** [subject] who were familiar with the mountain trail.

In this construction a singular verb is frequently used before a compound subject, especially if a plural verb would be un-idiomatic, as in the second example below:

> There **is food** and **drink** enough for everyone.
>
> There **was nothing** he could do and **little** he could say.

But notice that starting a statement with *there is* or *there are* is often wasteful and wordy:

Wordy	There is great narrative and dramatic power shown in the first part of this novel.
Revised	Great narrative and dramatic power is shown in the first part of this novel.
Wordy	There were at least a dozen hikers at our camp who were familiar with the mountain trail.
Revised	At our camp at least a dozen hikers were familiar with the mountain trail.

Verb and Complement

A verb agrees with its subject and not with its complement or its object:

> Our chief **trouble** [subject] **was** [not *were*] the black flies that swarmed about us on the trip.
>
> The black **flies** [subject] that swarmed about us on our trip **were** [not *was*] our chief trouble.
>
> The **material** [subject] that was most interesting to me when I worked on my reference paper **was** [not *were*] the books that stated the facts forcefully.

Inverted Word Order

When the word order is inverted, care must be taken to make the verb agree with its subject and not with some other word:

> Throughout the story **appear** thinly disguised **references** [subject] to the author's own boyhood.
>
> **Is** any **one** [subject] of these pictures for sale?

Accompanying the senator **were** her **secretary** and two **members** of her legal staff. [The verb has a compound subject.]

Subjects *series, portion, part*

Subjects like *series, portion, part, type* take singular verbs even when modified by a phrase with a plural noun:

A **series** of panel discussions **is** scheduled for the convention.

A substantial **portion** of the reports **is** missing.

The most interesting **part** of the investigations **was** the discovery and identification of the forged letters.

Exercise 5.E

Identify the subjects of the verbs italicized in the sentences below. Then decide whether the verb agrees in number with its subject. Revise if necessary.

Example   A part of the ceremonies and festivities *are* the athletic contests.

A part of the ceremonies and festivities is the athletic contests.

1. The students who received the trophy at the forensic tournament *were* proud of their accomplishment.
2. Their chief worry *were* not their many competitors, but a lack of experience and an abundance of nervous energy.
3. She is one of those people who never *gains* weight.
4. How any of those students *passes* the exams I'll never know.
5. It *were* the measles he came down with.
6. Josephine is not the only one of my relatives who *live* in Baltimore.
7. I want to know why all of the dozen *is* broken.
8. There *is* trouble and turmoil enough in this world.
9. In the theater on opening night *were* one of the actor's most vocal critics.
10. Her report on three separate accidents on three different expressways *was* not broadcast on the evening news. ∎

Exercise 5.F

Find the subjects of the italicized verbs in the following paragraph. If the subject is a pronoun, indicate what word or idea it refers to.

Epidemics *have taken* a great toll of lives in past generations. Death in infancy and early childhood *was* frequent and there *were* few families who didn't lose a member of the family at an early age. Medicine has changed greatly in the last decades. Widespread vaccinations *have* practically eradicated many illnesses, at least in western Europe and the United States. The use of chemotherapy, especially the antibiotics, *has contributed* to an ever decreasing number of fatalities in infectious diseases. Better child care and education *have effected* a low morbidity and mortality among children. The many diseases that have taken an impressive toll among the young and middle-aged *have been conquered.* The number of old people *is* on the rise, and with this fact *comes* the number of people with malignancies and chronic diseases associated more with old age.—Elisabeth Kubler-Ross, from *On Death and Dying* ■

Exercise 5.G

Determine the subject of each of the following sentences and select the verb form that agrees with it. If there is any problem of agreement, explain your choice of verb in terms of the points made in this section.

1. All (is, are) well.
2. Comparison of things that are unlike and that, by their uniqueness, (produces, produce) a sense of wonder in us, (show, shows) that the writer is just displaying his or her own cleverness.
3. Too many metaphors (is, are) a sign of a young writer.
4. "Patience and fortitude," though describing virtues, (is, are) a motto often used to counsel sloth.
5. These United States of ours (has, have) become a great nation.
6. He is one of those people who (is, are) always making trouble.

7. To have loved and lost (is, are) an experience most of humanity (has, have) suffered.
8. The bulk of our tax dollars (go, goes) to defense spending.
9. Neither metaphor nor simile (is, are) useful if the image is confused.
10. The series of programs on Hindu art (is, are) to run on six consecutive Monday evenings.   ■

Exercise   5.H

Compose sentences that include the following items:

1. *Three semesters*, meant as a single unit, used as the subject
2. The word *ethics* used as the subject in a plural sense
3. A singular subject followed by a phrase that includes a plural noun
4. *There are* at the beginning of the sentence
5. The expression *one of those who*
6. *A portion of the audience* used as the subject
7. The word *data* used as a subject in a plural sense
8. *The Three Musketeers* used as the subject
9. *It was* at the beginning of a sentence
10. *A series of group sessions* used as the subject   ■

6

VERBS

Vb **Change the verb form so that it conforms to standard usage.**

The words emphasized in these sentences are verbs:

The hunter **shot** a deer.

Our next speaker **will be introduced** by the presiding officer.

Are you ready?

In meaning, verbs indicate action *(run, manufacture, write)*, condition *(am, feel, sleep),* or process *(become, grow).* In form they may be one word *(do, see)* or a phrase *(should have done, will be seeing).* To indicate person, number, tense, and voice, they may add letters (prove*s*, prove*d*) or change internally (s*i*ng, s*a*ng, s*u*ng). Except in questions, verbs usually follow the subject.

The table on page 133 lists the terms used to describe the principal characteristics of verbs. See also 3, Verbals, and 5, Agreement of Subject and Verb.

6.1 Tense

T **Make the tense of the verb conventional in form or consistent with others in the passage.**

The tense of a verb indicates whether action has occurred in the past (she *spoke*), is occurring in the present (she *speaks*), or will occur in the future (she *will speak*). Tense also indicates the continuity of an action or an explanation (she *is speaking*, she *will be speaking*).

6.1
T

Tense Forms

The appropriate form of a verb should be used to indicate each of its tenses. Problems seldom arise with regular verbs, because they have only two forms:

1. the infinitive or base form used for the present tense (*walk, imagine, sleep*);

2. a form ending in *-ed, -d,* or *-t* for the past tense and past participle (*walked, imagined, slept*).

Except for the simple present and past tenses, English verbs show distinctions of time by various phrase combinations (*have walked, had walked, will walk,* and so on), often supported by adverbs (for example, "he is about to go" as future). The table on page 116 lists the most frequently used active tenses and the verb phrases most commonly associated with time distinctions.

Time and Tenses

The various tenses in English serve to indicate particular moments or periods in time:

PAST TIME

Tense	Use	Example
Past tense	Indicates something that happened at a particular time in the past	I **filed** a complaint.
Past progressive tense	Indicates something going on during a period of time in the past	I **was filing** a complaint when they came in.
Perfect tense	Indicates something that has happened at various times in the past	I **have filed** complaints many times in the past year.

PAST TIME

Tense	*Use*	*Example*
Past perfect tense	Indicates something that happened before some time in the past	I **had filed** many complaints before any action was taken.

PRESENT TIME

Tense	*Use*	*Example*
Present tense	Indicates something that happens or can happen in the immediate present	I **file** complaints.
Present progressive tense	Indicates something that is going on at the present time	I **am filing** a complaint.

FUTURE TIME

Tense	*Use*	*Example*
Future tense	Indicates something that can happen at some time in the future	I **will file** a complaint tomorrow.
Future perfect tense	Indicates something that will take place before some particular time in the future	I **will have filed** the complaint before the courthouse closes today.

Notice how the tenses are used to indicate differences in time in these sentences:

> He **has finished** [perfect] the novel and **is watching** [present progressive] television.

> He **had finished** [past perfect] the novel and **was watching** [past progressive] television.

> He **had finished** [past perfect] the novel when I **arrived** [past].

> He **finished** [past] the novel when I **arrived** [past].

Sequence of Tenses

The main verb in a sentence ordinarily determines what the tense of other verbs in the sentence can be. In most cases, you will know intuitively what tenses are appropriate in a sentence. For example, you can follow a main verb in the present tense with another verb in any other tense:

6.1

T

> I **see** that she **works** hard.
>
> I **see** that she **worked** hard.
>
> I **see** that she **will work** hard.
>
> I **see** that she **has worked** hard.
>
> I **see** that she **had worked** hard.
>
> I **see** that she **will have worked** hard.

Main verbs in past and future tenses are more restrictive, although many combinations are possible. When, for example, the verb of a main clause is in the past or past perfect tense, the verb in the subordinate clause is also ordinarily past or past perfect:

> They slowly **began** to appreciate what their teacher **had** [not *has*] **done** for them.
>
> Up to that time I **had** never **seen** Albert when he **hadn't** [or *didn't have;* not *hasn't*] an electronic calculator snapped to his belt.

However, with infinitives, the present (rather than the past) infinitive is conventionally used after a past verb in the main clause:

> I **would have liked** very much **to attend** [not *to have attended*] the seminar, but I was out of town.

With participles, the present participle is used to express action occurring at the same time as the main verb:

> **Reading** the abstract, he discovered the information he was seeking. [He discovers the information while he is reading.]

The present perfect form of the participle is used to express action occurring prior to that of the main verb:

> **Having read the abstract,** he sought for the information elsewhere. [First he reads the abstract, and *then* he turns elsewhere for information.]

Consistent Use of Tenses

Shift
Make the words or constructions consistent in form. Verbs should be consistent in tense; pronouns should be consistent in person and number.

Unnecessary shifts in tense (as from the present to the past, or the past to the future) confuse the sequence of your writing. In the following passage, the writer shifts inappropriately between present and past tenses:

Unnecessary shifts

I **sit** down at my desk early with intentions of spending the next four hours studying. Before many minutes **passed,** I **heard** a great deal of noise down on the floor below me; a water fight **is** in progress. I **forgot** about studying for half an hour, for it **is** quite impossible to concentrate on Spanish in the midst of all this commotion. [mixture of present and past]

A revised version uses the past tense consistently:

Consistent

I **sat** down at my desk early with intentions of spending the next four hours studying. Before many minutes **had passed,** I **heard** a great deal of noise down on the floor below me; a water fight **was** in progress. I **forgot** about studying for half an hour, for it **was** quite impossible to concentrate on Spanish in the midst of all that commotion. [past tense throughout]

In single sentences, problems of consistency can occur when a writer incorrectly shifts the tense of two or more verbs that should be parallel:

Shifted

For years I **have been attending** summer camp and **enjoyed** every minute of it.

Consistent

For years I **have been attending** summer camp and **enjoying** every minute of it.

Exercise **6.A**

Consider whether the italicized verbs in the sentences below show a consistent and appropriate use of tense. Revise the sentences whenever necessary. Treat all ten sentences as part of a single passage. In your final version, tenses throughout the selection should be consistent.

6.1
T

1. Since its beginning, the United States *was built* by people from all over the world.
2. For the past fifty years, however, immigrants *were welcomed* with less and less enthusiasm.
3. During this period, the only time the U.S. *has welcomed* immigrants with open arms *was* during the world wars and following Soviet invasions of Hungary and Czechoslovakia.
4. As soon as both world wars *had ended,* many of the previously employed *returned* to their jobs and consequently *displace* the immigrants who *work* in their absence.
5. One example of the resistance of the country to foreigners *can be seen* in the program "Operation Wetback," which *has been implemented* more than three decades ago to reduce the number of Mexicans in this country.
6. By the time "Operation Wetback" *was completed,* more than a million individuals of Mexican descent *have been expelled* from the U.S.
7. Even to the present day, waves of immigration *tended* to follow periods of business prosperity in the United States.
8. Whenever the American economy *was* on an economic upswing, the number of immigrants *increases,* and when the country *was* in an economic slump, the number of immigrants *would decrease.*
9. In the years following the Industrial Revolution, however, the development of industry and national resources *had continued* to slow, and accordingly the country *requires* fewer workers to fill the available jobs.
10. If an employer *has to choose* between hiring a firmly established native citizen and a newly arrived immigrant, he *would* often *hire* the immigrant, who very likely *demanded* significantly lower wages. ∎

6.2 Irregular Verbs and Auxiliaries

Some of the most commonly used verbs in English cause problems in writing because of their irregular forms or optional uses.

Irregular Verb Forms

The following list shows the principal parts of some troublesome irregular verbs. The first column lists the *infinitive* or base form. The second column gives the *past tense,* which expresses simple past (She *wrote* a letter). The third column lists the *past participle,* which is used with auxiliaries to form verb phrases (The jet *had roared* away; Soon these problems *will have been forgotten;* The chimes *are being rung*). The past participle cannot be used alone as a full verb in the past tense; it must be accompanied by some auxiliary:

Incorrect	It **blown.**	They **eaten.**
Revised	It **had blown.**	They **have eaten.**

When two forms are given in the list below, both are acceptable (He *lighted* a fire; He *lit* a fire). Verbs marked with an asterisk (*) are discussed in the sections following. For verbs not given here, consult a recent dictionary. Caution: If your dictionary labels a form in question *nonstandard, obsolete, archaic, dialect,* or *rare,* it is not suitable for most general writing.

Infinitive	*Past tense*	*Past participle*
arise	arose	arisen
bear (carry)	bore	borne
bear (give birth to)	bore	borne, born
become	became	become
begin	began	begun
bite	bit	bitten, bit
blow	blew	blown
break	broke	broken
bring	brought	brought
burst	burst	burst
buy	bought	bought
catch	caught	caught
choose	chose	chosen
come	came	come
dig	dug	dug

MOST FREQUENTLY USED
VERB TENSES

	I	he, she, it	we, you, they
■ **Present Tenses**			
Present (immediate present)	ask	asks	ask
Present Progressive (continuing present)	**am** asking	**is** asking	**are** asking
■ **Past Tenses**			
Past	asked	asked	asked
Past Progressive (continuing period in past)	**was** asking	**was** asking	**were** asking
Perfect (past time extending to the present; past participle plus *have* or *has*)	**have** asked	**has** asked	**have** asked
Past Perfect (a time in the past before another past time; past participle plus *had*)	**had** asked	**had** asked	**had** asked
■ **Future Tenses**			
Future (future time extending from the present)	**will** ask **am** going to ask	**will** ask **is** going to ask	**will** ask **are** going to ask
Future Perfect (past time in some future time; future tense of *have* plus past participle)	**will have** asked	**will have** asked	**will have** asked

dive	dived, dove	dived, dove
do*	did	done
drag	dragged	dragged
draw	drew	drawn
dream	dreamed, dreamt	dreamed, dreamt
drink	drank	drunk
drive	drove	driven
eat	ate	eaten
fall	fell	fallen
find	found	found
fly	flew	flown
forget	forgot	forgotten
freeze	froze	frozen
get*	got	got, gotten
give	gave	given
go	went	gone
grow	grew	grown
hang (a person)	hanged, hung	hanged, hung
hang (an object)	hung	hung
know	knew	known
lay (place)*	laid	laid
lead	led	led
leave	left	left
lend	lent	lent
lie (recline)*	lay	lain
light	lighted, lit	lighted, lit
lose	lost	lost
pay	paid	paid
prove	proved	proved, proven
ride	rode	ridden
ring	rang, rung	rung
rise	rose	risen
run	ran	run
say	said	said
see	saw	seen
set	set	set
shake	shook	shaken
shine	shone, shined	shone, shined
show	showed	showed, shown
shrink	shrank, shrunk	shrunk
sing	sang, sung	sung
sink	sank, sunk	sunk, sunken
sit	sat	sat
slide	slid	slid, slidden

6.2

Vb

speak	spoke	spoken
spring	sprang, sprung	sprung
stand	stood	stood
steal	stole	stolen
swim	swam, swum	swum
take	took	taken
tear	tore	torn
throw	threw	thrown
wake	waked, woke	waked, woken
wear	wore	worn
wring	wrung	wrung
write	wrote	written

Forms of the Verb *be*

The verb *be* has eight forms, three more than any other verb in English. In addition to the infinitive *(to be)*, there are three forms in the present tense, two in the past tense, the present participle, and the past participle:

	I	*he, she, it*	*we, you, they*
Present tense	am	is	are
Past tense	was	was	were
Present participle	being		
Past participle	been		

The forms of *be* are not troublesome in ordinary situations, at least not if you are reasonably well acquainted with edited American English. Some dialects do use *be* differently, for example, *she be singing.* These forms are usually not found in general written English, however.

Exercise   **6.B**

Fill in the proper forms of the verbs indicated in parentheses, including any necessary auxiliary verbs.

1. According to the sheriff, the lifeguard (past tense of *dive*) into the water and (past tense of *swim*) only a few yards before she (past tense of *become*) exhausted and nearly (past tense of *drown*) in the swift current.
2. The cruiser finally (past of *sink*) when the missile (past of *blow*) a gaping hole in its hull.

3. The ancient Greeks (past of *lead*) all other civilizations in the development of an alphabetic writing system.
4. We never (past of *dream*) that X-ray crystallography experiment would be so costly.
5. He (past of *choose*) to remain silent, repressing the evidence that might have saved the life of the youth who was (past of *hang*) by the mob.

Exercise 6.C

Rewrite the following paragraph, filling in the proper forms of the verbs indicated in parentheses, including any necessary auxiliary verbs.

As the action begins, it is clear that the old man (perfect of *rise*) and (perfect of *bid*) the young soldier enter. The audience is aware that the young soldier (perfect of *know*) for a long time that it was the old man who (past perfect of *slay*) his father. When the soldier (past perfect of *return*) from the war, his mother (past perfect of *forsake*) her deathbed to tell him how the old man (past perfect of *steal*) into the house, (past perfect of *find*) the loaded gun on the night table, and, even as the mother (past of *shrink*) into the corner of the room, (past perfect of *shoot*) her husband. Laden with this heavy sorrow, her heart (past perfect of *burst*). Within the next few moments of action the young soldier (future perfect of *bind*) the arms of the old man and (future perfect of *begin*) to lead him from the room.

Troublesome verbs

Choice of *can* or *may*

In all levels of usage, *can* is used to express the ability to do something:

> This car **can** do better than 125 miles per hour.
>
> I know she **can** do the work.
>
> He **can** walk now with crutches.

May expresses possibility and permission:

> That **may** be true.
>
> We **may** get there before dark.
>
> **May** I go?

Although spoken English increasingly uses *can* to express permission (*Can* I go? You *can* have any one you like), you should still use *may* in writing. You can sometimes distinguish between *can* and *may* by substituting *to be able* for *can* and *to have permission* for *may*:

Can he [Is he able to] play the piano?

May he [Does he have permission to] play the piano?

Correct Use of *do—did—done*

Some idiolects and dialects use *done* alone (He *done* his best to please her) when edited American English calls for other forms. Particular care should be given to the past tense and the past participle:

Present tense	I, we, you, they **do**; he, she, it **does**
Past tense	I, you, he, she, it, we, they **did**
Past participle	I, you, we, they have (had) **done;** he, she, it has (had) **done**

Using *don't, doesn't.* **Don't** is the contraction for *do not* (I *do not,* I *don't*); *doesn't* is the contraction for *does not* (he *does not,* he *doesn't*). The substitution of one form for the other (*Don't* she look pretty?) is not consistent with edited forms of the language.

Idioms with *do.* *Do* is used in many standard idioms (set expressions): *do* without, *do* away with, make *do.* *Do* is also used as the base in some slang and informal expressions that are better avoided:

When the lawyer finally arrived, she seemed **done in** [better: *exhausted*].

They **did** [better: *cheated*] the government out of $50,000.

Consult a dictionary whenever you are unsure about the appropriateness of a particular expression with *do* or *done.*

Correct Use of *get—got—gotten*

The principal parts of the verb *get* are *get, got,* and *gotten* or *got.* Both forms of the past participle are used in the United States:

He could have **gotten** [or *got*] more for his money.

Her efforts had **gotten** [or *got*] no results.

Used with *have* to show possession (see below), the form is always *got*. In other constructions, *gotten* is more common.

Using *have got*, *have got to*. *Have got* in the sense of possession (I *have got* a video recorder) or obligation (We *have got to* finish this experiment today) is widely used in speech and is acceptable in most kinds of writing. Some writers of formal English avoid the expression, regarding *got* as redundant and preferring *have* alone (I *have* a video recorder; We *have to* finish this experiment today). But while *have* by itself may convey a sense of possession or obligation, it functions so often as an auxiliary verb in English (*have* seen, *have* decided) that writers do not often think of it as a verb with its own meaning. Consequently most writers and readers accept both *have* alone and the admittedly redundant *have got*.

Idioms with *get*. In many common idioms *get* is standard usage for all levels of speaking and writing:

Standard	get up	get along with (someone)
	get away from	get over (an illness)
	get ahead	get tired

Other expressions with *get* are considered informal, and you may want to avoid them in college writing:

Informal	Long-winded discussions **get** on my nerves.
	This modern music **gets** me.
	Some people seem to **get** away with murder.
	A stray bullet **got** him in the shoulder.

When you are in doubt about the standing of an idiom with *get*, consult a recent dictionary.

Choice of *lie* or *lay*

This pair of verbs is especially troublesome, in part because the past tense of *lie* is the same as the present tense of *lay* (*lay/lay*).

Lie, meaning to recline, is an *intransitive* verb. That means it does not take a direct object. Its principal parts are *lie, lay, lain*:

You **lie** down for a rest.

Yesterday he **lay** in bed all morning.

The log had **lain** across the road for a week.

The present participle of *lie* is *lying:*

The log was **lying** in the road.

I found him **lying** in bed.

Lay, meaning to put or place, is a *transitive* verb. It takes a direct object. Its principal parts are *lay, laid, laid:*

He should **lay** down his cards.

She **laid** her purse on the table.

The cornerstone was **laid.**

The present participle of *lay* is *laying:*

He was **laying** the foundation.

The same forms are used when *lay* means "to produce an egg."

This chart may help you understand which form of these verbs to use:

	Infinitive	Past tense	Present participle	Past participle
LIE (to recline)	lie	lay	lying	lain (intransitive)
LAY (to place)	lay	laid	laying	laid (transitive)

For discussion of other verbs you may have questions about, see the Glossary of Usage.

Exercise 6.D

Supply the proper form of the verbs in parentheses in each of these sentences. Some of the constructions may call for an infinitive, participle, or gerund (see 3, Verbals).

Example   Last night the wind (whip) the leaves so that they (spin) like the arms on a windmill.

whipped, spun

1. In the saloon, the dark-bearded cowboy pushed aside his beer and slowly (draw) his gun.
2. Within a few minutes the carefree sheriff (ride) up to investigate.
3. A low moan was (wring) from the saloonkeeper's lips.
4. The sheriff had (rid) the town of many criminals before.
5. At the hitching post the horse (shake) his mane and nervously (paw) the ground.
6. Once she had (do) the exercises, she (do) her reading with much greater pleasure.
7. He could have (get) a higher grade if he had worked a little longer on the project.
8. The entire text of Handel's *Messiah* was (write) in less than a month.
9. Before he called, she had (lie) down to rest a few minutes.
10. Bartleby (choose) not to respond to his employer's questions. ∎

6.2

Vb

Exercise 6.E

Supply the correct verb form for the sentences below, choosing between some form of the pair of verbs in parentheses before each sentence.

Example   (lie/lay) Where had she _____ the checkbook yesterday?

Where had she _laid_ the checkbook yesterday?

1. (can/may) When you _____ do all the exercises in this section, you _____ go on to the next chapter.
2. (can/may) _____ I enter the laboratory if I prove I _____ conduct myself in a professional manner?
3. (can/may) It _____ be possible for NASA to launch an expedition to Mars, but _____ the scientists persuade Congress to fund such a mission?
4. (don't/doesn't) _____ the squad know where the field operations will take place?
5. (don't/doesn't) Frankly, it _____ seem likely that the economy will support so large an expenditure.
6. (have/have got) The City Prosecutor _____ all the evidence she needs to take the case to the Grand Jury.

7. (have/have got) All the children _____ colds in the last week. You had better check to see if they _____ temperatures now.
8. (lie/lay) The warrior's body _____ on the pyre where his kin had _____ their offerings for the protection of his spirit.
9. (lie/lay) We _____ the food near the spot where we had seen the big cat _____ last night.
10. (lie/lay) The cornerstone had been _____ decades before the edifice was finally completed. ■

Exercise 6.F

Write sentences following the instructions below.

1. a single sentence that uses both *can* and *may*
2. a sentence that uses the past tense of *get*
3. a sentence that uses the past participle of *do*
4. a sentence that uses the present participle of *lay*
5. a sentence that uses the present participle of *lie* ■

6.3 Active and Passive Voice

When the subject of a sentence is also the doer of the action, the verb is said to be in the *active voice:*

> Jane's father **gave** her a stereo.
>
> The quarterback **will autograph** the football.

When the subject is acted upon by someone or something else, the verb is in the *passive voice:*

> Jane **was given** a stereo by her father.
>
> The ball **will be autographed** by the quarterback.

A passive verb consists of a form of *be* plus the past participle of the verb. The following are all passive forms:

is begun	is being told
are chosen	had been thrown
was taken	will be approached

Although there are effective and appropriate uses of the passive voice (see below), the active voice is generally preferred because it promotes conciseness, encourages clarity, and helps the writer get to the point.

Appropriate Passives

The great majority of English sentences uses active verbs, but sometimes the passive is appropriate. Passive constructions are natural if the actor or agent is unknown or unimportant in the statement:

> We **were robbed!**
>
> The game **was postponed** because of rain.
>
> The expressway **will be completed** by spring.
>
> The entire fuel-handling operation **is conducted** by remote control, of course, and fresh fuel assemblies **can be delivered** to the storage rack or spent ones **removed** from it while the reactor is in operation.—T. R. Bump, "A Third Generation of Breeder Reactors," _Scientific American_

6.3
_Vb_

A passive verb may also be appropriate if the writer wants to emphasize the object or the act rather than the doer:

> The fire **was discovered** by the night watchman.
>
> The bill **is supported** by representatives of both parties.

Inappropriate passives

**Pass** Change the passive verb or verbs to active.

In many situations, passive constructions are weak or awkward and should be changed to the more direct active form:

Passive	The diet **was judged** ineffective by experts.
Active	Experts **judged** the diet ineffective.

As the following example demonstrates, to change a passive construction to an active one you must first identify who or what is doing the action in the sentence, and then rearrange the sentence so that the doer of the action is also in the subject position:

Passive	A modern atlas [subject] **was produced** [action] by Gerardus Mercator [doer] in the sixteenth century.

6.3

Vb

| *Active* | Gerardus Mercator [subject and doer of the action] produced [action] a modern atlas [object] in the sixteenth century. |

The examples above can be effective in either the active or passive voice, depending on the writer's purpose and emphasis. Often, however, the passive voice makes a sentence less clear and concise, and hides its main point. Sometimes weak passives simply result from a writer's failure to notice who is doing what to whom:

| *Passive* | The report **was prepared** by me. |
| *Active* | I **prepared** the report. |

However, you may sometimes find passive verbs employed as a way of deliberately obscuring who is doing what to whom. Politicians, public officials, lawyers, teachers, diplomats, and others often rely on the passive voice to deflect responsibility away from themselves or the actual doer of an action:

> The recession could not **have been foreseen or forestalled.** [By whom? Why not?]
>
> You **have been given** an *F* in the course. [By whom?]
>
> This form **is required to be filled out** by all applicants. [Who has made the requirement? For what reasons?]
>
> Appropriate measures **have been taken.** [By whom?]

You should examine and question such uses of the passive whenever you encounter them.

It is sometimes awkward to combine an active and a passive verb in the same sentence. If you can, make both verbs active:

| *Awkward* | The city **needs** more money to build schools, and it **will** probably **be raised** through a bond issue. |
| *Revised* | The city **needs** more money to build schools and **will** probably **raise** it through a bond issue. |

Sometimes, however, you may have to revise the entire sentence or retain the passive construction:

Acceptable but awkward	We **ordered** the package on Monday and it **was delivered** on Thursday.
Revised	The package we **ordered** on Monday **was delivered** on Thursday.
Revised	The package we **ordered** on Monday **arrived** on Thursday.

6.3
Vb

Exercise 6.G

Revise the sentences below so that they still mean the same thing, but are in the active voice.

Example   It has always been felt by me that the study of biology is boring.

I have always felt that studying biology is boring.

1. Biology is thought by students to be very time-consuming.
2. It is also felt that cutting up dead frogs is disgusting to some students.
3. Sometimes tests are given by biology professors which are thought to require too much memorizing.
4. Also, it is costly to some to pay the lab fees.
5. For these reasons, it is an opinion of mine that the abolishment of required biology should be considered by school authorities.
6. It was the belief of that particular candidate that our society is too willing to use and exploit technology which is not even fully understood by the experts.
7. The figures on population growth were gathered and analyzed by a team of statisticians.
8. The decision to sell half the holding of the corporation was arrived at by the Board of Directors during last week's meeting.
9. Several varieties of swallowtail butterflies were thought by the entomologists to be migrating to the jungles in Central America.
10. It is the contention of some linguists that more indirect questions and qualifiers are used by women than by men in everyday speech.
11. Whales are believed by some scientists to be as intelligent as human beings.

12. When readers' sympathies are aroused by pictures of baby harp seals about to be slaughtered, more contributions to the Save-the-Seals fund are likely to be made by the readers.
13. Computer science is believed by many people to be a field which demands a great deal of mathematical expertise.
14. In Samoa, dolls are more frequently played with by boys than by girls.
15. Universities are being attended by a much different population of students now than they were fifteen years ago. ■

6.4 The Subjunctive Mood

Mood is a grammatical term used to describe a writer's attitude toward a subject as it is expressed by the form of the verb. English has three such moods: the *indicative*, the *imperative*, and the *subjunctive*.

The indicative mood is by far the most common. Verbs in the indicative mood state facts and opinions or ask questions:

He **is** careful.

The museum **was designed** properly.

Have you **seen** the Sky Lab exhibit?

The imperative mood indicates a direct command or instruction:

Be careful!

When the liquid boils, **remove** it from the heat.

The subjunctive mood is used to express situations that are improbable or contrary to fact. It is also used with certain requests, demands, recommendations, and so on, and in certain set phrases:

I wish the house **were** mine.

It is recommended that the tests **be given** before the patient is admitted.

Could he swim better, he **would be** a lifeguard.

The *present subjunctive* is expressed by the infinitive (or base) form of a verb, regardless of the person or number of the subject.

> verb in the subjunctive: to pass
>
> It is essential that he **pass** the exam today. [third person, singular]
>
> It is essential that they **pass** the exam today. [third person, plural]

As you can see from the example, the third person singular does not take its characteristic *-s*.

The *past subjunctive* is the same as the simple past tense for all verbs except *to be*.

> I wish I **knew** more about calculus.
>
> We wish we **understood** the subjunctive.

For *to be,* the past subjunctive is always *were.*

> I wish I **were** older.
>
> I wish you **were** older.
>
> I wish she **were** older.
>
> I wish they **were** older.

Even in formal English, the subjunctive has a limited use today. The following sections discuss some of these uses.

Subjunctive in Conditions

The subjunctive is sometimes used, especially in formal English, to express contrary-to-fact, impossible, or improbable conditions:

> If only he **were** [not *was*] careful!
>
> If the museum **were** [not *was*] designed properly, the exhibits would be more popular.
>
> He said if he **were** [not *was*] president, he would veto the bill.

Subjunctive in *that* Clauses

The subjunctive is used in many *that* clauses (usually in a formal, often legal, context) following verbs which recommend, demand, or request:

Formal	It is required that the applicant **be** over twenty-one.
Standard	The applicant must be over twenty-one.
Formal	I ask that the interested citizen **watch** closely the movements of these troops.
Standard	I ask the interested citizen to watch closely the movements of these troops.

6.4
Vb

Subjunctive in Idioms

The subjunctive is found in numerous idioms and set expressions surviving from a time when the subjunctive was used freely:

If I **were** you	If only she **were** here	As it **were**
Be that as it may	Come what **may**	

Exercise   6.H

Identify the subjunctive verbs in the following sentences.

1. I wouldn't worry about rising tax rates if I were you.
2. If every assembly-line worker were involved in quality-control inspections, the quality of the final product would be improved.
3. The Duke of Ferrara pointed out that the portrait of his wife made her look as if she were alive.
4. The article will be completed, come what may.
5. The Animal Liberation League demands that animals be considered equivalent to human beings in their capacity to experience pain.
6. The Constitution requires that a candidate for the presidency of the United States be at least thirty-five years old.
7. Were it not for the Spanish Inquisition, the Mayan Libraries would not have been destroyed and we might know more today about how the civilizations of Central America came into being.
8. I ask that everybody be prepared to report on the progress of the committee.
9. Were you a woman in Israel, you would be required to serve in the armed services.

10. If we were living during the European Renaissance, we would very likely believe that the stars determine our fates. ∎

Exercise **6.I**

Complete the following sentences using subjunctive verb forms.

1. If I. . . .
2. She said if she. . . .
3. It is necessary that each student. . . .
4. What would you do if she. . . .
5. Safety regulations require that every employee. . . .
6. I wish that I. . . .
7. She wishes that she. . . . ∎

6.5 Idioms with Verbs

Id Change the word or expression so that it will be idiomatic.

An idiom is a usage that has been established through custom. Quite often, idioms make little obvious sense, especially to nonnative speakers of a language:

The manager of our office **got canned** today.

The caterers **are fixing** dinner now.

Linda **had** her heart **set** on a teak bookcase.

Verbs and verb phrases are often used idiomatically, but the idioms must be both correct and appropriate to the level of language being used by a writer. The Glossary of Usage lists some verb forms that should be avoided because they are clumsy or not appropriate to edited English. Others are acceptable in informal or general usage but are sometimes frowned upon in formal English.

Exercise **6.J**

Correct any faulty verb forms that you find in the following sentences. Some of the constructions call for verbals (see 3).

Example   She often had came to the same conclusion.

*She often **had come** to the same conclusion.*

1. The students were not use to seeing the chancellor in Duffy's Tavern, ordinarily a student hangout.

2. It was raining hard, and he had almost drownded before he come upon a place to find shelter.

3. He was wet through and through, and he said that his feet were nearly froze.

4. Having rode across the prairie all day, Lonesome Jim was thoroughly wore out and could not get his legs unbended.

5. Early in the day the TV stations broadcasted the news that the president was going to make a speech that night.

6. Having born a pack, a shovel, a canteen, a map case, and a notebook for thirty miles, Mike laid down and went to sleep immediately.

7. There don't seem to be any way to keep him from sleeping when he is tired.

8. Her grandfather believed that the family had originally came from northern Georgia.

9. Molly sat the overdue books on the counter and waited to pay the fine.

10. They got up before dawn, drunk coffee and ate rolls, checked the map, and taken back roads west for the next stage of their journey.

Review

TERMS USED IN DESCRIBING VERBS

Verb forms (6.1). English verbs have three principal parts:

Infinitive (the base form)	**Past tense**	**Past participle**
ask (to ask), go (to go)	asked, went	asked, gone

Regular and irregular verbs (6.1 and 6.2). Regular verbs add *-ed* to form the past tense and past participle (ask, asked, asked). Irregular verbs change form in other ways (sing, sang, sung; go, went, gone).

Tense (6.1). The "time" of a verb's action as expressed in the form of the verb:

Present: I go   **Past:** I went   **Future:** I will go
(For other tenses, see the table on p. 116.)

Transitive and intransitive.
A verb is **transitive** when it has an object: The teacher *demanded* (v) *order* (o).
A verb is **intransitive** when it does not have an object: He *slept* (v) well.

Active and passive voice (6.3). A **passive** verb is a form of *be* and a past participle: *is believed, was believed, had been believed, will be believed.* All other verbs are **active.**

Mood (6.4). The manner in which a statement is expressed:
The **indicative mood** expresses a fact or a statement: I *am* thrifty. The **imperative mood** is used to express a direct command or request: *Come* here! The **subjunctive mood** is used in some conditions and in clauses like this: It is necessary that he *be* twenty-one.

Auxiliary verb (6.2). A verb used in a verb phrase to show tense, voice, and so on: *am* going; *had* gone; *will* go; *should have been* gone.

Linking verb or copula (1.1). A verb that "links" its subject to a predicate noun or an adjective: She *is* a teacher. The days *became* warmer.

Finite and nonfinite verbs. A **finite verb** (from the Latin *finis*, meaning "end" or "limit") can be limited (5 and 6):

1. In **person** by a pronoun or subject (I *sing*, she *sings*);
2. In **time** by a tense form (she *sings*, she *sang*);
3. In **number**, singular or plural (he *sings*, they *sing*).

Finite verbs are full verbs in sentences and clauses: I *had gone* before he *arrived*.

The **nonfinite verb** forms (participles, infinitives, gerunds) are not limited in person or number and are ordinarily used in phrases (3): Before *leaving* I thanked our host. She needed a costume *to wear* to the party.

7

NOUNS

Nouns are words used in sentences chiefly as subjects of verbs, objects of verbs, of prepositions, or of verbals, as complements following a linking verb, as appositives, or as modifiers of other words. They change their form to show number (by adding -*s*, -*es*, and so on) and possession ('*s*, *s*'). A noun may designate a person (*George Washington, woman*), place (*Spain, home*), thing (*pencil, steak*), quality (*beauty, rage*), action (*hunting, logrolling*), or idea (*justice, reality*).

The table on page 144 shows the forms, functions, and customary ways of classifying nouns. The following sections focus on the common problems that writers have with nouns:

1. how to use plural forms conventionally;
2. how to use possessive forms correctly;
3. when to use *a* or *an* before nouns;
4. how to spot unidiomatic or clumsy noun modifiers.

7.1 Plurals of Nouns

P1 Change the noun to a standard plural form.

Most English nouns form the plural simply by adding -*s* to the singular form (*cats, girls, books, things*). If the plural makes an extra syllable, -*es* is added to the singular form (*bushes, churches, kisses, Joneses*).

A few nouns preserve older methods of forming the plural, adding -*en* (*children, oxen*) or changing the vowel (*feet,* _teeth, geese, mice)_. Some nouns have the same form for both singular and plural:

1. all words ending in _-ics_, such as _athletics, civics, mathematics;_
2. the names of some animals, such as _deer, fish, mink, sheep;_
3. a number of words rarely or never used in the singular, such as _barracks, headquarters, measles, pants, scissors._

Because there are few hard-and-fast rules for troublesome plurals, you should consult the dictionary whenever you are unsure of a plural form. If the plural of a noun is irregular, it will be shown under the entry for the singular form; if no plural is given, the plural is formed in the usual way, by adding _-s_ or _-es_. Ordinarily, you will not have trouble knowing when a plural noun form is needed. However, you may encounter some difficulty spelling some plurals. Section 17.2, Spelling Troublesome Plurals, deals with the most common spelling problems.

Exercise 7.A

Indicate the plural forms of the italicized words. You may want to consult a dictionary and Section 17.2, Spelling Troublesome Plurals.

1. the _fish_ in the well
2. the _wharf_ in San Francisco
3. his favorite _dish_
4. the cast iron _safe_
5. the troubled _industry_
6. the most popular _rodeo_
7. the troublesome _fungus_
8. the national _census_
9. the well-delivered _speech_
10. the wary _goose_

Exercise 7.B

Write sentences using the plural forms of the following words. You may use more than one word in a single sentence. Be sure to consult your dictionary whenever you are uncertain how a plural is formed.

father-in-law	datum
apparatus	antenna
sheaf	crisis
stimulus	medium
knife	analysis
phenomenon	louse
berry	aeronautics
handful	pro

7.2

Noun

7.2 Possessive Case

Case refers to the form a noun or pronoun takes to show its relationship to other words in the sentence. In English, nouns have only two case forms, the *common* form (*dog, book, John*) and the *possessive,* or genitive, which is the common form plus an *s* or *z* sound (*dog's, book's, John's*) or a plural form with no additional sound (*dogs', books'*). An *of* phrase (*of the dog, of the book, of John*) can function as a possessive and is usually regarded as an alternate form.

Uses of the Possessive

The possessive case of nouns is most commonly used to show possession (a *student's* book, a mannerism *of the professor*). But it also shows other relationships:

1. **Description:** a *day's* work, a drop *of oil, yesterday's* paper
2. **Doer of an act:** the *wind's* force, the *dean's* permission, the permission *of the dean*
3. **Recipient of an act:** the *bill's* defeat, the execution *of a spy*
4. **Subject of a gerund** (see p. 63): the *doctor's* warning, the *play's* closing.

Forms and Position of the Possessive

∨⁄ Insert an apostrophe or remove an unnecessary apostrophe.

In writing, the possessive case is signaled by an apostrophe. The position of the apostrophe ordinarily tells us whether a possessive is singular or plural:

Singular	officer's	niece's
Plural	officers'	nieces'

Position of the Apostrophe

Most singular nouns form the possessive by adding *'s*, as do the few plural nouns that do not end in -*s* (such as *men, women, children*):

> the **teacher's** remarks (the remarks *of the teacher*)
>
> a **day's** work (the work *of a day*)
>
> the **children's** playground (the playground *of the children*)

Plural nouns ending in -*s* form the possessive by adding an apostrophe alone:

> the **teachers'** meeting (the meeting *of teachers*)
>
> the **musicians'** union (the union *of musicians*)
>
> the **Joneses'** relatives (the relatives *of the Joneses*)

Singular nouns ending in -*s* may form the possessive by adding an apostrophe alone or by adding *'s*. Either is correct, but you should be consistent in whichever form you use.

> Mr. **Jones'** [or Jones's] business
> **Delores'** [or Delores's] father
> the **hostess'** [or hostess's] gown
> the **actress'** [or actress's] role

Group Words. With group words or compound nouns the *'s* is added to the last term:

> The **Queen of England's** duties
> the **attorney general's** job
> her **mother-in-law's** address
> their **mothers-in-law's** addresses
> **someone else's** responsibility

Nouns in Series. When two coordinate nouns (joined by *and, but,* or *nor*) are in the possessive, the apostrophe usually is added only to the last one if there is joint possession. But if there is individual possession, the apostrophe is used with both nouns:

Joint possession	**Barbara and Tom's** mother
Individual possession	**Barbara's and Tom's** bicycles
	neither Barbara's nor Tom's teacher

Plural Nouns as Modifiers. The apostrophe is not used in some expressions in which the plural noun is considered a modifier:

> **teachers** college
>
> **travelers** checks
>
> **Veterans** Administration
>
> United **States** Post Office

Substitution of plural noun modifiers for the possessive is increasing today, so you should carefully note letterheads, signs, official publications, and the like to determine customary usage.

Choice Between *of* Phrases and *'s* Forms

The *'s* form of the possessive is customarily used with living things (my *uncle's* house, *Hepburn's* films, a *cat's* paw, a *robin's* nest) and an *of* phrase with inanimate objects (the door *of the room*, an angle *of inclination*, the beginning *of the end*). But in many instances either form may be used, the choice depending largely upon the sound and intended emphasis of the expression (the *book's* cover, the cover *of the book*). Some idiomatic expressions are usually stated in one form only (a *week's* wages, a *moment's* hesitation, an embarrassment *of riches*, the wages *of sin*). With titles of books, plays, films, magazines, journals, and other works, you should employ an *of* form to express the possessive:

> the plot **of** *Star Wars*
>
> the first act **of** *Hamlet*
>
> the editors **of** *Atlantic Monthly*

Awkward Use of *'s* Forms. An *of* phrase is sometimes preferable to an *'s* form to avoid a clumsy or unidiomatic expression or a statement that may be ambiguous. When the modifying noun is separated from the word it refers to by a phrase or a clause, an *of* phrase should be used:

> The apartment **of the woman** who won the contest was ransacked last night. [not *The woman who won the contest's apartment* or *The woman's apartment who won the contest*]

The *of* phrase is useful in distinguishing between the recipient and doer of an act, particularly if the meaning is unclear in context. *John's photographs* might mean either photographs *of* him or photographs *by* him, but *the photographs of John* would ordinarily mean that John was the subject of the pictures.

The Double Possessive. In a few statements both the *of* and *'s* forms of the possessive are used, an idiom of long standing in English:

> those photographs **of John's** [meaning John owns or took them]
>
> that boy **of Henry's**
>
> some friends **of my father's**
>
> a remark **of the author's**

Exercise 7.C

Indicate whether the possessive forms italicized in the following sentences are correct. Revise whenever necessary.

1. The architect who lived in the *penthouse's* income was in six figures.
2. An aunt of *Sara's* managed the plant in *Miami's* suburbs.
3. The *President's* of the United States speech won the *press'es* approval.
4. A chapter of Joan *Didion's* book was reprinted by *Esquire's* editor.
5. The *county's* sheriff patrol car was damaged by the *pickup's* bumper.
6. The *coach's* remarks brought *anger's* tears to the *eye's* of the *quarterback's.*
7. We moved by the *flambeau's* light.
8. The *Hernandez's* legal firm specialized in real estate and corporate law.
9. We stopped briefly at the United *States'* Post Office on Pine Street.
10. The *strikers'* lost a *month's* income before negotiations resumed. ∎

Exercise 7.D

Indicate which of the italicized nouns in these sentences are correctly written with *s* endings and which should have *'s* or *s'.*

1. The *energies* of our system will decay, the *suns* glory will dim, and the earth will no longer tolerate the race which has disturbed *its* peace.

2. One of Sir James *Barries* humorous characters said, "Facts were never pleasing to him. . . . He was never on *terms* with them until he stood them on their *heads.*"

3. As flies to wanton *boys* are we to the *gods;* they kill us for their sport.

4. When the *childrens* laughter began to peal in the garden, the *Joneses* neighbors closeted themselves in the air-conditioned family room.

5. Barry *Manilows* success results from the American middle *classes* acceptance of the mass *medias* ability to create instant *heroes.*   ■

7.3 Use of *a* and *an* with Nouns

The choice between *a* and *an* before a noun or modifier depends on the initial *sound,* not the initial letter, of the word that follows *a* or *an.*

1. *A* is used before words beginning with a consonant sound (long *u* has the sound of the consonant *y*):

a car	a city
a *B*	a house
a one-eyed cat	a hyperbole
a manicure	a used car
a European country	a U-turn

2. *An* is used before words beginning with a vowel sound (the consonant *h* is sometimes silent):

an ape	an honor
an *F*	an hors d'oeuvre
an hour	an omission
an oar	an uncle

Abbreviations or acronyms occasionally cause a writer problems, but the rules above still apply. You should choose *a* or *an* according to the way the initial sound of the word that follows is actually *read,* not as it might be expanded. Some examples will help to clarify the matter:

an SAT proctor [SAT is treated as three separate letters with an initial vowel sound—*es*—rather than as "scholastic aptitude test" with an initial consonant sound—*sk*.]

an NET production [NET is treated as three separate letters with an initial vowel sound—*en*—rather than as "National Educational Television" with an initial consonant sound—*n*.]

7.4

Noun

a NATO weapon [Notice here that NATO is conventionally read as a single word with an initial consonant sound—*n*—rather than as four separate letters with an initial vowel sound—*en*.]

Exercise 7.E

Indicate whether *a* or *an* should be used before the following words or phrases.

1. _____ ogre
2. _____ NBC television show
3. _____ eucalyptus tree
4. _____ unique experience
5. _____ E. F. Hutton commercial
6. _____ Y-chromosome
7. _____ Xerox machine
8. _____ hieroglyph
9. _____ exhumation
10. _____ ewe
11. _____ android
12. _____ soliloquy of Macbeth's
13. _____ inalienable right
14. _____ eustachian tube
15. _____ I-30 motel
16. _____ unfortunate incident
17. _____ Huguenot
18. _____ history book
19. _____ historic event
20. _____ U.S. State Department official ■

7.4 Noun Modifiers

When an adjective is the customary form in an expression, it should be used in place of a clumsy or unidiomatic noun modifier:

After graduating from St. Olaf, Karen took her **medical** [not *doctor*] training at Northwestern.

After sparking his team to victory in the city championship, Les went on to play with a **Canadian** [not *Canada*] team.

But for words that do not have exact adjective equivalents, the noun forms are freely used as modifiers: a *murder* mystery, *kitchen* utensils, *radio* reception, *prison* walls. In some expressions either the noun or adjective form may be used: *atom* bomb, *atomic* bomb.

Noun forms used as modifiers—particularly units of measurement—are ordinarily singular: a ten-*ton* truck, a six-*foot* jump. (Used as nouns, the forms would be plural: ten *tons* of coal, a jump of six *feet*.)

Exercise 7.F

Noticing how nouns are used in what you read will acquaint you with their uses and help you discriminate among various styles. For each of the kinds of reading listed below, count and classify the nouns that appear in four paragraphs according to these categories: plural nouns, concrete nouns, abstract nouns, possessive nouns, and total number of nouns.

1. Article in a newsmagazine (*Time, Newsweek*, etc.)
2. Article in an opinion magazine (*Harper's, Atlantic*, etc.)
3. Article in a popular magazine (*Self, Sports Illustrated*, etc.)
4. Article in a newspaper
5. Editorial in a newspaper
6. One of your textbooks ∎

Exercise 7.G

Read each sentence below and then select the noun form you consider appropriate. If the choice is optional, explain the context in which each form would be used. Consult your dictionary if necessary to find the standard plural form.

1. Delicately the proud (man-of-wars, men-of-war) dipped their masts and fired (eight-gun, eight-guns) salutes.
2. Their (enemies, enemys) stood towering on the crests of the hills and then stormed thunderously into the unprotected (valleys, vallies).
3. The (atom, atomic) blast flowered evilly behind the desert dotted with pale (cactuses, cacti).

4. (A, An) awful explosion set the (axis, axes) of the earth quivering like a slackening top.
5. "The television (media, medium)," he said, "is responsible for our permissive attitude toward violence."
6. The two- (liter, liters) engine was powerful enough to propel the sport sedan to its first (victory, victorious) season.
7. Mardian is (a, an) eunuch in (*Antony and Cleopatra*'s first act, the first act of *Antony and Cleopatra*).
8. Her (finance, financial) degree was from Baylor.
9. It was a two-hundred- (yard, yards) plunge to the (ravine's bottom, bottom of the ravine).
10. She enjoyed Agatha Christie's (murder, murderous) mysteries. ■

Exercise **7.H**

The following sentences contain various errors in noun forms. Read the sentences carefully, as if you were proofreading your own composition, and make the necessary corrections. You may need to change the word order in some cases.

1. The father's-in-laws mood got worse as each bottle of wine was dumped into the punch, and soured completely when wine was spilled on the mother's of the bride dress.
2. The kingdom of vertebrae includes ourselfs and all beasts, birds, reptiles, frogs, and fishes.
3. The boy down the street's car was painted as brightly and strangely as a preening peacocks tail.
4. With a team of great black oxes he broke the soil to plant his first crop.
5. The doctor's last bill's effect upon the editor's-in-chief health was more than the medicine could cure.
6. It was the consensi of three generations of scholar's that the poetess's work was of the highest order.
7. All the babys had lost several of their teeth'.
8. Tennessee Williams' *Night of the Iguana*'s plot provided the story line for a ABC television mini-series.
9. It was the commander-in-chief's opinion that his generals were dumb as donkies.
10. The fire destroyed Andrew and Mary's clothes. ■

Review

FORMS, FUNCTIONS, AND CLASSES OF NOUNS

■ Forms

Singular and plural forms
Singular: boy, box, child, goose, hero, baby, phenomenon
Plural: boys, boxes, children, geese, heroes, babies, phenomena

Compound nouns or group words. Two or more nouns (written as one word, as two words, or hyphenated) that function as a single unit: bookcase, football; pine tree, high school; father-in-law, hangers-on

Possessive form: boy's, Harriet's, girls', cats'

Gender. A few nouns in English have one form for the masculine, one for the feminine: actor, actress. Many readers, however, now object to the use of some of the feminine forms: poetess, authoress, directress.

■ Functions

Subject of a verb: The *tires* squealed as the *motorcycle* skidded around the corner.

Object of a verb: The new company manufactured *thermometers*.

Complement: He became *vice-president*. A whale is a *mammal*.

Object of a preposition: The acrobats were performing inside the *tent*.

Object of a verbal: She tried to break the *record*.

Indirect object: He gave the *church* a memorial window.

Appositive: Mr. McDermott, the insurance *agent*, is here.

Modifier of a noun: She thought *cigarette* holders looked silly. *Tyler's* car was stolen.

Modifier of a statement: *Each year* we make new resolutions.

■ Classes

Proper nouns. Names of particular people, places, and things, written with capitals: Anne, George W. Loomis, London, Monday, Monroe Doctrine

Common nouns. In contrast with these proper nouns, all the other groups are common nouns and are written with lower-case letters

Concrete nouns. Names of objects that can be seen and touched: leaf, leaves, road, panda, manufacturer

Abstract nouns. Names of qualities, actions, ideas that are perceived mentally: kindness, hate, idealism, fantasy, concept

Collective nouns. Names of groupings of individuals: fleet, army, company, committee, bevy

Mass nouns. Names of masses or aggregates not definable as individual units: food, money, intelligence, justice

Count nouns. Names of things perceived as individual units: truck, shelf, pencil, cow, vase

8

PRONOUNS

A pronoun is a word that functions like a noun but does not name a specific person, place, or thing. Among the many pronouns are:

I	you	we
he	she	it
him	them	whom
who	which	that
myself	itself	themselves
all	either	some

A pronoun often substitutes for a previously stated noun called its *antecedent*. The antecedent provides the pronoun with its specific meaning:

> My **uncle** phoned last night. **He** is coming by plane. [*Uncle* is the antecedent of the pronoun *he*.]

> **Women** over forty are invited to join. **They** may apply by mail. [*Women* is the antecedent of the pronoun *they*.]

> **My friend and I** are invited to a **party** with her **cousins. We** are going to **it** with **them.** [*My friends and I* is the antecedent of the pronoun *we*, *party* is the antecedent of *it*, and *cousins* is the antecedent of *them*.]

When you use pronouns, you must be certain that they are in the form that indicates their function. You must also be sure that your readers are able to follow a pronoun's reference to its antecedent without confusion. The following sections discuss the most common problems in using pronouns. The table on page 171 lists the various kinds of pronouns and their forms.

8.1   Reference of Pronouns

Ref   Change the pronoun so that its reference will be exact and obvious; if necessary, substitute a noun for the pronoun or revise the sentence.

Pronouns Referring to a Definite Antecedent

The antecedent of a pronoun should be clearly stated, not merely implied. The pronoun should refer specifically to this antecedent:

Inaccurate	He had been vaccinated against typhoid, but **it** did not protect him. [no antecedent for *it*]
Accurate	He had a typhoid **vaccination,** but it did not protect him. [*Vaccination* is the antecedent of *it.*]

Instead of changing the antecedent, it is often better to substitute a noun for the inexact pronoun:

Inaccurate	She couldn't understand how to solve the problem until I wrote **it** out.
Accurate	She couldn't understand how to solve the problem until I wrote out the **solution.**

A simple test for accurate reference is to see whether the antecedent could be substituted for the pronoun. If not, the sentence needs revision.

Inaccurate	She talked a lot about the technique of horsemanship, although she had never ridden **one** [horsemanship?] in her life.
Accurate	She talked a lot about the technique of horsemanship, although she had never ridden a **horse** in her life.

The antecedent of a pronoun should not be a noun used as a modifier or a noun in the possessive form:

Inaccurate	To make an attractive **tulip** border, plant **them** close together. [*Tulip* is used as a modifier.]
Accurate	To make an attractive border of **tulips,** plant **them** close together.
Inaccurate	Bill provided a lot of excitement one afternoon when he was skipping rocks across the pond and hit a young **girl's** shoulder **who** was swimming under water. [A noun in the possessive functions as a modifier.]
Accurate	Bill provided a lot of excitement one afternoon when he was skipping rocks across the pond and hit the shoulder of a young **girl who** was swimming under water.

Exercise 8.A

In the following sentences, the antecedents of the italicized pronouns are implied, but not stated. Revise each sentence to include a clear antecedent.

Example I am a student of *photography*. More and more, they are regarded as works of art.

I am a student of photography. More and more, photographs are regarded as works of art.

1. Touring the aircraft plant, we saw *them* being manufactured.
2. Although we had analyzed the bacteria content of the stream thoroughly, *it* was not part of the final report of the committee.
3. Because they lost five pounds in two days, *it* was considered a great success.
4. The principal extolled the virtues of athletics even though, as far as we could tell, she had never been *one.*
5. In preparing the special effects for *Return of the Jedi*, I think *they* went overboard.
6. Although ether's effect is to put patients to sleep, *it* is rarely used as an anesthetic today.
7. If you find the glue pot, spread *it* on the kitchen wall.
8. After having photographed the dean, *it* was printed in the campus newspaper.

9. Although he had written several books on the UFO phenomenon and had produced several films, he had never seen *one*.

10. Whenever the temperature drops below freezing, the truck's battery goes dead and *it* refuses to move. ∎

Ambiguous Reference

Sometimes the meaning of a pronoun is unclear because the pronoun could refer to two different antecedents. To eliminate such ambiguity, either substitute a noun for the pronoun or clarify the antecedent:

Confusing	When Stanton visited the President in February, **he** did not know that **he** would be dead within two months.
Clear	When Stanton visited the President in February, **he** did not know that **Lincoln** would be dead within two months.

Sometimes ambiguous reference may be avoided by making one of the antecedents singular and the other plural:

Ambiguous	In the nineteenth century many businessmen [plural] exploited the workers [plural] at every point, not caring whether **they** were making a decent living wage, but only whether **they** were getting a lot of money.
Clear	In the nineteenth century many businessmen [plural] exploited the worker [singular] at every point, not caring whether **he** was making a decent living wage, but only whether **they** were getting a lot of money.

Using the same pronoun for different implied antecedents is particularly annoying to a reader and should be avoided:

Confusing	We pulled out our spare, which was under the seat, and put **it** on. **It** dampened our spirits for a while, but we decided to go on with **it**. [The first *it* refers to the tire, the second to the mishap, and the third to the trip.]
Revised	We pulled out our spare, which was under the seat, and put the tire on. The flat dampened our spirits for a while, but we decided to go on with the trip.

Identifying the antecedent by repeating it after the pronoun is a makeshift practice that should be avoided:

Clumsy	Boswell first met Johnson when **he** (Johnson) was fifty-four.
Revised	Johnson was fifty-four when Boswell first met **him.**

Ambiguity sometimes results from a careless use of possessive pronouns:

Ambiguous	Mrs. Hurst was a very popular woman and **her accusation** scandalized everyone in town. [Was Mrs. Hurst the accuser or the accused?]
Revised	Mrs. Hurst was a very popular woman and **the accusation she made** [or **the accusation made about her**] scandalized everyone in town.

Exercise **8.B**

In the following sentences you will find a variety of ambiguous pronoun references. Revise each sentence to clarify the relationship between pronoun and antecedent. You may have to add words or rearrange the sentence.

1. As the mob approached the demonstrators, they grew noisier and angrier.
2. When the President asked the Secretary of State for an assessment of the crisis, he looked worried.
3. Dr. Benson told Dr. Wood that she was now certain that she was wrong.
4. He found the blueprint in the manual and checked it carefully.
5. Many of the employees were unhappy that the board of directors had given the managers three paid holidays, but not them. They decided to complain to them about them.
6. While Ms. Wharton spoke to Mrs. Kelley, she leafed through the ledger on her desk.
7. If the students and the administrators cannot work out a compromise, they will just have to give in to them.
8. Give the manuscript and the typed copy to me, and after I finish proofreading this book, it will be done.

9. Many of us flew from Houston to Denver where everyone met.

10. He was a month premature, but when I saw my father lift him up and heard his first cries, I told him that I knew he was healthy. ■

Pronouns Referring to Ideas and Statements

This, that, which, and *it* are often used to refer to ideas or situations expressed in preceding statements:

> Always do right. **This** will gratify some people and astonish the rest.—Mark Twain

> Nor is the way in which a speech community rounds off its numbers haphazard; rather **it** is explainable as an interplay beween language and culture.—Peter Farb, *Word Play*

> Perhaps the enjoyment of music is always suffused with past experience; for me, at least, **this** is true.—Ralph Ellison, "Living with Music"

In such constructions, the idea to which the pronoun refers should be obvious. When it is not, the reader may be confused:

Ambiguous	The Supreme Court acted on the Gideon case after the accused had spent time in a Florida jail for a crime he had not committed, *which* is typical of American justice.
Revised	The Supreme Court acted on the Gideon case after the accused had spent time in a Florida jail for a crime he had not committed. *This judicial review* is typical of American justice.

You can usually eliminate a vague *this, that,* or *which* by specifying exactly what *this, that,* or *which* actually is:

Ambiguous	The film includes a kidnapping, a volcanic eruption, and a mountain rescue. *This* was especially well done.
Revised	The film includes a kidnapping, a volcanic eruption, and a mountain rescue. *The rescue sequence* was especially well done.

Exercise 8.C

Remove the ambiguous references in the sentences below by specifying what *this, that,* and *which* are. You may have to reword or rearrange the sentences.

1. The new, technically advanced and superbly engineered copier was heavily promoted, *which* was typical of the company.
2. The influx of new residents brings growth, new businesses, talented people, heavier traffic, and large housing developments. *This* is a problem.
3. The assembly booed loudly when it was announced that the academic counselor would speak. *This* was a surprise.
4. The invoice contained a list of items purchased, the number of items purchased, a coded wholesale price, and an uncoded retail price, *which* confused me.
5. *That*'s not certain. If she arrives today, she may decide to speak on the abortion issue. ∎

Use of *who, which, that*

Who refers to persons, *which* generally refers to animals or things, and *that* refers to either persons, animals, or things:

> Students **who** [or *that*] plan to enter the university in the fall quarter should forward transcripts of their records to the registrar.

> In five minutes he solved a problem **that** [or *which*] I had struggled with for nearly five hours.

> Dogs **that** [or *which*] are within the city limits must be vaccinated.

> This is a matter about **which** more information is needed.

Who is preferred to *that* when persons are referred to:

> the technician **who**   the machine **that**
> the composer **who**   the symphony **that**

The use of *which* to refer to persons is not usually desirable. *Which* is often used, however, to refer to impersonal organizations of people like groups, clubs, and companies:

> The state legislature, **which** [not *who*] passed the act despite the governor's protest, had its eye on politics.

The Maryland Company, **which** manufactured farm implements, has gone into bankruptcy.

That usually introduces restrictive clauses:

8.1
Ref

The state legislature **that** passed the act despite the governor's protest is still in session.

Who and *which* are used both restrictively and nonrestrictively. See 11.4, Commas with Nonrestrictive Modifiers.

Exercise 8.D

Decide whether the *who, which,* or *that* italicized in each sentence below is used correctly. Revise as necessary.

1. I wasn't sure whether the plumber *that* I hired was competent.
2. The mothers appealed directly to the state legislature *who* had originally rejected the proposal on day-care centers.
3. Gun control is a controversy *which* will not be resolved soon.
4. Bank clerks *that* are not trained to use word-processing equipment soon will be.
5. The seven major firms *who* manufacture automobiles in the United States compete fiercely. ∎

Use of *he* or *she*

The masculine pronoun *(he, him, his)* has customarily been used when referring to a noun or pronoun that includes persons of both sexes *(student, teacher, clerk, everyone, anyone, somebody):*

Each transfer student is required to submit a complete transcript of **his** grades.

Everyone who is eligible to vote should make certain that **he** has registered before the deadline.

Feminine forms are sometimes used as alternatives to the conventionally used masculine pronouns, especially in situations where females are the likely majority:

A nurse must carefully record **her** observations on each patient's chart.

Every aerobic dancer will have a chance to perform **her** routine before the group.

Using two singular pronouns to signify both sexes is sometimes an acceptable alternative:

Everyone who is eligible to vote should make certain that **he or she** has registered before the deadline.

However, this usage can quickly become awkward. Plural forms are sometimes employed to avoid the cumbersome overuse of the *he or she* combination:

Awkward   Each **owner** must pay **his or her** fine before **he or she** can get **his or her** pet out of the pound.

Revised   **Owners** must pay a fine before **they** can get **their** pets out of the pound.

Plural forms are also being used more frequently as an alternative to the generic *he:*

Every **student** who wishes to can get **his** textbooks at the Co-op immediately after registration.

All **students** who wish to can get **their** textbooks at the Co-op immediately after registration.

Another choice is possible. You may sometimes encounter *they (their, them)* employed as a common-gender singular form:

Each **applicant** submitted **their** plans.

Everyone who wishes to can get **their** textbooks at the Co-op.

Their used in this way is widespread in spoken English. However, the form is not universally accepted in formal written English. You may be able to avoid the problem entirely by omitting the plural pronoun:

Each applicant submitted [ ] plans.

Everyone who wishes to can get [ ] textbooks at the Co-op.

Exercise 8.E

Use pronouns to replace the repetitious nouns and make a single, smoother sentence. You may also have to change other words.

8.1
Ref

Example   John saw the sailboat. John knew at once that he must own the sailboat.

*John saw the **sailboat** and knew at once that he must own **it**.*

1. Christopher lit George's cigar. The cigar glowed brightly.
2. "My goodness, yes," Susan's husband said, "Susan's husband will tell you about Susan. Susan has left town."
3. The second baseman told the first baseman that the second baseman wanted to take the first baseman to dinner after the game. The first baseman said no.
4. When the teacher gave the students the students' assignment, the students groaned. Then the students did the work.
5. The owner of the newspaper demanded that the columnist write on less controversial topics. The columnist declared to the owner that the owner could not tell the columnist what to do. ■

Exercise 8.F

Revise each of the following sentences in which the reference of pronouns is inexact, misleading, or otherwise faulty.

Example   A general interest bookstore would probably do better in this town than an obscure one.

*A general interest bookstore would probably do better in this town **than a bookstore that specializes in obscure books.***

1. After he had studied *kung fu* for three months, he began to boast that he was an expert one.
2. An exercise room is available in the basement of the new physical education building which can be used by both students and faculty.
3. Tolliver's wildflower text is useful, but its descriptions of the high-plains ones are vague.

4. Football is a more complex game now than in the past, with its play books and game movies, but many are still brutally rough.
5. When the women were about to leave the exhibit of quarterhorses, they ran into their mates. ■

8.2 Agreement of Pronoun and Antecedent

Agr **Make the pronoun agree in form with the word to which it is related.**

To be clear in meaning, a pronoun must agree in number with its antecedent—the noun to which it refers. When a pronoun serves as subject, the number of the verb is determined by the antecedent of the pronoun. (See also 5, Agreement of Subject and Verb.)

Personal Pronouns

Personal pronouns, like nouns, have singular and plural forms, as listed in the table on page 171. A personal pronoun referring to a singular antecedent should be singular; one referring to a plural antecedent should be plural. Errors in agreement are most likely to occur when a pronoun is separated from its antecedent by some intervening element:

Inaccurate	Although the average **American** belives theoretically in justice for all, **they** sometimes fail to practice it. [*American* is singular; *they* is plural.]
Accurate	Although the average **American** believes theoretically in justice for all, **he or she** sometimes fails to practice it. [*American* and *he or she* are both singular, as are their verbs.]
Inaccurate	After reading his **arguments** in favor of abolishing property, I found that I was not convinced by **it**. [*Arguments* is plural; *it* is singular.]
Accurate	After reading his **arguments** in favor of abolishing property, I found that I was not convinced by **them**. [Both *arguments* and *them* are plural.]

When a pronoun's antecedent is a collective noun, the pronoun may be either singular or plural, depending on whether the collective noun is treated as singular or plural (see 5.2):

The **class** planned **its** next field trip.

The **class** had **their** pictures taken.

A pronoun referring to coordinate nouns joined by *and* is plural:

When **Linda** and **Gail** returned, **they** found the house empty.

Usually a singular pronoun is used to refer to nouns joined by *or* or *nor:*

Dick or **Stan** will lend you **his** skis.

Neither **wax** nor **acrylic** will hold **its** luster under these conditions.

In general, the principles governing agreement between pronouns and coordinate nouns are the same as those governing agreement between a compound subject and verb. See 5.1, Verbs with Compound Subjects.

Exercise 8.G

In the following sentences, decide whether the italicized pronouns agree in number with their antecedents. Revise as necessary.

1. Each member of the orchestra was responsible for *their* instrument.
2. Neither Phillip nor Mario had completed *his* course work.
3. Although his explanations of the ionization process were detailed and aided by charts, I did not follow *it.*
4. The drill sergeant put the squad through *its* paces.
5. None of the vineyards was up to *its* usual standards of excellence. ■

Relative Pronouns

When a relative pronoun (*who, that, which,* and so on) is used as the subject of a dependent clause, the antecedent of the pronoun determines the number of the verb and of all reference words:

George is one of those people who **have** trouble making up **their** minds. [The antecedent of *who* is the plural *people,* which requires the plural verb, *have; who* also requires the plural reference *their* for the same reason.]

George is a person who **has** trouble making up **his** mind. [The antecedent of *who* is *person.*]

Indefinite pronouns

A number of words that are indefinite often function as pronouns: *some, all, none, everybody, somebody, anybody, anyone.* As explained below, some of these words are considered singular; others may be singular or plural, depending on the meaning of the statement. In editing your papers be sure that verbs and reference words agree in number with indefinite pronouns.

everyone, anybody, somebody. Everyone, everybody, anyone, anybody, someone, somebody, no one, nobody are singular forms and are used with singular verbs:

Everyone **has** left.

Somebody **was** here.

Nobody ever **calls.**

all, some, none. All, any, some, most, more are either singular or plural, depending upon the meaning of the statement:

All of the turkey **has** been eaten.

All of these questions **were** answered.

Some of the dialogue **is** witty.

Some of the farmers **have** opposed price supports.

None may be either singular or plural, depending upon the context. In current usage it is commonly used with a plural verb, but formal usage still prefers a singular verb unless the meaning is clearly plural.

None of our national parks **is** more scenic than Glacier.

None of the charges **has** been proved.

None of the new houses **are** as well constructed as the houses built twenty-five years ago. [The sentence clearly refers to all new houses.]

The emphatic *no one* is always singular:

I have talked to the manager and three assistants, but no one **was** of any help to me.

each. *Each* is a singular pronoun. It usually takes a singular verb and singular reference words:

Each of the players on the football team **has his** own idea about physical training.

Each of the paintings **is** an original.

Although the use of the plural form to refer to *each* is considered informal (*Each* of the children ran as fast as *their* legs could carry *them*), this construction is sometimes found in writing when the plural idea is uppermost:

Each of these peoples undoubtedly modified Latin in accordance with **their** own speech habits.—Albert C. Baugh, *History of the English Language*

See also 9.3, Demonstrative Adjectives, for agreement of *this* and *that* (*this kind, that sort*).

Exercise **8.H**

Revise any faulty pronoun references in the sentences below and eliminate awkward constructions. Make all necessary changes, including those in noun and verb forms. Several acceptable versions may be possible.

Example   Each of the grocers were willing to lower their prices on meat.

*Each of the grocers **was** willing to lower **his** prices on meat.*

*All of the grocers **were** willing to lower **their** prices on meat.*

1. No one among the astronomers at the conference were ready to support the controversial hypothesis.
2. The corporation insisted that all their executives pass his or her physical fitness examination.
3. Everyone seemed to believe that their applications deserved priority consideration.
4. All of the hockey players was certain that he or she would play his or her best.

5. Some of the answers were challenged by the students.
6. All were invited; nobody are expected to attend.
7. Each of the mathematicians are presently working on his or her own approach to teaching calculus.
8. Whenever somebody reads the sign at the entrance to the bookstore, they snicker.
9. Every one of us have jobs lined up for the summer.
10. Some of the architecture is innovative; most of the interior fixtures is not. ■

Exercise 8.1

Rewrite the following sentences, changing the words indicated. Make all other changes that would naturally occur, including those in pronoun, noun, and verb forms.

Example   [Change *an athlete* to *athletes*.] When an athlete gets out of shape, he is probably insuring the end of his career and the end of his team's winning record.

*When **athletes** get out of shape, **they** are probably insuring the end of **their** careers and the end of **their** team's (or teams') winning record (or records, if teams').*

1. [Change *a person* to *people*.] When a person weaves in and out of traffic lanes, he is endangering the lives of other motorists as well as his own.
2. [Change *Another* to *Other*.] Another electronics store also reports that its computer sales have fallen off.
3. [Change *anyone* to *everyone*.] My sister wanted to be able to help anyone who looked insecure or troubled, and to make him feel at ease, no matter who it happened to be.
4. [Change *one* to *some*.] One actor may interpret the role of Hamlet one way, another another way: if one decides that the role is pathetic, another may decide that his view—the tragic one—is correct.
5. [Change *all* to *each*.] Until the law determining the age of legal majority was changed, all students were expected to provide their home address so that their grades could be sent to their parents. ■

8.3 Case of Pronouns

Case **Change the form of the pronoun to show its function in the sentence as a subject, object, or possessive form.**

Subject and Object Pronouns

Most personal pronouns and the relative or interrogative pronoun *who* have one form when they are used as subjects *(I, she, he, we, they, who)* and another when they are used as objects *(me, her, him, us, them, whom)*:

> **He** and **I** watched the film.
>
> They had recommended it to **him** and **me**.
>
> **Who** is speaking to **whom?**

A simple test may help you know which pronoun form to use. In a sentence like this—He left the books for Sarah and (I, me)—omit the words *Sarah and*. Then it becomes clear that *me* is the form to use: He left the books for *me*. Subject and object forms are listed in the table of pronoun forms on page 171.

After Prepositions

The object form of a personal pronoun is used after a preposition (a letter for *him;* among *us* three). When a pronoun immediately follows a preposition, there is seldom any question about the proper form, but when there are two pronouns, or when a noun is used with the pronoun, writers are sometimes tempted to use a subject form.

Incorrect	The work was divided between **she** and **I**.
Revised	The work was divided between **her** and **me**.
Incorrect	The same is no doubt true of what European and Asiatic nations have heard about **we** Americans.
Revised	The same is no doubt true of what Europeans and Asiatic nations have heard about **us** Americans.

After *than* in Comparisons

In written English, *than* is considered a conjunction, not a preposition. In comparisons, *than* is followed by the form of the pronoun that would be used in a complete clause, whether or not the verb actually appears in the construction:

> I am older than **she.**
>
> I like him better than **her.**
>
> I like him better than **she.**
>
> Alan dances better than **I.**

When you are unsure of the proper pronoun form to use in a comparison, check your choice by adding the implied verb to the sentence:

> I am older than **she** [is].
>
> I like him better than [I like] **her.**
>
> I like him better than **she** [does].
>
> Alan dances better than **I** [do].

Exercise 8.J

In the following sentences, choose the correct pronouns.

1. By (who, whom) was the class addressed?
2. I would rather have (she, her) as organizer of the festival than (he, him).
3. She works better with people than (he, him).
4. Among (we, us) four, there was little dispute.
5. (We, Us) New Yorkers should be proud of the diversity and size of our city. ∎

Choice of *it is I*, *it's me*

Formal English takes the subject form after the linking verb *be:*

> It is **I.**   That is **he.**

But most speakers and writers accept *"It's me"* or *"That's him."* *Me* is more natural in this expression because the pronoun stands in the object position, immediately after a verb. All authoritative grammars and dictionaries consider *it's me* acceptable general usage. Fortunately, this construction seldom occurs in writing, except in dialogue, where "It is I" would sound stilted.

The notion that *I* is somehow more "correct" or polite than *me* sometimes leads people to use the subject form even when the pronoun is the object of a verb. The object form should be used in such constructions:

Incorrect	Father took Jerry and **I** to the game.
Revised	Father took Jerry and **me** to the game.

Choice of *who, whom*

The distinction between *who* and *whom* has practically dropped from speech (the *Oxford English Dictionary* says *whom* is "no longer current in natural colloquial speech"), and it may eventually disappear in writing. For example, in this construction—*Who* are you taking to the concert?—most would agree that *who* seems natural, since it's in the subject position, although formal usage would require *whom*, as the direct object (You are taking *whom* to the concert?).

In most writing it is probably best to retain the distinction between *who* and *whom:*

1. Use *who* when the pronoun is the subject of a verb, even in subordinate clauses which may themselves be serving as objects.

   Who left early? [*Who* is the subject.]

   We did not know **who** left early. [*Who* remains the subject of the subordinate clause *who left early*, which functions as the direct object in the sentence.]

2. Use *whom* in objective constructions, especially when the pronoun is the object of a preposition and follows immediately after it.

   To whom are you speaking? [*Whom* is the object of the preposition *to.*]

   He was a man **in whom** we placed great trust. [*Whom* is the object of the preposition *in.*]

   Taxes will go up no matter **whom** we elect. [*Whom* is the direct object in the subordinate clause *whom we elect.*]

The easiest way to check your usage is to arrange the elements in the clause in a subject-verb-object order (we elect *whom; who* is elected); *whom* serves as object, *who* as subject. Sometimes intervening words cause problems, but the principle still holds:

He made a list of all the writers **who** [subject of *were*] he thought were important in that century.

Exercise 8.K

In the following sentences, choose the pronouns that would be correct in formal written English.

1. It is (she, her) (who, whom) prepared the slides.
2. (Who, whom) can we trust to provide a fair estimate?
3. I am uncertain (who, whom) administers the Smithsonian museums.
4. (Who, Whom) thinks (they, them) might be the plagiarists?
5. It is not (I, me).
6. He would have liked (whoever, whomever) we hired to manage the condominium.
7. (Who, Whom) are you attacking in this essay?
8. The animals knew (who, whom) was watching and caring for them.
9. Do you see (we, us) more often than you see (they, them)?
10. For (she, her) it would have been more fortunate if we, rather than (they, them), had been on her committee.

8.3

Case

Possessive Pronouns

Many writers have problems using the apostrophe correctly with possessive pronouns. Remember that an apostrophe is *not* used with the possessives of personal pronouns (a relative of *ours*; the tree and *its* leaves), nor with the possessive of the relative pronoun *who* (a boy *whose* name was Tom).

Possessive of Personal Pronouns

Personal pronouns have two forms for the possessive (see p. 171): one is used as a modifier before a noun (*my* roommate, *her* favorite hat); the other is used (by itself or in a phrase) after a noun (That pencil is *mine*; a friend of *hers*). While either form may be used in many statements (*our* government, this government of *ours*), there are some constructions in which one form is obviously better than the other:

| Clumsy | We decided to pool **their** and **our** resources. |
| Revised | We decided to pool **their** resources with **ours**. |

Confusion of *its*, *it's*. *Its* without the apostrophe is the possessive form of *it*; *it's* with the apostrophe is the contraction for *it is* or *it has:*

> Everything should be in **its** proper place.
>
> **It's** [it is] an ill wind that blows no good.
>
> **It's** [It has] been a long time.

One of the mistakes most frequently marked on student papers is using *it's* for *its*. If you tend to confuse these two forms you should check each instance of *its* (*it's*) when revising your papers. For example, if you've used *it's*, read the word as *it is* or *it has*; your meaning will reveal any errors.

Possessive of Indefinite Pronouns

The possessive of several indefinite pronouns is formed by using *of*, not *'s*. These pronouns are *all, any, each, few, most, none,* and *some:*

> It was the opinion **of all.** [not *all's* opinion]
>
> Adversity brought out the best side **of each.** [not *each's* best side]

The possessive of other indefinite pronouns is formed by using *'s*, just as with nouns:

> **Anyone's** guess is as good as mine.
>
> One man's meat is **another's** poison.
>
> **Somebody's** books were left in the classroom.

When indefinite pronouns are used with *else*, the apostrophe and *s* are added to *else* and not to the preceding word:

> These notes are somebody **else's.**
>
> Anyone **else's** offer would have been accepted.

Possessive of *who* and *which*

Whose is the possessive form of the relative pronoun *who*. *Who's*, the informal contraction for *who is* or *who has*, is not used in most formal writing:

> Best known of American primitive artists is Grandma Moses, **whose** paintings are familiar to thousands.
>
> It is the white-collar worker **who is** [informal: *who's*] least likely to be affected by seasonal unemployment.

Although *whose* usually refers to persons and *of which* to animals and things, *whose* is regularly used to refer to inanimate things when *of which* would be awkward:

> We each spent five dollars to see a film whose plot was predictable and whose characters were uninteresting.

> . . . we would cross a room in which no one ever sat, whose fire was never lighted, whose walls were picked out with gilded mouldings.—Marcel Proust, *Remembrance of Things Past*

Exercise 8.L

Read the following sentences and correct any pronouns used incorrectly.

Example   Would you like to leave a message with I?

*Would you like to leave a message with **me**?*

1. She divided what was left of the profits equally between Margaret and I.
2. A book in which a man and a woman collaborate should deal accurately with human nature, for between him and her they represent the two sexes.
3. Most of the other actors have had more experience than me and make fun of my stage fright.
4. A letter came for Paul and I inviting us to an investment seminar.
5. How could we be certain it's paint was original?
6. Their's and your calculators have the most functions.
7. Its a long way to Albuquerque.
8. She is the person who's most qualified to serve on the district court.
9. Somebody's attitude had better improve quickly!
10. We know its a gamble to combine their and our technology on the project, but each's approach has much to recommend it. ∎

8.4 Reflexive and Intensive Pronouns

The reflexive form of a personal pronoun is used to refer back to the subject in an expression where the doer and recipient of an act are the same:

> I had only **myself** to blame.
>
> He hurt **himself** skiing.

The same pronoun form is sometimes used as an intensive to make another word more emphatic:

> The award was presented by the governor **himself.**
>
> Life **itself** is at stake.

In certain constructions *myself* is mistakenly considered by some people as more polite than *I* or *me* (My wife and *myself* accept with pleasure), but in standard English the reflexive form is not used as the subject or as a substitute for *me:*

> Another fellow and **I** [not *myself*] saw the whole thing.
>
> Sam invited John and **me** [not *myself*] to the party.

Hisself and *theirselves* are not standard English forms.

8.5   Choice of Personal Pronoun Form

Personal pronouns indicate the person or persons speaking (first person: *I, we*), the person spoken to (second person: *you*), or the person or thing spoken of (third person: *he, she, it, one, they*). In writing, you can choose to refer to yourself as *I, one,* or *we*. The following sections examine questions that arise when you use personal pronouns.

Use of *I, we*

There is no reason to avoid the pronoun *I* in any situation where it is needed. Some writers think that using *I* makes their writing too personal and subjective. But remember that every piece of writing is written by some *I*; it is often better for the *I* to be presented plainly and honestly, rather than to try to get around the natural use of *I* by devices that only call attention to themselves.

Awkward	After exploring the subject, **the writer** finds that mass hysteria is a rather common occurrence.
Revised	After exploring the subject, **I** find that mass hysteria is a rather common occurrence.
Awkward	It seems evident based on personal experience that **one** succeeds according to effort as much as talent.

Revised   I have learned that success depends on effort as much as on talent.

We is useful for general reference (*We* are living in an atomic age), but as a substitute for *I,* the "editorial we" is out of place in most writing.

Awkward   The conclusions in **our** paper are based upon information **we** obtained from the local police.

Revised   The conclusions in **my** paper are based upon information **I** obtained from the local police.

In this case, the personal pronouns can even be eliminated entirely if an impersonal point of view is desirable:

Revised   The conclusions in the paper are based upon information obtained from the local police.

Use of *one*
One is used, particularly in formal writing, to refer either to people in general or to the writer:

> Watching the scene on television, **one** can sense the drama of the situation.

But this use of *one* is impersonal, rather stiff, and often ungainly, especially when *one* is repeated several times. General English characteristically uses personal pronouns in such expressions:

Revised   Watching the scene on television, **I** [or *you*] can sense the drama of the situation.

Awkward   When **one** has drunk to **one's** limit, **one** should avoid driving **one's** car.

Revised   When **you** have drunk to **your** limit, **you** should avoid driving **your** car.

In current American usage, it is standard practice to refer to *one* (meaning the writer or anyone) by the third-person *he* and *his* or *she* and *her:*

> **One** should be cautious if **he** wants to avoid offending **his** friends.

Use of *you*
You (meaning people in general) must be employed carefully

because many readers find *you* irritating or patronizing in some situations:

| *Awkward* | When **you** begin reading *The Waste Land*, **you** are totally confused. |
| *Revised* | When **I** began reading *The Waste Land*, **I** was totally confused. |

You can also be inappropriate or inaccurate when it inadvertently directs attention to some particular second person rather than to all readers or to the writer:

| *Too personal* | The booklet warns that **you** will be fined or imprisoned for not paying **your** federal income taxes. |
| *Revised* | The booklet warns that **citizens** will be fined or imprisoned for not paying **their** federal income taxes. |

Still, *you* is appearing more often in legal documents, warranties, insurance policies, and instructions because of its clarity and directness:

> **You** are required to make a payment by the fifteenth day of every month. If **you** do not make this payment on time, **you** will have to pay an interest penalty. . . .
>
> After **you** have glued Part G-1 to G-2, **you** should allow the joint to dry thoroughly.

You can also work well when a writer seeks to establish a close relationship with the reader.

Exercise 8.M

Decide whether the personal pronouns in the following sentences are appropriate. Revise when necessary. You may have to add nouns or pronouns, or rearrange the sentence.

1. As you enter the new Hyatt Regency, you are dazzled by the spectacular atrium rising thirty stories above you.
2. One can't help but be impressed by their accomplishments.

3. It is this writer's belief that Lord Byron was the best of England's so-called Romantic poets.
4. As soon as one completes the first part of the examinations, one should proceed immediately to the second part.
5. Should this Tebo Widget fail within a year of original purchase, purchaser may return the Widget to the manufacturer provided said purchaser has properly maintained the Widget and serviced it regularly. Tebo Widgets shall not be liable to purchaser for damages due to neglect or commercial use of the Tebo Widget. ■

8.6 Avoiding Shifts in Pronoun Form

Shift **Make the words or constructions consistent in form. Pronouns should be consistent in person and number; verbs should be consistent in tense.**

In using pronouns for general reference, be consistent. Do not make unnecessary shifts from singular to plural forms or from *we* to *you* or *one*:

Inconsistent	If **we** unearth any artifacts, **one** should be sure to label them carefully.
Consistent	If **we** unearth any artifacts, **we** must be sure to label them carefully.

Pronoun shifts are especially troublesome when they occur throughout a passage. Be sure your pronouns remain consistent as you move from sentence to sentence:

Inconsistent	After **one** has selected the boat **he** is going to learn in, it would be a good idea if **you** first learned the theory of sailing. Most of **us** have at least seen a sailing boat, but seeing one and sailing one are two different things. **One** might think that a boat can sail only with the breeze and not against it. Or **they** might think that a stiff breeze is necessary to sail a boat.
Consistent	After **you** have selected the boat **you** are going to learn in, it would be a good idea if **you** first learned the theory of sailing. **You** have probably seen a sailing boat, but seeing

one and sailing one are two different things. **You** may think that a boat can sail only with the breeze and not against it. Or **you** may think that a stiff breeze is necessary to sail a boat.

As the example above suggests, the pronoun *one* is more likely to lead to shifted constructions than are the other forms. Unless you intend to be impersonal and feel confident in your use of *one*, use *you, we, he, she,* or a noun substitute in these situations.

Exercise **8.N**

Revise the following sentences to correct the needless shifts in person or number and any errors in the use of reflexive and intensive pronouns.

Example	The modern car is very complex, and they are always breaking down.

*The modern car is very complex, and **it is** always breaking down.*

1. Some writers think teachers use grammar as a means to block your creative abilities.
2. When a person has worked for a year in Washington, one is reluctant to return home to an ordinary job.
3. When a student has spent a lot of time on his compositions, they are apt to be disgruntled if all they get is grammatical criticisms. Anybody would feel the same way if you had a teacher like mine.
4. Although a pocket dictionary can give some help, they cannot replace a standard desk dictionary.
5. Nobody in the class seemed very sure of their ability to analyze style.
6. One never knows what their future holds or where you'll be tomorrow.
7. They told us theirselves that they had lied.
8. Each of us felt uneasy knowing that one's work was slipshod.
9. His Honor hisself gave the commencement address.
10. Whenever you need a ballpoint pen, they can't be found. ∎

KINDS OF PRONOUNS

■ Personal Pronouns

	Subject	Object	Possessive
First person			
Singular	I	me	my, mine
Plural	we	us	our, ours
Second person			
Singular and plural	you	you	your, yours
Third person			
Singular			
masculine	he	him	his
feminine	she	her	her, hers
neuter	it	it	its (of it)
Plural	they	them	their, theirs

■ Relative Pronouns

who	whom	whose
that	that	
which	which	whose, of which

■ Interrogative Pronouns

who	whom	whose
which	which	whose, of which
what	what	

■ Reflexive and Intensive Pronouns

myself	yourself	himself	herself	itself
oneself	yourselves	ourselves	themselves	

■ Demonstrative Pronouns

this	these	that	those

■ Indefinite Pronouns

all	both	everything	nobody	several
another	each	few	none	some
any	each one	many	no one	somebody
anybody	either	most	nothing	someone
anyone	everybody	much	one	something
anything	everyone	neither	other	such

■ Reciprocal Pronouns

each other   one another

■ Numerical Pronouns

one, two, three . . .   first, second, third . . .

9

ADJECTIVES
AND ADVERBS

Adj/
Adv Use the appropriate form of the adjective
or adverb.

Adjectives are modifiers that relate to a noun or pronoun:

a **cheerful** smile [modifies the noun *smile*]

The child is **quick.** [modifies the noun *child*]

We are **alive.** [modifies the pronoun *we*]

Adverbs are modifiers that relate to a verb, an adjective, another adverb, or the whole sentence:

She smiled **cheerfully.** [modifies the verb *smiled*]

The engine is **barely** warm. [modifies the adjective *warm*]

The engine idled **very** roughly. [modifies the adverb *roughly*]

Happily, the mechanic found the problem. [modifies the entire sentence]

Adjectives and adverbs enable a writer to specify and to make distinctions (not shelf, but *lowest* shelf; not just happy, but *extremely* happy). These modifiers may add descriptive details, limit or make more definite the meaning of a key word, or qualify statements:

a room of **pleasant** memories [adds descriptive detail]

he laughed **loudly** [adds descriptive detail]

the **first** book [limits]

he left **immediately** [makes more definite]

perhaps you've had enough [qualifies]

Other examples of the uses of adjectives and adverbs are discussed in the sections that follow.

9.1 Position of Adjectives

Most writers have few problems with adjectives. The forms of adjectives are relatively simple, and they are usually easy to place in a sentence. The typical position of adjectives (and of participles and nouns used as adjectives) is immediately before the words they modify, though other positions are possible:

The **seated** audience grumbled in the **warm** auditorium.

Shaking off from my spirit what must have been a dream, I scanned more narrowly the **real** aspect of the building. Its **principal** feature seemed to be that of an **excessive** antiquity. The discoloration of ages had been great. **Minute** fungi overspread the **whole** exterior, hanging in **fine tangled** web-work from the eaves.—Edgar Allan Poe, "The Fall of the House of Usher"

I can see the woods in their **autumn** dress, the oaks **purple,** the hickories **washed** with gold, the maples and the sumacs **luminous** with **crimson** fires, and I can hear the rustle made by the **fallen** leaves as we plowed through them. —Mark Twain, _Autobiography_

Two or more adjectives are often placed after the word they modify to gain emphasis or to avoid a clumsy expression:

It was a striking house, **roomy** and **ornate.**

Except for a boy, **tall** and rather **gangly,** the room was deserted.

. . . the sailors thronged the streets in flapping blues and spotless whites—**brown, tough, and clean.**—Thomas Wolfe, _Look Homeward, Angel_

If an adjective is modified by other words, it often comes after the noun:

> The old man, exceedingly **weary** from his trip, lay down to rest.

Exercise 9.A

In the sentences below, make the adjective or adjective phrase in parentheses modify the italicized noun. You may have to rearrange other parts of the sentence.

Example   A luscious Pacific oyster *stew* served as the main course. (steaming)

A Pacific oyster stew, **luscious and steaming,** *served as the main course.*

1. The history *examination* lasted for three hours. (unusually difficult for Professor Smith's course)
2. Energetic *Richard Pryor* has been an assured box-office draw. (caustic)
3. The *Michael Todd Theatre* was one of the city's forgotten landmarks. (crumbling and decaying)
4. Barbara Walters built her reputation on asking tough *questions*. (probing and often embarrassing)
5. The confident *engineer* applied for the patent. (buoyed by her success)   ■

9.2 Predicate Adjectives

Predicate adjectives are adjectives that follow linking verbs. They refer back to the subject (see 1.1):

She is **envious.**	The child looks **sad.**
He seems **afraid.**	The dog smells **bad.**
The weeds grew **tall.**	

The common linking verbs are *be (am, is, are, was, were, has/have been), seem, appear, become, grow, prove,* and verbs describing sensations like *taste, feel, smell, look.*

Sometimes these same linking verbs are followed and modified by adverbs:

> The weeds grew **rapidly.**

The child looks **sadly** at the fire.

The dog smells **carefully.**

Writers often have trouble deciding whether the adjective or adverb modifier should be used with a linking verb. To determine whether a predicate adjective or an adverb should be used, see if the word modifies the subject or the verb. When it modifies or refers to the subject, use an adjective; when it modifies the verb, use an adverb:

9.2
Adj

> The children looked **unhappy.** [predicate adjective, describing *children*]
>
> As the rain continued to fall, the children looked **unhappily** out the window. [adverb, modifying *looked*]
>
> Overnight the weather turned **cold.** [predicate adjective, modifying *weather*]
>
> He turned **coldly** when he heard his name mentioned. [adverb, describing the way in which he *turned*]

Choice of *good, well*

Some writers have a problem choosing between *good* and *well*. Quite often, they use the adjective *good* when the adverb *well* is called for:

Incorrect	The motor ran **good.**
Correct	The motor ran **well.**
Incorrect	The team played **good.**
Correct	The team played **well.**

Either *good* or *well* may be used as a predicate adjective with the verb *feel*, but with different connotations:

> Don't you feel **well?** [referring to a state of health, not ill]
>
> It made her feel **good** to write her résumé and get it printed three months before graduation. [referring to a general attitude or bodily sensation—comfort, happiness, well-being]

Remember that *good* is an adjective (a *good* time; This pizza tastes *good*) and that *well* can be either an adjective (He is now a *well* boy; Are you feeling *well*) or an adverb (He writes *well*).

Choice of *bad, badly*

Bad is the accepted adjective form after a linking verb:

> She feels **bad.**   The situation looks **bad** to me.
>
> The milk tastes **bad.**

Some writers use *badly* when the emphasis is on the verb: I feel *badly* about your troubles. But the usage is not universally accepted and should be avoided in most writing.

Exercise 9.B

Choose the correct adjective or adverb choice in parentheses.

1. I feel (certain, certainly) that the grant proposal will win approval.
2. Doesn't she feel (good, well)?
3. How (unhappy, unhappily) the nurses seem knowing the young patient is not doing (good, well)!
4. The dog smells so (bad, badly) that it can't track a steak through the living room.
5. The signs appeared so (quick, quickly) that we couldn't read them (good, well).　■

Exercise 9.C

Create sentences following the directions given below.

1. Write a sentence using *good* as a predicate adjective.
2. Write a sentence using *bad* as a predicate adjective.
3. Write a sentence using *glad* as a predicate adjective.
4. Write a sentence using *good* as a predicate adjective and *well* as an adverb.
5. Write a sentence using both *bad* and *badly*.　■

9.3 Demonstrative Adjectives

This and *that* (called demonstrative adjectives) are the only adjectives with plural forms: *this* idea, *these* ideas; *that* project, *those* projects. *This* and *these* usually refer to something nearby, or something the writer is more closely associated with or more interested in. *That* and *those* usually refer to something farther away, or something the writer is less immediately interested in.

This cassette player produces good sound.

That cassette player is too expensive.

These books are required for the course.

Those books are recommended for further reading.

This and *that* are often used with *kind* and *sort*, which are singular nouns and should be preceded by singular modifiers:

> I like **this kind** of records best.
>
> Jokes of **that sort** annoy me.

9.4 Forms of Adverbs

Most adverbs are formed by adding *-ly* to an adjective: *accidentally, particularly, really, sincerely.* A few adjectives ending in *-ly (early, likely)* are also used as adverbs. A number of common adverbs *(now, quite, there)* have no distinctive forms.

Although adverbs can be made by adding *-wise* to a noun *(lengthwise, clockwise, otherwise),* this practice has been greatly overused. Adverbs produced by adding *-wise* are often clumsy: *budgetwise, weatherwise, economywise).* It is best to avoid such coinages.

Long and Short Forms of Adverbs

Some adverbs have two forms: one with an *-ly* ending (long form), the other without (short form): *slow—slowly, loud—loudly, tight—tightly.* Adverbs used with or without the *-ly* ending include these:

bright	direct	loud	sharp	tight
cheap	even	quick	slow	wrong
close	fair	rough	smooth	
deep	loose	second		

The long and short forms are often interchangeable:

> Go **slow.** Go **slowly.**
>
> Don't talk so **loud.** Don't talk so **loudly.**
>
> The rope was drawn **tight.** The rope was drawn **tightly.**

But in some situations the long and short forms are not interchangeable. The long forms are generally used between the subject and verb (They *closely* watched). The short forms are used more with short words: *new* found friends, but *newly* acquired rank. Formal writers tend to use the long forms; other writers prefer the short forms. But since comprehensive rules cannot be given, each writer has to choose between the forms largely on the basis of the tone and sound of the sentence:

The infant was **tightly** clinging to its mother.
The infant was clinging **tight** to its mother.

Bobtailed Adverbs

Do not drop the ending of an adverb that has only the *-ly* form. Some common, but incorrect, "bobtailed" adverb forms are *considerable, serious,* and *different:*

Incorrect	Twenty-five dollars is **considerable** more than I want to pay.
Correct	Twenty-five dollars is **considerably** more than I want to pay.
Incorrect	People told him to take his research more **serious.**
Correct	People told him to take his research more **seriously.**
Incorrect	She worked **different** from the others.
Correct	She worked **differently** from the others.

Even more common are the "bobtailed" adverbs *real, bad,* and *sure.* In general or edited English these words must have *-ly* endings to function as adverbs.

Incorrect	It was a **real** outstanding performance.
Correct	It was a **really** outstanding performance.
Incorrect	He danced **bad.**
Correct	He danced **badly.**
Incorrect	They were **sure** confident.
Correct	They were **surely** confident.

Dropping the *-ly* in such words is a characteristic of some dialects and of informal conversations. A dictionary will tell you what the standard adverb form is whenever you are in doubt.

Correct Use of *most, almost*

Almost is an adverb meaning "very nearly":

I **almost** lost my mind. [adverb, modifying the verb *lost*]

The train was **almost** always on time. [adverb, modifying the adverb *always*]

Most is an adjective meaning "the greatest number":

Most fishermen are optimists. [adjective, modifying *fishermen*]

You'll sometimes hear *most* used as an adverb in speech: This train is *most* always on time. When an adverb is needed in writing, use *almost*.

Exercise 9.D

Whenever necessary, rewrite the following sentences to eliminate awkward *-wise* expressions.

Example   Weatherwise, it was a perfect day.

The weather was perfect.

1. Turn the tap counterclockwise to release the detergent.
2. We were especially pleased with the new home, locationwise.
3. Though still a leader in advanced technology, the United States has slipped behind some other industrial nations educationwise.
4. Consumerwise, the stereo was an excellent bargain.
5. Talentwise, the rookie pitcher was the most promising player on the otherwise mediocre baseball club. ■

Exercise 9.E

Identify the correct adjective or adverb forms in the following sentences. If both of the forms in parentheses are acceptable, indicate both choices.

1. Play (fair, fairly)!
2. The massive crane (slow, slowly) raised the cross-members into position.
3. Kirk was (sincere, sincerely) about repairing the microwave oven (quick, quickly).
4. The grand jury (wrong, wrongly) implicated the banker in the embezzlement scheme.
5. It's (real, really) cold in Minnesota in January.
6. (Most, Almost) all the participants in the contest produced superior quilts.
7. We want to see the playoff game (bad, badly).
8. His lecture on Twain was so funny that it was difficult to take what he said (serious, seriously).

9. She (sure, surely) knows how to program that computer.
10. He announced that, hereafter, he intended to go (straight, straightly).   ■

9.5   Position of Adverbs

Adverbs Modifying a Single Word

Unlike adjectives, adverbs can have various positions in the sentence. Try to place them in a position that clearly indicates your meaning and emphasis.

When an adverb modifies a single word, its typical position is immediately before that word:

> a **quite** late party [modifies *late*]
>
> They **never** finished the job. [modifies *finished*]

This often puts the modifier of a verb between an auxiliary and participle:

> He had **quietly** withdrawn.

A modifier of a verb often follows the verb or comes after the verb and its object:

> He withdrew **quietly.**
>
> They finished the job **hurriedly.**

See also 3.2, Split Infinitives (pp. 67–68).

Sentence Adverbs

A good many adverbial modifiers—single word adverbs, phrases, or clauses—cannot sensibly be related to another single word in a sentence. It is conventional to say that these adverbs "modify the whole sentence" and to call them *sentence adverbs*. Their position is variable:

> **Unfortunately** they had already left.
>
> They had already left, **unfortunately.**
>
> They had **unfortunately** already left.

This flexibility makes it possible to shift the position of many sentence adverbs for variety as well as for emphasis.

Misplaced Adverbial Modifiers

MM Revise the sentence so that the expression
is clearly related to the word or statement
it modifies.

Be careful not to misplace a modifier so that the meaning of a
statement becomes ambiguous or even ludicrous:

Ambiguous	We had **almost** seen every painting in the Louvre. [*almost* seems to modify *seen*]
Clear	We had seen **almost** every painting in the Louvre.
Ludicrous	She was **almost** pregnant every year.
Clear	She was pregnant **almost** every year.

Modifiers are sometimes placed so that they could refer to
either one of two sentence elements. These are sometimes
called "squinting modifiers" (see p. 70):

> Lacquering the wood **beautifully** preserves it. [*Beautifully* might modify either *lacquering* or *preserves*. Shifting the position of the adverb will clarify the sentence: either *Beautifully lacquering the wood . . .* or *. . . preserves it beautifully.*]

> Although it was often said that the old boat would sink **somehow** it seemed blessed with unsinkability. [*Somehow* might modify the preceding verb *sink* or the following clause. Adding a comma after either *sink* or *somehow* would clear up the ambiguity.]

In some constructions, misplacing the modifier may alter the
intended meaning:

> The way I babble on **even** surprises me. [intended meaning: surprises *even* me]

For additional discussion of misplaced modifiers (and additional exercises), see 3.3, Misplaced Modifiers, and 3.4, Dangling Modifiers.

Position of *only* and Similar Adverbs

In formal usage, limiting adverbs like *only, merely, hardly, just*
are placed immediately before the element they modify:

> I need **only** six more to make a full hundred.

> The audience seemed **hardly** to breathe when the girl began speaking.

In spoken usage, limiting adverbs often stand immediately before the verb:

> I **only** need six more to make a full hundred.

> The audience **hardly** seemed to breathe when the girl began speaking.

This pattern, typical of spoken English, is acceptable in general writing, when no misunderstanding of the author's meaning will occur. In most cases, however, a sentence is clearer and more accurate with the adverb placed immediately before the word or phrase it modifies.

Exercise 9.F

Study the following sentences carefully and state where you would place the indicated modifier within each sentence. If more than one position is possible, explain what change of emphasis would result from shifting the modifier.

Example   Add *almost:* The fire had burned down to nothing.

> *The fire had burned down to **almost** nothing.*

1. Add *certainly:* The fields were carpeted with snow that had fallen in the night, for there had been none yesterday.

2. Add *scarcely:* Some had landed, oddly enough, on the back patio, where the wind was now blowing.

3. Add *almost:* Farther out in the yard, the doghouse was covered to the roof so that it looked like a small mound of cotton.

4. Add *even:* The garden walks were so obliterated by drifts that my father, who had laid out the garden, did not know where they were.

5. Add *more or less:* You could tell where one path went by following the clothesline, which had a ridge of snow that made it visible from the house.

6. Add *only:* Yesterday I had seen the yard with a few flowers growing.

7. Add *definitely:* "It's beautiful to look at," my father said, "but you'll have to shovel the walks because your mother will want to hang out the wash she did last night."

8. Add *better:* Picking up the old battered shovel, I went out into the bitter wind, knowing I would be able to get the job done before the snow hardened.
9. Add *hardly:* Although I walked on the white snow-blanket softly, I had taken a few steps when I fell in a position from which I could extricate myself.
10. Add *merely:* Because it was a moderate snowfall, I laughed and went on with my work. ■

9.6 Double Negatives

A statement in which a second negative needlessly repeats the meaning of the first negative is called a *double negative:* "The trip will *not* cost you *nothing.*" Such constructions do appear in other languages. In French, for example, two words (*ne* and *pas*) are needed to make a negative. In edited American English, however, one negative is sufficient: "The trip will cost you *nothing*" or "The trip will *not* cost you anything."

Obvious double negatives like *not* with *nothing* seldom cause problems. But watch for concealed double negatives, when *not* is combined with *but* or with adverbs of negative meaning such as *hardly, barely, scarcely:*

Double negative	There were **not but** three of us on the bus.
Revised	There were **but** three of us on the bus.
Double negative	They had **not barely** enough supplies to last two days.
Revised	They had **barely** enough supplies to last two days.

can't hardly, couldn't scarcely. Such common expressions as "I can't hardly hear you" and "There wasn't scarcely enough money left to pay the taxes" are double negatives, because *hardly* and *scarcely* in this sense mean *almost not.* The standard idioms that should be used in writing are "I *can* hardly hear you" and "There *was* scarcely enough money left to pay the taxes."

can't help but. The construction *can't help but* (or *cannot help but*) is an established idiom. Many writers, however, avoid it, using instead one of the expressions in the following sentences:

I **cannot but** feel sorry for him. [formal]

I **can't help** feeling sorry for him. [general]

irregardless. *Regardless* is the standard usage. The suffix *-less* is a negative ending; the addition of the negative prefix *ir-* in *irregardless* creates a double negative.

Double negative   Ohio State will play in the Rose Bowl **irregardless** of who wins today.

Revised   Ohio State will play in the Rose Bowl **regardless** of who wins today.

Exercise   9.G

Revise the following sentences to eliminate the double negatives or awkward uses of negatives.

1. After hearing the trucks shifting gears as they roared up the hill, I could not hardly believe that the city planners had assured the local residents that the traffic noise was acceptable.
2. It didn't seem to bother Pierre Curie hardly at all that his wife was more famous than he.
3. The auditorium was designed so that a speaker couldn't scarcely be heard by people in the back rows.
4. Americans today believe that a thin body is attractive, irregardless of whether it is healthy.
5. In Spanish, it does not make no difference if you use double negatives.
6. Because of her obsessive personality, Mary couldn't not step on cracks in the sidewalk.
7. It is inconceivable that major geological shifts will not occur in the Los Angeles area within this decade.
8. Sally Ride did not consider it a truism that women could not fly in space.
9. The government does not discount the possibility that the attack was unprovoked.
10. Not only did Anna not want to disbelieve David, but she also considered it not impossible that he spoke the truth. ∎

9.7 Comparison of Adjectives and Adverbs

Comp **Make the comparison more accurate, more appropriate, or complete.**

Forms of Comparison

Most adjectives and adverbs have three different forms to indicate degrees of comparison: the positive, the comparative, and the superlative. The positive form expresses no comparison; it is the simple form of the modifier *(red, slow, seriously)*. The comparative form makes a specific comparison between two things, indicating an increase or decrease over the positive form *(redder, slower, more seriously)*. The superlative form indicates the greatest or least degree among three or more objects (the *reddest* apple in the bushel, the *slowest* runner on the team, the *most seriously* presented argument).

Most adjectives and adverbs are compared in one of two ways: by adding *-er, -est* to the positive form, or by prefixing *more, most* (or *less, least*).

	Positive	*Comparative*	*Superlative*
Adjectives	hot	hotter	hottest
	brilliant	more brilliant	most brilliant
	expensive	less expensive	least expensive
Adverbs	near	nearer	nearest
	sincerely	more sincerely	most sincerely
	often	oftener, more often, less often	oftenest, most often, least often

In general, the *-er, -est* forms are used with words of one syllable *(longer, driest)*, and *more, most* with words of more than two syllables *(more interesting, most rapidly)*. With two-syllable words a writer often has a choice of either form *(abler, more able; easiest, most easy)*. The sound of the expression may determine which form is used:

> His step was **steadier** and **more elastic.** Even his bloodshot eyes looked **fresher,** and his hair and beard were **softer.**—
> Eyvind Johnson, *Return to Ithaca*

A few common modifiers form the comparative and superlative degrees irregularly:

bad	worse	worst
good, well	better	best
far	farther, further	farthest, furthest
little	less, lesser, littler	least, littlest
many, some, much	more	most

worse, worst. Worst is the appropriate form for the superlative: That was the *worst* [not *worse*] show I have ever seen.

farther, further. In formal English a distinction is sometimes made between *farther,* referring to physical distance (It was six miles *farther* to town), and *further,* referring to abstract degree or quantity (We will study these suggestions *further*). In general English, *further* is commonly used for both distance and degree.

Use of the Comparative Form

The comparative form of an adjective or adverb is ordinarily used when two things are compared:

> You're a **better** man than I am, Gunga Din!
>
> Blood is **thicker** than water.
>
> She works **more diligently** than her roommate.

But in some expressions the comparative form is used when no actual comparison is mentioned (*higher* education, the *lower* depths, *Better* Business Bureau). In others, the reader is left to supply the comparison (Look *younger,* live *longer* . . . than what?). Writers of advertising copy are particularly fond of this use of the comparative because of the favorable inferences the reader may draw: Smoke a *milder* cigarette; More protection for *fewer* dollars; Sudso gets clothes *cleaner.* This construction is meaningless and should generally be avoided.

Use of the Superlative Form

The superlative form ordinarily indicates the greatest degree among three or more persons or things:

> He was voted the member of his class **most likely** to succeed.
>
> Many critics consider *King Lear* the **greatest** of Shakespeare's tragedies.

In spoken English the superlative is sometimes used for comparing two things (Put your *best* foot forward). The same construction is occasionally seen in writing, but it is usually better to keep the superlative for comparisons among three or more.

Superlative forms also occur in expressions in which no direct comparison is implied (*best* wishes, *deepest* sympathy, *highest* praise, *most* sincerely yours). The form with *most* is frequently used as an intensive to signify a high degree:

> For example, Herbert Spencer (1820–1903), a **most** influential English philosopher. . . .—Melvin Rader, *Ethics and Society*

The informal use of a heavily stressed superlative to indicate only general approval should be avoided in serious writing:

> Hasn't she the **sweetest** voice? Better: Hasn't she a **sweet** voice?

Comparison of *unique* and Similar Words

Some people regard words such as *unique, perfect, dead, empty* as logically incapable of comparison or qualification because their positive forms express absolute states. Ordinarily, we wouldn't expect to say that something is *more unique, more perfect, deader,* or *emptier,* but in actual usage these terms are often qualified or modified by comparative forms, as in the following examples:

> We, the people of the United States, in order to form a **more perfect** union. . . .—Preamble to the Constitution of the United States

> . . . The **more unique** his nature, the more peculiarly his own will be the coloring of his language.—Otto Jespersen, *Mankind, Nation, and Individual from a Linguistic Point of View*

Whether words like *unique* should or should not be qualified is a matter that can be determined only by appropriateness. In college writing, they should ordinarily be used without qualification; invested with their full meaning, they are valuable words that say something precisely.

Qualifiers are acceptable in some instances. If you say that A is *more nearly unique* or *more nearly perfect* than B, you are not talking about absolute states that should not be qualified; you are saying that A is closer to being unique or perfect than B is.

Exercise   9.H

In the sentences below, use the appropriate form of the adjective or adverb in parentheses.

Example   August is the (warm) month of the year in Chicago.

*August is the **warmest** month of the year in Chicago.*

1. Of the two panelists, she answered the questions (intelligently).
2. We had seen (bad) plays in London than in New York.
3. Of the half-dozen apologies the teacher received, Ken's was (not sincere).
4. Among Beethoven's symphonies, the Ninth is (unique) for its choral finale.
5. The pilot seemed determined to push his plane (far) than he had before.
6. Isn't this puppy (cute)?
7. Of all the designers, she is the (able).
8. Look for the (expensive) fabric; we cannot afford the other.
9. His accident was the (bad) I have ever witnessed.
10. We doubted that the Porsche was the (swift) car in the field. The Renault, for one, was surely (fast).   ■

Comparing Comparable Things

When using comparison in your writing, make certain that the things compared are of the same kind and actually comparable:

Terms not comparable	America's cars are as good as the Japanese. [*cars* and *the Japanese* are not comparable]
Comparable terms	America's cars are as good as Japan's cars.
Terms not comparable	The rhinoceros has a hide almost as tough as an alligator. [*hide* and *alligator* are not comparable]
Comparable terms	The rhinoceros has a hide almost as tough as that of an alligator [or *as an alligator's*].

Completing Comparisons

Statements involving comparisons should be written out in full, particularly if any misunderstanding might arise through shortening one of the terms:

Ambiguous	I owe him less than you.	9.7
Clearer	I owe him less than I owe you.	*Comp*
	Or: I owe him less than you do.	
Ambiguous	He admires Eliot less than other modern poets.	
Clearer	He admires Eliot less than other modern poets do.	
	Or: He admires Eliot less than he does other modern poets.	

Double comparisons with *as . . . as, if . . . than* should be filled out in writing.

> He is **as** tall **as, if** not taller **than,** his brother. [not: *He is as tall if not taller than his brother.*]

> The styles vary **as** much **as, if** not more **than,** the colors.

Since the *if . . . than* construction tends to interrupt sentence movement, it is usually preferable to complete the first comparison and then add the second, dropping *than:*

> He is **as** tall **as** his brother, **if** not taller.

> The styles vary **as** much **as** the colors, **if** not more.

Use of *other* in Comparisons

Other is used when the comparison involves things of the same class, but not when the things being compared belong to two different classes:

> She is a better swimmer than the **other** girls.

> She swims better than any [not *any other*] boy in school.

> *Blithe Spirit* was more successful than the **other** plays we produced.

> I think movies are more entertaining than any [not *any other*] book.

Other is not used with superlative comparisons:

> Pavlova was the best of all the [not *all the other*] Russian ballerinas.

The Egyptians had attained the highest skill in medicine that had been achieved by any [not *any other*] nation up to that time.

Use of *like* or *as* in Comparisons

To introduce a prepositional phrase of comparison, *like* is standard usage:

They are **like** two peas in a pod.

He looks **like** his father.

Bicycle riding, **like** golf, can be enjoyed at almost any age.

Avoid substituting *as* for *like* or *such as* in prepositional phrases like this:

Incorrect	Some writers **as** Faulkner and Caldwell write about a particular region.
Correct	Some writers **like** Faulkner and Caldwell write about a particular region.

However, to introduce a clause with a definite subject and verb, *as, as if,* and *as though* are preferred to *like* in both formal and general English:

Incorrect	He acted **like** he didn't feel well.
Correct	He acted **as if** he didn't feel well.
Incorrect	He took to skiing **like** a duck takes to water.
Correct	He took to skiing **as** a duck takes to water.

Use of *so* and *such* as Intensifiers

In spoken English, *so* and *such* are commonly used as intensifiers:

You were **so** funny!

It was **such** an innovative proposal.

In written English, both *so* and *such* are regarded as too imprecise to serve as modifiers. Just how funny is *so* funny? How innovative is *such*? When you write, you should avoid using *so* or *such* as intensifiers; rather, substitute more precise modifiers or complete the comparison implied by the terms:

You were very funny. [*very* substituted for *so*]
It was an extraordinarily innovative proposal. [*extraordinary* substituted for *such*]

You were so funny we could not stop laughing. [comparison completed]

It was such an innovative proposal that the agency funded it immediately. [comparison completed]

Exercise 9.I

Some of the adjective and adverb forms and expressions of comparison in these sentences would be inappropriate in college writing. Revise each sentence to make it acceptable.

1. The ship lay in the harbor like it was a natural fixture.
2. It had been there so long that the weather had turned it more wharf-colored.
3. Many things would be needed to refurbish it, as caulking, paint, new masts, and glass for portholes.
4. All in all, it was the most 19th-century sight in the town.
5. The ship looked as much if not more pathetic than an old hound lying forgottenlike nearby a deserted farmhouse.
6. Still, the scene was real fine artwise, and camera enthusiasts were taking pictures most every clear day of the year.
7. Picturesque as the sight was, everyone agreed it was the saddest.
8. I thought wistfully of how trim and noble the ship must have been in its heyday, what with its tall masts and most every sail stretching out to catch the wind.
9. The reason for its being there was most unique; the owner had died of a sudden before he could make it into a museum.　■

Exercise 9.J

Fill in the modifiers in the paragraph below, choosing words that will help create a consistent tone for the paragraph.

Sometimes, late in the evening, when I have worked (adverb) and (adverb) at my desk, I stop and lean back in my (adjective) chair and hear night sounds (adjective) and (adjective) in the distance. Sometimes I hear a (adjective) car passing, or someone calling far away, or (adjective) music from some car radio, or a bird song, (adjective) and (adjective). Then I remember that there is a world outside my window (adjective) (adverb), and I go to the door and stand a moment, looking out (adverb).　■

PARTS OF SPEECH

Nouns: A noun designates a person, place, thing, quality, action, or idea: *plumber, France, piano, anger, studying, truth.* Nouns function in sentences chiefly as subjects, objects, complements, and appositives. (See p. 134.)

Pronouns: A pronoun functions as a noun but does not name a specific person, place, thing, or idea: *I, you, it, who, which, himself, this, everyone.* A pronoun usually serves as a substitute for a previously stated noun. (See p. 145.)

Verbs: A verb indicates action, condition, or process: *walk, is, become.* (See p. 109.)
   When forms of verbs are used in sentences as nouns or modifiers rather than as verbs, these verb forms are called *verbals.* (See p. 62.) Verbals are classified by form and function as: **Infinitives** *(to talk, to think),* which function either as nouns or modifiers; **Participles** *(talking, talked; thinking, thought),* which function as adjectives; **Gerunds** *(talking, thinking),* which function as nouns.

Adjectives: An adjective modifies a noun or a noun equivalent: *blue, glamorous, older.* (See p. 172.)

Adverbs: An adverb modifies a verb, an adjective, another adverb, or a whole statement: *soon, quietly, especially, incidentally.* (See pp. 172, 177.)

Prepositions: A preposition shows the relationship between a noun (or noun equivalent) and some other word in the sentence: *in, at, of, before.*
   A preposition introduces a *prepositional phrase,* which consists of the preposition followed by a noun (or noun equivalent), plus any modifiers of the noun: *in the tree, at me, of great importance, before dinner.* Prepositional phrases usually function as modifiers. (See p. 38.)

Conjunctions: A conjunction links together words, phrases, or clauses: *and, but, since, because, either . . . or.* (See pp. 39, 43.)

Interjections: An interjection is an expression of emotion that either stands alone or is inserted into a sentence without being grammatically related to the sentence: *oh, wow, help, no.* (See p. 197.)

Punctuation and Other Conventions

10

END
PUNCTUATION

Every complete sentence requires a mark of punctuation at the end, either a period, a question mark, or an exclamation mark. The great majority of sentences are statements, requiring a period (.). Direct questions are followed by a question mark (?), and emphatic or exclamatory statements are ended with an exclamation point or mark (!).

Periods and question marks also have several conventional uses in addition to their function as end stops.

10.1 Periods

⊙ **Insert a period at the place marked.**

Periods are the most common end stops; they mark the end of all sentences that are not direct questions or exclamations.

Periods After Statements

Madagascar is an island off southeast Africa.

"Where is he now?" she asked. "Tell me."

"Oh."

Periods After Indirect Questions and Courtesy Questions

An indirect question is really a statement *about* a question and is never followed by a question mark:

> He asked us where we got the money. (A direct question would be *Where did you get the money?*)
>
> They wanted to know what I had been doing since I graduated.

Periods are also used after courtesy questions although question marks are sometimes used in these situations:

10.1

⊙

> Will you please return this copy as soon as possible.
>
> May we hear from you when you return to our city.

Periods After Abbreviations

A period is conventionally used after most abbreviations:

Mr. H. L. Matthews	Oct.	Ph.D.
St. Paul, Minn.	D.D.S.	etc.

An abbreviation within a sentence may be followed by additional punctuation *(After she gets her M.A., she might go on to get her Ph.D.)*, but at the end of a sentence no additional mark is needed unless the sentence is a question or an exclamation:

> She already has an M.A.
>
> Does he have a Ph.D.?
>
> Don't go A.W.O.L.!

Periods are sometimes omitted from abbreviations, especially if they are made from initial letters: *UNESCO, GOP.* Consult an up-to-date dictionary for the preferred form of particular abbreviations. If usage is divided (*A.W.O.L., AWOL,* or *a.w.o.l.*), follow a consistent style throughout your paper. (See 16.1, Abbreviations.)

Periods with Figures

A period (decimal point) is used before fractions expressed as decimals and between whole numbers and decimals, and to separate dollars and cents:

0.5	4.6	3.14159	95.6%
$4.98	$.98	*but* 98 cents	*or* 98¢

See 14.2 for periods used as ellipses to mark the omission of words.

10.2 Question Marks

? Punctuate this sentence or sentence element with a question mark.

After Direct Questions

A question mark is used after a sentence expressing a direct question:

> What can we do?
>
> Did Napoleon dislike Elba?
>
> Really?

When a sentence begins with a statement but ends with a question, the ending determines the punctuation:

> Perhaps this explanation is poor, but is there a better one?
>
> We like his work, but can we trust him?

After Questions Within a Sentence

A question mark stands immediately after a question that is included within a sentence:

> Someone once remarked (wasn't it Mark Twain?) that old secondhand diamonds are better than no diamonds at all.
>
> "Are you engaged?" he blurted.

When a question mark and quotation marks occur together, the question mark goes inside the quotation marks if the quotation is a question. The question mark goes outside the quotation marks if the whole sentence is a question:

> He asked himself, "Is this the best of all possible worlds?"
>
> Do you agree that this is "the best of all possible worlds"?

To Indicate a Doubtful Statement

A question mark is used, with or without parentheses, to show that a statement is approximate or questionable:

Geoffrey Chaucer, 1340(?)–1400

Geoffrey Chaucer, 1340?–1400

Sometimes writers place a question mark in parentheses to indicate humor or mild sarcasm:

She gave him an innocent (?) wink over her menu.

If humor or sarcasm requires a signal for the reader to recognize it, it would probably be better to revise the entire passage.

10.3 Exclamation Marks

! **Insert or remove exclamation mark
at the place indicated.**

An exclamation mark is used after an emphatic interjection (*Oh! Ouch! Fire! Help! No, no, no!*) and after statements that are genuinely exclamatory:

The building had disappeared overnight!

What torments they have endured!

There is seldom a need for exclamation marks unless you are writing dialogue. Don't use an exclamation mark unless the statement is genuinely emphatic; it will not lend weight to a simple statement of fact, nor will the use of double and triple marks add anything.

Exercise **10.A**

Rewrite the following items, changing the end punctuation. Make any other changes you need in order to use different end signals.

1. My first job, as an elevator operator, was the most thrilling I've ever had! To me it was almost as if I were an actor, waiting my cue to speak and move!! My audience responded! How could they help it? They had to get off!!
2. What fear he must have felt while he swayed there!
3. He asked us where we got the money.
4. Win one of sixteen luxurious all-expense paid vacations to China!
5. How I hope we will win!
6. "Were you lost?" she asked.

7. Just where he learned to dance like that we didn't know.
8. Will you enter, please.
9. "Can he ever forgive me," she wondered to herself. "Not a chance," he responded silently as he strode across the yard. How dramatic these soap operas are!
10. He had no motive for the crime, so why, then, did he do it?

Exercise **10.B**

10.3

!

In the following passage, end punctuation has been omitted. Supply the appropriate marks.

Dear Abby: I am writing about a problem that is perplexing to me my husband is absolutely perfect in every respect except for one habit that I cannot seem to break him of

Instead of throwing out food containers after he has emptied them, he puts them back in the refrigerator I can't begin to tell you how many empty cartons, bottles and cans I have found in the refrigerator

No amount of scolding, pleading or nagging seems to help

He offers no explanation for this screwball behavior I think he's too lazy to walk to the trash can on the other side of the kitchen

Can you, or your readers, offer any kind of solution so that I can have a perfect husband—*Frustrated*

Dear Frustrated: You're crying with a loaf of bread under each arm and an empty ketchup bottle in the refrigerator if a man must have but one flaw in an otherwise flawless character, I can think of none so harmless, inoffensive and easy to forgive as your husband's cherish this paragon of virtue he's a candidate for sainthood—Abigail Van Buren, "Dear Abby"

11

COMMAS

⌒ **Insert a comma at the place indicated.**

Commas mark a slight separation between grammatical units, indicating various structural relationships between parts of sentences. They are highly important in determining the meaning, pace, and tempo of writing. About two-thirds of all punctuation marks used are commas.

To use commas well, you must know not only when to use them but also when to omit them. The principal uses of the comma are described in the following sections and summarized in the table on page 220. The table also lists some constructions in which commas should *not* be used, as discussed in 11.9, Misused Commas.

11.1 Commas Between Coordinate Clauses

A comma is usually used before the conjunction linking the coordinate clauses in a compound sentence, especially when the clauses are long or when it is desirable to emphasize their distinctness. The comma always comes *before* the coordinating conjunction, not after it:

> All the facts are in, **and** the accused seems guilty.

> This town does not actually exist, **but** it might easily have a thousand counterparts in America or elsewhere in the world.—Rachel Carson, *Silent Spring*

> The village was to the scale of the town of Lilliput, **and** I could have straddled over Toad Hall.—Aubrey Menen, "Dazzled in Disneyland"

Short Clauses Joined by *and, or, nor*

The comma may be omitted before the conjunctions *and, or, nor* in compound sentences if the coordinate clauses are short and closely related in thought:

> Life is short and time is fleeting.
>
> He had to get home or his father would be furious.
>
> Nancy didn't like her nor did I.

However, using a comma in such cases is always correct and prevents the risk of the sentence being misread.

11.2

⌃

Clauses Joined by *but, yet*

In both formal and general writing a comma is used between independent clauses joined by *but* or *yet* to emphasize the contrast:

> Life is short, **but** consider the alternative.
>
> This was not the man they had known, **but** ten perilous and eventful years had passed since their last meeting.
>
> It is an imperfect system, **yet** it is better than none.

Clauses Joined by *for*

A comma is necessary between clauses joined by *for* used as a conjunction, so that it won't be confused with the preposition *for*:

> He was an easy target, **for** anyone could pull the wool over his eyes. [*for* as a conjunction]
>
> He was an easy target **for** anyone who wanted to take advantage of him. [*for* as a preposition]

11.2 Commas After Conjunctive Adverbs

When two independent or coordinate clauses are linked by a conjunctive adverb (such as *however, therefore,* and so on), use a semicolon before the adverb and a comma after it (see also 4.2 and 12.1):

> I'll go to the party if you think I should; **however,** I'd rather be pecked to death by a flock of turkeys.

He tried it here but didn't like our ways; **consequently,** he's leaving for the back country.

You did not collect enough valid signatures; **therefore,** your petition has been ruled inadmissible.

11.3 Commas After Long Introductory Elements

Adverb clauses and long modifying phrases are usually set off by a comma when they precede the main clause. When these elements end a sentence, a comma may or may not be necessary.

Adverb Clauses

Adverb clauses (see 2.2) are often placed at the beginning of a sentence for variety or emphasis. In this position they are usually separated from the main clause by a comma:

> **When he said that we would be expected to write an essay every day,** I nearly collapsed.

> **Before penicillin and other antibiotics were developed,** pneumonia was often fatal.

The comma can sometimes be omitted when the introductory clause is short and closely related to the main clause, especially if both clauses have the same subject:

> **When I lived in New York** I went to the theater every month.

> **After he seized control** the situation changed drastically.

If in doubt, however, use a comma.

When an adverb clause *follows* the main clause, no comma is used if the subordinate clause is closely related to the meaning of the sentence:

> I nearly collapsed **when he said that we would be expected to write an essay every day.**

> Pneumonia was often fatal **before penicillin and other antibiotics were developed.**

If a following subordinate clause is only loosely related to the main clause, it is separated from the main clause by a comma:

> The new wing will be finished by spring, **unless, of course, unexpected delays occur.**

I have known readers who find Huxley unreadable, **although they have found it impossible to explain why.**
—Colin Wilson, "Existential Criticism"

Long Modifying Phrases

Long modifying phrases are generally punctuated in the same way as adverb clauses. When they come before the main clause, they are followed by a comma:

> **To understand fully the impact of Einstein's ideas,** one must be familiar with those of Newton. [infinitive phrase]
>
> **Leaning far out over the balcony,** he stared at the waves below. [participle phrase]
>
> **In such a situation,** speakers of the creole often deny their mother tongue. [prepositional phrase]—Peter Farb, *Word Play*

11.3

When the phrases are relatively short and closely related to the clauses they modify, the comma is often omitted:

> **In this context** the meaning is entirely different.
>
> **To evade the IRS** he moved to Costa Rica.

When the modifying phrase *follows* the clause, commas are unnecessary if the thought seems to flow smoothly from one to the other:

> One must be familiar with Newton's ideas **to understand fully the impact of Einstein's.**
>
> Special treatment may be necessary **in case of severe malnutrition.**

Exercise 11.A

Complete the sentences started below, punctuating wherever necessary.

1. When she hit. . . .
2. If I can. . . .
3. Although he. . . .
4. . . . yet we didn't.
5. . . . however profitable the company might be.
6. . . . moreover, the taxes were not paid.
7. At this particular location. . . .

8. . . . when he promised to revise the entire estimate downward.
9. . . . for he was not prepared for the rehearsal.
10. . . . and so did I. ■

Exercise 11.B

Read the following sentences carefully. In which of the places marked with brackets would you insert a comma? In which do you consider a comma optional? Not appropriate? Give specific reasons for your choice of punctuation.

1. When a man assumes a public trust [1] he should consider himself as public property.—Thomas Jefferson
2. Let us all be happy and live within our means [1] even if we have to borrow money to do it.—Artemus Ward
3. Whenever punctuation problems arise [1] it is a good idea to consult the text [2] and determine the proper usage.
4. Walk right in [1] and sit right down.
5. I laughed [1] and I cried [2] and I waved [3] all at the same time. ■

Exercise 11.C

Punctuate the following sentences, supplying commas and semicolons (see 11.2) as needed.

1. Until the Renaissance Western science assumed that the earth was the center of the universe however when Copernicus advanced the theory of heliocentrism science began to undergo what Thomas Kuhn would describe as a "paradigm shift."
2. According to Kuhn's *Structure of Scientific Revolutions* paradigm shifts occur when existing scientific theories can no longer explain the observed facts.
3. When enough unexplained facts accumulate science goes through a period of uncertainty and finally new bases for scientific investigation supplant those which have become obsolete.
4. In pointing out the importance of "paradigm shifts" Kuhn explains that paradigms determine the shape and extent of scientific knowledge.

5. In simple terms paradigms dictate the kinds of questions scientific researchers can ask and the ways in which these questions can be answered.

6. Kuhn describes scientific paradigm shifts as "revolutions" for they involve an overthrow of old beliefs and their replacement by new ones.

7. In some cases scientific revolutions may be almost as violent as political revolutions.

8. For instance today we accept as common knowledge the idea that the earth revolves around the sun yet when Copernicus first advanced his heliocentric theories he was in danger of losing his life on the charge of heresy.

9. In essence a paradigm shift is a change in perspective or point of view.

10. For instance before Einstein advanced his theory of relativity scientists viewed matter and energy as two separate entities.

11. Einstein's theory however offered a new way of looking at the relationship between matter and energy.

12. Our physical senses only allow us to perceive matter and energy separately but the theory suggests a point of view beyond time and observable reality from which the two entities are indistinguishable.

13. We find it hard to understand how such a theory could be true bound as we are by the constraints of time and our own physical senses.

14. To our common sense Einstein's theory sounds absurd but because its application has made possible many sophisticated technological developments we must accept its validity for the time being.

15. Kuhn's doctrine of scientific revolutions invites us to view science as a matter of intellectual fashion nevertheless most of us prefer to think of science as a purely objective search for truth. ∎

11.4   Commas with Nonrestrictive Modifiers

Rest   If the modifier marked is nonrestrictive, set it off with a comma or commas; if it is restrictive, do not separate it from the term it modifies.

Subordinate Clauses and Phrases

A *nonrestrictive* modifier is a subordinate clause or a phrase that does not limit or define the term it modifies. In other words, it does not *restrict* the term's meaning; if it were omitted, the meaning of the sentence would not change much:

> The satellite, **which resembled a giant washtub,** was placed into orbit by the shuttle. [nonrestrictive modifier]
>
> The satellite was placed into orbit by the shuttle. [modifier removed]

Nonrestrictive modifiers are set off by commas:

11.4 ↑

> Last night's audience, **which contained a large number of college students,** applauded each selection enthusiastically.
>
> The people of India, **who have lived in poverty for centuries,** desperately need financial and technical assistance.
>
> Vasari's history, **hovering between fact and fiction,** is not a reliable source of data.

Notice again that the modifiers in the three preceding sentences are not essential to the terms they modify. Although some information would be lost if they were removed, the central meaning of each sentence would not change.

A *restrictive* modifier limits or defines the meaning of a term; without it, the sentence would take on a different meaning or become difficult to understand. Since it is essential to the sentence, it is *not* set off by commas:

> He is a man **who thinks for himself.**
>
> Ortiz discovered many temples **which were pre-Toltec in origin.**
>
> The questions **that she did not answer** were the most interesting ones.

Removing the restrictive clause seriously alters the sentence, leaving it vague or significantly different in meaning:

> He is a man.
> Ortiz discovered many temples.
> The questions were the most interesting ones.

Almost all clauses beginning with *that* are restrictive. All clauses in which the relative pronoun can be omitted are restrictive (the questions *he failed to answer;* the book *I read*).

In distinguishing between restrictive and nonrestrictive modifiers, consider the nature of the term modified and the context in which it occurs. If the term is fully defined in itself and cannot be confused with another, the modifier that follows is nonrestrictive. But if the term is vague or ambiguous without the modifier, the modifier is restrictive. Compare the function of the modifier in each of these passages:

11.4

> Children **who can't swim very well** should stay off the diving board.
> Children, **who can't swim very well,** should stay off the diving board.
> While in Rome, I took photographs in the vicinity of St. Peter's. The square, **designed by Michelangelo,** is perfectly symmetrical.
> While in Rome, I took photographs of squares designed by Michelangelo, Bernini, and Borromini. The square **designed by Michelangelo** is perfectly symmetrical.

Appositives

Appositives—nouns or noun equivalents that "rename" or extend the meaning of a preceding expression—are usually nonrestrictive and are set off by commas:

> The All-American pastime, **baseball,** is becoming less popular than football.
>
> Thomas Malthus, **author of the first serious study of population growth,** foresaw one of our greatest modern problems.
>
> Lincoln delivered a famous address at Gettysburg, **site of a crucial Civil War battle.**

Notice that such appositives, like nonrestrictive modifiers, must be set off by *two* commas when they occur in the middle of the sentence.

Restrictive appositives and those used as part of a person's name require no commas:

> I thought the question referred to Lewis **the novelist** rather than to Lewis **the union leader.**
>
> William **the Conqueror** invaded England from Normandy.

Exercise 11.D

The following sentences contain both restrictive and nonrestrictive modifiers and appositives. Punctuate each sentence appropriately. If the sentence makes sense either way, explain the difference in meaning between the restrictive and the nonrestrictive modifier.

Example   The alligator which was often hunted for its hide was in danger of becoming extinct.

The alligator, which was often hunted for its hide, was in danger of becoming extinct.

1. The wall that was built by Hadrian served its purpose for many years.
2. Abraham Lincoln sometimes called "The Great Emancipator" has become a symbol to many groups which crave independence.
3. Diamonds that are synthetically produced are more perfectly formed than natural diamonds which have serious flaws.
4. American movies exported abroad are popular in countries that have no native movie industry.
5. The French chef whose accomplishments are well known is eagerly sought by expensive restaurants and hotels.
6. Cockfighting outlawed by the Mexican authorities still takes place in areas where the police seldom turn up.
7. The oboe which is a woodwind instrument is played by means of a reed inserted in the mouthpiece.
8. The early settlers who were exposed to severe winters and who expected Indian attacks usually constructed forts many of which can still be found.
9. Drunk drivers who are responsible for many traffic fatalities obviously do not consider the value of human life.
10. The common belief that science can solve everything is another example of the naive optimism that most people are prey to. ■

11.5

11.5 Commas to Set Off Interrupting, Parenthetical, and Contrasting Elements

A word, phrase, or clause that interrupts or changes the movement of a sentence is usually set off by commas or other appropriate marks (see 13, Dashes, Parentheses, and Brackets):

> There are, **however,** few college subjects in the humanities and the social sciences in which forty-five hours of the teacher lecturing and the students listening can be useful. —Nathan Glazer, "The Wasted Classroom"

> I believe, **even though the market has rallied,** that this is a good time to sell.

Whether the degree of interruption is sufficient to require commas depends on tone and emphasis. Formal English uses commas more frequently than general English for this purpose.

11.5

⌃

Adverbs that Compare or Contrast

Adverbs that compare or contrast some preceding idea *(however, therefore, consequently, too, also)* are generally set off by commas when they occur within a sentence:

> It was in Paris, **too,** that we felt the spirit of the American expatriots of the twenties.

> The largest single group of terms in the dictionary, **however,** is that in the general vocabulary, which belongs to all speakers of American English—Patrick E. Kilburn, "Ruckus in the Reference Room"

When such words appear at the beginning of a sentence, they may or may not be followed by a comma, depending on the emphasis desired:

> **Thus** the way was cleared for further explorations.

> **Nevertheless,** work did not always proceed according to plan.

When a clause beginning with such an adverb is joined to a preceding clause, the *semicolon* must be used, since these words are weak connectives. They relate ideas to one another but do not join them grammatically (see 4.2, page 83, Comma Splice, and 12.1, page 223, Semicolons Between Main Clauses Linked with a Conjunctive Adverb):

> Business recessions take place periodically; **however,** they are generally short-lived.

The natives are incredibly poor; **moreover,** they have little hope of bettering their lot.

When adverbs that closely modify the verb or the entire sentence *(perhaps, so)* begin the sentence, they should not be followed by a comma. Similarly, conjunctions are part of the clauses they introduce and should not be set off from them:

> **Perhaps** a solution can still be found.

> **But** the average American cannot afford such luxuries.

Expressions of Contrast

Commas are used to set off expressions that indicate a contrast or contradiction. Such expressions are often introduced by *not* or *but:*

> We ordered thirty feet of brocade, **not thirty yards.**

> He is not going with you, **but with me.**

> The life so short, **the craft so long to learn.**

Weak Exclamations

Weak exclamations *(well, oh, say)* and *yes* and *no,* when used as modifiers, are conventionally separated from the rest of the sentence by commas:

> **Well,** not much can be done about it now.

> **Yes,** times have changed.

> **Oh,** I neglected to mention that in my letter.

> It is doubtful whether the ordinary city-dweller is more grasping than the French peasant, **say,** or even the sturdy New Englander.—Herbert Muller, *The Uses of the Past*

Names in Direct Address

Names used in direct address are also set off by commas:

> I firmly believe, **fellow citizens,** that justice will prevail.

> It seems to me, **George,** that your attitude is poor.

> **Workers of the world,** unite!

> Make sure the contract clearly states, **Joan,** that we are not liable for loss due to theft or vandalism.

Exercise **11.E**

Repunctuate the following sentences, correcting faulty marks and adding punctuation wherever needed.

1. Computer executives occasionally hire liberal arts majors as programmers-in-training, in fact many of these liberal arts graduates are adept at technological jobs.
2. Ladies and gentlemen I implore you to consider the consequences of approving this too-hastily-drafted piece of legislation.
3. We found nevertheless that people would buy products with higher prices if the labels were fancy.
4. Autopsies performed on schizophrenics reveal moreover that their brain cells are wildly disordered, but, scientists have not discounted the effect of emotion on the development of mental illness.
5. Well some people including me believe that the 1969 moon landing was a scenario concocted by Hollywood producers. ∎

11.6 Commas to Separate Items in a Series

Words, Phrases, or Clauses in a Series

A comma is the mark ordinarily used to separate coordinate words, phrases, or clauses in a list or series:

> He remembered these feelings as precisely as he remembered the **clothes,** the **cars,** the **furniture,** the **songs,** the **slang.**—Arthur Mizener, *The Far Side of Paradise*

> We were taught **how to sit gracefully, how to walk, how to converse politely.**

Although usage is divided, most writers prefer to use a comma before a connective joining the last item in a series:

> We had **hot dogs,** potato **salad,** soft **drinks, and watermelon** at the class picnic.

> It was left to the House of Representatives to decide whether the Presidency should go to **Jackson, Adams, or** Crawford.

In some informal writing, especially in newspapers, the final comma is omitted if no misinterpretation is possible. However, because there is quite often the possibility of misreading, it is generally better to use a final comma:

> The lot was littered with trash, dented barrels, parts from discarded machines and abandoned cars. [Are there abandoned cars on the lot, or just parts of them?]

> At the rock concert we heard Blackberry Wine, Golden Gate Bridge, Red Eye and the Bull Dogs. [Is Red Eye and the Bull Dogs one group or two?]

If each of the items in a series is joined by a conjunction, commas are ordinarily omitted:

> We combed the bookstores in London for early editions of famous old novels and first editions of less valuable items and any Protestant hymns we could find.

11.6

The following sentence illustrates series with and without connectives:

> Scenes down on the farm or among raftsmen poling their flatboats or among the prairie schooners and Indians of the West were present in the canvasses of painters like George Caleb Bingham, William Sidney Mount, and Alfred Jacob Miller.—Holman Hamilton, "The American Renaissance"

See also 12.1, page 224, Semicolons to Separate Elements Containing Other Marks.

Coordinate Adjectives

Commas are used to separate adjectives in a series when they modify the same noun. Since each performs the same function, such adjectives are called *coordinate.* In a coordinate series each member could sensibly be joined by *and* instead of a comma, or the order of modifiers could be reversed:

> He spoke of the **violent, exciting, challenging** era that followed the Civil War.

Commas are not used when the adjectives are arranged so that each one modifies the entire following expression. Such items cannot be joined by *and* or reversed in order:

> She made a **tasty Hungarian** goulash.

> He spoke longingly of the **good old prewar** days.

Notice that a comma is never used between the last adjective in a series and the noun it modifies.

Exercise 11.F

In which of the places marked with brackets would you insert a comma? In which do you consider a comma optional? Not appropriate?

11.6

↑

1. If a man can write a better book [1] preach a better sermon [2] or make a better mousetrap [3] than his neighbors [4] though he builds his house in the woods [5] the world will make a beaten path to his door.—Ralph Waldo Emerson

2. Put your trust in God [1] my boys [2] and keep your powder dry.—attributed to Oliver Cromwell

3. When I was a child [1] I spake as a child [2] I understood as a child [3] I thought as a child: but when I became a man [4] I put away childish things.—I Corinthians

4. Professor Tillman [1] author of several books [2] gave a series of lectures on the Depression.

5. The manager explained several methods for improving the availability [1] flexibility [2] and cost-effectiveness [3] of the company's [4] telephoning network.

6. A few American folktales depict women as dependable [1] responsible [2] and insightful individuals, but more commonly they present women as evil [3] schemers and malicious [4] dangerous [5] gossips.

7. We could hardly believe how well he was managing [1] cleaning the house [2] and fixing meals [3] and washing clothes [4] and driving his two young sons to and from their daily [5] baseball practices.

8. Venus has been described as a dry [1] gaseous [2] scorching [3] planet [4] obscured by clouds [5] oppressed by a heavy [6] carbon dioxide atmosphere [7] and hotter than molten lead.

9. He described the wine as having a tangy [1] impudent [2] bouquet.

10. She was smoking heavily [1] she hated herself [2] and she wondered why she hadn't simply given up her disgusting [3] tobacco [4] habit. ∎

11.7 Commas to Separate for Clarity

Commas should be used wherever necessary to prevent misreading. They are useful in the situations described below.

1. **When the subject of a clause may be mistaken for the object of a verb or a preposition that precedes it:**

   As far as I can see the results have not been promising. [confusing]
   As far as I can **see, the results** have not been promising. [comma inserted to prevent *the results* from being misread as the object of *see*]

   When the rains are over the fields are plowed. [confusing]
   When the rains are **over, the fields** are plowed. [comma inserted to prevent *fields* from being misread as the object of a prepositional phrase]

2. **When a word has two possible functions.** Words like *for, but,* and *however,* for example, may be used in several ways:

   The surgeon's face showed no emotion, **but** anxiety and a little nervousness must have been hiding behind that impassive mask. [. . . showed no emotion but anxiety. . . .]

   Sharon was thoroughly embarrassed, **for** her parents treated her like a child. [. . . was thoroughly embarrassed for her parents. . . .]

   However, I interpreted his remarks liberally and continued my work. [However I interpreted his remarks. . . .]

3. **When one expression might be mistaken for another:**

   After he broke his **hand, writing** was very difficult for him.

4. **When the same word occurs consecutively** (although usage is divided on this):

   Whatever **is, is** right.

Exercise 11.G

Repunctuate the following sentences whenever necessary.

1. When Agatha began to run a mile left her breathless.

2. Oil field exploration requires the technological ability to lower a drill bit bit by bit.

3. Most psychiatrists believe that in the development of childhood autism, no one is to blame but mothers often suffer severe guilt.

4. When the chemistry students have finished their experiment will yield significant data.

5. When Louis Armstrong felt like playing his horn seemed to become a magical instrument. ■

11.8 Commas in Conventional Places

Commas are often used in conventional ways to set off distinct units of information.

Numbers. Commas are conventionally used to group numbers into units of threes in separating thousands, millions, and so forth:

> 2,853   84,962   3,542,869

Commas are not generally used in round numbers of four figures, serial numbers, or street addresses:

> There were about 2000 words in the article.
>
> The serial number of my typewriter is 11-6445793.
>
> He lives at 11085 Champagne Point Road.

Dates. Commas are used to separate the day of the month and the year:

> February 8, 1928   November 21, 1975

When only the month and year are given, a comma is not necessary, although it is frequently used:

> October 1929 *or* October, 1929

The form favored in military usage—16 March 1984—is more common in British than in American writing.

Addresses. Commas are used in addresses to separate towns, counties, states, and districts; they are not used between state and ZIP code, however.

Toledo, Ohio 43601

Hamilton, Madison County, New York

He was born in Washington, D.C., in 1937.

Titles. Commas are used to separate proper names from titles and degrees:

Marshall Field, Jr.

Jerome Blum, M.A., Ph.D.

Gen. H. L. Matthews, U.S.M.C., Ret.

11.8

Notice that the final element in dates, addresses, and titles is followed by a comma if it falls within a sentence:

He was born on December 7, 1929, twelve years before we entered World War II.

She was born in Miami, Ohio, and lived there for seven years.

Sammy Davis, Jr., followed his father into show business.

Letters. Commas are conventional after the salutation of informal letters *(Dear Shirley, Dear Uncle Joe,)* and after the complimentary close of most letters *(Yours truly, Sincerely yours,).* A colon is used after the salutation of a formal or business letter *(Dear Mr. Miller:).*

Quotations. A comma is customarily used after expressions that introduce direct quotations:

Sherman said, "Only a fool would carry on like that."

If the phrase interrupts a sentence in the quotation, it is set off by two commas:

"Only a fool," Sherman said, "would carry on like that."

No comma is needed with very short quotations, exclamations, or phrases closely built into the structure of the sentence:

Father always said "Time is money."

She began to scream "Fire!" as soon as she saw the smoke.

One famous writer called slavery a "peculiar institution."

Exercise 11.H

Add commas wherever necessary in the following sentences.

1. We lived at 2853 East 97th Street in Medford Oregon before we moved to Washington D.C. in winter 1984.

2. Ms. Rhoades estimated that roughly 1000 of the 5304 students taking the placement exam would pass it.

3. On February 20 1963 John Glenn Jr. U.S.M.C. became the first American to orbit the earth.

4. "The Congress of the United States is tangled in a web of problems" the newscaster observed "and the President is playing the spider."

5. Carol said "No! I won't do it." ■

11.9

No ⌣

11.9 Misused Commas

No⌣ **Remove the unnecessary comma.**

Too many commas may be as bad as too few. Be prepared to justify every comma you use. The most common errors in using commas are described below.

No Comma Between Main Sentence Elements

Since a comma is a mark of separation, it should not be used between those elements of a sentence that naturally go together: subject and verb, verb and object (or complement), preposition and object. There should be no commas where the brackets stand in the following sentences:

Subject and verb   Sometimes students who have attended expensive preparatory schools [ ] have trouble adjusting to large public universities.

Verb and object   I have often noticed [ ] that a person's physical characteristics may influence his personality.

Verb and _complement_	Whenever the dogs in the kennel appeared [ ] restless or hostile, the trainer took steps to pacify them.
Preposition and _object_	Nothing troubled her except [ ] that her friendship with Swift was causing gossip.

No Comma Between Two Words or Phrases
Joined by _and_

Two items joined by _and_ or by one of the other coordinating conjunctions are not ordinarily separated by a comma. Commas would be out of place in the following compound constructions:

> Primitive agricultural tools [ ] and bits of clay pottery were found. [compound subject]
>
> He either talked too much [ ] or else said nothing at all. [compound predicate]
>
> In his senior year he was captain of the football team [ ] and secretary of his class. [compound complement]
>
> She wanted more time for study [ ] and contemplation. [compound object of preposition]

A comma is appropriate, however, when a coordinating conjunction is used to join two independent _clauses_ (see 11.1):

> The fence was repaired, **and** new sod was laid.
>
> He was offered full amnesty, **but** he resolved to serve the sentence given to him.

No Comma between Main Clauses
Without a Connective

A comma alone is an inadequate mark of separation between two main clauses:

Comma splice	Advertisers first try to identify what people want to achieve in life, **then** they create ads to make people believe they can achieve their goals by buying certain products.
Comma splice	I grew apprehensive as the jump approached, **the** cliff was higher and steeper than I had anticipated.

If clauses are not joined by a coordinating conjunction, they must be separated by a semicolon or punctuated as individual sentences:

Revised   Advertisers first try to identify what people want to achieve in life, *and* then they create ads to make people believe they can achieve their goals by buying certain products. [coordinating conjunction *and* added]

Revised   I grew apprehensive as the jump approached. The cliff was higher and steeper than I had anticipated. [two separate sentences created]

11.9
No ⌃

For a fuller discussion of this problem, with more examples and exercises, see 4.2, Comma Splices.

Commas can be used to join two main clauses on rare occasions when those clauses are very short:

I laughed, I cried, I waved.

You got lost, he got rescued.

No Comma with Restrictive Modifiers

A restrictive modifier is one that is essential to the meaning of the sentence (see 11.4); it should not be separated from the element it modifies by a comma. The boldface elements in the following example are restrictive and should stand as they are here, without commas:

The conenose, or kissing bug, is an insect **whose painful bite can draw blood.**

The book **that I left at home** is the one I need for class.

No Comma After the Last Item in a Series

A comma is never used between the last adjective in a series and the noun it modifies:

He imagined himself as a **rich, handsome, successful [ ] man** of the world.

A comma is not used after the last item in other kinds of lists or series:

The work of such modern masters as **Picasso, Matisse, van Gogh, and Gauguin [ ]** shocked conservative critics when it was introduced at the famous New York Armory show in 1913.

Exercise **11.I**

Commas have been omitted from the following passages. Copy the paragraphs, punctuating with commas wherever you think appropriate; be prepared to account for the commas you insert. The first passage is from a version of "Rapunzel" and the second from an issue of *Glamour*.

1. There was once a man and his wife who had long wished in vain for a child and at last they had reason to hope that heaven would grant their wish. There was a little window at the back of their house which overlooked a beautiful garden full of lovely flowers and shrubs. It was however surrounded by a wall and nobody dared to enter because it belonged to a witch who was feared by everybody.

2. If we really want to *get our act together* for the 80's to be sure we *maintain our space* and *stay well and truly centered the reality of it* is that it's time to admit that some of the language we are taking with us into this shiny new decade has lost its vigor. Idiom if it is used to salt and pepper what we say has to be fresh has to convey an immediate unexpected image. When *mellow* and *laid back* begin to sound more like candy bars than states of mind they aren't working any more.

   So we will if you will try very hard to prune the following out of our vocabularies:

   We will try never again to *set priorities;* we absolutely refuse to *prioritize.* We will try to avoid being *prepped out* or *California'd out* or *grossed out* or *burned out.* Prepositions have been carrying too heavy a burden— we will try to enjoy things without *getting into them* we will try to retreat with decorum before we become *out of it.* We will look for ways to convey understanding without having to assure anyone that *we know where he or she is coming from.* ■

Review

COMMAS

■ **Commas Are Used:**

1. Between coordinate clauses (11.1)
   a. When they are joined by *and, or, nor* if the clauses are long or not closely related
   b. When they are joined by *but* or *yet*
   c. When they are joined by *for*
2. After conjunctive adverbs that link coordinate clauses (11.2)
3. After long introductory elements (11.3)
   a. When an adverb clause precedes the main clause (usually optional if the introductory clause is short and closely related)
   b. When a long modifying phrase precedes the main clause (usually optional if the phrase is short and closely related)
4. With nonrestrictive modifiers (11.4)
   a. To set off subordinate clauses and phrases that do not limit or restrict the meaning of the term they modify
   b. To set off appositives
5. To set off interrupting and parenthetical elements (11.5)
6. To separate coordinate items in a series (11.6)
   a. In a series of words, phrases, or clauses not joined by conjunctions (optional before *and* joining the last item in a series)
   b. In a series of coordinate adjectives, all modifying the same noun
7. To separate constructions for clarity (11.7)
8. In certain conventional places (11.8)
   a. In numbers, dates, addresses
   b. With titles and degrees
   c. In correspondence
   d. With phrases identifying direct quotations

■ **Commas Should Not Be Used (11.9):**

1. Between main sentence elements
2. Between two words or phrases joined by *and*
3. Between main clauses without a connective
4. With restrictive modifiers
5. After the last item in a series

12

SEMICOLONS
AND COLONS

Both semicolons and colons are strong marks of punctuation, but their functions are different and should not be confused; they cannot be used interchangeably. The constructions requiring each mark are well defined and relatively few, yet some students have trouble with them, particularly semicolons. The semicolon is a mark of separation between coordinate sentence elements. The colon is a mark of anticipation directing the reader's attention to what follows.

12.1 Semicolons

∧
; Use a semicolon at the place marked to separate coordinate sentence elements.

As a mark of separation, the semicolon is much stronger than a comma and almost as definite as a period. As you read the following passage, you will probably come to a complete stop after *crossroad* and after *tumble-down:*

> Our haunted house was not strictly in the best haunted-house tradition. It was not a ramshackle pile standing at a lonely crossroad; it was on a street inside the town and was surrounded by houses that were cheerfully inhabited. It was not tumble-down; it was a large, well-built mansion of

brick, and it still stands, good as new.—Frank Sullivan, *The Night the Old Nostalgia Burned Down*

Periods could have been used instead of semicolons in this passage, but semicolons more clearly indicate the contrasts in the closely related examples.

The few constructions in which a semicolon is required are listed below. Notice that in all its uses the semicolon marks a separation between *coordinate* elements—expressions of equal rank.

12.1

⌃
;

Semicolons Between Main Clauses Without Coordinating Conjunctions

A semicolon must be used to separate main clauses that are not joined by one of the coordinating conjunctions *(and, but, for, or, nor, yet):*

> The penalty for not turning work in on time is a lowered grade; the penalty for not turning it in at all is failure.

These clauses are clearly separate in thought and structure and could be punctuated as separate sentences. A semicolon is used to combine such clauses when the writer considers them parts of one idea. Sometimes the second clause continues the thought of the first:

> The cathedral was Romanesque; its columns were thick and its nave dark.

> Alfred Hitchcock was probably the first director to place *himself* at a slightly ironic distance from the action of his films; his own subtle mockery helped him confect high-gloss thrillers that serious people might enjoy without losing their sense of identity.—Jacob Brackman, "Onward and Upward with the Arts"

Sometimes the second clause presents a contrasting idea:

> You're not disturbing us; we welcome the break.

> But however immature they are, these lovers are not dull characters; on the contrary, they are hauntingly and embarrassingly real.—Arthur Mizener, *The Far Side of Paradise*

The use of a comma rather than a semicolon or period between main clauses without an expressed connective is considered a serious error in writing. (See 4.4, Comma Splices.)

Semicolons Between Main Clauses Linked
with a Conjunctive Adverb

A semicolon is used before conjunctive adverbs like *however,*
therefore, consequently, and *nevertheless* when they occur between clauses:

> On your income tax return you can deduct the cost of meals
> and lodging for business trips; **however,** you cannot deduct
> the cost of meals if you were not away overnight.

> And, in fact, absence of intellectual content is the mark of
> the sentimental genre; **conversely,** it is because of her intel-
> lect that Jane Austen is never sentimental.—Brigid Brophy,
> "A Masterpiece, and Dreadful"

12.1

The use of heavy conjunctive adverbs *(nonetheless, conversely)*
between long clauses is probably more characteristic of a formal style, as the second example above may indicate. They
do appear in other places, of course, as in the less formal first
example.

Many writers use these adverbs as transitions between
sentences rather than as transitions between clauses:

> This is not the place to conduct a full evaluation of the bi-
> ological family. **Nevertheless,** some of its important virtues
> are, nowadays, too often overlooked.—Leon R. Kass, "The
> New Biology"

Note that a comma follows the conjunctive adverb. (See also
11.2, Commas After Conjunctive Adverbs.)

Semicolons with Coordinating Conjunctions

A semicolon is sometimes used between main clauses connected by coordinating conjunctions if:

1. the clauses are unusually long,
2. the clauses are not closely related,
3. one or more of the clauses contain commas, or
4. the writer wishes to show an emphatic contrast between
    statements:

> I have known many black men and women and black boys
> and girls who really believed that it was better to be white
> than black, whose lives were ruined or ended by this belief;
> **and** I myself carried the seeds of this destruction within me

for a long time.—James Baldwin, "Unnameable Objects, Unspeakable Crimes"

Semicolons to Separate Elements Containing Other Marks

Semicolons are often used in lists and series to separate elements that contain commas or other marks. In the following sentences the semicolons are necessary for clarity:

12.1

$\hat{;}$

> The course will survey all the Shakespearean dramatic genres: in the first month, the comedies, including *Taming of the Shrew* and *As You Like It*; in the second month, several history plays; in the third month, the tragedies, notably *Hamlet* and *Coriolanus*; in the last month, the romances, excluding *Pericles*.

> In response to a request for information from columnists Helen and Sue Bottel, the following changes were volunteered by young readers: "groovy" to "gravy baby"; "right on" to "right there" or "left arm"; "out of sight" to "out of state"; "scram" to "make like a banana and split."—Mario Pei, "The Language of the Election and Watergate Years"

Notice that here, just as with main clauses, the semicolon separates *coordinate* elements. It is never used between elements of unequal rank, such as phrases and clauses or main and subordinate clauses.

Exercise 12.A

Commas and semicolons have been omitted from the sentences below. Insert the appropriate punctuation.

1. In the summer she visited Munich Heidelberg Frankfurt and Salzburg and in early fall she went on to Albania Greece and Egypt.
2. The weather was hot humid and miserable all day however a west wind cooled the air after dark.
3. Orchestra rehearsal begins at seven she will be there even though she needs to study.
4. The storm knocked out the electricity consequently we could not read or watch television.
5. She knew her parents were worried about her and so she called in to let them know she was all right.

6. In the past scientists assumed that memory was a brain function widely distributed among the cells of the cerebral cortex however Richard Thompson's claim that he has pinpointed the site of the memory in the cerebellum may cause them to modify their beliefs.
7. The main load-carrying parts of a suspension bridge the cables are made of high-tensile steel which provides maximum flexibility and the anchor rods are generally embedded in concrete which provides maximum stability.
8. The guiding principle in her household was entropy consequently as the days passed the perishable foods she had lost in the depths of her crammed refrigerator eluded her searches despite the pungent evidence of their decay.
9. Leonardo da Vinci a man of great mechanical genius coupled with artistic imagination recorded what has been described as a "one-man industrial revolution" in his notebooks yet his efforts were marred by his inability to communicate his ideas clearly to others.
10. The cities included as stops on the tour were Geneva Switzerland Heidelberg Germany Vienna Austria Sophia Bulgaria and Belgrade Yugoslavia. ∎

12.2

12.2 Colons

Insert a colon, or change the misused colon.

A colon is a mark of anticipation, directing attention to what follows:

> The directions are simple: insert Tab A into Slot B and fold on the dotted line.

> Molecular biologists have now provided a fairly complete picture of how genes carry out their primary function: the specification of protein structure—William B. Wood and R. S. Edgar, "Building a Bacterial Virus"

Students sometimes confuse colons and semicolons, but their functions are entirely different. The distinction is simple: a colon introduces or indicates what is to follow; a semicolon separates coordinate elements. The following passage illustrates the correct use of both marks (as does the sentence of the text immediately above):

> Smaller birds were less elusive: a pair of blue-winged warblers scolded us for coming so close to their nest, as the juncos had along the higher trail; a winter wren, reminiscent of the Long Trail in Vermont, lit up the woods with song; a kingfisher shot downstream with his loud rattle.—Paul Brooks, "The Great Smokies"

12.2 Anticipatory Use of Colons

A colon may be used after a main clause to indicate that a list, an illustration, or a summation is to follow:

> Many standard food words mean money in nonstandard use: cabbage, kale, lettuce.—Stuart Berg Flexner, "American Slang"

> Other gems of military gobbledegook are seemingly non-deliberate: *accidental delivery of ordnance equipment* to indicate shelling of our own or allied troops by mistake; *combat placement evacuator* for a shovel; *aerodynamic personnel accelerator* for a parachute.—Mario Pei, "The American Language in the Early '70's"

The colon is used as an anticipatory mark only after grammatically complete expressions. Do not use a colon between verbs and their objects or complements, or between prepositions and their objects:

Colon	He visited the following cities: Boston, Dallas, Chicago, Miami, and Seattle.
No colon	He visited Boston, Dallas, Chicago, Miami, and Seattle. [objects of verb]
Colon	The string section consists of four instruments: violin, viola, cello, and bass.
No colon	The four instruments in the string section are violin, viola, cello, and bass. [complements of verb]

Ordinarily you do not need a colon after expressions that, in themselves, anticipate or point out the significance of items in a series. These expressions include *such as* and *for example:*

The boys carefully avoided strange-sounding vegetables, **such as** okra, zucchini, and kohlrabi.

Albert always gave glowing reviews to horror and science-fiction films, including, **for example,** *Halloween, The Thing, Return of the Jedi,* and *Superman.*

Colons Between Main Clauses

A colon may be used between two main clauses when the second clause is an illustration, a restatement, or an amplification of the first:

The plan was ingenious: we would rob them after they had robbed us.

12.2

Colons Before Quotations

A colon is generally used between an introductory statement and a grammatically complete quotation, especially if the quotation is more than one sentence:

Within the past two years, there have been an increasing number of references by Negro writers and speakers to the *Through the Looking Glass* episode where Humpty Dumpty says: "When I use a word it means just what I choose it to mean—neither more nor less."—Haig A. Bosmajian, "The Language of White Racism"

When a short quotation is built closely into a sentence, it may be preceded either by a comma or by a colon, depending on how it is introduced:

As Alexander Pope said, "A little learning is a dangerous thing."

She reminded him of the words of Pope: "A little learning is a dangerous thing."

Colons in Conventional Places

A colon is customary in the following places:

1. after an expression introducing examples or a large body of material (as after *places* in the preceding sentence);

2. between hours and minutes expressed in figures: 11:30 A.M.;

3. in references to books and periodicals:

    Between volume and page: *The Nation,* 98:295

    Between chapter and verse of the Bible: Matthew 4:6

    Between the title and subtitle of a book: *China: A Modern Enigma*

4. after the salutation in a business letter:

    Dear Sir: Dear Professor Jones:

See 15.1 for the use of capital letters after colons.

12.2

Exercise **12.B**

Decide whether the colons used in the sentences below are appropriate. Correct any faulty punctuation.

1. As Jessica was preparing to leave for a bicycle tour of the French countryside, she packed: four pairs of knee-length khaki shorts, three cotton T-shirts, an extra pair of walking shoes, and a light beige sweater.
2. Many steps go into the production of a business computer program: the need for the program is perceived, the programmer writes instructions based on the type of hardware and the desired outcome, and a technical writer translates the program into a user-friendly instruction manual.
3. Since Walter was an opera enthusiast: he attended the three performances of *La Traviata* during his stay in New York.
4. Good nutrition involves: eating food daily from the four food groups: bad nutrition is a hastily gulped cheeseburger with fries.   ◼

Exercise **12.C**

Write sentences following the directions below.

1. a sentence with a colon preceding a list of information or examples
2. a sentence with a colon between two main clauses
3. a sentence that cites a chapter and verse from the Bible
4. a sentence that lists the title and subtitle of a book
5. a sentence with a colon before a quotation   ◼

13

DASHES, PARENTHESES, AND BRACKETS

Dashes, parentheses, and brackets are all used to separate interrupting elements from the main thought of the sentence. Dashes are ordinarily used when the interruption is abrupt or emphatic; parentheses are used when the interruption is an aside or explanatory remark; and brackets are conventionally used when an editorial comment interrupts quoted material.

13.1 Dashes

/--/ **Use a dash or dashes to set off the expression marked.**

Dashes are used to set off phrases which are added to sentences or which interrupt them:

> The instructions for assembling the wagon neglected to mention one essential tool—**a skilled mechanic.**

> William donated the painting—**worth more than $50,000—** to the wildlife fund auction.

On the typewriter, a dash is made with two unspaced hyphens. No space is left between the dash and the words it separates:

```
the painting--worth more
```

Use of dashes is often a matter of stylistic choice, but dashes are customarily used in the situations explained below.

1. To set off emphatic and abrupt interruptions:

   Can we berate the average citizen for relying too heavily on credit when the politicians in Washington—**and we might as well include professional economists and financial experts**—have failed to balance a budget in years?

2. To mark sharp turns in thought:

13.1
/--/

   He praised Ann's intelligence, her efficiency, her enthusiasm—**and then announced that she was fired.**

   He is a humble man—**with a lot to be humble about.**

3. To enclose added elements (usually to give greater emphasis to elements that could also be set off with commas):

   Still we do condemn—**we must condemn**—the cruelties of slavery, fanaticism, and witch-burning.—Herbert Muller, *The Uses of the Past*

   With our love of record keeping—**doubtless a mark of our business society**—the origin of almost everything is known or easily discoverable.—Jacques Barzun and Henry Graff, *The Modern Researcher*

4. To set off an expression that summarizes or illustrates a statement that precedes or follows:

   He founded a university, and devoted one side of his complex genius to placing that university amid every circumstance which could stimulate the imagination—**beauty of buildings, of situation, and every other stimulation of equipment and organization.**—Alfred North Whitehead, "The Idea of a University"

   Bunker Hill, Gettysburg, Iwo Jima—these battlefields have become a part of the American consciousness.

5. To serve some special uses:
   a. To precede a credit line, as at the end of the quoted passages in this book.
   b. After introductory words that are to be repeated before each of the lines following:

We pledge—
To uphold the Constitution.
To obey the laws of this state.

c. To separate questions and answers in testimony:

Q.—Did you see him?
A.—No.

d. To indicate interrupted dialogue (usually *two* dashes separated by a space are used):

"Well, I had always assumed that — —"
"I don't care what you assumed," John snapped.

Exercise 13.A

Add dashes and any other necessary punctuation wherever appropriate in the following sentences.

1. The push to upgrade national standards of education at least according to the latest government report is motivated by a need to compete intellectually and technologically with other industrial nations.

2. Luis' insights were brilliant but his method of investigation if in fact it could be called a method was far from scientific.

3. Artificial intelligence that is to say the part of computer science which focuses on making computers perform tasks that require intelligence has had a profound influence on the field of cognitive psychology.

4. His philosophical position was based on a strictly mechanistic view of human psychology a human being as an information-processing system.

5. Mr. Valdes began his report by explaining the scope of his work and what aspects of the problem he would include and deliberately exclude from his presentation.

6. His final words uttered in a wheezing gasp from his deathbed were "The money is hidden in my"

7. Dr. Goldstein who emerged from the swim center wearing his shirt inside-out and his pant leg tucked into his dingy sweatsock summoned a cab and headed in the direction opposite to the one he intended a perfect example of the absent-minded professor.

8. The institute of science and technology subscribed to a

utilitarian rather than to a humanistic philosophy of education and instruction.

9. "Some snakes in the wild are fast and efficient" Nancy Ratner, "Dormitory Dialogues"

10. The new shopping mall must be able to meet all reasonable environmental standards, offer convenient access to all shoppers in the western suburbs, allow for future expansion, and avoid causing significant traffic problems in the adjacent neighborhoods. ∎

13.2 Parentheses

(/) **Use parentheses to enclose the expression marked.**

Parentheses are curved marks used to enclose incidental or explanatory remarks. These functions are discussed below.

1. To enclose incidental remarks:

   He was adored **(I have spent some time looking for the right verb, and that's it)** by the members of the *Journal* staff, who greeted him each afternoon, in a sudden silence of typewriters, as if they hadn't seen him for a long time. —James Thurber, "Franklin Avenue, U.S.A."

2. To enclose details and examples:

   For seven long years **(1945–52)** austerity was the key word in British economic life.

   The changes can be seen by comparing the profits made before 1929 **(upper diagram)** with those made after 1929 **(lower diagram)**.

   The book has a complete discussion of causes of the Cuban revolution **(pages 165–87).**

3. To enclose figures or letters used to enumerate points:

   The main questions asked about our way of life concern **(1)** the strength of our democracy, **(2)** our radical practices, **(3)** our concept of modern economy, and **(4)** the degree of materialism in our culture.—Vera Dean and J. B. Brebner, *How to Make Friends for the U.S.*

No punctuation marks are used before a parenthetical statement that occurs within a sentence. If a comma or period is needed after the parenthetical material, it is placed *outside* of the closing marks:

> There is talk with music (tapes and records), talk with film and tape (movies and television), talk with live public performance (demonstrations and "confrontations").—William Jovanovich, "A Tumult of Talk"

However, when the parenthetical statement stands alone or occurs between other sentences, the appropriate end punctuation is placed inside the closing mark:

> The agricultural agent advised us to plant cottonwoods and live oaks. (Live oaks have the advantage of retaining their foliage through the winter months.)

13.2
(/)

> After a six-hour delay, we flew out of New York at dusk. (What a magnificent sight!) Yet Mike and Cindy were still waiting patiently at the airport in Minneapolis when we arrived.

Exercise **13.B**

Identify the parenthetical sentences or phrases in the following passages and punctuate accordingly.

1. By 1919, when Earle P. Halliburton had moved to the oil-rich area around Wilson, Oklahoma, to start a well-cementing business Halliburton had always been an enterprising fellow he had been experimenting with the then-newfangled two-plug cementing system.

2. Operators using this system would estimate the well casing's fluid capacity and then try to determine when the top plug stopped whether the right amount of fluid had been pumped figure 1.1.

3. Halliburton's conviction that the cementing process could be improved by more exact downhole measuring techniques led him to experiment with running marked clothesline downhole too stretchy with lowering flat steel measuring line too bulky and almost as stretchy, and finally, with reeling off from the surface the earliest round steel wireline.

4. During the following years about 1921 to 1940 Halliburton and other oil patch innovators continued to perfect wireline measuring methods. ■

13.3 Brackets

[/] **Use brackets to set off any insertion
in quoted material.**

Brackets are used to insert brief editorial comments and explanations in material quoted from other writers:

> Lest it be thought that I am exaggerating, listen to Mencken: "The impact of this flood **[of common-speech, non-fashionable Americanisms]** is naturally most apparent in Canada, whose geographical proximity and common interests completely obliterate the effects of English political and social dominance."—Eric Partridge, *Slang Today and Yesterday*

Comments or directions may be bracketed in conversation or in other quoted material to show that the speaker didn't actually say the enclosed words:

> For the first few minutes the practiced speaker, therefore, fills in time with his "Thank you" to the chairman introducing him. . . . Then come his formal salutations, "Mr. President, honored guests **[if there are any]**, ladies and gentlemen."—*Amy Vanderbilt's Complete Book of Etiquette*

The Latin word *sic* (meaning *thus* or *so*) is sometimes inserted in brackets within quoted material to mark an error in spelling, usage, or fact that appeared in the original:

> The author's next letter was headed "Danbury, Conneticut **[sic]**, Oct. 6, 1854."

Sic is used in scholarly writing whenever it is necessary to reproduce an original text exactly—errors and all. The *sic* assures a reader that some obvious error, unusual usage or spelling, or other discrepancy has not been introduced by a subsequent writer or editor:

> The folio text of the *The Tempest* reads: ". . . all dedicated / To closenes **[sic]**, and the bettering of my mind."

Sic may also be used in less formal situations when a writer wants to underscore an error for some illustrative purpose:

> The young woman wrote to us, demanding to know why we had denied her advanced placement credit after she had taken "four years excellerated **[sic]** English in high school."

In this book brackets are used with examples of writing to enclose words that might better be left out of a sentence, to suggest an improved expression, and to comment on a construction. These special uses are illustrated below:

> At the end of an hour and a half we arrived at **[the spot where]** the red flag **[was situated].**
>
> He looks similar to **[like]** his father.
>
> Most fishermen are *optimistic.* **[adjective, modifying** *fishermen***]**

Occasionally brackets are used for parenthetical material that falls within parentheses—thus ([ ])—but such constructions are awkward and can usually be avoided. Consult the preceding section to be sure that you don't confuse the normal uses of parentheses and brackets.

13.3

[/]

Some students ignore brackets because most typewriters do not include the characters for typing this piece of punctuation. When typing, it is necessary to leave a space before and after the bracketed expressions and to draw in the marks manually. Don't simply substitute parentheses for brackets. They are not interchangeable. (See 13.2, Parentheses.)

Exercise **13.C**

In each numbered space in the following sentences, which mark of punctuation would you consider most appropriate: a comma, a semicolon, a colon, a dash, a bracket, or a parenthesis? Is punctuation necessary in all cases? If more than one choice is possible, list the marks in order of your preference.

1. Let us begin by looking [1] at the two countries where population pressures are most severe [2] India and Pakistan.
2. The finalists in diving were [1] Wilkins [2] U.S.A. [3] and Oyama [4] Japan [5] no one else had qualified.
3. To Ahab, the white whale became an obsession [1] even Starbuck [2] the first mate [3] could do nothing to shake him out of it.
4. Reisman divides behavior into two major classes [1] inner-directed [2] directed toward pleasing the self [3] and other-directed [4] concerned with pleasing others [5].

5. The Edsel was [1] the most carefully planned and lavishly promoted new car in automobile history [2] but it was a total failure.

6. Someone [1] was it Carlyle [2] ironically used a truss factory [3] as a symbol [4] of modern [5] industrial progress.

7. Some industries have established good relations with their unions by increasing benefits [1] vacations, insurance, pension plans [2] but many manufacturers feel that there is only one permanent solution to their chronic labor problems [3] increased automation.

13.3

[/]

8. The key word in the essay [1] *faction* [2] is carefully defined by Madison at the beginning [3] then he goes on to explain [4] what forms it may take.

9. An audience is basically one of three things [1] although various mixtures are also possible [2] friendly, hostile, or indifferent.

10. When Cadwallader quit talking [1] the chairman snorted [2] tugged at his ear [3] and spoke [4] "If you ladies and gentlemen [5] there were no ladies present [6] believe that I will support this recommendation [7] then you have lost your minds."

11. The dictionary [1] thesaurus [2] and encyclopedia are now back on the shelves in the library.

12. When our younger daughter was about six [1] it's a little hard to tell since she was usually several things at once [2] and her brother was about twelve [3] he taught her all about golf.

13. Their original home lies off the main route between Fort Worth and Lubbock [1] Texas [2] about 225 miles from here [3] in a county that for many years had the lowest per capita income in the state.

14. Sometimes [1] even at my age [2] I can't say curse words because I'm afraid my mother [3] she has an ear that's accurate up to 1,000 miles [4] will hear and come get me.

15. The professor projected my design [1] my first ever [2] onto the screen and began the critique.

14

QUOTATION MARKS,
ELLIPSIS MARKS,
AND ITALICS

In general, the more common punctuation marks—periods, question marks, commas, semicolons—show how a writer wants words grouped together for meaning and emphasis.

The three marks discussed in this section—quotation marks, ellipsis marks, and italics—are somewhat different in purpose. They are visual guides that tell the reader at a glance such things as whether the words are a writer's own and whether they are being used in a special way. Compare the following pairs of sentences:

> He said I was a fool. [He accused the *writer* of being a fool.]
> He said, "I was a fool." [He called *himself* a fool.]
>
> He spoke of Watson's moral decline. [the moral decline of Watson]
> He spoke of Watson's *Moral Decline.* [a book by Watson]

Although quotation marks, ellipsis marks, and italics are used less often than other punctuation, it is important to know how to use them correctly. They are often necessary in research and writing that contains references to the work of others.

14.1 Quotation Marks

" / " **Make the quotation marks and accompanying punctuation conform to conventional usage.**

Quotation marks are necessary to set off direct speech and material quoted from other sources. They are also used around some titles and around words used in special ways.

Usage varies, but double quotations (" ") are the usual marks in American publications. Use single marks (' ') only for quotations within quotations—see page 273. (Single quotation marks are made on the typewriter with apostrophes.) Whether double or single, quotation marks are always used in *pairs*, before and after quoted material.

Quotation Marks to Enclose Direct Discourse

Statements representing actual speech or conversation—which is called *direct discourse*—are enclosed by quotation marks. The following passage illustrates typical punctuation for direct discourse. Notice not only the quotation marks but the punctuation used with them:

> When we got home, Cathy asked, "Did you win the game?"
> David said, "You'd better believe it. I got four hits, and we won 8 to 5."
> I hobbled to my chair.
> "And Daddy hit a triple," Mindy said. "You should have seen him run."

In dialogue, a new paragraph is begun with every change in speaker, as in the example above. But when statements or brief remarks are quoted directly to illustrate a point, they are usually not set off typographically. Instead they are incorporated within the paragraph of which they are a part:

> It was during that second year that I began to dislike having students tell me they enjoyed my class. "You're a good teacher," they kept saying. "You're so free about things." On my course evaluations most of them gave me top grades in every category and then wrote something like, "This was a great class because the teacher understood

that the students in this university have a lot of other things to worry about besides his particular course."

By my third year of teaching freshman composition I was wondering whether the educational theorists I had trusted knew what they were talking about. That year when students asked me, "Will spelling count?," I equivocated. Sometimes I found myself saying, "I'm not sure. What do you think? Should spelling count?"—Jack Connor, "Will Spelling Count?"

Only *direct discourse*, which represents the actual words of the speaker, is enclosed by quotation marks. *Indirect discourse*, which gives the substance of what the speaker said but not the exact words, is *not* enclosed in quotes:

Direct	The coach said, "Get in there and fight."
Indirect	The coach told us to get in there and fight.
Direct	"At the present time," the senator replied, "I haven't made up my mind about the bill."
Indirect	The senator replied that he had not yet made up his mind about the bill.

Quotation Marks Around Quoted Material

Words taken directly from another writer or speaker must be clearly set apart, either by quotation marks or by some other conventional typographic device such as setting them in reduced type. Whether you are quoting a phrase or several paragraphs, make certain that you follow the exact wording and punctuation of your source—even down to any errors in grammar and mechanics (see p. 234). Quote everything exactly as your author wrote it.

Short Quotations

Quotation marks are used around quoted phrases and statements that are included within the body of a paragraph. The quoted material may be worked into the structure of a sentence or may stand by itself:

Another immortal pun is Eugene Field's comment on the actor Creston Clarke that "he played the king as though we were in constant fear that somebody else was going to play the ace."—Max Eastman, *The Enjoyment of Laughter*

Long Quotations

When quoted material is relatively long—more than one full sentence from the original source or more than four lines in your paper—it is usually indented ten spaces (three more for the beginning of a new paragraph) but not enclosed in quotation marks:

> A British member of Parliament, A. P. Herbert, also exasperated with bureaucratic jargon, translated Nelson's immortal phrase, "England expects every man to do his duty":
>
> > England anticipates that, as regards the current emergency, personnel will face up to the issues, and exercise appropriately the functions allocated to their respective occupational groups.
> >
> > —Stuart Chase, *The Power of Words*

14.1
« / »

A Quotation Within a Quotation

Use single quotation marks around quoted material that appears within a quotation which is itself enclosed in double marks:

> If they depended solely on economic theory to guide them, they would be in the position of the man John Williams mentions: "About the practical usefulness of the theory, I have often felt like the man who stammered and finally learned to say, 'Peter Piper picked a peck of pickled peppers,' but found it hard to work into conversation."—C. Hartley Grattan, "New Books"

In the rare instances when a third quotation occurs within a second, double and single marks are alternated, like this:

> In the next passage he gives an example of Mill's uncontrolled temper: "Mill attacked Beaton with a poker after reading his comment that 'A work of genius is not, as Mr. Mill says, "a spontaneous outflowing of the soul"; it is the product of intellectual discipline, a quality Mr. Mill notably lacks.' "

Such a proliferation of quotation marks is confusing and can usually be avoided, either by indenting and single-spacing the main quotation or by paraphrasing some of the material:

> In the next passage he gives an example of Mill's uncontrolled temper, telling how Mill took after Beaton with a

poker for writing that "A work of genius is not, as Mr. Mill says, 'a spontaneous overflowing of the soul'; it is the product of intellectual discipline, a quality Mr. Mill notably lacks."

Quoted Verse

You may incorporate a phrase or line of verse directly into a sentence by enclosing it in quotation marks, as in this sentence which borrows a phrase from *Romeo and Juliet:*

"A plague on both your houses" was the general attitude toward the parties in any conflict, no matter what the outcome.—Percy Finch, *Shanghai and Beyond*

If two or three lines of verse are incorporated into a paragraph, the passage is enclosed in quotation marks and the line breaks are indicated by diagonal slashes (/) with a space left on each side:

Milton opens *Paradise Lost* by announcing that he will write "Of Man's first disobedience, and the fruit / Of that forbidden tree whose mortal taste / Brought death into the World."

If the quoted passage extends over several lines of the poem, it is best to line it off exactly as it appears in the original, and indent ten spaces. Quotation marks are unnecessary:

Milton opens *Paradise Lost* by announcing that he will write

> Of man's first disobedience, and the fruit
> Of that forbidden tree whose mortal taste
> Brought death into the World. . . .

Quotation Marks Around Titles

Quotation marks are used to set off the titles of short written works such as single poems, essays, short stories, and magazine articles. The titles of books and the names of newspapers and magazines are italicized (in typed or handwritten work, italics are indicated by underlining):

The Oxford Book of English Verse includes only two poems by Oliver Goldsmith: "Women" and "Memory."

Judith Blake and Kingsley Davis have contributed an article titled "Norms, Values, and Sanctions" to *The Handbook of Modern Sociology,* edited by Robert E. L. Faris.

See 14.3, Italics, for a chart, and 33, The Research Paper.

A few titles are neither set off by quotation marks nor italicized:

the Bible
Old Testament
the Constitution of the United States
Lincoln's Gettysburg Address
Montgomery Ward Catalogue
the Denver Telephone Directory
    (or any other catalogue or directory)

Do not put quotation marks around the titles of papers you write.

Quotation Marks to Set Off Words

Words used in some special way within a sentence are often set apart by quotation marks or by italics.

A Word Used as a Word

A word used as a word or as an example rather than for its meaning in a passage is either italicized or enclosed by quotation marks. Use one or the other consistently:

> People often confuse the meanings of words that sound alike, such as **"allusion"** and **"illusion."**

> I have trouble typing *artificial* and *expectation.*

Apologetic Quotes for Slang and Colloquial Expressions

In serious writing, an expression associated with unedited or colloquial forms of English is sometimes put in quotation marks to show that the writer knows it is not considered appropriate in formal usage:

> The disheartening outcome of recent international conferences has convinced some of our statesmen that certain nations consider us as little more than **"fall guys."**

> **"Klutz"** was the only word we could think of to describe this well-intentioned but befuddled manager.

The trouble with apologetic quotes is that they focus the readers' attention on the expression and make them wonder why the writer chose to use it. If you think a word or phrase is right for what you are saying, it is best to use it without apology. You should especially avoid employing quotations as an apology for clichés:

> His **"bird in the hand"** proved to be a **"horse of a different color."**

Most readers will be aware of your retreat to a trite expression without your effort to underscore it.

Nicknames

When a real or imaginary person is frequently referred to by his or her nickname, the nickname is not set off by quotation marks:

Abe Lincoln	Huck Finn	Babe Ruth
Liz Taylor	Boy George	Tennessee Williams

However, if a nickname is shown with a real name, it is often set off by quotation marks:

> Tony "Big Tuna" Accardo

Words Used Derisively

Sometimes a writer may use quotation marks around a term to show derision or sarcasm:

> This remarkable piece of "art" consists of a large canvas covered with mud and old bus transfers.
>
> She was so "genteel" that she avoided any reference to the human body.

It's generally better to try to make the whole tone of the passage derisive rather than to rely on quotation marks as signposts. Yet the technique used judiciously can be effective.

Quotation Marks with Other Punctuation

The following conventions govern the use of other punctuation with quotation marks:

1. Commas and periods are always placed _inside_ the closing quotation mark:

   > "Yes," Roger agreed, "it's too late to worry about that now."
   >
   > Her watch case was described as "waterproof," but "moisture-resistant" would have been more accurate.

2. Semicolons and colons are placed *outside* the closing quotation mark:

This critic's attitude seems to be "I don't like any movie"; on a few occasions, though, he has had kind words for a travelogue or a documentary film.

Fully a third of the railroad passengers were what conductors call "deadheads": people who ride on passes and never tip.

3. Question marks, exclamation points, and dashes are placed inside *or* outside the final quotation mark, depending upon the situation. They come *inside* when they apply to the quotation only:

14.1

" / "

Mother looked at me and asked, "Why do you say that?"

He gave me a skeptical look which seemed to mean "Look who's talking!"

Terrence interrupted, "No, listen to this—" and proceeded to recite a poem none of us had ever heard before.

They are placed *outside* the final quotation mark when they apply to the entire statement:

Who was it who said that "good guys finish last"? [The whole sentence is a question.]

And to top it all off, she refers to her automatic dishwasher as "essential equipment for gracious living"!

End punctuation marks are never doubled. If a quotation ends your sentence, the end punctuation within quotation marks also indicates the end of the sentence:

Ever since I moved to Boston to conduct symphony concerts exclusively, one of the principal questions put to me in interviews is "How much do you miss opera?" [not " . . . in interviews is "How much do you miss opera?".]
—Erich Leinsdorf, "What Makes Opera Run"

No period is added after the final quotation mark, even though the sentence is a statement, not a question. Occasionally it is necessary to use double marks *within* a sentence to avoid a possible misreading, but such instances are rare:

Mind you, not "Do you miss opera?", because the questioner takes it for granted that it is impossible for one who

has conducted so much opera to live without it, but "How
much?"—Erich Leinsdorf, "What Makes Opera Run"

Exercise 14.A

Write sentences according to the directions below.

1. a sentence that includes the names of two poems
2. a sentence that includes a short quotation from a book
3. a sentence in which you identify a speaker and the
   speaker says something as direct discourse
4. the sentence above converted to indirect discourse
5. three sentences giving dialogue between two speakers
   as direct discourse
6. the three sentences above converted into indirect discourse ■

14.1

" / "

Exercise 14.B

All quotation marks and indentations have been omitted from
the following passage of dialogue. Rewrite the passage, supplying quotation marks and indentations to identify the
speakers.

I don't know, said Miss Grimes, speaking more to
herself than to the others. I don't regret teaching. You see
something grow when you are with children. And as María
says, it's helping. She turned briskly back to the girl. I'll tell
you what, she said. If you want to go ahead studying and
learning while you think about being a teacher, I'll help you
and you can help me. You can be the schoolhouse house-
keeper, if you like, and help with the sweeping and cleaning up, and I'll give you lessons in return. Would you like
that? Yes, said María. She drew a deep breath, and stood
up. There was a lot to think about, all of a sudden. I think
I'd better go home now, please, she said. That's right, said
Miss Grimes, standing up herself like one lady saying
goodbye to another. You go home and tell your parents
about it, and talk it over with them. Then, if they give you
permission, we'll do it. Good-bye, then, said María. Good-
bye, answered Miss Grimes.—adapted from Alice Marriott,
María: The Potter of San Ildefonso ■

From *Maria: The Potter of San Ildefonso,* by Alice Marriott. Copyright 1948 by
the University of Oklahoma Press. Reprinted by permission.

14.2 Ellipsis Marks

/ . . . / **Use an ellipsis mark to indicate any omission in quoted material.**

A punctuation mark of three spaced periods, called an ellipsis mark, indicates that one or more words have been omitted from quoted material. If the ellipsis comes in the middle of a sentence, a space follows the last word before the first period in the ellipsis:

> "All government . . . is founded on compromise and barter."—Edmund Burke

If an ellipsis comes at the end of a sentence, the sentence period (or other end punctuation) is retained, and the three periods of the ellipsis follow it. There is no space between the last word and the end punctuation:

> Fourscore and seven years ago our fathers brought forth upon this continent a new nation . . . dedicated to the proposition that all men are created equal. Now we are engaged in a great civil war. . . . We are met on a great battlefield of that war. . . .—Abraham Lincoln, Gettysburg Address

> Does this sound harsh today? . . . Yes, but I cannot sell my liberty and my power, to save their sensibility.—Ralph Waldo Emerson, "Self-Reliance"

To indicate that an entire paragraph or more or an entire line or more of poetry has been omitted, a full line of ellipsis marks is used:

> That's my last Duchess painted on the wall,
> Looking as if she were alive . . . [two words omitted]
> . . . . [two lines omitted]
> Will't please you sit and look at her?
> —Robert Browning, "My Last Duchess"

Ellipses are sometimes used, especially in narrative, to indicate interruptions in thought, incompleted statements, or hesitation in speech, as in this description of the dying words of John Wilkes Booth, the assassin of Lincoln:

Water was poured into his mouth. He blew it out feebly, opened his eyes and moved his lips to shape the words: "Tell . . . mother. . . ." Then he fainted again. When he came to, he finished his sentence: "Tell . . . mother . . . I . . . died . . . for . . . my country."—Eleanor Ruggles, *Prince of Players*

Exercise **14.C**

Practice using ellipsis marks by rewriting the following sentences, omitting material either from the middle of the sentences or from the end. Be sure your versions still make sense and are grammatically correct after you have inserted the ellipsis marks. Punctuate carefully. All the sentences are from George Orwell's essay "Politics and the English Language."

14.2

/ . . . /

Example   Most people who bother with the matter at all would admit that the English language is in a bad way, but it is generally assumed that we cannot by conscious action do anything about it.

Most people . . . would admit that the English language is in a bad way, but it is generally assumed that we cannot . . . do anything about it.

1.   It follows that any struggle against the abuse of language is a sentimental archaism, like preferring candles to electric light or hansom cabs to aeroplanes.

2.   Modern English, especially written English, is full of bad habits which spread by imitation and which can be avoided if one is willing to take the necessary trouble.

3.   The political dialects to be found in pamphlets, leading articles, manifestos, White Papers and the speeches of undersecretaries do, of course, vary from party to party, but they are all alike in that one almost never finds in them a fresh, vivid, home-made turn of speech.

4.   This invasion of one's mind by ready-made phrases *(lay the foundations, achieve a radical transformation)* can only be prevented if one is constantly on guard against them, and every such phrase anaesthetizes a portion of one's brain.

5.   Silly words and expressions have often disappeared, not through any evolutionary process but owing to the conscious action of a minority.

14.3 Italics

Ital Underline the word or expression marked to correspond to the conventions for using italic type.

Words are set off or emphasized in most published works by printing them in slanting type called *italics*. In handwritten or typed papers, such words are underlined:

```
The article first appeared in Harper's Magazine
and was reprinted in The Reader's Digest.
```

Italics for Titles and Names

In general, the titles of long or complete works of art or of certain objects are italicized; shorter pieces conventionally appear in quotation marks. The following chart will help you to identify the proper forms.

ITALICIZED	"IN QUOTATIONS"
Titles of books *The Brothers Karamazov* *Roman Life* *Jude the Obscure*	**Chapters or sections of books** "The Grand Inquisitor" "Roman Religion"
Names of magazines and journals *Time* *Road & Track* *PMLA*	**Articles and essays in magazines, journals, and newspapers** "The Economy: More Good News"
Names of newspapers *The Cleveland Plain Dealer* *The Chicago Tribune* [or the Chicago *Tribune*]	**Names of sections in magazines or newspapers** "Modern Living" "Sports"
Titles of plays *Amadeus* *The Tempest* *The Glass Menagerie*	**Titles of short stories** "The Lottery" "Everything That Rises Must Converge"
Titles of long poems or collections of poetry *The Miller's Tale* *Don Juan* *Leaves of Grass*	**Titles of short poems or individual poems within a collection** "Jabberwocky" "She Walks in Beauty"

ITALICIZED	"IN QUOTATIONS"
Titles of long musical works	**Titles of songs**
Verdi's *Requiem*	"Lord Randal"
Das Rheingold	"Night and Day"
Abbey Road	"She Came In Through the Bathroom Window"
Titles of television or radio shows	**Titles of episodes or segments of television or radio programs**
Dallas	"My Mother, My Roommate"
60 Minutes	
All Things Considered	
Titles of paintings, sculptures, and other works of art	
the *Martyrdom of St. Matthew*	
The Thinker	
the *Mona Lisa*	
Names of ships	
Intrepid	
U.S.S. *Arizona* [note that the prefix U.S.S. is not italicized]	
Nautilus	
Names of trains	
the *Tom Thumb*	
the *Orient Express*	
Names of aircraft	
the *China Clipper*	
Enola Gay [note that types of aircraft are not italicized: Boeing 767, B-1, DC-8]	
Names of spacecraft	
Mariner 4	
Challenger	

Special Cases

Certain very familiar works, important documents, and religious works are neither italicized nor placed in quotations:

the Bible	the Declaration of Independence
the Koran	Magna Carta

Names of individual books of the Bible are also given without italics or quotation marks:

> Book of Exodus
> Revelation
> 1 Corinthians

See 14.1, page 241, Quotation Marks Around Titles, and 33, The Research Paper.

14.3
Ital

Italics for Words and Phrases Used as Examples

Words used as words or as examples rather than as parts of a sentence should be italicized or set off by quotation marks. (See also 14.1, p. 242, Quotation Marks to Set Off Words.)

> Even on a sophisticated level there is some variation in word usage. For instance, what in other parts of the country is called a *sidewalk* was and may still be called in my native section of Maryland a *pavement,* and what is elsewhere called a *pavement* was in our usage the *street* if in town and the *road* if in the country.—Thomas Pyles, *Words and Ways of American English*

Italics for Foreign Words

Words from foreign languages that have not been absorbed into English should be italicized, not set off by quotation marks:

> In Antiquity every tree, every spring, every stream, every hill had its own *genius loci,* its guardian spirit.—Lynn White, Jr., "The Historical Roots of Our Ecological Crisis"
>
> Sometime soon after he arrives in Hawaii, a sweet lassitude creeps over the *malihini* (newcomer).—*Time*

Foreign expressions that would ordinarily be underlined for italics include terms like *coup d'état, Weltschmerz, deus ex machina,* and *mañana.* In most books and formal writing, the accents and other marks are retained.

Scientific names for plants, insects, and so forth are also italicized:

The mistletoe *(Phoradendron flavescens)* is the state flower of Oklahoma.

Words from other languages that are now widely used in general English are not considered foreign terms and so are not underlined or otherwise set off:

bourgeois	debut	laissez-faire	sputnik
chalet	debutante	prima donna	status quo
chic	fiancee	slalom	vice versa

Although dictionaries usually designate words that are now anglicized (have become part of the English language) and those that are not, their usage tends to be conservative. If you are certain that an expression marked "foreign" is familiar to your readers, you need not underline it.

Abbreviations of the less common Latin words and phrases used mainly in reference works are sometimes italicized, but Latin abbreviations in general use are not:

e.g.   et al.   etc.   ibid.   i.e.   vs.   viz.

Italics for Emphasis

Italics are used in printed material to indicate an emphatic word or stressed statement:

> Since we cannot have our fill of existence by going on and on, we want to have *as much life as possible* in our short span.—Susanne K. Langer, "Man and Animal: The City and the Hive"

Italics should be used sparingly for emphasis. When used excessively or with words that do not deserve stress, this device may strike a reader as artificial or pompous.

Exercise **14.D**

Write sentences following the directions below:

1.   a sentence in which you quote two lines of a poem
2.   a sentence in which you use quotation marks to set off a single word
3.   a sentence in which you quote something you have read with ellipsis marks to indicate that you have omitted something

4. a sentence that includes a word or phrase italicized for emphasis
5. a sentence in which you use a foreign word or phrase

■

Exercise **14.E**

All the quotation marks and indentions have been removed from the following passage from a short story. Rewrite the passage, using quotation marks and indentions to show dialogue and changes in speaker.

They do say, Mr. Adams said to Old Man Warner, who stood next to him, that over in the north village they're talking of giving up the lottery. Old Man Warner snorted. Pack of crazy fools, he said. Listening to the young folks, nothing's good enough for *them*. Next thing you know, they'll be wanting to go back to living in caves, nobody work any more, live *that* way for a while. Used to be a saying about Lottery in June, corn be heavy soon. First thing you know, we'd all be eating stewed chickweed and acorns. There's *always* been a lottery, he added petulantly. Bad enough to see young Joe Summers up there joking with everybody. Some places already quit lotteries, Mrs. Adams said. Nothing but trouble in *that*, Old Man Warner said stoutly. Pack of young fools.

—Adapted from Shirley Jackson, "The Lottery"

■

Exercise **14.F**

Write passages as suggested below:

1. a sentence in which you quote the opening line of a popular song or a poem
2. a short paragraph in which you quote the opening paragraph of an editorial from a local paper
3. a short passage in which you quote an entire stanza of a popular song or a poem
4. a single sentence in which you mention the name of a current magazine and the names of two articles it contains
5. a sentence in which you quote a question

■

Exercise   **14.G**

All of the quotation marks have been omitted from the following paragraph. Rewrite the passage, using quotation marks
and italics where appropriate.

> Sneer words are those adjectives that put some distance
> between the speaker and the subject by saying, I'm us-
> ing this next word under protest. Examples of sneer
> words are self-proclaimed, self-styled, would-be, pur-
> ported, and that Soviet favorite, so-called.—William Sa-
> fire, "Sneer Words," _The New York Times Magazine_, Jan-
> uary 13, 1980   ■

Exercise   **14.H**

In the sentences below, add quotation marks and/or italics as
needed.

1. Many readers think that William Faulkner's story Barn
   Burning is as great an achievement as his novel Absalom! Absalom!
2. England's Turmoil, Chapter 14 of Barbara Tuchman's A
   Distant Mirror, describes the political situation in England during the fourteenth century.
3. Alicia enjoyed Gene's company somewhat, but she felt
   he lacked the panache of her previous beau.
4. He proposed as the senior class motto, Readiness is all.
5. Are you familiar with the Browning poem that contains
   the line Oh, to be in England?
6. Isn't I'm Called Little Buttercup a song from Gilbert and
   Sullivan's operetta H.M.S. Pinafore?
7. An editorial in the Herald-Tribune entitled Going Too
   Far stated that the new fair housing statutes violated the
   rights of property protected by the U. S. Constitution
   and the Bill of Rights.
8. In one Agatha Christie mystery, Hercule Poirot rides the
   Orient Express.
9. We had to memorize Poe's The Raven and portions of
   Chaucer's Canterbury Tales.
10. I thought the review of A Streetcar Named Desire was
    naive.   ■

15

CAPITAL LETTERS, HYPHENS, AND APOSTROPHES

Capital letters, hyphens, and apostrophes function as signals. Writing in which capital letters are improperly used may seem inept to readers; words incorrectly hyphenated may be difficult to read and can cause faulty modification; misuse of apostrophes can cause confusion between contractions and possessive forms.

15.1 Capital Letters

Cap Capitalize the word marked; be consistent in use of capital letters.

lc Write the word marked with a lowercase (small) letter.

Convention dictates when capital letters are used; writing in which capitals are used inconsistently or unconventionally may focus attention on the wrong words and interrupt the natural flow of thought.

The following sections describe the most frequent uses of capital letters. A complete listing of all forms is obviously impossible. Consult a recent dictionary or style manual if you are in doubt whether to capitalize a particular word.

Capitals to Mark Units of Expression

Capital letters are used to draw the reader's attention to the beginning of a statement or to individual words in titles.

First Word of a Sentence. Capitalize the first word of every sentence or expression punctuated with an end stop (period, question mark, or exclamation mark):

> Has the change helped? Not much. The reason is obvious.

15.1
Cap

First Word of a Line of Poetry. In traditional verse style, the first word of each line is capitalized:

> Full many a gem of purest ray serene,
>   The dark unfathomed waves of ocean bear;
> Full many a flower is·born to blush unseen,
>   And waste its sweetness on the desert air.
>   —Thomas Gray,
>   "Elegy Written in a Country Churchyard"

Some contemporary poetry does not follow this convention:

> anyone lived in a pretty how town
> (with up so floating many bells down)
> spring summer autumn winter
> he sang his didn't he danced his did.
>   —E. E. Cummings

First Word of a Quotation. The first word of a direct quotation that is in itself a complete sentence is capitalized:

> He said, "The future of mankind cannot be left to chance."
> "The crisis is here," she said. "We must act now."

But no capital is used when the quotation is fragmentary or built into the structure of the sentence, or when the second part of a quoted sentence is interrupted by an expression such as *he said:*

> According to the advertisement, it was the "most spectacular picture of the year."
> "The argument is based," he said, "upon a false premise."

In Parentheses. A complete sentence enclosed in parentheses is always capitalized when it stands alone, but when enclosed *within* another sentence, it usually is not:

> The broadcast, sponsored by a local bank, was frequently interrupted by lengthy commercials. (**A**pparently the sponsor doesn't believe that silence is golden.)

> Fitzhugh was the member of a prominent family (**h**is mother was the granddaughter of Sir Thomas Wyatt) and was received in the highest circles.

15.1
Cap

After a Colon. A complete sentence standing after a colon is not usually capitalized when the connection with the preceding clause is close:

> Indeed, if Galileo had not been so expert an amateur theologian he would have got into far less trouble: the professionals resented his intrusion.—Lynn White, Jr., "The Historical Roots of Our Ecological Crisis"

The sentence after the colon is often capitalized when it is distinctly separate or when the writer wants to give it emphasis:

> We knew one thing for sure: **T**he swimming meet had not been judged fairly.

In Titles of Written Material. The first word, the last word, all important words (nouns, pronouns, verbs, adjectives, and adverbs), and all prepositions of more than five letters are capitalized in the titles of books, magazine articles, essays, and so forth:

> "The **B**attle **H**ymn of the **R**epublic"
> *Pottery Through the Ages*
>
> *Of Mice and Men*
> *Tender Is the Night*

I **and** *O*. The pronoun *I* and the exclamation *O* are always capitalized to prevent reading them as parts of other words:

> *Emilia.*   **I** do beseech you
>   That **I** may speak with you, **O** good my lord!
>   —*Othello*

The exclamation *oh* is not capitalized unless it stands first in a sentence.

Exercise **15.A**

Review the following sentences, capitalizing whenever needed.

1. Dr. Glass intended to write an article entitled "the fallacy of statistical evidence."
2. She decided to write the article because both her students and her colleagues were overly influenced by statistics: they seemed to believe that numbers made any measurement accurate.
3. When writing term papers, for example, few of her students dared to question the statistics they encountered (even when their intuitions suggested that conclusions drawn from these statistics might be wrong).
4. Dr. Glass recalled a term paper entitled "a rational solution" written by a student who had investigated neighborhood protests against a proposed shopping mall.
5. The student had described the residents' opposition to the mall as "emotionally charged hysteria against community development."
6. To illustrate the irrationality of the residents, the paper quoted one angry homeowner: "this noisy, cluttered, ugly scar will bring noise and traffic to our quiet area every day of the week; oh, i have read the studies, but they don't promise us a thing."
7. "But if the resident who had made this charge had actually read the preliminary studies," the student's paper went on to say, "he would have realized that his fears were unfounded."
8. The student who had written the paper had not questioned the validity of the developer's studies. (nor had he considered the possibility that what was an "acceptable noise level" to a developer might not be so to a resident.)
9. Dr. Glass hoped her article would clarify the issue by explaining a crucial point: some phenomena cannot be quantified without serious distortion.
10. She used the outline of her article in a class lecture (she found that it helped her clarify the argument) before she finished the final draft.

_15.1_
Cap

Capitals for Proper Nouns and Their Derivatives

The names of specific people, places, and things, and the words derived from them are conventionally capitalized (*Karl Marx—Marxism; Africa—African sculpture; Lent—Lenten menu*). Examples of the most frequent types of proper nouns are given in the following sections.

In a few cases, words originally derived from proper nouns have dropped the capital in the course of frequent use (*pasteurized milk, a jersey blouse, french fries*). Usage differs about the capitalization of others (*diesel, levis*). Up-to-date dictionaries provide a guide in such matters, as do the practices of current publications.

15.1

Cap

Names and Titles of People. A person's name or nickname is capitalized:

Abraham Lincoln	Eudora Welty	Hank Aaron
Barbara McClintock	Mindy	Dizzy Gillespie

A title should be capitalized when it is used as part of a person's name, but not when it is used as a descriptive term. A few titles of high rank are usually capitalized whether or not the officeholder is named: *the President (of the United States), the Pope, the Queen of England, the Chief Justice of the Supreme Court.* Titles referring to a position or an office rather than to the specific person holding it are not capitalized:

Capitals	*No capitals*
Professor Townsend	Francis Townsend is a professor.
Sergeant Anne Moore	A sergeant maintains discipline.
Judge R. A. Snow	She was elected judge.
The President [of the U.S.] vetoed the bill.	The president of the company resigned.
The Queen addressed the opening session of Parliament.	England has had several queens.

Names of family relationships are usually capitalized when used with a person's name or when used as proper nouns standing for the name. They are not capitalized when used as common nouns or when preceded by a possessive:

Capitals	_No capitals_
Grandma Lowell	She is a grandmother.
Aunt Sarah	My aunt's name is Sarah.
I showed Mother the card.	I showed my mother the card.
Whatever Father said, we did.	His father was demanding.

Names of Groups. Names referring to racial, national, linguistic, political, or religious groups are capitalized:

Chilean	Swede	Democrat	Catholic
English	Italian	Republican	Jew
French	Indian	Communist	Muslim

Names of social and economic groups are not capitalized (except occasionally for stylistic emphasis):

the middle class   the intelligentsia   the bourgeoisie

Names of Organizations. Names and abbreviations of business associations, clubs, fraternities, and other voluntary organizations are capitalized:

National Association of Manufacturers **(NAM)**	Boy Scouts
Rotary International	League of Women Voters
National Organization for Women **(NOW)**	United Auto Workers **(UAW)**
	Phi Beta Kappa

The words _freshman, sophomore, junior, senior_ are capitalized only when they refer to organized groups and their functions _(the Freshman Class, the Junior Prom)_, not when they refer to an academic status _(She is a_ sophomore; _The_ seniors _must write a thesis)._

Names of Places. Words that designate specific geographical divisions or particular places and areas (and words derived from them) are capitalized:

Asia	Egypt	Hyde Park
European	Texan	the Bowery
Latin America	Boston	Third Avenue

When the names of directions are used to identify geographic areas, they are generally capitalized. When they merely indicate direction, they are not:

15.1
Cap

Capitals	*No capitals*
the old **West**	**w**est of Suez
a **S**outherner	a **s**outhern exposure
the **Far E**ast	**e**astern Tennessee

Names of Institutions. The names of specific public and private institutions and their divisions and departments are capitalized. Names that apply to a whole class of institutions are not:

15.1

Cap

Capitals	*No capitals*
Chicago Public Library	a public library
U.S. Public Health Service	public health problems
Rock Falls High School	our high school
College of Business	a business major
Department of History	a history examination

Specific high-school or college academic courses are capitalized; general subjects are not, except for language courses:

Capitals	*No capitals*
Modern French Literature	literature
Advanced Narrative Writing	composition
Chemistry 101	chemistry
Abnormal Psychology 410	psychology
German 101	

Names of Specific Objects. Names of specific objects, such as ships, planes, structures, famous documents and artifacts, and brand-name products are capitalized:

the **S.S.** *Independence*	the Golden Gate Bridge
the **S**uper **C**hief	the Lincoln Memorial
a **C**utlass	Magna Charta

Names of Units in Time. Capitalize words designating specific periods, events, months, days, and holidays:

the **S**tone **A**ge	the Norman Conquest	Thursday
the **R**enaissance	the Battle of Waterloo	Labor Day
the **C**ivil **W**ar	January	

Names of seasons are not generally capitalized:

winter	summer	spring	fall	autumn

Sacred Names. References to deities and to sacred texts are capitalized. Pronouns referring to the Christian Trinity are also usually capitalized:

God	Holy Ghost	Talmud
the Savior	Bible	Koran
Virgin Mary	New Testament	Buddha

Abstractions. Abstractions like ideas, qualities, or conditions may be capitalized, especially in formal and sentimental writing, to show that they are being discussed in some ideal or absolute state. Sometimes abstractions are personified, particularly in poetry:

> Throughout recorded history, Man has responded to the challenge of Nature.

> The pursuit of the Good Life is a persistent human preoccupation.

In earlier centuries, it was common for writers to use capitalization more heavily than we do today:

> So large a Part of human Life passes in a State contrary to our natural Desires, that one of the principal Topics of moral Instruction is the Art of bearing Calamities.—Samuel Johnson, *Rambler*

Quite often, every noun in an essay was capitalized, as in the example above. In contemporary prose, capitalized abstractions are seldom appropriate. College students should confine them to formal papers of critical analysis or philosophical theory and follow the practices found in readings assigned in the course for which the papers are written.

Distinguishing Proper and Common Forms. Some words can be spelled either with or without capitals. These forms must be distinguished because they often have different meanings:

Capitals	*No capitals*
a Democrat (a member of the Democratic Party)	a democrat (one who believes in democracy)
A Republican principle (of the Republican Party)	a republican principle (of a republic)
Orthodox beliefs (of the Greek Orthodox Church)	orthodox beliefs (conventional)
Catholic sympathies (of or with the Catholic Church)	catholic sympathies (broad; universal)
Romantic poetry (of the Romantic Period)	romantic poetry (concerning romance or love)

Exercise **15.B**

Review the following sentences, capitalizing as needed.

1.   Last summer I took a university course called aesthetic principles: classical and romantic.
2.   Antiquity is sometimes described as the "golden age" because it was a time when reason seemed to prevail and civilization was ordered by a natural pursuit of truth.
3.   The secretary of state preferred to listen to beethoven's *ninth symphony* and to read nineteenth century english poetry, especially shelley's odes and byron's *don juan*.
4.   The kings of the french and english nations were, with a few exceptions, inept chief executives.
5.   For financial reasons, sophomores were welcomed to attend the junior cotillion.
6.   The middle ages was an historical era weakly covered by the collection of books in the public library, but the chief librarian intends to enlarge the collection by late spring thanks to a generous gift from the medieval history society.
7.   The democrats doubted that their presidential candidate would have wide support in the south and the west.
8.   Despite a strong background in philosophy, he could not graduate until he had taken philosophy 101.
9.   It surprised professor saldivar that none of his sophomore students in the american literature course had read either *moby dick* or *the scarlet letter*.
10. The department of agriculture is located in the calloway building, just east of the memorial street bridge. ∎

15.2 Hyphens

Hyph Insert or remove hyphen to conform to current usage.

Hyphens are used to connect two or more words used as a single expression *(heavy-hearted, will-o'-the-wisp)* and to keep parts of other words distinct *(anti-inflation)*.

Hyphens are needed in some instances to prevent misreading *(un-ionized)* or to differentiate between the same words used in different ways (a _drive in_ the evening, a _drive-in_ theater). But generally they are used as a matter of convention (_brother-in-law, hocus-pocus_).

In printed matter the use of hyphens varies considerably: newspapers and general English use relatively few hyphens; formal English uses more. The important thing to look for in proofreading is consistency. If an expression is hyphenated the first time it occurs in your essay, it should be hyphenated throughout.

This section lists the most common uses of hyphens. See also 18.2, page 319, Spelling and Word Division.

Hyphens for Word Division

One of the most common uses of the hyphen is to divide a word at the end of a line when there is inadequate space to complete it:

> The proposal for a modification of curriculum was supported unanimously.
>
> Both candidates were eager to win the endorsement of organized labor.

Words must be divided between syllables. While certain rules apply to the division of words, you may find it helpful to consult a dictionary whenever you are uncertain about where to divide a word:

dis / sev / er	knowl / edge
he / ma / to / poi / e / sis	Pe / king / ese

Avoid dividing short words or leaving a single letter at the end of a line:

Incorrect	We were excited about our trip to O-hio.
Revised	We were excited about our trip to Ohio.
	We were excited about our trip to Ohio.

Hyphens in Compound Words

A hyphen is used between two or more words considered as a single unit in certain expressions, as discussed below.

Names for Family Relationships. Some compound names for family relationships are hyphenated; others are not:

Hyphenated	father-in-law, great-grandfather, sister-in-law
One word	stepson, stepmother, grandfather
Two words	half brother, second cousin

Compound Numbers. A hyphen is used in numbers from twenty-one to ninety-nine. Fractions are hyphenated except when the fraction already contains a hyphenated number:

thirty-three	**four-fifths** of a box
one hundred **twenty-eight**	**one-half** inch
twenty-first birthday	one **thirty-second** of an inch

Compounds with *self*. Most group words beginning with *self* are written with hyphens (*self-contained, self-pity, self-support, self-government*); some may be written with a hyphen or without (*self support, self government*). A very few words beginning with *self* are written as one word: *selfsame, selfless, selfhood*. Consult a recent dictionary to find out which form is preferred.

Standard Compound Nouns. A number of compound nouns are regularly written with a hyphen: *bull's-eye, good-for-nothing, jack-o'-lantern, secretary-treasurer.* Other similar compounds are written as one word (*beeswax, newsprint*) or as two words (*intelligence test, labor union, shipping point, water cooler*).

Since practice is likely to vary with many of these forms, you often have the option of using or not using a hyphen. Where no confusion of terms is apt to arise, most writers would omit the hyphen. If you are in doubt whether a hyphen is necessary, consult a good recent dictionary.

Hyphens in Group Modifiers

When two or more words act as a closely linked modifier immediately before another word, they are often hyphenated to suggest the close relationship:

gray-green eyes	a **nineteenth-century** poet
a **well-kept** lawn	an **all-out** effort

A hyphen should always be used to prevent a possible misreading:

> a **slow-motion** picture   a **pitch-dark** room
> a **navy-blue** suit   a **high-voltage** warning label

When the first word of a group modifier is an adverb ending in -*ly*, no hyphen is used after it:

> **richly deserved** praise   **openly antagonistic** attitude

Compound modifiers formed with present or past participles are usually hyphenated when they precede a noun:

> a **good-looking** man   a **well-planned** attack

Such phrases are not usually hyphenated in other positions:

> Her father was **good looking.**
>
> The attack was **well planned.**

Long phrases or clauses used as modifiers are hyphenated:

> Watching him play Oedipus was a **once-in-a-lifetime** opportunity.
>
> . . . and he offers dramatic recitals about guerrillas (whom he didn't meet) and possible ambushes (which he didn't find), all of it pretty much in the **gosh-we-could-even-hear-the-guns-in-the-distance** school of war reporting.—G. Barrett, "Korean Scenario"

This type of construction is most often found in informal writing. It is not effective if overused.

Hyphens with Prefixes

Hyphens are used between certain prefixes and the root word either as a matter of convention or to prevent ambiguity. Dictionaries list most of these forms.

1. Between a prefix and a proper name:

    pre-Renaissance   post-Civil War
    ex-President Truman   un-American
    anti-Semitic   pro-German

2. Between some prefixes that end with a vowel and a root word beginning with a vowel, especially if the root word begins with the same vowel:

semi-independent   re-ink   co-option

When the parts have become merged in general use, no hyphen is necessary, though it is often still found:

reelected   coordinate   preexistent

3. To prevent possible confusion with a similar term or when the prefix is stressed:

to **re-cover** a sofa (to *recover* from an illness)

a **run-in** with the police (a *run in* her stocking)

to **re-sort** buttons (a seaside *resort*)

Suspended Hyphens

Occasionally, more than one single-hyphenated modifier may precede a word or phrase. In such cases, a hyphen may still be used to indicate the suspended modifying connection:

neither the **one-** nor the **two-humped** camel

Two-word forms first acquire the hyphen, later are printed as one word, and not infrequently the transition is from the **two-** to the **one-word** form, bypassing the hyphen stage.
—*GPO Style Manual*

Unnecessary Hyphens

Don't hyphenate a term that is currently written as a single word or as two words. Even if your dictionary lists as alternatives such old-fashioned forms as *to-night* and *post-man*, use the first or preferred form. Here is a brief list of words that writers are sometimes tempted to hyphenate:

One word	*Separate words*
anybody (pronoun)	all right
basketball, baseball, football	class president
bookkeeping	high school
himself, myself, ourselves	"How do you do?"
outdoor	motion picture
overlooked	no one
percent	report card
semicolon	school days
throughout	second in command
uphold	six o'clock
whatever	tax rate

Exercise **15.C**

Indicate which of the following expressions should be written as separate words, which should be one word, and which should be hyphenated. The words in parentheses indicate the sense in which the expression is intended.

1. a lot (of work to do)
2. anti Islamic
3. base ball
4. dark horse
5. every one (is present)
6. flame thrower
7. gilt edged
8. give and take
9. hydro therapy
10. in so far as
11. jet black
12. left overs (food)
13. man hunt
14. man of war (a ship)
15. may be (perhaps)
16. never the less
17. non communist
18. not with standing (a conjunction)
19. over look (to slight or neglect)
20. out and out (outright)
21. Ping Pong
22. re written
23. school board
24. self satisfied
25. semi colon
26. some body (is missing)
27. space craft
28. ten word (telegram)
29. three quarters (of an inch)
30. where abouts (at what place)

Exercise **15.D**

Add hyphens as needed in the sentences below.

1. Science is in part a fact finding discipline and in part a concept making enterprise.

2. Scientists operate from the time tested premise that naturally occurring events in the universe can be described by physical laws and that evidence of these laws is discernible to the senses.

3. The nineteenth century naturalist Charles Darwin, for instance, derived his now famous theory of evolution from his observations of fossilized life forms as well as from studying present day organisms.

4. Fossil records, he believed, indicated a natural occurrence over long time spans, of the same type of selective breeding process that is well known to modern day plant and animal breeders.

15.3

5. This selection process favors well adapted individuals—those plants and animals which are best suited to survive in their environments.

6. One thought provoking concept which the work of Darwin calls to mind is the relationship beween an organism and its environment.

7. A species which, in keeping with a gradually changing food supply, evolves from a plant eating to a flesh eating creature becomes a part of the environment to which other life forms must adapt.

8. Smaller animals which now might serve as prey to the recently evolved carnivorous species would need to develop self protective capabilities to enable them to cope with the life threatening addition to their environment.

9. They must, for instance, become fleet of foot, like rabbits, or they must develop body protecting shields, like porcupines or armadillos, in order to reestablish the ecological balance.

10. Such changes, of course, must be multi generational; once born, an individual creature does not alter its essential characteristics, but its genetic make up, passed on to future generations, may contribute to essential changes in the species.   ■

15.3 Apostrophes

Insert an apostrophe where it belongs or take out the unnecessary apostrophe.

An apostrophe (') is used in contractions, to mark the plural form of some expressions, and to indicate the possessive case of nouns. Although it is a minor mark that seldom affects the reader's interpretation of a statement, its omission or misuse is noticeable.

Apostrophes in Contractions

Contractions are an attempt to represent the rhythms of speech. They are appropriate in dialogue, informal writing, and much general writing. They appear often enough in formal and academic writing to indicate that most writers consider them appropriate in such situations. You should be aware, however, that many teachers, editors, and readers think that contractions are out of place in formal and academic prose.

15.3 ∨

When a contraction is appropriate in writing, an apostrophe is used to indicate the omission of one or more letters:

can't	I'll	it's (it is)	we're
don't	she's	o'clock	won't

Notice that *till* (as in "from morning till midnight") is not a shortened form of *until* and no apostrophe is used with it.

An apostrophe is used with dates from which the first figures are omitted *(the class of '59, the spirit of '76).* In formal writing, dates should usually be written in full.

Apostrophes with Possessive Case Forms

An apostrophe is used with the singular and plural forms of nouns and indefinite pronouns to indicate possession:

John's car	children's games
New York's parks	your parents' permission
a stone's throw	anybody's guess

An apostrophe is not used with the possessive forms of the personal pronouns *his, hers, its, ours, yours, theirs:*

the city and **its** suburbs

these seats are **ours**

The position of the apostrophe can indicate whether a possessive is singular or plural:

Singular	architect's	boy's
Plural	architects'	boys'

It is conventional for the *'s* form of the possessive to be used with living things and the *of* form to be employed with inanimate objects or concepts:

Dr. Witte's thesis

the puppy's checkup

the design **of** the building

the eye **of** the needle

15.3
∨

For additional discussion of apostrophes and possession, see 7.2, page 136, Forms and Position of the Possessive, and 8.3, page 163, Possessive Pronouns.

Apostrophes for Plurals of Letters and Figures
An apostrophe is generally used before an *s* to form the plurals of figures, letters of the alphabet, and words considered as words, but the apostrophe is sometimes omitted:

the early 1900's [*or* 1900s]

several size 16's [*or* 16s]

a .44 pistol and two .22's [*or* .22s]

Note that words used as words, letters used as letters, and so on, are also italicized, but the *s* is not:

Lucille tried to cut out all the *that*'s in her sentences.

There are four *s*'s, four *i*'s, and two *p*'s in Mississippi.

Apostrophes for Letters Dropped in Representing Speech

An apostrophe is commonly used to indicate the omission of sounds in representing speech:

"But J. C. he wouldn't let me be until I brought him over. Just kept on sayin', Mamie I'm not a-goin' to move until I see where I'm goin'."—Ann Petry, *The Narrows*

When frequent apostrophes make for difficult reading, it is not necessary in representing conversation to indicate all such omissions.

Exercise **15.E**

Add apostrophes as they are needed in the sentences below.

1. In America its sometimes possible to identify peoples national origins by their patterns of speech.
2. Each region of the country has its own characteristic vocabulary, phrase structures, and pronunciation.
3. In northern Iowas hinterlands, for instance, some peoples German background influences a speech pattern that changes the order of words in sentences and does not always differentiate between *ch*s and *sh*s.
4. The people who speak this dialect dont sound at all like speakers of the so-called Kings English.
5. A typical expression in this dialect is the following remark made by a wife to her husband at the dinner table: "Don eat y self over, Leonhardt, theres pie back yet."

15.3
∨⁄

Exercise **15.F**

In the two paragraphs below, capital letters, apostrophes, and hyphens have been omitted. Insert them where you think they are appropriate.

1. i arrived at eau clair in late april with my wife, who had joined me at the end of spring training. we rented a single room with a tiny kitchenette on the second floor of an old two family house. it disturbed me that, unlike most baseball wives, carol knew nothing about the game to which i had devoted my life. she took her cues solely from my enthusiasms and despairs. whenever i pitched decently—a rarity—i had to tell her so, and then she would smile and say, "thats nice, dear." when i was knocked out of the box in the first inning and she saw my dejection, she commiserated with me: "well, its certainly not your fault. its hard to do good when you only play a little bit . . . why doesnt your manager let you play as much as the other pitchers?"—Pat Jordan, *A False Spring*
2. "but sir, i dont think i really deserve it, it was mostly bull, really." this disclaimer from a student whose examination we have awarded a straight "a" is wondrously depressing. alfred north whitehead invented its only possible rejoinder: "yes sir, what you wrote is nonsense, utter nonsense, but ah! sir! its the right *kind* of nonsense."—William G. Perry, Jr., *Examining in Harvard College*

16

ABBREVIATIONS,
ACRONYMS,
AND NUMBERS

Abbreviations, acronyms, and numbers are useful and appropriate in technical, business, and legal documents, as well as in other specialized kinds of writing, in reference works, and in footnotes. In most general writing, however, words and figures are usually written out. This chapter discusses the conventions followed in using abbreviations, acronyms, and numbers in most general writing.

16.1 Abbreviations

Ab Write in full the abbreviation or, if an abbreviation is appropriate, change it to the correct form.

Dictionaries list most current abbreviations, either as regular entries or in a separate section, but they don't indicate when these forms should be used. The following sections discuss the kinds of abbreviations that are appropriate in formal and general writing as well as some forms that should not be used. If you are in doubt whether a particular abbreviation is appropriate, you will usually do better to avoid it.

Abbreviations for Titles, Degrees, and Given Names

The courtesy titles *Dr., Mr., Mrs.,* and *Mssrs.* are always abbreviated when used with proper names, as are *Jr.* and *Sr.:* *Dr.* Kathy H. Holt, *Mr.* Claude C. Sampson, *Jr.* The convenient *Ms.,* used as a courtesy title equivalent to *Mr.* in addressing a woman without regard for her marital status, must remain an abbreviation, since it was devised as an abbreviation and does not stand for any word. Academic degrees are also generally abbreviated: *M.A., Ph.D., LL.D., M.D., D.D.S.* If a degree or title is added after a name, it is the only title used:

> William Carey, **M.D.,** *or* **Dr.** William Carey [not *Dr.* William Carey, *M.D.*]
>
> James T. Holloway, **Esq.,** *or* **Mr.** James T. Holloway [not *Mr.* James T. Holloway, *Esq.*]

16.1
Ab

In formal writing, titles like *Reverend, Professor, President, Senator, Admiral* are usually written out in full. In most other styles they may be abbreviated *if* the first name or initials of the person are used:

Standard forms	Forms to avoid
The Reverend James T. Shaw	The Rev. Shaw
The Reverend Mr. Shaw	Rev. Shaw
Rev. J. T. Shaw	The Reverend delivered a sermon.
Professor John Moore	Prof. Moore
Professor Moore	John Moore is an English Prof.
Prof. John R. Moore	
General Westmoreland	Gen. Westmoreland
Gen. William Westmoreland	The Gen. was given a new command.

Spell out given names (sometimes called Christian names) or use initials. Avoid such abbreviations as *Geo., Thos., Chas., Wm.:*

> **George** Harriman *or* **G. F.** Harriman [not *Geo.* F. Harriman]

Saint is almost always abbreviated when it is used with a name. The feminine form *(Ste.)* does not appear regularly. *SS.* is the plural form:

St. Francis	**Ste.** Catherine
St. Lucy	**SS.** Peter and Paul
Sault **Ste.** Marie	

Abbreviations for Agencies and Organizations

If a government agency or other organization is known primarily by its initials (or by some other shortened name), the writer should generally use the familiar abbreviation rather than the full name:

16.1

Ab

FBI	TVA	AFL-CIO	NBC Network
CIA	GOP	SPCA	MGM Studios
FHA	ROTC	4-H Club	*GPO Style Manual*

See 16.2 for a discussion of *acronyms* and page 277 for explanations of how to capitalize and punctuate abbreviations.

Abbreviations for Place Names and Dates

The names of countries, states, cities, months, and days are usually written out except in journalistic writing and reference works:

United States	Ghent, Belgium	Wednesday, May 3
South America	Portland, Oregon	Christmas [not *Xmas*]

Words like *street, avenue,* and *boulevard* should be written out in general writing, not abbreviated as they might be in addressing a letter.

A few unusually long place names are customarily abbreviated even in rather formal writing: the *USSR;* Barbados, *B.W.I.* (for British West Indies); Washington, *D.C.*

Abbreviations for Units of Measurement

In ordinary writing, most expressions for time, weight, and size are customarily written out:

Standard usage	*Forms to avoid*
in a minute	in a min.
hour	hr.
several pounds	several lbs.
four grams	4 gr.
weight	wt.
a half inch	½ in. or ½″
sixty centimeters	60 cm.

These units are abbreviated in directions, recipes, references, and technical writing when they are used with figures: ¼ _lb._ butter, _16 ft. 3 in._ In technical writing, the period is usually omitted after an abbreviation unless the abbreviation spells a word:

3 **ft** _but_ 3 **in.**

Abbreviations for Scientific and Technical Terms

Some scientific words, trade names, and other expressions are referred to by their abbreviations when they are familiar to readers and would be needlessly long if written out:

Rh factor (**Rh**esus factor)

DNA (**d**eoxyribo**n**ucleic **a**cid)

FM radio (**f**requency **m**odulation radio)

EDB (**e**thylene **dib**romide)

In chemistry, the elements are assigned specific symbols:

Gold—Au   Silver—Ag   Iron—Fe
Nitrogen—N   Lead—Pb   Tin—Sn

When an unfamiliar abbreviation is to be used repeatedly, explain it the first time it is introduced either with a phrase or by using the full name followed immediately by the abbreviation in parentheses:

The International Phonetic Alphabet, commonly known as the IPA, provides a more precise method of recording speech than does our conventional alphabet.

The writing lab uses **computer-assisted instruction (CAI)** to increase its efficiency.

Measurements expressed in technical terms are abbreviated when they are used with figures:

Tests show the car's highest speeds to be 34 **mph** [miles per hour] in low gear, 58.7 **mph** in second, and 93.5 **mph** in third.

The turntable can be adjusted to play records at either 78, 45, or 33⅓ **rpm** [revolutions per minute].

Expressions of this kind are written with either three periods or none _(m.p.h._ or _mph)_ with the usage consistent throughout a paper. These terms are not abbreviated when used without figures:

The speed of a ship is usually given in knots rather than in **miles per hour.**

Other Standard Abbreviations

There are a few standard abbreviations that are used in all kinds of writing:

a.m., p.m. The expressions *a.m.* (*ante meridiem,* "before noon") and *p.m.* (*post meridiem,* "after noon") are always abbreviated: 6:00 *a.m.,* 12:24 *p.m.* Current usage prefers small letters for these abbreviations, but they may be capitalized.

16.1

Ab
The abbreviations *a.m.* and *p.m.* are used only in referring to a specific time:

Incorrect	He had an appointment in the **p.m.**
Correct	He had an appointment at **3:00 p.m.**

B.C., A.D. The abbreviations B.C. and A.D. are used to distinguish dates in history in reference to the birth of Christ. They are always abbreviated and capitalized. B.C. means "before Christ" and follows the date; A.D. stands for *anno Domini,* "in the year of our Lord," and precedes the date. When neither form is used with a date, the A.D. form is implied:

454 B.C.   A.D. 76   1985

You may sometimes encounter the forms B.C.E. (Before Common Era) and C.E. (Common Era) as alternatives to B.C. and A.D. respectively.

Commonly Used Latin Expressions. English has absorbed a number of Latin expressions that are conventionally abbreviated. The following are in common use and should not be italicized:

cf.	*confer*—compare (with another source)	
e.g.	*exempli gratia*—for example	
etc.	*et cetera*—and so forth (never *and etc.*)	
i.e.	*id est*—that is	

Many writers prefer the English equivalents for these and similar expressions. The overworked catchall *etc.* should generally be avoided. Substitute *and so forth (and so on, and the like)* or rephrase the list, introducing it with *such as* or a similar qualifier. See also 33.4, Abbreviations in Endnotes.

The Ampersand. Generally the ampersand (&) should not be used as a substitute for *and* unless it appears in an expression or title that you are copying.

> *U.S. News* **&** *World Report*
> Doubleday **&** Company, Inc.

Capitals with Abbreviations

Abbreviations are capitalized when the words they stand for are capitalized or when the abbreviation represents a title:

> DAR (**D**aughters of the **A**merican **R**evolution)
> USAF (**U**nited **S**tates **A**ir **F**orce)
> Lt. Col. Edward Brown
> St. Matthew
> St. Joan
> 100 degrees F (**F**ahrenheit)

When an abbreviation stands for words that would not be capitalized if they were written out, no capitals are needed unless the abbreviation begins a sentence.

> Add 3 **tsps.** salt.
> more than 40 **lbs.**

Periods with Abbreviations

A period should be put after the abbreviation of a single word and usually between the letters of abbreviations for longer terms:

> p.   Lt.   e.g.
> ch.   hp.   c.o.d.
> Nov.   B.A.   P.S.

Usage is divided about the punctuation of abbreviated names made of two or more letters written as a unit. Some publications prefer periods *(P.T.A., B.B.C.)*, but a growing number are using the solid form *(PTA, BBC)*, especially when the abbreviation is generally used instead of the full name. Some dictionaries list optional forms. It doesn't make much difference which form you use as long as you are consistent throughout your paper.

When an abbreviation falls at the end of a sentence, only one period is used: Send the letter to Canon, U.S.A., Inc.

Plural and Possessive Forms of Abbreviations

Plurals of abbreviations are generally formed by adding an *s:*

1 min.	30 mins.
1 lb.	28 lbs.
PTA	dozens of PTAs across the country

However, some abbreviations do not change to indicate the plural:

1 cm.	40 cm.
1 mph	70 mph
1 ft.	36 ft.

16.1

Ab

Others change their form irregularly:

p. 312	pp. 312–65
St. Luke	SS. Cosmos and Damian

Possessives, when required, can usually be formed by adding *'s* or by using the preposition *of:*

The FBI's Internal Affairs Division
The Director of the FBI

Exercise 16.A

Decide whether the abbreviations in the sentences below are appropriate. Indicate those abbreviations that should be spelled out completely or explained for a reader who might not understand them.

1. Many business execs. still believe that what is good for GM is good for the U.S.A.
2. New cars coming off the assembly lines in Detroit, Mich., no longer have to conform to the 5 mph bumper protection standard.
3. I was surprised to discover that the man who signed his name "Mr. Wm. F. Brayton, Esq." was actually my bro. Bill, who now lives in Mt. Vernon, Ia.
4. It is not true that college profs. have to have a Ph.D or even an M.A. or M.S.
5. During the experiment, for which she received a payment of $20, she allowed herself to be injected with THC.

6. A cheap place to stay in NYC is the YMCA on 64th St.
7. Dr. Wells wanted to add a P.S. to the letter to Rev. Jas. Hoffman before her husband took it to the P.O. at 3 P.M. EST.
8. If the indoor temp. rises above 80° F, the a/c will switch on automatically.
9. The KKK's plans to march down Constitution Ave. in Washington, D.C., prompted a number of groups—e.g., the NAACP, NOW, and DAR—to organize a march.
10. The ratings showed that for the 2nd year in a row, people watched more programming on ABC than on CBS, NBC, MTV, NET, & CNN. ■

16.2
Acr

16.2 Acronyms and Initialisms

Acronyms are abbreviations formed from the initial letters of the words in a lengthy name or expression. They are pronounced as single words:

NATO—North Atlantic Treaty Organization
VISTA—Volunteers in Service to America
HUD—Department of Housing and Urban Development
SADD—Students Against Drunk Driving

Initialisms, like acronyms, are abbreviations formed from the initial letters of the words in a name or expression. But initialisms are pronounced letter by letter:

SAT—Scholastic Aptitude Test
IRS—Internal Revenue Service
HBO—Home Box Office

In some cases, acronyms and initialisms have all but replaced the formal or technical names of objects, concepts, and organizations:

UNESCO   SEATO
CARE   AFL-CIO

Some acronyms have become so common that they are treated as actual words and no longer require capitals:

laser   radar
scuba   Amvets

When acronyms and abbreviations are used as a shorthand for technical phrases or expressions within a specialized field, you may need to define them briefly or write them out fully when they first occur in order to assist readers who might be unfamiliar with them:

CRT (cathode ray tube)
MIRV (multiple independently-targeted reentry vehicle)
IV (intravenous)
CAI (computer-assisted instruction)

16.3

Num

It is increasingly common in technical fields to coin words or phrases to serve as corporate and product names or as designations for new systems, languages, and concepts. Two such familiar coinages are the brand names *Kodak* and *Xerox.* Many such coinages have appeared in recent years to describe computer-related languages and data bases:

ERIC   BASIC   PLATO
CONDUIT PASCAL

Like acronyms, these alphabetical coinages should be explained to audiences who are not familiar with them.

Acronyms, initialisms, and coinages generally form plurals by adding -*s* and possessives by -'*s* or *of:*

thirty CRTs
the MCAT's importance
the difficulty of COBAL

16.3 Numbers

Num Follow conventional usage for words or figures
for numbers; be consistent in the treatment
of numbers.

There are few firm rules about using figures or words for numbers occurring in most writing. In general, books and magazines write out all numbers through one hundred and also larger numbers that can be written in two words (*six thousand, three million*). This style is usually appropriate for college papers and for most other kinds of general and formal writing. Newspapers and informal writing generally use figures for all numbers over ten, and some scientific and technical publications use figures exclusively.

General and formal	Informal
four	four
ten	ten
fifteen	15
ninety-four	94
114	114
22,500	22,500
thirty thousand	30,000
five million [but usage varies]	5,000,000 (or 5 million)

There are a few special situations (described in the section following) in which figures are always customary. In other cases, use the form that is appropriate not only for your audience but for your material. In general, write out all simple one-digit and two-digit numbers as well as round numbers that can easily be read; use figures for numbers that cannot be written in two words and for series of numbers that are to be compared.

Words appropriate	He shot three quail and one rabbit.
Figures appropriate	The next ship unloaded 3500 pounds of king salmon, 947 pounds of chinook salmon, and 200 pounds of crab.
Words appropriate	Five votes were cast for the class president's proposal, twenty-one against it.
Figures appropriate	In Colorado 10,547 farmers voted for controls; in Indiana, 17,003; in Minnesota, 10,750. The nationwide total was 87.2 percent in favor.
Words appropriate	If I had ten dollars for every time I've broken one of my resolutions, I would have at least a thousand dollars by now.
Figures appropriate	Dresses in the $35–$50 range were selling well, those from $51–$75 fairly well, and those over $75 hardly at all.

Whichever form you use, be consistent. Don't change needlessly from words to figures or from figures to words in the same piece of writing:

Inconsistent	When I was 15, I thought anyone over thirty-five was old.
Consistent	When I was fifteen, I thought anyone over thirty-five was old.

Conventional Uses of Figures

Use figures for dates, except in formal social correspondence, such as wedding invitations. The forms *1st, 2nd, 3rd,* and so on are sometimes used in dates, but only when the year is omitted:

> October 10, 1985   Oct. 10, 1985
> October 10   October 10th

Use figures for hours before a.m. or p.m.; hours are spelled out before *o'clock:*

> 7 a.m.   1800 hours (military usage)   twelve noon
> 11:35 p.m.   one o'clock   twelve midnight

Use figures for mathematical and technical numbers, including percentages:

> 3.14159   longitude 74°02′E.
> 99.8 percent, 99.8%   .410 gauge shotgun

Except in dates and street numbers, a comma is used to separate thousands, millions, etc., although it may be omitted in four-digit figures:

> 1,365 (or 1365) pounds   8,393,624   17,016

Use figures for page numbers and similar references:

> pp. 183–86   page 12
> chapter iv   Genesis 39:12
> Ch. 19   Act III, scene iv, line 28 (III, iv, 28)

Use figures for sums of money, except sums in round numbers or, in formal style, sums that can be written in two or three words:

Figures	*Words*
a bargain at $4.98	two thousand a year
The British pound was once worth $4.85.	a dollar a dozen

Use figures for street numbers (with no commas between thousands):

> 6907 Old Post Loop   Apartment 3C, 1788 Grand North

Use figures for statistics and series of more than two numbers, especially when the numbers are to be compared:

> The survey showed that the class contained 24 Democrats, 21 Republicans, and 3 Libertarians.

Plurals of Figures. The plural of a figure is written with either 's or -s.

> six nines: six **9's**, six **9s**   by tens: by **10's**, by **10s**

Numbers at the Beginning of Sentences. These numbers are written out unless they are dates:

> **Two** to 3% of loading and up to 10% is common and 20 to 30% in specially surfaced papers. . . .—"Paper Manufacture," *Encyclopaedia Britannica*
>
> **1960** was a year of devastating drought in China.

Arabic and Roman Numerals

Arabic numerals (1, 2, 17, 96) are used in almost all cases where numbers are expressed in figures. Roman numerals, either lowercase or capitals (i, ii, cxlvi; I, II, CXLVI), are occasionally used to number outlines, chapters, acts of a play, or formal inscriptions. They are almost always used to number the front matter of a book (such as title page, acknowledgments, preface); a new pagination in Arabic numerals begins with the body of the book.

In Roman numerals a small number preceding a larger is to be subtracted from the larger (ix = 9, xc = 90). The following table shows the common Roman numerals (lowercase):

1	i	10	x	50	l	200	cc
2	ii	11	xi	60	lx	400	cd
3	iii	15	xv	70	lxx	500	d
4	iv	19	xix	80	lxxx	600	dc
5	v	20	xx	90	xc	900	cm
6	vi	21	xxi	99	xcix	1000	m
7	vii	30	xxx	100	c	1500	md
8	viii	40	xl	110	cx	1066	mlxvi
9	ix	49	xlix	199	cxcix	1985	mcmlxxxv

Cardinal and Ordinal Numbers

Figures that indicate number only (1, 2, 3, 75, 135) are *cardinal numbers*. Numbers that indicate order (first, second, third, seventy-fifth) are *ordinal numbers*. Except in routine enumeration, ordinals should be spelled out rather than abbreviated to 1st, 2nd, 3rd, 75th.

Ordinals can be either adjectives or adverbs:

> She took **first** prize. [adjective]
>
> He will speak **first.** [adverb]

16.3

Num

Ordinal forms ending in *-ly* (*firstly, secondly*) are unnecessary and are now rarely used.

Exercise   **16.B**

Read the following sentences carefully, keeping in mind the principles stated in the preceding section. Rewrite faulty sentences, making whatever changes are necessary. In some cases there is a choice in usage; remember that one principle of using numbers and abbreviations is to be consistent.

1. When we arrived at the theater on 8th St., we found that the evening's performance would start an hr. late.
2. The university recently added 2 new members to its faculty—Jos. Blumenthal, MA, and Mary Persons, Doctor of Philosophy.
3. 6 members of the OAS conferred recently with the U.S.A.'s U.N. representative at her office in N.Y.
4. Fifty-five to 60% of USC students approved the 2 o'clock curfew; about 30% were violently opposed.
5. His monument to St. Francis, a remarkable piece of sculpture, weighed over 2500 lbs. and rivaled his monument to Saint Peter.
6. P. 237 of the manual lists the home addresses of U.S. senators & p. 298 lists their D.C. addresses.
7. On Dec. 23 CBS will dramatize the most celebrated Xmas story of recent times: "A Christmas Carol" by Chas. Dickens.
8. Dr. Roscoe Caries, D.D.S., reported that in an experiment involving two thousand and forty-four children, tooth decay was not significantly reduced.

9. Lee had 4 sisters (ranging in age from sixteen to 31 yrs.) and a widowed mother.

10. After 10 months the FBI agent finally tracked Groark to Ogden, Miss., where he found him suffering from d.t.'s in the barn of the Rev. John Gantry, D.D..

11. Julius Caesar observed that Gaul was divided into iii parts.

12. The population of the town had declined steadily for over 20 yrs. so that by 1980 fewer than 500 people, a population less than ¼ of its size in Nineteen Forty, lived in Gray's Landing.

13. The new commuter train will run between the three major cities in the state at a speed well over one hundred and thirty five m.p.h.

14. Do you know that the highest point in Alberta, Can., is Mt. Columbia, which has an altitude of 12,294 ft?

15. The plainest address I ever sent a letter to was 100 Main St., Normal, Ill.

16. Back in the 60's I used to believe that no one over thirty could be trusted; now that I'm over 30 myself, I'm willing to trust people all the way up to 55 or sixty yrs. old.

17. If we're going to finish the project by 6 o'clock, we have to get 5 more two-by-fours before the lumber yd. closes at 1.

18. According to a recent poll, the ethnic distribution at the university is 50% Caucasian, 23 percent Hispanic, ten % black, seven percent Oriental, and 3% American Indian.

19. You can fly from here to Denver for $95 if you don't mind a 45 min. layover from 2:30 A.M. to 3:15 A.M. in Dallas.

20. I can remember being paid a wage of one dollar and twenty-five cents per hr. back in Nineteen Seventy-One. ∎

ABBREVIATIONS

■ Titles, Degrees, and Names

The following titles are always abbreviated when used with proper names and always precede the name, except as noted:

Dr.	Mrs.	Sr. [follows name]
Mr.	Ms.	Jr. [follows name]
Mssrs.		

The following titles and degrees are usually abbreviated and ordinarily follow a name:

M.A.	B.A.	D.D.S.
Ph.D.	B.S.	
M.D.	LL.D.	

The following titles are generally written out in full when used with last names only. They may be abbreviated when a full name is used:

President Reagan	*Pres.* Ronald Reagan
Senator Kennedy	*Sen.* Edward Kennedy
Reverend Graham	*Rev.* Billy Graham
Professor Soellner	*Prof.* Rolf Soellner
General Washington	*Gen.* George Washington

■ Agencies and Organizations

Institutions known primarily by their initials are usually abbreviated and capitalized:

FBI	AFL-CIO	GPO [Government Printing Office]
CIA	NOW	

■ Place Names and Dates

Countries, states, cities, months, days, and street designations are usually written out in full in general writing, but abbreviated in technical and referential material and in addresses:

General writing	**Technical or special circumstances**
United States	U.S.A.
New York	NY
Wednesday	Wed.
Lamontier Boulevard	Lamontier Blvd.

■ Units of Measure and Technical Terms

In most writing, units of time, weight, and measure are written out:

> in a minute [not _in a min._]
>
> half a quart [not _half a qt._]

Measures are regularly abbreviated in technical material, reference books, reports, and recipes:

> 3 tsp. flour
>
> 100 lbs.
>
> mpg, m.p.g.

Technical terms are commonly abbreviated in many fields:

> DNA
>
> Rh factor
>
> AM radio
>
> DAI
>
> OED

■ **Standard Abbreviations**

These abbreviations appear in all levels of writing:

> a.m./p.m.
>
> B.C./A.D.
>
> etc.

17

SPELLING

From the most able, to him that can but spell:
There you are number'd.
    —*John Heminge,* HENRIE CONDELL

Sp **Correct the spelling of the word marked.**

Good edited writing is characterized by accurate spelling. Readers seem to be more offended by misspelled words than by any other mechanical error; misspellings may distract readers from what you are trying to say or may convey an impression of carelessness and incompetence. Out of regard for yourself and your readers, see that whatever you write is as free from error as possible.

This chapter will first examine some of the principles of spelling and the most common causes of spelling errors. Then you will find a number of tactics for eliminating errors and improving your spelling.

17.1 Some Principles of Spelling

English spelling would be easier if each sound used in speaking were represented in writing by a single letter or combination of letters. But the way an English word is pronounced and the way it is spelled do not always match. Consider the variety of sounds represented by *a* in the first column of words and *ou* in the second:

fare	though
war	bough
hat	enough
many	through
lay	
far	
human	

A single English sound may be represented in a variety of ways: b*ee*, bel*ie*ve, prec*e*de, s*ea*, mach*i*ne. As an additional complication, many English words are written with silent letters: lam*b*, *p*sychology, *k*nife, r*h*ythm, *w*rote. Others, called *homonyms*, sound alike but are spelled differently:

17.1

Sp

write	sight	meat	to	its	peace
right	site	meet	too	it's	piece
rite	cite	mete	two		
wright					

Chaotic as spelling can seem in English, some principles are helpful for spelling common words. Following are guides to spelling you are probably familiar with already; a review of them may be timely. You can find more detailed information by consulting the spelling section in your dictionary.

Retaining or Dropping Final *-e*

Words ending in a silent *-e* generally retain the final *-e* before suffixes or additions that begin with a consonant (*-ment, -ly, -some, -ness):*

arrange + **m**ent = arrange**m**ent
nine + **t**y = nine**t**y

Other examples:

awe—aw**es**ome	require—require**m**ent
definite—definite**l**y	shape—shape**l**ess
hope—hope**l**ess	spite—spite**f**ul
place—place**m**ent	safe—safe**t**y

There are exceptions to this guideline:

argue—arg**um**ent	nine—nin**th**
awe—aw**f**ul	true—tru**l**y
due—du**l**y	

Words ending in a silent *-e* generally drop the *-e* before suffixes and additions beginning with a vowel (*-ing, -able, -ous, -ary*):

argu**e** + **ing** = argu**ing**   imagin**e** + **ary** = imagin**ary**

Other examples:

arrive—arri**val**   shape—sha**ping**
conceive—conceiv**able**   value—val**uable**
grieve—grie**vous**   write—wri**ting**

In a few words the silent *-e* is retained before a vowel to avoid confusion with other forms:

dy**e** + **ing** = dy**eing** (compare *dying*)
sing**e** + **ing** = sing**eing** (compare *singing*)

Words ending in *-ce* or *-ge* retain the final *-e* before additions beginning with *a, o,* or *ou* (so that the final *-c* or *-g* will not suggest the "hard" sound):

chang**eable**   notic**eable**   unmanag**eable**
courag**eous**   outrag**eous**   veng**eance**

Words with *-ie-* and *-ei-*
The familiar jingle learned by most schoolchildren is helpful in spelling *-ie-* and *-ei-* words: "Write *i* before *e* except after *c,* or when sounded as *a* as in *neighbor* and *weigh.*"

Words with *-ie-*. Words with *-ie-* are more common than words with *-ei-*. The typical sound of *-ie-* is *ē:*

achieve   chief   grievous   niece
believe   field   hygiene   siege

Other *-ie-* words are *mischief, sieve,* and *view.*

Words with *-ei-*. After *c,* and also to spell the sound *ā, -ei-* is generally used:

ceiling   perceive   eight   reign
conceive   receipt   freight   vein
deceive   receive   neighbor   weigh

The long *ē* sound is spelled *-ei-* (rather than *-ie-*) in a few words: *either, leisure, neither, seize, weird.* Other sounds spelled *-ei-: counterfeit, foreign, height, heir.*

Doubling the Final Consonant

Double the final consonant before a suffix beginning with a vowel (*-able, -ed, -er, -ing*) with (1) words of one syllable ending in a single consonant after a single vowel (*brag, hit, sit*) and (2) with words of more than one syllable, ending the same way and accented on the last syllable (*commit, forget, prefer*):

One-syllable words

bat	batter	batting
grip	gripping	gripped
pin	pinned	pinning
spot	spotty	spotted
wet	wetter	wettest

Words of more than one syllable

commit	committed	committing
control	controllable	controlled
occur	occurrence	occurred
omit	ommitted	omitting
prefer	preferred	preferring

The consonant is *not* doubled (1) in words with two vowels before the final consonant (*daub, daubing; keep, keeper; spoil, spoiled*), or (2) in words ending with two consonants (*help, helped; peck, pecking; lurk, lurked*), or (3) when the accent of the lengthened word shifts to an earlier syllable (*infer', in' ference; prefer', pref' erable; refer', ref' erence*).

Usage is divided about doubling the final consonant of some words not accented in the last syllable, but American spelling generally favors the single consonant:

bias—biased	quarrel—quarreling
counsel—counseled, counselor	travel—traveler, traveled
diagram—diagramed	worship—worshiped,
kidnap—kidnaping, kidnaper	worshiping

Words with Final -y

A final *-y* preceded by a consonant regularly changes to *i* before all suffixes except those beginning with *i*:

body—bodies	duty—dutiful
busy—business	easy—easily
carry—carried, carrying	envy—envious

happy—happiness	mercy—merciful
lonely—loneliness	study—studious, studying
marry—marriage, marrying	Tory—Tories

Final -*y* preceded by a vowel remains unchanged when a suffix is added:

boy—boys, boyish
delay—delayed, delayer
enjoy—enjoyable, enjoyment, enjoying
play—playful, playing, played

17.1

Sp

See also 17.2, Spelling Troublesome Plurals.

Words That End with *-cede, -ceed, -sede*

Only one word ends in -*sede: supersede.* Only three end in -*ceed: exceed, proceed, succeed.* All other words of this sort end in -*cede: precede, recede, intercede, secede,* for example.

Words That End with *-able, -ible, -ance, -ence, -ant, -ent*

Words with these endings should be carefully checked for correct spelling. Words ending in -*able* (like *advisable, desirable, improbable, suitable*) are much more common than those ending in -*ible* (such as *audible, divisible, horrible, visible*). But since no rules govern the formation of these endings, consult a dictionary if you are in doubt.

A few words are spelled with either -*able* or -*ible* endings. Dictionaries indicate the more common or preferred spelling by putting it first *(collapsible, collapsable; preventable, preventible).*

The spelling of words ending in -*ance, -ant; -ence, -ent* must also be watched, since pronunciation does not distinguish them (attend*ance,* confid*ence;* defend*ant,* exist*ent*).

Variant Spellings

When a word is currently spelled in two ways *(extol, extoll),* use the more common form. Many words have secondary spellings, usually British or simplified forms generally labeled in dictionaries as *Brit., Variant, Archaic,* and so on, so that you can choose the form appropriate to your subject and style. Most people writing today, and certainly anyone who has difficulty with spelling, will ordinarily prefer:

1. The more modern of two equally reputable spellings: *draft, mold, plow* instead of *draught, mould, plough.*

2. The simpler form of a specialized word if it has attained currency among the people who use it most: *anesthetic, medieval, program, sulfur* rather than *anaesthetic, mediaeval, programme, sulphur*. Although it is possible to simplify the spelling of many common words (such as *thru* for *through, enuf* for *enough, nite* for *night*), conventional spelling is expected in most kinds of writing.

3. American rather than British spellings: *center, labor, pajama* rather than *centre, labour, pyjama*. For the spelling of proper names (the British *Labour* Party) and for direct quotation (the Prime Minister described it as "a *humourless* affair"), British spelling should be followed, but in other situations the American forms should be used.

17.1
Sp

Exercise **17.A**

This exercise should help to fix some of the general principles of spelling in your mind. Copy the words in each of the following groups, making the additions or changes indicated:

1. Supply *-ei-* or *-ie-* as required for correct spelling:

all—d	for—gn	n—ther	th—r
bel—ve	fr—ght	p—ce	v—l
conc—ve	h—ght	s—ve	w—rd
counterf—t	l—sure	s—ze	

2. Add *-ed* to the following verbs to show whether the final consonant is doubled or not. If there is a choice of forms, indicate both of them:

bargain	dine	list	refer
bias	droop	play	travel
chide	drop	quarrel	whelp
clot	kidnap	question	

3. Add *-ing* to each of these words, making any necessary changes in the root form of the word:

become	endure	prove
control	hope	use
dine	hurry	write

4. Change each of these words to an adjective ending in *-ous:*

continue	dispute	mischief
courage	glory	outrage
courtesy	grieve	sanctimony

5. Add *-able* or *-ible* to the following words, changing letters wherever necessary to conform with accepted spellings:

accept	digest	repair
advice	force	sense
contempt	justify	train

6. Add *-ance, -ant* or *-ence, -ent* to these words, making any other necessary changes:

ascend	dally	provide
compete	defend	revere
confide	maintain	vigil

7. Indicate which of the following words might be considered a secondary, unconventional, or British spelling. Use a dictionary to check your answers.

naive	colour
judgement	hobo
encyclopaedia	tonite
realise	tuff
nebula	connexion

17.2 Spelling Troublesome Plurals

Plural forms can be especially difficult to spell correctly. Some helpful guidelines for spelling plurals follow.

Nouns Ending in *-y, -o, -um, -us,* and *-f*

Nouns ending in *-y* following a vowel form the plural regularly by adding *-s:*

toy—toys	bay—bays
monkey—monkeys	tramway—tramways

But nouns ending in *-y* preceded by a consonant change the *-y* to *i* and add *-es:*

apology—apologies   ferry—ferries
company—companies   curiosity—curiosities
library—libraries   study—studies

There is an exception to this principle. In forming the plural of proper names, the -*y* is retained and -*s* added:

all the **Kellys**   both **Marys**

Nouns ending in -*o* preceded by a vowel form the plural by adding -*s:*

folio—folios   studio—studios
tattoo—tattoos   cameo—cameos

If the final -*o* is preceded by a consonant, the plural is usually formed by adding -*es,* but a few nouns add -*s* only:

17.2

Sp

echo—echoes   *but:*   piano—pianos
hero—heroes   solo—solos
potato—potatoes   banjo—banjos
tomato—tomatoes   soprano—sopranos
veto—vetoes   tobacco—tobaccos
                         Eskimo—Eskimos

A few nouns ending in -*o* add either -*s* or -*es* to form the plural: *cargos, cargoes; hobos, hoboes; zeros, zeroes.* Because no rule can be given for adding -*s* or -*es,* a writer must either memorize the plurals or consult a dictionary.

Some nouns ending in -*um* preceded by a consonant form the plural by replacing -*um* with -*a:*

addendum—addenda   curriculum—curricula
datum—data   medium—media

Similarly, some nouns ending in -*us* form the plural by replacing -*us* with -*i:*

syllabus—syllabi   octopus—octopi   cactus—cacti

Nouns that form their plural by replacing -*um* with -*a* or -*us* with -*i* always contain two or more syllables. But beyond this general guideline, there are no dependable rules for these plural formations. In many cases, a regular plural form can also be used: *curriculums, cactuses, octopuses.* To form the plurals of these noun forms correctly, you must either memorize the accepted forms or consult a dictionary.

Nouns ending in -*f* or -*fe* often form the plural regularly (*beliefs, chiefs, fifes, roofs*). But some common words ending in -*f* form their plurals by changing -*f* to -*ves:*

calf—cal**ves**	knife—kni**ves**	self—sel**ves**
half—hal**ves**	leaf—lea**ves**	thief—thie**ves**

The plural of a few nouns ending in -*f* may be either -*s* or -*ves:*

elf—el**fs**, el**ves**	scarf—scar**fs**, scar**ves**
hoof—hoo**fs**, hoo**ves**	wharf—whar**fs**, whar**ves**

17.2

Sp

Group Words and Compound Nouns

Most compound words and group words form their plurals by adding -*s* to the last word of the group, whether the expression is written as one word or two:

baby sitter—baby sitter**s**
cross-examination—cross-examination**s**
major general—major general**s**

But when the significant word is the first term (as it often is in hyphened compounds), that word is the one made plural:

daughter-in-law—daughter**s**-in-law
man-of-war—**men**-of-war
passer-by—passer**s**-by
president-elect—president**s**-elect

The plural of nouns ending in -*ful* is made by adding -*s* to the last part of the word; two cup*fuls,* three tablespoon*fuls.*

Exercise 17.B

In the following sentences, supply the correct forms of the nouns within parentheses.

1. Professor Novak was annoyed when she discovered that her work-study students had consumed two (plural of *carafe*) of coffee during their extended lunch. She wanted (plural of *apology*) from both of them for their tardiness.

2. "You act like disreputable (plural of *hobo*)," she sighed in disgust as they took up their (plural of *knife*) to resume their dissections.

3. "But we needed a break," they protested, angry at this

latest of her constant complaints and (plural of _cross-examination_).

4. Professor Novak softened, recalling that her previous assistants had been clumsy (plural of _oaf_) who had destroyed several irreplaceable culture (plural of _medium_).
5. After a series of scathing (plural of _memorandum_) they had been replaced. They retaliated by tasteless (plural of _memo_) of their own which had been distributed even to (plural of _passerby_) in the hall outside the laboratory.
6. The confrontation had been a nasty (singular of _phenomena_), one which Professor Novak did not wish to repeat.
7. Her recollections were abruptly interrupted by excited (plural of _cry_) from her current work-study students.
8. "Dr. Novak! Look at the (plural of _ovum_) we've discovered!"
9. Dr. Novak was excited. She had thought both (plural of _platypus_) being dissected were male.
10. All her annoyance vanished as she foresaw the impact this single (singular of _data_) would have in her Australian mammal study. ■

17.3 Common Spelling Errors

Spelling problems are often idiosyncratic. Yet certain kinds of errors trouble many writers and certain words are persistently misspelled. You may find it useful to know what situations and what words should make you especially careful about your spelling.

Errors Caused by Faulty Pronunciation

Although faulty pronunciation is not a major cause of misspelling, it is responsible for some very common mistakes:

Misspelling	_Correct spelling_
ath**a**letics	**ath** let ics
priv**l**ege	priv **i** lege
envir**o**ment	en vi **ron** ment
mischie**vi**ous	mis chie **vous**
perscribe	**pre** scribe

Pronounce each syllable to yourself when writing longer words (_ac-com-pa-ny-ing, par-tic-u-lar-ly, stud-y-ing_). Also notice that many longer words contain letters that are blurred or lost in speech: tem-per-*a*-men-tal, ac-ci-den-*tal*-ly, lab-*o*-ra-to-ry.

Omission of Final -*ed*

One of the most common spelling errors is the omission of -*ed* at the ends of words:

Incorrect	He is **prejudice.**
Correct	He is **prejudiced.**

This kind of spelling error often occurs because of analogy to speech, where the -*ed* sound is often lost in rapid conversation or is assimilated by the following sound. To catch such errors in writing, you will have to rely on your eye rather than your ear. There are three principal trouble areas:

In Verb Forms. Regular verbs form their past tenses and past participles by adding -*ed*. Be careful not to drop these letters, especially before words beginning with *t*, like *to*. *Used to* and *supposed to* are commonly misspelled:

> I **used to** [not *use to*] misspell words.
>
> He is **supposed to** be [not *suppose to* be] an authority.

In Verbal Modifiers. The past participle is often used as a modifier *(stewed prunes, raised platform)*. Here too the tendency in pronunciation is to drop the -*ed*, and many such shortened forms have become established: *grade school, oilcloth, cream cheese, roast chicken*. Others are sometimes found in print, but are not yet regarded as conventional: *bottle beer, whip cream, advance headquarters, ice tea*. In college papers it is better to use only shortened forms that are generally accepted. In less formal writing, more latitude is allowed, but dictionaries, current written practice, and appropriateness to the paper should serve as guides.

In Modifiers from Nouns. Adjectives are often formed by adding -*ed* to nouns: *long-haired, heart-shaped, two-faced*. When the -*ed* is dropped in such forms—a growing tendency in current English—the result is a noun modifier (see 6.4): *king-size bed, hard-surface road, high-heel shoes*. Established forms like these are acceptable in all writing. It's usually better, however, to keep the -*ed* (as in *advanced courses, middle-aged, old-fashioned*).

Separate Words and Combined Forms

Observe the distinctions between expressions that are written as one word and those written as two. These forms frequently need to be checked in revision:

> **all ready** [adjective phrase]: The girls were at last **all ready** to leave.
>
> **already** [adverb of time]: It was **already** dark when they arrived.
>
> **all right** [adjective phrase, conventionally written as two words]: The seats seemed **all right** to me. (The forms _alright_ and _alrite_ are not accepted in edited usage.)
>
> **all together** [adjective phrase]: We were **all together** at the depot.
>
> **altogether** [adverb, meaning _wholly_]: That's **altogether** another matter.
>
> **a while** [noun]: They talked for **a while.**
> **awhile** [adverb]: Can't you stay **awhile** longer?
>
> **may be** [verb phrase]: She **may be** the next mayor.
> **maybe** [adverb, short for _it may be_]: **Maybe** you'll have better luck next time.

Certain phrases may be mistakenly written as one word through analogy with other forms or because they are often run together in speech:

> The assignment was **a lot** more difficult than I expected. [not _alot_]
>
> The judge **threw out** his testimony. [not _throughout_]
>
> We live in a **dog-eat-dog** world. [not _doggie-dog_]

Confusion of Words That Sound Alike

Be careful not to confuse words of identical or similar sound. It is easy when writing rapidly to put down _their_ for _there_, _its_ for _it's_, _maybe_ for _may be_, but conscientious writers will check their finished work closely for errors of this sort. Substituting one form for another may suggest an idea that the writer did not intend:

> Psychiatric treatment changed Bobby from a withdrawn, unhappy child to a normal, happy boy **excepted** [should be _accepted_] by his group.

The following pairs of words are often confused in spelling. In most cases, writers are aware of the differences between these words when they are paying attention. Check a dictionary if you cannot distinguish between them.

accept—except	holy—wholly—holey
access—excess	human—humane
advice—advise	its—it's
affect—effect	lead—led
aisle—isle	loose—lose
allude—elude	moral—morale
allusion—illusion	of—off
altar—alter	passed—past
angel—angle	peace—piece
ascent—assent	personal—personnel
assistance—assistants	plain—plane
bare—bear	presence—presents
berth—birth	principal—principle
born—borne	prophecy—prophesy
breath—breathe	quiet—quite
capital—capitol	reign—rein—rain
censor—censure	stationary—stationery
choose—chose	straight—strait
cite—sight—site	than—then
coarse—course	their—there—they're
complement—compliment	to—too—two
conscience—conscious	waist—waste
council—counsel	weak—week
elicit—illicit	we're—were—where
envelop—envelope	whether—weather
fair—fare	who's—whose
forth—fourth	write—right—rite
gorilla—guerrilla	your—you're
hear—here	

Difficult or Troublesome Words

A list that contained all the words which—at one time or another—give writers difficulty would quickly swell to dictionary size. Yet some words are clearly more troublesome than others. The following list contains words frequently misspelled in student papers. Use it either as a study guide or as a means of identifying those words that typically give you trouble. Use the list to construct a spelling list of your own made up of the common errors you share with others plus the individual words that you typically misspell. (The following can also serve as a challenging vocabulary list.)

absence	benign	council
acceptable	bizarre	counsel
accessible	boulevard	cynicism
accommodate	bourgeoisie	
accustomed	breath	dealt
achieve	breathe	deceive
acquainted	Britain	decision
acquire	bulletin	defense
across	bureau	definite
address	bursar	dependent
adolescent	business	description
aggravate		desert
agreement	camouflage	desperate
all right	catalogue	dessert
all together	[*or* catalog]	develop
a lot	category	device
already	cede	devise
altogether	cemetery	difference
analysis	censure	dining room
analyze	changeable	dinosaur
annals	characteristic	disappearance
annihilate	choose	disappoint
apology	clientele	discipline
appearance	colloquial	dormitory
argument	column	drunkenness
article	committee	
assassinate	comparative	ecstasy
athlete	competent	effect
athletics	complement	effervescent
attendance	compliment	effete
augment	conceive	egress
authentic	concession	eighth
authoritative	conscience	embarrass
	conscientious	emergence
baroque	conscious	empirical
beautiful	consensus	entrepreneur
beginning	continuous	environment
believe	convenience	equipment
benefited	coolly	espresso
[*or* benefitted]	correlate	exaggerate

17.3
Sp

exceed
excel
except
exercise
exhilaration
existence
exonerate
extol [*or* extoll]
extraordinary
extremely

facetious
facsimile
Fahrenheit
fallible
familiar
fascinate
February
felony
feudalism
fixation
flamboyant
flammable
fluorescent
fluorine
foreign
forestall
formaldehyde
formerly
forty
fraternize
friend
fulfill
furlough
fuselage

gaiety
gaseous
gauche
gauge
gelatin
ghetto
governance
government

gradient
graffiti
grammar
grimace
guarantee
guard
gubernatorial
guerrilla
    [*or* guerilla]
gyrate

hackneyed
handkerchief
harangue
harass
hegemony
height
hemorrhage
hindrance
hors d'oeuvre
humorous
hurriedly
hygiene
hypocrisy
hypocrite
hypothesize

ideally
idiosyncrasy
idyllic
illicit
illiterate
imaginary
immediately
imminent
impede
impostor
inaugural
incalculable
incidentally
incredible
indefatigable
independent
inedible
initiate

innocuous
inoculate
inseparable
insurance
integer
integrate
intelligent
interference
intermural
interpret
interrupt
intramural
iridescent
irrelevant
irresistible
irritable
isotope
itinerary

jealousy
jeopardy
judgment
    [*or* judgement]
jurisprudence
juror
juxtapose

kerosene
knowledge
knowledgeable

laboratory
labyrinth
laissez faire
laryngitis
lecherous
leisure
lenient
library
license
lien
likable
    [*or* likeable]
loath
loathe

loneliness
lozenge
luminance

macabre
maelstrom
maintenance
malfeasance
malleable
manageable
maneuver
manufacturer
medicine
mediocre
memorandum
meningitis
mileage
minuscule
miscellaneous
mischievous
misogyny
missile
misspelled
mnemonic
monotonous
mysterious

nadir
naiveté
   [_or_ naivete]
nascent
necessary
neighbor
neurosis
nevertheless
niece
noticeable
nuclear

obedience
oblique
obscene
obsolescence
occasionally
occurrence

ombudsman
omission
omitted
omniscient
opportunity
oppression
oscillate
ostracize

paid
pageant
pamphlet
pantomime
parallel
paraphernalia
parliament
particularly
pasteurize
pastime
peasant
perceive
peremptory
perform
permanent
pharmaceutical
pheasant
phosphorescence
physiology
possession
posthumous
preceding
predominant
preferred
prejudice
prerogative
prevalent
privilege
probably
procedure
proceed
professor
pronunciation
propaganda
proportion

prurience
psychology
publicly

quadriplegic
quandary
quantity
quark
query
questionnaire
quiescent
quiet
quite
quixotic
quizzes

rapport
realization
recede
receipt
receive
reciprocity
reconnaissance
recurred
reference
referent
referring
register
registrar
registration
rehearsal
reimburse
reiterate
reliance
relieve
remembrance
reminisce
renaissance
repertory
repetition
reprieve
rescind
resemblance
reservoir

17.3
_Sp_

residence
restaurant
resuscitate
reversible
rhetoric
rhyme
rhythm
rudimentary

sabotage
sacrilegious
sanguine
satellite
satirize
scenery
schedule
scheme
schizophrenia
secession
secretary
seige
seize
sergeant
significance
silhouette
similar
skiing
soliloquy
sophomore
souvenir
sovereign
subtlety
succeed
succession

sufficient
summary
superfluous
supersede
supplementary
suppress
surreptitious
susceptible
syllabus
symmetry
sympathize
synapse
synonymous
synthesize

tableau
tangential
temperament
temperature
theoretician
therefore
thorough
till
tomorrow
tortuous
tragedy
transferred
truly
tyranny
tyrant

ubiquitous
unalienable

unanimous
unconscionable
unconscious
undoubtedly
uniformity
unnecessary
until
usually
usury

vacuum
vague
valence
validity
valuable
vengeance
veracity
veterinary
viscous
villain
vinyl
viscose
vitamin
voyeur

weird
wherever
wiener
wondrous
writhe
writing

zoological
zucchini
zygote

17.3

Sp

Exercise 17.C

Make up sentences that will illustrate the differences in meaning in the pairs and trios of words on page 300. If possible, use the pair of words in a single sentence.

Examples   Everyone **except** Sam **accepted** the invitation.
It's difficult for the leopard to change **its** spots.

■

Exercise **17.D**

Words in the following sentences have been confused with words that are similar in sound or meaning. Other sentences mistakenly run together two or more words that should be separate. Still others wrongly separate a single word. Identify and correct these and all other spelling errors.

1. James became irritated when his room mate, Oscar, returned from a trip to Britian with an affected Cockney acsent.
2. When June and Mike asked thier proffessor if they could go a head with thier chemistry experiment on the affects of hydrochloric acid on regular rain water, the proffessor replied, "Alright, but be sure to keep tract of the amount of acid you pore into the beaker."
3. The American computor industry has decided to step up micro electronic research; otherwise, the industry stands to loose it's competative edge in the world computor market.
4. To insure the personnel touch, Aunt Ida enjoyed writting notes on embossed stationary.
5. Because Sigmund Freud's theories dominated pyshoanalytic practice in the early ninteenth century, innovators such as Carl Jung sometimes wondered weather thier own theories would ever be excepted.
6. Do to the increase in alcohol-related accidents, Mr. Schwinn's insurence agency began offering cheaper policies to tea totalers.
7. Because the oceanography final contained alot of questions on edible plankton, a subject she had forgotten to review, Agatha felt that she had studied tonoavail and feared she would fail the coarse.
8. Water-flooding was long the principle method of tertiary recovery in the oilfield, but by the mid-seventies fireflooding had also become quiet common.
9. By the time Wally arrived at the picnic sight, he was two hours late; his freinds had all ready eaten and left.
10. He was a briliant musician, but his temperament was uneven and his rappore with his colleagues was meager. ■

17.3

_Sp_

17.4 Improving Your Spelling

Absolute correctness in spelling is not easy to achieve in English. But there are a variety of techniques you can employ to overcome spelling problems and reduce the number of errors you usually make. They are discussed in this section.

Eliminate Careless Mistakes

If you are like most writers, many of your misspellings are likely to be of words you actually know well: *it's* for *its*, *there* for *their*, *who's* for *whose*. Such errors may result from writing under pressure (an essay exam in school) or failing to proofread your final copy. Though careless misspellings are understandable, they nonetheless detract from the accuracy and competence of your writing.

Accurate proofreading requires careful word-by-word reading. Journalists often catch mistakes by reading what they have written backwards, thereby focusing attention on each word. Some writers use a pencil to pinpoint every word separately as they search for the misspelling that can slip through even a careful reading. Other people read their papers aloud, pronouncing each word distinctly. One caution: When you have found a misspelling, be sure to check the words immediately after it carefully. Many writers have a tendency to miss errors that follow immediately after mistakes they have caught.

Learn to Visualize Words

People who do a good deal of reading tend to be better spellers than those who read little, for seeing a word on the printed page tends to fix it in the mind. Sometimes, however, we learn to recognize a word in reading without really noticing how it is spelled. Very few Americans, for example, ever learned to spell the last names of the late Soviet premiers, Nikita Khrushchev and Leonid Brezhnev, though they saw those names in their newspapers every day for years. Many people have a similar problem with such common English words as *occasion, occurrence,* and *precede.* When you meet a new word—or when you have to look up a familiar one—look at it carefully, noticing each syllable, and try to fix it in your mind for future use. Don't shy away from mnemonic devices if they help you visualize a difficult word:

> There's **a rat** in sep**arat**e.
>
> People who **govern** are in **govern**ment.

Learn New Words

Learn to spell new words correctly as you find them in your college courses. You can't use a new or unfamiliar expression in your writing until you can spell it with confidence. Make a note of the words you will probably have to write in reports or in examinations. Underline key words in textbooks and observe their spelling on the blackboard. Then write them out in syllables, pronouncing them as you do so:

ba cil lus	Gen ghis Khan
bi par tite	me tath e sis
car bon if er ous	pro pri e tar y
de men tia prae cox	u ni cel lu lar

When instructors in various courses complain that their students can't spell, they are usually referring either to very common words or to special words in the essential vocabulary of their subject.

Use a Dictionary

If you are uncertain about the spelling of a word, consult your dictionary. The trial-and-error method of writing a word several ways until it "looks right" *(curiousity? couriousity? curosity?)* is unreliable.

For papers written outside class, it's probably best to check spelling in *revision*. If you stop to look up the spelling of every doubtful word while you are writing a first draft, you may lose the flow of thought or interrupt the sentence movement. Put a check in the margin or over the word as you are writing; then when you are ready to revise, look up each word you have marked.

Look for Patterns in Your Misspellings

Try to identify what kinds of words typically give you problems. When you have to look up a relatively familiar word, ask yourself, what does it have in common with the other words you have to rely on a dictionary to spell? You may discover that you have a consistent difficulty with plurals, words which end in *-cede, -ceed,* or *-sede,* or words with double consonants *(embarrass; parallel).* At the least, you will know to be cautious when words in these configurations appear in your writing. Better yet, you can review those principles of spelling which may make it easier for you to get such words correct without consulting a dictionary.

Practice Spelling Troublesome Words

17.4

Sp

If you are willing to take the time, you can often get the spelling of troublesome words straight in your mind by writing them until you spell them right without hesitation. It sounds like a tedious process, but it's probably worth the time if it enables you to become comfortable with words so that you can use them. If you are uncertain about the spelling of *embarrass,* for example, write or type the word ten, twenty, or more times, in its various forms, until the spelling becomes automatic: *embarrass, embarrassed, embarrassment, embarrassing.*

Separate into syllables words that you find difficult to spell (consult your dictionary for the proper division). Stress those letters or combinations of letters that trouble you:

em baR Rass	par aL Lel
oC Ca sion al ly	preJ U dice
o MiT Ted	rep E ti tion
op tI mist	sep A rate

It helps to say the word as you write it, either aloud or to yourself. The combination of (1) seeing a word letter by letter, (2) writing it carefully, and (3) pronouncing it will overcome some spelling problems.

Keep a Personal Spelling List

You can help yourself in proofreading if you will keep a list of words you have misspelled or that you have trouble spelling. The words should be spelled correctly and should be easy to find so that you can refer to them when proofreading your papers. The purpose of such a list is to prevent the same mistakes from occurring in one paper after another.

Such a list can also be a means of eliminating errors. Use your personal list as a tool for categorizing your typical misspellings. Then work on eliminating each category of mistakes. Or rank your errors according to your perception of their frequency or seriousness. Systematically attempt to learn how to spell the words that have given you the most trouble. A little writing and copying practice now may save you endless trips to the dictionary later.

Exercise 17.E

Read the following paragraph, correcting the misspelled words. Feel free to consult a dictionary; you may want to see how many mistakes you can find and correct without a dictionary first, however.

The principal that every great man is a national calamity is easily defensable. It is difficult to concieve that strong men will not irresistably impose upon their countrymen their own eccentricities and prejadices. Napoleon, for example, beleived that he had a definate destiny to succede, a mysterous "star" guiding him and France to great heighths. He did not dream of any hinderance from the other nations of Europe. His plans were to seperate them one by one and to sieze all power and priveledge. Only Britian refused to acommodate itself to his grandiose schemes. His temperment was characteristic of his enviroment; massively fasinated by Romantic psycology, he had an exagerated consciousness of the independant existance of his charisma. Napoleon was tradgically dissappointed in his hopes, as were his spiritual forebears, Alexander the Great, Caesar, and Louis XIV, and his inheritors, Hitler and Mussolini. ■

SPELLING

■ Edit Carefully for Spelling Problems When:

1. A word has a homonym or another word that sounds like it: *tail—tale, here—hear, accept—except.*
2. A suffix is added to a word ending in *-e: ninety, conceivable, garageable.*
3. A word contains *-ie-* or *-ei-: believe* or *receive.*
4. A word contains a double consonant: *embarrass, omitting, occasion.*
5. A suffix is added to words ending in final *-y: marrying, easily.*
6. A word ends with *-cede, -ceed,* or *-sede: precede, proceed, supersede.*
7. A word ends with *-able, -ible, -ance, -ence, -ant, -ent: debatable, incredible, performance, persistence, coolant, correspondent.*
8. A word has variant spellings: *labor, labour; gray, grey.*
9. A word forms its plural irregularly: *phenomena, thieves.*
10. A word is spelled differently from the way it is pronounced: *plumber, enough.*
11. An expression might be written as one or two words, depending on the intended meaning: *all ready—already, a while—awhile, may be—maybe.*

■ To Improve Your Spelling:

1. Eliminate careless errors by
   —reading your sentences backwards to focus your attention on individual words.
   —using a pencil to read and edit word-by-word.
   —reading your work aloud.
2. Learn to visualize words by
   —reading carefully.
   —breaking troublesome words into syllables.
   —devising mnemonic devices.
3. Learn new words, particularly those in your major field.
4. Use a dictionary.
5. Identify patterns in your misspellings.
6. Practice spelling troublesome words by
   —writing or typing them repeatedly.
   —separating them into syllables.
   —pronouncing them aloud.
7. Keep a personal spelling list.

18

USING A
DICTIONARY

A dictionary is a writer's most useful general reference book. While it probably is more reliable than any single one of us, a dictionary is not a supreme authority that can be quoted to settle all arguments about words and their meanings. Rather, it is a record of the ways language is actually used, and any dictionary is an incomplete record. The pioneer lexicographer Samuel Johnson concluded long ago that it was foolish for a man to attempt to "embalm his language." But the notion still persists that a dictionary is—or should be—a code of law for language use.

For this reason there has been considerable debate, and some heated argument, about whether a dictionary should *prescribe* or *describe* language use. Some people want a dictionary to tell us which pronunciation is right, which meaning is proper, which use of a word is legitimate.

Other people, including the editors of many dictionaries, declare that dictionaries are not intended to rule our use of language. Almost any rule that a dictionary could offer to govern pronunciation or definition would have originated in observation of how people at some time in the past actually pronounced and defined words. If a dictionary, then, sets out to be a system of law, the editors would be converting the *habits* of some past time into *rules* for the present.

The editors of most recently published dictionaries want to *register* how the language is used. To that end, many offer a variety of acceptable pronunciations for many words, with no effort to dictate what is "best." Some editors, too, omit usage labels (which declare that some words are *colloquial* or *vulgar* or *erroneous*) on the ground that the correctness or appropriateness of a word can seldom be determined out of context.

Contexts change, and language changes. Sometimes a unique or precise meaning of a word is lost. A *tragedy* today is any unhappy event rather than the catastrophe with moral significance that the word signalled in the past. *Parameter,* a technical term in mathematics, is now used vaguely to mean limits or boundaries and is even confused at times with *perimeter*. But changes can also improve and enrich the English tongue. For centuries our language has been enlarged by the addition of words from other languages: *sky, leg, scowl* (Norse); *cheese, bishop, oyster* (Latin); *parliament, scarlet, flower* (French); *guacamole, mesa, stevedore* (Spanish); *zombie* (Kongo); *karate* (Japanese); *gumbo* (Bantu).

Since language changes, both for the better and the worse, a dictionary can only record the way words are used. It cannot control language. The standards for determining what good language is rest in other hands (see Introduction, pp. 1–23).

18.1 Selecting a Good Dictionary

A good dictionary, though not a final authority, is an indispensable reference tool for every college student. Dictionaries answer questions about the meanings, spellings, origins, and pronunciations of words. They also give information about the forms of words (plurals, past tenses) and idiomatic constructions (what preposition, for example, is commonly used with a particular noun or verb). One of the most valuable habits a writer can acquire is the regular use of a dictionary.

Dictionaries differ in size and purpose, but certain criteria apply in evaluating any dictionary for general use. First of all, it should be up-to-date. New words and expressions are continually coming into the language (*online, trickle-down, microchip, garageable, access channel, floppy disc, aspartame*) and old words are always being used in new senses (*user-friendly* computers, a *crash* program, a publicity *handout,* the *Silicon* Valley). Even spelling and pronunciation can change with time

(catalog, catalogue; ab' də men, ab dō' men). In addition, most dictionaries are somewhat encyclopedic, including information about prominent people and places. There are always new names to be added *(Chernenko, Zimbabwe)* and new facts to be recorded.

In an effort to keep their entries up-to-date, most dictionaries make limited changes every year or so. Check the copyright dates before you buy a dictionary to find out when it was last revised. You might also want to look up some words that have recently come into use to see if they are included.

A good dictionary of current English is not simply an updating of earlier word books; it reflects the research and judgment of a large staff of experts who record and analyze hundreds of thousands of examples of words in actual use. It is the responsibility of the lexicographer to make certain that the language has been sampled adequately and that all the most common uses of even uncommon words have been found. Then all these raw materials must be carefully gone through, some discarded and some reworked. Eventually the result should be a concise yet accurate description of the words that constitute the great bulk of our language. Whatever "authority" a dictionary has, then, depends on the scholarship, discrimination, and judgment of its editors.

18.1
Dict

Dictionaries for General Use

The most complete descriptions of contemporary English are to be found in the various unabridged dictionaries. Though not practical for desk use, these large dictionaries are invaluable for reference, and at least one of them is available in every college and public library:

The Oxford English Dictionary. Often referred to by its initials, the *OED* is in thirteen volumes with supplements published to update the original edition (1888–1928). Its more than 500,000 entries provide an historical record of how words and phrases have been used in English since A.D. 1150. The dictionary attempts to record the first appearance of a word in written English and provides illustrative quotations from writers to show its typical use at various times in history. A dozen or more columns are sometimes devoted to a single word. In many kinds of studies, the *OED* is a basic source for research. It is also considered to be among the greatest dictionaries in any language. *The Shorter Oxford English Dictionary* (two volumes) is an abridgment of the larger work and somewhat easier to use. In 1971, the unabridged *OED* was published in a compact, miniaturized-print edition. This two-volume set comes with a magnifying glass.

Webster's Third New International Dictionary of the English Language. First published amid controversy in 1961 and updated since, *Webster's Third* is a descriptive rather than prescriptive dictionary. It describes how words are used in English, but makes few recommendations about appropriate usage. It is regarded as the most authoritative and complete record of the English language currently available, with 450,000 entries and many illustrative quotations. Definitions are listed chronologically rather than according to their significance in current usage.

18.1

Dict

The Random House Dictionary of the English Language. This unabridged dictionary, first published in 1966, contains 260,000 items—somewhat fewer than other comparable volumes. Yet its entries are notably up-to-date and it includes biographical and geographical names within its main listing.

Two older dictionaries continue to be very useful:

The Century Dictionary and Cyclopedia. Although this ten-volume work, the most comprehensive dictionary ever published in the United States, has not been reprinted since before World War I, it contains much information not available in more recent dictionaries. *The New Century Dictionary* is basically an abridgment of this work.

Webster's New International Dictionary of the English Language. The second edition of the unabridged Webster, first published in 1934, is no longer in print but remains available in most libraries.

For everyday use, the most practical dictionary for a student to own is one of the shorter "college" dictionaries listed below. Each of these dictionaries has its own special strengths, but all are well edited and adequate for general use:

American Heritage Dictionary

Random House Dictionary, College Edition

Webster's New World Dictionary of the American Language
Webster's Ninth New Collegiate Dictionary

Sample entries from one of these dictionaries, labeled to show some of the features of a dictionary, are reproduced on page 317. Pocket dictionaries are convenient in size, but lack the information and comprehensiveness most students need.

Special Dictionaries

Supplementing the general dictionaries—unabridged and abridged—are numerous specialized dictionaries that give more technical or specialized information.

18.1
Dict

Historical Dictionaries

Good dictionaries for general use are based in part upon scholarly dictionaries made over long periods of time. _The Oxford English Dictionary_ discussed above is one such record of the development of the English language. Another work, made on the same plan as the _OED,_ is _The Dictionary of American English._ This four-volume set gives the history of words as they have been used by American writers from 1620 to 1900. _A Dictionary of Americanisms_ (two volumes) gives the history of words that originated in the United States and brings the record of American English up to 1944.

Dictionaries in Special Subjects

Dictionaries of slang, usage, and other specialized language uses are available, and most fields have dictionaries of their specialized vocabularies. It is a good idea to know the titles of those in any fields you are going to work in. The following list merely suggests the range of such books. Most of them are revised from time to time.

Backhouse, D., et al. _Illustrated Dictionary of Photography._ New York: International Publications Service, 1974.

Baker, Cyril C. _Dictionary of Mathematics._ New York: Hart, 1970.

Bennett, Harry, ed. _Concise Chemical and Technical Dictionary._ 3rd ed. New York: Chemical Publications, 1974.

Brander, Michael. _Dictionary of Sporting Terms._ New York: Humanities, 1968.

Chaplin, J. P. _Dictionary of Psychology._ New York: Dell, 1975.

Clark, Donald T., and Bert A. Gottfried. *University Dictionary of Business and Finance.* New York: Apollo, 1972.

Clason, W. E. *Elsevier's Dictionary of Chemical Engineering.* 2 vols. New York: Elsevier-North Holland, 1969.

Dorian, A. F. *Dictionary of Science and Technology.* 2nd rev. ed. 2 vols. New York: Elsevier-North Holland, 1982.

Good, Carter, ed. *Dictionary of Education.* 3rd ed. New York: McGraw-Hill, 1973.

Graf, Rudolf F. *Modern Dictionary of Electronics.* 5th ed. Indianapolis: Howard Sams, 1977.

Granville, Wilfred. *Theater Dictionary: British and American Terms in the Drama, Opera, and Ballet.* Westport, Conn.: Greenwood, 1974.

Gray, Peter, ed. *Student Dictionary of Biology.* New York: Reinhold, 1973.

Greenwood, Douglas. *The McGraw-Hill Dictionary of Modern Economics: A Handbook of Terms and Organizations.* 2nd ed. New York: McGraw-Hill, 1973.

Martin, Michael, and Leonard Gelber. *Dictionary of American History.* Rev. ed. Totowa, N.J.: Littlefield, 1978.

Monkhouse, F. J. *A Dictionary of the Natural Environment.* Ed. John Small. Rev. ed. New York: Halsted, 1977.

Myers, Bernard S., and Shirley D. Myers, eds. *Dictionary of Art.* 5 vols. New York: McGraw-Hill, 1969.

Oppermann, Alfred. *Dictionary of Modern Engineering.* 3rd ed. 2 vols. New York: International Pub. Service, 1974.

Scholes, Percy A. *Concise Oxford Dictionary of Music.* 2nd ed. New York: Oxford, 1964.

Shipley, Joseph T., ed. *Dictionary of World Literature.* Rev. ed. Totowa, N.J.: Littlefield, 1972.

Thewlis, J., ed. *Concise Dictionary of Physics.* 2nd ed. Elmsford, N.Y.: Pergamon, 1979.

18.2

Dict

18.2 Learning to Use Your Dictionary

Dictionaries differ not only in the information they include but also in the way they present it, and the best dictionary in the world will be of little value to you unless you know how

Sample Dictionary Entries

entry and word division ⎯⎯⎯⎯⎯

mo·ment \'mō-mənt\ *n* [ME, fr. MF, fr. L *momentum* movement,

etymology ⎯⎯⎯⎯⎯⎯
particle sufficient to turn the scales, moment, fr. *movēre* to move]

definition, with examples
showing use of the word
in context

1 : a minute portion or point of time **:** INSTANT **2 a :** present time <at the ~ he is working on a novel> **b :** a time of excellence or conspicuousness <he has his ~ s> **3 :** importance in influence or effect **:** notable or conspicuous consequence **4** *obs* **:** a cause or motive of action **5 :** a stage in historical or logical development **6 a :** tendency or measure of tendency to produce motion esp.

usage label
about a point or axis **b :** the product of quantity (as a force) and the distance to a particular axis or point **7 a :** the mean of the *n*th powers of the deviations of the observed values in a set of statistical data from a fixed value **b :** the expected value of a power of the deviation of a random variable from a fixed value *syn* see IMPOR-TANCE

mo·men·tar·i·ly \ˌmō-mən-'ter-ə-lē\ *adv* **1 :** for a moment **2**

part-of-speech labels
: INSTANTLY **3 :** at any moment
mo·men·tary \'mō-mən-ˌter-ē\ *adj* **1 a :** continuing only a moment **:** TRANSITORY **b :** having a very brief life **:** EPHEMERAL **2 :** operative or recurring at every moment *syn* see TRANSIENT *ant*

synonyms and antonyms
agelong — **mo·men·tar·i·ness** *n*
mo·ment·ly \'mō-mənt-lē\ *adv* **1 :** from moment to moment **2 :** at any moment **3 :** for a moment

entry of variant spelling
mo·men·to \mə-'ment-(ˌ)ō\ *var of* MEMENTO
moment of inertia : the ratio of the torque applied to a rigid body free to rotate about a given axis to the angular acceleration thus produced about that axis
moment of truth 1 : the final sword thrust in a bullfight **2**

pronunciation guide ⎯⎯⎯⎯⎯
: a moment of crisis on whose outcome much or everything depends

"run-on" entries, words
mo·men·tous \mō-'ment-əs, mə-'ment-\ *adj* **:** IMPORTANT, CONSE-QUENTIAL — **mo·men·tous·ly** *adv* — **mo·men·tous·ness** *n*

whose meaning is clear
from main entry
mo·men·tum \mō-'ment-əm, mə-'ment-\ *n, pl* **mo·men·ta** \-'ment-ə\ *or* **momentums** [NL, fr. L, movement] **:** a property of a moving body that determines the length of time required to bring it to rest when under the action of a constant force or moment;

cross reference
broadly **:** IMPETUS
mom·ma \'mäm-ə, 'məm-\ *var of* MAMMA
Mo·mus \'mō-məs\ *n* [L, fr. Gk *Mōmos*] **:** the Greek god of blame and mockery

abbreviation
¹mon \'män\ *dial chiefly Brit var of* MAN
²mon *abbr* **1** monastery **2** monetary
¹Mon \'mōn\ *n, pl* **Mon** *or* **Mons 1 :** a member of the dominant native people of Pegu in Burma **2 :** the Mon-Khmer language of

homographs, entries spelled
the Mon people
²Mon *abbr* **1** Monaghan **2** Monday **3** Monmouthshire

alike but different in
meaning, derivation,
or pronunciation
mon- *or* **mono-** \under stress the (1st) "o" is sometimes ō *although not shown at individual entries*\ *comb form* [ME, fr. MF & L; MF, fr. L, fr. Gk, fr. *monos* alone, single — more at MONK] **1 :** one **:** single **:** alone <*mono*plane> <*mono*drama> <*mono*phobia> **2 a :** containing one (usu. specified) atom, radical, or group <*mono*hydrate> <*mono*oxide> **b :** monomolecular <*mono*film> <*mono*layer>

prefix entry

pronunciation key

ə abut	ᵊ kitten	ər further	a back	ā bake	ä cot, cart
aù out	ch chin	e less	ē easy	g gift	i trip	ī life
j joke	ŋ sing	ō flow	ò flaw	òi coin	th thin	th̲ this
ü loot	ù foot	y yet	yü few	yù furious	zh vision

to read and interpret the information it provides. Before using a new dictionary, read the front matter carefully. It will explain the organization of entries, the method of indicating pronunciation, the use of restrictive labels, and the meaning of abbreviations and symbols used in the definitions and etymologies. Then look carefully at a page of entries to see how words and phrases are handled. Test your understanding of the pronunciation guide by using it to pronounce some familiar words. Look through the table of contents to see what sections of information your dictionary provides in addition to the main alphabetical list of words. You may find a short grammar of the English language, a discussion of punctuation, a table of signs and symbols, a list of colleges and universities in the United States, and a guide to the preparation of manuscript copy.

A little time spent in learning to use your dictionary can make it immensely useful to you. The following sections describe the kinds of information found in most dictionaries; the sample entries on page 317 show how one dictionary presents this information, but most dictionaries are similar.

Exercise   18.A

To help you become acquainted with your dictionary, write out the following information about it for discussion in class or to be handed in.

1. The title, the name of the publisher, and the most recent copyright date. This date may be found on the back of the title page.

2. A list of the sections following the introduction and preceding the dictionary entries (such as "How to Use the Dictionary," "A Guide to Pronunciation," "Usage Levels").

3. A list of the material in the appendix (if any), such as "Signs and Symbols," "Biographical Names," "Colleges and Universities in the United States."

4. How the words are listed. Do the words appear in one alphabetical list or in separate lists (for biographical names, geographical names, abbreviations, etc.)?

5. The location of derived forms. Are derived forms (*cynical* and *cynicism* from *cynic*, for example) listed separately as main entries in the alphabetical list, or are they listed under the base word?

6. The location of etymologies. Do the etymologies come at the beginning or at the end of an entry?

7. The order of the definitions of the words. Does the older meaning or the current meaning come first in such words as *bibulous, cute, ghastly, shrewd, liquidate, souse* (noun), *recession, fulsome?* ■

Spelling and Word Division

Develop the habit of using your dictionary to check the spelling in your papers. If you are unable to find a word because you are uncertain of one of the beginning letters, try to think of other possible spellings for the same sound. (Is it *gibe* or *jibe?*) Remember that dictionaries give the spelling not only of the base form of a word but also of distinctive forms—the principal parts of verbs, the plurals of nouns, the comparative and superlative forms of adjectives and adverbs—that are in any way irregular.

Your dictionary may give two spellings for a word when usage is divided *(hemoglobin—haemoglobin; although—altho).* Use the spelling that the editors have indicated is the more common one. (The method of listing variants will be explained in the front matter of the dictionary.) Avoid spellings labeled British (such as *colour, gaol*) in favor of the usual American spellings.

18.2

Dict

Dictionaries divide words into units (usually corresponding to spoken syllables) by means of small dots or spaces: *de·mar·ca·tion, de light ful.* This device will enable you to see each part of the word clearly and to notice if you have omitted or transposed any letters. In writing, divide a word at the end of a line only where your dictionary shows a division. The word *reorganization,* for example, might be divided at the end of a line in any one of five places: *re·or·ga·ni·za·tion.* Not all dictionaries divide every word in exactly the same way, but by following the practice of any good dictionary you will avoid such careless blunders as dividing *bedraggled* into *bed-* and *raggled.* See also 17, Spelling, and 23.4 Manuscript Form.

Exercise **18.B**

What information do you find in your dictionary on the spelling of these pairs of words? Are the spellings interchangeable? If so, which form would you use and why?

aesthetic—esthetic	draft—draught	licorice—liquorice
carat—karat	favor—favour	sac—sack
catalog—catalogue	gaol—jail	traveling—travelling
catsup—catchup		

Pronunciation

Because English spelling is not consistently phonetic (there are over 250 ways to spell the forty-odd sounds in English), dictionaries use a system of special symbols to show how words are pronounced. The word *bamboozle*, for example, might be respelled this way after the entry word: *băm bōō′ zəl.* The pronunciation key at the bottom of the page will illustrate, with familiar words, the sound represented by the symbols *ă, ōō,* and *ə.* Since the consonants *b, m, z,* and *l* have no special marks over them, you may assume that they are pronounced in the usual way. The accented syllable in *băm bōō′ zəl* is indicated by a heavy stress mark. Phonetic spellings also indicate secondary stress, when appropriate, usually by a lighter mark (′) but sometimes by a different symbol. Since the system for showing pronunciation varies somewhat from dictionary to dictionary, you should study carefully the explanatory notes in the front of your own book before attempting to use its pronunciation key.

18.2
Dict

Dictionaries often list two or more pronunciations for a word when usage is divided. Although the first pronunciation is usually the more common one, it is not necessarily "preferred," and you should use whichever pronunciation is customary in your own community.

Exercise   **18.C**

To become familiar with the pronunciation key in your dictionary, write out the answers to the following questions.

1.   What pronunciations does your dictionary list for each of these words? Is the first pronunciation given the one you hear most frequently? If not, tell how it differs, including the stress (accent):

address	creek	greasy	pianist
adult	decadent	herb	poinsettia
Celtic	drama	impotent	research
coupon	gibberish	leisure	Oedipus

2.   How is each of these words pronounced when used as a noun? As a verb?

confine	consort	exploit	impact	misuse
conflict	escort	ferment	import	refuse

Meaning

Dictionaries are perhaps most important for what they tell us about the meanings of words. Dictionaries begin each definition or group of definitions with an abbreviation showing whether the word is being defined as a noun *(n.)*, adjective *(adj.)*, verb *(vb.)*, transitive verb *(v.t.)*, intransitive verb *(v.i.)*, or other part of speech. This information is important, for words usually have different meanings in different grammatical contexts. Sometimes the meanings are closely related (for example, the meanings of *advance* as a verb, a noun, or an adjective) but sometimes they are completely different (the meanings of *fly, plant,* and *court* as verbs or as nouns).

In looking for the meaning of a word in context, therefore, you must ordinarily isolate the right group of definitions before you can find the particular meaning you are looking for. Then you should look over all of the definitions included in that group. Some dictionaries give the oldest meaning first. (*The Oxford English Dictionary,* for example, defines *kindness* as "kinship, near relationship; natural affection arising from this" in its first definition of the word since *kindness* had this specific meaning before the more general sense of "kind behavior" we are familiar with today.) Other dictionaries do give the most common meaning first. But often you will want neither the oldest nor the most common usage, but a more specialized meaning that comes late in the entry. At the end of the entry, or at the end of a group of definitions for one part of speech, you may also find one or more idioms listed.

In using dictionary definitions, you should keep two general principles in mind:

1. A dictionary does not *require* or *forbid* a particular meaning or use of a word; it merely *records* the most common ways in which a word has actually been used. Therefore you must exercise judgment in deciding whether a particular word will be appropriate in a particular context.

2. A dictionary definition is for the most part a record of the *denotation*, or specific meaning, of a word; at best, it can only suggest the *connotation*, or suggestive qualities, which varies with context and with use. (See 29.1.) In general, it is better not to use a word until you have heard it or read it and know at least some of its connotations.

18.2
Dict

Exercise 18.D

Answer the following questions by referring to the definitions given in your dictionary:

1. In what kind of writing would it be appropriate to use the word *gimmick?*
2. In what profession would the word *dolmen* most likely be used?
3. Where would you be most likely to hear the word *legato?*
4. When a woman *rests on her laurels,* what is she doing?
5. Which of the expressions below would be underlined in a paper to indicate they belong to a foreign language?

Realpolitik	sarong	toccata
de facto	savoir-faire	vice versa

Exercise 18.E

Consult your dictionary and choose the best definition for the italicized word in each of these sentences:

1. At ten he became a printer's *devil.*
2. His *fellowship* expired at the end of the year.
3. Luther objected to the sale of *indulgences.*
4. The entrance fee was *fixed* at twenty dollars.
5. She has extremely *catholic* reading tastes.

Areas of Usage and Special Labels

Some words (or particular meanings for some words) are labeled in a dictionary as *dialectal, obsolete, archaic, foreign, colloquial, slang, British, United States,* or are identified with some particular activity or field—medicine, law, astronomy, music, sports, manufacturing, electricity. One of the college dictionaries *(American Heritage)* even includes a separate section on usage. Words unlabeled in a dictionary are considered part of the general vocabulary.

Usage labels can serve as rough guides, but you should bring your own observation to bear on individual words. Certainly you would ordinarily avoid words marked *obsolete* or *archaic,* but many words that carry no label *(albeit, perforce)* would be equally out of place in most college writing. On the other hand, many words marked *dial.* or *colloq.* (such as *high-*

brow) might fit perfectly well into both informal and general English. The label _colloquial_, which many people mistake to mean nonstandard, simply suggests that a particular usage is more characteristic of speech than it is of writing. The label _U.S._ means that the usage is found in the United States but not in other parts of the English-speaking world.

Most dictionaries of the English language include frequently used words and expressions from foreign languages. Some dictionaries indicate that such terms are generally considered foreign by listing the language in parentheses: _(It.)_, _(Fr.)_. Some also use an identifying mark, such as a dagger or an asterisk, before all foreign-word entries. Such labels are useful because they help distinguish between foreign words that are now considered part of the English vocabulary _(chalet, aria, mesa)_ and those that are still considered distinctly foreign _(dolce far niente, Weltanschauung, enceinte)_ and must be underlined in a paper. (See 14.3, Italics for Foreign Words.)

Exercise 18.F

Answer the following questions by consulting the grammatical information given in the dictionary entry for each word:

1. What is the past participle of _shear?_
2. What is the past tense of _bear_ in the sense of _carry?_
3. What does _feign_ mean when it is used intransitively?
4. What does _gull_ mean when followed by a direct object?
5. What is the plural of _ghetto?_
6. What is the plural of _stratum?_　　　　　　　　　■

Exercise 18.G

Use a dictionary to determine what special labels, if any, are attached to the words in the following list. Discuss when it would be appropriate to use such terms. Also indicate whether those words that lack a special label would be appropriate in all types of general writing. It may be necessary to consult more than one dictionary.

OK	hanky-panky	to-do
dumbbell	maitre d'hotel	Mafioso
harangue	hickey	harum-scarum
equine	whence	slugabed

　　　　　　　　　■

Synonyms and Antonyms

Most dictionaries list words of similar meaning *(synonyms)* with the basic or most comprehensive word of a group and explain how these various related words differ slightly in meaning, especially in connotation. Sometimes the entry for a word will also list an *antonym,* a word of opposite meaning *(cowardly* would be an antonym for *courageous).*

There are several specialized books containing lists of related words: *Webster's Dictionary of Synonyms,* Fernald's *Standard Handbook of Synonyms, Antonyms, and Prepositions,* Soule's *A Dictionary of English Synonyms, Webster's Collegiate Thesaurus,* and Roget's *Thesaurus.* The *Thesaurus* is probably the most widely used book of synonyms, but since it does not give definitions, its chief use is to remind writers of words they recognize but do not use regularly. If you find words that appear to be appropriate but you are not completely sure, check their definitions in a dictionary.

Etymology

A dictionary not only tells how a word is used and pronounced but also gives its origin, or *etymology.* Sometimes the etymology is merely a notation of the language from which the word was borrowed (as *decor* is from French and *Gestalt* is from German) or a statement of how it was coined. But often the etymology is fairly complicated; the development of the word *advance,* for example, can be traced back through Middle English to Old French and finally to Latin. The explanatory notes at the front of your dictionary include a discussion of etymology and a key to the abbreviations and symbols used in tracing a word's origin.

Knowing how a word originated will often help you understand and remember it. Knowing that *philanthropy,* for example, comes from the Greek words *philein* (to love) and *anthropos* (man) may help fix its meaning in your mind. It may also help you figure out other words by analogy *(philology, anthropocentric).*

Etymologies often illustrate how word meanings have changed from their original to their present use and are interesting as records of human thought and experience.

Exercise **18.H**

Consult the etymologies in your dictionary to answer the following questions:

1. What is the origin of each of these words?

   sandwich farm tulip semester
   robot assassin lecture geology

2. Which of the following words have retained most or all of their original meanings? Which have retained some? Which none?

   curfew fiasco pedigree silly
   fecund miscegenation pilot tragedy

Exercise **18.I**

The following questions can be answered by finding the special information they require in the dictionary. In some cases it is attached to the regular word entry; in others special sections at the back or front of the dictionary must be consulted.

1. Write sentences using the words below. Be sure your sentences distinguish among the similar words put together as sets:

   deviate—digress—diverge—swerve
   slim—thin—slender—skinny
   fictitious—legendary—mythical
   giggle—titter—snicker—chuckle
   latent—potential—dormant

2. Give antonyms for the following words: *authentic, chaste, devout, futile, venial.*
3. Who was John Huss? When did he live?
4. Where are the Carpathian Mountains?
5. How large is a lemming?
6. Is Mexico City smaller or larger than Paris in population?
7. Where is Miami University?
8. How long is a furlong?
9. What does the symbol B/L mean in business and commerce?
10. What does the sign ∴ mean in mathematics?

COMPOSITION

Part

TWO

A WRITER'S

CHOICES

19

THE PROCESS
OF WRITING:
PURPOSE AND
AUDIENCE

Everything you write involves choices. You may have to decide what your subject will be, whom you intend to include in your audience of readers, how you will arrange your ideas, and what tone you will take to convey your feelings. You may need to decide on an appropriate length for your piece, an effective opening line, subtle but strong transitions, a satisfying conclusion, and much more. Quite often many of these choices will be made for you. When your teacher asks for a 500-word comparison of two works of art for a college writing class or your boss requests a one-page confidential assessment of your firm's marketing manager, you face assignments which close some important options (subject, audience, length) but leave others open (development, organization, tone).

The writing you do, then, involves many situations, choices, and options. For example, the patterns, techniques, and conventions you employ in preparing a biology lab report may differ from those you use when your campus newspaper editor asks you to compose an editorial on the growing problems in world banking. The two situations differ, as do the problems and opportunities you face in addressing them in words. Both situations will produce writing: a lab report and an editorial. But those written products will result from processes involving dozens of judgments and decisions, no two of which may be exactly alike.

Yet if it isn't possible to anticipate every choice you'll make as a writer, it is possible to examine what writers typically do when they write, to sketch out the processes they go through in identifying their options, developing their plans, and setting their words down on paper or on a word-processor screen. In the following chapters, we will explore in detail a sequence of choices which approximates the steps writers may follow in doing their work. Our major concerns will be:

1. defining and understanding your purpose in writing,
2. recognizing the needs of your audience,
3. discovering what you have to say about your subject,
4. developing and arranging your material,
5. using outlines effectively, and
6. drafting, revising, and editing your writing.

The writing process outlined above may seem deceptively simple to you and suspiciously linear, moving neatly from the choice of a subject to the editing of a final draft. Yet the path to a successful report, editorial, or essay is often meandering and poorly marked. Most writers get lost or sidetracked occasionally; they may find themselves wandering in circles, unhappy with the drafts they've written or unable to start at all.

In fact, good writing evolves out of getting stuck and looking back to where you've been before pushing forward again. It is a process that survives ideas that don't sail, outlines that collapse, paragraphs that have to be poked and prodded before they say what you want them to say. Quite often it includes the excitement of watching an idea grow, change, and mature right on the page or screen in front of you—an idea you didn't even know you had until you started turning words and phrases into sentences and paragraphs.

19.1 Defining and Understanding Your Purpose

In planning a writing project, you must address two basic questions:

Why am I writing this?

For whom am I writing?

The answers to these closely related questions provide you with a framework for making many subsequent decisions about an assignment. If you have only a topic—abortion or taxes, let's say—you are on an ocean of limitless possibility and are probably drowning. You have no direction or purpose, no shore to swim to.

But once a purpose and audience are determined—either by you or by a teacher or employer—the subject and what you must do with it snap into sharper focus:

> Write a position paper **to persuade** [purpose] a **local chapter of the National Organization of Women** [audience] to support a constitutional amendment banning abortion.

> Write a letter to **the editor of a conservative midwestern newspaper** [audience] to **correct the facts** [purpose] in an editorial she has written condemning government funding of independent relief agencies in Central and South America.

Simply knowing what your purpose and audience are does not automatically make your writing easy. In both of the situations above, a writer faces a formidable task. He may not succeed with either audience. But with the audiences and the purposes clearly spelled out, he has a much better chance of making intelligent choices about his subjects. He knows what to research, what to emphasize, perhaps even how to organize the piece. A clear understanding of audience and purpose gives you criteria by which to judge how effectively a writing project is developing.

In most professional circumstances, you will be presented with assignments where the purpose of a piece is stated explicitly:

> **to assess** the environmental impact . . .

> **to summarize** the decisions of the committee . . .

> **to lay off** two hundred employees . . .

> **to report** on the progress of the agency . . .

> **to defend** the record of the school board . . .

> **to welcome** new residents to the community . . .

> **to ask** for funds . . .

When the instructions are this clear, you can usually begin to plan your writing by measuring what you want to achieve against certain characteristics of your readers. What level of expertise do those readers expect in your environmental impact statement, how much detail do they require in the summary, how much compassion in the lay-off notice?

In academic and other situations, you will often be given assignments for which the purpose of your writing is not so explicitly named. Your history professor asks for a paper on the Russian revolution, but does not suggest whether the paper should be merely informative or whether it should explore the subject, perhaps leading toward an argumentative stand. Your English teacher wants your reaction to *Macbeth*, but does not state the criteria she'll use to assess your "reaction." Your friend on the college newspaper asks you for a piece on the student health service; "Be creative," he says.

In situations like these, you have two options. The first is to ask for more specific instructions. No teacher, editor, or supervisor should object to your asking the question: *What is my purpose in writing this piece?* If better instructions are not offered or the choice of purpose really is up to you, then you need to decide what you intend to do with your subject. Any decision you make initially can, of course, be modified as you move through the planning and drafting stages. But starting off with a confident sense of your aim can save you time and energy.

Although the actual occasions for writing are almost without number—including everything from a note thanking Aunt Martha for a birthday gift to a fifty-page senior honors thesis—it is possible to classify the reasons for writing in a relatively simple, useful fashion. For example, when it is up to you to determine what the purpose of a given essay will be, you may want to know some of the consequences of your decision. Or if you are told to be informative or persuasive, you may want a clearer, more technical sense of what those terms mean. One way to classify the writing most students and professionals do is according to the relationships among three key components in any act of composition:

1. the writer
2. the subject matter
3. the audience

We can use a triangle to present these relationships graphically:

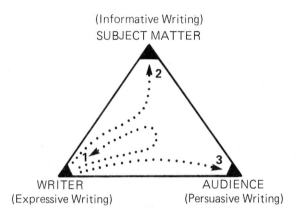

(Informative Writing)
SUBJECT MATTER

WRITER   AUDIENCE
(Expressive Writing)   (Persuasive Writing)

The dotted lines inside the triangle suggest something about the different kinds of writing discussed below.

Expressive Writing

Some kinds of writing are about you. You dominate the piece, writing about yourself and for yourself. As line 1 in the diagram shows, writing with this purpose leaves the author and returns to the author. It is called *expressive writing* because its primary aim is to allow an author to express himself or herself. Expressive writing can begin with a meditation on a small object, incident, or feeling that circles outward to state a more universal problem:

> Right there is the usefulness of migraine, there in that imposed yoga, the concentration on the pain. For when the pain recedes, ten or twelve hours later, everything goes with it, all the hidden resentments, all the vain anxieties. The migraine has acted as a circuit breaker, and the fuses have emerged intact. There is a pleasant convalescent euphoria. I open the windows and feel the air, eat gratefully, sleep well. I notice the particular nature of a flower in a glass on the stair landing. I count my blessings.—Joan Didion, "Migraines"

You should note two things about expressive writing. First, there are many different kinds of expressive writing. Personal letters, diaries, and journals often seem intended chiefly as personal expression; some descriptive writing is the author's account of learning to see. Some expository and argumentative writing turns out to be expressive writing when the author, instead of seeking to explain or to persuade—that is, to reach an audience—uses the occasion for meditative purposes to work out personal thoughts about a subject. Second, expressive writing offers some opportunities and sets some limits that other kinds of writing don't. You are probably free, for example, to write more informally than you might otherwise and to use looser forms of organization. You are your own prime object of attention in this kind of writing; you must first of all be honest with yourself. The measure of a successful piece of expressive writing is how well and how honestly it expresses your feelings, hopes, and dreams.

Informative Writing

In other kinds of writing, the subject deserves primary attention. As line 2 in the triangle indicates, the author and, to a lesser extent, the audience fade into the background when your attention is on the subject. This is *informative writing;* it focuses on things other than the author, exploring a topic clearly, accurately, and comprehensively. In college and professional life, you will be asked to do a great deal of informative writing. Many business letters are informative, as are most reports, whether a trip report, book report, laboratory report, or research paper. Most answers on essay exams and most papers on literary topics are also guided by this aim of writing.

When you are asked to write informatively, you may be dealing with subjects ranging from highly technical investigations to theoretical or exploratory work. Much informative writing is concerned with material facts, observations, numbers, and statistics. Sometimes you need only report the facts, clearly and well:

> Almost from the first, Strauss had his cloth dyed the distinctive indigo that gave blue jeans their name, but it was not until the 1870's that he added the copper rivets which have long since become a company trademark. The rivets were the idea of a Virginia City, Nevada, tailor, Jacob W. Davis, who added them to pacify a mean-tempered miner called Alkali Ike. Alkali, the story goes, complained that the

pockets of his jeans always tore when he stuffed them with ore samples and demanded that Davis do something about it. As a kind of joke, Davis took the pants to a blacksmith and had the pockets riveted; once again, the idea worked so well that word got around; in 1873 Strauss appropriated and patented the gimmick—and hired Davis as a regional manager.—Carin C. Quinn, "The Jeaning of America—and the World"

When your purpose is to inform readers, you don't have the same kind of freedom that you might with expressive writing. You are obligated to be accurate, to be as comprehensive as you reasonably can be, and to present facts without bias. You must use technical language accurately and organize your work carefully. Sometimes you will find that your work must follow the patterns set by other writers in your area or field. Newspaper reports are expected to present the most important information in the first few paragraphs. Articles you intend to send to magazines or journals should follow the conventions of the publication, conventions you may have to become familiar with.

19.1
Pur

Committing yourself to an informative aim also means that your writing will have to be relatively formal and clear—that is, an intended reader should be able to follow what you are saying without struggling with the way you say it. The measure of good informative writing is how accurately and comprehensively it presents your subject to your designated group of readers.

Persuasive Writing

Line 3 in the triangle points to the audience, the proper target of attention in *persuasive writing*. When you commit yourself to a persuasive purpose you want to move an audience to think or act in a particular way:

Young people should have the right to control and direct their own learning, that is, to decide what they want to learn, and when, where, how, how much, how fast, and with what help they want to learn it. To be still more specific, I want them to have the right to decide if, when, how much, and by whom they want to be *taught* and the right to decide whether they want to learn in a school and if so which one and for how much of the time.—John Holt, "The Right to Control One's Learning"

Many forms of writing are designed to move or persuade an audience. Sermons belong to this group, as do advertisements, letters of recommendation, critiques, all forms of argument, and letters to the editor.

When you have taken on a persuasive task, you will need to have a clear sense of who you are trying to convince. You will need to find arguments likely to move your audience to act, arguments that are close, lucid, and reasonably easy to follow. You will need to gather evidence to support all of your major assertions. Most demanding of all, a commitment to persuasion will require you to be believable to others in a way not demanded by expressive or informative writing. Your readers must trust you.

Persuasive writing opens up many options for you in the way you appeal to an audience. You can use both logic and emotion in honest ways when you believe in an idea. In the best persuasive writing, you will often find a powerful tension between the style of the logician and the emotive language of the heart. Effective persuasive writing moves your audience to think and act the way you want them to.

As you undertake a writing project, you may want to begin with an assessment of what purpose you intend to serve. Will your piece be mainly expressive, informative, or persuasive? As your ideas develop, you will probably find that your general statement of aim will narrow into something much more specific. You will discover that any given piece of writing can contain elements of all three aims: a persuasive editorial may contain paragraphs of facts; a medical study based on facts may come to an argumentative conclusion; a primarily informative autobiography may contain many expressive passages. Understanding your dominant aim should help you gain a clear idea of the options you have in reaching your audience, developing your material, finding an appropriate style. It should not limit your possibilities or creativity.

19.1

Pur

Exercise **19.A**

1. Examine a newspaper or a popular magazine from the point of view of the three purposes of writing discussed

in this section. How many examples of expressive, informative, and persuasive writing can you find? Do some features in the magazine or journal not fit into these categories?

2. Consider how each of the following subjects might be handled if it were the subject of an expressive essay, an informative essay, a persuasive essay. Do any of the subjects lend themselves more readily to one purpose than to others? Assume that the readers for your imagined essays are the students in your writing class.

the federal budget	Aristotle
roses	labor unions
soybeans	Christmas
the Korean War	Freudian psychology
homesickness	quantum mechanics
computer graphics	violins
the existence of God	the Dewey decimal system
Aztec art	Mother's Day

19.2 Recognizing the Needs of Your Audience

The better you understand whom you are writing to, the clearer your sense of purpose will be. You can tailor your writing to the interests and abilities of very specific groups when you know that most of your readers will be, for example, wealthy, successful business people, or angry, politically active tax reformers, or motivated freshman English students. Or you can avoid the mistake of being too particular, specific, or technical when you are addressing a general audience not restricted to a particular age, profession, income level, political orientation, or other group.

You should think about your audience throughout the entire process of planning and writing an essay. You want to choose a subject likely to interest your readers and develop it in ways that will inform or amuse them, neither repeating what they already know nor leaving out what they are ignorant of. You want your diction and sentence structures to be suited to the level of your audience's ability. You don't want to be too difficult or condescending. In short, as you compose, you want to acquire the habit of thinking the way your readers do and revising to anticipate their needs so that, finally, you are able to achieve your purpose.

Relating to an Audience

Most of the time, you will be addressing what is called a "general audience." You might be intimidated if you think of this immense group as consisting of all reasonable men and women in a given area, such as a city, a university, a country, perhaps the entire world. Consider it, instead, as the largest group with which you share a common vocabulary, general interests, and a roughly equivalent level of education. This general audience is *you* when you pick up *Time*, or read *The New York Times*, or browse the best-selling nonfiction section at your bookstore. A general audience is a reasonably literate, relatively neutral, and generally sympathetic group of people who will listen to you if you write about interesting subjects in language that is relatively formal (but not stuffy) and lively (yet not silly). Of course, you will never be able to please every individual reader in a general audience, and it is probably not wise to try.

19.2

Aud

Not all audiences are as large as a general one. Some may contain only a single person, as in the case of a diarist writing to himself or one friend writing to another. But single-member audiences can be just as tricky to deal with as larger ones. You may have to address personally someone you know little or nothing about: the admissions director at a law school, the congressional representative in your district, the complaint manager at Sears. In such cases, you have to write according to your perceptions of what their jobs and positions entail. You wouldn't want to be chatty or careless with the admissions director or tactlessly abrupt with the complaint manager who reads dozens of angry letters a week. For students, the most important single-person audiences may be teachers who read their work and immediately assess their performance.

Writers also address audiences that consist of small groups—from two to approximately fifteen or twenty people. Perhaps the most important small groups for most students and professionals are the class and the office. (Families are important small groups too.) Communication at this level is usually more impersonal than in one-on-one situations, but smoothed by the familiarity that develops in any group involved in a common activity. Small groups often share common vocabularies, conventions, routines, rituals, and styles, all of which make it easier for you to find appropriate words for a memo, essay, report, letter, note, or other communication. But the dynamics of a small group also impose greater expectations on you and require more immediate judgments than a larger group might.

Large groups come in many shapes and sizes. Some of the classes and offices already mentioned may actually involve communications among hundreds of individuals. Yet while these may be large groups, it is still possible to identify common interests and purposes that writers can start with. The administration of a college with twenty thousand students can still address its "student body" knowing that, despite enormous differences, those thousands of individuals who make up the campus student population have a common interest in the institution's policies, routines, traditions, history, and problems.

19.2

Aud

Addressing Special Audiences

Many times you can pinpoint your audience by defining them according to areas of specialization or attitudes and beliefs. Finding your common ground with these specialized audiences may be easier when you know what they believe in, how they act, or what they expect from you.

Specialized Backgrounds

In the academic and professional worlds, it is important for you to know the level of knowledge an audience is likely to have about a given subject. This information is particularly important to you as you prepare to do research or consider how you are going to handle technical terms or complex ideas. We use such terms as *specialists, experts, generalists, amateurs, students, novices,* and *dilettantes* to describe persons with varying degrees of knowledge in any given field. A specialist in nuclear energy can write in the technical language of her profession when discussing theory with other colleagues, but must simplify her language and approach when talking to undergraduates in a physics course or interested citizens at a town meeting. Just as complex is the author-audience relationship running in the opposite direction: the less-knowledgeable person addressing the expert. This is the rhetorical situation students face daily, and it is not an easy one—as anyone who has taken an essay exam knows. Students must display a reasonable degree of knowledge and a grasp of the vocabulary and conventions of a discipline. And yet, because they are students, they aren't expected to have mastered the idiom of the subject. In fact, attempting to sound too much like an expert in an essay may hurt a student who is not yet in command of his subject. The balance is a delicate one indeed.

Beliefs and Attitudes

You can usually break a large audience down into more manageable and predictable special interest groups. These may be based on beliefs (Protestant, Catholic, atheist, Marxist), racial or ethnic heritage (black, white, Chicano, Indian), nationality (Canadian, American, Slovak, Polish, Peruvian), political party or inclination (Republican, Democrat, Tory, conservative, liberal, anarchist), sex (male, female, gay, lesbian, straight), economic condition (poor, middle-class, rich, ultrarich, *nouveau riche*, laborer, blue-collar, white-collar, bourgeois), hobbies and interests (boating, skydiving, photography), and thousands of other categories. These audiences share certain important assumptions, proclivities, backgrounds, and vocabularies—all of which may make it easier for you to know what to say, but also more difficult to say it with the authority and sense of identification each group demands from someone attempting to speak to it.

19.2

Aud

Knowing what background your readers share may help you make important assumptions about the attitudes they are likely to have toward you and your ideas. You will often find yourself judging whether what you intend to say will be received favorably, unfavorably, or indifferently by a given audience. Then you must come up with strategies to deal with the anticipated attitude. And you may find friendly audiences as troublesome as an unfriendly one. Consider the plight of a politician trying to keep the interest of supporters who have heard her write about the same issues dozens of times. Good writers don't take friendly audiences for granted, bend before hostile ones, or underestimate neutral ones.

Age

Age is an important consideration for writers sizing up an audience. Not only can it help determine the level of development of any group (preschool, elementary school, early teen, senior citizen), age can also reveal much about the ideas, experiences, and social and historical phenomena shared by the members of a given group. Allusions to the Depression, FDR, and WWII have a poignant immediacy to the men and women who knew them as experiences, not history. A younger audience may not have the same understanding of such allusions. It is very easy for writers—especially student writers—to address the larger world only from the perspectives of their own time (or their youth), in constant allusions to their cherished beliefs, music, language, and entertainments. To some extent this tendency is both inevitable and creative. Yet good writers are aware of more than just themselves and their own views. They try to be as knowledgeable about the audiences they address as those to which they belong. As a writer, you must be able to look forward and backward, to see the world through the eyes of childhood sometimes and also through the eyes of the aged.

How can you learn to address specific audiences, especially in difficult situations where intense feelings are involved? There is no easy way. As suggested at the beginning of this section, you can try to step into the shoes of your audience. You can begin by looking at an issue from your audience's point of view. You can, for example, try to describe something as another person might see it—some scene or object, say, that is displeasing to you but pleasing to another. Or you can try to impersonate another and write an explanation or argument as the other person would. You can acknowledge opposing views and work to understand them.

If people disagree with us, it's usually because they see good in a different way, and we can try to see it as they do, without sacrificing our own views. It takes time and patience to search for the common ground where you and an audience can meet, but that is the grace we owe each other.

Exercise 19.B

For this exercise, use a paper you have already written, if possible. If none is available, use an article from a popular magazine.

1. Rewrite the opening paragraphs for an audience of ten-year-olds.
2. Rewrite the opening paragraphs as they might be if you were farther from the subject in time or space or remote from it emotionally.
3. Rewrite the opening paragraphs so that they address a group of readers who dislike you personally.
4. Rewrite the opening paragraphs for a group very different from the ones you identify with—for example, for a different age group or for a group with a different social, ethnic, or religious background.
5. Rewrite the opening so that it is significantly less formal than you think appropriate for an academic audience.

■

Exercise **19.C**

Attempt to describe the audiences of the following publications according to some of the perspectives described in this section: distance, size, specialization, beliefs and group identifications, attitude, and age. (Not all perspectives can be applied to each publication.) You will probably not be immediately familiar with all of the publications, so you'll have to look at them in your library or local newsstand.

The New York Times	*The Reader's Digest*
The Daily Worker	*Road & Track*
Conservative Digest	*The Saturday Evening Post*
Cosmopolitan	*Obbservatore Romano*
American Journal of Physics	*Scientific American*
Humpty-Dumpty	*Popular Mechanics*
Paris Match	*The New Yorker*
Town and Country	*Tiger Beat*

■

20

20.1

Plan

DISCOVERING
WHAT YOU
HAVE TO SAY

20.1 Techniques for Generating Ideas

As the previous chapter makes clear, your purpose and audiences limit the scope of any given writing project. If you are in business, you must define strategies, analyze personnel, answer correspondence. If you work in a laboratory, you must report your findings, draw conclusions, propose new experiments. If you are in a history class, you must respond to questions on exams and prepare research papers. But now, to our first two basic questions,

> Why am I writing this?
>
> For whom am I writing?

we add a third that completes the set of major considerations when planning your writing:

> What is my subject?

There are two aspects to this question. Sometimes you really are free to choose a subject, especially in academic situations where teachers in courses require "a paper" but do not get much more specific. Often, though, a specific assignment is given to you, which eliminates the work you must do to find a topic but not the responsibility to develop it fully.

Much of the advice in this section (20.1) is designed to help you when you must actually find a subject. The material in the remaining sections of this chapter (20.2–20.5) should help you when you are given a subject or assignment.

Keeping a Journal

Journal writing, a technique usually associated with expressive prose, can provide you with materials and ideas for all kinds of writing. Effective journal writing requires daily attention over a long period of time. Some composition teachers require their students to keep a daily journal; if your teacher doesn't, you might try it on your own. Commit yourself to making regular entries. The entries may be words, phrases, sentences, paragraphs, essays, poems, bits and pieces. The point is to record things that matter to you or puzzle you or cause you to wonder. Put down what you see and learn and feel and know. Copy into your journal things you have read or heard that move or entertain you. A journal can get you in the habit of expressing yourself on paper.

20.1

Plan

To make a journal work, you need to make regular entries: saving up for a week and writing a group of entries won't give you an account of what you were conscious of on *different* days. Don't be hesitant, and don't imagine that every entry should be something important. If a song you hear on the radio moves you, try to say why and how it moved you. If something goes sour in one of your classes, try to figure it out by recalling what different people said and did.

Making Abstractions Concrete

A second thing you can do requires some practice and could be a part of your journal. Try writing concrete phrases and sentences about abstract ideas and impressions that come to you. The purpose in doing this is for you to get in the habit of putting your ideas and impressions into quite specific settings or terms, as in the following examples:

Ease and relaxation	an unhurried visit to the Wagon Wheel Art Gallery in Colorado
Fear	the whir of a rattlesnake when you can't see it; the taste of brass in your mouth after an out-of-control car just misses you
Comfort	some good chocolate and some exciting books on a Friday evening with the weekend still ahead
Anxiety	a message to call home without any indication of what it's about

Creating particular scenes and terms to describe ideas and impressions may help you avoid falling back on standard phrasings and clichés when you are trying to put yourself on paper. (See also Abstract and Concrete Words, p. 552.)

20.1

Plan

Neither writing in a journal nor making abstractions concrete will guarantee that you will find a good subject whenever you want one. Both may help you by letting you see which way your thoughts and impressions are likely to run, which topics appear and reappear in journal notes, and which kinds of topics seem to matter to you most.

Seeing Patterns and Connections

Freewriting

Another way to find a subject is to try *freewriting*, composing nonstop for a specific length of time (five or ten minutes, or more). It is important to keep writing for the full time, putting down whatever thoughts, ideas, images, and impressions occur to you. If you can think of nothing to say, write "I can't think of anything to say" and keep writing. Just the physical act of writing in this way can warm up your brain and overcome writer's block.

Equally important, as all those words and ideas hurry onto your page, you may begin to see patterns or expressions developing. A chance phrase, an unexpected juxtaposition of words, a startling sentence may contain the seed of an idea worth planting and growing. You can continue your freewriting on the topic, composing nonstop on the idea. Or you can develop it through brainstorming, asking questions, or one of the other techniques discussed below.

Observing and Questioning

Looking for patterns and connections in your ideas, experiences, and reading is yet another way of coming up with topics likely to satisfy both you and potential audiences. Here are some questions and concepts to ponder:

1. Do you notice which things seem to recur in your experience or reading? Actions, attitudes, emotional reactions, and other experiences may never be *exactly* repeated, but there are probably recognizable likenesses and patterns among your experiences. These may help you find a subject or see an assigned subject in a new way.

2. How do you look at your experiences? What do you focus on? How and when does your focus change? When you first entered your composition class, did you see and hear individuals, or did you respond to the class as a whole? How do you look at it now? Shifting your focus from long-range to close-range, looking at one part, then at another, then at both in relation to each other enables you to see what's around you and what happens when your focus shifts.

3. How do your experiences differ from the experiences of others? How varied is your experience or reading? How do the things you are familiar with appear to other people? Answering questions like these may help you understand your own ideas and impressions and learn what there is in them that has significance for you.

4. What can you learn about an idea, an event, or an experience by looking at it in three different ways? If you regard a subject as something fixed, you can examine its parts. If you regard your subject as changing and dynamic, you may see the relationships among the parts. Or, your subject may be part of a larger context, and you may want to see how it fits into this larger scene.

5. What is there in your experience that can be shared with another? Can you find a way of presenting your experience that will make it possible for another to share? How can you use the knowledge and values that others have so as to connect them with you and your subject?

20.2   Exploring Your Subject

Just finding a subject is not usually enough to make you feel confident about writing on it. You may need to examine it further to decide what you know about it, what you need to say about it, and what you need to learn about it. Some of the techniques for exploring a subject resemble the techniques for finding a topic explained in the previous section and the suggestions for developing and organizing material offered in the next chapter. That's because the processes of finding, developing, and then actually writing about ideas are interrelated. Thinking about a subject may suggest a pattern of development and organization. When you begin using that pattern to write the essay, you may discover new aspects of the subject itself, which in turn may modify your arrangement of ideas. Like a healthy blaze, writing may require a little kindling to encourage the initial spark, but once the fire is roaring, it will sustain itself. Consider the techniques suggested below as striking the match.

Brainstorming

Brainstorming is a colorful word to describe intense, purposeful thinking. You can brainstorm just about any subject— even those you think you know well. For five or ten or twenty minutes, list all the thoughts you have on a subject. Don't be too critical or too careful about what you include on that roster initially. Push yourself to name as many parts and aspects of the subject as you can think of. Sometimes it helps to number the items in your list to see how much you already know about a subject.

The list becomes your catalogue of ideas. You can begin categorizing them, linking those that are similar or creating pairs of opposites. You can throw out aspects of the subject you don't intend to develop, and rank the remainder according to your sense of their importance.

You may find that brainstorming with a group is even more stimulating and inventive than working alone. Volunteer to help your classmates or colleagues think through their ideas if they'll help you with yours. Keep an open mind in such sessions and a playful willingness to listen to seemingly absurd suggestions. Some of them may contain the key to a great notion.

Asking the Journalist's Questions

When your purpose is to inform, the most direct way of exploring your subject may be to ask what have become known as the journalist's questions:

1. Who?   4. When?
2. What?   5. How?
3. Where?   6. Why?

Though elementary, these questions can help determine the range, significance, and dimensions of any topic. Not every question is relevant to every topic; part of your task as a writer is to choose which aspects of a subject must be developed and which can be appropriately ignored in a given situation.

1. **Who?** This question asks who is involved, who is to blame, who deserves credit, who is likely to be affected by an action or idea. In explaining or examining _who?_ you may need to probe into biography, autobiography, history, documents, records, and other such materials. You may have to consider personal interviews or even personal experience.

2. **What?** This question explores what happened, what is involved, and what the consequences might be. The answers may be factual and simple, or the facts themselves may be what are under scrutiny. _What?_ may entail narrating a process, describing an object, defining a phenomenon, or classifying an event.

3. **Where?** The question _where?_ is obviously concerned with the locale of an event or situation, but it also suggests inquiries into the effects of particular environments. Why did such and such a thing happen here and not there?

4. **When?** This question examines the various timeframes in which an event, idea, or phenomenon can occur, from the actual minute-by-minute reporting of a sequential action to the larger question of how something fits into vast historical patterns. How does time affect or alter the event? What would have been the consequence

20.2

Plan

of a given idea occurring five years (or five centuries) earlier? Why did something take so long to be reported? Why was action so swift in one instance and so slow in another? Questions relating to time are numerous and complex.

5. **How?** This is a question that may require an exploration of the mechanics of an object, process, or event. What made what you are examining possible, probable, or inevitable? What are the conditions necessary to make what happened possible? Can the conditions and event be duplicated? How does something work? What made possible its success or failure?

6. **Why?** This may be the most abstract and difficult question of all. It may inquire into the mysteries of physical processes *(Why does iron rust while aluminum does not?)*, or into the motivations of human actions *(Why does Othello kill Desdemona?)*. The answer to *why?* may require an inquiry first into many other aspects of a problem and an answer to questions of sequence, time, and agency *(Who did what to whom when?)*. *Why?* is the question of the child, the philosopher, the poet, and the scientist.

20.2

Plan

You may have to ask each of these questions twice: once for yourself and once for your audience. Thinking about your readers and what they know about a subject will broaden your perspectives and make it less likely that you will have to reconsider your work at a later stage.

When the subject you are exploring is argumentative or involves an investigation of facts, you may find a classical version of the journalist's questions useful. It provides a sequence for the questions that can help you understand your subject and organize your thoughts:

1. What happened? [entails narrating and describing]
2. What is its nature? [entails defining and classifying]
3. What is its quality? [entails evaluation]

If you took "Hunger in America" as your general subject, this series of questions would suggest that you must first present the evidence that hunger does indeed exist. You could do this by carefully describing conditions that you have seen or read about. Then the classical model would lead you to define and classify the kinds of hunger you are concerned with. You could distinguish between those people who actually do not have enough to eat to preserve life and those suffering from malnutrition as the result of ample but poor diets, for example. The last step in the process would be to evaluate the problem you have documented, to argue that it is or is not serious or that one group or another is to blame for the situation. These journalistic questions, considered in this sequence, can be applied in interesting ways to many potential topics, especially persuasive ones.

Exploring Patterns and Relationships

Some of the patterns of organization you may later use to develop your topic are really ways of thinking about a subject. We list the most common patterns here and then discuss them in greater detail in the next chapter to remind you how interconnected the process of planning an essay can be.

20.2

Plan

1. **Description.** What does the object or structure look like? What is it made of? What are its colors, shapes, dimensions, weight, properties, textures, densities? What makes it different from other objects? What are its special qualities?

2. **Narration.** What happened? How does the event unfold? In what order? What is the history or biography of the subject? What is the main event? Can you narrate events in some unusual way—through flashbacks, reversed order, associational order? Will readers be able to follow you?

3. **Process.** How does a thing work? What makes a complex system (such as a corporation, a bodily organ, a government agency) operate? Are there subsystems within the larger system that readers need to know about? What can cause a system to stop functioning? What terms do readers need to know to understand a process?

4. **Cause and Effect.** Why did something happen or fail to happen? What are the direct causes? What are the indirect or contributory causes? Do you know who is responsible? Can you find out? What facts, figures, and

background information must you provide your readers for them to understand what happened?

5. **Classification.** What does the object or system look like in relationship to other objects? How is it similar to them? What are its differences? What is it that links the objects within a group: shared parts, beliefs, activities? What helps you place an object into one group and not into another? Will your readers find the classification consistent, complete, and useful?

6. **Division.** Can you divide your subject or topic into parts? Are some parts more important than others? Can you arrange the parts in ways that make your subject clearer to your readers?

20.2

Plan

7. **Comparison and Contrast.** What is your subject like? How does it differ from other similar objects, ideas, or proposals? What are its advantages and disadvantages, strengths and weaknesses?

8. **Definition.** How can you distinguish one object from all others? What is its general class or *genus?* What are its identifying characteristics or *species?* Will your readers understand your definition best if you explain it in terms of the way it works, by examples, by some other means?

9. **Evaluation.** What is the thing, idea, or proposal supposed to do or achieve? How would you measure its success or failure? How would your audience? Does the subject meet the criteria for success? Can you convince your readers that it does?

Drawing on Personal Resources

You already know enough about some subjects to develop them well. Your own experience will provide ideas and material for many college essays: what you have done in school and out, the jobs you have held, your hobbies, the people you know, the places you have visited, the courses you are taking. Consider this brief list of topics and see how many you could write on from your own experience:

Considerations in Buying a Car
A Successful Amateur Play

Building a Movie Library
Overcoming Self-Consciousness
A Job I Disliked
Advice to a High-School Student About to Enter the University
Living Within a Budget

The techniques and questions in this section are designed to stimulate your thinking about an idea or a subject, not provide you with a complete outline for your finished piece. The questions overlap and reinforce each other partly because the process of invention is rarely clean and sequential. One idea generates another which leads to a third which negates the first, and so on. And this process does not end once you have located a subject or narrowed it to a thesis or begun writing; it continues through every sentence and paragraph you write and is an important aspect of revision.

Exercise **20.A**

Following is a list of general topics. For each topic, define an audience and purpose ("I am going to write a letter to _the Secretary General of the United Nations_ [audience] _urging the world body to protect human rights in Uganda_ [purpose]."). Then use one of the techniques for invention and focus outlined in sections 20.1 and 20.2 to suggest approaches to your general subject appropriate to that purpose and audience. With each general topic, vary your purpose, audience, and technique for exploring an idea.

Career choices	Identity crises
Study habits	IQ testing
College entrance requirements	Sex roles and expectations
Private/public education	Peer pressure
Competition	Medical ethics
Athletic scholarships	Environmental issues
Photography	Electronic age
Graffiti	Nuclear deterrence
Television news	Terrorism
Trends in music	Sports heroes
Adolescence	Animal rights

20.3   Limiting Your Subject

When your purpose and audience are clearly defined, there is little danger that any subject you select will be too narrow. More likely, you will have selected too large a subject and will have failed to limit it to those aspects which you are interested in and which your readers might be willing to learn about. With noble but enormous subjects like "American Foreign Policy," "The Aims of Higher Education," or "The Role of Women in American Society Today," most writers can only repeat commonplace judgments and empty generalities. After writing a paragraph or two, they find they have little to say to keep readers attentive:

> American foreign policy is complex. It deals with the relationship between the United States and all the major foreign powers as well as all the minor powers. The United States must deal with its powerful rival, the Soviet Union, its traditional European allies, its Central and South American neighbors, its client states throughout the world, and that group of states known as the "Third World." As you can see, foreign policy encompasses a great deal. . . .

Limit the subject you select so that you can develop it fully according to the requirements of your assignment. Most college papers are short—a thousand-word essay would fill only one newspaper column. Because even ten thousand words would not be enough to cover most large subjects ("Justice," "Preventing Computer Thefts," "Forestry"), divide such subjects into topics you can handle. Using the techniques of invention described in 20.1 and 20.2 is one way to discover aspects of a subject worth serious and extended treatment.

A subject like "American Foreign Policy" might be broken down in many ways. You might want to consider limiting your study to a particular time and place: "U.S. Foreign Policy Toward Latin America in 1941–45." You might examine foreign policy in terms of the individuals who controlled it: "The Foreign Policy of Henry Kissinger." Even this narrowing is not of much use when you are limited to a thousand words, so you might want to break the subject down by imposing restrictions of time, place, and cause: "The Effect of the

Nixon/Kissinger Policies of Detente on the Strategic Arms Control Talks in the Early 1970's." When you have reached this point, you have already gone substantially beyond limiting your subject. You know what sources you need to explore and what information you must gather, and you may even have a rough idea of how to organize your projected essay. You are much more in control and aware of your options than when you faced the subject "American Foreign Policy."

In general, then, it is best to concentrate on a single, well-defined aspect of a subject rather than on the subject as a whole:

General subject	*More specific topic*
Voting as an obligation of citizenship	Arousing student interest in voting
Sportsmanship	How sportsmanship differs in tennis and baseball
Smog control	The effectiveness of smog control devices for cars

As you gather information, your topic may change slightly—and it may continue to change through all the preliminary stages of your thinking. The important thing to remember at first is to keep the topic specific and to avoid falling back on a general subject.

Yet there is one danger you should be aware of, especially when writing personal experience narratives. You can be so specific and so personal that you never link your topic to more challenging and universal ideas. An essay that goes into endless specific detail about what happened on a ski trip or during a tour of Europe without ever generalizing or considering wider connections is apt to seem self-centered and empty. Similarly, even very technical or theoretical articles may sometimes benefit from an occasional look at wider or practical implications and applications. Erring on the too-specific side is rarer than on the too-general, but it does happen.

Exercise 20.B

Following is a list of general topics. For each topic, specify a purpose and an audience, and then narrow the subject to a well-defined aspect that would satisfy your audience and purpose.

China	Contraceptives
Boat-building	Air safety
Vikings	Orchestras
Corn	Foreign movies
Engineering	Modern architecture
Freud	Sports

20.4 Locating a Thesis

When you have found at least tentative answers to these questions,

Why am I writing this?

For whom am I writing?

What is my subject?

you may be in a position to compose a *thesis statement*, when one is called for. (Not all kinds of assignments require explicit theses.) A definite statement of the main or central idea of your paper is useful for three reasons:

1. it will help you see just where you are going and why;
2. it will give you a single focus for the development of your paper;
3. it will help you select the material you will use in the paper.

Usually a single declarative statement, the thesis should normally be either a simple or complex sentence.

The thesis statement is not the topic of your paper or its title; it is a sentence that answers the question "What is the main idea that I am trying to present to the reader?" A statement of the central or controlling idea of a paper titled "The Honor System" might read "The honor system works only as well as the students want it to work" or "The honor system at this college is popular with the faculty but not with the students." In a paper explaining a process or activity, the thesis statement might be "Learning to play the violin demands patience as well as talent" or "Performance is more important than appearance when you are buying a used car."

To write a thesis statement, you must decide what it is you can say about your *subject* that will achieve the *purpose* you have for writing and that will satisfy the needs and expectations of your *audience*. Thesis statements are particularly important when you are writing to explain something or to argue a point. In complex essays, no single sentence may serve as a thesis. Instead the main point or central idea develops cumulatively as the essay progresses. Don't expect everything you write or read to have a thesis statement.

Exercise   **20.C**

Each of the following topics has a thesis statement that can lead to an interesting paper, but some of the points listed don't have any bearing on the controlling idea and should be changed or eliminated. Arrange the ideas in groups that belong together, eliminating or changing them as necessary.

20.4
Plan

1. **Language instruction** (part of an essay intended to convince those in control of educational funding that foreign language instruction in the United States is important)

   Thesis: The American educational system is doing students a disservice by placing minimal importance on foreign language instruction.

   a. Because language represents ways of viewing the world, de-emphasizing language education encourages students to be ethnocentric in their thinking.
   b. Many liberal arts programs in state universities have dropped foreign language requirements.
   c. Many citizens of other countries subscribe to the stereotype of the "ugly American."
   d. Some students object that they "do not have a head for learning languages."
   e. Americans are frequently at a disadvantage in understanding foreign business issues because of their unfamiliarity with other languages.
   f. Language learning requires memorization and frequent review.
   g. American students are limited in their opportunities because they cannot go abroad to study unless they have a command of other tongues.

h. Educators are beginning to challenge the traditional belief that women are better language learners than men.

i. American schools rarely provide language instruction to children under twelve years of age, the period of time during which an individual is most facile in acquiring language.

2. **Small farms** (a paper informing city dwellers of the economic difficulties forcing many small farm operators out of business)

Thesis: Small farms may soon disappear from the American scene.

a. Art and fiction often contrast the serenity and wholesomeness of country life with the vice and corruption of the cities.

b. Farming is a business that involves great financial risk: farmers cannot control weather or growing conditions or the stability of farm prices.

c. Modern farm equipment is so expensive that single-family farms do not yield enough annually to cover the necessary investment in equipment.

d. Some farms specialize in crop production while others produce livestock.

e. Much of the profit in food production goes to those who process farm products into the consumer items we find in the supermarkets.

f. While many people think of rural life as romantic, there is actually little glamour in the day-to-day business of raising hogs.

g. Today, less than 10 percent of the United States' population is actively engaged in farming as a business.

h. Small farmers are finding it difficult to compete with corporate farmers who can afford to invest in expensive equipment and advanced techniques of fertilization.

i. Unlike many labor groups, farmers have never organized into strong, centralized labor unions.

j. The United States produces a surplus of agricultural products, many of which are sent to foreign markets

20.4
Plan

to feed people who live on infertile, arid, or otherwise unproductive lands.

k. During a bad year, small farmers may not earn enough profit to pay their property taxes. ∎

Exercise 20.D

1. Use the title of one of the courses you are taking this school term as the starting point for a paper. In this paper, you are to tell your classmates about an idea or concept you have recently encountered in the course. You should begin with the course title itself ("The History of Astronomy"; "Introduction to Auditing"; "Experimental Food Science") and then brainstorm for a short while, listing the ideas, concepts, and terms that have been a part of class discussion or reading during the last week or so.

20.4

Plan

Example   **The History of Astronomy**

Galileo
Copernicus
The heliocentric universe
Galileo's telescope
The Office of the Inquisition
Galileo's trial before the Inquisition
Galileo's condemnation

Then attempt to shape your thoughts into phrases and finally into sentences that might serve as the main point or thesis statement for a paper:

> Once he had made a telescope, it was only a matter of time before Galileo found evidence in the heavens to support Copernicus' belief in a heliocentric universe.

> When the Inquisition condemned Galileo for supporting the Copernican belief that the earth orbited the sun, it also effectively stifled science in Catholic Europe for years to come.

Finally, use these topic sentences as the focus for group

discussions in which you compare your statements with those of your colleagues. Which topics seem worth pursuing? Which of the ideas you have introduced seems to interest your potential readers the most? How might you develop it?

2. Repeat the preceding assignment (1), this time using the headlines on the front page or editorial page of your college or local newspaper as your initial subject ideas. Brainstorm one of the more intriguing headlines, and work it up into several thesis statements. Discuss the statements with your classmates. Then pursue the most promising one: write an essay.   ■

20.4

Plan

21

DEVELOPING AND ARRANGING YOUR MATERIAL

Once you have a subject, audience, and purpose, you are also likely to have ideas about how to present the material you are considering to your readers. You begin thinking about what you should include (and exclude), what emphasis you want to give different parts of your piece, and what order you want your material to follow.

21.1 Patterns of Development

What follows is a list of some familiar ways of organizing material in an essay. These patterns can give structure to entire essays or just to parts of them. As you plan to write, you should treat these designs as ways of thinking about a subject. When, for example, you consider a comparison/contrast pattern for an essay, you are encouraging yourself to think about the similarities and differences in objects or ideas. When you recognize the need to describe something, you are also obligating yourself to look at it closely and identify its distinctive features. Organizing a piece of writing often resembles the process of finding and exploring a subject examined in the preceding chapter.

When you find that you need to structure an essay with special care or that you have a great deal of material to organize, you may want to put your plan down on paper in the form of an outline. Each of the patterns explained in the following pages can be the framework for a simple scratch outline or for a more detailed formal one. (Outlines are discussed in Chapter 22.)

Description

You *describe* when you want your readers to see an object, person, or scene the way you see it. Description figures in every kind of writing, from poetry to technical reports.

Descriptive writing succeeds only when you show your audience the specific, identifying details of an object or scene. The details you select will depend upon your purpose as well. Effective description requires that you see an object or scene clearly yourself, that you understand what you see, and that you say precisely what you see:

21.1
Dev

> I know how a prize watermelon looks when it is sunning its fat rotundity among pumpkin vines and "simblins"; I know how to tell when it is ripe without "plugging" it. I know how inviting it looks when it is cooling itself in a tub of water under the bed, waiting; I know how it looks when it lies on the table in the sheltered great floorspace between house and kitchen, and the children gathered for the sacrifice and their mouths watering. I know the crackling sound it makes when the carving knife enters its end and I can see the split fly along in front of the blade as the knife cleaves its way to the other end; I can see its halves fall apart and display the rich red meat and the black seeds, and the heart standing up, a luxury fit for the elect.—Mark Twain, *Autobiography*

No two people look at a scene in exactly the same way. What makes one writer's descriptions more vivid than another's is the kind of details selected and the way they are arranged.

Good descriptive writing is precise. Notice how lifeless the description is in this paraphrase, from which the specific details have been removed:

> After Lincoln became a lawyer, he started to pay more attention to his appearance. But even though he wore his

hair in the accepted fashion of the time, he still wasn't well dressed. As a result, he acquired the reputation of being one of the most careless dressers in town, along with another local man, who was a judge, and who was equally careless about the way he looked.

Contrast that paraphrase to the description as it was written:

> And though Lincoln had begun wearing broadcloth and white shirts with a white collar and black silk cravat, and suggestions of sideburns coming down three-fourths the length of his ears, he was still known as one of the carelessly dressed men of Springfield, along with Stephen Logan, who wore unbleached cotton shirts and had sat two years as a circuit court judge wearing an unbleached cotton shirt with no cravat or stock.—Carl Sandburg, *Abraham Lincoln: The Prairie Years, I*

The details you select for a descriptive passage should contribute to a central impression. Often a few well-selected details will give a sharper picture than a large number of ill-assorted ones:

> The way you can recognize a local boy's pickup is by what we call "Hardin County racing stripes." That is, dried tobacco juice, slipstreamed back along the driver's door. You can also tell by the gun racks, which carry plastic-stocked Remingtons or a J. C. Higgins shotgun. Loaded, of course.—Gordon Baxter, "Peterbilt Pickups"

Descriptions should be organized so that your readers can follow the way your eyes are moving across your subject: from left to right, far to near, or top to bottom. In technical descriptions, you may want to include an illustration, diagram, or figure to help your readers follow you more closely.

Narration

You narrate to show readers what is happening over a period of time. Narratives can be autobiographical, historical, journalistic, even fictional.

A narrative often reflects your point of view on a subject; you may be an observer or part of a story. Whether participant or observer, you should try to keep the focus on what is happening—unless, of course, the piece is self-expressive and the narrative really is designed to tell the reader about you.

In narrative writing, events are typically written down in chronological order and in the past tense. However, the order can be varied, and the present tense is sometimes employed to create a sense of events actually occurring, as in this paragraph:

> At the storm's crest, the bulging cloud creeps over the Hawksbill peak. The sky is a nest of electrical charges. Lightning makes tracks across the sky like a lost skier over new snow. The bolts flash from cloud to cloud, from cloud to earth, from cloud to atmosphere, always followed by the sharp report of thunder, the hot air's response to the searing lightning. The rain comes, so hard it strips great chunks of bark off the trees, tears away clumps of rock along the exposed ridge.—Harry Middleton, "Storm"

21.1

Dev

Whether a narrative is written in the present or past, one tense should usually be kept throughout.

Just as you seek out the most outstanding features when writing a description, in preparing a narrative you usually want to build upon the most important events, deleting the insignificant or distracting ones. You can't report everything that happens, and in most cases you wouldn't want to. Your readers would simply be bored. So it is important to choose events and details that will make a narrative understandable and lively. Avoid statements that leave your readers asking "Who?" "Why?" "When?" or "What?" Choose those details that illuminate the most important actions. You can usually make your point and still keep the action moving by selecting two or three lively incidents.

Process

When you need to explain how something works, you follow a pattern called *process narrative*. To prepare an effective process essay, you want to list events or steps in a simple, clear order:

> If your new lamp was purchased prefilled with lamp oil, unscrew the burner. Thread the wick into the burner, and remove the plastic plug with a knife or screwdriver. Screw the burner back on the base and light the wick. Replace the chimney. If your lamp was not prefilled, the fount or base

must first be filled with lamp oil, and there would be no plug to remove.—"Instructions for Enjoying Your Oil Lamp," Lamplight Farms

When appropriate, you can number the steps in a process or use some other device (such as underlining) to highlight important features. Many technical explanations include simple illustrations and figures. Be sure to explain any terms that your readers might not understand. Note how the writer in this example pauses briefly to define _capillaries:_

> Filtering the blood begins the process of urine formation. All oxygenated blood is transported to the kidney by the renal artery. Once within the kidney, the artery begins to break up into smaller vessels which divide further to form networks of capillaries—minute blood vessels which connect the ends of arteries to the beginning of veins. In the capillaries the blood pressure increases, since the same amount of blood being forced through the arteries is now pushed through the narrower-diameter capillaries. The higher pressure forces water and other small molecules in the blood through the capillary walls in the kidney. . . .

21.1
Dev

Cause and Effect

Whenever your readers need to know how or why something happened, you may choose to employ a cause and effect analysis. Quite simply, you trace responsibility for an action or idea to its roots. In many cases, you will find several possible explanations for a phenomenon. Why, for example, have student SAT scores been declining for so long? You could easily list and discuss a dozen reasons. But a good cause and effect paper does more than just list reasons. It separates accurate explanations from inaccurate ones and it avoids oversimplifying complex problems. Cause and effect essays require you to study events and their causes carefully so that you can explain accurately how or why something happened:

> What are the Japanese doing right? And how have they done it on a crowded group of islands, without enough coal and oil, without significant natural resources, without adequate farmland?
> The rather chilling answer is that they have done it by a social process—by a kind of group behavior modification.

An average Japanese who goes to work for a company is there for life. He works throughout the day in an atmosphere in which consensus is always the goal. If, as his career progresses, he needs retraining, the company will retrain him, so he need not get involved in the protection of rights that American unions strive for. The company's goals are his. The people he sees socially are from the company.—Adam Smith, "The Japanese Model"

Classification

You may find that the best way of studying or explaining large groups of things (colleges, trucks, planets) is to break them down into smaller classes. These classes should help define those things included in them in some important way:

Colleges { State-supported
Church-supported
Private, non-denominational

Trucks { Front-wheel drive
Rear-wheel drive
Four-wheel drive

Planets { With thick atmospheres
Without thick atmospheres

Categories such as these should be inclusive—every item in the larger group should fall into one of the smaller groups. The groups themselves should not overlap.

A classification essay usually begins with a rationale for the general system of categories, the writer explaining how his system makes a concept clearer or more manageable. Then the essay discusses each of the classes in some detail. Quite often, the first paragraph of a classificatory piece provides a direction for all that follows, indicating the order in which each class will be discussed:

Inanimate objects are classified into three major categories—those that don't work, those that break down and those that get lost.—Russell Baker, "The Plot Against People"

Division

Sometimes you will have a large subject that needs to be broken into parts, not separate classes, in order to be explained to your audience. In discussing the anatomy of a flower, for example, you may decide to give a paragraph or two to each of the major components: stem, leaf, petal, sepal, and so on. Many subjects become more manageable when you pause to divide them into parts or look for logical divisions or breaks. You can create a rough organization for your piece by listing the divisions and then arranging them in some way useful to your readers: by chronology, by size, and so on.

Definition

You will often be called upon to define words, ideas, and concepts. You can satisfy these sorts of assignments in a number of ways. The most familiar pattern is what is called the *logical definition.* In it, you first explain what general class an object belongs to and then examine some of the features which distinguish it from other objects in the general class:

> *schnauzer:* a breed of dog [general class] developed in Germany, having a blunt muzzle and wiry gray coat, and trained to control rodents [distinguishing features]

21.1
Dev

Most dictionary entries are examples of logical definitions. A logical definition can be extended to essay length if you go into detail about both the general class and the distinguishing features. But *extended definitions* often use other techniques for defining an object. Things can be defined by what they are, what they are not, what they do, what they do not do. You can even define an object by giving examples:

> A gadget is nearly always novel in design or concept and it often has no proper name. For example, the semaphore which signals the arrival of the mail in our rural mailbox certainly has no proper name. It is a contrivance consisting of a bamboo pole, two copper right-angles, some wire and a piece of shingle. Call it what you like, it saves us frequent frustrating trips to the mailbox in winter when you have to dress up and wade through snow to get there. That's a gadget!—John J. Rowlands, "Gadgeteers"

Comparison and Contrast

Among the patterns of development you will use most often is comparison and contrast. Strictly speaking, comparisons list the resemblances between objects or ideas:

> The Ukrainians are the Texans of Russia. They believe they can fight, drink, ride, sing, and make love better than anybody else in the world, and if pressed will admit it. Their country, too, was a borderland—that's what Ukraine means—and like Texas it was originally settled by outlaws, horse thieves, land-hungry farmers, and people who hadn't made a go of it somewhere else. Some of these hard cases banded together, long ago, to raise hell and livestock. They called themselves Cossacks, and they would have felt right at home in any Western movie. Even today the Ukrainians cherish a wistful tradition of horsemanship, although most of them would feel as uncomfortable in a saddle as any Dallas banker. They still like to wear knee-high boots and big, furry hats, made of gray or black Persian lamb, which are the local equivalent of the Stetson.—John Fischer, *Why They Behave Like Russians*

21.1

Dev

Contrasts are studies of differences:

> The Rolls-Royce and Mercedes-Benz are both prestigious, very expensive automobiles. But the Rolls appeals to buyers interested in what is old, familiar, and traditional. The styling is simple and dignified, almost sedate, and the engineering, while up-to-date, pushes no new frontiers. The Mercedes is likewise a car with a tradition, but it is one with an emphasis on innovation and development. Its styling is often controversial, reflecting leading-edge technology that cares more that the vehicle work right than look right. Both luxury cars find all the eager buyers they want.

Many essays of this type include elements of both comparison and contrast, as the previous example demonstrates. There are comparisons in the first and last sentences, although the paragraph as a whole focuses on contrasts.

You can organize comparisons and contrasts by first discussing all the features of one idea or subject and then discussing the features of the second object. Or, if such a plan seems to make the analysis break awkwardly in the middle, you can present a sequence of comparisons and contrasts on each major point. The two plans might look like this for a paper contrasting public and private schools:

Plan 1
A. Public schools
   1. Cost of attendance
   2. Curriculum
   3. Facilities
B. Private schools
   1. Cost of attendance
   2. Curriculum
   3. Facilities

Plan 2
A. Cost of attendance
   1. Public school
   2. Private school
B. Curriculum
   1. Public school
   2. Private school
C. Facilities
   1. Public school
   2. Private school

Analogy

You may sometimes want to organize an entire essay, or a portion of one, by using an extended comparison called an *analogy*. In an analogy you explain a new or difficult idea by referring to another idea your readers are more familiar with:

> I love the artist or scholar whose activity is like the bee pursuing the delicious nectar of the flowers. The bee has no mind to become a renowned authority on which flowers contain the best nectar; the bee simply loves nectar. In all probability, the bee, through his actual experience, will soon have a *fantastic* knowledge of the flower geography of his neighborhood—as good perhaps as any human scholar who "studies" botany. And I say the bee really knows the flower much better than the botanist. The botanist merely knows *about* the flower; the bee knows the flower directly.—Raymond Smullyan, "Bees and Scholars"

21.1

Dev

Analogies can work just as well explaining why certain comparisons should not be made or why certain systems should not serve as models for others:

> . . . we must recognize that human biology often provides a poor model for the struggles of other organisms. Humans are slowly growing animals. We invest a great deal of energy in raising very few, late maturing offspring. Our populations are not controlled by the wholesale death of nearly all juvenile members. Yet many organisms follow a different strategy in the "struggle for existence": they produce

vast numbers of seeds or eggs, hoping (so to speak) that a few will survive the rigors of early life. These organisms are often controlled by their predators, and their evolutionary defense must be a strategy that minimizes the chance of being eaten.—Stephen Jay Gould, "Of Bamboos, Cicadas, and Adam Smith"

You must exercise caution whenever you structure an entire essay around an analogy. Be certain that the extended comparison does not introduce more problems than it solves. If your readers, for example, strongly object to the analogy or if they find that your comparison only complicates matters, you may want to try another strategy. But analogies can provide exciting ways of conceptualizing ideas and shaping papers.

Support and Illustration

One of the simplest patterns of organization can also be one of the most effective if you use it well. All *support and illustration* involves is making statements and supporting them with specific explanatory examples, details, facts, or reasons. This tactic is particularly effective when you are developing topics that require lists of "reasons why": "The Value of Studying Foreign Languages," "The Problems of Using Robots in Industry," "Why Freshman Writing Courses Should Not Be Required." In papers of this kind, the individual items supporting the main point should be arranged according to some strategy, with the better arguments presented first to raise interest, and the very best saved until the end to conclude forcefully and convincingly. The following selection shows how an assertion ("Americans should be more optimistic about the future") is supported by one example after another:

> Moreover, American society has often gone beyond tolerance. It increasingly treats people on a basis of equal moral worth. Many examples suggest themselves, and, though each is a story of incomplete revolution, the steps taken so far merit recognition. The increasing provision of lawyers for the poor in criminal and civil cases in both federal and state courts is a case in point. Another is the impressive record of school desegregation which finally took place during the 1970s in the South. Despite talk of white flight and desegregation, 80 percent of all Southern white

children attend public schools. There whites and blacks learn to make their peace with each other and, in some cases, go on to achieve reciprocal genuine respect. This marks an enormous change—part of a set of changes regarding the races that have affected the South in a decade and a half and that have brought us closer to the American dream of mutual respect.—Booth Fowler and Saul Brenner, "In Defense of Optimism"

Exercise 21.A

For each of the topics below, write out several sentences to show how you might develop the subject according to the suggested pattern of development, as shown in the example. Each of the topics should be developed for a general college audience.

Example *topic:* New artists change our musical tastes. *pattern:* support and illustration

1. In the mid-1950's, Elvis Presley changed the direction of pop music with "Blue Suede Shoes" and other hits.
2. By the early 1960's, folk musicians like Bob Dylan and the Kingston Trio brought different sounds to the attention of the nation.
3. The Beatles took the spotlight in the later '60's, and spawned an entirely "new" sound, which many other groups imitated.
4. The early 1970's found a new and "slicked-up" country sound which brought country music onto the popular music charts in a big way.
5. Many singers and groups have come and gone in the past twenty years, but it is interesting that some artists have not only been able to change with the times, but they have also helped shape and change our musical tastes, making way for new styles, including acid rock, punk rock, and other new forms of music.

a. *topic:* Building a new silicon chip factory near a residential neighborhood. *pattern:* analogy
b. *topic:* Opinion is divided on the virtues of smog-control devices in autos and factories. *pattern:* comparison/contrast
c. *topic:* The discovery that the world is round changed both science and everyday life. *pattern:* cause and effect
d. *topic:* A library (or some other institution) offers many practical services. *pattern:* division
e. *topic:* Computers have created a host of new words. *pattern:* definition
f. *topic:* The typical college curriculum includes a variety of courses. *pattern:* classification
g. *topic:* Great heroes must often deal with adversity. *pattern:* support and illustration ∎

21.2 Strategies of Argumentation

21.2

Arg

In school and in the workplace, you will likely encounter situations in which you are expected to prove something or to persuade others to think or act in a particular way. To succeed, you will have to provide your reader with good reasons for agreeing with you.

Locating the Argument

An argumentative paper *proposes* something. Whether it attempts to demonstrate a truth or makes a call for action, it centers on a proposition that the writer must be prepared to prove:

> Cities need old buildings so badly it is probably impossible for vigorous streets and districts to grow without them.— Jane Jacobs, "Cities Need Old Buildings"

In planning a persuasive paper, you must take the time to formulate your proposition carefully. As your thesis statement, your proposition gives direction and unity to your argument. Ordinarily it needs to be simple—composed ideally of a single subject and a single predicate. If you argue, for example, that "County government must be put into new hands on election day and reformed to keep state and federal agencies from encroaching on local authority," you have, by using a double predicate, introduced two arguments, both of which must then be proved.

You should find the suggestions in 20.4, Locating a Thesis, helpful in formulating an arguable proposition.

Using Resources and Evidence

When we state our opinions in informal situations, we often give little or no evidence to support them: "John is a reckless driver"; "The cost of living is going up every day"; "Divorce is the main cause of juvenile delinquency." This does not mean that we have no good reasons for believing as we do, but simply that our reasons are usually known and accepted by our listeners. On occasions when our opinions are questioned, we may attempt to support them with facts drawn from our experience and reading: "John had two accidents last month, and he always drives too fast"; "Steak is up sixty cents a pound, and a refrigerator costs almost twice as much today as it did six years ago"; "Psychologists say that emotional stability depends on a secure family life." Such evidence is considered acceptable or even convincing in informal situations, usually because the listener's personal regard for the speaker lends some weight to the evidence.

In writing, however, the relationship with your audience is far more impersonal; authority must rest much more on the facts themselves. Readers who know neither John nor you will want to know what kind of accidents John had and who was at fault; they will wonder whether "too fast" means in excess of speed limits; they may suspect that "always" is an exaggeration. Before accepting what you have asserted about the relationship between divorce and delinquency, they may want to read what the psychologists have actually said to be sure you are not misinterpreting their remarks or ignoring opposing opinions.

The more facts supporting your opinion that you can gather from experience or from the written statements of others, the more reason you can give your readers to accept that opinion. You will not be able to present absolute *proof,* but the greater the weight of your evidence, the more probable it will seem to your audience that your belief is the best one.

21.2

Arg

Documentation

When your own observations form the basis of an argumentative paper, be sure to tell the readers why you consider your statements to be fairly authoritative. Otherwise they may not be sure how much value to attach to them. Somewhere near the beginning of the paper, state the circumstances under which you gathered your facts:

> Since I was sixteen I have spent my summer vacations working in a local department store, first as a stock clerk and later as an assistant display manager. During that time, I have become familiar with the typical organization of a large retail store. . . .

> My home is only nine miles away from the Menominee Indian reservation, and I have had frequent opportunities to meet and talk to members of the Menominee tribe. . . .

> In gathering examples for this paper, I spent ten hours listening to radio programs featuring rock-and-roll records and copied down the lyrics of a dozen of the current favorites. . . .

21.2
Arg

When you incorporate published material into your paper, be sure to reproduce it accurately and to credit the sources, whether you quote them directly or not. It is not fair or honest to present someone else's experiences or observations as if they were your own. In a research paper, credit is given formally by means of notes (33.4, Step Five: Documenting the Paper), but in a general paper mention may be made informally. The following are some typical examples of how such informal acknowledgments can be handled:

> Franklin Soames, the author of *Zapotec Culture*, found that. . . .

> At a recent medical convention, H. L. Matthews, the noted urologist, was quoted as saying. . . .

> But according to Jean Lafontant, in a recent article in *Time*. . . .

Sources which have been used extensively may be given credit in a note at the beginning or at the end of a paper:

> Much of the material for this paper was taken from C. D. Darlington, *The Evolution of Man and Society* (New York: Simon & Schuster, 1969).

Using Induction and Deduction

In most cases you will be guided by your own good sense in selecting arguments strong enough to convince your readers. It really won't matter whether you can identify your arguments as *inductive* or *deductive*, so long as your work is clear, convincing, and suited to your audience and purpose.

Still, in discussing logic and argument, you may want to know what the terms *induction* and *deduction* mean. Defined simply, *induction* involves a movement of thought from individual facts and observations to general conclusions. *Deduction* moves from generalizations already existing (called *premises*) to conclusions about particular cases. These processes of thought are closely interrelated, induction supplying the premises for subsequent deductive arguments.

For example, let us say that in a controlled scientific study of two hundred recovered cancer patients, one hundred are fed an extremely low-fat diet while the remaining hundred are fed a traditional American diet high in fats. After several years, a detailed analysis of these two hundred individual cases shows that only 12 percent of those in the low-fat group had a recurrence of their disease while 36 percent in the regular-diet group suffered relapses. These facts suggest a carefully qualified inductive conclusion: a low-fat diet seems to be a factor in preventing the recurrence of cancer. Shortly after this study is published in a medical journal, a doctor is treating a patient who has recently recovered from cancer. The doctor draws a conclusion based on two premises, the first one supplied by the journal article:

> *Premise 1:* A low-fat diet seems to be a factor in preventing the recurrence of cancer.
>
> *Premise 2:* Her patient has recently recovered from cancer.

The deduction the doctor makes is simply that her patient should go on a low-fat diet to improve chances of a sustained recovery. The doctor's deduction is based upon a premise validated (in a limited way) by the inductive experiment.

As you might suspect from this short example, the process of induction involves more than casual observation. In order for an inductive conclusion to be true, it must be based upon valid and reliable facts; the experiments must be repeatable; and the populations studied must be representative, random, and sufficiently large. The method of gathering information or observing phenomena must follow recognized conventions and procedures within a given field, whether the study be a medical one involving research on cancer patients or a literary one involving the way a poem ought to be read. (See 33.2, The Components of Research Reports.) In much of your academic writing, your inductive arguments are likely to be based on relatively little firsthand information or on only limited observations. It is always important, then, that your conclusions note all the limitations of your sources.

Deductive arguments are as complex as inductive ones. You probably are familiar with the basic unit of deductive reasoning, the *syllogism*. It consists of three statements, two of which are premises and the third a conclusion drawn from the premises:

1. All stars are fusion engines.
2. The sun is a star.
3. The sun is a fusion engine.

21.2

Arg

A full explanation of syllogistic reasoning is too complicated to treat here; you may want to pursue such a study in a logic course. The fact is, however, that few writers think or write syllogistically.

Instead they pay good common-sense attention to their premises—to the statements and beliefs they present as *givens* in an argument. Sometimes you can argue from premises that most of your readers tend to agree with, in which case you can proceed with your demonstration without explaining or defending each value or belief. In arguing to an audience of conservative Republicans, for example, you would not have to pause to argue that:

—government is the problem, not the solution;

—spending cuts are preferable to tax increases;

—the first responsibility of government is to maintain a strong defense.

With a different audience, say of liberal Democrats, the same statements would be the bones of contention, the very questions under debate, not the principles a writer could safely take for granted.

In many fields, the *givens* are numerous. Without prior agreement on the meaning of certain terms or the acceptance of certain principles, argument would be almost impossible. In some cases, however, where the basic differences between antagonists are fundamental, you may have to look for the common ground or partially create it. Capitalists and communists might argue endlessly over theories of production, the meaning of human rights, or the liberties of the press, but they can probably see a common good in avoiding nuclear war. Similarly, believers and atheists may base their ethical standards on different premises, but members of both groups will denounce murder, rape, theft, and treachery.

Finding Arguments

Consider some of the following tactics when you are looking for ways of making a strong case for what you believe in.

21.2
Arg

Argument from Nature. You may want to appeal to an audience to accept things the way they are. In such a case, you can present an *argument from nature,* studying the way things are conventionally defined and presenting the *status quo* as a healthy and reliable norm. For example, the young man who decides to run for homecoming *queen* might be denied on the grounds that a queen is, by nature, a female.

Argument from Analogy. People cannot always agree on the nature of things, of course, and for that reason they have often turned to other kinds of argument. The *argument from analogy* brings a subject and argument into a reader's knowledge by suggesting its similarity to something better known, as in the fairly common—but often ineffective—analogy of government and business. The evidence you bring to this kind of argument must show that the comparison is both significant and accurate. In the following example, the author argues that city life does not alienate man or alter his basic character; he points out by analogy that domestication has not "denatured" the cat:

> . . . I can see no evidence that frequent contact with nature is *essential* to human well-being, as the antitechnologists assert. Even if the human species owes much of its complexity to the diversity of natural environment, why

must man continue to commune with the landscapes in which he evolved? Millions of people, in ages past as well as present, have lived out their lives in city environs, with very little if any contact with "nature." Have they lived lives inherently inferior because of this? Who would be presumptuous enough to make such a statement?

The common domestic cat evolved in the wild, but a thousand generations of domesticity do not seem to have "denatured" it in the least. This is not the place to write the ode to my cat that should someday be written. Suffice it to say that although she never goes out of doors, she plays, hunts, loves, and eats with gusto, and relaxes with that sensuous peace that is uniquely feline. I submit that she is not more "alienated" than her wild sister who fights for survival in some distant wood.—Samuel C. Florman, "A Rebuttal of Antitechnologists"

21.2
Arg

Argument from Consequence. The *argument from consequence* enforces a proposition by examining cause and effect, antecedent and consequence. This is a useful kind of argument, but it is limited by the fact that human affairs are not ordered by certain laws of causality. Poverty *sometimes* breeds crime; prolonged tyranny *frequently* leads to revolution; honesty is *occasionally* rewarded. Before expressing an opinion about the outcome of some course of action, or about the cause of some event, make sure that the weight of evidence lends probability to your statement. In the following example, George F. Will argues from consequence that psychiatry is to blame for the verdict exonerating a man who attempted to kill the President:

> The Hinckley verdict illustrates three perversities: The most morally indefensible crimes are becoming the most legally defensible. The idea of the individual is being obliterated in order to maximize the rights of the individual. And the quest for the chimera of perfect justice is subordinating the social good, including the rule of law, to the quicksilver axioms of a "science" that is long on pretenses and short on testable assertions.—"Psychiatry, Law at Cross-Purposes"

In effect, he is arguing for a greater separation of the principles of law from the idiosyncrasies of psychiatric analyses. Note, too, how Will attacks the premises of psychiatry, describing them as "quicksilver" and "untestable."

Argument from Authority. A final argument is the *argument from authority*. It depends upon the testimony of respected persons, the authority of institutions, the weight of important documents. While a simple appeal to authority no longer carries much weight, this argument can be powerful when you handle it skillfully. The "back to basics" movement in education is supported at least in part by appeals to an older tradition of learning which seemed to work better than contemporary schooling. The testimony of credible witnesses and experts remains a key to legal processes. And in the political realm, the argument from authority and tradition can be logically appealing. Arguments that depend upon appeals to the stability or integrity of the U.S. Constitution, for example, carry considerable weight because of the authority of the document, its age, and its demonstrated success in organizing a government.

21.2
Arg

Taking Your Argument to Your Audience

Whatever kind of argument you use (those above are only samples), remember that your readers have some confidence in their own intelligence and judgment and will likely resent a writer who attempts to make up their minds for them. (See the discussion of author-audience relationships in 19.2.) State your facts as specifically as possible so that your readers can check them for themselves if they want to, and give your reasons for whatever conclusions you draw. Compare the following statements for effectiveness:

Vague	A few years ago, the president of a large corporation said that taxes were too high.
Specific	In a speech to the Toledo Chamber of Commerce on April 14, 1974, Oscar Winslow, president of the Winslow Steel Corporation, said, "Corporation taxes today are so high that they are destroying business incentive."
Vague	In many of his newspaper articles, H. L. Mencken made slighting references to democracy. Anyone can see that he despised it.

Specific   In his articles for the Baltimore *Sun*, H. L. Mencken frequently referred to democracy in terms such as these: "the domination of un-reflective and timorous men, moved in vast herds by mob emotions" (July 26, 1920); "it may be clumsy, it may be swinish, it may be unutterably incompetent and dishonest, but it is never dismal" (July 14, 1924).

In trying to persuade readers to accept your opinion, you will naturally want to gather facts that will support your position. It is not fair to your readers, however, to suggest that *all* evidence reinforces your belief. They may be familiar with contrary evidence; even if they are not, its absence may make them suspect that you are stacking the deck in your favor. In a court of law, an attorney who deliberately suppresses evidence damaging to his or her case may be disbarred from future practice. The consequences to writers are usually not so serious, but they may also lose the case.

21.2

Arg

When you come across facts that do *not* support your opinion, give them as careful consideration as you do those that do. Is their source authoritative and relatively free of bias? Do they offer serious and relevant reasons to question your present opinion? Do they outnumber the facts you can find to support it? It may be that you will want to alter or modify your proposition after taking opposing facts into account. You may decide that your original opinion was wrong; many writers are unaware of the flimsy basis of their beliefs until they begin trying to substantiate them.

Even if the facts you gather do not change your opinion, it is unfair simply to discard those that fail to support it. In fact, it will strengthen your position in the readers' eyes if you frankly admit unfavorable evidence along with your reasons for being unpersuaded by it. The readers are your jury. If you have arrived at an opinion by weighing opposing evidence sensibly, they should be able to do the same.

Testing the Argument

One way to test your argument, or to examine the argument of another writer or speaker, is to scrutinize it for flaws in reasoning and in the use of evidence. Probably the most common flaws are these:

Hasty Generalization. In informal situations, we often overgeneralize from the facts: "She's *never* on time"; "Advertising is *only* a pack of lies." A little consideration shows us that all-or-none, black-or-white situations are rare; reality is more accurately described in terms of finer shadings and degrees. Most readers are aware of this, and although they will accept and make statements like the above uncritically in conversations, they are suspicious of them in writing.

Be especially cautious in using terms like *all, always, everybody, nobody, never, none, only,* and *most.* Before making such all-inclusive statements, make sure that they are justified. If there are any exceptions to some assertion you make, modify your language to make it more accurate. Don't say that *all* young people want a home and family: *some* or *many* might be more accurate. Before you say that *most* early marriages end in divorce, ascertain from some reliable source whether more than 50 percent actually do; otherwise you are not justified in using *most.* Keep in mind that the English vocabulary provides a wealth of qualifying terms (*some, seldom, often,* to name only a few), and choose those that most accurately describe the number, extent, and frequency of the facts you are asserting.

Compare these two statements for precision of expression. Both are based on the same facts (of the delinquents in the State Training School, 75 percent come from low-income families, 45 percent have used narcotics at some time, and 20 percent have IQ scores over 100):

Overgeneralization	**Almost all** delinquents in the State Training School come from families **on the verge of starvation. Most** of the delinquents are **dope addicts,** and **very few** are **brilliant.**
Accurate statement	**Three out of four** delinquents in the State Training School come from **low-income homes. Almost half** of them have **at least experimented** with narcotics. **A significant minority** are **above average mentally.**

False Analogy. Comparison and analogy are effective means of arguing, but only if there is really a basic similarity between the compared terms. If, for example, a university administrator sets out to argue for new rules and economies in his or her school on the basis that it should be run like a business, we should probably reject that argument on the grounds that the analogy is not valid, for similarities between a business and a university seem only incidental, not essential. Indeed, almost any analogy reveals weaknesses if examined carefully. It is good advice to limit your reliance on arguments by analogy to what is obvious and fairly sound. Pushing an analogy too far can quickly undermine your own case.

Post Hoc, Ergo Propter Hoc. This fallacy (literally, "after this, therefore because of this") is the fairly common one of assuming that two events or things are causally related simply because they are related in time. The ancients sometimes blamed problems in the state on comets and other astral events that preceded them. In more recent times, serious questions have been raised and statistical battles waged over the relationship between various phenomena (the Three Mile Island accident, the rise of rock music, the human intrusion into space, the increased use of pesticides) and subsequent occurrences (increases in infant mortality, shifts in morality, damage to the atmosphere, decline in bird populations). In some cases, convincing links have been demonstrated; in others the relationships suggested are probably examples of the *post hoc, ergo propter hoc* fallacy.

21.2
Arg

Non Sequitur. The label *non sequitur* ("it does not follow") applies to errors of reasoning in which the conclusion does not follow from the evidence presented. Sometimes a step in reasoning has been omitted, and the fallacy can be corrected by supplying the missing link. But sometimes the conclusion is drawn from evidence that has no bearing on the issue: that Mary Starr uses a particular toothpaste has nothing to do with its quality; that a man does not beat his wife has nothing to do with whether he is a good husband; that the army teaches useful skills has nothing to do with the wisdom of sending troops to other countries.

Begging the Question. This term applies to an argument that assumes the truth of what needs to be proved. A politician who argues "Our feeble county government, desperately in need of reform, must be placed in new hands on election day" is begging the question unless he *proves* that the present government is feeble and in need of reform. Similarly, the student who challenges the C grade he received on a paper on the grounds that he is an "A student" is unconvincing since his premise is exactly what is under question.

Ignoring the Question. This is a broad term that applies to all arguments that are irrelevant, as when a governor argues that his administration is not corrupt because the state budget is balanced. Another way he might ignore the issue would be to resort to an *argumentum ad hominem* ("argument against the man"), attacking the integrity of his opponents rather than the charge of his own corruption. Or he might use *glittering generalities* such as "my devotion and dedication to the fine people of this great state" to draw his audience into acquiescence by the weight of good words.

Either/Or. An easy fallacy to fall into is the division of a complex issue into two sharply opposing parts: either we rapidly build up our military strength or we capitulate to the Eastern Bloc; either we unilaterally disarm or we face nuclear oblivion; either the manager goes or the whole office staff quits. Such ultimatums possess rhetorical drama and undeniable audience appeal. Yet they usually get in the way of more serious and more sophisticated analyses based on other alternatives.

21.2
Arg

When you have finished the first draft of an argumentative paper, examine it carefully for flaws. Have you weighed the available evidence? Are your generalizations supported by fact? Are your inferences valid? Make sure that your argument is both honest and sound.

Exercise 21.B

Look for several pieces of argumentation and bring them to class for discussion. In each, try to determine just what the central topic of debate is and what kind of evidence the writer uses. Notice what kind of relationship the writer tries to establish with the audience. Test the argument against your own judgment and common sense and against the fallacies listed above. You may find it helpful to look at newspaper editorials, letters to editors, advertisements, television commercials, graffiti, bumper stickers, political and social commentary in magazines. ◼

Exercise **21.C**

Examine the following premises. Which might be acceptable to a "general" audience? For premises that would not be widely accepted, describe the specific audience to which they might appeal or serve as the starting point of arguments.

1. Bigger is better.
2. What's good for General Motors is good for the U.S.A.
3. A fetus is a developing human being.
4. Give me liberty or give me death.
5. The right of the worker to strike is inalienable.
6. Chemicals are unnatural.
7. A point is a location in space without length, width, or depth.
8. A good dramatic plot is unified in time, location, and action.
9. Plagiarism is unacceptable academic behavior.
10. Haste makes waste.

21.2
Arg

Exercise **21.D**

Examine the following statements for logical or argumentative flaws. Identify any fallacies you detect in them.

1. It always rains on Good Friday.
2. Men are aggressive and insensitive.
3. "I couldn't have stolen that watch; I'm an honest person."
4. We have to choose between a clean environment and a healthy economy.
5. Of course we lost. The team was out on the town last night.
6. Professors are like eggs; they come hard-boiled or scrambled.
7. A little hard work never killed anyone.
8. He's not a good carpenter, but he is a nice man.
9. She must be a good teacher. Her classes are always full.
10. He's a bigot. He wouldn't sign the petition.

22

USING
OUTLINES

An outline should never be a mere exercise. Instead it should represent your effort to think through your subject, breaking your essay into its components so that you can judge how the whole will satisfy your purpose and audience. The following sections discuss the major types and traditional forms of outlines, explaining how they can serve you at various stages in the writing process.

22.1 Types of Outlines

Four kinds of outlines are widely used: the scratch outline, the thesis statement outline, the topic outline, and the sentence outline. Sometimes your instructor will tell you which form to use. When you have no specific instructions, select the form that best suits your method of working and the kind of paper you are writing. In planning a long paper, especially one involving research, you will probably want to make a topic or sentence outline. For short papers and extemporaneous writing, informal notes or a scratch outline will generally serve the purpose. Even for long papers, you may find it useful to work informally for some time before committing yourself to a final, detailed plan. It is not uncommon, for example, for writers at work on long projects to draft key passages—an opening paragraph, a closing paragraph, a passage developing the central idea—and then to fit these bits of writing into a more formal plan, along with jotted notes, sentences, and other scraps of ideas. Whatever techniques you use, the important thing is to develop a plan that will guide you in writing your paper.

Scratch Outlines

A scratch outline is a series of notes—single words or phrases—jotted down to refresh your memory as you write. An outline of this sort is useful when time is limited, as when you are writing examinations or brief papers in class. The following is a sample scratch outline for a lengthy paper on telescopes.

The Development of the Telescope
1. Galileo and the basic refractor
2. The multi-element telescopes of the eighteenth and nineteenth centuries
3. Newton and the reflecting telescope
4. The construction of massive reflecting telescopes
5. The advantages and limitations of refracting and reflecting designs

22.1
Out

The exact form of a scratch outline is unimportant since ordinarily you will be the only one who sees it. You can modify or rearrange the list in any way to suit your purposes.

Thesis Statement Outline

If the essay you are writing calls for a thesis statement (p. 354), you may find that the statement itself provides the terms for an outline that organizes the entire paper. A thesis statement which gives structure to your entire effort can also be helpful in writing essay exams and other short papers. It can also serve as an extension of some of the invention techniques discussed in Chapter 20.

Suppose, for example, you are asked to write a short paper on the topic of *mass media*. A combination of brainstorming and asking exploratory questions (see pp. 346–49) leads you to develop the following list of ideas on this general subject:

Influence of Mass Media on Our Lives
—Can increase our range of knowledge and awareness

—Influence begins early: young children learn commercial jingles or wear T-shirts with media heroes printed on them

—Serves as a common pool of information, a national unifying force. Power of national news networks

—Our political awareness may be shaped by selective news coverage and media bias

—Media programming may influence our taste in movies, dress, food, etc.

—Media (radio, TV, films) are passive entertainments, perhaps replacing one-to-one human relationships

—Media advertising shapes our notion of the "good life" and influences our values

It is possible to arrange these notes as a scratch outline, as suggested above. Further work, however, might enable you to exercise tighter control over your topic by formulating a thesis statement such as this:

22.1

Out

While the mass media, especially television and radio, have extended our awareness of the world and provided us with a common pool of cultural understanding, they may also be blamed for weakening our individuality and depersonalizing our contact with our own culture.

This thesis statement can then serve as a guide for the rest of the essay; it suggests some of the directions the subsequent essay might take. Here is a brief conceptual outline suggesting how an idea might develop from random thoughts reshaped into a thesis.

Part 1: Opening
I'll introduce the essay by providing several specific examples of media influence on American life—for example, of sports fanatics gathering to watch *Monday Night Football*.

Part 2
In this part I'll point out some of the ways media bring us ideas and events we might otherwise miss—for example, foreign news events.

Part 3
Here I'll talk about the ways television and radio bring us together by increasing the cultural expectations we share with others—for example, children across the country

know the same cartoon characters and adults discuss the same soap operas.

Part 4

This will be the pivotal section of the essay, where my focus shifts from the good done by the media to the problems caused by television, radio, and so on.

Part 5

Here I'll get at the heart of the problem: our passive role of receiving but not directly responding to media communications makes us particularly receptive to media standardization and regimentation—for example, except in the most limited way (telephone call-ins, telephone polls, some limited two-way cable service), we cannot challenge positions espoused by news analysts or media politicians in a face-to-face manner.

Part 6

Here I'll make the major point my essay seems to have been leading to: we are allowing media to depersonalize our thinking and recreation. Maybe I'll use the example of Hal the computer from the movie *2001* to illustrate the fears we might have about machines penetrating our lives.

Part 7: Conclusion

I'll probably conclude by admitting that the mass media have, indeed, extended our awareness of the world and made most of us more intelligent and sophisticated. But I'll also suggest that the quality of life we experience has diminished because of the media: we think and act as large groups do, not as creative, unpredictable individuals.

22.1

Out

Thinking through how you might develop a given thesis idea in this way allows you to detect the strengths and weaknesses of your position. Your observations might even lead you to revise the thesis statement substantially:

> Although the mass media may be blamed for weakening our individuality and depersonalizing our contact with our own culture, by and large the influence of television, radio, and other forms of communication has been positive, extending our awareness of the world and providing us with a common pool of cultural resources.

A short essay developed from this sentence would have a totally different emphasis from the one outlined above.

Topic Outlines

The topic outline, the most frequently used kind of formal outline, is helpful in organizing longer papers. It consists of brief phrases or single words (not sentences) that are numbered or lettered to show the order and relative importance of the ideas.

While topic outlines often seem precise and formal, they should be treated as part of the writing process. Developing such an outline can help you arrive at a satisfying plan for developing your ideas. The first thing to do in preparing a topic outline is to get all your ideas on paper. Let's say you have brainstormed the subject "The Army as a Career for College Men and Women" and produced this rough, unsorted list of ideas:

Security
Promotion slow but steady
Many different branches appeal to different interests
Low pay
Commissioned ranks open to men and women graduates
Can't be fired
Cost of uniforms
Discipline often annoying
Frequent moves hard on soldier's family
See interesting places and people
Social life restricted to small circle
Good retirement benefits
Annual vacation with pay
Military job training useful in civilian careers

22.1
Out

Determining the Central Idea

Looking at your list, you discover that some points stress the advantages of an army career, others the disadvantages. The next step is to divide the notes into two columns:

Advantages

Security
Promotion slow but steady
Many different branches appeal to different interests
Can't be fired
See interesting places and people
Good retirement benefits

Annual vacation with pay
Commissioned ranks open to men and women graduates
Military job training useful in civilian careers

Disadvantages

Low pay
Cost of uniforms
Discipline often annoying
Frequent moves hard on soldier's family
Social life restricted to small circle

In this form the relationship between the various ideas is not shown (What is the relationship between "Promotion slow but steady" and "Many different branches appeal to different interests"?) and there is no clear balance between the two columns (Is "Security" supposed to balance "Low pay"?). In analyzing the columns, however, you can see that there are two main ideas in each—the financial aspect of an army career and the living conditions that go with army life. You might then balance the notes in this way:

22.1

Out

I. Financial aspect
   A. Disadvantages
      1. Low pay
      2. Cost of uniforms
   B. Advantages
      1. Security
      2. Promotion slow but steady
      3. Commissioned ranks open to men and women graduates
      4. Can't be fired
      5. Good retirement benefits
      6. Annual vacation with pay
      7. Military job training useful in civilian careers
II. Social aspect
   A. Disadvantages
      1. Discipline often annoying
      2. Frequent moves hard on soldier's family
      3. Social life restricted to small circle
   B. Advantages
      1. Many different branches appeal to different interests
      2. See interesting places and people

Arranging the notes in some system may help you decide on a main point you want to make in your paper. "The Army as a Career for College Men and Women" doesn't tell what you are going to say about the subject; it is a title, not a central idea.

At this stage you can see that there is more and stronger material on the financial advantages of a military career than on its disadvantages. On the other hand, the disadvantages of living conditions seem to outweigh the advantages. Assuming that you want to treat the subject fully and in a favorable light, you could frame a tentative statement of purpose: "Although there are definite disadvantages to an army career, the advantages outweigh them." This statement will now govern the reworking of the outline. At this stage it is still tentative and can be changed as the purpose becomes clearer in your mind.

Revising the Outline

With the central idea as your guide, you can arrange the outline so that every part of it contributes directly to the purpose of the paper. Examine each heading to see if it needs to be strengthened or elaborated upon, if it repeats or overlaps another heading, or if it is unrelated to the central idea.

In the first part of the outline "Cost of uniforms" seems to be a weak point. Aren't officers given allowances for their uniforms? Possibly "Expense of frequent entertaining" is a stronger point, so substitute it for "Cost of uniforms."

The financial advantages of an army career seem to stand out, but looking at these entries carefully, you will see that some overlap or are actually minor parts of other points. The heading "Security" obviously covers "Slow but steady promotion," "Commissioned ranks open to men and women graduates," and "Can't be fired." Closer examination reveals that "Annual vacation with pay" is an aspect of living conditions rather than of finances; it should therefore be shifted to the second main heading.

Under "Advantages" in the second main heading, the first entry, "Many different branches appeal to different interests," seems out of place or else incorrectly phrased. Perhaps the point is that military people may be able to find jobs they like or are best fitted for.

As the plan now stands, the first part seems stronger. To make the argument more convincing, it would be a good idea to reverse the present order: begin with "Living conditions," and then end the paper on an emphatic note—the training that the army affords for success in other fields. After these changes have been made, and after some headings have been reworded to make them parallel in form, the final outline might be:

Thesis statement: Although from the standpoint of living conditions and finances there are some disadvantages to an army career for college men and women, the advantages outweigh those disadvantages.

   I. Living conditions
      A. Disadvantages
         1. Discipline often annoying
         2. Frequent moves hard on family
         3. Social life restricted to a small circle
      B. Advantages
         1. Opportunity to find the job one is suited for
         2. Annual leaves with pay
         3. Chance to travel, to see new places, and to meet new people
  II. Financial considerations
      A. Disadvantages
         1. Low pay
         2. Frequent entertaining expensive
      B. Advantages
         1. Security
            a. Slow but steady promotion, including commissions for men and women graduates
            b. Permanent employment
            c. Good retirement benefits
         2. Preparation for success in civilian careers after retirement

The outline now can be the basis for an orderly paper that makes a definite point. It can also serve as a guide for a reader of the finished essay.

Sentence Outlines

A sentence outline is developed in the same way as a topic outline, but the ideas are more fully stated. Each heading is expressed as a complete sentence, usually consisting of just one main clause:

Thesis statement: Although from the standpoint of finances and living conditions there are some disadvantages to an army career for college men and women, the advantages outweigh those disadvantages.

I. Living conditions are a major consideration in choosing a career.
  A. Army life has several shortcomings in this respect.
    1. The strict discipline imposed is often annoying.
    2. Frequent moves are hard on an officer's family.
    3. Social life is usually restricted to a small circle of army families.
  B. On the other hand, there are certain advantages to life in the army.
    1. The military, with its wide range of occupations, gives one an opportunity to find the job he or she is best suited for.
    2. There are generous annual leaves with pay.
    3. Wide travel opportunities can introduce one to new places and people.
II. Financial considerations are also of major importance.
  A. Two disadvantages are apparent.
    1. Army pay is low compared to that in many civilian jobs.
    2. Officers are burdened with the cost of frequent entertaining.
  B. The advantages, however, are more striking.
    1. The army offers a high degree of job security.
      a. Promotions are slow but steady, with commissions open to men and women graduates.
      b. There is almost no danger of dismissal.
      c. Retirement benefits are good.
    2. An army career is an excellent preparation for success in civilian careers after retirement.

22.1

Out

Note these three criteria of a sentence outline:

1. Each heading is a complete, single sentence, not two or three.
2. Each sentence is in the form of a statement, not a question.
3. All the sentences are in the same tense.

The chief advantage of a sentence outline is that your ideas will have to be relatively clear and well-conceived before they can be stated in complete sentences. For this reason, instructors sometimes assign sentence outlines as a prelude to writing long formal reports, such as the research paper, or as final outlines developed from longer papers.

Exercise **22.A**

1. Choose three of the following general subjects, narrow them to a topic specific enough for a short in-class paper, and write a scratch outline for each.

Population growth	College admissions
Study abroad	standards
Student summer work	Computer literacy
Television standards	Foreign cars
Automobile safety	Medical ethics
standards	Religion in America today
Automation	High school athletic
Popular myths	programs

2. Write a scratch outline on any one of the following topics that appeals to you, or choose your own. When you have jotted down all your notes, frame a thesis statement and put the notes in the form of a topic outline.

Why People Watch Excavations
Should Physical Education Be Required in College?
Income Is Not the Primary Goal of Education
Speaking in Public
Unusual Place Names
Forecasting Election Results
I Prefer Bach
Our Local Parking Problem
Mass Transit in America
How the American Family Has Changed
Why People Go to Boxing Matches
Why Soap Operas Are So Popular
College Is Not the Only Path to the Future
The Distribution of Wealth in My Hometown

3. Choose one of the topics in the exercise above and develop it more fully into a complete sentence outline.

4. Examine a published essay. Can you extract an outline from it? Does it follow a coherent plan? Does it have to follow a rigid pattern to communicate effectively? Discuss. ∎

22.2 Standard Outline Form

Numbering, indention, punctuation, and other physical aspects of outlines follow certain conventions, particularly when the outlines are to be read by someone other than the writer. When you are required to turn in an outline with your paper, use the type of outline your instructor specifies and put it in standard form.

Numbering and Indention

Make the numbering of your headings consistent throughout. This is the typical method for numbering and indenting a topic or sentence outline:

Thesis statement: _____

I. _____   (sentence statement)
    _____   (roman numeral for main
    _____   head)
    A. _____   (capital letter for subhead)
        1. _____   (arabic numeral for sec-
        2. _____   ond subhead)
            a. _____   (lowercase letter for third
            b. _____   subhead)
    B. _____
II. _____

The main heads (I, II, III . . .) are set flush with the left-hand margin. The subheads are indented four or five spaces in typed copy and about three-quarters of an inch in longhand, or they may be indented so that they are directly under the first word of the preceding heading, as shown in this book.

When a heading runs over one line, the second line is indented as far as the first word of the preceding line:

I. The photoelectric cell, known as the "electric eye," has been put to a variety of practical uses.
    A. It is used in elevator floors to enable the elevator to stop at exactly the right level.

When you make an outline, avoid overelaborate and confusing systems. There is rarely any need to go farther than the third subhead (a, b, c . . .). Two levels of headings are often enough for a short paper.

Punctuation and Capitalization

In a topic outline, capitalize only the first letter of the word beginning the heading (and all proper nouns), and do not put any punctuation at the end of the entry because these headings are not complete sentences.

> I. Present need for physicists
>   A. In private industry
>   B. In government projects

Punctuate every heading in a sentence outline just as you would punctuate the sentences in your paper: begin with a capital letter and end with a period. Except for proper nouns, other words in the heading are not capitalized (a heading is not a title).

> I. The advantages of specialization in college are many.
>   A. Students can set goals for themselves.
>   B. They can obtain more knowledge about their subjects.

Content of Headings

Each heading in an outline should be specific and meaningful. Headings like "Introduction," "Body," and "Conclusion" aren't useful unless you indicate what material belongs in the sections. Instead of using general labels such as "Causes" and "Results," indicate what the causes or results are.

Putting headings in the form of questions or in statements that will have to be filled in later is not an efficient practice. The necessary information will have to be supplied when you write, so you might as well supply it in the planning stage.

Indefinite

> I. The Wars of the Roses
>   A. When they began
>   B. Why?

Definite

> I. The Wars of the Roses
>   A. Started 1455
>   B. Caused by rivalry between Houses of Lancaster and York

Dividing the Material

Generally, if a heading is to be divided at all, it should be divided into more than one part. When there is only one heading under a topic, it usually repeats what is in the topic and should therefore be included with it:

Unnecessary division

The Smithsonian Institution
I. Established by an Englishman
  A. James Smithson
    1. In 1846

Accurate division

The Smithsonian Institution
I. Established by James Smithson,
  an Englishman, in 1846

22.2

Out

The heads of an outline should represent equally important divisions of the subject as a whole, and should be parallel in grammatical form and tense. In a topic outline, if *I* is a noun, *II* and *III* are also nouns; if *I* is a prepositional phrase, so are *II* and *III*. The same principle applies to subdivisions. A sentence outline should use complete sentences throughout and not lapse into topic headings.

Unequal headings	*Equal headings*
Growing Roses	Growing Roses
I. Preparing the soil	I. Preparing the soil
II. Planting	II. Planting
III. Growing the plant	III. Watering
IV. Mildew	IV. Fertilizing
V. Insect pests	V. Spraying
VI. Using a spray gun	

The subdivisions should also designate equally important and parallel divisions of one phase of the main divisions:

Unequal subheads	*Equal subheads*
I. Job opportunities in Wisconsin	I. Job opportunities in Wisconsin
A. Raising crops	A. Agriculture
B. White-collar work	B. Business
C. Dairy farms	C. Industry
D. Factory jobs	
E. Breweries	

Headings of equal rank should not overlap: what is in *II* should exclude what is covered in *I; B* should be clearly distinct from *A*.

22.2

Out

Overlapping	*Accurate*
Ways of transporting freight	Ways of transporting freight
I. Water	I. Ship
A. Ships	A. Passenger ships
B. Freighters	B. Freighters
II. On the ground	II. Truck
A. Trucks	III. Railroad
B. "Piggyback" in trucks	A. Loaded into cars
III. Railroads	B. "Piggyback" in trucks
IV. In the air	IV. Airplane

Exercise **22.B**

Check the following outlines from the standpoint of effective and useful planning. Then state specifically what you consider to be the unsatisfactory aspects of each one, in form and content. Revise the outlines accordingly.

1.   Types of American schools

    I. Schools open to everyone
       A. Elementary schools
       B. There are many colleges and universities
       C. Secondary or high
       D. Providing technical instruction
       E. Private schools

2.   Why everyone should be able to swim.

     I. Everyone should learn to swim.
       A. As early as possible.
         1. Children have been taught as young as three years
    II. The ability to swim may save your life.
       1. never swim alone
       2. don't show off in the water
       3. Many schools require students to pass swimming tests.
         a. my experiences
         b. Red Cross lifesaving test

3.   Increasing automation in industry presents many problems.

22.2
Out

     I. Unemployment
       A. Permanent layoffs
       B. Shorter working hours
       C. Decreases job opportunities
    II. What is automation?
       A. Definition
       B. Uses
         1. Where it cannot be used
       C. there are many advantages to automation
    III. Increased leisure time
       A. Recreation
         1. Hobbies
         2. Traveling
         3. Adult education classes
    IV. New skills are required.
       A. Trained technicians
       B. The unskilled workers are laid off.
         1. Providing government benefits
         2. Providing added training
     V. Is automation here to stay?

4.   Computer literacy

     I. What is computer literacy?
       A. Computer languages
       B. Learning to read and write computer languages

      C. Knowing how to talk about computers
         1. acronyms
         2. technical jargon
         3. overcoming fear of computers
      D. Example of COBOL language
      E. Job prospects for computer programmers
         1. salaries
         2. job security and benefits

5.   Ways of earning money in a pinch

    A. Donating blood
    B. Participating in medical experiments
    C. Selling used books and records
    D. Careful budgets can prevent problems
    E. Consider taking a part-time job

23

DRAFTING,
REVISING,
AND EDITING

The preceding chapters examined some of the major questions you face as you prepare to write: What is my purpose? What is my audience? What do I know about my subject? How can I find out more about it? How do I develop and arrange what I want to say? These issues do not disappear the minute you begin to write your first draft. Instead they remain the questions that will guide you as you draft, revise, rewrite, and edit a piece. This chapter is about writing the essay itself, the whole complicated process of getting words down on paper or up on a word processor screen in a form that suits you, your assignment, and your readers. It provides you with strategies and suggestions for handling the choices and problems you face when you write. The next chapter is the "real-life" version of this one: it shows how one student went about writing a paper. His process does not always match the procedures recommended here because, as you probably know, every assignment poses different challenges and writers address them in different ways. But the two chapters taken together should give you some practical tips for making your own writing process more skillful and efficient.

23.1 Getting Started: The First Draft

For many assignments, getting started means acquiring a workable notion of what the assignment is, for whom it is being written, and how the subject can be developed and organized. These concerns are addressed in Chapters 19–22.

But getting started can also mean finally getting some words on paper—not an easy task for either the student or the professional writer. Most of us can find a dozen reasons for putting off the writing we have to do: We decide that we just have to wash the car, for example. Or, taking our task more seriously, we convince ourselves that we must do more background reading and research. We pretend to have writer's block. We wait for some spirit to move and inspire our composition.

Bad strategies, all of them. Don't wait for inspiration or the proper mood—start writing while the ideas and information you have gathered from adequate (not exhaustive) preparation are still in your mind. You will learn as much about your subject by writing about it as you have by reading about it. Writing is a way of learning.

Beginning the Draft

The beginning of a paper is often the most difficult part to word effectively. If you can't think of a good opening sentence, begin with some other part; if the wording of a good first paragraph doesn't come to you at once, start with a part that comes more easily. You shouldn't waste time trying to get an ideal opening; as you work, a good start will often occur to you. Many beginnings are written last. (See 25.5, Opening Paragraphs.)

Once you have broken the ice by writing two or three sentences, you'll often find it easier to go on, even without that elusive "inspiration." Writing, like many other activities, calls for a warm-up, and you may have to do a few laps and some wind sprints before you're ready to go.

As a rule, write the first draft as rapidly as you can. Your paper will have more life if you put your ideas down one after the other without pausing to worry about correctness. At this stage you should concentrate on getting down the gist of what you have in mind.

Plan to write your rough draft uninterrupted, if possible. When you are working on a paper that is too long to be written in one sitting, it sometimes helps to stop in the middle of a paragraph or a passage that is going easily and well, perhaps even in the middle of a sentence. This ordinarily makes it easier to get started again when you come back to your work. Take time to read over what you have already written before you begin writing again.

Leave plenty of space in the first draft for making corrections and changes. There should be ample margins on both sides of the page and space between lines for insertions and corrections.

Make the first draft as complete as possible. Write down more than you will probably use in your final paper; be generous with explanations and illustrative examples. It is much easier to cut out material in revision than it is to look for more to satisfy the requirements of length or completeness of presentation. Papers that are heavy with material added at the last moment always seem disjointed. Those that have been pruned down from, say, fourteen hundred to a thousand words are likely more compact and to the point.

Put in any good ideas that occur to you while you are writing the first draft, even though they might not have appeared in the original plan. If you are using an outline, you need not follow it down to the last minor subdivision. Frequently a sentence written on paper will bring to mind an aspect of the topic you overlooked when your material was in note form. If the new idea turns out to be irrelevant, it can be omitted in revision; but if it is important, you can alter your plan to include it.

23.1

Draft

Framing a Title

The title of your paper should give a definite and accurate idea of the subject matter in as few words as possible. Especially in informative writing, a title need not mystify or startle readers, although it may perhaps arouse their curiosity or appeal to their sense of humor. Interesting titles are usually welcome, but one that is brief, simple, and exact will serve the purpose. Consider how important a clear, descriptive title is to you when you search a card catalogue, index, or bibliography.

A title should not suggest more than the paper actually covers. If you are discussing your tastes in music, avoid such sweeping titles as "Modern Jazz" or "Music of Today"; use instead "Music I Like" or "Why I Prefer Billy Idol Over Billy Joel." A report on the experiences of a baby-sitter scarcely deserves the title "Child Psychology" or "The Care of Infants"; "Experiences of a Baby-Sitter" will be good enough if you cannot think of a better title.

Unnecessarily long titles are not satisfactory, especially those that merely repeat the assignment: "An Experience in Childhood That Left a Lasting Impression on Me." The thesis statement of your paper is not intended to serve as a title. Instead of writing "Reading Taught by Sound Should Replace Sight Reading," name the subject: "Reading by Sound."

The title is not part of the paper, and it should not be referred to by a pronoun in the first sentence. If you want to mention the title in your opening, rephrase it slightly.

23.2 Revising

When you have completed a rough draft, you may want to consider the advice E. B. White, a great essayist, gives in *Elements of Style:*

> Do not be afraid to seize whatever you have written and cut it to ribbons; it can always be restored to its original condition in the morning, if that course seems best. Remember, it is no sign of weakness or defeat that your manuscript ends up in need of major surgery. This is a common occurrence in all writing, and among the best writers.

His words should be some comfort to anyone who fears that a good writer is someone who gets it right the first time. In truth, a good writer may be someone who gets it right the second or third or fourth time.

When you have finished that first draft, try putting it aside for a while before you think about it any more or check it over or revise it. Most people find it difficult to look at their own writing carefully and critically while the ideas they have tried to express are still running about in their minds. For this reason, it's helpful to write a first draft as early as possible, so that you can wait a day or two (or at least several hours) before examining it. If the assignment gives you time to write a draft and put it aside for a week or two, you may be astonished to discover how perceptive a critic you are when you return to it for revision.

Substituting, Adding, Cutting, and Rearranging

Many students believe that revising a paper means simply repairing faults of grammar, spelling, and punctuation and improving word choice. They like to think that they can adequately revise a paper by making a few marks on the original version and rewriting or retyping the essay. Often they simply incorporate the comments and corrections a teacher or colleague has made in the margin of their draft and think they have done enough.

To revise adequately, you must be willing to do far more than just substitute one word or phrase for another. Often an early draft is underdeveloped: it does not present its ideas fully enough for readers to appreciate them. When this is the case, you are not likely to improve a draft much if you only correct the more obvious mechanical errors and fail to add more examples, more evidence, and more detailed arguments. How much is the following paragraph improved when only the surface errors are taken care of in version 2?

23.2
Rev

1. American foreign policy is a concern of each and every American citizen. Truly, we must except the fact that what is done by the foreign policymakkers in our goverment influence our daily lifes. Foreign policy is a big factor in our American political system as it is in every political system in the world.

2. American foreign policy is a concern of each citizen. We must accept that what is done by the foreign policymakers in our government influences our lives. Foreign policy is a big factor in our political system, just as it is in every political system in the world.

The improvement is insignificant. Version 2 may have fewer errors than _1_, but both paragraphs lack a mature subject, interesting details, an issue worth discussing. Real revision in this case means making major _additions:_

American foreign policy becomes a concern of each citizen when the President decides he must intervene in the affairs of another country by introducing American marines or naval forces, or when Congress approves a treaty that deals with the security of the United States. At such times—frequent in our history—the lives and treasure of ordinary citizens are in the hands of the decision makers in Washington. What controls do we have over these officials, many of them unelected bureaucrats in the state department, to assure that citizens have a voice in shaping the way the U.S. government faces the world?

Sometimes, your first draft may be too long, or too thorough in presenting facts to an audience already familiar with them. Or perhaps some of your paragraphs veer away from a main point. Or maybe you just ramble. In these cases, you may have to cut what you have written, a process as painful for many writers as losing weight. You shouldn't become so attached to what you have written that you cannot bear the thought of cutting words, sentences, or even whole paragraphs and sections when your readers are better served by a leaner, more direct text:

23.2

Rev

> By the second day of our Alaskan cruise, I felt like a Roman emperor, reveling in daily banquets. ~~The emperors of Rome were famous for their elaborate feasts and gustatory orgies that often lasted days.~~ They fed us food as if they had never heard of fat and we had never heard of cholesterol and heart attacks. ~~Although some medical studies now suggest that a certain amount of cholesterol may be useful to the body.~~ There were apples and oranges in our rooms, and lush purple plums. The meals were beyond believing. And the dessert table sent me into ecstacy.

Perhaps the most difficult revision to make is one involving the rearrangment of your text. You may discover that the lead sentence of a paragraph serves better as its conclusion, or that the order of examples is stronger if you place the more common ones first and the more intriguing ones later to keep readers interested. Such alterations can be made relatively easily, but revision often goes beyond tinkering with sentences or individual examples. Sometimes you may have to move whole paragraphs or rethink the overall plan of the essay. In these cases the rearrangement you commit yourself to may be felt in every part of the essay, like the aftershocks of a minor earthquake. Writers are often reluctant, understandably, to consider major rearrangements of their drafts, yet such changes may be needed if a piece is to succeed. There is more risk involved when you make major changes, but there are also greater opportunities.

When you revise, you must be as willing to add, cut, and rearrange as you are to substitute one word or phrase for another. Revision is not an incidental, optional part of composing—it is the key to the entire process.

Getting Feedback

At times you will be the only person who sees the drafts you prepare for an assignment and, consequently, you may have to rely on your judgment alone to guide revisions. However, writers at all levels and in all professions often seek comments and opinions about the writing they are working on. In many professional situations, writing is a collaborative effort undertaken by teams or committees to capitalize on their members' individual strengths. In academic situations, you are usually expected to be responsible for your own work. But that should not prevent you from soliciting the honest advice and assistance of colleagues, reputable tutors, instructors in a writing laboratory, and, most important, your teachers.

23.2
Rev

You should ask for advice and opinions—not corrections. Tutors and friends who "fix up" your prose can involve you in serious situations of scholastic dishonesty, possibly leading to failure in a course or expulsion from a college or university. What you want to know when you hand a draft to someone for review is how well the essay works. Where is it unclear or dull? What are its strengths and weaknesses? Is it informative or persuasive? Does it reach its intended audience? If the essay needs improvement, it is up to you to initiate and make the changes. Getting feedback as you produce an essay is both appropriate and useful. The writing won't be read in a vacuum; it needn't be produced in one either.

In an increasing number of writing courses, teachers are putting their comments on drafts of essays rather than on final versions. Doing this allows the students to understand their problems and opportunities early on and to incorporate improvements into the final version, not find out their weaknesses when it is too late to do much about them.

When you get a draft back, approach your job of revising systematically. Don't try to change everything at once. The questions listed in the following sections may help you organize your revision process.

Revising for Purpose and Audience

Your first two concerns when reviewing a draft should be how well the piece fits your assignment and how well it suits the audience who will read it. Returning to the original assignment sheet is a wise practice whether you are following a teacher's instructions, a foundation's specifications for a grant proposal, or a journal, magazine, or newspaper's criteria for submitting an article. Review your essay with the intended audience in mind.

Trying to read your draft once through the eyes of potential readers can be a practical exercise. Ideally, you may find someone from that group willing to read your draft and comment on it.

1. Does your work satisfactorily meet the expectations of the assignment?
2. Have you explained difficult concepts at a level appropriate to your audience? Is your vocabulary too specialized or not technical enough?
3. Have you defined terms that almost everyone in your audience will recognize, but left difficult words and concepts unexplained?

Revising for Content

When you have finished a draft, check to see whether you have provided all the information, answered all the questions, made all the arguments, or refuted all the objections you intended to. Even if you have done what you hoped to, you need to ask yourself, "Is it enough?"

1. Have you shown the significance of your facts sufficiently, or do you leave a reader asking, "So what?"
2. Have you explained the reasons behind your statements, or do you leave your readers asking, "Why?"
3. Have you ignored an important perspective, given too few examples and illustrations, or relied on weak or inappropriate sources?

4. Are all your facts, figures, references, and dates accurate?
5. Have you presented your ideas adequately and those of others fairly?
6. Have you included only information that is relevant to your subject, or have you rambled?

Revising for Organization

Putting a draft aside for a day or two is a great help in detecting flaws in organization. Once again, you must try to put yourself in the position of a reader who is coming to your material fresh, someone who does not know beforehand what your pattern of development is or what reasons you had for inserting examples, arguments, transitions, and so on.

1. Will it be clear to a reader what your paper is about? Does each paragraph add something to the subject?
2. Can you point to explicit words that help a reader see the outline that underlies your paper? Have you indicated which ideas are of major importance and which are subordinate? Is there a logical progression in your piece?
3. If you are listing points (for example, advantages or reasons), have you listed them in an order that makes the best impression on readers, such as from most to least important or least important to most, or in an order determined by logical necessity, such as cause and effect? If you are comparing or contrasting, have you selected the most suitable pattern for your material?
4. If appropriate, does your paper move smoothly toward a climax? Is the conclusion logical?

Revising for Coherence and Cohesion

The material in your draft should fit together in a way that makes sense to your readers. Your audience should detect a cohesion in the links between sentences and paragraphs and find the entire piece readable. (For a more complete discussion of cohesion within and between paragraphs, see 25.4.)

1. Are there gaps in your thinking or between the ideas expressed at the end of one paragraph and the beginning of another?

23.2
Rev

2. Does each paragraph grow out of the topic of the preceding one? Will the linkages be clear to your readers?
3. Have you used transitional words and phrases to signal various relationships within and between paragraphs?

Revising for Style

Good style, the concern of Chapters 25–30, is important in any draft, but becomes progressively more important in your final versions, as you look for opportunities to add grace and polish.

1. Have you gotten rid of awkward phrases, bothersome repetitions, and wordy expressions?
2. Is the language of your essay natural? Does it sound like you?
3. Does the language suit the demands of your audience? Have you avoided jargon and clichés?
4. Is your essay readable?

23.2

Rev

Revising the Opening, Closing, and Title

Your opening and closing paragraphs and your title are worth more than a second glance, because the title and the opening should catch the interest of your reader, and the closing should leave the reader with a sense of satisfaction that you've rounded to a close. (For a more complete discussion of opening and closing paragraphs, see 25.5 and 25.6).

1. Does your opening paragraph get into your subject as directly as possible? If your first sentence is weak, does the second or third sentence, or even the second paragraph, make a better opening?
2. Is your conclusion emphatic, interesting, or forceful, or does it seem to trail off?
3. Is the conclusion an extension of your opening paragraph rather than a restatement of it or an abstract of your entire paper?
4. Does the title give a definite and accurate idea of the subject matter in as few words as possible? Is it brief, simple, and exact?

Exercise 23.A

1. Examine the draft of an essay you have written or a draft written by a colleague, asking four questions:
   a. How can this draft be improved by *substitutions,* that is, by replacing words, phrases, sentences, or whole paragraphs with better material?
   b. How can this draft be improved by *adding* new material?
   c. How can this draft be helped by *cutting* some of what it already contains?
   d. Can this draft be improved by some *rearrangements* of its material?

   Revise your draft in light of your answers or indicate to your classmate how his or her draft might be reworked.

2. Give a draft you are working on to several different people, asking for their general reaction to the piece and for some particular reactions. Be sure to tell them what your assignment is and who you expect your readers to be. Compare their reactions. Do they find the same strengths and weaknesses? Is it always possible to account for any disagreements in your reviewers' opinions? Be willing to serve as a critic for your colleagues' drafts. When you are a critic, be honest, helpful, and tactful.

3. Experiment with revision by taking a draft you have written in response to an assignment or by finding a short piece in an anthology or magazine and then shifting the audience, the purpose, or both. What changes would have to be made in the essay to accommodate the new purpose and audience? Would the changes be major or minor?

4. Examine a draft you have written from the point of revising the content. Can you defend your reasons for including some material and excluding other ideas, examples, illustrations, and so forth? How has your choice of audience influenced your decisions about content? How might your content change with a change of audience?

5. Examine the organization of a draft you or a classmate have written. Make at least one major change in organization, moving an entire paragraph, or reordering the major examples, or rearranging any pattern of develop-

23.2
Rev

ment you may have used. What are the consequences of
that change? Does it improve your piece?

6. Find a short essay in an anthology or magazine, make a
    copy of it, and underline every device in it that contrib-
    utes to its coherence. Look for ties between sentences
    and paragraphs. Look for the repetition of key words
    and phrases. Underline all transitional words. How
    much of the essay contributes to tying the piece to-
    gether?

    Do the same thing with a draft or essay you have
    written. Are your transitions adequate? How might the
    coherence and cohesion of your essay be enhanced?

7. Rewrite the opening and closing of an essay you have
    written or a draft you are working on. Show the original
    and revised versions to classmates. Which do they pre-
    fer? Which do you?

8. Work with several classmates on separate rewrites of the
    opening or closing paragraph of a single essay or draft
    you have all read. Compare your versions. Which seems
    to be the most effective revision? Can you explain why?
    Would several of the versions be acceptable, given dif-
    ferent audiences or purposes?

9. Come up with five or more titles for a draft you are
    working on. Which do you like best? Which is most ap-
    propriate in describing what you have done? Which
    might be most attractive to your readers? Show your ti-
    tles to classmates for their opinions.

23.3 Editing and Proofreading

Anything you compose, from a one-paragraph memo to a
forty-page senior thesis, may go through many versions before you feel confident that you've got it right. You may prepare multiple drafts of the entire effort, or work and rework
certain parts over and over again, leaving other portions com-
paratively untouched after the first draft. At some point,
though, you must decide that your work is finished: you have
done the best you can in the time available to you.

At this stage, you can begin to edit seriously. Editing is
the cleaning up of surface errors, everything from slips in
grammar and spelling to the correction of typographical er-

rors. Too much attention to these matters in the drafting and revising stages can get in the way of formulating ideas effectively. But you must eventually give concentrated attention to the mechanics of your writing.

If you have the time, put a clean version of your final draft aside for a while—several days are ideal, but several hours are often more practical. Then proofread the text carefully, line by line. No matter how perfect your final version may appear, give it this final check. Errors somehow creep into even the most careful writing.

Here are some of the things to look for as you proofread your essay:

1. Check spelling (see p. 288).
   —Look for transposed letters.
   —Look for slips of the pen.
   —Look for illegible words.
   —Look for omitted endings, especially *-ed* and *-s*.
2. Check possessive forms (see pp. 136, 163).
   —be sure not to forget the apostrophe (') before or after the *-s: boy's, boys'.*
   —Don't confuse *its* (possessive form) with *it's* (contraction for *it is).*
3. Check capitalization (see p. 254).
4. Check punctuation (see pp. 83, 194, 216, 221).
   —Make sure all sentences have end punctuation.
   —Check for comma splices.
   —Examine all semicolons for appropriateness.
5. Check to see that the title of your paper is in proper form (see pp. 241, 256).
   —Make sure that major words are capitalized.
   —Do not underline your title or capitalize each letter in it unless this is the form your teacher or institution requires.
6. Check to see that titles of books, articles, plays, television programs, works of art, songs, and other works mentioned in your paper are properly handled.
   —Titles of books, plays, and other long or major works are underlined (see p. 248).
   —Titles of articles, songs, short poems are set between quotation marks (see p. 248).
7. Check to see that you have used quotation marks and

parentheses properly and in pairs (the closing quotation marks and parenthesis are often forgotten).

8. Check the numbering of your pages.
9. Check subject/verb agreement (see p. 94).
10. Check agreement between pronouns and antecedents (see p. 155).
11. Check for dangling modifiers (see p. 72).
12. Check your parallel structures for consistency (see p. 497).
13. Check for unintentional fragments (see p. 77).
14. Check for words or phrases that have been omitted from your text, or words that have been inadvertently repeated.
15. Check for those errors that you have found in your previous work.

Making Corrections in the Final Copy

If you are using a word processor, you can correct errors easily on the screen before printing your page. When you are typing or handwriting your copy, changes and corrections should be kept to a minimum, particularly on important papers. When you have to make major changes in the final copy (rewording sentences, revising paragraphs), do the page over. For minor changes (spelling, punctuation, adding or striking out a word), make the corrections neatly and according to standard practices.

To add a word, use a caret (/\) and write the missing word directly above it:

Manuscript should easy to read.

To strike out a word, draw a straight line through it (don't use parentheses or brackets):

Final copy should be as ~~as~~ accurate as possible.

To indicate the beginning of a new paragraph where you have failed to indent, write the symbol ¶ immediately before the first word of the new paragraph:

So ended my first day away from home. The second day. . . .

To correct a misspelled word, draw a line through it and write the correct form directly above. This makes a neater and more legible correction than an erasure:

```
                                  quantity
Quality is more important than  qunity.
```

To indicate in typed copy that two letters should be reversed in order (transposed), use a curved line:

```
bewteen    recieve    Smiths' novel
```

23.4 Manuscript Form

Your teacher or employer may specify a particular form for the writing you do: the size and kind of paper; the width of margins; the numbering of pages; the kind of spacing, and so forth. Be sure to follow all such directions carefully. Typical college manuscript form is described in the following pages.

Typed Papers

If you have a typewriter and know how to use it, it is a good practice to type all papers prepared outside class. Typed manuscript is easier to read than most handwriting and makes a stronger impression. Most teachers are willing to accept papers done by printers attached to word processors provided that the quality of both print and paper is adequate. Check with your instructor beforehand to be sure.

In typing your final version, use unlined white 8½-by-11 inch paper, but not onionskin that lets the type show through.

Use double spacing throughout except for triple spacing before and after long (more than four lines) quotations.

Follow standard conventions in typing. For the figure 1 use lower case l (not capital I). For a dash use two hyphens with no space between the words and the dash:

```
The book--a first edition--was missing.
```

Check your work carefully for typographical errors. Uncorrected typing mistakes are usually considered errors.

Handwritten Papers

If you cannot type, you need not worry. With reasonable care, handwritten papers can be made just as acceptable as those that are well typed.

Use lined white paper, 8½ by 11 inches, with lines at least one-half inch apart. Writing done on closely lined paper is hard to read and difficult to correct. Do not use pages torn from spiral-bound notebooks, because their rough edges stick together. Use black or dark blue ink.

Handwritten papers should be easy to read. If a word looks misspelled or is difficult to decipher, it may be marked as an error. Handwriting that is too small puts an unnecessary strain on the eyes of the reader; handwriting that is excessively large is no less difficult to read. Try to strike a happy medium in size. If you have developed what you consider to be an individual style of penmanship, make certain that it will be as legible and attractive to others as it is to you. You might ask your teachers if they prefer you to double-space handwritten papers just as you would a typed one. The space between your lines of prose makes your handwriting more readable and leaves room for comments and revisions.

23.4

Form

Margins and Spacing

Leave ample margins on both sides of the page. An inch and a half on the left and an inch on the right are customary margins in handwritten and typed papers. Leave at least an inch and a half at the top and an inch at the bottom of every page.

Indent paragraphs uniformly. Five spaces from the left-hand margin is an acceptable indention for typed papers, and about an inch for those written in longhand. Don't indent any line that is not the beginning of a paragraph, even though it is the first line on a page. The last line on a page should not be left partly blank unless it is the end of a paragraph.

Don't crowd your writing at the bottom of a page. Start a new page, even if it will contain only a line or two.

Division of Words

Div **Divide the word marked according to the syllabication given in a reliable dictionary.**

If you leave plenty of room at the right-hand side of your page, you will not have to divide many words at the ends of the lines. It is a good idea to divide words only if writing them out or putting them on the next line would make the lines conspicuously uneven.

Words of one syllable should not be divided at all: *through, played, bright.* Also avoid breaking a word if a single letter will be left at the beginning or end of a line. There is no point in dividing a word like *a-lone;* the single letter at the end of the line is less attractive than the space left by carrying the whole word over to the next line. See 18.2, Spelling and Word Division.

Words spelled with a hyphen *(self-confidence, mother-in-law)* should be divided only at the hyphen.

Form of the Title

The title appears on the first page of your paper. On unlined paper, place it in the center about two inches from the top of the page or double-spaced from your name, course title, and so on (as instructed by your teacher); on lined paper, write the title on the top line. Leave a blank line between the title and the first line of the text.

23.4

Form

Capitalize the first and last words in your title and all others except short words like *and, the, a, an,* and prepositions of fewer than six letters:

> Breaking and Training a Horse
> How Not to Become Overweight
> The Art of Making Friends
> Strength Through Community

No period should be put after a title. However, if the title is expressed as a question or as an exclamation, it should be followed by the proper end punctuation.

> Why not ERA?   Man Overboard!

Titles are not enclosed in quotation marks. Even when familiar quotations are used as titles, no marks are needed:

> Blood, Sweat, and Tears   The Home of the Brave

Numbering Pages

The first page of a manuscript is not numbered. Begin with the second page, using Arabic numerals (2, 3, 4 . . .) for paging. Numbers are customarily put at the top of the page in the right-hand corner or in the center. Make certain that the pages of your paper are in the right order before you turn the paper in.

Long tables, diagrams, charts, and other material supplementary to the text itself are usually put on separate pages, placed near the part that refers to them, and numbered consecutively with the other pages.

It is not necessary to write *more* at the bottom of each page or to put *Finis* or *The End* at the conclusion.

Endorsing the Paper

Sign your papers as you are expected to. Include all the information that is asked for, and put it in the right order. Clear and uniform endorsement is a real convenience to the teacher who must handle the papers.

Ask your instructor how the papers should be submitted, whether folded, flat, or otherwise, and how they should be held together. Use binders only for longer papers.

23.4

Form

Exercise 23.B

1. Edit the following student essay. Write a helpful comment at the end, and assign the paper a grade. Compare your suggestions and evaluations with those made by others in the class.

"The Farmers and Food Prices"

When people complain about high food prices, the blame always ends up in the farmer's lap. "Those farmers are making a fortune and we're almost starving!" I hear people say. Well, I can tell you that the farmers do not make a fortune, and that compared to any other workers, farmers are overworked, underpaid, and have jobs with the most risk and least security.

Labor unions have decreed that laborers can work no more than forty hours a week without being paid overtime, which is time-and-a-half. And if you ask a laborer to work on Sundays or holidays, they get double-time. But the farmers have to work every day, often from sunup to sundown (which in the summer is over fourteen hours). Cows must be milked everyday. Sundays and holidays included.

And when the crops are ripe, the farmer's must work to harvest them seven days a week until all are in. There is no forty-hour week, no overtime, no double-time, for farmers.

Laborers have unions which negotiate wage contracts for them. Members of the most powerful unions get longevety and cost-of-living raises yearly. But farmers get paid what the food processors feel like paying them. They cannot strike for higher wages. The only thing they can do is withhold their crops from the market until prices rise to where they think they should be. But if they do that, people think their just being greedy, when really their only doing what laborers are doing, trying to get a living wage.

If you asked a laborer to work at a job where all the products he works on, through no fault of his own, can disintegrate over night and where he will get no pay if this happens, he will just laugh at you. But farmers do just that. They must work to get out a product which may or may not materialize, depending on purely outside influences, particularly inclement weather. If there is a too-wet spring, they cannot plant in time. If there is a too-wet fall, the harvest is delayed or sometimes even ruined. If there are shortages of gasoline or fertilizer, farm work will be held up. The farmers are at the mercy of the elements and the various chemical shortages that can happen at any time.

So, its not the farmers who make a killing while your food bill goes up. Any money they make can never fully pay them for the risk they take and the hard work they do day in the day out, year after year.

2. Edit one of your own recent drafts, paying particular attention to the proofreading checklist on pages 411–12.

_23.4_

Form

24

AN ESSAY IN PROGRESS

This chapter traces an actual student essay as it develops from an assignment sheet to a final version. Presented to you are the records of the writing process, the rough notes, drafts, comments, and revisions that contributed to the final piece. The writing was done for an English course by a freshman named Ken Duncan, an engineering major and gymnast from San Angelo, Texas. As part of a regular course assignment, he was asked to play the role of art critic, evaluating what he observed at one of the galleries in the Harry Ransom Center at the University of Texas at Austin. If his notes, drafts, and resulting paper sometimes seem imperfect or sketchy, it is precisely because composing does not ordinarily follow an ideal "handbook" model. What we hope the materials and commentary do show you is how—given the right effort and adequate time—ideas can be coaxed into appropriate language. Your writing process might not be the same as Ken Duncan's; it may be more systematic or less so. Compare what you do to what he's done here and find out.

24.1 Getting Started

About midway through a summer session freshman English course, Ken Duncan received this assignment sheet from his instructor:

English 306
Rhetoric and Composition
Essay of Evaluation

First draft: June 20
Final version: July 1

The Harry Ransom Center here on campus houses several
collections of art. You have received an invitation
(engraved, of course) to view the collections and to
critique one or more of the paintings or sculptures you
find especially intriguing. Your review is intended to
serve as a guide for your classmates, helping them to
understand why the work(s) you've chosen to discuss
deserve acclaim, or something less. Your readers do not
have a great knowledge of art, but they do expect your
review to be sensibly argued. They will want to know the
criteria you are using to evaluate the paintings or
sculptures, and they will expect you to describe the
pieces in sufficient detail for them to visualize what you
are examining. (All the artworks in the galleries have
names; be sure to use them.) Stated simply, your readers
want to know why you liked or disliked a given work. If
you are ambitious, you may try to evaluate an entire
collection or selected groupings of paintings and other
works.

Your readers expect a relatively short piece, but one that
is adequately developed and laden with precise details.

Enjoy your trip to the Harry Ransom Center!

24.1

Essay

Ken's first set of notes don't indicate whether he enjoyed his expedition to the gallery, but he clearly understands the assignment. Two sculptures catch his attention immediately and he sets down some preliminary descriptions:

> Solon H. Borgham   1868 – 1922
>
> <u>The Horse Wranglers</u> or <u>Bronco Busters</u>
> The sleek body of a fine American
> Quarterhorse Bronze adds the rustic
> look of an American Cowboy.
> holding rope in left hand
>
> Frederic Remington 1861 – 1909
> <u>Mountain Man</u>
> long hair, rifle, traps, sleeping
> bag. buckskin clothes. some
> animal skin as a cap, musket,
> powderhorn, large skinning Knife,
> sturdy horse going down a steep
> incline

Almost at the same time he is describing the objects he intends to evaluate, he begins brainstorming, jotting down phrases that define the criteria he will use in his paper. The notes are rough and preliminary. He starts with single sentences and words, but then begins generating tentative paragraphs as he explores the topic to see whether it will work. The notes (p. 421) indicate that Ken feels he has found his subject. His major technique for developing his material and focusing on his topic seems to be brainstorming (see 20.2). He does just a little freewriting and draws on his personal experiences as a way of understanding why he likes western art (see 20.1). Ken might have benefited from more extended freewriting at this stage since he clearly has some thoughts

Evaluation
Realistic

I want in my living room. It must be of the outdoors. It must be representational. It must have animals

To appreciate the art it helps to have seen the place that it is supposed to represent.

Make you understand the life it is supposed to represent.

Detail Powerful Moving

Western art is so easy for me to appreciate because I own two horses, have galloped through the thick brush of my grand-mother's ranch, have rounded up cattle, have gone down the steep rim rock.
   I can easily understand the excitement, the fear, the lonliness and power. These sculptures ~~easily~~ represent. I have experienced all these emotions cowboying on my grandmother's ranch. Few ~~the~~ art works from other times can make me understand the atmos-phere of that time. Paintings that can tell a viewer how the place smelled, how the earth felt, how the people felt are the true works of art.

worth exploring. But his initial notes are limited to what you have seen; he probably was eager to get a draft on paper. Although he does not work up even a scratch outline (see 22.1), it seems likely he'll proceed by discussing his criteria for evaluating the sculptures and then he'll examine each work individually.

24.2   The First Draft

Ken Duncan's first draft opens with a straightforward paragraph lacking polish but delivering the basic facts:

> My criteria for good art is that I would want to display it in my living room and that it would reflect my interests of hunting, fishing, skiing, and riding horses, or my proud heritage of living in West Texas. Therefore, I knew exactly what kind of art I wanted to see in the Harry Ransom Center, the Western Art. Located on the second floor in the obscure southwest corner, the Western art seemed to be hidden from the general public, as if the University of Texas were ashamed of its small collection. Although the collection was small, it included some beautiful pieces of Western art. My favorite pieces were the two bronze sculptures, The Horse Wranglers (also called Bronco Buster) by Solon H. Borghum and Mountain Man by Frederic Remington.

The final version will need to be more sophisticated, but a paragraph of this kind gets the draft going. The last sentence in the paragraph is as close as Ken gets to a thesis statement. It tells us that he likes both *The Horse Wranglers* and *Mountain Man* and suggests that he'll probably talk about the works in

that order. But it conveys little hard information at this stage. Ken hasn't done much to evaluate the sculptures or make his readers interested in what he has to say about them. He needs to think about his subject a good deal more.

The remainder of the first draft looked like this when he turned it in for the comments of his teacher and classmates:

The Horse Wranglers depicts a pair of cowboys and their horses colliding into one another. One horse has stumbled to the ground while the other is suspended above the ground. The rider of the fallen horse is grabbing the front and back of the saddle in an attempt to stay on the horse. The other rider holds a rope that is looped around the neck of the fallen horse. The sculpture shows the power and elegance of the sleek American quarterhorse and the courage and skill of the American cowboy.

In contrast, Mountain Man shows the tranquility and lonliness of a man and his horse descending a steep hill.

The man has all the equipment of a typical mountain man. He

wears buckskin clothing and an animal hide for a cap. He

carries a musket, powder horn, large skinning knife, and

traps. The animal he rides is a sturdy quarterhorse. The

graceful horse is carefully gliding down the rocky path.

I would be proud to display these sculptures in my

home. I appreciate both The Horse Wranglers and Mountain

Man because I have felt the power and seen the elegance of a

fine quarterhorse, and I have felt the lonliness and

tranquility of riding a horse by oneself. Borghum and

Remington achieve their objectives of expressing simple

emotions felt by people in the Old West.

24.2

Essay

You will note that Ken Duncan is rather cautious about what he includes; rather than write a draft filled with examples and illustrations, he starts with a draft that will need development and amplification. His structure is very simple—perhaps too simple—consisting of an introductory paragraph that outlines his criteria of evaluation, two short paragraphs of description, and a conclusion. There are some interesting transitions. Note how the paragraphs of development open with roughly parallel sentences that indicate a contrast between the two works of art:

> *The Horse Wranglers* depicts a pair of cowboys and their horses colliding into one another.
>
> In contrast, *Mountain Man* shows the tranquility and lonliness of a man and his horse descending a steep hill.

Notice too how the opening paragraph is tied in to the concluding one:

My criteria for good art is that I would want to display it in my living room. . . .

I would be proud to display these sculptures in my home.

But despite these nice touches, Ken's draft needs more work, as he no doubt realizes. In his class, he has the opportunity to get advice from both his instructor and his classmates.

Exercise 24.A

1. Review the rough notes Ken Duncan wrote before preparing his draft of "Western Art" (see pp. 420–21). What words and phrases found their way into his first version? What did he leave out? Do you agree with his choices?
2. Before turning to the next section, evaluate Ken's draft. What advice would you give him to improve it? What are the major strengths of his piece? The major weaknesses? How well does his draft serve its purpose and audience? What would you add? Take out? Rearrange?
3. How good are Ken's criteria for evaluating the sculptures? Are you convinced by them? Are they likely to satisfy the audience described in the assignment?
4. Make a scratch outline of Ken's first draft. Does it follow a particular pattern? Does the outline indicate a need for additional development? ■

24.3

Essay

24.3 Comments and Revisions

After they read his draft, Ken's classmates praised his descriptions, but told him to do more evaluating. His teacher was more specific and made comments on Ken's draft. Notice that the remarks focus on the major problems of "Western Art" but do not correct the paper or rewrite it for Ken. Revision is the writer's responsibility.

Western Art

More specific title?

Are these criteria absolute? Would you reject a work of art just because it didn't match your interests?

My criteria for good art is that I would want to display it in my living room and that it would reflect my interests of hunting, fishing, skiing, and riding horses, or my proud heritage of living in West Texas. Therefore, I knew exactly what kind of art I wanted to see in the Harry Ransom Center, the Western Art. Located on the second floor in the obscure southwest corner, the Western Art seemed to be hidden from the general public, as if the University of Texas were ashamed of its small collection. Although the collection was small, it included some beautiful pieces of Western Art. My favorite pieces were the two bronze sculptures, The Horse Wranglers (also called Bronco Buster) by Solon H. Borghum and Mountain Man by Frederic Remington.

More development

Tighten

The Horse Wranglers depicts a pair of cowboys and their horses colliding into one another. One horse has stumbled to the ground while the other is suspended above the ground. The rider of the fallen horse is grabbing the front and back of the saddle in an attempt to stay on the horse. The

More description. Talk about the material, the masses, forces, energies in the pieces. How does the artist convey power and elegance?

other rider holds a rope that is looped around the
neck of the fallen horse. The sculpture shows the
power and elegance of the sleek American quarterhorse and the courage and skill of the American
cowboy.

What are your Responses to the Work?

        In contrast, <u>Mountain Man</u> shows the
tranquility and lonliness of a man and his horse
descending a steep hill. The man has all the
equipment of a typical mountain man. He wears
buckskin clothing and an animal hide for a cap.
He carries a musket, powder horn, large skinning
knife, and traps. The animal he rides is a sturdy
quarterhorse. The graceful horse is carefully
gliding down the rocky path.

Remind your readers that Mountain Man is a sculpture. Name the artist again?

Good details here, but you need more development.

        I would be proud to display these sculptures
in my home. I appreciate both <u>The Horse Wranglers</u>
and <u>Mountain Man</u> because I have felt the power and
seen the elegance of a fine quarterhorse, and I
have felt the lonliness and tranquility of riding
a horse by oneself. Borghum and Remington achieve
their objectives of expressing simple emotions
felt by people in the Old West.

*24.3
Essay*

Develop this idea.

*A good first draft, but you need
to describe and evaluate more. Opening
is abrupt. Conclusion deserves amplification.
A lot of work remains to be done, but
you've found subjects worth talking about.*

Ken begins revising. Like many writers, he hopes to salvage as much of his original work as he can. His initial changes are mostly substitutions (see 23.2); he tries to find better words and phrases to put in place of weak or unclear expressions. Here are his first revisions:

Western Art

In the Harry Ransom Center, the modern art is fun to look at; the Egyptian, Greek, and medieval art reveal the talent of ancient painters and sculptors; but my favorite art is western art

~~My criteria for good art is that I would want~~
~~to display it in my living room and that it would~~

Western art
 reflect my interests ~~of~~ *in* hunting, fishing, skiing,

and
and riding horses, ~~or~~ my proud heritage of living

in West Texas. ~~Therefore, I knew exactly what~~ *I would display a good western painting or sculpture before I would* ~~think about~~ *consider*

displaying any other kind of art. In the Harry Ransom Center, the western art, I
~~kind of art I wanted to see in the Harry Ransom~~
~~Center, the Western Art.~~ Located on the second

floor in the obscure southwest corner, ~~the Western~~

Art seemed ~~to~~ be hidden from the ~~general~~ public,

as if the University of Texas were ashamed of its

small collection. Although the collection was

small, it included some beautiful pieces of

Western Art. My favorite pieces were the two

bronze sculptures, The Horse Wranglers (also

called Bronco Buster) by Solon H. Borghum and

Mountain Man by Frederic Remington.

The Horse Wranglers depicts a pair of cowboys

and their horses colliding ~~into one another.~~ One

horse has stumbled to the ground while the other

is suspended above the ground. The rider of the

fallen horse is grabbing the front and back of the

saddle in an attempt to stay on the horse. The

other rider holds a rope that is looped around the

neck of the fallen horse. ~~The~~ sculpture ~~shows~~ the
Viewing   *I could see*

power and elegance of the sleek American quarter-

horse and the courage and skill of the ~~American~~
two

~~An horses muscles.~~ *The large muscles of the horse are prominently*
~~cowboys~~ *displayed ~~which~~ the smooth bronze finish gives*
the appearance of the horse having a shining summer coat.
In contrast, <u>Mountain Man</u> shows the

tranquility and lonliness of a man and his horse
atop
~~descending~~ a steep hill. The man has all the

equipment of a typical mountain man. He wears

buckskin clothing and an animal hide for a cap.

He carries a musket, powder horn, large skinning

knife, and traps. The animal he rides is a sturdy
that
quarterhorse. The ~~graceful horse~~ is carefully
balanced on
~~perched~~ gliding down the rocky path.
either of
I would be proud to display these sculptures

in my home. I appreciate both <u>The Horse Wranglers</u>

and <u>Mountain Man</u> because I have felt the power and

seen the elegance of a fine quarterhorse, and I

have felt the lonliness and tranquility of riding
myself?
a horse by (oneself.) Borghum and Remington achieve

their objectives of expressing simple emotions

felt by people in the Old West.

These surface revisions help the piece a bit, but Ken needs to think about his work more deeply. Examined from the perspective of his purpose (in this case, his teacher's assignment), the draft is marginally acceptable: it both describes and evaluates two works of art. But while the descriptions have some merit, and the criteria of evaluation are spelled out in the first paragraph, the instructor makes it clear in his comments that the criteria aren't sufficient and the descriptions need more work.

From an audience perspective, Ken is more successful. The language of his draft is simple, clear, and reasonably detailed. It contains no technical terms or concepts that his classmates would not understand. And he talks about his feelings, if only briefly, in a way that is likely to interest his readers: "I have felt the power and seen the elegance of a fine quarterhorse. . . ."

As for his subject matter, Ken Duncan has decided to rely chiefly on personal experience in developing his essay. It would be easy to imagine his piece expanding to include a section on the reputation of western art in art circles. Or he could include short biographies of Solon Borghum and Frederic Remington. These developments of his subject would require some research in the library, but the essay would be stronger and more authoritative as a result. However, as you will see, he does not expand his material in this direction.

24.3
Essay

From the standpoint of organization and cohesion, the draft is adequate. It is, of course, very short. Its pattern of organization is so simple as to seem almost artless: the two sculptures are examined one after another in mild contrast. Yet this simplicity contributes to clarity and cohesion. It would be possible to maintain this basic structure even if the essay were greatly expanded. On the other hand, Ken could attempt a new structure, perhaps a comparison-contrast design that compares the sculptures feature by feature instead of looking at them one at a time. Once again, Ken, like many students, chooses a conservative approach and sticks with his original structure when he rewrites his essay.

Finally, there is the style of the draft to consider. It is occasionally rough. The opening sentence is a bit clumsy, for example. It is not easy to follow because of the lengthy clauses, and it rambles before coming to the main point. But most of Ken's writing is admirably free of wordiness and generalities. He is good at describing physical objects with some precision ("The other rider holds a rope that is looped around the neck of the fallen horse") and likes to list details ("He wears buckskin clothing and an animal hide for a cap. He carries a musket, powder horn, large skinning knife, and traps."). His revision should build upon the simple grace that is the hallmark of his style. (For a review of the preceding revision criteria, see pp. 402–13.)

In working his way from a first draft to a second version, Ken Duncan spends most of his time revising his opening paragraph. In his notes, he comes up with several versions. One is short and direct:

```
     Of all the different kinds of art in the Harry Ransom

     Building, my favorite is the small collection of Western Art,

     specifically the bronze statues of horses.
```

Another is a slightly expanded variation of the same paragraph:

```
     Of all the different works of art in the Harry Ransom

     Building, Egyptian, Greek, Roman, Medieval, American, and

     modern, my favorite are the two bronzes of Western Art hidden in

     the obscure southwest corner of the second floor--specifically

     the . . .
```

This version trails off, unfinished. It is followed by a bold departure, a substantially new paragraph emphasizing the criteria that will operate in the evaluation. Note here the opening sentence that is rejected before the new paragraph begins:

```
In-my-view

A-good-piece-of-art-should-reflect-my-what-I-my

My only criteria for a good piece of art is that I would could

pay money for it and proudly display the-piece it in my living

room. However, to be displayed in my living room, a piece of

art must reflect my heritage, experience, and or interests.  The

art must be-of-nature have                  because I enjoy

hunting and fishing and just-being riding horses in a peaceful

place away from any city.  The art must be-of-Texas have

something to do with the West because I have lived all my life

in West Texas.  The art must be of nature pertaining to West

Texas because my heritage is that of a boy brought-up exposed-to
```

the-wonders-of-nature who has lived his entire life in a-small
West Texas town-and-on-a-large-West-Texas-ranch.--Accordingly,
And because, my interests are hunting, fishing, riding horses,
and just being away from civilization.

This is an awkward, but reflective, paragraph. The criteria
Ken sets down for judging art are too personal to apply generally (a criticism his instructor made on his first draft), but
he seems determined to mention them, at least at this stage.
The opening paragraph leads to a second, related paragraph:

Consequently, I knew exactly what kind of art I want to see
in the Harry Ransom Center. The modern art in the Ransom Center
was fun to look at, but the bright, colored patterns and
pictures reminded me of the-excitement-in of a large city and
the, not of the peacefulness of nature. The Egyptian, Greek,
and Medieval art looked intriguing, but I am not interested in
having the distant past in my living room. The art that I was
looking for was, of course, the Western art, located in the
second floor in the obscure southwest corner.

By this time you have no doubt noted how certain phrases
and expressions appear over and over again in Ken's work
and how ideas from one version merge with those in another.
For example, a paragraph that does not appear in the final
version includes a short expansion of the assertion that "I am
not interested in having the distant past in my living room";
the passage circles back, almost predictably now, to living in
West Texas:

I appreciate art that depicts places and emotions that I have
seen or felt. European art loses its appeal because I have
never seen Europe. However,-I-have-traveled-throughout-Western
America. Traveling to these Europe and seeing the places where
the artists were inspired would possibly make me appreciate the
art.

These sentences are an example of the way writing helps us to think out loud, to explore the _why_ of an idea we may have had for a long time but have never questioned. Even though the lines do not appear in Ken's second version, they help him understand the limits of his criteria.

Ken's notes show that he spent less time working on the conclusion of his short essay. Indeed, the concluding paragraph in his second version is almost identical to what appears in his first draft, despite his instructor's appeal for more development. He does take the time to change his title from the too-general "Western Art" to the far more specific and appealing: "Horses and Men: Two Bronzes in the University of Texas Collection."

Ken does some additional revising, but all in all makes relatively few major alterations. He does not, for example, rethink his organization or go to outside sources to expand his knowledge of western art. He concentrates, as many students do, on polishing his language and making some of his assertions more specific and clearer.

_24.4_

Essay

Exercise **24.B**

1. How do Ken's efforts to salvage his draft (pp. 428–29) compare with your typical attempts to revise a paper? Would it be possible to rework this paper adequately if the revisions were limited to substitutions?
2. What do you think Ken Duncan does best in his essay? What strengths does he have to capitalize on? Do you agree with the assessment of his draft offered on pages 426–27? What would you add to this evaluation?
3. What kinds of comments on an essay do you usually find most helpful? What sorts of comments do you tend to ignore? Why? ∎

24.4 A Final Version

The edited and proofread version of Ken Duncan's evaluative essay looked like this after his instructor had read and commented on it:

Horses and Men:

Two Bronzes in the University of Texas Collection

      Walking through the Harry Ransom Center, I

gazed at the bright colors and odd patterns of the

Modern Art; I pondered the talents of Egyptian,

Greek, and Medievel artist and sculptors; but I   *sp* / ∧ ^s

was captivated by the Western Art. Located on the

second floor in the obscure southwest corner, the

Need
subjunctive:
"Were"

Western Art seemed hidden from the public, as if

the University of Texas was ashamed of its small

               have

collection. I would proudly display any piece of   *"ed" omitted*

Western Art from the University's small collection

24.4

Essay

in my home because the Western Art reflected my

interests in hunting, fishing, and riding horses   *Criteria of*

and my proud heritage of living in West Texas. *evaluation*

But my favorite pieces were the two large bronze *still need*

                            more

sculptures, <u>The Horse Wranglers</u> (also called *explanation*

<u>Bronco Busters</u>) by Solon H. Borghum and <u>Mountain</u>

<u>Man</u> by Frederic Remington.

    <u>The Horse Wranglers</u> depicts a pair of cowboys

and their horses colliding. One horse has

stumbled to the ground while the other is sus-   *Mood*

pended above the ground. The rider of the fallen *description*

horse is grabbing the front and back of the saddle

in an attempt to stay on the horse. The other

rider holds a rope that is looped around the neck

of the fallen horse. The large muscles of the
horses are prominently displayed while the smooth
bronze finish gives the appearance of the horses

awkward

having shiny summer coats. The bronze riders give

the viewer the impression of a weather-beat, dirty

s / have

cowboy who has spent the whole day on a horse in

the sun. The sculpture wonderfully illustrates
the power and elegance of the sleek American

develop

quarterhorse and the courage and skill of the
American cowboy.

In contrast, the rough bronze sculpture,
Mountain Man, shows the tranquility and loneliness
of a man and his horse atop a steep hill. The man
has all the equipment of a typical mountain man.
He wears buckskin clothing and an animal hide for
a cap. He carries a musket, powderhorn, large

*Good
description
again*

skinning knife, and traps. The animal he rides is
a sturdy quarterhorse that is carefully balanced
on the rocky path. At first glance, the long-
haired, bearded mountain man seems contently
perched on the top of the world, making the viewer
envious of the man and his horse. But a closer

*repetition
"mountain
man"*

look at the bronze sculpture and the expression-
less mountain man makes the viewer understand that

*Good
point
expand*

a mountain man's life was an extremely tough,
harsh, lonely way to make a living.

I would be proud to display either of these

sculptures in my home. I appreciate both The

Horse Wranglers and the Mountain Man because I

have felt the power and seen the elegance of a

fine quarterhorse, and I have felt the loneliness

and tranquility of riding a horse by myself.

Borghum and Remington achieve their objectives of

expressing the simple emotions felt by people in

the Old West.

Several more sentences here explaining, perhaps, the value of art that expresses simple emotions.

Evaluation of "Horses and Men"

24.4

Essay

As you can see, Ken Duncan's essay still has some problems, despite the time he spent revising. He could have proofread more carefully to catch obvious mistakes such as *Medievel* and *weather-beat,* but these slips are minor; a more significant omission is his failure to describe or analyze fully the criteria he is using in evaluating the two sculptures. The essay proves that Ken has a strong attachment to nature and an attraction to art depicting those aspects of western life he loves; in fact, his early notes and drafts hint at more details about the sources of his emotions than his final version contains (from his notes: "I have experienced all these emotions cowboying on my grandmother's ranch."). Both the instructor and most of his readers would like him to expand his discussion of his feelings and to view them in a slightly larger context. His opening talks about Egyptian, Greek, Medieval, and modern art, and at least one draft version explores his difficulty in appreciating European art ("I am not interested in having the distant past in my living room"), but unfortunately a discussion of the universality of his values does not emerge, even in a brief way. The result is an essay that seems narrower and less convincing (in terms of the criteria of evaluation it offers) than it otherwise might have been.

Yet the piece has its strengths too. The author's selection of bronzes that depict contrasting emotions turns out to be an effective technique to structure the essay now that the descriptions are somewhat fuller and a viewer's reactions to the pieces more interestingly explained. The essay is organized from the second paragraph to the conclusion by the contrast between the power and elegance of *The Horse Wranglers* and the loneliness and tranquility of *Mountain Man*. Most readers would probably want still more commentary, and maybe more inquiry into the pieces themselves (why the alternative title for *The Horse Wranglers?*) and the artists who produced them. But the descriptions are satisfying even in this version, and the feelings expressed by the writer are sincere and believable.

Because his teacher allowed opportunities for extensive revision before the final essay was due, Ken Duncan was not given the chance to revise "Horses and Men" again. Yet it is easy to see the direction such a new version might take. The current version does many things right. Its language is clear, controlled, and generally accurate, and its subject matter is appealing. The paper is ripe for exactly those kinds of revisions—mostly additions and amplifications—that make a good piece excellent.

24.4

Essay

Exercise **24.C**

Below are several writing assignments. Prepare an essay in response to one or more of them and keep a full record of your writing process, saving everything from your earliest brainstorming lists and scratch outlines to your final, carefully edited version.

1.   Your grandparents are about to celebrate their fiftieth wedding anniversary. The grandchildren have all been assigned jobs to do in preparation for the celebration. One of your cousins is catering the anniversary dinner, another is preparing a commemorative photo album. Your task is to compile a brief history of the family to append to the photo album, a short piece that touches on most of the family members—children and grandchildren—important to your grandparents.

The problem, of course, is the tone. Neither of your grandparents is particularly sentimental. In fact, they are realistic enough to be offended by saccharine accounts of the family's accomplishments. On the other hand, too much honesty might offend those members of your line whose achievements have been less than sterling. Your job is to present your family in a way that is interesting and honest without offending any of those liable to attend the anniversary party and read your essay in the photo album.

2. After several years of intense preparation, you are finally applying for medical (dental, law, graduate) school. You have done everything right: gotten straight A's, worked at summer jobs tied in to your career, earned the respect of your supervisors, joined all the appropriate campus organizations, been a big brother/sister, given blood regularly. You have even practiced your writing to be sure you can handle a professional school application with skill and polish.

    The fill-in-the-blanks portion of the application to your chosen school gives you no problems. You proudly relay all the biographical information and list your numerous accomplishments, beginning with your election as class president in the first grade. But then the application form hurls a change-up. It demands an essay. You anticipated as much, but the topic of the statement is to be your *weaknesses*. To quote exactly:

    > Every year we receive hundreds of applications from qualified candidates for our profession. Almost all applicants possess unusual strengths and talents. We would like you, in a short essay, to assess not the strengths you doubtlessly have, but your weaknesses and how you deal with them. Limit your essay to approximately 1000 words.

    How do you handle this rhetorical situation? After all your years of developing skills, talents, and virtues, the screening board is interested in your failures! After carefully examining your less remarkable characteristics, write the essay the board wants. Be honest. Keep in mind the strategies of aim and audience that apply here. What is the admissions board looking for? Can you present your weaknesses as strengths—or will that tactic look cagey? Do the faults you have seem real? Are any serious enough to disqualify you as a candidate for medical (dental, law, graduate) school?

3. In cooperation with the State Department, the College of Communication at your university has set up an exchange program with a university in the Soviet Union.

24.4

Essay

As part of that program, you have been asked to prepare a twelve-hour video cassette sampler of American television for a radio/television/film class at the Russian school. They have already done the same for your class, sending along several videotapes of Soviet news, sports, and entertainment programs, all of it a bit more serious and sober than your American classmates might have liked, but reflecting well on life in the U.S.S.R.

You work hard on your American television sampler, including a little of everything, from the *CBS Evening News, Mister Rogers' Neighborhood,* and *Nova* to *Monday Night Football, Dynasty,* a smattering of blue jeans commercials, and an *I Love Lucy* rerun. Your class, your teacher, and the State Department representative think you have represented the United States well in your tape without glossing over problems or faults in American television programming. You take the tapes home for one more review before mailing them to your Russian videopals.

24.4

Essay

Unfortunately you have a run-in with your thirteen-year-old brother that evening when you refuse to drive him to see the latest Kung-Fu space epic at the local Bijou. He plots revenge. Unbeknownst to you, he carefully unwraps your U.S.S.R.-bound package, removes your video tapes, and replaces them with his own cassettes. The next morning you send the tapes, airmail, firstclass, and special delivery, to Leningrad— twelve uninterrupted hours of MTV rock videos. Your cover letter assures your Russian friends that they are about to view the kind of TV most Americans would regard as "typical."

It doesn't take long for an infuriated State Department official to lodge an angry protest with your dean, who contacts your teacher, who contacts you. The three of them sit down with you to discuss the problem which even they think is a bit funny after you explain what must have happened. (Your brother, however, will have to deal with the CIA.)

But the damage has been done. Even after the error has been explained, twelve hours of MTV are in Soviet hands, being viewed over and over again by students and faculty convinced now that everything they have been told about a corrupt and decadent West must be true. The State Department liaison finally decides that you are going to write to the Soviet students, explaining rock videos to them in a way that undoes some of the damage. But what will you say to account for the strange images, bizarre techniques, peculiar music (remember that your kid brother selected the material), and incredible people who appear on the screen? How will you reconcile mom, apple pie, and rock videos to readers who prefer borscht and Tchaikovsky? That, the State Department official says, is your problem. Write the piece.

4. You are a passionate believer in _____. You have argued the cause at home, in class, at your employer's, and have even become active in a local _____ organization. Your town newspaper has decided to run an entire page devoted to the _____ controversy. Your allies decide that you are the one to represent their side of the argument in the paper because of your abilities as a writer. You take up the challenge, glad to have this opportunity to argue your position. But then you learn who is going to pen the opposing article: an intelligent and polished writer you know well from the several impromptu debates you have had in the student union, on street corners, and in the city hall lobby. Your opponent on the _____ issue is no pushover.

    Of course neither you nor he will see what the other has written until the paper comes out. All you can do is anticipate the arguments he is likely to make, counter them, and present better arguments of your own. You know one thing: your adversary has a fondness for emotional appeals. He can play audiences like a fiddle when he gets going, getting them to laugh, cry, smirk, or frown almost at will. But he tends to overdo it at times and the tactic then becomes transparent. Perhaps you can anticipate both his strength and his weakness in your article, while at the same time making your own formidable case for _____. Write the article.

5. Hard times have arrived at the Tebo Widget Corporation in Dimebox, Texas. You have just joined the company as a public relations officer. Corporate profits are down and layoffs are deemed necessary by a tough manage-

ment. The Japanese are producing top-quality widgets at rock-bottom prices. Moreover, their widgets have several innovative design features which the Tebo Corporation has been slow in adopting. As a result, many former Tebo customers are turning to the more advanced and less costly Japanese widgets.

To meet this stiff competition, Mr. Tebo and his board of directors have undertaken a massive program of reorganization and modernization which, they hope, will improve the company's widgets and raise productivity at their sprawling Dimebox facilities. But to finance the retooling (which has forced the company to borrow heavily), costs have to be cut to the bone in all areas. One cost-cutting measure is the layoff of almost 500 employees for an indefinite period of time. There is a possibility that the furloughs may become permanent, a rumor fueled by the Tebo Corporation's order for seventy Japanese-built assembly-line robots.

Although the Tebo management is largely to blame for the company's decline, its workers share some of the responsibility. Employees at Tebo Widget have enjoyed comfortable jobs at wages roughly 30 percent higher than the national average for widget workers and almost 50 percent higher than their Japanese counterparts. The Tebo employees have not, however, kept pace in productivity or quality control. Absenteeism has been high—especially on Friday afternoons and Monday mornings. Younger workers show little loyalty to the company or its products; they are also the ones who will be most heavily affected by the layoffs.

Your job as public relations officer is to write the layoff announcement explaining the company's action, admitting the corporate difficulties (without overtly criticizing management or hinting that Tebo is in deep financial trouble) and also making it clear that employees share a portion of the blame for the action the company has taken. You must do this in language acceptable to both management and labor, yet honest enough to satisfy the aggressive local news media eager to uncover Tebo Corporation's "real" problems. Your boss has emphasized how important it is for the Tebo Corporation to maintain the goodwill of the citizens of Dimebox.

24.4

Essay

PARAGRAPHS, SENTENCES, AND WORDS

25

PARAGRAPHS

A paragraph can be viewed as a form of punctuation. The indention of the first line of a paragraph tells your reader that you are making a new point, shifting your attitude, turning to a new feature of your subject, looking at some part of your subject in a different way. Paragraph indentions are signs to help your readers follow what you are saying. At the same time that paragraphs are separating ideas for emphasis, reading ease, and transition, they are also serving as part of the overall design of a piece of writing.

There are no absolute rules about paragraphing and no general models of ideal paragraphs. Some good paragraphs have topic sentences (see 25.2, Topic Sentences) and some equally good ones lack them. Some paragraphs follow specific patterns of development, but most, in fact, do not. Some paragraphs develop a single idea in a unified and coherent way; others are not strictly unified but manage to be coherent anyway. The fact is that the effectiveness of any paragraph depends on how well it serves its readers, not how closely it adheres to abstract models and concepts.

Most writers have some point in mind when they mark a paragraph break, and most want to be sure that their readers can follow their thinking from the first sentence in the paragraph to the last one. Few writers achieve these purposes by consciously patterning their work or following formulas for paragraph development. Yet some of the traditional ways of looking at paragraphs can be of use to you when your writing is not going so well and you have to find out why your ideas seem underdeveloped, confusing, or unemphatic. The following sections examine aspects of paragraphing and are offered to you as suggestions for improving your paragraphs, not as dies for stamping them out.

25.1 Paragraph Length and Development

¶ *dev* **The paragraph marked is not adequately developed. Your readers may need additional information or more illustrations and examples.**

You can express some ideas in a few simple statements; others may require many additional sentences of explanation or illustration to make a point.

Appropriate Paragraph Length

¶ 25.1
dev

Sometimes you want your paragraph indentions to signal a separation. They can indicate that you are moving from one stage in the development of a topic to another. A paragraph that attempts to cover more than one stage of the topic can often be divided in ways that make it more readable. For example, in the following selection, it would make sense to start a new paragraph at the point indicated, even though the entire passage is about rules people live by:

> How many times have you stopped at a red light late at night? You can see in all directions; there is no one else around—no headlights, no police cruiser idling behind you. You are tired and you are in a hurry. But you wait for the light to change. There is no one to catch you if you don't, but you do it anyway. Is it for safety's sake? No; you can see that there would be no accident if you drove on. Is it to avoid getting arrested? No; you are alone. But you sit and wait. [new paragraph] At major athletic events, it is not uncommon to find 80,000 or 90,000 or 100,000 people sitting in the stands. On the playing field are two dozen athletes; maybe fewer. There are nowhere near enough security guards on hand to keep the people from getting out of their seats and walking onto the field en masse. But it never happens. Regardless of the emotion of the contest, the specta-

tors stay in their places, and the athletes are safe in their part of the arena. The invisible barrier always holds.—Bob Greene, "How Unwritten Rules Circumscribe Our Lives"

In fact, the author did start another paragraph when he turned to athletic events as a new example.

Inexperienced writers, however, tend not to write paragraphs that are too long, but too short, breaking up related statements into many paragraphs. This distracts the reader and gives the writing a choppy effect:

> The day of the game finally arrives and the first thing you do is look out the window to check on the weather.
>
> As the paper predicted, it is a beautiful sunny morning with very little wind—real football weather. You try to pass the morning by reading about the game, while you are counting the hours and the minutes until the game starts.
>
> Finally you start for the game, only to find the nearest available parking over a mile from the stadium. You begin the long walk across the campus, joining the thousands of people all as eager as you are, all hurrying in the same direction.
>
> As you pass the impressive Gothic buildings, memories of your college days come back to you, and you wish for a moment at least that you were back in school again.

ℙ *25.1*

dev

The first two paragraphs concern the morning of the game and should be written as one; the last two paragraphs also deal with one topic—the trip to the stadium—and should similarly be combined.

Ordinarily if there are more than two or three indentions on a single page of one of your papers, you should look at your writing carefully to determine whether you have separated into different paragraphs things that belong together in the same paragraph.

This does not mean that a short paragraph is automatically a poor one: even a one-sentence paragraph can sometimes be used to good effect. In fact, single-sentence paragraphs that serve as transitions between one part of the discussion and another are fairly common in papers that have several main divisions. The one-sentence paragraph following is used to shift from a discussion of American accomplishments to a presentation of some American problems:

. . . No society has ever been so well nourished, so well bathed, so well doctored. No civilized society, furthermore, has ever worked such short hours to produce and distribute the necessities of life.

Two dark spots in this otherwise bright picture must be noted.

America's affluent society does not adequately care for its old people. The elderly have. . . .—Stuart Chase, "Two Cheers for Technology"

The real test of paragraph length is not in the number of words or lines, but in the answers to these questions: Does the indention help the reader to understand or read the piece more easily? Will any of the paragraphs be clearer or more emphatic if it is broken up? Should any of the paragraphs be combined to emphasize a relationship or to avoid choppiness?

Exercise 25.A

P 25.1
dev

Take a good sampling of the length of paragraphs in various kinds of writing: newspapers, textbooks, magazines, professional journals, novels, reports, and so on. Take special note of paragraphs that are unusually long or short. How do you account for the atypical length? What functions do paragraphs have in these different materials? Can you determine a writer's indention strategy in any given piece? ■

Typical Content of Paragraphs

No rule exists that says a paragraph *must* do this, or that, or the other. Paragraphs may have one sentence or many. One paragraph may state a point and amplify it with explanation and illustration. Another paragraph may be nothing but illustration of a point made in a preceding paragraph. A whole series of paragraphs may contain only episodes and illustrations to explain an earlier point.

Still, it may be helpful to consider that many fully developed paragraphs are composed of three kinds of statements: general statements, specific statements, and details. Examine the following paragraph:

(1) The ordeal and spectacular death of King Kong, the giant ape, undoubtedly have been witnessed by more

Americans than have ever seen a performance of *Hamlet*, *Iphigenia at Aulis*, or even *Tobacco Road*. (2) Since RKO-Radio Pictures first released *King Kong*, a quarter-century has gone by; yet year after year, from prints that grow more rain-beaten, from sound tracks that grow more tinny, ticket-buyers by thousands still pursue Kong's luckless fight against the forces of technology, tabloid journalism, and the DAR. (3) They see him chloroformed to sleep, see him whisked from his jungle isle to New York and placed on show, see him burst his chains to roam the city (lugging a frightened blonde), at last to plunge from the spire of the Empire State Building, machine-gunned by model air-planes.—X. J. Kennedy, "Who Killed King Kong?"

The first sentence in this paragraph is a *general* one, setting the scene for what follows. The first part of sentence 2 is more *specific*, restricting the first sentence somewhat by explaining why so many people have seen the movie *King Kong* (because it has been in release for over twenty-five years). The rest of that sentence gives *details* about the condition of the movie and what the viewers see. And sentence 3 gives still more details about the plot of the movie. It is not likely that the author began this paragraph with the intention of following any pattern from general statement to particular detail; in-stead, it reflects the tendency of writers to make assertions and then to support them with details.

¶ 25.1
dev

1. **General statements** may range from opinions to large generalizations. They may even serve as restatements, summaries, or conclusions:

   Maxine's is the better plan.

2. **Specific statements** are subtopics of the general state-ment, expanding, defining, qualifying, conceding, refut-ing, evaluating, or dividing it:

   Her plan has three advantages.

3. **Details** are the particular observations and facts that support the general and specific statements, sometimes by describing, narrating, exemplifying, particularizing, and comparing and contrasting:

It will cost $25,000 less than Steve's proposal; it will have wider support among the sales representatives; it can be implemented immediately.

Generalizations and statements of opinion are most convincing when supported by details, because details can usually be checked for accuracy. Much effective writing, in fact, is made up of *details,* with *general statements* to hold them together and show their meaning, and with *specific statements* to direct the reader's attention. In the passage that follows, note how a doctor uses general and specific statements and details to explain *coronary thrombosis,* a term unfamiliar to many readers:

> (1) The diagnosis of "heart disease" is feared by all of us, and not without reason. (2) As long as the heart beats there is hope, but we all realize that if the heart stops beating we will die.
>
> (3) The ability of the heart to function depends primarily on the state of the heart muscle or myocardium, as it is technically known. (4) Our existence, therefore, depends largely on the state of the blood vessels that bring nourishment to the myocardium—the coronary arteries. (5) The heart can, of course, be damaged by other disease processes. (6) For instance, the heart may fail because it is irreparably damaged by an infection as in rheumatic disease, or by poisons, or toxins, as in diphtheria.—William A. R. Thompson, M.D., "Coronary Thrombosis," *Today's Health*

¶ 25.1
dev

The first five sentences are general or specific statements about the heart and the importance of having healthy blood vessels to nourish it. The last sentence lists some of the specific threats to the proper functioning of the heart.

When you are revising paragraphs that seem underdeveloped to you, consider the relationship between the general and specific statements in your work and the supporting details. Do you provide enough details to explain or prove what you are asserting? Do the details support statements that are adequately qualified? Will your readers understand the general point you are trying to make in the paragraph?

Exercise 25.B

Examine several paragraphs in a magazine, textbook, or journal, or use the selection provided below. Number the sentences in the paragraphs you have chosen and then try to determine if the sentence is a general statement, a specific statement, or a statement which presents details. Do these categories account for all the sentences in the paragraphs? What other kinds of statements do you find?

Example (1) Surprisingly, non-runners are very much like you and me. (2) They include people from every walk of life. (3) And there are not only walkers. (4) There are sitters, leaners, nappers, starers, procrastinators, TV-watchers, popsicle-lickers, readers, sneezers, yawners, teasers, stumblers, lechers, stamp collectors, static-electricity gatherers, and, of course, the totally immobile.—Vic Ziegel & Lewis Grossberger, "The Non-Runner"

(1) general statement
(2) specific statement
(3) specific statement
(4) statement of detail

(1) It is sobering to compare the first six American Presidents with recent American Presidents. (2) When the United States was a new nation, it had from four to ten million inhabitants scattered over an immense territory, with no major cities, no great universities, no national newspapers or journals, and, as Henry James observed, with barely a national capital. (3) Yet its voters (at a time when only adult white males had the vote) had the wisdom and good fortune to elect Washington, John Adams, Jefferson, Madison, Monroe, and John Quincy Adams to the Presidency.

(4) Now we are a great world power of some 225 million persons, with a dozen major cities and a genuine world capital, scores of great universities and research institutions, the most elaborate system of communications extant, and the longest tradition of participatory democracy of any people. (5) Yet in recent years our leaders were Harry Truman, Dwight Eisenhower, John Kennedy, Lyndon Johnson, Richard Nixon, and Gerald Ford—estimable men all (except one), but not one of world stature.—Henry Steele Commager, "Presidents Then and Now"

¶ 25.1
dev

■

25.2 Topic Sentences

You can often enhance the clarity and completeness of a paragraph by stating its point or main idea in what is called a *topic sentence:* a key sentence to which the other statements in the paragraph are related. The topic sentence sometimes comes at the start of the paragraph, as in this example:

> **A faith is not acquired by reasoning.** One does not fall in love with a woman, or enter the womb of a church, as a result of logical persuasion. Reason may defend an act of faith—but only after the act has been committed, and the man committed to the act. Persuasion may play a part in a man's conversion; but only the part of bringing to its full and conscious climax a process which has been maturing in regions where no persuasion can penetrate. A faith is not acquired; it grows like a tree. Its crown points to the sky: its roots grow downward into the past and are nourished by the dark sap of the ancestral humus.—Arthur Koestler, *The God That Failed*

Another method is to work *toward* the topic sentence, using it as a summary or a conclusion for the details in the paragraph:

> In order for a political coalition to work well, people do not have to love one another; they do not have to share the same life style or cherish the same values. They have to be realistic enough to pursue limited goals in line with their own self-interest. Lower-middle-class blacks and white ethnics share more self-interests in common than either group does with any other. **It is on the basis of shared self-interests that lasting political coalitions are built, and on no other.**—Michael Novak, "Further Reflections on Ethnicity"

There is no rule requiring topic sentences to be either first or last. They may appear in the middle of a paragraph, or they may appear both first *and* last, as when writers return at the end to their initial point. And, of course, not every paragraph will have a statement that can be identified as a topic sentence.

You may want to have a topic sentence:

1. when it is important that your reader focus on a single idea in the paragraph;

2. when such a statement helps you organize the details and other material in each section of your essay;

3. when such a statement is useful in tying each paragraph to the overall design of an essay.

Exercise 25.C

1. Identify topic sentences in the passage that follows. Discuss the function they have in the selection.

All about us, living in our very families, it may be, there exists a race of curious creatures. Outwardly, they possess no marked peculiarities; in fact, at a hasty glance, they may be readily mistaken for regular human beings. They are built after the popular design; they have the usual number of features, arranged in the conventional manner; they offer no variations on the general run of things in their habits of dressing, eating, and carrying on their business.

Yet, between them and the rest of the civilized world, there stretches an impassable barrier. Though they live in the very thick of the human race, they are forever isolated from it. They are fated to go through life, congenital pariahs. They live out their little lives, mingling with the world, yet never a part of it.

They are, in short, Good Souls.

And the piteous thing about them is that they are wholly unconscious of their condition. A Good Soul thinks he is just like anyone else. Nothing could convince him otherwise. It is heartrending to see him, going cheerfully about, even whistling or humming as he goes, all unconscious of his terrible plight. The utmost he can receive from the world is an attitude of good-humored patience, a perfunctory word of approbation, a praising with faint damns, so to speak—yet he firmly believes that everything is all right with him.

There is no accounting for Good Souls.

They spring up anywhere. They will suddenly appear in families which, for generations, have had no slightest stigma attached to them. Possibly they are throw-backs. There is scarcely a family without at least one Good Soul somewhere in it at the present moment—maybe in the form of an elderly aunt, an unmar-

₽ 25.2

dev

ried sister, an unsuccessful brother, an indigent cousin. No household is complete without one.

The Good Soul begins early; he will show signs of his condition in extreme youth. Go now to the nearest window, and look out on the little children playing so happily below. Any group of youngsters that you may happen to see will do perfectly. Do you observe the child whom all the other little dears make "it" in their merry games? Do you follow the child from whom the other little ones snatch the cherished candy, to consume it before his streaming eyes? Can you get a good look at the child whose precious toys are borrowed for indefinite periods by the other playful youngsters, and are returned to him in fragments? Do you see the child upon whom all the other kiddies play their complete repertory of childhood's winsome pranks—throwing bags of water on him, running away and hiding from him, shouting his name in quaint rhymes, chalking coarse legends on his unsuspecting back?

Mark that child well. He is going to be a Good Soul when he grows up.—Dorothy Parker, "Good Souls"

¶ 25.2
dev

2. Examine a short article in a magazine, journal, or anthology to see how regularly professional writers rely on topic sentences. Keep a tally of how often:

a. you can identify a topic sentence at all;
b. the topic sentence is the first sentence in a paragraph;
c. the topic sentence occurs at the end of a paragraph;
d. the topic idea or point of the paragraph is stated more than once within the paragraph unit.

Compare your results with your colleagues' findings. Be sure to discuss how different aims and purposes in writing might affect the regularity of topic sentences: in what kinds of writing do clear statements of ideas seem to appear most often?

3. Use the ideas listed here as starting points for paragraphs or short essays. Then check to see where you have placed your topic sentences. Can you give sharper focus to your draft paragraphs by stating a thesis more clearly or by repositioning your topic sentence? Experiment.

The Presidency of the United States is a tough job.
Most freshmen don't know what they want to gain from their college educations.
You simply can't get by without a car.
A good product alone doesn't guarantee a company's success.
Sometimes you _can_ judge a book by its cover.
Math anxiety is not a laughing matter.
Music is for more than just listening. ▪

25.3 Paragraph Unity

If the paragraphs you write tend to head off in more than one direction, making it difficult for readers to follow your train of thought, you need to work on paragraph unity. Paragraphs can be made easier for your readers to understand if you arrange your general statements and details in sequences that move toward a single point. It is not unusual for good paragraphs to say more than one thing or to make several points; your job is to make your readers understand the relationships between these ideas. And, of course, you don't want your audience to be distracted by material that doesn't contribute to your purpose.

¶ 25.3
dev

Some Patterns of Development

The following are some familiar patterns for arranging paragraphs. They may be useful to you when you want to be certain that your readers see the relationships between your assertions and your supporting details.

Deductive and Inductive Development

Two basic patterns for developing the main idea in a paragraph are _deductive development,_ supporting a main point made at the beginning of the paragraph, and _inductive development,_ moving toward a main point at the end. Deductive and inductive development are often referred to as the methods of _support_ and _climax._ A deductive or support paragraph will often have a topic sentence at or near the beginning. An inductive or climax paragraph will often have a topic sentence at or near the end.

In the following inductive paragraph, the early sentences provide the data on which the conclusion—the last sentence—is based:

> Tomes of research are not needed to conclude that the necessity for brainwork in ordinary day-to-day matters has substantially diminished in recent years, pretty much in step with the declining test scores. For both customer and clerk, the simple exercise of calculating change has been eliminated widely by the electronic cash register. Hand-held calculators make it possible to do household arithmetic with scarcely any investment of brainpower, or even much attention. Kids witness that and eventually take part in it themselves. Soaring sales of even smarter electronic devices are hailed widely by the computer trade as the beginning of a new age of grander, intellectual horizons for ordinary folks. For many, it may turn out that way. **But for many more, the new gadgets will mean a decline in the need to think hard, just as the revolution in mechanical machinery produced a decline in the need to work hard.**—Daniel Greenberg, "Electronic Gizmos Make Us Stupid"

The more common deductive pattern, illustrated in the following paragraph, has the primary assertion or main point first, followed by supporting details:

P 25.3
dev

> **It is a town not wholly without traditions.** Residents will point out the two-hundred-year-old Manor house, now a minor museum; and in the autumn they line the streets on a scheduled evening to watch the volunteer firemen parade. That is a fine occasion, with so many heads of households marching in their red blouses and white gloves, some with flaming helmets, some swinging lanterns, most of them genially out of step. There is a bigger parade on Memorial Day, with more marchers than watchers and with the Catholic priest, the rabbi, and the Protestant ministers each delivering a short prayer when the paraders gather near the war memorial. On the whole, however, outside of contributing generously to the Community Chest, Manorites are not addicted to municipal get-togethers.—Phyllis McGinley, "Suburbia, of Thee I Sing"

Notice that the central thought in both of these paragraphs is focused in a topic sentence, its position depending on the pattern the writer has used to develop the main idea.

Development by Illustration

Illustration is a way of developing a paragraph by adding illustrative examples to explain or support a general statement:

> Of the world's exaggerators, none surpasses the Arabs, whose language is a symphony of poetical excess. A Cairo gas station attendant greets his co-workers in the morning: "May your day be scented with jasmine." Sometimes the exaggerations that are inherent in Arabic can be dangerous. Saudi Arabia's late King Saud once told a visiting group of Palestinian journalists that "the Arabs must be ready to sacrifice a million lives to regain the sacred soil of Palestine." It was rhetoric, a flourish; Arabs hearing it would no more take it literally than would an American football crowd hearing "Rip 'em up, tear 'em up." But the words made headlines all over the world as a statement of bloody Saudi intent.—Lance Morrow, "A World of Exaggeration"

Development by Definition

You may need to develop a paragraph by explaining a term through logical definition, that is, by assigning the term to its general class and then distinguishing it from other members of the class. Definitions appear often in informative and argumentative writing. Note how, in the paragraph following, the author first places _ballet_ in its class—dance—and then begins a longer definition by discussing the derivation of the term:

¶ 25.3
dev

> Ballet is a word that can cause some confusion when one is talking of dance. It is used in various contexts to mean different things. It originates from _ballo_ in Italian and _bal_ in French, meaning dance in the sense of "a dance" or "a ball"; that is to say, a social occasion at which people dance. The Italian word _balletto_ was used in the sixteenth century for a series of social dances usually performed by, but not limited to, couples.—Dame Margot Fonteyn, "Ballet"

A definition can also be given in a less formal or obvious way, as in the following example, in which the author defines the "meaning" of the play _When We Dead Awaken_ to place it in a larger social context:

> Ibsen's _When We Dead Awaken_ is a play about the use that the male artist and thinker—in the process of creating cul-

ture as we know it—has made of women, in his life, and
in his work; and about a woman's slow struggling awak-
ening to the use to which her life has been put. Bernard
Shaw wrote in 1900 of this play "[Ibsen] shows us that no
degradation ever devized or permitted is as disastrous as
this degradation; that through it women can die into luxu-
ries for men and yet can kill them; that men and women
are becoming conscious of this; and that what remains to
be seen as perhaps the most interesting of all imminent social developments is what will happen 'when we dead
awaken.'"—Adrienne Rich, *"When We Dead Awaken:* Writing as Re-Vision"

Development by Comparison, Contrast, and Analogy

A paragraph can be developed by showing how its subject
resembles or differs from another subject. Quite often a paragraph may examine both similarities and differences:

P 25.3

dev

> So Grant and Lee were in complete contrast, represent-
> ing two diametrically opposed elements in American life.
> Grant was the modern man emerging; beyond him, ready
> to come on the stage, was the great age of steel and ma-
> chinery, of crowded cities and a restless, burgeoning vital-
> ity. Lee might have ridden down from the old age of chiv-
> alry, lance in hand, silken banner fluttering over his head.
> Each man was the perfect champion of his cause, drawing
> both his strengths and his weaknesses from the people he
> led.—Bruce Catton, "Grant and Lee: A Study in Contrasts"

An analogy is a comparison designed to explain an unfamiliar
object by referring to a more familiar one. An entire paragraph may be based on a single comparison, as in this example:

> Because of the way it came into existence, the solar sys-
> tem has only one-way traffic—like Piccadilly Circus. The
> traffic nearest the centre moves fastest; that further out
> more slowly, while that at the extreme edge merely
> crawls—at least by comparison with the fast traffic near the
> centre. It is true that even the furthest and slowest of the
> planets covers nearly three miles every second, which is
> about 200 times the speed of an express train, but this is a
> mere crawl in astronomy. The planets Mercury and Venus,

which constitute the fast traffic near the centre, move, the former ten and the latter seven, times as fast. We shall find the reason for all this later; at present we are merely concerned with the facts.—Sir James Jeans, *The Stars in Their Courses*

Development by Cause and Effect

When you are explaining how or why something happened, you may want to organize a paragraph according to a cause and effect sequence. The paragraph might begin with a statement naming a cause (for example, an unanticipated shift in the jet stream), and subsequent sentences might then list the effects (for example, ice storms in Florida, balmy December weather in Minnesota). Or the pattern might be reversed, with various effects identified, leading up to a general statement naming a possible cause. Here is a paragraph which is developed according to a cause-effect sequence:

> Overpopulation would drive wildlife to the wall; the eagle and the elk would become memories; the smell of pine already is synthesized and marketed in pressurized cans for use in deodorizing our apartments and—who knows—perhaps some day our cities. Many would eat fish-flour, but few would know the taste of brook trout or fresh-caught salmon.—Stewart L. Udall, "Our Perilous Population Implosion," *The Saturday Review*

¶ 25.3
dev

Development by Classification

A paragraph can be developed by examining how a given subject can be classified. First, the classification is explained, and then the characteristics of the class can be discussed. In the following example, the writer announces his intention to divide reading into four types according to "manner and purpose," and then spends the rest of the paragraph listing the particulars of his first class, "reading for information":

> It seems to me possible to name four kinds of reading, each with a characteristic manner and purpose. The first is reading for information—reading to learn about a trade, or politics, or how to accomplish something. We read a newspaper this way, or most textbooks, or directions on how to assemble a bicycle. With most of this sort of material, the reader can learn to scan the page quickly, coming up with

what he needs and ignoring what is irrelevant to him, like the rhythm of the sentence, or the play of metaphor. Courses in speed reading can help us read for this purpose, training the eye to jump quickly across the page. If we read *The New York Times* with the attention we should give a novel or a poem, we will have time for nothing else, and our mind will be cluttered with clichés and dead metaphor. Quick eye-reading is a necessity to anyone who wants to keep up with what's happening, or learn much of what has happened in the past. The amount of reflection, which interrupts and slows down the reading, depends on the material.—Donald Hall, "Four Kinds of Reading"

Development by Division

A paragraph may be organized around a simple division of a subject into its parts or characteristics. The parts are usually named, and then the rest of the paragraph can examine each one in a little more detail, as in the following example:

P 25.3

dev

There are three essential qualities for vulture country: a rich supply of unburied corpses, high mountains, a strong sun. Spain has the first of these, for in this sparsely populated and stony land it is not customary, or necessary, to bury dead animals. Where there are vultures in action such burial would be a self-evident waste of labor, with inferior sanitary results. Spain has mountains, too, in no part far to seek; and the summer sun is hot throughout the country. But it is hottest in Andalusia, and that is the decisive factor.—John D. Stewart, "Vulture Country"

Development by Chronological Order or Sequence

One of the most basic ways of organizing a paragraph is to list events as they occurred:

To compress my next 25 years: When I was 17 Dad let me enlist as a mess boy in the U.S. Coast Guard. I became a ship's cook out in the South Pacific during World War II, and at night down by my bunk I began trying to write sea adventure stories, mailing them off to magazines and collecting rejection slips for eight years before some editors began purchasing and publishing occasional stories. By 1949 the Coast Guard had made me its first "journalist"; finally with 20 years' service, I retired at the age of 37, determined to make a full time career of writing. I wrote mostly magazine articles; my first book was "The Autobiography of Malcolm X."—Alex Haley, "My Furthest-Back Person—'The African' "

The same step-by-step structure is essential in paragraphs that explain how something works or how to do something:

> The actual process of riveting is simple enough—in description. Rivets are carried to the job by the rivet boy, a riveter's apprentice whose ambition it is to replace one of the members of the gang—which one, he leaves to luck. The rivets are dumped into a keg beside a small coke furnace. The furnace stands on a platform of loose boards roped to steel girders which may or may not have been riveted. If they have not been riveted there will be a certain amount of play in the temporary bolts. The furnace is tended by the heater or passer. He wears heavy clothes and gloves to protect him from the flying sparks and intense heat of his work, and he holds a pair of tongs about a foot-and-a-half long in his right hand. When a rivet is needed, he whirls the furnace blower until the coke is white-hot, picks up a rivet with his tongs, and drives it into the coals. His skill as a heater appears in his knowledge of the exact time necessary to heat the steel. If he overheats it, it will flake, and the flakes will permit the rivet to turn in its hole. And a rivet which gives in its hole is condemned by the inspectors.—Editors of *Fortune*, "Riveters"

¶ 25.3
dev

Development by Spatial Order

Much descriptive writing relies on the recording of objects in some systematic spatial arrangement so that readers are able to understand where the writer is and what the writer is trying to depict. Common spatial arrangements you might use in a paragraph are *near to far, high to low, east to west,* and so forth. Notice how carefully the author of the following paragraph provides readers with reference points (the summit of a mountain, the west, a ridge) as he leads them through this description of an oncoming storm:

> The cumulus clouds begin rolling into one another, meshing, building. The wind stops, even here on the summit of Hawksbill Mountain looking out over the Blue Ridge Mountains of Virginia and the fertile Shenandoah Valley. In an hour the clouds to the west are enormous, angry

combinations of black and violet, chalk white and cobalt blue. The clouds resemble gigantic misshapen mushrooms, skillet-flat on the tops and bottoms. These are the storm's heralds: the thunderheads, what meteorologists call cumulonimbus clouds. The ridge where I sit waiting for the storm becomes a show of flat, slow-moving shadows until the wind, all of a sudden, picks up again with a roar, bending the tasseled boles of old white oaks halfway to the forest floor. The same angry wind sends the shadows scampering down the greenstone into the dark, damp safety of the hollows.—Harry Middleton, "Storm"

Combining Patterns of Development

The patterns of development outlined on the previous pages rarely appear in such pure forms. In most cases, several patterns converge in a single paragraph. The following short paragraph illustrates three patterns of development: By *defining* a conventional internal combustion engine in the first sentence, the writer is then able to *contrast* the diesel engine with it. The explanation of the diesel engine is then further developed by telling in *chronological order* how it works:

P 25.3

dev

> The conventional gasoline engine functions by drawing a vaporized mixture of gasoline and air into itself, compressing the mixture, igniting it and using the resulting explosion to push a piston down a cylinder. In the cycle of the diesel, only air is drawn in; the air is then very highly compressed so that it heats up naturally. In the next stage, a very accurately timed and measured quantity of fuel is injected into the cylinder, and because of the heat of the air, the mixture explodes spontaneously, which is why the diesel is sometimes referred to as a compression-ignition engine.—Tony Hogg, "That Old-time Ignition," *Esquire*

A paragraph, like a full paper, should follow the form of development that best suits the subject and that will be clearest to the reader. For a fuller discussion and additional examples, see 21.1 Patterns of Development.

Exercise 25.D

Discuss how the patterns examined in Section 25.3 might be used to develop some of the following topics into one-paragraph articles for the editorial or feature pages of your school newspaper. Then write two different versions of an article, experimenting with different ways of developing the topic. Discuss with your classmates which of the two versions would be more likely to satisfy the readers of the newspaper.

> Much of the flavor of this campus (city, neighborhood) comes from its architecture.
> Movies are better (worse) than ever.
> Suppose the telephone had never been invented.
> Space exploration has changed the way we think.
> Education cannot solve every problem our society faces.

■

Eliminating Irrelevant Ideas

Paragraph unity is damaged by the introduction of irrelevant and unrelated ideas. These break the chain of thought and make a paragraph seem unfocused and immature:

> Among the oddities of the plant world, Venus's-flytrap is one of the most interesting. **Venus is the mythological goddess of love.** It is a carnivorous plant that catches and devours insects and occasionally even small birds. This is done by means of paired lobes that resemble the halves of an oyster or clam, **scientifically known as bivalves.** When the lobes are open, they expose a colorful interior that attracts insects in search of nectar. Once it is disturbed, the powerful lobes snap shut, and strong digestive juices go to work to break down and assimilate the body. **Some people have successfully grown these plants in their homes.**

¶ 25.3
dev

The boldface statements in this example are not directly related to the subject of the paragraph, and in revision they should be omitted or transferred to another paragraph. The last sentence above, for example, might be appropriate in a paragraph telling how to grow Venus's-flytrap, but it is out of place in a description of the plant's physical qualities.

When a paragraph has a clearly stated topic sentence, you can assess the relevance of any questionable material by asking what it adds to the thesis. If you find that you can delete a sentence without appreciably altering the sense of a paragraph, you probably should omit the sentence. But reread your material carefully to be certain that no material before or after the deleted sentence refers to it.

Exercise 25.E

Rewrite the following student paragraphs, eliminating any irrelevant sentences, phrases, or words.

1. Composition textbooks never take the time to praise the lowly pencil, which, despite the dawn of electronic typewriters and word processors, remains the essential tool of composition. I always use a pencil when I write a draft. Most of my friends do too, though some rely on felt-tipped markers. The standard yellow pencil is made of wood, aluminum, graphite, and rubber. Its long, slender, hexagonal body is easy to hold and its yellow color is appealing to the eyes. Scientists have determined that certain colors, especially greens and yellows, are soothing and tranquil. The outer casing of the pencil is made from two pieces of wood cut and shaped symmetrically and then glued together around a piece of lead. The rubber-tipped eraser is connected to the trunk of the pencil by an attractive strip of gold-colored aluminum banded by handsome ridges and serrations. There's hardly a more handsome or practical tool in any discipline than the lowly pencil.

2. It is hard to find a rational argument on the virtues and drawbacks of electricity production with nuclear power plants. The prophets of doom across this nation look at a nuclear plant and, in their minds, superimpose a mushroom cloud over it. Most of these professional pessimists make a tidy profit from publishing gloomy books about how terrible life is. Most of them are paranoid. Without a glance at engineering or technical reports, they begin spouting about how all nuclear power plants are constantly on the verge of explosion or meltdown. (More likely, their brains are on the verge of meltdown.) Every time there has been a mishap at a nuclear plant, the anti-nuke demonstrators have screamed hysterically about how close we are to a catastrophe, no matter how remote the chance of injury to the public may have been. They are silent, however, when workers are killed on oil derricks or miners are buried procuring fuel for coal-burning plants. Only recently have nuclear engineers begun the catch-up battle of teaching the public of

the impossibility of a major accident in a nuclear power plant which might endanger large numbers of the public. ■

25.4 Paragraph Coherence and Cohesion

₱ *coh* **Rewrite the paragraph to make the relationships between ideas clear.**

A paragraph represents a chain of thought: it is a series of statements that are associated in your mind and that you want the reader to see in the same relationship. The elements in most paragraphs should be related as closely as the elements in a sentence, where presumably the parts fit each other to make a whole.

Ways of Achieving Coherence Within Paragraphs

Among the more common techniques for achieving coherence and cohesion between statements are the following:

1. **Repetition** of an important word from a previous sentence.

    Women are being seen in a wider range of **jobs.** These **jobs** include some that were previously male-only: astronaut, coal miner, mechanic, and police officer.

    ₱ *25.4*
    coh

2. **Use of a synonym,** a different word or phrase of much the same meaning as one already used.

    The crowd in St. Peter's Square noisily awaited the appearance of the **pope.** Finally, after a delay, the **pontiff** strode onto the balcony.

    Eagerly the passengers waved from the decks of the *Queen Elizabeth II.* The **massive vessel** buzzed with the excitement of another memorable voyage.

3. **Use of a pronoun** referring to a word or idea in the preceding sentence.

    The most loyal college football fans are **ex-students. They** are the ones who buy the season tickets, remember all the fight songs, and cheer for every big play. **Football** is the world to **them. It** keeps **them** warm on the coldest Saturdays in autumn.

4. **Use of a connecting word or phrase,** an adverb or conjunction that points out explicitly the relationship between statements or thoughts.

He won the last three presidential primaries. **Yet** his party doubted his ability to win the general election.

As European economies moved toward mercantile structures in the sixteenth and seventeenth centuries, they began to experience the growth and vitality of capitalism. They **also** felt the growing pains. **For the first time in centuries,** inflation was rampant and formerly stable or stagnant systems were shaken by alternating periods of prosperity and recession.

5. **Use of parallel structures,** sentences or phrases that share or repeat a particular grammatical form.

The contract should be terminated immediately. **The firm has failed to** survey the property **as stipulated in article** 7. **The firm has failed to** come up with a suitable design for the building by November 15, **as stipulated in article** 13. And the company **has failed to** obtain the permits from the city necessary to begin clearing the acquired lots **as they are required to in article** 20. [Parallel structures often allow for some variation for the sake of variety, so that the fourth sentence here does not match the second and third exactly.]

¶ 25.4
coh

6. **Use of chronology,** devices that indicate sequence *(first, second, third; before, after)* or time *(in the morning, later, then).*

First we applied the primer. **Then** we were ready to spray the rust inhibitor.

He appeared listless **in the morning. Later,** he was the image of the bustling executive.

We are inclined to overlook the absences of guides to the reader in our own writing because the relationship of ideas is already clear to us, but we notice immediately when other writers forget to show the connection between ideas. Consider how the following unconnected paragraph is improved by showing the relationship between the statements:

Unconnected version

Many people today believe that objectionable movies should be censored by federal or local agencies. The recent emphasis in American films on immorality and violence is outrageous. They are undermining our nation's morals and our prestige abroad, according to many people. There may be some truth here. I agree with the diagnosis, but I cannot accept the cure. Censorship poses a greater threat to a democracy, in my opinion.

Relationships shown

Many people today believe that objectionable movies should be censored by federal or local agencies. **These critics** have been outraged by the recent emphasis in American films on immorality and violence. **Such films,** according to **them,** are undermining our nation's morals and our prestige abroad. **This** may be true. **However,** although I agree with **their** diagnosis, I cannot accept **their** cure. It seems to me that censorship poses a greater threat to a democracy **than objectionable entertainment.**

Achieving Coherence Between Paragraphs

When your draft has problems with connections between paragraphs, you can try linking them by relating the topic of a new paragraph to the topic of the preceding one. This is easier than it may sound; it is usually natural to phrase the opening statement of a paragraph so that it grows out of what you have just said. In the paragraphs below, linking words are in boldface type:

Putting **food** into the **weightless body** has always been a special challenge for NASA. For a while no one was sure if a human could eat normally in **zero-g.** There were those who worried that when John Glenn made the first American around-the-world space flight he wouldn't be able to swallow his **food** in **weightlessness** and would choke to death. Once Glenn returned to earth, his stomach full, his throat clear, **extraterrestrial meal planning** began in earnest. **Space meals** have progressed from such items as gelatin-coated coconut cubes and peanut cubes to complete heat-and-serve **meals** on board **Skylab** and the space shuttle.

Space meals are not prepared so much as assembled. All the **food** is precooked and is either canned, dehydrated, or **packed** in aluminum-backed plastic envelopes called flex pouches. Because it's impossible to pour water in **zero gravity** (it congeals into silvery balls that drift around in a spacecraft), **dehydrated food** is revived by squirting water through a needle into the sealed plastic **pouches.** Each **pouch** has a flexible plastic top that lets the cook knead the water into the dried **food.** Liquids are drunk through a straw with a clamp attached to keep the straw pinched shut when not in use. **All** are in containers shaped to fit neatly into a compartmentalized and magnetized food tray, where they are anchored in place by Velcro tape.

Weightlessness affects not only how food is **packaged,** but also what kind of **food** is inside. Even **without gravity,** it is possible to eat some **foods** off an open plate with a fork or spoon. **Meals** with sauces or gravies work especially well because they tend to stick to the plate and not float away. The **Skylab** astronauts, who tested out many **space meals,** found some were disasters. In one report to earth, the first crew crossed chili off their eating schedule. Every time they opened a container of it, there was an explosion of **food:** "Great gobbets of chili go flying all over; it's bad news."— Douglas Colligan, "The Light Stuff"

Connections from paragraph to paragraph are established here by repeating key words (*food, space meals,* and *weightless*) and by synonyms of key words (*zero-g, zero gravity, weightlessness*).

P 25.4

coh

The familiar *transitional words* may be used at the junctures between paragraphs to signal various relationships. Here is a sampling of useful words and phrases:

and	still
also	so
in addition to	therefore
moreover	consequently
yet	in summation
after all	hence
but	and then
however	until
nevertheless	before
on the contrary	afterwards

Transitional words are strong signals of direction that need to be used cautiously in an essay. If you rely only on transitional words, your piece may seem heavy-handed.

For major transitions, such as from one main section of a long paper to another, a brief paragraph (sometimes just one sentence) will often serve to prepare readers for what is coming next. Notice the middle paragraph in this passage:

> But nothing in that end of town was as good as the dumpground that scattered along a little runoff coulee dipping down toward the river from the south bench. Through a historical process that went back, probably, to the roots of community sanitation and distaste for eyesores, but that in law dated from the Unincorporated Towns Ordinance of the territorial government, passed in 1888, the dump was one of the very first community enterprises, almost our town's first institution.
>
> More than that, it contained relics of every individual who had ever lived there, and of every phase of the town's history.
>
> The bedsprings on which the town's first child was begotten might be there; the skeleton of a boy's pet colt; two or three volumes of Shakespeare bought in haste and error from a peddler. . . .—Wallace Stegner, *Wolf Willow*

Ordinarily the subject matter of successive paragraphs is so closely related that separate transition paragraphs are not needed, and in short papers they are usually out of place.

Exercise 25.F

¶ 25.4
coh

Many of the connective devices have been removed from the following paragraph. Rewrite it to improve its cohesion.

> I seem to spend all my life in transit. Constant travel to and from school and work keeps me in transit. I have a choice of vehicles, a truck and a motorcycle. I am forced to choose between them on the basis of speed, handling, mileage, comfort, safety, and ease of parking. The motorcycle has some advantages. It is nimble in traffic. It has instant acceleration. Instant acceleration is ideal for short jaunts. A truck gets tied up in traffic. A cycle squeaks right through. It is downright enjoyable. The parking problems on any campus are likely to be numerous. The motorcycle is compact. This is an advantage. I can ride the bike right on campus and park near classes. Lots suitable for the truck are far away. On rainy days I prefer the truck. A cozy seat next to a blasting heater beats an open ride through icy rain. Cycling in the wet

is uncomfortable and dangerous. The rain slickens oil on the road and reduces the efficiency of brakes. The chance of a spill doubles. The truck offers the protections of size and weight. If a motorcycle hits a pickup, the rider is in trouble. The driver of the truck experiences a minor delay. I have had several friends crippled in motorcycle-truck collisions. I have hit a motorcycle myself. They can be very hard to see. I use the motorcycle out of necessity. I did not intend to use it in the city when I bought it. I must choose between the economy of riding a bike and the safety of driving a truck. ■

Exercise 25.G

In the sample paragraph below, each sentence picks up a word, phrase, or idea from the preceding sentence. Using the topic sentences provided, write paragraphs following this model.

P 25.4
coh

Example   Lots of Americans talk about "getting in shape," but few do much about it. By "getting in shape" I don't mean taking a walk now and then or wearing a girdle. There is only one way to get in shape, and that is with regular exercise. And regular exercise means setting aside some time of the day, every day, for strenuous physical activities. Among the useful activities are jogging, push-ups, and sit-ups.

1.   The road to riches is usually a muddy path, not a freeway.
2.   The registration system at this college is incredibly complicated.
3.   Tax policy in the United States is ripe for reform.
4.   The media has now created fad diseases.
5.   Keeping energy conservation a major issue has not been easy. ■

Exercise 25.H

Each of the following two paragraphs lacks continuity. Rewrite them, making whatever rearrangements, additions, or omissions are needed to make the continuity clear.

1. By 1937 Americans began to grow aware of the menace of fascism. The United States government extended the Neutrality Act to cover the war in Spain. This prevented the republicans from getting American guns and supplies. Up until 1937 Americans had paid more attention to domestic than to foreign problems because they had not been dramatized. But tensions were mounting in Europe, and the Spanish Civil War attracted a great deal of interest. A Gallup poll taken in 1937 showed that 65 percent sided with the republican forces against the fascist Franco. It was 75 percent in 1938. Of course Hitler represented fascism at its worst, as we all know.

2. When I got about thirty feet out into the lake, I saw that the water was rougher than I had thought. Several large breakers hit me full in the face, and I took in too much water for comfort. There are techniques good swimmers use to avoid getting swamped by breakers, but I had never learned them because I didn't think it was important at the time. I decided to head back toward the rocks, but I couldn't see the flat shelf where I had entered. In desperation, I headed toward a jagged group of rocks nearby. Just as I got close to it and was groping for a foothold, a large breaker threw me against a sharp edge and knocked me breathless. Being thrown against rocks in rough waters is a danger many inexperienced swimmers overlook. ■

25.5
Intro

25.5 Opening Paragraphs

The first paragraph of a paper usually has two functions: to introduce the subject and to catch the reader's interest. Plan your paper so that you can get into your subject as quickly as possible. The shorter the paper, the more direct your beginning should be.

If, after finishing your first draft, you find that you have written an obviously weak beginning, see if the second or third sentence, or even the second paragraph, may not provide a better starting point. Often the first few lines of writing are simply a warm-up, and the paper actually begins a few sentences later.

Effective Openings

The job of most opening paragraphs is to introduce a subject and to interest the reader. Some of the ways to meet these tasks are discussed on the following pages.

A Statement of Purpose or Point of View. In some kinds of writing—chiefly reports—you can open with a direct statement of purpose:

> In this paper, I will present the results of three recent experiments on behavior modification and examine the research design flaws I have discovered in each experiment.

In other kinds of writing, or in many academic essays, you should open with something more subtle than a mechanical statement of purpose. Rather than beginning abruptly—*In this paper I am going to give you my reasons for majoring in political science*—you might provide some background or explanation to lead a reader into your subject:

> When I decided to enter the university, like most freshmen I had only the vaguest notion of what subject I intended to major in. But now after two quarters of haphazardly chosen course work, and after a good deal of self-analysis, I have decided that **there are at least four good reasons why I should major in political science.**

25.5

Intro

If your purpose is to discuss one aspect of some general subject, the first paragraph can make the limits of your paper clear:

> The Great Lakes are one of the major lake systems of the world. Through the centuries many large cities have grown up along their perimeter as people recognized their value for inland navigation, water supply, and recreation. Pollution of their waters by industrial wastes has also inevitably increased through the years, until now it presents a serious threat. **The pollution problems in Chicago are typical of those of the Great Lakes area as a whole.**

A Definition. If your paper deals with some subject which has a variety of meanings for different readers, it is good to make your definition clear at the outset. There is no need to start with a flat and stereotyped statement like "According to Webster, a hobby is 'an engrossing topic, occupation, or plan,

etc., to which one habitually returns.' " Give a definition that
fits your own approach to the subject:

> A hobby, as I see it, is an activity that takes up most of
> your spare time and all of your spare money. At least that
> has been my experience since I became interested in pho-
> tography. . . .

An Important Fact. One of the quickest and clearest ways to
open a paper is with the statement of an important fact that
will lead to the general topic. This is a natural opening for a
narrative and can also be good for a discussion of ideas:

> There have been two downright attempts by govern-
> ments to curb freedom of the press in America since Plym-
> outh Rock. The first took place when John Peter Zenger, a
> New York publisher, was jailed in 1735 for criticizing the
> British colonial governor, but through a brilliant defense by
> Andrew Hamilton, a salty old Philadelphia lawyer, was ac-
> quitted. In the second instance, 63 years later under our
> own young Constitution, the accused was less fortunate.—
> Alvin Harlow, "Martyr for a Free Press," *American Heritage*
>
> Publishers estimate that there are approximately 800
> books-only bookstores in the entire United States. This is
> the rough equivalent of the number of bookstores in the
> city of London alone.—Marya Mannes, "Empty Bookstores
> Equal Empty Minds," *Fort Worth Star Telegram*

A Reference to Personal Experience. If your subject is one
with which you have had some personal experience, a reference to your connection with it provides an appropriate beginning. In an essay on the complex problems of leading a
university, for example, the author, a university president,
begins in this way:

> Before Clark Kerr went through the revolving presiden-
> tial door at Berkeley, he defined the modern multiversity
> president's job. It was, he said, to provide "sex for the stu-
> dents, football for the alumni, and parking for the faculty."
> Eight years later, after my own maiden year as president of
> the University of Cincinnati—whose 36,104 students make
> it the largest urban multiversity in the country after New
> York City's—I can report: The parking problem is worse.
> College football is being energetically chased by man-eating
> tigers (in our case the Bengals). Sex is so taken for granted

as to rate no priority.—Warren Bennis, "The University Leader," *The Saturday Review*

A Lively Detail, Anecdote, or Illustration. A good way to arouse the reader's interest and curiosity is to begin with a lively detail—perhaps with an anecdote, an apt quotation, or an allusion to some current topic. Such material should of course be related to the subject of the paper, as is this beginning of an article on the conservation of natural resources:

> Millions of years ago, a volcano built a mountain on the floor of the Atlantic. In eruption after eruption, it pushed up a great pile of volcanic rock, until it had accumulated a mass a hundred miles across at its base, reaching upward toward the surface of the sea. Finally its cone emerged as an island with an area of about 200 square miles. Thousands of years passed, and thousands of thousands. Eventually the waves of the Atlantic cut down the cone and reduced it to a shoal—all of it, that is, but a small fragment which remained above water. This fragment we know as Bermuda.
>
> With variation, the life story of Bermuda has been repeated by almost every one of the islands that interrupt the watery expanses of the oceans. . . .—Rachel Carson, *The Sea Around Us*

25.5

Intro

A Question. One of the easiest ways of opening a paragraph (or an entire essay) is to lead off with a question. The question puts the focus on exactly what it is you want to talk about. As you might expect, paragraphs of definition can open this way quite naturally:

> What is chance? Dictionaries define it as something fortuitous that happens unpredictably without discernible human intention. Chance is unintentional and capricious, but we needn't conclude that chance is immune from human intervention. Indeed, chance plays several distinct roles when humans react creatively with one another and with their environment.—James H. Austin, "Four Kinds of Chance"

Openings to Avoid

The opening paragraph should mark the actual beginning of the paper and be clearly related to the subject. If it does not create interest in the subject or get it under way, it probably does not belong in the paper. These common mistakes make poor beginnings:

Beginning Too Far Back. If you are discussing the organization of the United Nations, there is no need to begin with the reasons for the failure of the League of Nations, nor is there any reason to begin a paper on Lincoln as President with an account of his legislative career. The shorter your paper, the more direct should be your beginning. A statement of your purpose or a rewording of your central idea is the simplest way to begin a paper written in class.

An Apology or a Complaint. A statement such as this is discouraging to most readers: "Being a mere freshman, I'm afraid that what I have to say on this topic won't be of much value. . . ." Complaints are also better left unwritten: "Before I started to write this essay, I thought I could find some interesting material on my subject in the library, but there wasn't any. . . ." Remember that readers are interested only in the ideas that you present, not in the difficulties or disappointments you may have had while writing the paper.

Too Broad a Generalization. "Science in the last fifty years has made more progress than any other branch of knowledge" is a generalization far too sweeping to explain or prove in a five-hundred-word or even a five-thousand-word paper. Statements such as this are likely to be more impressive to the writer than they are to the reader. Wherever possible, begin with a specific statement: "Though smaller than your thumb, an electronic device called the transistor has had a tremendous effect on radio and television sets."

A Self-Evident Statement. Avoid starting a paper with a remark so obvious that it need not be mentioned: "America has a great number of resorts and parks situated in many scenic localities." And resist the temptation to open your paper with some commonplace observation that gives no hint of your subject: "It has been said that the only thing constant in life is change." If you have started your paper with a self-evident remark, see if the sentence immediately following is a good beginning for your paper.

Exercise 25.1

Revise the following opening statements so that they at least tell readers what the paper is about. Try also to make the statement lively enough to catch the readers' interest.

Example   In your modern world of today, personal hygiene has become very important for success in the modern complex world of business.

Good opening These days, if you want to get ahead, it probably helps to look good and smell good.

Better   Each year, Americans spend billions on creams, deodorants, aftershaves, soaps, and other products designed to make them look and smell good. It is a sad reality that one's success in the world is probably determined as much by grooming as it is by talent.

1. There are many topics of importance in the news these days. One of the many important topics is how we are going to control inflation.

2. I have always liked certain kinds of hobbies. One of the most interesting hobbies I enjoy writing about is training guinea pigs, which is a very interesting hobby.

3. The abolishment of capital punishment and the reasons why I favor it is the subject of this paper.

4. The morning was dark and gray. A fog enshrouded the dormitory and reflected my mood as I approached the delicate topic of required physical education.

5. "There are two sides to every question," says the proverb. This is not so in the case of the controversy over whether or not to register handguns. Only one opinion can be substantiated with facts. According to my dictionary, a handgun is a "gun which can be held in one hand easily, usually a pistol." ∎

25.6
Concl

25.6 Closing Paragraphs

In informative essays, the concluding paragraph has the task of summarizing what you have said and drawing out the important implications. In persuasive writing, your conclusion may determine what ideas the audience takes away with them. If they leave favorably disposed to what you have argued for, they may take the action or adopt the position you have been recommending. Precisely because it is "the end," a concluding paragraph represents one of the most important parts of an essay. You should take the time to assess carefully all the choices you have when you reach this point.

Effective Conclusions

Your final paragraph should tie together the ideas you have been developing and emphasize the main point of the paper. Some suggestions for effective conclusions follow.

A Climax. Make your final paragraph the culmination of the ideas you have been developing, or save the most important idea for the last. The concluding paragraph thus becomes the climax of the paper. A student paper of about a thousand words, which has described in detail the operation of a large used-car lot, brings all the details to a focus in this conclusion:

> This used-car lot was sponsored by an organization which sells over a million cars a year, so it was by no means a fly-by-night affair. Although no sloppy repairs were done, and no highly crooked deals were tolerated, there was just a slight suspicion that the company was getting the best of every customer on every deal. This company, however good or bad, is representative of many similar organizations in the United States.

25.6
Concl

A Suggestion for Action. If you have been criticizing some situation (parking on the campus, the price of textbooks, daylight saving time), end your paper with a positive suggestion for action, or at least a clear call for action, as in this paragraph:

> At the end of her freshman year in college a girl I know wrote home to her mother, "Hooray! Hooray! Just think—I never have to take English any more!" But this girl had always been an excellent English student, had always loved books, writing, ideas. It seems unnecessary and foolish and wrong that English teachers should so often take what should be the most flexible, exciting, and creative of all school courses and make it into something that most children can hardly wait to see the last of. Let's hope that we

can and soon will begin to do much better.—John Holt, "How Teachers Make Children Hate Reading," *Redbook*

A Summary Statement. Longer and more formal papers are sometimes concluded by restating the main points of the discussion. But for most papers written in composition courses, it is seldom necessary or advisable to summarize what has been said. The result is often a weak and mechanical ending.

Tying the Ending to the Beginning. The final paragraph may repeat, in different wording, the opening idea. This method is useful in longer papers, both to remind the reader what the main subject is and to give it final emphasis. It is also helpful (if not overdone) in shorter papers, where the repetition of key ideas, key words, or key figures may give the reader a sense of a circle neatly closing. The two paragraphs following are the opening and closing of an essay in which the author reminisces about his instructor in writing:

> When I was a freshman, *Gulliver's Travels* taught me more about writing than any other book. Other freshmen might find little to learn from it, but that is because they do not have Craig LaDriere for a teacher. . .
>
> Freshman English is not supposed to be a source of innocent merriment. Its object all sublime is to make thought yield to words. Nobody quite learns how, but I went farther with Jonathan Swift and Craig LaDriere than ever before or since.—Francis G. Townsend, "A Freshman in Lilliput," *College Composition and Communication*

25.6

Concl

Endings to Avoid

Avoid unemphatic, inconclusive, or contradictory endings. Here are some typical pitfalls to avoid in your closing paragraphs.

An Apology. Ending a paper with an apology for its shortcomings only serves to emphasize them:

> I am sorry this paper is so short, but I always have a difficult time putting my ideas on paper.

If you carefully work out your ideas before writing and then present them as effectively as you can, you will not need to apologize for your efforts.

A Qualifying Remark. If the last sentence of a paper is an exception or a qualifying remark, it weakens everything that has been said before:

> Although I haven't answered why some people refuse to face facts, I have come to the conclusion that not facing facts may be a natural part of human nature. Of course this can be carried to extremes.

There may be two sides to every subject, but when the purpose or scope of your paper is limited to the arguments for one side only, don't suddenly shift to the other side in your conclusion. If, for example, you have been presenting every argument you can think of in favor of price controls or strict ecological legislation, don't end like this: "Of course, there is much to be said for the other side also." If you feel such a qualifying statement is necessary, make it earlier in the paper.

Minor Details or Afterthoughts. A paper describing the role of the pitcher in baseball shouldn't end with a remark about other aspects of the game:

> Baseball is one of America's favorite sports, and to spend an afternoon at Wrigley Field watching two great pitchers battling for a victory is an exciting experience. What I have said about pitching gives you an idea what a pitcher must keep in his mind while out there on the mound, or as a substitute on the bench. **There are eight other players on the team besides the pitcher and the same can be written about each individual player and his position.**

25.6
Concl

Some concluding statements make a reader wonder whether the writer actually finished his paper or abandoned it in the middle of an idea:

> I could go on for pages describing the other interesting people I met on the ship, but the length of this paper doesn't permit it.

Instead of putting a sentence such as this at the end of your paper, round out the description fully, or if the topic is already developed sufficiently, see if the next to the last sentence might make a respectable conclusion.

Exercise 25.J

Below are five sample beginnings and endings from student papers. For each one, write two or three sentences criticizing the writing, including the title, if necessary (see Framing a Title, p. 401). Point out effective writing, too. Then, pick two from the five and rewrite them yourself.

Example *Beginning paragraph from a paper called "Good Neighbors or Bad"*

Since I myself have never been outside of the United States, it may be foolish of me to think I can make any useful suggestions about our Latin American policy. However, I have read about recent events in the Caribbean and South America with great interest, and, if you will bear with me, I would like to comment at some length on our present policy.

Critique (1) Writer doesn't really complete his thesis statement until the last two words of the paragraph. (2) Writer needlessly emphasizes his own weaknesses, which turns off the reader. (3) The title might be too general.

25.6
Concl

Rewrite Recent events in the Caribbean and South America have stirred up a great deal of interest in the press about our neighbors to the south. It seems to me that we should take this opportunity to reexamine our country's role in these events, and perhaps our entire Latin American policy.

1. *Beginning paragraph from a paper called "The Utility of Cats"*

When the California Gold Rush was at its height, grain supplies were so devastated by rats that prospectors eagerly paid $100 and up for cats. One enterprising merchant is said to have made a fortune by bringing a shipload of stray cats from New York to San Francisco via Cape Horn. Although the cat has not always been so highly prized, its usefulness to human beings has been recognized since the days of Pharaohs. Its continuing popularity in the United States is certainly due to its utilitarian as well as to its decorative qualities.

2. *Beginning paragraph from a paper called "Modern Chicken Farming"*

   The world today is not what it was fifty years ago. Just think of all the amazing technological changes that have taken place. The automobile has replaced the horse and buggy; radio and televison have revolutionized communications; modern medicine has conquered disease. And in 1945 the atomic age was born. Chicken farming, too, has changed drastically from what it was in 1930. I would like to describe some of those changes in the pages that follow.

3. *Closing paragraph from a paper called "What a Liberal Education Means to Me"*

   But the greatest value of a liberal education is a personal one; it goes beyond politics and economics. Besides helping the individual to live in his world, it helps him to live with himself. Liberal studies stimulate a love of reason and a flexible, inquiring attitude toward the great questions of mankind. They keep the mind strong and alert and stimulate a well-rounded intellectual development which is as essential to a full life as physical development. A liberal education, in the deepest sense, is an education for life.

4. *Closing paragraph from a paper called "The Population Explosion"*

   All the statistics indicate that the future is bleak for the human race if the population explosion is not checked. Food, water, and other essential resources are even now inadequate. Living space is dwindling fast. Of course the picture may not be as dark as it looks. Maybe science will find a solution before long, or maybe the explosion will just taper off.

5. *Closing paragraph from a paper called "Population Pressures"*

   An architect recently suggested that cities could be built in the sea to house the extra millions. They would consist of concrete buildings like silos attached to pontoon islands and could extend as far below the water as they do above. People who lived on the lower levels could then watch the fascinating underwater world through their living-room windows! People have never even begun to exploit the sea and know very little of its hidden wonders.

25.6

Concl

26

SENTENCE DEVELOPMENT

I gained an immense advantage over the cleverer boys. . . .
I got into my bones the essential structure of the ordinary
British sentence—which is a noble thing.—Winston
Churchill, ROVING COMMISSION: MY EARLY LIFE

26.1

Comb

To develop sentences suited to your audience and purpose in any writing assignment, you must begin with a confident understanding of sentence grammar. You may want to review those sections earlier in this handbook that deal with clear and appropriate sentence structure:

However, grammatical correctness is only one quality of effective sentences. Good writing is made up of sentences developed in an appropriate style. And style is a matter of *choice*, not rules.

Among the most important stylistic choices you make while writing and revising sentences are those which relate to length and structure. This chapter is about how you can develop effective sentences by combining sentences, by coordinating and subordinating ideas appropriately, and by using parallel structures correctly.

26.1 Combining Related Sentences and Ideas

Sentence length varies somewhat according to the fashion of the times. Early nineteenth-century writers built their ideas into sentences that averaged thirty to forty words. Writers today tend to use somewhat shorter sentences, averaging between twenty and thirty words. These figures are only averages; individual sentences vary greatly in length. The essential point is that there is no special virtue either in long sentences or in short ones. Far more important is your ability to write a sentence—long or short—that suits both you and your readers at any given point in a piece.

You may have a tendency, however, especially in college, to keep your sentences short because it seems like a safe strategy. Errors in punctuation and difficulties in structure are less likely to show up in short sentences. But there are some things that you can't say briefly. There are some times when a leisurely accumulation of insight and observation in a sentence will let you be more thorough, more honest. John Erskine, the novelist, remarked some time ago that "When you write, you make a point, not by subtracting as though you sharpened a pencil, but by adding." As you add to sentences, more often than not they become more specific. Start with a base sentence, for example:

The geologist unpacked the rocks.

The statement is generalized. The geologist is given no identity; the rocks have no particular significance. But consider what happens when we add to the statement:

The nervous geologist unpacked the precious rocks.

> Awed and eager, the nervous NASA geologist unpacked the precious red rocks.
>
> Awed and eager, the nervous NASA geologist unpacked the precious red rocks, the first objects ever brought from Mars to Earth.
>
> Under the glow of TV cameras, the nervous NASA geologist, awed yet eager, unpacked the precious red rocks, the first objects ever brought from Mars to Earth.

With each addition the scene is more clearly specified. The fourth version packs far more information than the much shorter first one.

Students often wrongly equate long sentences with wordiness (see Chapter 28, Sentence Economy). But in fact, long sentences often prevent wordiness by eliminating unnecessary words and needless repetitions of information. If we broke the fourth sentence above into shorter sentences, it might look like this:

> TV cameras glowed. The NASA geologist worked under them. The NASA geologist was nervous and awed. But the NASA geologist was also eager. The geologist unpacked the rocks. The rocks were red. The rocks were precious. The rocks were the first objects ever brought from Mars to Earth.

26.1

Comb

Although the sentences in this new version are shorter, most readers would find it wordier than the original and far more choppy and difficult to follow. The same information is repeated over and over again. Readers have to backtrack to earlier sentences before moving on to later ones. And every item is treated in its own sentence, suggesting that each statement (. . . *the geologist was . . . eager. The rocks were . . . from Mars . . .*) is of equal value. The longer versions avoid these problems by combining related ideas, thus helping readers understand the relationships between ideas and their relative importance.

Linking Related Ideas

When you write, look for opportunities to combine short sentences into longer ones that put related ideas closer together. Be on the alert for the need to combine sentences when a draft you have written contains one of the following kinds of repeated information:

1. A series of sentences with identical or similar subjects (pronouns or synonyms).

> **An American sailing team** had held the America's Cup for 132 years. **The American team** was surprised in 1983 when it was defeated by the Australians. **The Americans** had been confident.

Combined
> Having held the America's Cup for 132 years, the confident American team was surprised in 1983 when it was defeated by the Australians.

2. A series of sentences in which the last item of one sentence is the same as the first item of the next sentence.

> For 132 years, the America's Cup had been held by **the American team. The American team** was surprised **in 1983. In 1983** it was defeated by the Australians.

Combined
> Having held the America's Cup for 132 years, the American team was surprised in 1983 to be defeated by the Australians.

3. Successive sentences which employ some form of *to be* as the main verb.

> The American team **had been** the winner of the America's Cup for 132 years. In 1983, however, the team **was** surprised. The Australian team **was** the winner of the cup. The Australian victory **was** unexpected.

Combined
> Having held the America's Cup for 132 years, the American team was surprised by the unexpected Australian victory in 1983.

26.1
Comb

Adding to Basic Sentences

As you combine ideas and add details to your sentences, you move readers away from general experiences toward a visualization of things as *you* see them. With each addition and combination, the texture of detail in a sentence becomes richer. Some of the many ways of adding to your basic sentences are discussed below.

1. Make the subject, the verb, or the complement compound. (See Sections 1.4 and 5.1.)

Compound subject   **Both the Cardiff Giant and the Piltdown Man** were at one time considered the remains of prehistoric human beings.

Compound predicate   Such discoveries **tantalized** a gullible public and **enriched** unscrupulous showmen.

Compound object   The showmen were fond of exhibiting **"scientific" oddities and human wonders.**

2. Insert appositives into the subject-verb-object structure.

Appositive   The Cardiff Giant, **allegedly a petrified man of immense proportions,** was exposed as a hoax.

3. Use verbals or verbal phrases.

Verbals   Similarly, the Piltdown Man, **discovered in Sussex County, England, in 1912,** was later found to be a composite skeleton, **assembled from the bones of nonhuman primates.**

4. Use noun clauses for the subject or the complement.

Noun clause   In both cases, scientists were for a time convinced **that the discovery of the fossilized human remains shed new light on our understanding of human history.**

5. Use adjective clauses to modify the subject or the complement.

Adjective clause   **Believing the Cardiff Giant to be evidence for the biblical text about "giants on the earth,"** many people interpreted the petrified man as a refutation of evolutionary theory.

6. Use adverb clauses to modify the verb.

Adverb clause   **Although the creator of the Piltdown Man has never been convincingly identified,** researchers speculate that it may have been Sir Arthur Conan Doyle, author of the Sherlock Holmes stories.

7. Add adjectives, adverbs, or prepositional phrases.

| *Prepositional phrases* | Fantasies **in the guise of scientific discoveries** seem to attract people **with a need** to believe **in something.** |

With each addition—and there are others you can devise by reviewing the sections on the grammar of sentences—you are modifying the length of your sentence to add detail.

Exercise 26.A

Five short sentences follow. Rewrite each one of them in four ways, adding constructions such as those suggested in the preceding list (pp. 484–85).

| *Example* | The singer looked surprised. |

The singer, a woman no longer young, looked surprised.
The singer, looking surprised, turned toward the orchestra behind her.
The singer, tall and stately, looked surprised.
The singer, who is best known for her recordings of Schubert, looked surprised.
The singer looked surprised when the bassoonist called out to her.

26.1
Comb

1. The third baseman hit a double.
2. Mrs. Merriwether took the job.
3. The book is interesting.
4. The class inspired her.
5. Joe fell.   ■

Exercise 26.B

Combine the following short sentences into one or two longer ones.

1. The Soviets have a killer satellite.
   The United States also has an anti-satellite weapon.
   These and other such weapons will move war into space.
   The prospect is a bleak one.

Only prompt action may stop war in space.
Only a treaty may stop war in space.

2. The Soviet anti-satellite system rides in space.
   It is an orbiting satellite.
   It has demonstrated the ability to shoot down other spacecraft.
   It is vulnerable itself.
   Its orbit can be tracked.

3. The American anti-satellite device is mounted on a fighter aircraft.
   The fighter aircraft can be launched from anywhere in the world.
   The anti-satellite device can be mounted in several hours.
   It is less vulnerable than the Soviet killer satellite.

4. Alcohol abuse is a serious problem.
   This problem includes an alcohol-involvement in half the murders committed in the United States.
   This problem also includes an alcohol-involvement in half the traffic fatalities in the United States.
   Alcohol also ruins families.
   It ruins health.
   It undermines the process of education.
   Many college students drink.

5. Alcohol does not kill brain cells.
   That is a myth.
   It does damage brain cells.
   The damage takes place over a period of time.
   Alcohol also inhibits the brain cells from manufacturing proteins and ribonucleic acids.
   These proteins and acids play a role in learning and memory. ■

26.2
Coord

26.2 Effective Coordination

Coord **Show the intended relationship between independent clauses by using appropriate coordination, or correct the faulty coordination.**

An important aspect of sentence development is coordination. Coordinate sentence structures link independent clauses that are roughly equal in importance:

I won the medal, **but** you won the affection of the crowd.

The staff is in disarray; the office must be reorganized immediately.

In such constructions, coordinating conjunctions (such as *and, but, or, nor, yet, for, either . . . or,* or the semicolon) are used to link *independent* clauses:

The space shuttle *Columbia* landed **and** *Challenger* was launched.

We admire your creativity, **but** we have no position for you now in the corporation.

Either interest rates will fall **or** sales of homes and automobiles will decline sharply.

You can use coordinate structures to indicate that the independent clauses in a sentence are related or balanced:

High productivity means high profits **and** high profits mean better wages for workers and increased dividends for investors.

The United States grew from a minor outpost on the Atlantic Ocean to a continental empire, **and** its Constitution developed along with it.

Coordination also effectively emphasizes contrasts:

Modern medical technology has produced miracles, **but** expensive machines and equipment have also driven health care costs to astronomical levels.

Democratic nations care but little for what has been, **but** they are haunted by visions of what will be.—Alexis de Tocqueville, *Democracy in America*

You must be careful, however, not to use a coordinate structure where a subordinate one would be more precise (see 26.3, Effective Subordination). This is often the case when independent clauses are linked by the coordinating conjunction *and.* The sentence can often be improved by changing the coordinate relationship into a subordinate one:

26.2

Coord

Coordinate statement

A falling apple brought the issue to his attention **and** Sir Isaac Newton formulated the law of universal gravitation.

One statement subordinated	**After a falling apple brought the issue to his attention,** Sir Isaac Newton formulated the law of universal gravitation.
Coordinate statement	"I, Too, Sing America" is one of Langston Hughes' best-known poems, **and** it has been reprinted in many textbooks.
One statement subordinated	"I, Too, Sing America," **which is one of Langston Hughes' best-known poems,** has been reprinted in many textbooks.

Care should also be taken when employing *so* or *and so* as a coordinating conjunction. In many cases, your sentence will be clearer if you replace the coordinate construction with a subordinate one:

Inexact	She couldn't find a job, **so** she decided to go to summer school.
Revised	**Since she couldn't find a job,** she decided to go to summer school.
Inexact	He was new to the neighborhood, **so** he had few friends.
Revised	**Because he was new to the neighborhood,** he had few friends.

<table>
<tr><td>26.2</td></tr>
<tr><td>*Coord*</td></tr>
</table>

The inexact sentences are not wrong; in both, *so* means *therefore* or *consequently*. But the revised sentences are better; *since* and *because* are signals alerting the reader at the outset that cause-effect relationships occur in the sentences.

Exercise 26.C

Replace any inexact coordinate constructions in the following sentences with more precise ones, or revise the sentence, subordinating one clause to another (see 26.3 if necessary). Not all the sentences require revision.

Example	Nine million Americans suffer from alcoholism, and the state governments are doing little about the problem.
	*Nine million Americans suffer from alcoholism, **but** the state governments are doing little about the problem.* [revised with a coordinate construction]

Although nine million Americans suffer from alcoholism, the state governments are doing little about the problem. [revised with a subordinate construction]

1. All college athletes share the same "dumb jock" stigma, and many are top-notch students.
2. They needed money for groceries at the end of the month, and they pawned his old pocket watch.
3. They had lived on the plains for forty years, and so they knew what to expect of the weather.
4. I don't like the new longer zip codes, so the mail service might be faster because of them.
5. Beaver was constantly in trouble, and the Cleavers were regarded as the ideal family.
6. It cost him a sore back, and he got the garden planted by April 15.
7. The Comanches had gathered and camped deep in Palo Duro Canyon, and MacKenzie's troops found them.
8. Keep trying; he must be home.
9. We are logical creatures, so we can shape our destinies, and so we can avoid the consequences of nuclear war.
10. The shutter of the camera clicks at an ultrafast 1/1000 of a second, and the resulting pictures are not fuzzy or distorted by the movement of divers off the board. ■

26.3
Sub

26.3 Effective Subordination

Sub Show the intended relationship between ideas by using appropriate subordination, or correct the faulty subordination.

Another way of developing and structuring sentences is to use subordination. Subordinating conjunctions (such as *because, although, since, after, if,* and so on) and relative pronouns *(that, who, which)* link dependent or modifying clauses to main ones, focusing the action on a particular statement:

After Columbia landed, Challenger was launched.
Columbia landed **before** Challenger was launched.

Although I won the medal, you won the affection of the crowd.

Although you won the affection of the crowd, I won the medal.

Statements that describe or explain other statements should be made subordinate if doing so makes the relationship of the ideas clearer. This also holds true for statements that tell how, when, where, or why something happened. For example, these three sentences are too closely related to remain separate in most contexts:

Mozart made his first trip to Italy in 1769. He was thirteen years old. His father went with him.

One of the statements can be emphasized while the other two are made subordinate to it:

1. In 1769 Mozart made his first trip to Italy
2. when he was thirteen years old
2. accompanied by his father

Then the sentence would look like this:

In 1769, **when he was thirteen years old** [subordinate clause], Mozart made his first trip to Italy [main clause], **accompanied by his father** [verbal phrase].

26.3

Sub

When ideas deserve equal emphasis, you can phrase them in grammatically coordinate ways (as explained in 26.2, Effective Coordination). But when you want to show the relative importance of ideas or to define precisely the relationship between statements, you should consider using subordinate sentence constructions. You may find many opportunities in your writing to improve the maturity and the sound of your sentences by combining short but related sentences into longer ones with subordinate conjunctions indicating how the separate clauses are related to each other:

Simple An ice skater is the picture of confidence. He glides across the ice. He controls every movement with the precision of a ballet dancer.

Improved As he glides across the ice with the precision of a ballet dancer, an ice skater is the picture of confidence.

Showing the Relative Importance of Ideas

In a given sentence, the material in the subordinate clause is usually less important than the material in the main clause. When you write a sentence, you need to know what point you want to emphasize in the whole passage so you can decide what parts to subordinate. For instance, in joining the two statements "The lightning struck the barn" and "Mother was setting the table for supper," the first would be the main statement in a general account of the event:

> The lightning struck the barn [main clause] just as Mother was setting the table for supper [subordinate clause].

But if the point to be emphasized is what Mother was doing when the lightning struck, the sentence would probably be written like this:

> When the lightning struck the barn [subordinate clause], Mother was setting the table for supper [main clause].

The paragraph would then probably go on to tell what Mother did in the crisis.

Exercise 26.D

Combine each of the following groups of sentences in two ways. Be sure each version includes a subordinate clause. Do not hesitate to alter verb tenses. Be prepared to discuss the different emphases evident in each version.

Example   The swirling waters rose alarmingly. We sought high ground.

> **Before the swirling waters rose alarmingly,** we sought high ground.
> **As we sought high ground,** the swirling waters rose alarmingly.

1. Inflation plummetted.
   Interest rates rose.
2. The city government campaigned to remove vehicular traffic from a downtown shopping corridor.
   Most merchants vigorously opposed the measure.

3. I worked at a department store.
   I made a lot of money.
   I hated the job.
4. *Rip-off* is a general term.
   It can refer to a bad call in sports.
   It can refer to a bad grade in school.
   It usually means a fraud of some kind involving money.
5. Members of the electoral college are not legally bound to vote for the candidate who won the majority of votes in the district they represent.
   It is customary for their votes to reflect the wishes of their constituencies.
6. He left.
   We arrived.   ■

Faulty Subordination

Faulty subordination usually occurs when a writer strings together ideas uncritically, as they happen to come to mind. Consider, for example, the haphazard use of dependent constructions in the following sentences:

> Because her mother died when Barbara was five years old, and since her father lived a solitary life, Barbara had a very unhappy childhood, having no family to confide in.

> Because most computers operate in special languages, people who want to use them must learn to speak C-BASIC, FORTRAN, COBOL, or other special languages, although more and more computers, which are sometimes described as "user-friendly," take simpler commands.

The elements in these cluttered statements need to be rearranged for clarity:

> Barbara had a very unhappy childhood. She was five years old when her mother died, and since her father led a solitary life, she had no family to confide in.

> Because some computers operate in special languages, people who want to use them must learn C-BASIC, FORTRAN, COBOL, or other languages. More and more computers, sometimes described as "user friendly," now take simpler commands.

When you go over the first draft of your papers, revise any subordinating elements that weaken your sentences or obscure their meaning.

Tandem Subordination

It is usually best to avoid statements in which a series of dependent clauses are strung together. Too many clauses beginning with similar connectives *(who, which, that; when, since, because)*, each built upon the preceding one, are called tandem subordination, or "house-that-Jack-built" constructions:

Tandem subordination	He had carefully selected teachers **who** taught classes **that** had a slant **that** was specifically directed toward students **who** intended to go into business.
Revised	He had carefully selected teachers who specifically slanted their courses toward students intending to go into business.
Tandem subordination	The recordings **which** I bought last week were scarce items **that** are essential to people **who** are making collections of folk music **which** comes from Spain.
Revised	Last week I bought some scarce recordings that are essential to collectors of Spanish folk music.

Inverted Subordination

Putting the main idea of a sentence in a subordinate clause or phrase ("inverting" the proper relationship between statements) may result in an awkward or incongruous statement:

Inverted	She was eighteen when her hands were severely burned, which meant that she had to give up her goal of becoming a concert pianist.
More accurate	When she was eighteen, [main clause:] **her hands were severely burned.** As a result, [main clause:] **she had to give up her goal of becoming a concert pianist.**
Inverted	While the cautious president and the worried premier signed the delicately worded agreement, crystal chandeliers glowed above them.

26.3

Sub

More accurate	Crystal chandeliers glowing above them, the cautious president and worried premier signed the delicately worded agreement.

Inverted or "upside-down" subordination frequently occurs in sentences that trail off into weak participle phrases:

The emphasis was wrong, **causing us to rewrite the entire book.**

Such sentences can be improved by putting the less important statement in an adverb clause:

We rewrote the entire book **because its emphasis was wrong.**

Problems with *as*

You should be careful not to rely too heavily on the subordinating conjunction *as*. *As* may introduce various kinds of adverb clauses:

Degree or manner	I went as fast **as I could go.**
Time	Our guests arrived **as the clock struck nine.**
Cause	**As it was getting dark,** we made for home.
Comparison	Silver is not as expensive **as gold is.**
Attendant circumstance	**As the fire spread,** the sky grew darker.

The variety of its meanings makes *as* a word to be watched in writing. In some instances it is the proper and only connective to use—to express comparisons, for example (We went as far *as the others did),* or in clauses of manner (*As Maine goes,* so goes the nation). But in many other constructions, *while, when, since,* or *because* would be more exact and emphatic:

While [not *as*] we were walking, he told us stories.

The war was almost over **when** [not *as*] he was drafted.

A sentence may be significantly misread if a writer means *because* but uses *as*:

As Peter altered the document, the police arrested him.

Because Peter altered the document, the police arrested him.

The first version could mean that Peter was arrested *while* altering a document. The second version makes it clear that Peter was arrested *as a consequence* of altering the document—a major difference. To introduce clauses of reason, purpose, or result, *since* or *because* is better than *as* in most writing:

> He refused to join in the square dancing **because** [not *as*] he was afraid of making a fool of himself.

Exercise 26.E

Combine the following sentences as the directions indicate, using coordination (see 26.2) and subordination.

Example   The hurricane approached.
We fastened the screens.
We taped the windows.
[subordinate with *as*]

As the hurricane approached, we fastened the screens and taped the windows.

The hurricane approached as we fastened the screens and taped the windows.

1. For centuries, Newton's explanation of gravity seemed sufficient.
   Einstein corrected it.
   [coordinate]
2. Horror movies retain their popularity.
   They have become more gruesome.
   They have become stomach-turning.
   They have less interesting plots than older films.
   [subordinate]
3. Carl Jung regarded the dream as a mirror of human actuality.
   He regarded the dream as a mirror of human potential.
   Sigmund Freud tended to treat the dream as a disturbed state.
   [subordinate]
4. *Future shock* is a term.
   It was coined more than a decade ago.
   It describes the inability of people to cope with rapid change.

26.3

Sub

It may only describe the desire many people have to stagnate.
[coordinate]

5. Loyalty may be the dog's most highly touted trait.
His real loyalty is to his stomach.
[subordinate]

6. The equipment used in cross-country and downhill skiing looks similar.
It is markedly different.
[coordinate]

7. Winters in Madison mean six months of ice, snow, and bitter temperatures.
We moved.
[subordinate]

8. The Trans-Am is great to look it.
It handles brilliantly.
It rides well.
It uses a lot of gas.
It weighs more than a sports car should.
[coordinate]

9. He stepped off the corner.
He was hit by a bus.
[subordinate with *as*]

26.3

Sub

10. He did not watch the traffic.
He was hit by a bus.
He stepped into the street.
[subordinate with *because* and *as*]

■

Exercise 26.F

The following paragraph contains many problems with subordination. Revise it so that it reads more clearly and accurately. You will have to rearrange clauses, add words, change connectives, and alter punctuation. Compare your version with that of a colleague.

Although he sold his idea to the U.S. Navy, John Ericsson, who was a Swedish-born inventor, after he designed the *Monitor*, which was to be the Union's first ironclad ship, had trouble raising capital to build it. But some New York businessmen financed the project. After he met all the construction specifications in only 100 days, Ericsson launched the *Monitor*, which measured only 172 feet in length and 41 feet in width, having a hull set low in the water and a turret rising above it. This radical design, which allowed the two 11-inch guns to fire in any direction, provoked comments on the vessel's odd appearance, sometimes referred to as a "cheesebox on a raft." Meanwhile, after they realized the superiority of the conventional U.S. Navy, which had successfully bottled up the major Southern ports, officials of the Confederacy authorized the rebuilding of a burnt-out warship so that it could be transformed into an ironclad vessel which could break the Union blockade. After it had been armored with plate that had been fabricated from flattened railroad tracks, the Southern ironclad, which was known both as the *Merrimack* and the *Virginia*, and which was almost a hundred feet longer than the *Monitor*, was equipped with ten guns. But it weighed a great deal because of its heavy armor, a sturdy ram, fuel, and guns, causing it to maneuver poorly. When the *Monitor* and the *Merrimack* finally met in battle, it was March 9, 1861. The *Merrimack* had spent the previous day shooting at wooden vessels in the Union blockade fleet stationed off Hampton Roads, Virginia. Volleys aimed at the *Merrimack* bounced off its iron hull. Two Union vessels were destroyed before the *Merrimack* retired on March 8, because it expected to do more damage the next morning. On March 9, the *Monitor* appeared to challenge the *Merrimack* which opened fire on the smaller ship which presented so small a target that it was difficult to hit. The *Monitor* returned the fire, failing to damage the stoutly-built sides of the clumsy but formidable Confederate vessel. After four hours had passed, and since neither ship was able to sink the other, the battle ended in a draw, even though it had historic consequences and the two ships would never fight again. ▪

26.4

//

26.4 Parallelism

// Make the sentence elements marked parallel in form.

Ideas of equal value in a statement can be made parallel—that is, they can be expressed in the same grammatical form. Putting coordinate ideas in parallel constructions shows the reader that you regard two or more things as related and equal in importance; the *appearance* of parallel passages is a signal that they are closely related. Parallelism also helps the reader see in which direction the statement is going and makes for smoother writing, since it helps prevent unnecessary shifts in person and number and in the tense and mood of verbs.

Elements in Series

Words, phrases, and clauses in series are best stated in parallel form. The boldface words in the following sentence are parallel because each is the object of the preposition *with:*

> His mind was filled with artistic **projects, schemes** for outwitting his creditors, and vague **ideas** about social reform.

The compound predicates in this sentence are also parallel:

> His dramatic attempt to take over the conduct of his own case **alienated** him from his counsel, almost **broke up** the trial, and probably **helped** to cost him his life.—Joseph Kinsey Howard, *Strange Empire*

26.4

//

When coordinate ideas are not stated in parallel form, the statement is likely to seem awkward and unpolished:

Not parallel	We were told **to write** in ink, **that we should use** but one side of the paper, and **we should endorse** our papers in the proper manner. [an infinitive phrase and two clauses]
Parallel	We were told **to write** in ink, **to use** but one side of the paper, and **to endorse** our papers in the proper manner. [three infinitive phrases]

A preposition or other connectives should be repeated between the items of a series when necessary for clarity:

Preposition not repeated	These problems are currently of great concern **to** the school system, teachers, and many parents.
Clearer	These problems are currently of great concern **to** the school system, **to** teachers, and **to** many parents.

Connective not repeated	The opposing citizens argued **that** the increased tax rates were exorbitant and the commissioners should find some other way to raise the money.
Clearer	The opposing citizens argued **that** the increased tax rates were exorbitant and **that** the commissioners should find some other way to raise money.

Exercise 26.G

Create sentences in which you use the following elements in parallel series. You may have to alter the phrasing of some items and you may rearrange them as you see fit.

Example	to play soccer to star at track being a baseball player _It was his dream to play soccer and baseball and to star at track._

1. junior high school
   senior high school
   freshman year in college
2. win
   losing
   to draw
3. the British Parliament
   the United States Congress
   West Germany's Bundestag
4. in the house
   around the house
   under the house
   in front of the house
5. carrying on trade
   to allow military shipments
   share technically sensitive equipment
   to carry on diplomatic dialogue
6. though it was cold
   although the roads were treacherous
   even though the winds and blowing snow reduced visibility
   despite warnings of more bad weather

26.4

//

7. presidential hopefuls
   former presidents and vice-presidents
   powerful party bosses
   inexperienced delegates
   pushy, arrogant newspeople eager to upstage each other
   delegates who had been to many conventions
   local and state party officials ■

Elements Being Compared or Contrasted

Elements that are compared or contrasted through the use of pairs of conjunctions such as *either . . . or, neither . . . nor, not only . . . but* (or *but also*) are usually clearer and more emphatic when they are stated in parallel constructions:

> This is the life of a musician in which are recorded **not only the events of his life, but also details of all his works,** which are analyzed and described fully.—Lionel McColvin, *The Wonderful World of Books*

Since readers expect similar constructions to follow pairs of conjunctions, they may be momentarily confused or sidetracked if the pattern is shifted:

26.4
//

Shifted	You may go to the ski jump either by special train or a chartered bus may be taken.
Parallel	You may go to the ski jump either by special train or by chartered bus.
Shifted	He admired the senator not for his integrity, but because of his political cunning.
Parallel	He admired the senator not for his integrity, but for his cunning.

Exercise 26.H

Create sentences with parallel contrasts beginning with the sentence elements provided below. Where possible, add more than one parallel item.

Example	. . . either taxes had to be raised or . . .
	It was clear to the congressional panel that either taxes had to be raised or new sources of revenue had to be found.

1. . . . neither the Empire State Building nor . . .
2. . . . neither California wines nor . . .
3. . . . not only the finest engineering but also . . .
4. . . . not only to win additional support for nuclear disarmament proposals, but . . .
5. . . . either embracing the principle of equal justice under law or . . .   ■

Elements in a List

Elements in a list are usually stated in parallel form to show that they are equal in importance and to make the list easier to read. Lists of instructions, for example, usually rely on parallel sentences:

> If your dishwasher does not operate properly,
> 1. **Check to see whether it is plugged in.** Installers sometimes forget this last step in installing your machine.
> 2. **Check to see whether a fuse has blown.** Replace the blown fuse or trip the breaker. However, you may need to call an electrician if your machine persistently blows its circuits.
> 3. **Check the position of the On/Off Switch.** The machine will not begin to operate until the timer dial has rotated to the start position. This may take several minutes. The power light, however, should glow even before the machine actually starts.

26.4

//

Notice how the parallel phrases in this example are the focus of attention. A reader is drawn first to the basic point, and then to the more specific information which follows each direction. In this way, the parallel phrases help organize and emphasize information. The same technique of listing elements in parallel form may be useful to you in answering certain kinds of examination questions. If you are asked to name, enumerate, or list and then to explain aspects of a topic, you may find using parallelism an efficient way to organize your answer.

Question: Name and discuss some of the causes of inflation.

Response: Inflation is caused by:
1. An increase in the amount of unencumbered wealth available to consumers.
2. A decrease in the amount of goods available for consumption.
3. A refusal on the part of the central banking powers or individual banks to restrict credit.
4. A willingness on the part of the central government to print money.

Simple lists also should follow parallel structures:

All participants are asked to bring the following items:
—binoculars
—boots
—adequate rain gear
—35mm cameras

Students listed their favorite activities as:
1. watching television,
2. listening to the radio,
3. eating,
4. sleeping,
5. going out.

26.4

//

Exercise **26.1**

Rewrite the following instructions, turning the prose passage into a clear set of steps (follow the model on p. 501, "If your dishwasher does not operate properly"). You will have to delete some material and rearrange other portions of the original instructions.

Microwaving a Cornish Hen

You can prepare a delicious cornish hen in about ten minutes using a microwave oven. All you have to do is clean the bird, removing the little packet of heart, liver, and other entrails packed inside, and then wash it thoroughly. If you are a perfectionist, you can trim away the fat, but if you are in a hurry, leave the fat on. No one will notice. Be sure the little bird is fully defrosted when you wash it. You can defrost a cornish hen by putting it in a deep bowl of

water for several hours. (The sink works well here.) Be sure
to change the water a few times to keep the hen cold as it
defrosts. You don't want it to spoil. You can also defrost it
in the microwave in about ten minutes. I usually start the
defrosting in the microwave at one-third power, and then
complete the job in the sink. Once the hen is defrosted and
washed, sprinkle pepper in the cavity to flavor it. Don't use
salt. Then prick the hen all over its skin with a fork to prevent the skin from popping while it cooks. Smear the hen
with melted butter and then sprinkle on some paprika for
color. If you are in a hurry, you can skip the butter. It
doesn't make much difference. Don't forget the paprika;
leave it off and the hen comes out of the oven looking pale
as Ohioans in April. Make a tent of wax paper, place it over
the hen (which should be on a microwave-safe roaster), and
stick your masterpiece in the oven for about eight minutes
at full power. Some ovens may take longer. Rotate the bird
one or twice to assure even cooking. Lots of recipe books
say you should start by cooking the bird on its back, and
then flip it over after about four minutes, but I have found
that to be a lot of trouble and messy to boot. Just be sure
the bird cooks thoroughly. Take it out of the oven. Slit the
skin at the base of the drumsticks to drain the grease. Let
the bird cool for several minutes. Then serve. ◼

26.4
//

Balanced and Antithetical Sentences

When parallel constructions, especially clauses, are noticeably
equal in length and similar in movement, the sentence is
called _balanced._ Balance is useful for emphatic statements and
for comparing and contrasting ideas:

> Abbé Dimnet, in _The Art of Thinking,_ was teaching the
> American how to think in a few easy lessons, just as ten
> years later Mortimer J. Adler was to teach him how to read
> in a few somewhat harder ones.—Leo Gurko, _The Angry
> Decade_

> The best model of the grand style simple is Homer; perhaps
> the best model of the grand style severe is Milton.—Mat-
> thew Arnold, _On Translating Homer_

When contrasting clauses occur in parallel constructions in a
single sentence, the sentence is called _antithetical._ Such a construction fittingly emphasizes a striking or important contrast:

You may eat without danger our canned food, fresh and hot, from your own campfire, but you will drink in peril the dirty water, polluted and foul, from the nearby stream.

Antithetical sentences can easily be overused, but they are occasionally effective to mark turning points in an essay—the first half of the sentence pulling together what precedes, the contrasting second half forecasting what follows.

Exercise 26.J

Rewrite the following sentences, eliminating unnecessary words and making related elements parallel in form.

1. I wrote because it amused me, and I enjoyed correcting the work, too.
2. The town turned out to be hard to reach, a bore, and very chilly in the evening.
3. He trudged his way through his homework, and finished off his notes, then turning on the TV.
4. The house was charming and a real buy, but it was not near enough public transportation nor quite large enough for our family.
5. People who haven't been to Alaska ask questions about the prices, how cold it gets in winter, and what is worth seeing.
6. I am tall and bald and have an ungainly gait.
7. This report is exceptionally complete and a fine example of concise writing.
8. She longed to throw herself at her piano teacher's feet, would promise never to touch the instrument again, and of course ask his forgiveness for abusing Chopin so horribly.
9. Worst of all was the way the cat always wanted to sit on his papers when he was writing, but there were other distractions too, such as the neighbors playing their stereo at top volume and wanting to go swimming and his desire to plant some shrubs in the backyard.
10. The friends and relatives wept with joy as the miners emerged from the collapsed shaft, alive, hungrily, and having been scared.

26.4

//

27

SENTENCE
VARIETY AND
EMPHASIS

When writing and revising, you want to be sure that your sentences are *varied*—to avoid monotony—and *emphatic*—to focus on your ideas. This chapter describes some of the choices you can make in designing your sentences to be more readable and powerful.

27.1 Sentence Variety

Var **Vary the sentence patterns in the passage marked to avoid monotony or to make your meaning clearer or more emphatic.**

We rarely notice the sentence patterns of good writing. It is only when the prose is clumsy or monotonous that we begin to detect awkwardness and repetition. When something you have written is dull or hard to read, you may want to consider varying your sentence openings, varying the patterns of your sentences, or varying the kinds of sentences you are using.

Varying Sentence Beginnings

When several consecutive sentences begin the same way—
with a noun subject, for example—the passage is likely to be
monotonous and to lack impact:

> **Meteorology** has made many advances in recent years.
> **Weather observation balloons** have been developed to
> gather data from the upper stratosphere. **Time-lapse pho-
> tography** has improved the study of cloud formations and
> patterns. **Barometric instruments** of greater sensitivity are
> widely used. **Radar** is useful in detecting the approach of
> storms and precipitation.

Such monotony can be easily relieved by simple variations:

> **In recent years** meteorology has made many advances.
> **Weather observation balloons** have been developed to
> gather data from the upper stratosphere, and time-lapse
> photography has improved the study of cloud formations
> and patterns. **Gaining wider use** are barometric instru-
> ments of greater sensitivity. **Radar** is proving essential in
> detecting the approach of storms and precipitation.

27.1

Var

Sentence beginnings can be varied and made more interesting
by occasionally starting with a modifier—a word, phrase, or
clause—as in this passage from an essay on the Grand Canyon:

> **We** have almost come full circle. **Once** those who had
> seen the Canyon thought of it as useless. **Then came** those
> who thought it might be useful because of the river which
> flowed through it. **They** were in turn followed by men like
> Theodore Roosevelt, who saw the Canyon as a precious
> heritage of wonder and beauty. **Now, today,** it is threat-
> ened again by men interested only in exploitation, men
> who unfortunately have the means to destroy what no age
> before ours was "technologically advanced" enough to
> transform and mar.
>   **"Human needs come first"** is the all too specious slogan
> of those for whom the words of Theodore Roosevelt carry
> no weight. **They** do not like to admit that those primary
> needs in which they happen to be interested are the "hu-
> man needs" of temporary economic advantage. **That the
> Grand Canyon, the sublime "great unknown" of John
> Wesley Powell,** might fall victim to the manipulations of

sloganeers should be unthinkable; that it is not unthinkable should be our shame.—Joseph Wood Krutch, "The Eye of the Beholder"

To begin sentence after sentence with the same kind of modifier would be no less monotonous, of course, than to begin every sentence with the subject. The emphasis you wish to make and the general movement of the passage should determine your sentence beginnings.

Varying S–V–O Order

A less common means of varying sentence patterns is changing the usual order of subject-verb-object or subject-verb-complement in declarative statements. This is called *inversion:*

> Supplementing the guitars and drums are a solo cello, a ragtime piano, an Indian sitar, sound effects of barnyard animals, and a complete symphony orchestra.—Peter Schrag, "Facing the Music"

But except in questions and requests, inversion should ordinarily be used only when the words put first really deserve special emphasis by withholding the subject. Inversion used solely for variety may have painful results, as in this reversal:

27.1
Var

> A garden city, with one of the most delightful climates in the world, is Victoria.

Cumulative and Periodic Sentences

Sentence patterns may also be varied if you use both cumulative (also called *loose)* and periodic sentences.

Cumulative Sentences

In cumulative or loose sentences, the main statement comes first, followed by subordinate elements that explain, amplify, or alter its meaning. This pattern is the one most commonly used both in speech and writing, for we characteristically make our points by adding on meanings.

He broke the vase,
    a costly piece from China.

We caught two bass,
    hauling them in briskly
        as though they were mackerel,

pulling them over the side of the boat
in a businesslike manner
without any landing net, and
stunning them
with a blow on the back of the head.
—E. B. White, "Once More to the Lake"

Diagramming E. B. White's cumulative sentence in this way shows how he expands his basic idea *(We caught two bass)* by adding on a series of modifiers, in this case three parallel clauses *(hauling, pulling, stunning)*.

You can often create an effective cumulative sentence by starting with a general statement and then amplifying it with particular details, as in these two examples:

Once on the mound,
he was a most unlikely looking pitcher,
slouching,
tangle-footed,
absent,
with the aspect of a lost goose.

Modern homes are hectic,
governed by the television schedule, and
disrupted by conflicting commitments
to jobs,
school, and
clubs.

27.1

Var

Exercise 27.A

Make cumulative sentences by adding to the ten simple sentences below. Try to add at least three additional units to each, as in the example. Be sure to review your sentences carefully, checking for comma splices, run-ons, or awkward phrases. Compare your finished sentences with those of your classmates.

Example   It was a depressing day.

It was a depressing day, with black clouds obscuring the sun, a cold wind whipping through the trees, and even the birds hiding from the weather.

1. Engineering is a demanding major.

2. Columbus faced obstacles before and during his voyage of discovery.
3. Some television commercials irritate me.
4. It was a dark and stormy night.
5. Keeping a journal is a personal commitment.
6. Despite the tangled traffic, Washington, D.C., was an exciting experience.
7. On her first try, she couldn't get the stick shift Escort to move more than four feet.
8. Trailing 25–10 at halftime, the football players glared at each other in the locker room.
9. The skyscraper was on fire.
10. _Liberation_ can mean many different things. ■

Periodic Sentences

Cumulative sentences give the impression of a writer thinking through an idea as he adds to, modifies, specifies, or even contradicts an initial statement. A _periodic_ sentence has the opposite effect. It gives the impression that a writer is stating a completed thought, one he has developed fully before setting it into words. The modifiers ordinarily precede the main statement or interrupt it in such a way that the main idea is held in suspension until the end of the sentence. Notice in these examples of periodic sentences how the modifying phrases build up to the main clause:

Terry,
    acting on impulse,
    showing no fear,
rescued the trapped motorist.

    Like animals furious to defend their young,
    or an angry sea hurling itself against an intruding shoreline,
the villagers attacked the bandits.

27.1

Var

Although periodic sentences occurred frequently in writing before this century, they are now much less common than cumulative sentences. They require planning beforehand and are more typical of a formal than of a general style. The very fact that periodic sentences are not widely used, however, gives the pattern all the more value as a means of achieving emphasis.

When you are framing a periodic sentence, make certain that the suspension is not awkward or unnatural, as it is in this example:

The reader will probably agree after reading this essay **that Pearl Buck's example** of the woman who, after being married for a number of years and raising a family, gradually loses interest in most of her former outside activities, **is true.**

Exercise   27.B

Make periodic sentences by completing the sentences started below, as in the example.

Example   After he found the candlestick on the rug

After he found the candlestick on the rug, and after he learned that the fingerprints were not those of the dead woman, and after he found the scratches on the lock, the inspector became convinced that this was a case of murder.

1. When the sun went down
2. After finals were over for the seniors
3. Although regular class attendance is important
4. While others might need lots of money
5. If you have followed the map carefully up to this point

27.2

Emph

■

27.2   Sentence Emphasis

Emph   **Rewrite the passage so that the position and expression of the ideas will show their relative importance.**

In composing your sentences you should help your reader to see your ideas in the same relative importance as you do—to distinguish among the more important, the less important, the incidental. Although the emphasis given to particular ideas depends in large part upon the way the whole paper is put together, individual sentences can weaken or strengthen this effect. The sentences in the following paragraph, for example, are unemphatic because they are haphazardly constructed. They are wordy, the beginnings are weak, and the endings are dull:

> There are some interesting points about contemporary American life in "The Mobile Society" by Herman Matthews. Some of the things he notes are the paradoxes in it. The way a person often reduces his independence by relying more on mechanical devices is one example the author gives. A man may actually become the machine's slave instead of its master, as he thinks he is.

To make the statements more forceful and concise, the writer might have revised the sentence structure in this way:

> In his essay "The Mobile Society," Herman Matthews points out some of the paradoxes in contemporary American life. He notes, for example, that increasing reliance on mechanical devices often reduces a person's independence. Thinking he is the machine's master, he may actually become its slave.

Exercise **27.C**

Rewrite the following paragraph, rearranging and combining the sentences so that the position and expression of the ideas will show their relative importance. You may want to structure the sentences and rearrange the material to emphasize the comparison and contrast between the space stations of science fiction and the ones planned by NASA. You may supply additional transitions and material as needed.

27.2

Emph

> Often predicted by science fiction are real scientific achievements. Science fiction stories have often featured space stations. They have done this for more than a hundred years. Now plans for a space station are being made in real life by scientists and technicians who work for NASA. The space station will resemble something built from an erector set. It will not look like a wheel. The wheel-shaped station is popular in science fiction. In these fictional accounts, the giant space station is usually spinning to simulate gravity. The real space station will not spin. Centrifugal imitation of gravity is not necessary in space. This was discovered by NASA scientists. They examined

data brought back by astronauts on previous missions into space. These astronauts voyaged in the Apollo and Skylab vehicles. Science fiction stories tend to locate space stations in deep space. Some are located at points where their rotation matches the earth's. They seem to be stationary at a point approximately 22,500 miles above the Earth. Real space stations will also orbit the Earth. They will orbit at a height of approximately 700 miles. They will not seem to be stationary. The real space stations will be permanent vehicles. Teams of astronauts will shuttle back and forth. They will exchange duties with astronauts on board. Fictional space stations were also regarded as permanent structures. The dream of writers is about to come true. The dream is a century old.   ■

Emphasis by Position in the Sentence

Important ideas can be stressed by putting them in emphatic positions in the sentence. In longer statements the most emphatic position is usually at the end, the next most emphatic position at the beginning:

> If it was the workings of our democracy that were inadequate in the past, **let us say so.** Whoever thinks the future is going to be easier than the past **is certainly mad.** And the system under which we are going to have to conduct foreign policy is, I hope and pray, **the system of democracy.**— George F. Kennan, *American Diplomacy, 1900–1950*

27.2

Emph

Sentences—particularly those that introduce or sum up the main points of a topic—should end strongly. Statements that are qualified by a phrase or a word at the end are usually weak:

Unemphatic	The work at the mill was hard and often dangerous, but the mill hands were not quick to complain.
Improved	The work at the mill was hard and dangerous, but the mill hands didn't often complain.
Unemphatic	These songs are dull and unoriginal, with few exceptions.
Improved	With few exceptions, these songs are dull and unoriginal.

Because the main statement is not completed until the end, periodic sentences are frequently more emphatic than cumulative sentences (see 27.1):

Cumulative Sociology 101 should interest every thoughtful student with its discussion of the theoretical as well as the practical aspects of human behavior.

Periodic Sociology 101, with its discussion of the theoretical as well as the practical aspects of human behavior, should interest every thoughtful student.

A particular kind of periodic sentence, the _climax_ sentence, directs the reader through phrases and clauses arranged in ascending order to the most important element at the end:

We shall fight on the beaches, we shall fight on the landing-grounds, we shall fight in the fields and in the streets, we shall fight in the hills; **we shall never surrender.**—Winston Churchill, Speech following Dunkirk, 1940

Sentences that begin with _There is_ or _There are_ tend to be emphatic as well as wordy; frequent use of these constructions will make your writing seem flat and uninteresting.

27.2
Emph

Flat There were several people who objected to the commission's plan.

Improved Several people objected to the commission's plan.

Exercise 27.D

Combine the following sets of sentences in two ways: first arrange them to form periodic sentences; then rearrange the same material into cumulative sentences. When you have finished both versions of all seven sets, compose a complete paragraph, selecting the revised sentences which seem to be the most effective way of relaying the information. If neither sentence in any set sounds right to you, reassemble the information in a way that does sound effective. You may want to use compound subjects, parallel or contrasting structures, or some short sentences. Pay attention to transitions.

Example   Erika tried to be a perfect guest.
                 She participated in all the family activities.
                 They were unfamiliar activities.
                 She ate every type of food her hosts offered her.
                 Some of the food was strange.
                 There were unappetizing things about it.

*Participating in all the unfamiliar family activities
and eating even the strange and unappetizing foods
her hosts offered her, Erika tried to be a perfect guest.*
[periodic]

*Erika tried to be a perfect guest, participating in all
the family activities, even though they were unfamiliar, and eating every type of food her hosts offered her,
even though some of it was strange and unappetizing.*
[cumulative]

1.   She ate pumpkin-flower tacos.
      She ate chili peppers.
      They made her eyes water.
      They made her mouth burn like fire.
      She even ate tortillas stuffed with fried sheep brains.
      She did not know if she could stomach *huitlacoche*.

2.   Her generous hosts explained to her what *huitlacoche*
      was.
      They said it was a great delicacy.
      They assured her she would like it very much.
      They described it as "mushrooms of corn."

3.   She had never heard of mushrooms of corn before.
      She didn't know what they were exactly.
      She had a hunch.
      She had grown up on a farm in Iowa.
      She had an idea what they might be.

4.   She and her brothers used to play in the cornfields.
      They would run up and down the rows of corn.
      They would play hide-and-seek.
      They would sometimes encounter ears of corn with a
      disease.
      Their father called the disease "corn smut."

5.   They would find corn smut in the field.
      They would recoil in horror.

They would end their game.
They would hurry home.
6. Corn smut made the kernels swell.
The husk could no longer contain them.
The husk would burst open.
The kernels became huge and disfigured.
They became black.
Corn smut was the ugliest thing on earth.
That's what she believed.
7. Her hosts proudly placed the *huitlacoche* on her plate.
They waited for her to take the first bite.
They were proud of their special meal.
She understood at that moment what cultural differences were all about. ■

Emphasis by Repeating Key Words

Statements can be made emphatic by repeating important words or phrases:

> These and kindred questions **need** discussion, and **need** it urgently, in the few years left to us before somebody presses the button and the rockets begin to fly.—George Orwell, *The Orwell Reader*

> His highest hope is to **think** first what is about to be **thought,** to **say** what is about to be **said,** and to **feel** what is about to be **felt.**—Bertrand Russell, *Unpopular Essays*

27.2
Emph

In your reading you will sometimes see a word or phrase repeated deliberately for effect at the beginning of consecutive clauses or sentences:

> I believe this government cannot endure permanently half slave and half free. **I do not expect** the Union to be dissolved—**I do not expect** the house to fall—but **I do expect** it will cease to be divided.—Abraham Lincoln, "House Divided" speech, 1858

The Declaration of Independence illustrates this same kind of repetition. Occasionally you will also see a word or phrase repeated at the end of consecutive clauses, as in Psalm 136, where each verse concludes "for his mercy endureth forever." In the hands of a skilled writer, these techniques can be highly effective, but they should be used very sparingly, and only when a serious subject can be honestly and appropriately conveyed in the deliberate manner they suggest.

Effective (and intentional) repetition should be distinguished from careless repetition, as discussed in 28.3.

Emphasis by Mechanical Devices

The least effective way to emphasize ideas is by italicizing, underlining, or capitalizing words; by setting them off in quotation marks; or by using emphatic punctuation marks (!!!). Certain kinds of advertising rely heavily on such devices:

> "Oh, of course," you may reply, "it's just a matter of calories." But IS it? Suppose you had to choose between a larger glass of orange juice and half a sirloin steak? You would probably reach for the orange juice. Actually, *the steak would give you 15 times as many ENERGY-stimulating calories.* Yet *the total number* of calories in each is roughly the same! So, you see, it ISN'T "just a matter of calories." It's the KIND of calories that makes the big difference.

In most writing, mechanical devices for emphasis should ordinarily be avoided; the wording of a statement or its position in a sentence should give it the emphasis it deserves.

Exercise 27.E

Rewrite the following sentences so that the important points are correctly emphasized.

1. Television programs today are very adolescent in content, at least most of them.

2. There were two magnificent volcano peaks which towered over the valley.

3. Students on the campus were completely unaware that under the abandoned stands of Stagg Field scientists had produced, through concentrated day-and-night effort under rigid security precautions, the first controlled atomic chain reaction.

4. There is something the average voter doesn't realize— that his ONE vote really *can make a difference;* in fact, it can change the outcome of the WHOLE ELECTION!

5. Thumbing frantically through his catalogue and clutching his registration cards in his sweaty hands while he stands in line is the typical freshman.

6. Sculpture is an excellent hobby, although it can be expensive and not everyone has the skill to pursue it.
7. Outside his office there were several customers waiting, and they insisted there were other matters they had to attend to.
8. Many juvenile delinquents (you'd be surprised *how* many) have parents who refuse to try to *understand* them. ∎

Avoiding Stringy Sentences

Avoid stringing together (with *and, but, so, and then)* statements that should be written as separate sentences or as subordinate elements. Sentences carelessly tacked together in this manner are not only monotonous to read but lose all their emphasis because every idea seems to be of equal importance:

> About fifty feet away I saw a buck deer running for safety **and so** I kneeled on my right knee **and then** I brought the rifle to my right shoulder. He was still running, **so** I fired one shot at him, **but** I missed, **but** he stopped and looked at me, **and then** I had a much better target to shoot at.

Reading such sentences aloud should reveal their weaknesses and help you revise them for better organization.

> About fifty feet away I saw a buck deer running for safety. Kneeling on my right knee and bringing the rifle to my shoulder, I fired once, but missed. He stopped to look at me, providing a much better target.

27.2

Emph

Avoiding Misrelated Ideas

When ideas are haphazardly related, your sentences will be puzzling and unemphatic. Don't leave it to your readers to figure out why you have linked ideas together:

> As Byron is the poet of youth, it is appropriate that the new and completely reset edition of his poems should be published on March 1. [What is the relation between *youth* and the date of publication?]

> Nassau has a delightful climate that attracts hundreds of tourists every year, and some historians think that Columbus landed in this area in 1492. [If there is any relationship between Nassau's climate and Columbus, it should be stated.]

Exercise 27.F

Revise the following passages to clarify the meaning and to eliminate ambiguities and contradictions.

1. My high school days are over and I realize I cannot turn back time, so I must now make the best of my future. Now that I am continuing my education, I am also trying to improve on the mistakes I made in high school. One by one I am ironing out the deep wrinkled problems and solving them.

2. There is a lot of evidence that great scientific discoveries do not happen by chance, but usually involve thinking on the part of the scientist.

3. There are two major factors that help a person mature, heredity and environment. Although my heredity was good, my environment was a different matter. The friends I had were by no means juveniles, nor were they scholars. Since I spent most of my spare time with my buddies, I adopted the same habits they had concerning studying. We did not excel or fail in school, but we could have done a lot better.

4. As time passes, many complexities in our environment result from scientific and technological advancements which create new branches in every field of activity, thus causing the youth of today to seek out a more thorough education.

5. The body goes through certain changes between youth and old age, whether a person realizes it or not. ■

27.2
Emph

Exercise 27.G

In the following paragraphs too many simple sentences are used to convey the ideas represented. Rewrite the paragraphs by combining the sentences when necessary to show the interrelationships between ideas and to show their relative importance. You may vary the order of sentences in your revision if you wish.

1. The powder dissolved. It was a mixture of bauxite and sodium. The chemist stirred it. She used a glass rod to stir it. She stirred it into a beaker of water. The solution was poured into another beaker. This beaker was larger.

The chemist stirred the mixture again. She watched the solution turn milky. The solution changed as the chemist stirred.

2. England was once the home of Germanic tribes. These tribes spoke a dialect we call Old English. Old English was the ancestor of Modern English. Modern English is a Germanic language. It is in the same language family as German, Dutch, and Swedish. English is not a Romance language. It has many Romance words. Romance languages include French, Spanish, and Italian. These Romance words came to English during the eleventh century. The Norman Conquest in 1066 brought the French language to England. French was the language of the conquerors. French became the language of the upper class. English speakers began to adopt French words and phrases. They intermingled these French words and expressions with their native English tongue.

3. The effects of the Norman Conquest continue to this day. They survive in our English language. The French influence still remains. Today we use many Romance words in Modern English. We use these words along with Germanic words. Our language is a record of our past. It retains history. The history belongs to a civilization. The civilization is composed of speakers. They all speak the language. They all partake of its history. They all contribute to its history. Language is an on-going record of civilization. ∎

27.2
Emph

Exercise 27.H

This and the previous chapters explore ways to arrange sentences to give them the effect you want them to have. For additional work in composing sentences, practice some of the special arrangements below, either by composing your own sentences or by copying sentences from your reading that illustrate the arrangements.

1. A sentence with three parallel units
   Example: He was disappointed with his car, mad at the salesman, and disgusted with himself.
2. An antithesis, in which contrasting or opposite terms occur in successive clauses

Example: I admire your courage, but I question your judgment.

3. A sentence in which the normal order (S–V–O) is inverted
    Example: One poll does not an election make.
4. A sentence in which conjunctions occur between each of the elements in a series
    Example: A loaf of bread and a jug of wine and thou may be all right with him, but I want a loaf of bread and a jug of wine and thou and air conditioning.
5. A group of sentences with repeated openings or a sentence with repetition at the beginning of successive clauses
    Example: ". . . We shall fight on the beaches, we shall fight on the landing-grounds, we shall fight in the fields and in the streets, we shall fight in the hills. . . ."
    —Winston Churchill
6. A group of sentences with repeated endings or a sentence with repetition at the end of successive clauses
    Example: "The world will little note, nor long remember, what we say here, but it can never forget what they did here."—Abraham Lincoln
7. A group of sentences in which the last word in one sentence is the first word in the next
    Example: Excellence is our standard. Standard, we think, is substandard. Substandard is not permitted.
8. A sentence in which the words in the first clause are reversed in the second clause
    Example: ". . . Ask not what your country can do for you; ask what you can do for your country."—John F. Kennedy ■

Exercise 27.1

The following sentences constitute the text of a letter. Combine and restructure the sentences to make the piece read more smoothly. In deciding how to combine and organize the material, assume the following conditions: the letter is from a panel of individuals who are in charge of assigning study cubicles to students. The panel has written this letter to defend firmly and politely its assignment policies against complaints that it has shown favoritism and has become lax in carrying out its duties.

January 15, 1985

To Whom It May Concern:

We try to make everyone happy. The assignment system has its shortcomings. We admit that. It is not a perfect system. The arrangements we make cannot be acceptable to everybody. Some students have their own private study places. Some students are on waiting lists. They have no cubicles at all. We have a limited number of cubicles to assign. Some students have priority over others. Private cubicles are assigned to those who have priority. The ones who have priority are upper-division students: seniors and juniors. In that order. They have shared cubicles in the past. They need private cubicles to write their SENIOR RE-PORTS!!! Other students have earned no priority. They must share their study space. We regard seniority as one of the inescapable facts of life.

Occasionally there are empty cubicles. These cubicles may go unused for quite some time. The students assigned to them don't use them. They pick up the keys at the beginning of a term. A key that has been picked up tells us that a cubicle is occupied. We have NO OTHER WAY OF CHECKING!!! We respect students' privacy. We choose not to monitor the cubicles personally. We try to run a humane system. We are not machines. We are not police either. A humane system is not always the most efficient system to run. We listen to students who have special needs—unusual projects, health problems, and so on—for private cubicles. We make some exceptions. That is a necessary part of the system as we see it.

The Committee on Cubicles

27.2

Emph

Now rewrite the letter from the perspective of some dissatisfied students who wish to direct a polite but firm complaint to the panel in charge of assigning study space. Change the *we*'s to *you*'s and recombine, rearrange, and revise the material as needed so that the letter reads smoothly and conveys the proper emphasis. You may want to add to or delete portions of the text. ■

28

SENTENCE
ECONOMY

28.1

Wdy

Sentence economy means wording statements so that their meaning can be grasped by the reader without unnecessary effort. No one likes to listen to a speaker who talks too much and says too little, and no reader likes to cut a path through a tangle of useless words or constructions to get at a relatively simple idea.

Practicing sentence economy doesn't mean that you should strip your sentences down to the bare minimum, as you might in composing a telegram or writing a classified ad. The shortest words and simplest constructions are not always the most economical, for they may fail to convey your exact or complete meaning. Economy of expression requires rather that you state your ideas in the most accurate and direct way possible.

28.1 Avoiding Wordiness

Wdy Make the sentence or passage marked less wordy and more direct.

You can minimize wordiness in a variety of ways:

1. Look for opportunities to reduce a sentence or clause to a phrase or single word:

   The snow lay like a blanket. It covered the countryside. [two sentences]

   The snow, **which lay like a blanket,** covered the countryside. [one sentence contains the other reduced to a clause]

   The snow covered the countryside **like a blanket.** [one sentence contains the other reduced to a phrase]

   The snow **blanketed** the countryside. [one sentence contains the other reduced to a single word]

2. Eliminate unneeded and ineffective verbs and their modifiers:

Wordy	He crawled slowly over the river bank, looking for the flint chips **which would mean that he had found a campsite.**
Reduced	He crawled slowly over the river bank, looking for flint chips **marking a possible campsite.**

3. Eliminate unnecessary passive verb constructions:

Passive	It **was observed** by all the student mechanics that the wires **had been crossed** by the teacher.
Active	All the student mechanics **observed** that the teacher **had crossed** the wires.

4. Eliminate forms of the verbs _to be_ and _to have_ whenever you can without a loss of meaning:

Wordy	**He is a native of the plains** and knows the value of water conservation.
More economical	**A native of the plains,** he knows the value of water conservation.
Wordy	A few of the fellows **who were less serious** would go into a bar **where they would have** a steak dinner and a few glasses of beer.
More economical	A few of the **less serious** fellows would go into a bar **for** a steak dinner and a few glasses of beer.

28.1

Wdy

5. Eliminate constructions such as *there is, it was,* and *it seems* whenever you can without altering your meaning:

Wordy	There are two plays in our anthology, and I like them both.
More direct	I like both plays in our anthology.
Wordy	There is a suggestion box in almost all big business houses where employees may put ideas.
More direct	Most big business houses provide suggestion boxes for their employees.
Wordy	It seems likely that she will be our next editor.
More economical	She is likely to be our next editor.
Wordy	There is only one excuse that is acceptable, and that is, "I have a class this hour."
More economical	Only one excuse is acceptable: "I have a class this hour."

6. Eliminate *that, which,* and *who* whenever you can without sacrificing clarity or precision:

28.1
Wdy

Wordy	I was sure that he borrowed the calculator.
Tighter	I was sure he borrowed the calculator.
Wordy	I enjoyed the story which she wrote and which *Esquire* published.
More economical	I enjoyed the story she wrote and *Esquire* published.
Wordy	Jack was the one who wrote the manual.
More direct	Jack wrote the manual.

Exercise 28.A

Revise the following passages to minimize wordiness. Combine sentences as needed.

1. It seems to me that many first-time college students have great difficulty in making the adjustment from high school behavior to college behavior. The classroom maturity level of the average freshman is far below what I had been led to expect. The classroom attitudes of the

freshman students seem to be better suited to a less mature format of study than for college-level work. During serious lectures on important class material it is not infrequent that laughing or loud talking can be heard by the entire class. The professor will stop the class only long enough to remind the guilty parties of the severe consequences involved when they are asked to leave the room, which usually means that they may not be allowed to finish the course.

2. Americans of every generation have been exposed to corrupt government officials who abused their powers in order to promote their own interests or beliefs that they have. There was a senator named Joseph McCarthy who was a prime example. This self-appointed guardian of democracy established a senate committee devoted to the seeking out and exposing of communists who lived in America. In a period of time when the fear of communism had already been heightened by the Cold War, the American public was intimidated by Senator McCarthy who bullied them. Innocent citizens and public officials were harassed by McCarthy until he was censured by the Senate.

3. The question over whether or not school lunches should or should not be paid for by an agency of the government is a long-standing debate. As part of a government that is for the people and by the people, I am going to exercise my right to express my opinions on this subject. I feel that it is time for the federal government to finance lunches for all school children as a much-needed social service. ∎

28.2 Removing Deadwood

Dead Revise the sentence or passage to eliminate deadwood.

Deadwood is a term for a particular kind of wordiness: "lazy" words and phrases that clutter up a statement without adding anything to its meaning.

> Anyone acquainted with violin construction knows that the longer the wood is seasoned, the better **the result will be as far as** the tone of the instrument **is concerned.**

Empty expressions like those in boldface above do nothing to further communication. They find their way into first drafts because they come easily to mind. You must prune them out in revision. Eliminating deadwood will make a statement neater and more direct without changing its meaning, as these examples illustrate (deadwood in brackets):

> Every thinking person these days seems to agree [with the conception] that the world has gone mad.
>
> Because [of the fact that] she had been ill, she missed the first two weeks of classes.
>
> After a delay of forty-five minutes, the audience [got to the point that it] became restless and noisy.

The wordy formulas that serve as fillers in casual conversation are more noticeable and annoying in writing than they are in speech. Roundabout expressions should be replaced in revision by more direct terms:

get in touch with	*means*	call *or* see
due to the fact that	*means*	because *or* since
in this day and age	*means*	now *or* today
at the same time that	*means*	while

28.2

Dead

Certain words, generally in stereotyped phrase combinations, account for much of the deadwood found in student writing. Here is a list of some common deadwood words and phrases:

Word	*As deadwood*	*Deadwood eliminated*
case	**In many cases** students profit from the research paper.	Many students profit from the research paper.
character	The gossip was **of a sordid and ugly character.**	The gossip was sordid and ugly.
exist	The crime conditions **that existed** in Chicago became intolerable.	The crime in Chicago became intolerable.
fact	In spite of **the fact that** he is lazy, I like him.	In spite of his laziness, I like him.

factor	Speed is also **an important factor.**	Speed is also important.
line	He always thought he would be successful **along agricultural lines.**	He always thought he would be successful in agriculture.
manner	He glanced at her **in a suspicious manner.**	He glanced at her suspiciously.
nature	She seldom talks on any subject **of a controversial nature.**	She seldom talks on any controversial subject.
seems	**It seems that** we have not lost a daughter, but gained another icebox-raider.	We have not lost a daughter, but gained another icebox-raider.
tendency	When I am supposed to be working, **I have a tendency to** eat popcorn and dawdle.	When I am supposed to be working, I eat popcorn and dawdle.
type	His father had an executive **type of** position.	His father had an executive position.

28.2

Dead

These words have definite meanings in some expressions (a *case* of measles, a minor *character* in the play, a *field* of clover, and so forth), but as used here, they are meaningless and unnecessary.

Exercise **28.B**

Read the following sentences carefully, looking for roundabout expressions and deadwood. Then rewrite them into direct and economical statements.

1. In college one must put away the childish thoughts of her girlhood and begin thinking of the future that lies ahead with adult ideas and responsibilities.
2. Throughout my previous school days I have been the

type of person who hasn't had to study a great deal to get grades above those obtained by the average student.

3. One of my bigger excuses was the fact that I claimed there were too many social activities currently in progress.

4. The method used to detect the approach of other ships is radar.

5. The total and complete lack of meaningful television programming on the major television networks is a situation that disgusts me and that sickens me.

6. Habits can be classified into two distinct types: one is the useful, progressive, uplifting kind while the other is of the nature that deteriorates character and often damages the physical body.

7. My scholastic averages show, in my opinion, a rather distorted picture of my true knowledge.

8. I have chosen this road of higher education to reach my goal, which is that of teaching children.

9. To reach this goal I must be well educated and have a thorough understanding of my subject.

10. The income from the tourist business is an important source of revenue for people who own businesses in Florida. ■

28.2
Dead

Exercise 28.C

Revise the following passages to minimize deadwood and wordiness. Combine sentences as needed.

1. Stemming from a lack of responsibility and self-control, the major factor in the problems faced by many college-aged students is in the area of academic preparation. Once, I sat down in my mathematics class when a scruffy, blond-haired boy asked whether or not I had worked number twenty-five of the homework problems. I replied that I had toiled for three hours on them, and had indeed worked that particular one. He then asked if he could compare his answer with the one that I had; I agreed. I handed him my complete assignment. He produced a sheet of paper which was blank and proceeded to copy every answer that I had worked on onto his paper. I was furious—but not in a position to indicate my displeasure since I had volunteered my answers—and

felt cheated. When students fail to do the preassigned homework assignments, they should accept the consequences in a mature fashion.

2. There are several reasons why the United States needs a military draft, even during times of peace. One of the most evident is due to the fact that the military must have a sufficient level of manpower to defend sufficiently our country. The volunteer-type force will simply not be able, in troublesome times, to bring in enough people. Another ill-effect caused by the volunteer factor is the lowering of standards in all branches of the military. Instead of raising the standards to cope with the sophisticated character of many modern weapon systems, the services have lowered their standards progressively to get the numbers of recruits they need. ■

28.3 Avoiding Careless Repetition

Rep **Eliminate the ineffective repetition of words, meanings, or sounds.**

Unless repeated for a definite reason, a word or a phrase should not be made conspicuous by too frequent use in the same passage.

28.3
Rep

Effective Repetition

Sometimes repetition is essential for meaning or for sentence structure; intentional repetition may also be effective for emphasis:

> There is no way of becoming **inaccurate** by industry, and if you deliberately try to be **inaccurate** you fail. **Inaccuracy** is perhaps the most **spontaneous** and the **freest** of **gifts** offered by the Spirit to the wit of man. It is even more **spontaneous** and more **free** than the **gift** of writing good **verse,** or that rarer **gift** which I have also written of here—the **gift** of writing abominably **bad verse;** exceptionally **bad verse;** criminally **bad verse;** execrable **verse.**—Hilaire Belloc, *On*

Some kinds of words must of course be used over and over again: articles *(a, an, the)*, conjunctions *(and, but, or)* prepositions *(of, in, at)*, and pronouns *(it, that, my, which)*. Because their purpose is strictly functional, these words are usually not noticed.

Useless Repetition

Unintentional, unnecessary, and ineffective repetition of words is illustrated in this passage:

> When I was in high school, I would take a book home once or twice a week and maybe read it two or three hours at a **time. Most of the time** I would read **most** of my homework just in **time** to have it ready before class began. It was very easy **most of the time** to read the assignment and have it prepared when my **time** came to be called upon for recitation.

Repetition of this kind is weak and ineffective, for it focuses attention on words rather than on ideas. It also suggests that the writer may be careless and unconcerned with what he or she is saying.

Repetition of Words

Repeat words in a passage only when you have good reason for doing so. Key words (such as the subject) may sometimes be repeated for clarity or emphasis, but less important terms should not be used more often than necessary.

28.3

Rep

Careless repetition	The **problem** of feeding its ever-increasing population is one of India's most acute **problems.**
Revised	Feeding its ever-increasing population is one of India's most acute problems.
Careless repetition	Many people think **that** if a **product** is endorsed by a prominent person **that** it is a good **product** to buy.
Revised	Many people think that a product endorsed by a prominent person is a good one to buy.

Especially to be avoided is repetition of the same word in two different meanings:

Confusing repetition	If I **run,** I'll get a **run** in my stockings.
Revised	If I run, I'll **tear** my stockings.

Confusing repetition	Astrology is so popular in Hollywood that many movie **stars** won't sign a contract unless the **stars** are favorable.
Revised	Astrology is so popular in Hollywood that many of the movie stars won't sign a contract unless their **horoscopes** are favorable.

Repetition of Meanings

Avoid adding words and phrases that repeat meanings already stated or implied. The bracketed expressions in the following sentences are a form of deadwood (28.2). They should be omitted because they merely repeat ideas already in the sentences:

> In the modern world [of today], time has a meaning different than it had when transportation was slower.

> It is believed that the age of the earth is about two billion years [old].

> She decided to trim the family room in bright red, but the [resultant] effect was not what she had anticipated.

Words like *color, size,* and *shape* often needlessly repeat a meaning that is already clear:

Unsatisfactory	His hair was brick red **in color.**
Revised	His hair was brick red.
Unsatisfactory	**The length** of the locks is about two thirds of a mile **long.**
Revised	The locks are about two thirds of a mile long.
Unsatisfactory	Behind the house was an enclosed court which was rectangular **in shape.**
Revised	Behind the house was an enclosed rectangular court.

28.3
Rep

The abbreviation *etc. (et cetera)* means "and so forth." To write "*and* etc." is equivalent to saying "and and so forth." Avoid this nonstandard expression.

Repetition of Sounds

Avoid carelessly repeating sounds. Pay special attention to the sounds of suffixes like *-ly, -ment,* and *-tion:*

> The concept of such sanctu**ary** immun**ity** unquestiona**bly** predominant**ly** influenced the ene**my** to enter into the conflict.

Written permission of the administration is required for re-registration of those students who are on probation.

Alliteration—the repetition of the same sound at the beginning of words in a series—is out of place when it attracts attention to the words at the expense of the ideas:

> I am looking for a shop that still has pleated pants for poor and paunchy professors.
>
> She then made herself comfortable in a rather rickety rattan rocker.

Exercise 28.D

Revise the following sentences to eliminate careless or ineffective repetition of words, meanings, or sounds. If the repetition in any statement seems intentional and effective, explain what purpose it serves.

28.3

Rep

1. The hazy figures in the background are vague and indefinite, and they add a sinister note to the painting.
2. The advantage of getting a broader perspective through travel is only one of the advantages of spending a summer traveling through the United States.
3. Many people live so compulsively by the clock that they have a fixed time for eating, a fixed time for bathing, and a fixed time for everything but enjoying life.
4. An application of lotion to the area of inflammation should relieve the pain.
5. Concrete and steel have both been used successfully in skyscraper construction, but buildings of concrete must have much thicker walls at the lower levels that those of steel. On the other hand, concrete has a far greater decorative potential than steel.
6. Camping in a camper near Canyon Cascade was considered by all to have been a most unique experience.
7. The real truth is that the culprit's cycle was maroon in color.
8. He blamed his cold on the cold weather, sighing that his nasal blockage was totally complete. ■

Exercise **28.E**

The following passage is wordy, repetitious, and indirect. Rewrite it, eliminating unnecessary material and combining sentences as needed.

Morris Dancing

In England and in Canada and also in other British territories, or places which at one time or another used to be influenced by British rule, Morris dancing is a popular entertainment which many people participate in. The tradition of Morris dancing goes back centuries to a time before the Renaissance when Morris dancing was a fertility-type ritual which the Moors used to practice in Spain and which was eventually introduced to England where it continues to survive to this very day. It seems that traditionally Morris dancing teams were comprised totally of all men and no women, though in the United States and Canada, women are now dancing on Morris dance teams. Morris teams usually consist of six members who dance in what is called a set. A set is a formation of dancers that is a little bit like the formations that dancers are in who are doing square dances. The dancers in a Morris dance do traditional steps to English folk tunes, and often they do these steps to English folk tunes while performing hand movements at the same time, and when they perform these hand movements they usually proceed to hold either handkerchiefs or wooden sticks from trees which have the bark stripped off of them. In the process of dancing, they clap the sticks together. At this point in time, Morris dances are most commonly performed at Renaissance festivals, Madrigal dinners, or special events such as Shakespeare festivals. Dancers dress in costumes called kits and they usually consist of white pants or knickers and white shirts and straw hats decorated with flowers and ribbons. They also wear leather bell pads. These bell pads are tied around the lower leg. They are covered with small sleigh bells so that they jingle with the movement of the dancers as they dance to the music. The music is a factor of a variety of instruments including such traditional instruments as the recorder, pipes, whistles, and drums. Morris dancing is of a colorful and noisy character. ∎

28.3
Rep

SENTENCE ECONOMY

■ To Minimize Wordiness:

1. Look for opportunities to reduce a sentence or a clause to a phrase or a single word.

2. Eliminate unneeded and ineffective verbs and their modifiers.

3. Eliminate unnecessary passive verb constructions.

4. Eliminate forms of the verbs *to be* and *to have* whenever you can without a loss of meaning.

5. Eliminate constructions such as *there is, it was,* and *it seems* whenever you can without altering your meaning.

6. Eliminate *that, which,* and *who* whenever you can without sacrificing clarity or precision.

7. Cut out stereotyped phrases.

8. Check for carelessly repeated words or phrases.

9. Check for tautologies *(end result, totally complete).*

10. Check for carelessly repeated sounds.

29

THE MEANING
OF WORDS

A word is dead
When it is said,
Some say.
I say it just
Begins to live
That day.—Emily Dickinson

We usually take for granted that we know the meanings of the words we use, except when there is a question of accuracy (*infer* or *imply?*) or of appropriateness (*boss* or *supervisor?*). But if you are to use the words that will best convey your meaning, you need to know what choices are available to you.

29.1 Words in Context and Situation

Words do not actually have "meaning" until they are used in speaking or writing. Then their meaning derives partly from the *context,* or the words around them, and partly from the *situation* in which they are used, which involves the attitudes and purposes of either a speaker and listener or a writer and reader.

It is easy to see how the context limits the meaning of a word. A word like *deck, run, fly,* or *match* can be used in several senses, but usually in a particular sentence it can have only one meaning:

> Tomorrow we'll take a **run** up to the lake.
>
> You will have to **run** to catch the train.
>
> Frowning, she noticed the **run** in her stocking.
>
> Aaron scored the third **run** after two were out in the seventh.
>
> He did a **run** of scales and decided that was enough practice.
>
> When the store opened on the morning of the sale, there was a **run** on video cassettes.

The situation in which a word is used also helps clarify its meaning. The word *bill* in "The bill is too large" would mean one thing if the speaker were trying to identify a bird and another if he were discussing family finances.

Exercise 29.A

29.1

Mng

The meaning of a word often depends on the context in which it is used. Write two sentences using each of the following words to show how the meanings of the words can change as they move from one context to another.

course	field	cup	stack
studio	pitching	book	feedback

Denotation: The Core of a Word's Meaning

When we first think about the meaning of words, we usually think of their *denotation,* what they have come to represent as a result of the ways they have been used. This is the meaning that dictionaries record and describe for us. The thing that a word refers to or suggests is called its *referent.*

Some kinds of words have more definite denotations than others because their referents are more limited or more exact. Depending on their definiteness, words may be classified into three groups:

1. **Concrete words,** words that name people, places, or objects, are the most exact in meaning: *man, Walt Whitman, Lake Erie, my bicycle, the library, reindeer, a Boy Scout knife.*

2. **Relative words,** words that describe qualities, are less definite than concrete words and frequently depend for their meanings on the situation or on the writer's past experience with a term: *hot, pretty, honest, angry, silly, impossible.* In New York City, a *tall* building might mean any structure over twenty stories, but in a city with no skyscrapers, *tall* might refer to any building higher than five stories. Relative words that are terms of evaluation (*good, bad, strange, effective, worthless*) often take their meaning from the writer's point of view—which readers may or may not share. A *healthy* economy may mean one thing to a Republican, and an entirely different thing to a Democrat. When you use evaluative terms, you need to take into account the possibility that readers may not share your opinions. Consequently you may need to explain how or why you have used a given relative word.

3. **Abstract words,** words that refer to general concepts— acts, situations, relationships, conditions—are the least definite: *reasoning, citizenship, education, intelligence, culture, objectives, art.* Since these words have a range of referents (think of all the activities that may be included in *education,* for example), rather than a specific referent, they are more difficult to use exactly than concrete words. When you use abstract words, you need to keep your audience in mind, being certain to define or explain any terms readers are apt to find difficult or ambiguous. (See also 30.1, Abstract and Concrete Words.)

29.1
Mng

Connotation: The Power to Suggest Meaning

Most words have acquired associations and suggestions that go beyond their denotation. The associations and suggestions are called the word's *connotations.* The word *soapbox* has been so long associated either with ranting politicians or home-made racers (the Soapbox Derby) that we don't think of it as describing a carton for soap. And, as someone has suggested, only a tone-deaf ornithologist might be able to ignore all the mystery and romance associated with the word *nightingale.*

Very often the chief difference between words of closely related denotation is in their connotation. Both *inexpensive* and *cheap* refer to low price, but *cheap* may also connote poor quality; *average* and *mediocre* both refer to the middle of a range, but *mediocre* suggests dispraise; *belief, faith, creed, dogma* all refer to ideas held, but they differ widely in suggesting how they are held. It is easy to see why some students of language say that there are no true synonyms.

Dictionaries try to suggest the shades of meaning that words may have, but the best way to find the exact connotations of a word is to observe how it is actually used in current writing and speech. The connotative value of a word often changes over time. *Sly,* for example, once meant *skillful,* but as it is generally used now it would fit into the same context as *devious* or *tricky;* it may even suggest *criminal* or, sometimes, *lecherous.* Words like *genteel* or *elitist* have lost their favorable connotation as the values they represent have lost much of their appeal. Certain words, usually those whose referents arouse very different responses, are extremely variable in connotation: *punk rock, feminist, right-winger.* When you use such words, be cautious, making sure that your attitude is clear to your reader and that you are being fair to your subject. Words with high connotative value, like words that are associated with prickly controversies, may create special problems for you.

Exercise   29.B

The connotative value of words is important in determining their use: for example, if you say "I am *plump;* you are *heavy;* he is *fat,*" three different pictures emerge. Arrange the following groups of words into columns, according to their connotation: favorable, neutral, or unfavorable.

1. student, scholar, bookworm
2. stubborn, firm, pigheaded
3. counterfeit, replica, copy
4. racy, obscene, blue
5. unusual, bizarre, unique
6. tolerant, flexible, wishy-washy
7. caustic, penetrating, sharp
8. reserved, aristocratic, snobbish
9. buffoon, wit, comic
10. officer, police, copper
11. svelte, anorexic, thin
12. literary artist, hack, writer

Exercise 29.C

Without using a thesaurus, come up with a list of words with various connotations for each of the terms listed below.

Example calm: *sluggish, easy-going, phlegmatic, laid-back, lethargic*

independent	tolerant	suave
famous	careful	ugly
poor	neat	vigorous
ambitious	intelligent	ill
frugal	pacifist	sexy
chaste		

■

29.2 Fair Words and Slanted Words

It is often difficult to distinguish between connotative words used fairly to represent a writer's thoughts and connotative words presented with a slant to manipulate a reader's point of view. Which of the following sentences or phrases is fair, and which slanted? Can such distinctions be made out of context?

29.2
Slant

> A long-time supporter of extreme left-wing causes. . . .
>
> The ACLU might be described as a criminal's lobby. . . .
>
> The Soviets reported that Korean Airlines Flight 007 had been "terminated."
>
> The Supreme Court has guaranteed a woman's right to choice in the matter of abortion.
>
> The Supreme Court has denied the unborn child's right to life.

We may be clever enough to recognize the biases in political rhetoric or propaganda, but unable to detect subtler slanting of words used to shape our beliefs. It may not be possible to speak or write in completely neutral, objective language about anything that has fully engaged our interest. To write well about some subjects—especially those involving political, social, and ethical issues—we must usually care enough about the subject to take a stand or make firm judgments. When we use highly connotative language to strengthen arguments, our adversaries may regard this "fair" use of charged or suggestive words as blatant slanting.

Examine, for example, the first sentence of this paragraph:

> Earth-dwellers now have the choice of making their world into a neighborhood or a crematorium. Language is one of the factors in that option. The right words may not automatically produce the right actions but they are an essential part of the process.—Norman Cousins, "The Environment of Language," *Saturday Review*

The passage occurs in an essay pleading for ethical uses of language, and the author clearly wants to sway us. The word *earth-dwellers* cancels differences arising from sex, race, creed, or nationality, and reminds us instead of our common character and interdependence. The word *neighborhood* suggests security and companionship, weighting the argument in favor of that choice, while the word *crematorium* conjures up the unspeakable horrors of genocide. Slanting here appears to be fair: it is plain that we are getting Norman Cousins' opinion. But a reader suspicious of Cousins' views on the desirability of an international community might regard *earth-dwellers* as a cagey term inserted to gloss over the realities of national differences. And the pairing of the highly connotative *neighborhood* and *crematorium* might be seen as an example of an either/or argumentative fallacy weakly concealed by emotional language. No writer can satisfy and please all readers in a general audience, yet no writer can afford to ignore the connotations in the language he or she chooses.

29.2

Slant

Recognizing and Avoiding Slanted Language

The story is told of a harvester of enormous appetite who shortened the legs of the dining table on the side where he sat so that the food would slide toward him. By exploiting the suggestive power of words, writers can similarly tilt arguments and meanings in their favor.

Sometimes slanting occurs only because writers, in their enthusiasm, allow words that are too intense to intrude in statements presented as fact. To say "All television programs are designed for the twelve-year-old mind" is allowing a personal distaste for television programming to make the writer careless. Superlatives such as *all* or *most, only* or *nothing but* should often be reduced to less extreme words to allow for exceptions and other possibilities. Not *all* television programs are designed for twelve-year-olds.

Much unfair slanting occurs in statements of opinion where a writer, knowingly or not, assumes that he or she is the only reliable resource. There is nothing slanted in a simple statement of one's likes or dislikes *(I can't stand bleating, timorous conservationists)*. But the same opinion stated as a general fact in slanted wording *(Most conservationists are noisy, timorous eggheads who wouldn't recognize a moose if it sat on them)* implies that the writer expects the reader to share that opinion without thinking about it.

Just as writers who unfailingly trust themselves as the only reliable resource are likely to slant their writing, so are writers who, in their enthusiasm for their own position, fail to consider more than one possibility. In the following passage, the author ruthlessly attacks wilderness lovers, using a variety of questionable techniques.

> The trumpeting voice of the wilderness lover is heard at great distances these days. He is apt to be a perfectly decent person, if hysterical. And the causes which excite him so are generally worthy. Who can really find a harsh word for him as he strives to save Lake Erie from the sewers of Cleveland, save the redwoods from the California highway engineers, save the giant rhinoceros from the Somali tribesmen who kill those noble beasts to powder their horns into what they fondly imagine is a wonder-working aphrodisiac?
>
> Worthy causes, indeed, but why do those who espouse them have to be so shrill and intolerant and sanctimonious? What right do they have to insinuate that anyone who does not share their passion for the whooping crane is a Philistine and a slob? From the gibberish they talk, you would think the only way to save the bald eagle is to dethrone human reason.—Robert Wernick, "Let's Spoil the Wilderness"

From one point of view, the passage contains unexamined assumptions (wilderness lovers are hysterical) and unsubstantiated assertions (they speak gibberish)—the sources of much slanting in writing on social or political topics. Yet, to complicate the issue somewhat, the essay can be read from another perspective, one that sees it as deliberately and obviously exaggerated (the "trumpeting voice of the wilderness lover"; "their passion for the whooping crane") to draw attention to the excesses of nature lovers. Is the writer guilty of failing to consider alternative views in his attack, or is onesidedness the fault he is trying to point out in wilderness lovers? This confusion is precisely the kind of dilemma readers often face in evaluating highly connotative prose and the sort of interpretive risk writers run when they produce it. In general, heavily slanted writing can be objected to on at least four grounds:

1. it doesn't accurately represent the situation being discussed;
2. it suggests that the writer is at the very least careless of what he or she says and more probably willing to distort the facts for his or her own purposes;
3. it stands in the way of an intelligent and constructive approach to problems that affect the public interest;
4. it is likely to antagonize the readers (unless they are similarly prejudiced) and so prevent clear communication.

Exercise 29.D

29.3
ww

Practice shifting the values expressed in writing by rewriting the opening three paragraphs in two newspaper articles so as to slant the account one way or another. Discuss the slant, if any, in the original version. Bring to class for discussion some items you find in newspapers or magazines that seem slanted to you. ■

29.3 Choosing the Right Word

WW Replace the wrong word with one that accurately conveys your intended meaning.

In most factual prose, words should be used in their established forms and senses; if they are not, the reader may be misled or confused. An expression such as "The scene *provoked* his imagination" (in which *provoked,* commonly meaning "angered," is inaccurately used instead of *stimulated*) interferes with communication. In revising your papers, check any words that you are unsure of, especially those that are not part of your regular vocabulary. Be particularly alert to words that are easily confused.

Distinguishing Words of Similar Spelling

In English there are many pairs of words that closely resemble each other in sound or spelling but have quite different meanings: *moral* and *morale, personal* and *personnel, historic* and *histrionic.* When writing hastily, you may accidentally substitute one word for another, but you can easily eliminate such errors by proofreading your work and by referring to a dictionary when necessary. When words of identical pronunciation, called *homonyms,* are confused in writing, the mistake may be called a spelling error (*bear* for *bare; there* for *their*). But your instructor is likely to label it WW (wrong word) if he or she suspects that you may not know the difference in meaning (*principal* for *principle; affect* for *effect*).

The following words are frequently confused in college papers. If you are not sure of the distinction between them, remember your dictionary.

accept—except	detract—distract
adapt—adopt	formally—formerly
affect—effect	human—humane
allusion—illusion	imply—infer
censor—censure	persecute—prosecute
cite—site	precede—proceed
complement—compliment	principal—principle
conscientious—conscious	respectful—respective
credible—creditable—credulous	stationary—stationery

29.3

WW

Exercise 29.E

Write sentences using the words listed above. Be sure that your sentences show clearly the differences in meaning. ▪

Distinguishing Words of Similar Meaning

Word errors frequently occur because the writer has failed to distinguish between words of similar meaning. A synonym is a word of *nearly* the same meaning as another:

angry—annoyed—indignant
frank—candid—blunt

      multitude—throng—crowd—mob

      strange—peculiar—quaint—bizarre

A few words have identical meanings and are therefore inter-changeable *(flammable—inflammable; ravel—unravel; toward—towards)*. But most synonyms, while they refer to the same idea or object, differ somewhat in denotation or connotation and thus cannot be substituted for each other without affecting the sense or tone of the statement. One term may be more formal than another *(coiffure—hairstyle)*; more concrete *(tango—dance)*; more exact *(charitable—kind)*; or more personal *(dad—father)*. A useful source of synonyms is a thesaurus—an extremely valuable book to writers who use it judiciously. Be sure you fully understand the denotations and the connotations of any words you select from a thesaurus' ample lists of synonyms.

    Writers sometimes use strings of fanciful synonyms to avoid repeating the same expression for an idea or object *(cats, felines, furry beasts, tabbies, nine-lived creatures)*. Such "elegant variations" are pretentious and are usually more annoying than simple repetition. Readers expect key words to be repeated when they cannot be replaced by pronouns *(cats . . . they)*. Factual synonyms *(these animals)* are also unobtrusive and will seldom strike the reader as repetitious.

29.3

WW

Distinguishing Words of Opposite Meaning

Some pairs of words are confused even though they have contrasting or wholly opposite meanings. Make sure that you know the meanings of the following commonly confused antonyms:

concave—convex	inductive—deductive
condemn—condone	physiological—psychological
explicit—implicit	prescribe—proscribe
famous—notorious	subjective—objective
former—latter	temerity—timidity

Confusing such pairs may result in your saying the very opposite of what you intend. Half-knowing a word is often more dangerous than not knowing it at all.

Exercise **29.F**

Write sentences using the words listed above. Make sure that
your sentences show clearly the differences in meaning. ■

Vocabulary Building

Although many word errors are caused by confusion or carelessness, it's easy to use the wrong word (or settle for the
almost-right word) simply because you do not know another
one. College papers are likely to deal with complex ideas and
precise distinctions that may demand a larger vocabulary than
you have needed in the past.

Most people use only about a third as many words as
they recognize. Thus, an obvious way to enlarge your working vocabulary is through conscious exercise. In making an
effort to say precisely what you mean you should search not
only among the words in your active vocabulary, but also
among those you have learned to recognize. Frequently we
find new words in reading *(cybernetics, rhetoric, apartheid)* and
learn their meanings from the context or from a dictionary.
Using these words in writing or speaking helps make them
more readily available for future use.

It is sometimes possible to guess the meaning of a word
by knowing its parts. Many scientific words, for example, are
formed with suffixes and roots from Greek or Latin:

29.3

ww

mono- (one)	-graph (writing, written)	poly- (many)
bi- (two)	bio- (life)	macro- (large)
tele- (at a distance)	photo- (light)	micro- (small)

Since the combined meanings of the parts may only approximate the meaning of the whole, however, it is usually safer
to use a dictionary and learn the entire word.

Exercise **29.G**

The first word that comes to mind is not necessarily the best
one, even if it means approximately what you intend. Read
each of the following sentences carefully and choose the word
in parentheses that most *exactly* expresses the intended meaning. Use a dictionary if necessary.

1. The latest statistics (dispute, refute, rebuke) his claim that the economy is expanding.
2. In time Einstein (convinced, persuaded, showed) most physicists that his theory was correct.
3. Most states have laws that (stop, deter, prohibit) gambling.
4. We stopped in our stroll on lower Main Street to (give, donate, contribute) some money to a blind man.
5. The remarks at the end of his speech (implied, inferred, insinuated) that he had some financial support for his plan.   ■

Exercise 29.H

Rewrite the following sentences to correct any term or terms used incorrectly, inappropriately, or inexactly.

1. The jury ruled that building a sewage disposal plant so near a residential area constituted an infraction of the rights of homeowners.
2. Although he claimed to enjoy caring for his elderly parents, Song Li unconsciously wanted to be out in the world, starting his own life.
3. Mr. LeFevre was uneasy about his students' reactions to the lecture he planned since he realized that Latin grammar was disinteresting to most college freshmen.
4. Like all first-year students, Michael and Roxanne were paranoia about their grades.
5. The journalist knew that her story inferred that the nurse had perpetuated the crime.
6. Although laws now protect equal rights, individuals and institutions continue to discriminate towards minorities.
7. The social workers devised a questionnaire which they hoped would illicit the facts about the quality of housing in rural environs.
8. Because he had become such an imminent figure in his field, Dr. Czagyi had become a notorious speaker at conventions and workshops.
9. I was so impelled by the violence in that movie that I extirpated myself from the theater.
10. The children in the academy had been so orientated towards competition that they couldn't except the new principle's philosophy of cooperative learning.   ■

29.3

WW

30

THE EFFECT
OF WORDS

Because you can't judge the effect of words out of context, you must rely on your judgment to choose words that will convey your meaning accurately and reveal your attitude toward a subject. You can do three things to make your word choice more effective. First, you can choose the words that best suit your purpose from your present vocabulary. Second, you can sharpen your judgment by paying closer attention to the language around you and noticing the differences in usage you encounter. Third, you can read widely to experience the range and variety of writing. All written English is a bank you can draw on.

30.1 Formal Words

We call a piece of *writing* formal—even if its vocabulary is largely from the range of general English—when its sentences are unusually complex, its organizational patterns tight and demanding. We call *vocabulary* formal if it ranges much beyond the characteristic spoken vocabulary, from words slightly more characteristic of writing than of speaking to such specialized words as *moribund, educand, genotype,* and *ailurophobe.*

Appropriate Use of Formal Words

In using formal language, you run the risk of sounding remote from your subject and from your reader. Unless you are at ease with formal words, you also run the risk of seeming pretentious. But some situations demand and deserve the precision of good formal usage. Some things cannot be said easily, or at all, otherwise. If the nature of your subject requires a formal vocabulary, as the following passage does, use it:

> Through the centuries (if not millennia) during which, in their retelling, fairy tales became ever more refined, they came to convey at the same time overt and covert meanings—came to speak simultaneously to all levels of the human personality, communicating in a manner which reaches the uneducated mind of the child as well as that of the sophisticated adult. Applying the psychoanalytic model of the human personality, fairy tales carry important messages to the conscious, the preconscious, and the unconscious mind, on whatever level each is functioning at the time.—Bruno Bettelheim, *The Uses of Enchantment*

Formal words are appropriate to writers and speakers who use them easily and naturally and to situations that require them for precision. As always, you must be sure that your vocabulary is suited to the audience you are addressing.

30.1
Stilt

Stilted Language

Stilt   **Replace the stilted word or words marked with words from the general vocabulary.**

Stilted language refers to any and all expressions that are too heavy or too formal for the situation. Such words sound artificial, whether they are short or long, common or uncommon. A typical fault of inexperienced writers is the use of "big words" in a misguided effort to sound impressive:

> It is difficult to filter out one specific cause for a social problem. Most often there are many minute factors interrelated and closely correlated. Our conception of a social problem today possesses more magnitude than that of two or three decades ago. We now consider the world as a unit rather than an aggregation of component entities.

Ideas are easier to understand and are more convincing if the wording is natural. It should be exact, not inflated beyond the requirements of the subject or the expectations of the reader. The language of the sentences just cited, for example, might be simplified as follows:

> A social problem can seldom be traced to a single, specific cause. Today we are much more aware of the complexity of social problems than we were twenty or thirty years ago, for we have come to see that all societies are interrelated.

Writers are most likely to use stilted language when they aren't certain what attitude they should take toward their material or toward their readers. They may use inflated diction because they wrongly believe that certain papers should be as formal and impersonal as possible, or that big words will impress the reader, or that inflated diction is humorous ("a fair damsel garbed in the mode of the moment" instead of "a fashionably dressed young woman").

Extremely stilted language is sometimes called *gobbledygook*—inflated diction that seems to have lost all contact with the matter being discussed. Writing full of such jargon is often found in print today, especially in specialized journals and government publications, but this does not make it good English.

30.1
Stilt

The remedy for pretentious language is simple: Review what you have written, preferably some time after you have written it; if you find the language markedly different from what you would use in conversation, look at the words carefully to see whether you can find simpler substitutes.

The trouble with gobbledygook is that people who talk and write that way get to thinking that way. When that happens, they lose connection with the world where humans live, a language machine spins on and on, and the sound of human voices fades.

Technical Words

In writing intended for a general audience, unfamiliar terms not made clear by the context should be defined or explained. Technical terms or unfamiliar expressions that often need explaining include:

1. scientific terms *(isotope, lobotomy, gneiss)* and other expressions restricted to a specialized activity *(a cappella, heroic hexameter, escrow, chiaroscuro, farinaceous, binary);*
2. words used in special senses rather than in the usual way (the *spine* of a book, to *justify* a line of type, the *recorder* as a wind instrument;
3. foreign words and phrases not customarily used by most people *(lex talionis, pourboire, eisteddfod, Walpurgisnacht).*

You should not use an inexact or wordy expression in place of a necessary technical term. If, for instance, the subject of a paper is mountain climbing, it is better to define and use a word like *piton* than to say "those little metal gadgets that ropes are tied to." Do not use unfamiliar words just to show off, but do use and explain all terms essential to your subject.

Often a simple definition or explanation can be worked into the sentence where the technical term is introduced, as in the following examples:

> The ability of the heart to function depends primarily on the state of the heart muscle, or myocardium, as it is technically known.

> In cold weather the Eskimos wear mukluks (fur boots) and parkas (short fur coats with fur hoods).

30.1
Stilt

As a rule, do not simply quote a dictionary definition, which may be too narrow, but compose one that fits the style and scale of your own paper. Compare a dictionary definition of *oligarchy* with this description of the term:

> I mean by "oligarchy" any system in which ultimate power is confined to a section of the community: the rich to the exclusion of the poor, Protestants to the exclusion of Catholics, aristocrats to the exclusion of plebeians, white men to the exclusion of colored men, males to the exclusion of females, or members of one political party to the exclusion of the rest. A system may be more or less oligarchic according to the percentage of the population that is excluded; absolute monarchy is the extreme of oligarchy.—
> Bertrand Russell, *The Impact of Science on Society*

The crucial thing in defining a term is to give an adequate description of the way *you* are using it, with details and concrete illustrations to clarify the meaning.

Exercise **30.A**

Rewrite the following passages in clear and effective English.

1. Our high school was eminently well-equipped for various recreational pursuits. For those of sportive inclination, there was the capacious gymnasium, which resounded to multitudinous roars when our champions engaged a challenging contingent.

2. This film demonstrates the progress of an idealized date, from the ideational impetus to the request, acceptance, the dating experience itself, and the final leavetaking, in the process raising some significant questions regarding dating and suggesting partial answers as discussional guides.

3. Is the love of monetary remuneration such that it acerbates all else into obliviousness? Can we not conjure into our configurations and substratums of consciousness some other destination than the almighty dollar?

4. The utilization and heightened availability of systems of word-processing capability should substantially enhance our current scribal methodologies and significantly alter our modes of perceiving compositional behaviors.

5. It may be a budgetary requisite to seek augmentation of federal receipts through incremental enhancements of the current revenue-generating instruments in order to adequately fund the implementation of new programs of social assistance.

_30.1_

Stilt

Exercise **30.B**

1. Check magazines, newspapers, professional journals, and other sources for examples of writing that is pompous or deliberately obscure. Rewrite the examples that seem most in need of revision.

2. Take a common phrase or expression and translate it into gobbledygook. Give it to a classmate or colleague to translate back into English.

Example Walk. [at a street crossing]
  It is necessary that you perambulate as you traverse this signal-protected pedestrian crossing area; it is strictly forbidden to attempt to cross at any increased rate.

Abstract and Concrete Words

Abst **Replace the abstract expression with one that is more specific.**

Formal writing may tempt you to use words that tend to be more abstract than concrete (see p. 547). Abstract words usually refer to ideas, qualities, acts, or relationships. Concrete (specific) words refer to definite persons, places, objects, and acts. This list suggests the differences between the two kinds of words:

Abstract (general)	*Concrete (specific)*
school	Boston College
men's organization	Lions Club
a politician	the senator from Kentucky
food	cheesecake
an educator	my history teacher
creed	Westminster Confession
east	the East
labor	running a ditching machine

30.1

Stilt

Good writing relies on both concrete and abstract language. The specifics add energy and evidence to a piece, and the abstractions reveal the writer's thoughts. Yet many writers think that serious or formal writing demands a difficult and abstract vocabulary. Others mistakenly assume that the more general their writing, the more convincing and impressive it is. The fact is that even papers on abstract topics ("The Importance of Education," "The Principles of Democracy") can be factual, concrete, convincing, and intellectually rigorous if written in words that represent the writer's experiences and beliefs.

Exercise 30.C

The sentences below are general statements, and they may be somewhat vague. Rewrite each of them so that they use more concrete words and name more specific things. Don't worry about the length of your sentences—think instead about making them as specific as you can.

1.   City noises are sometimes raucous and distracting.

2. Individuals who live in an urban metropolis can engage in more leisure activities.
3. Fuel conservation will require some changes in our way of living.
4. More people now are interested in keeping fit.   ■

Exercise 30.D

Sometimes you may need to generalize without citing specific information. Keep track of the information in each of the items listed below and then write out your generalization from each.

1. one week's daily weather reports in a local newspaper
2. one episode of a soap opera
3. any three hours of listening to the same disc jockey on a radio station you are familiar with
4. the letters to the editor in any three days' issues of a local newspaper   ■

30.2 Informal Words

Informal words include those marked *colloquial* in dictionaries and most of those marked *slang*. *Colloquial* words are those more often found in speech than in writing; *slang* words are likewise more characteristic of spoken language and are apt to be short-lived. Informal words are part of general English, but may not be appropriate to all kinds of writing.

30.2

Inf

Appropriate Use of Informal Words

Informal words are often appropriate in discussions of informal or humorous situations and activities such as sports. They are also sometimes fitting in discussions of more important topics, where the language is typically general English. You will find such words used, without apology or quotation marks, in many reputable publications. Note the boldface words and phrases in these passages:

> Even so, these two bits of intellectualistic slang are preferable to certain other clichés so commonly heard as to be allowed to befoul the language almost unnoticed. No study is **worth its salt** unless it is *in depth;* no memorandum can

be taken seriously unless it is a *position paper;* and everyone is **at sea** until he is *orientated.*—Russell Lynes, "Dirty Words," *Harper's*

It is about 40 years since the pioneer feminists **raised such a rumpus by rattling the cage bars** that society was at last obliged to pay attention.—Brigid Brophy, "Women Are Prisoners of Their Sex," *Saturday Evening Post*

If you are tempted to apologize for informal words by putting them in quotation marks, ask yourself whether they are genuinely appropriate. If they are, use them without apology, but if not, replace them with words from the general vocabulary.

Inappropriate Use of Informal Words

Inf **Change the informal expression to one that is more general.**

It is disconcerting to a reader to encounter an informal expression in relatively formal writing:

The displaced persons in Europe experienced many **tough breaks** after the end of the war. [more appropriate: *hardships*]

The natives believe that they can expiate certain offenses against tribal customs by **throwing a feast.** [better: *giving a feast*]

In formal writing, informal words not only indicate a shift in variety of usage but may also suggest that you've grown careless toward your subject:

When Desdemona failed to produce the handkerchief, Othello began to suspect that she **wasn't on the level.**

Be particularly careful about certain expressions so widely used that you may not realize (until the slip is called to your attention) that they are considered informal rather than general usage:

Plays of this sort are seldom seen **in our neck of the woods.**

Faulkner had **a funny habit** of writing long, rather complicated sentences.

Exercise 30.E

Revise the following passages to increase or decrease the level of formality as indicated in the directions in brackets.

1. [*Increase the level of formality.*] Pain is so unbelievable. It's the kind of thing you don't understand. You just hurt. What actually makes or constitutes pain? How do muscles get sore just from lifting something up? They tell you it's because you put so much stress on them. But then why don't you hurt just from walking around or doing ordinary stuff? Why does the pain come only after working out? I mean you do the same thing to them, move them in the same way. I guess it's just one of those things you have to take for granted.

2. [*Lower the level of formality.*] The significance of the kidney within the framework of human organic functions is that it participates in the removal of materials constituting waste in our blood and it facilitates the achievement of a balance in the amount of acids and bases necessary for the normal operation and functioning of the human organism. The primary function of the organ known as the kidney is the expulsion of metabolic wastes by the forming of the bodily excretion known as urine. The attainment of this goal by the kidney is achieved through the sequencing of three steps: the filtering of the blood, the adding of organic wastes to the nephron tubule, and the reabsorbing of water and minerals. ■

30.3
Trite

30.3 Lively Words vs. Tired Expressions

Good writing, whether factual or fictional, captures a reader's interest and holds attention; other writing, concerned with similar facts or ideas, may strike a reader as lifeless and boring. In either instance the wording may be correct, but in the more enjoyable and memorable reading, the words are fresh and direct:

> Then a tremendous flash of light cut across the sky. Mr. Tanimoto has a distinct recollection that it travelled from east to west, from the city toward the hills. It seemed a sheet of sun.—John Hersey, *Hiroshima*

> Supper was a young squirrel who had nevertheless achieved an elder's stringiness, roasted in foil on the embers, and a potato baked in the same way.—John Graves, *Goodbye to a River*

The search for fresh and direct expression does not require that you strain obviously for effect, by searching for unusual expressions or words, any more than it requires that you use eccentric punctuation or unconventional sentence structure. It does mean that you should take an interest in the freshness of your expression and that you should take sufficient time and thought to put aside worn and tired language in favor of lively words. You want to avoid the momentarily fashionable phrase (vogue words), the too-familiar saying (trite expressions and clichés) and the word afraid of its own meaning (euphemisms).

Vogue Words

All of us from time to time resort too easily to "vogue words," words that our society has currently adopted as signals of value. *Meaningful* is such a word, *dialogue* is another, and *ambience* is a third. These words and others like them come into popular use in a number of ways, and then suddenly they are everywhere. The problem is that when we start using words and phrases such as *the bottom line,* or *relevant,* or *scenario,* then the vogue words begin to take the place of thinking, and we use them automatically.

30.3
Trite

Other vogue words can be listed: *game plan, flat out, lib* (short form of *liberation*), *participatory democracy, pick up on, interface, prioritize, disincentive, victimization, sourcing,* words with *-wise (profitwise, timewise).*

Trite Expressions

Trite   **Replace the trite expression with one that is fresher or more direct.**

Trite expressions, or clichés, are pat phrases so familiar that, given the first words, we can usually finish the expression without thinking:

> This is going to hurt me more ——————
> He is down but not ——————

The problem with trite expressions is that you can use them without thinking. They are there in the air, and you can fill a gap on your page by plucking one. They are part of a community language; using them quickly becomes habitual. But when you use trite expressions, they replace your own words and thoughts, and so they mask your own meaning.

Figurative language (30.4) adds interest to writing when it is fresh and appropriate, but stale comparisons and personifications only bore the reader. It will not make anything seem cooler, hotter, or neater if you describe it as *cool as a cucumber, hot as a two-dollar pistol,* or *neat as a pin.* Here is a short list of trite figures of speech; you can probably think of many similar expressions:

quick as a wink	at the drop of a hat
lost in thought	a watery grave
sly as a fox	run like a deer
rotten to the core	like a shot from a cannon
white as snow	brave as a lion
in a nutshell	Mother Nature

Similarly, many quotations have lost their vividness through overuse:

a sadder but wiser man	all the world's a stage
stone walls do not a prison make	water, water, everywhere

30.3

Trite

If you wish to enliven your writing with quotations, there are many fresher, less-quoted lines.

Euphemisms

A euphemism is a polite expression used in place of a more common term which the user fears might be offensive. Euphemisms are often employed in conversation out of consideration for the listener's feelings: a salesperson is more likely to tell a customer that he has a *problem figure* than that he is *overweight* or *fat.* But although euphemisms are often necessary in social situations, they ordinarily sound evasive or affected when they appear in writing. A great many euphemisms are used in political, social, economic, and military prose to win approval for ideas or concepts that might be rejected or looked upon unfavorably if described more directly:

Euphemistic expression	Direct expression
a pre-owned automobile	a used car
underprivileged, disadvantaged	poor
senior citizens	old people
halitosis	bad breath
unmentionables	underwear
expecting	pregnant
pass away	die
revenue enhancement	tax
strategic withdrawal	retreat
negative incentive	punishment
negative growth	decline

Exercise   30.F

The following sentences contain clichés and trite expressions. Rewrite them in more direct language or, if you can, fresh figurative language.

1. If he wins the election—and he may—we are all up the creek without a paddle.

2. Silence reigned supreme among us as the principal gave us a piece of his mind.

3. When he got to the campus post office and found his failure notice, it was a bitter pill to swallow.

4. Armed to the teeth with notes and coffee, he started to work on his research paper.

5. The chief executive nipped the squabble in the bud and got the discussion down to brass tacks.

6. Each and every man should take out life insurance so that his loved ones will be well provided for when he goes to his eternal reward.

7. I told him straight from the shoulder that his work was no longer acceptable.

8. If it didn't mean showing my hand too soon, I would tell the newspapers that I intend to throw my hat in the ring.

9. A teacher is called upon to render services beyond the call of duty time and time again. His unselfish devotion to the youth of America goes a long way toward making this a better world to live in.

10. The investigators didn't leave a stone unturned in their relentless search for the fugitive from justice.   ■

30.3

Trite

30.4 Figures of Speech

Figures of speech are expressions of comparison, personification, or association used to intensify statements or to make them more expressive and vivid, usually by shifting from the ordinary uses and meanings of words. This is a literal, nonfigurative statement:

> The fewer words a person uses, the more quickly his or her meaning will be understood.

The same idea can be expressed in a more memorable way by a well-chosen figure of speech:

> . . . meaning is an arrow that reaches its mark when least encumbered with feathers.—Herbert Read, _English Prose Style_

Notice how the use of well-chosen figures of speech enlivens this description of a summer morning in New York:

> Heat has an effect on sound, intensifying it. On a scorching morning, at breakfast in a cafe, one's china cup explodes against its saucer with a fierce report. The great climaxes of sound in New York are achieved in side streets, as in West 44th Street, beneath our window, where occasionally an intestinal stoppage takes place, the entire block laden with undischarged vehicles, the pangs of congestion increasing till every horn is going—a united, delirious scream of hate, every decibel charged with a tiny drop of poison.—E. B. White, _The Second Tree from the Corner_

_30.4_
Fig

The use of figurative language is not limited to purely descriptive passages or to "literary" subjects. You will find figures of speech used freely and effectively in such diverse material as financial articles, literary criticism, advertising copy, sports writing, and political discussions. The review on pages 562–63 defines some of the more common types of figurative expressions.

Effective Figures of Speech

Fig   **Change the figure of speech marked to an expression that is more appropriate to your subject and your style; avoid inconsistent figures.**

Although figures of speech, if they are fresh and perceptive, clearly have an appeal, they are *not* mere ornaments. Indeed, when they seem to be ornaments, they are usually being used unnaturally and ostentatiously. Figurative expressions should be in keeping with your subject and your style, and they should be accurate enough to contribute to the meaning. Expressions that are too strong or that strive too hard to be picturesque only confuse or irritate the reader:

> As fall comes in with its gentle coolness, Mother Nature **launches her chemical warfare,** changing the leaves into their many pretty colors.

> My grandfather's barn was **like a medieval fortress shrouded in legend.**

Straining for unusual expressions seldom results in effective writing. The figures to use are those that actually come to mind when you are trying to give an exact account of the subject. They should be fresh, if possible; even more important, they should fit their context and sound natural.

Consistent Figures of Speech

30.4
Fig

A figure of speech should not begin with one kind of picture and switch to another wholly unrelated one. These *mixed metaphors*, as they are usually referred to, often present a ludicrous picture instead of the fresh insight the writer intends:

> When he **crossed that bridge,** he **bit off more than he could count on.**

> The nineteenth century **became a door** opened by some of the braver authors, through which many of the earlier ideas of writing for children, which had been **crushed or discarded, again sprang to blossom,** and spread into the many branches of children's literature that we have today.

If you can look at your own writing with some degree of objectivity, you can usually determine whether a figure is consistent or not. Sometimes an expression that seemed very vivid at the moment of writing proves, upon rereading, to be confusing or even ridiculous.

Exercise **30.G**

The critic I. A. Richards has speculated that we use figurative language more than we are aware. He maintains that we can barely get through three sentences without it. Try confirming this claim in any magazine you have handy. Go through an article or two, copying the figurative language that you find. Classify it according to the types of figures listed in the review on pages 562–63.

Example   There were nine *hands* on the ranch (synecdoche) who tended the cattle and also the fields of wheat that *rippled like waves* (simile) in the wind. ■

Exercise **30.H**

Modify the following sentences by employing the figure of speech indicated in brackets.

Example   He scored low on the exam. [hyperbole]

    If he had scored any lower on the exam, he might have struck oil.

1. That Mercedes cost a lot of money. [hyperbole]
2. Rural life isn't easy. [simile]
3. The stereo receiver made some noises before it blew up. [onomatopoeia]
4. Suzie showed her parents the ribbon she had won at camp for dutifully cleaning toilets and shovelling horse manure. [euphemism]
5. History is a puzzling concept. [metaphor]
6. I love liver. [litote]
7. The computer didn't work well on Mondays or on sunny days. [personification]
8. It was cold. [hyperbole]
9. The 40,000 seat stadium had been built with three restrooms. [irony]
10. He wanted to be a minister, but he became a sports announcer instead. [metonymy] ■

Review

TYPES OF FIGURATIVE LANGUAGE

Hyperbole   Deliberate exaggeration for interest and emphasis.

It was a day **to end all days.**
He's the **greatest** second baseman **in the world.**

Irony   Use of a word or phrase to signify the reverse of its literal meaning.

For Brutus is an **honourable man.** . . . Shakespeare, *Julius Caesar*
That's just **great.** [expression often signifying disgust]

Litotes   Deliberate understatement.

Hemingway was **not a bad writer.**
Golly, what a **gully!** [said of the Grand Canyon]

Metaphor   Implied comparison between two unlike things, often used to show some unexpected likeness between the two.

. . . . Out, out, **brief candle!**
Life's but a walking shadow, a poor player
That struts and frets his hour upon the stage
And then is heard no more. . . . Shakespeare, *Macbeth*

Metonymy   The use of a word associated with a concept to evoke the concept itself.

Suited to the **plow** [to be a farmer], he sought to live by the **pen** [to be a writer].
He's a **jock.**

Onomatopoeia   Use of words to create a sound appropriate to the sense.

The bees **buzzed.**
It was a hot day in late July when I sat with Uncle Miles at Belting beside the **strippling ream.** The deliberate Spoonerism was Uncle Miles's, and it did seem to express something about the stream that rippled beside us as we sat on the spongy grass.—Julian Symons, *The Belting Inheritance*

Oxymoron   Coupling contradictory terms.

At age eleven she **enjoyed the fright** of reading *Dracula*.

Periphrasis   Substitution of a descriptive phrase for a name,
                    sometimes of a name for a descriptive phrase.

Be true to the **red, white, and blue.**

From the baseball stories of my youth, I remember the **Splendid
Sprinter** and the **Yankee Clipper.**

Personification Attribution of human qualities to nonhuman or
                   abstract things.

They turned and waved, and then the jungle **swallowed** them.

Simile   Comparison between unlike things, stated
                   through the use of a word such as *like*, *as*, or
                   seem (see *Metaphor*).

My mistress' bosom **is as white as the snow, and as cold.**—Joseph
Addison, *The Spectator*

Synecdoche   Naming a part when the whole is meant, or
                   naming a whole when a part is meant.

The poor man had twelve **mouths** to feed.

Wisconsin meets **Oregon** in the Rose Bowl.

SPECIAL

ASSIGNMENTS

Part

THREE

A WRITER'S WORK

31

WRITING

FOR THE

PROFESSIONAL

WORLD

If I err, I'd rather err on the side of getting my point across in a human way. . . . Bennett Bidwell

Almost every job in every profession will at some time require writing. Engineers write proposals or reports of specifications. Doctors prepare case histories and instructions. Business people correspond with others both inside and outside their organizations, and they write progress reports, recommendations, and so on. Some organizations specify the formats their writers are to use. Even when this is not the case, most writers in business and professions follow certain conventions—conventions that don't differ much from the standards recommended throughout this handbook.

This chapter discusses some of what is expected in various forms of professional and practical writing, including business letters, memoranda, résumés, and reports. It also includes a brief discussion of word-processing equipment.

31.1 Business Letters

To write an effective business letter, you must know your purpose, understand your audience, organize and convey the content clearly, and present it in an attractive and conventional format. The following sections explain these criteria.

Purpose and Audience of Business Letters

Business letters are the means by which firms communicate with people outside of the organization and with other organizations. People write business letters to organizations to request information, to complain about a product, and so on. In most cases, the writer has both a primary purpose—to order something or inquire about something—and a secondary purpose—to establish a beneficial business relationship. Your purpose in writing a business letter, then, is likely to be both specific and general, informative and persuasive.

A successful business letter may have to make sense to and satisfy several potential audiences. You will want to present yourself as reasonable, competent, and accurate to readers who (you hope) share the same characteristics. As the situation dictates, you will want to be precise yet cordial in making your presentation, avoiding the personal remarks and intimacies that might be found in a personal letter without making your business letter cold and distant. The reader of your business letter is likely more concerned with how your request will affect him or her than with your needs.

Similarly, if you are writing for a company, institution, or agency, the letter you write represents the organization. If you seem curt, remote, disorganized, or inaccurate, so does your employer. And even though you and your company may write hundreds or thousands of letters annually, you are addressing people who may be writing to you for the first time. They expect to be treated as individuals. The standard advice given in many business writing texts is to cultivate a "you-attitude" in your letters. That is, always put yourself in the reader's position no matter how negative your message might be; try to show that you have your reader's interests in mind. Assume good will, not stupidity or malicious intent, on the part of your reader.

The Content and Organization of Business Letters

The content of business letters varies according to your purpose: you may be making a complaint, asking for data, replying to an advertisement, or addressing some other concern. In all situations you need to be as thorough and accurate as possible in assembling information and anticipating your readers' questions. Additional letters of inquiry cost both time and money.

Be sure your readers are aware of the context in which a letter is being written. They should understand why a letter is necessary, what its origins are, or what the letter is a response to. They must see your connections and follow the sequence of your thoughts.

Here is a list of information you may want to include in a business letter. Obviously, not every letter will require all of these elements:

Basic Information

1. Your name.
2. Your address, including *zip code*. If you are a student, you may want to include campus and permanent addresses.
3. Your phone numbers (home/campus/office), including *area code*. You may want to indicate convenient times for calling, if a telephone response is appropriate.
4. Your position or title, when relevant (a student at Tulane; Dr.; D.D.S.; a long-time customer of Montgomery Ward).

31.1

Let

Particular Information

1. Your specific request, complaint, decision, action, and so on. Include all pertinent information—dates, times, quantities, amounts. Be accurate. Indicate when any figures you use are estimates. With certain kinds of inquiries or complaints, you may want to include relevant serial numbers, identification codes, part numbers, account numbers, or catalogue numbers. In many situations, you may be asked to provide your social security number.

2. Important background information.
3. The accurately spelled names of everyone involved.
4. The specific action you are requesting, expecting, or taking.
5. Any conditions that have a bearing on the situation ("If the part is unavailable, please let me know").
6. Any time restraints operating ("If we do not hear from you by December 10, we will have to offer the position to another candidate").

All the information in a business letter should be accurate or verifiable. When appropriate, you may indicate the means by which a reader can check your account:

> My full dossier is available upon request at the Ball State Placement Office. . . .
>
> I have asked the university to forward a copy of my course transcripts.
>
> The figures are those reported in the most recent issue of _The Journal of Petroleum Technology_.
>
> I have enclosed copies of cancelled checks indicating payment [or so that you can check your records].

Do not send your original documents to verify information unless circumstances specifically require them. Rely, instead, on copies you can afford to lose.

A business letter should be clearly organized and should get to the point immediately. There is usually no need for a rambling preamble or chatty introduction. Identify your purpose as quickly as possible:

> I am applying for the position of communications officer announced by Alcoa in its _Wall Street Journal_ job listing on May 12.
>
> I am asking you to investigate a misunderstanding I have had with Mr. James Barlow, your service representative in the McLean, Virginia, region, about the Skinner Corporation's responsibility for the costs of labor in repairing my defective Skinner vacuum sweeper, model 2-TM3 (serial #631473B). I ordered the sweeper through your catalogue on September 27, 1984; it is still covered by your full three-year warranty (copy of warranty and sales receipt enclosed).

Use the paragraph structure of your letter to organize and separate different kinds of information and requests. Each paragraph can focus on a single aspect of the issue. For example, the paragraph above to the Skinner Corporation introduces the writer's concern. Subsequent paragraphs would then provide the explanatory details. For example, if the customer encountered Mr. Barlow three times, three separate paragraphs might follow, each explaining one service problem. A separate paragraph would outline what the customer is requesting. A concluding paragraph may or may not be necessary. (See the sample letter on p. 578.)

Paragraphs in business letters are usually shorter than those in essays and reports. Single-sentence paragraphs are both common and appropriate.

The Tone and Style of Business Letters

Business letters should be clear and unpretentious. Too many business letters—especially letters of recommendation and job applications—are written in stiff, impersonal styles. Or they lapse into the jargon of a particular trade or profession, or fall into strange bureaucratic dialects, where simple things become complex and complex things become impossible:

> Regarding your recently forwarded request, attached please find the application form which should be completed and submitted in accordance with the instructions affixed. Please sign the document and return promptly to the address indicated above.

31.1

Let

Business and professional letters should not rely on faddish language and vogue expressions such as the following:

Poor	Improved
parameters	limits
dialogue with	talk with
prioritize	set priorities
implement [v]	carry out, accomplish
causative factors	causes
viable	workable; possible
optimize	perfect [v]; improve
interface with	meet with; work with
in-depth study	study
bottom line	profit; most important (feature)

Nor should they employ formal, obsolete expressions that tend to deaden communication:

Poor	*Improved*
at your earliest convenience	soon
avail yourself of this opportunity	try
enclosed please find	here (is)
in accordance with	as (we) agreed
pursuant to	regarding
as per our conversation of	as
contents duly noted	thank you
due to the fact that	because

Business letters should be edited according to those guidelines for eliminating wordiness and deadwood that apply to other kinds of writing (see p. 523).

A business letter should be brief and precise, but it should not be cold and impersonal. You may, for example, use personal pronouns and contractions (sparingly) in business letters when they make your writing sound natural and clear. You want to give an impression of concern and interest, particularly when you are writing for an institution that deals with hundreds or thousands of people:

Not   Received in this office your communication pursuant to complaint concerning Skinner Vacuum Sweeper 2-TM3.

But   I have read your letter concerning the warranty service you've received on our Skinner Vacuum Sweeper (Model 2-TM3).

31.1

Let

Whether you are writing *to* an institution or *for* one, you should strive to be polite and positive, tactful and sympathetic, not surly and negative:

Not   That pile of junk you call a vacuum sweeper vibrates and wheezes like an asthmatic steam engine and couldn't suck up a feather if you stuck it down its throat. I don't suppose you'll do anything about it.

But   My Skinner vacuum vibrates, wheezes, and has virtually no suction. Please help me obtain the appropriate service.

Not	This company refuses to repair any of their implements subjected to abuse by their operators or employed in commercial applications.
But	Our warranty covers only vacuum sweepers used for purposes they were designed to handle. From your description, your vacuum sweeper was used for purposes clearly beyond the scope of our warranty.

A human being ought to show up even in the most routine business letters. Impersonal language is not more accurate or official than natural, human language.

Assembling the Business Letter

Companies and large institutions often adopt particular formats for their communications, specifying everything from the shape of paragraphs and the size of margins to particular style preferences. You should follow any guidelines provided by your employer. When you write a business letter for yourself, you can choose among the formats illustrated in the section of sample letters (pp. 578–89). Whatever your format, most business letters have to take into account the following features and components.

Format of the Letter

Paper. Use good quality paper. The standard sheet for business letters is 8½ by 11 inches—the same size as ordinary typing paper. Businesses and institutions often provide letterhead paper with the name and address of the firm printed at the top.

31.1

Let

Typing. Business letters should be typed. Use single spacing within each section of the letter, including addresses. Double space between divisions and paragraphs. Type on one side of the paper only. Retype heavily corrected letters.

Margins and white space. Margins vary, but they should always be wide enough all around the sheet to present a handsome appearance, like the frame around a picture. Try to keep the right-hand margin reasonably straight; one or two words stretching noticeably past that margin can detract from the professional appearance of a letter. Avoid typing all the way to the bottom of a page.

Very short letters should be centered slightly above the middle of the sheet and arranged to fill the page as attractively as possible. Lengthy letters should not be crowded. Try to break up long paragraphs at logical divisions to increase the white space and enhance readability. A page of uninterrupted single-spaced typing is not inviting.

Pagination. There are advantages to keeping a business letter to a single page. But if a letter runs to more than one sheet, number the pages (after the first) at the top, preferably in the right-hand corner.

The Components of the Business Letter

The Heading. The heading supplies the address of the letter writer and the date of the correspondence:

> 902 Luther Place
> Duluth, Minnesota 55804
> January 5, 1985

Its position in the letter depends upon the format selected (see sample letters). If letterhead stationery is used, only the date needs to be provided, its position determined by the design of the letterhead. The heading is always single-spaced. Dates may be given in either of these forms:

> May 28, 1984   28 May 1984

Do not use fully numerical dates (5/28/84) in the heading.

31.1

Let

Inside Address. The inside address gives the full name and address of the person or firm to whom the letter is directed. The inside address should correspond exactly with the address on the envelope in which the letter will be mailed. Include any titles and positions used by the person to whom you are writing:

> Naomi Leventhal, Ph.D.
> Research Associates, Inc.
> 10815 North Lamar Boulevard
> Austin, Texas 78744

Never allow titles and degrees to overlap:

Not	Dr. Naomi Leventhal, Ph.D.
But	Naomi Leventhal, Ph.D.
Or	Dr. Naomi Leventhal

The inside address is typed flush with the left-hand margin of your letter, from one to six lines below the last line of the heading. No punctuation is used at the end of the lines. The inside address should match the address on the letterhead of material you may have received from the company or institution to which you are writing.

Greeting. The greeting or salutation appears below the inside address, separated from it by a line of space. In business letters, it is followed by a colon. If the letter is addressed to a particular individual in a firm, you may use either the name or an impersonal greeting:

Dear Mr. Kaiser:	Dear Sir:
Dear Miss Jenkins:	Dear Madam:

Until recently it was customary to use the masculine form of address *(Gentlemen:* or *Dear Sir:)* if the letter was addressed to the firm as a whole or to an individual whose name was unknown. Since the recipient is just as likely to be a woman as a man, however, alternative salutations are becoming more widely used. One acceptable salutation is simply the name of the company or, if appropriate, the title of the individual or department:

Dear Sir or Madam:

Dear Editor:

Dear Matthews Camera Company:

When titles are employed in a greeting, they are ordinarily spelled out in full, with the exception of the most common ones *(Mr., Mrs., Ms.,* and *Dr.):*

Dear Dr. Soellner:	*but*	Dear President Reagan:
Dear Mrs. Beasley:		Dear Senator Metzenbaum:
Dear Ms. Frost:		Dear Professor Altick:

In some business correspondence, the greeting may also include an *attention line* or a *subject line*. These special lines may be located above the greeting or after it. An attention line identifies a particular person in a firm who might take special note of your letter, although the letter itself is directed to the company, not to the individual:

> Dear Ross, Ernst, and Wherry:
>
> Attention: Ms. Sandra Brown, Comptroller

A subject line identifies the particular concern of your letter. It is useful in directing your letter to the right department or person:

> Subject: Your Order #201
>
> Dear Mr. Krebs:

Both of these devices are likely to be used only in relatively formal business communications.

The Body. The body of a letter should be attractively arranged to highlight the important information. The various paragraph formats for the body are illustrated in the sample letters.

Closing. A conventional expression called the *complimentary close* is used at the end of the letter. Only the first word of the close is capitalized; a comma follows the last word. The general tone of the letter will suggest how formal the close should be:

Formal	*Less formal*
Yours truly,	Sincerely yours,
Yours very truly,	Sincerely,
Respectfully yours,	Yours sincerely,

The close can be either flush with the left-hand margin or in the middle of the page, depending on the chosen letter format.

The Signature. The signature is always written in longhand below the closing. For clarity, however, you should type your name below your signature. It is also a common practice in business letters to indicate your position:

Sincerely yours,

Randolph Garcia

Randolph Garcia
Director of Admissions

Some firms also include the name of the company in the signature:

Yours truly,
WYOMING BOX, INC.

Ethel Hazelton

Ethel Hazelton
Production Manager

Be sure to allow enough space—usually four lines—between the closing and your typed name for an uncrowded signature.

Below the signature, you may find a number of notations in a business letter. Sets of initials in the lower left-hand corner indicate that the letter was typed by someone other than the writer, usually a secretary. The first initials belong to the person who dictated the letter, the second to the person who typed it. Forms for this notation vary:

JR/cr   GM:dw
JR/CR   GM:DW

Identifying initials may be followed by a line indicating that something has been included with the letter. Again, this *enclosure line* may take one of several forms:

JR/cr
Enclosure

JR/cr
Encl.

GM/dw
Enclosures 2

SJ/kl
Enclosures 2
      1. Annual Report
      2. Product Catalogue

A notation may also indicate that copies of a letter have been sent to someone other than the person it is addressed to:

AC/pl
cc: Mary Trachsel
    Roger Cherry

31.1

Let

The Envelope

Both the address of the person to whom you are writing and your own address should be clear and complete on the front of the envelope. A block style—with the left-hand margin even—is the standard form for both addresses.

No punctuation is used at the end of the lines in this form. A comma is used between the name of a city and the state if they are put on the same line, but not between the state and the ZIP code:

Chicago, Illinois 60611

When you abbreviate street designations, use the standard forms *(St.* for *Street, Ave.* for *Avenue, Blvd.* for *Boulevard).* For names of states, use only those abbreviations given in your dictionary *(Penn., Okla.)* or the ZIP code directory (PA, OK).

Use an envelope that matches your stationery and fold the letter to fit. With long business envelopes, a standard sheet (8½ by 11 inches) is folded horizontally into three sections. With short business envelopes, it is folded once across the middle and then twice in the other direction.

```
Alice B. Clink
2914 West Lynn
Morgantown, West Virginia 26505




                        Personnel Director
                        Data Management Corporation
                        201 Andrews Building
                        Westover, West Virginia 26504
```

31.2
Job

31.2 Résumés and Job Application Letters

When you apply for a job, you are usually expected to introduce yourself to a prospective employer through a résumé and a job application letter. The résumé is a one-page sum-

Sample Letter in Modified Block Format: Complaint

1204 Robert Lane
McLean, Virginia 22101
February 15, 1985

Skinner Corporation
Electric Appliance Division
One Renewal Plaza
Ypsilanti, Michigan 48197

Dear Skinner Corporation:

I am asking you to investigate a misunderstanding I have
had with Mr. James Barlow, your service representative in
the McLean, Virginia, region, about the Skinner
Corporation's responsibility for the costs of labor in
repairing my defective Skinner vacuum sweeper, model 2-TM3
(serial # 63147313). I ordered the sweeper through your
catalogue on September 27, 1984; it is still covered by
your full three-year warranty (copy of warranty and sales
receipt enclosed).

Approximately three months after I purchased the Skinner
sweeper, it failed to operate and was repaired by
Mr. Barlow on December 28, 1984, at his shop in McLean at
no cost to me.

A month later, the machine again failed, having lost all
power. On January 23, 1985, Mr. Barlow replaced the
on/off switch at no charge. The switch showed evidence of
corrosion. The machine ran weakly for another two weeks,
wheezing and vibrating.

I returned the machine for service on February 8, 1985.
Mr. Barlow called me later that day to report that when he
opened the machine for a thorough inspection, he found the
motor and most internal metal parts corroded or water-
damaged. He indicated that he had replaced the motor and
refurbished other damaged components, but that since the
machine showed evidence of abuse, he would have to charge
me $76.00 for labor. He claimed that the machine was no
longer covered by the three-year warranty because it had
been subjected to conditions it was not designed for.

31.2
Job

HEADING

In modified block form, the address and date, as well as the closing and signature, are centered on the page. Paragraphs are <u>not</u> indented, however.

INSIDE
ADDRESS

GREETING

A colon always follows the greeting in a business letter.

BODY

Notice that the writer is careful to provide the name of the service representative, the model and serial numbers of the defective machine, and the date of purchase. Supporting evidence is also enclosed.

The writer narrates the sequence of events in his complaint. Each incident is described in its own paragraph.

The first two paragraphs provide background information.

The major issue is addressed in detail in this longer paragraph.

31.2
Job

While it is true I used the sweeper in an emergency
shortly after purchase to vacuum up some water that had
leaked onto the carpet in my office during a heavy
rainstorm, I do not believe that action constituted abuse.

I am grateful Mr. Barlow was willing to cover the cost of
a new motor, but I believe I am entitled to a full
reimbursement of the labor charges which I was forced to
pay to get my machine out of Mr. Barlow's shop. The terms
of your _full_ warranty promise replacement or repair of all
defective parts without cost to the purchaser.

I await your prompt reply.

Sincerely,

Patrick J. Williams

Patrick J. Williams

Enclosures 2
cc: Virginia Consumer Protection Agency
     FTC

The customer indicates exactly what action he expects. Note that he underlines full since that term has particular significance in this complaint.

CLOSING   In the modified block format, both the closing and signature are
SIGNATURE   centered.

These notations acknowledge the enclosure of copies of the warranty and sales receipt and indicate that the writer has sent duplicates of his letter to two government agencies.

Sample Letter in Full Block Format:
Adjustment of Complaint

One Renewal Plaza
Ypsilanti, Michigan 48197

February 23, 1985

Mr. Patrick J. Williams
1204 Robert Lane
McLean, Virginia 22101

Dear Mr. Williams:

I have read your letter of February 15, 1985, in which you
ask to be reimbursed for the costs of labor charged to you
for the repair of your Skinner vacuum sweeper, which is
still under warranty. I have talked to our service
representative in McLean, Mr. James Barlow, about your
problem.

Based on your description and on our own examination, the
sweeper was used for purposes that are beyond the terms of
Skinner's full warranty. Our warranty covers only vacuum
sweepers used for purposes they were designed to handle.
Both the instruction manual and warranty expressly warn
against the hazards of using the machine in wet conditions. Mr. Barlow indicates that water corrosion was
responsible for all three failures of your machine. We
have no obligations under warranty to pay for parts or
labor in these circumstances.

Yet because we value you as a customer, Skinner Corporation is willing to cover half of your labor costs for the
third repair. I am enclosing a check for $38.00.

31.2
Job

HEADING   The company letterhead provides the address. In full block form, the address and date, as well as the closing and signature, are aligned with the left-hand margins. Paragraphs are <u>not</u> indented. Full-block form is customarily used only with business letterhead.

INSIDE   The inside address is aligned with the left-hand margin.
ADDRESS

GREETING

BODY   Paragraphs in full block form are <u>not</u> indented.

The body of this reply to Mr. Williams' complaint first acknowledges the previous letter (see p. 672). Then, in a separate paragraph, it establishes the company's position. The third paragraph offers a compromise.

31.2
Job

Used for appropriate purposes, your Skinner sweeper will,
I am sure, give you dependable service in the future.

Yours truly,

Kirk Rodgers

Kirk Rogers
Consumer Affairs Director

KR/dj
Enclos.

CLOSING

SIGNATURE

In full block form, the closing and signature are aligned with the left-hand margin. The signature here also indicates the writer's position with the company.

These notations indicate that Mr. Rogers' letter was typed by a secretary with the initials D. J. and that one item (a check) is enclosed.

Sample Letter in Indented Format:
Letter of Recommendation

2914 West Lynn
Morgantown, West Virginia 26505
April 7, 1986

Personnel Director
Data Management Corporation
201 Andrews Building
Westover, West Virginia 26504

Dear Personnel Director:

    Andrea Leonardi, an employee at my restaurant, Night
Out, for the past three summers (1983-85), has asked me
for a job recommendation. I understand that she is
seeking a position as a computer management specialist
with your firm.

    Of course, the kind of work Ms. Leonardi did for me
during her summer vacations differed considerably from the
profession she was being trained for at the University of
Michigan, from which she will be shortly receiving her
B.S. degree. She started initially as a waitress, but by
the end of her last summer with me, I would have been
pleased to hire her permanently as my manager.

    Specifically, Ms. Leonardi is an exceptionally
talented employee who has a sharp eye for detecting
problems and eliminating them. Less than a month after
she began working at Night Out, she suggested a reorganization of table responsibilities that led immediately to
swifter service and created less friction among waitresses
and waiters. During her second summer I encouraged her to
analyze and reform my buying procedures--and the result
was a noticeable improvement in the quality of our produce
and meats at a 15 percent savings.

HEADING   In the indented format, the heading, closing, and signature are centered.

INSIDE   The inside address is aligned with the left margin.
ADDRESS

GREETING

BODY   Paragraphs in the indented format are indented between five and ten
spaces. This is the difference between the indented format and the
modified-block format, which does not use indention.

A good letter of recommendation describes the specific qualifications
and attributes of a job candidate.

Particular examples of a candidate's ability can provide convincing   *31.2*
evidence of merit.
                                                                     Job

As you can see, Ms. Leonardi has enormous potential
in management. Just as important, though, she gets along
superbly with her colleagues who might well have envied
her talents and rapid advancement as a summer employee.
Instead, they actually anticipated her return each May,
knowing that her work was likely to contribute to their
own security and well-being. Andrea has all the qualities
an employer looks for: reliability, honesty, good nature,
and, most of all, intelligence.

I can recommend her to you without exception or qualification. Andrea Leonardi may be the best employee I
have had in the seventeen years I have owned Night Out.
My only regret is that her training and interests have
prepared her for more challenging and financially rewarding work than I can offer her. Please call me if you
would like additional information.

Sincerely,

Alice B. Clink

Alice B. Clink
Proprietor, Night Out
421-4848

31.2
Job

The letter addresses specific concerns any employer might have about a job candidate.

CLOSING

SIGNATURE

31.2
Job

mary of pertinent information about yourself, including personal data, educational background, and employment record. It is a general statement, suitable for circulation among a number of potential employers. The job application or cover letter accompanying the résumé is more specific. It explains to the employer why you are interested in the job and why he or she should examine your résumé and ask to interview you. The résumé and letter should be carefully prepared since they represent your foot in the door and convey to employers the first impression they will have of you.

The Résumé

There is no standard form for the résumé. The sample on p. 592 is only one of many acceptable designs. A good format is any that presents information clearly and neatly, in statements that are reasonably parallel. Divisions and subdivisions should be logical and a reader should be able to locate information quickly. The most important details (such as major degrees, work experience, and achievements) should be highlighted so that your qualifications are apparent at a single glance. Résumés ought not ordinarily exceed one page—especially early in a career.

Personal Information. You should include your name, address (including zip code), and phone numbers (including area codes). If you are a student, you may want to provide both campus and home addresses. If you are already employed, you may want to do the same with business and home locations. You are not expected to furnish information about age, sex, marital status, number of children, or physical characteristics (height, weight) on a résumé. Nor should you have a photograph printed on it.

Education. Employers are always interested in the education and training you have had. You need not mention elementary and junior high experience. Depending on the job, high school work may or may not be significant. College, vocational, professional, graduate, and postgraduate experiences should be listed in an appropriate sequence, usually chronological. Be sure to name the degrees you have received, the institutions granting them (with city/state location if not well

31.2
Job

known), and the year the degrees were conferred, as well as any academic scholarships or honors you received.

Employment. Potential employers will want to know what kinds of work experience you have had and when. You should list jobs relevant to the position you are seeking. For some applications you would want to list only important, full-time work you have had. In others, it may be important to show that you have had a diversity of experience. Students might want to list, for example, summer jobs they have held. Be sure to give the names and (when needed) the addresses of previous employers. Try not to leave unexplained gaps in your employment or academic records; potential employers often look for a steady pattern of education and employment in your background.

Awards, Achievements, Interests. Depending on the position you are seeking, you may want to list major awards you have won or positions and offices you have held. The key here is selection. An employer obviously will be eager to interview a job candidate who can present evidence of significant accomplishments or community service. But you must assess your achievements through the eyes of the employer, not your own. You may be very proud of 4–H ribbons, scouting medals, or high school academic prizes, but they may seem less impressive to a company or institution hiring on a regional or national scale. Many employers like to see evidence of community involvement or outside interests and hobbies, but these matters can usually be left off the résumé and saved for the interview.

31.2
Job

Recommendations, Credentials, and Placement Services. A résumé may include the names and correct titles (Professor, Dr., Ms., Mrs.) of people who have agreed *in advance* to provide you with educational, personal, or employment references. It is also acceptable to include one line—"References Available on Request"—but be sure your references will agree to recommend you. The résumé may also indicate whether your full credentials (all letters of recommendation, transcripts of grades, lists of course work) are available as a package through some placement office or job-finding service. Be sure to furnish complete addresses.

Sample Résumé

Irene Tremain
856 East Oceanside Drive
Los Angeles, California 90016
(213) 267-1927

OBJECTIVE   Position in applied bacteriological
                 research, especially in some area of
                 disease control or prevention

EDUCATION   1982-84
                 Ohio University, Athens, Ohio
                 M.S., Bacteriology

                 1978-82
                 Duke University, Durham, North Carolina
                 B.S., Biology

                 Summer 1981
                 The University of Chicago
                 Seminar in microbiology and statistical
                 techniques

EXPERIENCE   June, 1984--present
                 Los Angeles Board of Health
                 Specialist in epidemological studies.
                 Liaison with Los Angeles Elementary Schools
                 Health Services.

                 Summer 1982
                 Froude Institute, Chicago, Illinois
                 Assistant to Dr. Joseph Roth in preparing
                 his <u>Tropical Diseases: A Casebook</u> (1983).

                 Summer 1980
                 Laboratory assistant, Department of
                 Bacteriology, Duke University

AWARDS   Outstanding Employee Award, Los Angeles
                 Board of Health, 1985

REFERENCES   Academic dossier available from the
                 Academic Placement Service, Ohio
                 University, Athens, Ohio 45701

                 Dr. Lucille Lesiak
                 12 Cannon Road
                 Los Angeles, California 90018

                 Dr. Joseph Roth
                 Froude Institute
                 Chicago, Illinois 60637

31.2
Job

Printing and Duplication. If you need many résumés, you might consider having them professionally printed. But handsomely typed résumés reproduced on good quality paper are always acceptable. Be sure to proofread your résumé meticulously; a misspelled word or awkward expression can sink your entire application. Have someone—preferably an interested teacher or friend—read over your résumé carefully before you have it duplicated. A résumé should contain no errors, strikeovers, or mechanical irregularities (such as inconsistent headings, or punctuation). Take whatever time you need to produce a flawless page.

The Job Application Letter

A job application letter accompanies a résumé. The job or cover letter should explain what position you are interested in and why. Since your résumé explains your general qualifications, the cover letter can focus on your specific strengths and provide information tailored to a prospective employer. A letter of application complements a résumé; it does not simply repeat it.

Like résumés, job application letters rarely exceed one page. Employers or personnel officers may grow impatient with applications that go into too much detail—especially when they must review dozens or even hundreds of such letters. They are looking for the reasons to select your application above all the rest, not for an account of your life story. Consequently, your letter should point out the strongest features of your candidacy and the reasons for your interest in an advertised position.

Your letter should be direct and honest. If you are applying for a specific job, be sure to respond to the qualifications and experience required; indicate how your background matches the desired qualifications. If the job listing you are responding to is general, or when you are inquiring about the possibilities of employment at an institution not listing positions, make it clear in your letter what kind of work you are interested in and capable of doing. In some situations, you may want to discuss acceptable salary ranges, though money and fringe benefits are often treated as items to be negotiated at the interview or later. Still, if you have specific criteria about job authority, location, conditions, and salary, you may

31.2

Job

Sample Letter of Application
in Modified Block Format

856 East Oceanside Drive
Los Angeles, California 90016
December 6, 1985

Dr. Irwin Postle
Columbus Board of Health
101 High Street
Columbus, Ohio 43214

Dear Dr. Postle:

I am interested in the position of Disease Control Manager
advertised by the Columbus Board of Health in the current
issue of <u>Bacteriological Reviews</u>.

I already have substantial experience in disease management, having worked for almost two years with the Los
Angeles Board of Health, most recently as associate
director of the influenza-control program. My contributions to that unit earned me the board's "Outstanding
Employee Award."

As my enclosed résumé indicates, both my academic and my
professional responsibilities have prepared me for a
managerial position in epidemological research and applications. I am versed in current research and theory and
understand the logistical problems involved in applying
research findings to the health care systems of a large
metropolitan community.

My job here in Los Angeles has been satisfying and rewarding, but I am seeking a more demanding position and I
am also eager to return to Ohio where I grew up and
received a portion of my education. I would be available
for an interview in Columbus with several days' notice.

Thank you for considering my application. I look forward
to hearing from you.

Sincerely,

Irene Tremain

Irene Tremain
(213) 267-1927

31.2

Job

want to mention them discreetly in your application letter if only to prevent you and a prospective employer from wasting time pursuing an impossible hiring goal. Be sure to indicate in your letter your willingness and availability for interviews.

A job application letter uses the same format as any business letter. It should be neat, well arranged, and mechanically flawless.

31.3 Memos

Memos are a common, practical form of communication within institutions and businesses. They resemble business letters in that they are designed to present material clearly, schematically, and briefly, and to transmit and record policies, information, actions, and recommendations. The form memos take varies from institution to institution; many firms and agencies print up their own memo forms. In general, the heading of a memo indicates *to whom* it is addressed, *whom* it is from, the *subject,* and the *date.* Memos are not ordinarily

Sample Memo

```
To:         Carl Sontel, Marketing Director

            Meredith Hall, Advertising Manager

From:       Jane Manfred, Production Manager   JM

Date:       February 6, 1984

Subject:    Fall Catalogue


May we please meet briefly on Monday, February 13, in
Conference Room A to discuss the production schedule of
our fall catalogue?  Since we are increasing the cata-
logue's length and adding four-color photographs of our
new product lines, the design, layout, and printing will
take longer than they have in the past.  Therefore, we
must plan the work schedules of our groups as soon as
possible.

If Monday is not convenient for you, please suggest an
alternative time for us all to meet.
```

31.3

Memo

signed, but the author line may be initialled (see sample memo).

Memos should state their purpose clearly and make their major points forcefully. For this reason, memos often contain lists of actions or recommendations phrased in reasonably parallel form. While such communications tend to be less formal than business letters and more abrupt in their exposition, memos should be written with an awareness of the audiences to whom they are directed. A memo that is tactless or unclear may cause significant problems within an organization.

31.4 Reports

Reports of various kinds are among the most significant communications within businesses and institutions. They influence or determine policy, summarize and present information, or record the results of past actions or policies. Even within a single institution, there may be many different kinds of reports. Some may be periodic, done on a regular schedule, such as evaluations of employee performance, sales reports, inventory reports, and progress reports. Other reports address needs as they arise in an agency or firm: reports on particular problems or opportunities, market surveys, opinion surveys (see sample report, p. 599), reports on new or revised policies, comparative reports, task force reports, commission reports.

This great variety of purposes makes it difficult to set down any but general criteria for effective reports in the professional world. These considerations, however, may be helpful:

31.4
Rept

1. **Reports should be informative.** The criteria applied to informative writing (see pp. 333–34) are appropriate measures for many kinds of reports. Although an author of a report may be deeply and personally involved with a subject, a report is not the occasion for self-expression. More often than not, a report examines and discusses a subject; decisions or actions are sometimes left to others, but frequently recommendations are made. Reports are often argumentative or persuasive, but they should avoid the "hard sell" approach.

2. **Reports are based on research.** Personal opinion or general knowledge is rarely sufficient material for a report, although a progress report, for example, may be based on one employee's thorough knowledge. Reports are often based on facts either gathered for the report or analyzed in it. A task force may examine U.S. census figures, for example, to determine the movement of population and the consequent need for corporate expansion or retrenchment in certain areas. Or an agency may authorize its own, more specific, demographic studies.

3. **Reports are clearly presented.** An effective report packages its ideas in a convenient and logical way. Figures and tables are often used to support or document statements; indeed, some reports are chiefly made up of statistics in tabular form, such as annual reports to stockholders. The overall arrangement of the report should aid readability. Key points or recommendations ought to be easily located, and headings should be clear and precisely descriptive of what follows. Documentation should be apparent and methods of gathering information adequately explained. If the report is lengthy, it should include a table of contents and a list of figures.

4. **Reports are clearly organized.** The occasions on which reports must be written are so diverse and the kinds of reports that may be called for are so many that no single guide can show you how to write every kind of report. If you must write reports for your work, you might examine earlier reports in your company's files. Libraries can also provide you with texts on business and professional writing that go into some depth on the structure and format of different kinds of reports. There is, however, a basic organizational pattern common to many reports which you may find useful:

31.4
Rept

Introduction
A statement of the problem
The occasion or need for exploring the problem
The anticipated or proposed method for exploring the problem

Middle

An account of the procedures followed in exploring the problem

An account of the information resulting from the investigation, including tests, samplings, interviews, questionnaires, statistical investigations, and so on

End

A presentation of the findings, suggestions, or proposals; a display of results, conclusions, and possibly recommendations

Not all reports will have all these parts, and not all reports will follow this order. Many reports do follow a pattern much like this, but some have special requirements. A *progress report*, for example, may present the middle steps suggested above. A progress report is an account of what has been done so far in a given investigation or undertaking. A *briefing report* is meant, usually, to anticipate what is going to happen, to outline what should be known or done first, last, and in between to anticipate problems. A *briefing* is intended to prepare someone for what is to come. A *critique* or *evaluation* looks at an enterprise or piece of work after it is over or completed. One way to perform an evaluation is to closely examine the beginning and middle of the enterprise to see if a given conclusion can be validated.

5. **Reports are clearly written.** Because reports are often addressed to relatively narrow audiences of specialists, professionals, or experts, they are often filled with technical terms, concepts, and language that might not be readily understood by the general public. Given the audience of specialists, this technical language is often appropriate and even necessary. But experts and technocrats appreciate and expect clarity and brevity in technical communications. And many reports have audiences that include nonspecialists. Engineers making recommendations to corporate managers, for example, must translate their proposals into terms the managers can understand. If the body of a report must be technical, the introduction and conclusion can often be put

into less formidable language to spell out the initial issues and to explain potential solutions.

Sample Report

The sample report on the next few pages summarizes the results of a study performed by The Gallup Opinion Index and published in the February 1983 issue of *The Gallup Report*. The relatively short report precedes ten additional pages of detailed statistics in *The Gallup Report* supporting each major finding about public opinion on the issue of electoral reform. Notice how the information in the report itself is carefully arranged under clear headings, how simple tables are used to summarize some information, and how the authors of the report avoid making any personal judgments about their findings.

Electoral Reform: Both General Public and "Opinion Leaders" Support Changes in Political System

In the wake of the costliest congressional election in U.S. history, and with the 1984 presidential campaign getting under way, a majority of Americans favor major changes in political campaigns and far-reaching electoral reforms.

When asked if they want changes in the way political campaigns are conducted, 55 percent replied affirmatively, with the proportion rising to 71 percent among persons with a college background. Leading the list of gripes are the enormous cost of the campaigns, mudslinging, and the length of the campaign period.

The changes sought by U.S. adults extend to the entire electoral process, including the *selection* and *election* of the President and members of Congress.

Search committees favored by many

Fully half of the electorate, among those with views on the matter, think a better way is needed to *select* presidential candidates. And a majority of voters back a proposal to use search committees to seek out the most highly qualified candidates, following the procedure used by large corporations, foundations, and universities in filling vacancies.

A total of 54 percent of survey respondents think this process should be followed by the Republican and Democratic parties as a way of finding exceptional potential candidates. Rank-and-file party members could then choose the one they prefer in the primaries.

31.4
Rept

Large pool of talent available

The views of "opinion leaders" on electoral reform were also sought in a special survey among some of the nation's most prominent citizens. This survey was based on a national sample of 1,346 persons listed in *Marquis's Who's Who In America* who represent many fields of endeavor, including business, government, science, education, religion, and the arts.

Results of this opinion leader survey suggest that search committees would have a large pool of talent upon which to draw. As many as three in 10 (29 percent) leaders say that if a committee were to come to them and ask them to run on their party's ticket for the United States Senate, while offering to pay all campaign expenses, they would accept the offer.

Favor other changes in selection process

Not only does the public as a whole (and, to some extent, opinion leaders) favor the idea of search committees, but they would support changes in other stages of the nomination procedure.

A recent Gallup survey shows voters, by the ratio of 44 percent to 33 percent, in favor of changing the present primary-election system to a *regional* system in which four individual regional primaries would be held in different weeks of June during a presidential election year.

A 1980 Gallup survey found an even larger proportion of the public (66 percent) in favor of a plan that would replace the many state nomination races (there were 37 in the 1980 campaign) with a single *national* primary, allowing voters in all 50 states to choose the nominees by direct popular vote.

Opinion leaders vote 50 percent to 30 percent in favor of regional primaries and 47 percent and 42 percent in favor of a nationwide primary election instead of the present system.

31.4

Rept

Regional primaries

	Good idea	Poor idea	No opinion
General public....................	44%	33%	23%
Opinion leaders	50	30	20

Nationwide primary

	Favor	Oppose	No opinion
General public	66%	24%	10%
Opinion leaders.............	47	42	11

Government to place limits on spending

One of Americans' chief complaints about the way political campaigns are run is the enormous expenditure of money needed to get elected or to stay in office. To this end, a 55 percent majority of the general public would like to see the Federal government provide a fixed amount of money for the election campaigns of candidates for Congress, prohibiting all other contributions.

Among opinion leaders, views on the issue are evenly split, with the same percentage supporting the limit as opposing it (46 percent).

Government funding of congressional campaigns

	Good idea	Poor idea	No opinion
General public	55%	31%	14%
Opinion leaders.................	46	46	8

Opinions divided on six-year presidency

When asked their views on a single six-year term for the President with no re-election, opinion leaders are divided with 49 percent in favor of the proposal and 47 percent opposed.

A 1981 Gallup survey showed the general public rejecting a six-year term 61 percent to 31 percent. However, among informed individuals—that is, those who had heard or read about the proposal and could name at least one advantage and disadvantage—opinion was split between people who favored the proposal (47 percent) and those who opposed it (49 percent).

One six-year term

	Favor	Oppose	No opinion
General public	31%	61%	8%
Informed public	47	49	4
Opinion leaders	49	47	2

**Public wants
house term changed**

Another major electoral reform, which wins support from both the general public and opinion leaders, is a proposal to change the term of members of the House of Representatives from two years to four years.

The public votes 51 percent to 37 percent in favor of such a change, while opinion leaders lean 58 percent to 36 percent in support of a four-year term.

Change house term to four years

	Favor	Oppose	No opinion
General public	51%	37%	12%
Opinion leaders	58	36	6

The public also backs limiting members of the House of Representatives to three four-year terms, or a total of 12 years by a 2-to-1 vote, 59 percent to 32 percent. Opinion leaders, however, lean to the opposite view, 51 percent to 43 percent.

31.4

Rept

Limit to house terms

	Favor	Oppose	No opinion
General public	59%	32%	9%
Opinion leaders	43	51	6

Voter apathy

Proponents of electoral reform maintain that basic changes will help overcome apathy among Americans and encourage them to become more involved in the political process.

Only slightly more than half of U.S. adults vote in presidential elections, while the proportion drops to four in 10 in congressional elections. Fewer than half of Americans can name the Congressman or -woman from their district. Furthermore, politics ranks very low on the list of career choices of teenagers today. In addition, politicians do not fare well in terms of their public image. Elected officials at the national, state, and local level tend to score poorly in surveys of the public's perceptions of the honesty and ethical standards of people in various professions.

31.5 Using Electronic Typewriters and Word Processors

Electronic typewriters and word processors have made composing easier and quicker. These powerful tools are now widely available in schools, businesses, and homes. Although it is not possible here to explain all their features, they do change the way we write in ways worth noting.

Electronic Typewriters

Electronic typewriters feature keyboards with some capacity for memory. Consequently they can be programmed to handle functions not available on standard electric or manual typewriters. Most significantly, electronic typewriters have the ability to quickly erase large portions of a line—sometimes an entire line of text. In some machines the line is displayed on a small screen, allowing a writer to correct any errors before the line is printed. Electronic typewriters can also easily vary pitch (the distance between typed letters), underline words automatically, repeat almost any function, and move the printer (usually a daisy wheel) to the left margin when it reaches the end of the last word that will fit on a line.

Electronic typewriters greatly increase the speed of typing and, to an extent, make composing drafts on a machine somewhat easier. They are also significantly quieter than standard electric machines and very easy to learn how to use.

31.5

Type

Word Processors

Word-processing systems are much more powerful, versatile, and expensive than electronic typewriters. Some word processors are self-contained units built only, or primarily, for word-processing; but microcomputers can also serve as word processors with the right program, or software. A full system consists of four basic components:

1. **A central processing unit (CPU) and a keyboard.** The CPU is the brains of the computer, containing the chips that make it work. You control the computer through a keyboard which resembles that of a regular typewriter, but has additional keys and functions. Some computers also employ a pointing device—called a *mouse*—to speed commands to the CPU.

2. **The monitor.** The monitor is the screen, usually capable of handling lines of up to 80 characters, on which the text you produce is displayed. A block of pulsing light called a *cursor* indicates where you are on the screen or where you want to make some addition, change, or deletion.

3. **The printer.** This is the device that turns the words (and, in some cases, images) you view on the screen into a printed text. Following the directions for format you give it, the printer will produce a letter or report with the requested margins, spacing, pagination, and so forth. Printers vary in their quality. Dot-matrix printers shape letters from many small dots; daisy-wheel printers provide typewriter-quality lettering.

4. **Software.** The word-processing functions of a system depend upon the software program it uses. Programs vary significantly in what they can do. Some powerful software programs can be difficult to learn, but once mastered they enable a writer to produce very professional texts.

31.5

Type

Word-processing greatly enhances your capacity to revise a text easily. Although careful and thorough revision is the key to effective writing, many writers are reluctant to significantly alter a text when they know that such changes may mean reworking and retyping pages of material. Much of the drudgery is eliminated on a word processor. You make changes to your text on a screen where words are just dots of light waiting to be manipulated. If your changes entail large additions or rearrangements, the computer takes care of the text, realigning paragraphs, closing up spaces, doing all the work in seconds that might have taken hours of old-fashioned cutting and pasting.

The printer enables you to print out a text at any time so that, if you choose, you can have neat versions of your first draft, intermediate drafts, and final document as a record of your composing. But to an extent the need for separate drafts is eliminated because the constantly changing version on the monitor screen is your draft until you give the command to print. Among the many functions a word processor can handle (depending upon your equipment and program) are the following:

1. **Scrolling the text.** You can move through your text letter-by-letter, word-by-word, line-by-line, paragraph-by-paragraph, or page-by-page.
2. **Deleting** by letter, word, line, paragraph, or block. In some problems, deleted material is stored so that you can retrieve it and put it back in your text.
3. **Adding material.** You can add material to your text at any point.
4. **Rearranging material.** You can move words or larger blocks of material to new positions in a document.
5. **Automatic formatting.** You can determine margins, spacing, line length, pagination, and so on. When your text is printed, it will meet your specifications. With some programs you can have the computer align (or justify) the right-hand margin to give your text a professional look. Word processors can also center, underline, create boldface, and otherwise change the look of the type.
6. **Search.** You can instruct a word processor to find for you all uses of a particular word. Or you can automatically substitute one word for another—a useful way to correct misspellings. Some word processing programs can signal and correct misspelled words.

31.5
Type

The actual functions of word-processing equipment are more numerous and complex. In the future, almost any person who must write in his or her profession will become acquainted with these machines. Once you learn how to use them, word processors allow you to spend more time writing and revising than you otherwise might have done, since the actual production of the text is automatic. They greatly improve the opportunities you have for proofreading and editing a text. But the machines can only do so much. You are still responsible for the ideas, their arrangement, and their style. Only you can judge when a text is satisfactory.

32

WRITING IN
THE ACADEMIC
WORLD

The basic skills you need to write well in the professional world are the same ones you need in college. Assignments and audiences, however, can be markedly different. This chapter considers some of the special kinds of writing you may need to do in the academic world.

32.1 Abstracts

An *abstract* is a brief summary or condensation of a complete article, chapter, or other lengthy piece of writing. An abstract provides, in effect, a prose outline of a piece, naming its major argument or points but leaving out the supporting details and evidence. Here are two abstracts that precede lengthy articles in professional journals:

The Impact of Mass Media Violence on U.S. Homicides

DAVID P. PHILLIPS
University of California, San Diego

The impact of mass media violence on aggression has almost always been studied in the laboratory; this paper examines the effect of mass media violence in the real world. The paper presents the first systematic evidence indicating that a type of mass media violence triggers a brief, sharp increase in U.S. homicides. Immediately after heavyweight championship prize fights, 1973–1978, U.S. homicides increased by 12.46 percent. The increase is greatest after heavily publicized prize fights. The findings persist after one corrects for secular trends, seasonal, and other extraneous variables. Four alternative explanations for the findings are tested. The evidence suggests that heavyweight prize fights stimulate fatal, aggressive behavior in some Americans.

Dropping Out of High School:
The Influence of Race, Sex, and Family Background

RUSSELL W. RUMBERGER

Stanford University

This paper examines the extent of the high school dropout problem in 1979 and investigates both the stated reasons students leave school and some of the underlying factors influencing their decision. Particular attention is focused on differences by sex, race, and family background. Data for this research come from a new, national sample of youth who were 14 to 21 years of age in 1979. A multivariate model is developed to estimate the effects of family background and other factors on the decision to drop out of school. Several results emerge from the study: The reasons students cite for leaving school vary widely, with women more likely to leave because of pregnancy or marriage and men more likely to leave to go to work; family background strongly influences the propensity to drop out of school and accounts for virtually all the racial differences in dropout rates; various other factors, including ability and aspirations, also influence this decision.

3.1
Abst

Both abstracts define the nature of the issue to be discussed:

1. the impact of mass media violence on aggression;
2. the high school dropout problem in 1979.

They briefly explain the evidence or methods of investigation:

1. the first systematic evidence;
2. a multivariate model is developed.

And they both then present the conclusions reached in the paper:

1. heavyweight prize fights stimulate fatal, aggressive behavior;
2. the reasons students cite for leaving school vary widely.

Abstracts of this type serve to summarize material and to assist a reader in examining a research article. The summary tells a reader what to expect from the complete piece and draws attention to the main ideas.

Many journals require the authors of submitted material to provide abstracts of their articles. One way to practice preparing abstracts is to write them for the reading you are required to do in your courses—for instance, for a course that refers you to library materials kept on reserve.

When preparing an abstract, you should do the following:

1. Name the thesis, major arguments, or major points in the piece.
2. Describe in a general way the methods or evidence used to support the argument.
3. Describe the major conclusions and any necessary qualifications.
4. Avoid direct quotation of the original article. You may want to borrow some terms or key phrases (particularly when they are used in a new or technical way by the author), but you should avoid lengthy word-for-word quotations from the piece itself.
5. Keep the wording natural. Abstracts should be readable. Although most abstracts must be kept short, they should not sound like telegrams. Avoid sentence fragments and clipped phrases. Use transitional words and phrases to tie the piece together.
6. Follow the organization of the original article when preparing your abstract. Do not try to rearrange items to satisfy your sense of how the argument should develop.
7. Revise and proofread your abstract carefully, especially if it is to accompany an article. Be sure you have not omitted key ideas. Look for ways to make your wording more concise.

32.1

Abst

Some people prefer to prepare abstracts as they read an article, pulling out the topic ideas or main headings as they go along. Others choose to read the article through completely, constructing the abstract after they have a feel for the complete argument. Both methods can work well, but the best method of preparing an abstract (especially for a novice) may be to combine the techniques: a quick reading for the major argument followed by a more detailed analysis to discover the significant components, details, or evidence.

The abstract itself may be organized according to different developmental patterns, depending on the structure of the original piece. An abstract or plot summary of a novel is likely to be arranged chronologically; a research report may require a classificatory design in its precis; an abstract of a comparison/contrast article would probably follow a similar comparison/contrast design.

Most journals set limits on the length of abstracts they publish to accompany articles. Obviously, the length of your abstract will determine how detailed you can be in summarizing a given piece.

Exercise **32.A**

As practice in preparing summaries, write abstracts not exceeding 200 words of major articles from three of the following journals or magazines.

Scientific American	*Modern Photography*
Fortune	*Electrical Engineer*
Naturalist	*Consumer Reports*
College English	*Journal of African Studies*
Field and Stream	*College Composition and Communication*
Sports Illustrated	*Better Homes and Gardens*
Journal of Nutrition	*Rolling Stone*
Time	*Newsweek*
Psychology Today	*U.S. News & World Report*
Ms.	*Film Quarterly*
National Review	*Commonweal*

32.2

Notes

32.2 Taking Lecture Notes

Students rarely think of their lecture or reading notes as a form of writing. Yet such notes, if well prepared, can be of value to you not only during the course which generates them, but also months or years later when you may need to review what you have learned—perhaps in preparing for a professional school admissions examination or in working at your job. Good notes can serve as a permanent record of what you have learned.

Plan to keep your class notes in some durable form. Loose-leaf notes or cards tend to become scattered. A sturdy notebook is an intelligent choice—one notebook per course. If you put all of a semester's or quarter's labor in just one large notebook, those courses are bound together for good. You may find such an arrangement inconvenient at some later time when you are trying to organize three years of biology notes or four years of engineering labs. Or you may find that half the notebook is left empty because some of the courses you are taking generate few notes.

Separate notecards are excellent for reading notes, especially when you are responsible for large numbers of books or articles which you may later have to organize into a bibliography or use for a longer paper. Such cards can be kept in small folders or file boxes.

How you actually take notes depends upon the type of course you are involved in. Classes that consist of a series of lectures probably require the most systematic note-taking while those organized around discussion sessions or lab work will entail different procedures. In the latter kind of course, you may have to record significant information immediately after the class session.

Here is some general advice on taking lecture notes:

32.2

Notes

Follow a Pattern. At the beginning of a class, try to determine whether the lecture will follow a pattern. Use that pattern to organize your notes, employing an outline form whenever possible with headings, subheadings, and supporting evidence. A history presentation might follow a narrative structure, focusing on a sequence of significant events, dates, or movements. A lecture on government or economics might have a cause/effect design or rely on a set of classifications. A literature or fine arts lecture might begin with definitions and then employ a structure of evaluation. (See Chapter 21 for discussions of these and other patterns of development.) The topic headings in your notes might be conceived as the subject headings and divisions in the outline of an essay on the subject.

A word of caution: Lectures are not always faithful to a consistent structural pattern, even when a teacher intends that they be carefully organized. Digressions may occur spontaneously, or students may ask questions which reshape the original design. In your notes, you may need to accommodate such shifts of direction and emphasis. You may have to determine whether a digression is relevant to the topic and worth incorporating in your notes.

Focus on Main Ideas or Points. Too many students begin a semester trying to record every word or detail the teacher mentions. This is usually an exhausting mistake, especially when lectures cover approximately the same ground as assigned textbook material. Rely on the textbook for the facts, details, dates, and specifics; look to the lecture for the *concepts* a teacher chooses to emphasize or for clarifications of textbook materials: how to work a given formula, the practical applications of a theory, and so on.

Focus on Key Words and Concepts. Use headings and other devices of emphasis to underscore what are clearly the major concepts or new terms introduced in the lecture. Be sure you understand any terms an instructor uses. Ask questions at the appropriate time. Get the titles and authors of works mentioned right. Names, dates, or phrases that a teacher considers important enough to put on the blackboard should probably appear in your notes.

Read the Textbook. If a lecture is to coincide with textbook materials or an assigned reading, do the reading before the lecture. You may want to reread a difficult piece again after an instructor has discussed it. But don't go into a lecture cold whenever a teacher intends to refer to supporting materials for amplification or discussion. You will be lost.

Don't Crowd Your Notes. Leave space in the margins and between items for additional commentary or emendations.

Review Your Notes. As soon as possible after class, go over your notes, highlighting key points, adding headings, filling

32.2

Notes

in key points (dates, formulas, examples). If you annotate your notes in this way immediately after a class, you'll have the important concepts fresh in your mind and you will know which ones to emphasize for future reference. You may save yourself hours of work when it comes time to study for a comprehensive final examination. Check your notes with those of a colleague for accuracy, comparing facts, interpretations of concepts, and emphases.

Keep Your Notes Neat and Legible. Notes that you can't decipher a month later are a waste of time.

32.3 Taking Essay Exams

Answering an examination question in essay form is similar to writing a short expository or argumentative paper. In studying for a course, you have become familiar with a fairly wide range of information; to answer a specific question, you must recall the relevant material, organize it, and present it in essay form.

Reading the Questions

Because most examinations have a time limit, students often begin writing feverishly after no more than a glance at the questions. The results of such frantic haste are usually disappointing. You can use the allotted time far more profitably if you take a few minutes at the start to read all the questions and directions. If a choice is offered, decide which questions you are best prepared to answer and cross out the others. If the questions have different values, plan the amount of time to spend on each: a question worth 10 percent, for example, should not take up 30 percent of your time. Try to save a few minutes at the end to check your answers.

Before beginning to write, be sure to read the question thoroughly. Many answers are unsatisfactory simply because students misinterpret or forget the question in their hurry to fill the paper with words. Examine each question carefully and decide what kind of answer it requires. Don't misread or overlook key words. Notice in the following questions how a change in one word would affect the whole question:

Explain the *effect* [*causes*] of the Spanish-American War.

Describe the reproductive *cycle* [*structures*] of the frog.

Discuss the *structure* [*sources; significance*] of Moby Dick.

Since the verb often determines the nature of the answer, take particular care to interpret it properly. Here are some of the verbs instructors commonly use in essay questions.

analyze: give main divisions or elements, emphasizing essentials

classify: arrange into main classes or divisions

compare: point out likenesses (and sometimes differences as well)

contrast: point out differences

criticize: give your opinion as to good and bad features

define: explain the meaning, distinguish from similar terms

describe: name the features in chronological or spatial order

discuss: examine in detail

evaluate: give your opinion of the value or validity

explain: make clear, give reasons for

illustrate: give one or more examples of

interpret: give the meaning or significance

justify: defend, show to be right

review: examine on a broad scale

summarize: briefly go over the essentials

Writing the Answers

Before beginning to write an answer to a question, remember that the instructor expects you to demonstrate *specific* knowledge on the subject. A succession of vague generalities will not be acceptable. Even if you are discussing a fairly broad general topic, support whatever generalizations you make with specific illustrations. Do not omit essential particulars because you assume the *instructor* is familiar with them already; the main purpose of the examination is to find out what knowledge *you* have acquired.

A scratch outline (see 22.1) of the main points you plan to develop in your answer may be useful as a guide in writing. But whether you make an outline or not, make a concentrated effort to set your thoughts down in some logical order:

32.3

Exam

all the sentences should relate to the question asked, and each should lead to the next in an orderly fashion. Many essay answers are unsuccessful because students, although well-informed, present information in a haphazard, unrelated fashion, giving the impression that they are thoroughly confused on the subject. It is often useful to repeat the key terms of the questions and the main points you'll be making about the terms in a thesis statement at the beginning of your answer. This can serve as an organizational guide for your writing.

Remember that the *length* of the answer is not the criterion of its worth: choosing the right facts and organizing them sensibly will impress the reader far more. Avoid throwing in unrelated material just to demonstrate your knowledge or to disguise your ignorance of more pertinent information. Since the time you have to write your answer is limited, you should confine yourself strictly to what you know about the specific question asked. Your instructor is not likely to give you much credit for a short essay on the wrong subject, no matter how good it may be.

Examination answers should be written in acceptable general English. Although instructors do not expect an essay written in class to be as fully developed and as polished in style as one written at home, they do expect it to be adequate in grammar, usage, and the mechanics of writing. Even if a paper is otherwise accurate, frequent misspellings do much to lower the reader's opinion of it. Take particular care to spell and use correctly any technical terms or names that have been used in the course: *myosis, mercantile, assize, neurosis, imagery,*

32.3

Exam

Lamarck, Malthus, Schopenhauer. Instructors are understandably disturbed if they think you have paid scant attention to terms you have heard in class and read in the text numerous times. Careful proofreading of the answers may help you eliminate any careless errors you may have made and will also give you a chance to fill in gaps in information.

Examples of Essay Answers

Printed below are essay answers in biology and history. Read each question carefully, decide what sort of answer is required, and compare the two student answers. Then read the criticisms that follow. The sentences in the answers are numbered to facilitate discussion.

Question: Define *dominant* as it is used in genetics.

Answer A: (1) In genetics, dominant is the opposite of recessive. (2) Different characteristics are inherited by the individual by means of genes acquired from the male and female parents. (3) These genes are arranged, or carried, on
chromosomes, and are paired, one from each parent. (4) A
good deal is still unknown about the behavior of genes, although the science of genetics is making rapid progress. (5)
Gregor Mendel, a monk, made discoveries in heredity by
doing experiments with sweet peas. (6) He found that certain traits are stronger (dominant) and others are weaker
(recessive). (7) Therefore, if two genes carry the same characteristic, one will be dominant over the other. (8) Examples of this are dark eyes, normal color vision, etc.

Answer B: (1) The term *dominant* as used in genetics refers
to that situation in which one gene in a pair takes prece-
dence over another in determining a given characteristic in
the individual. (2) For example, if a child inherits a gene for
blue eyes from one parent and for brown eyes from the
other, he will have brown eyes. (3) This is because the
brown-eyed gene is *dominant;* the blue is *recessive.* (4) He
still carries both genes and may transmit either to his offspring, but one has masked the effect of the other in his
physical appearance. (5) Clear dominance does not occur in
all pairings, however. (6) Sometimes *mixed dominance* occurs, as in the case of sweet peas, where a cross between a
red and a white parent produces pink offspring. (7) Some
cases of dominance are *sex-linked;* the gene for color blind-
ness in humans, for instance, is dominant in the male and
recessive in the female.

Criticism: Answer A contains irrelevant general information (sentences 2–5) and does not give a clear definition of
dominant. You cannot explain the meaning of a word simply
by naming its opposite (sentence 1). "Stronger" and
"weaker" (sentence 6) are poor synonyms because they
have such a variety of meanings. The answer also misleads
by oversimplification: sentence 7 implies that complete
dominance occurs in *all* pairings of genes. It is also not clear
to what species of life the two examples in the last sentence
(dark eyes and normal color vision) refer.

Answer B is satisfactory. The term is clearly defined in
the first sentence. Sentences 2–4 give an example of its use,
distinguish it from its opposite, and add an important qual-

32.3

Exam

ification. Sentences 5–7 note two important variants in the meaning of the term. There is no irrelevant material.

Question: Compare and contrast English and Spanish colonial methods in the New World.

Answer A: (1) The Plymouth colony suffered many hardships in the early years of its existence. (2) This was also true of the Roanoke colony, but it eventually failed and did not survive. (3) The climate was more promising there, but it seemed as if the kind of people it included, like gentlemen unused to work, adventurers, and renegades, did not have the patience and religious fervor of the New England settlers. (4) The same was true of the Spanish colonies in Florida and elsewhere—the climate was good, but the men were selfish and had no direction. (5) The Spanish were more cruel toward the Indians than the English, and there was nothing constructive in their aims.

Answer B: (1) The Spanish generally thought of the New World as a reservoir of riches to be tapped. (2) The great Spanish conquerors, like Cortez and Pizarro, were explorer-adventurers whose main aim was to subjugate the native population and wrench from them whatever riches and power they possessed. (3) The Spanish method was usually to impose a military dictatorship upon a restive populace; the domination depended on military force. (4) The English, on the other hand, thought of the New World colonies as a *permanent* extension of English civilization. (5) Their methods were not to immediately extract native riches, but to plant the seeds of English life in the new continent. (6) Unlike the Spaniards, the English generally emigrated in family units, placated rather than subdued the native inhabitants, invested labor and capital in the New World soil, and awaited long-term fruits. (7) Settlement was their aim rather than exploitation.

32.3
Exam

Criticism: More than half of answer A (sentences 1–3) contrasts *two English colonies* rather than *English and Spanish colonial methods*. Mention of climate in sentences 3 and 4 is also irrelevant to a question dealing with methods. "Selfish" and "had no direction" need further explanation, as do "cruel toward the Indians" and "nothing constructive."

Answer B is much more satisfactory than A. The basic differences in aim and the consequent differences in method are fairly well stated. The first section of the answer (sentences 1–3) describes Spanish methods; the second (sentences 4–7) presents the significant differences in English aim and method.

32.4 Writing About Literature

In college English courses students are often asked to write about literature—to examine, interpret, and discuss fiction, poetry, drama. Literary analysis and interpretation are not radically different from the close reading and interpretive writing you might do in history, philosophy, and sociology courses or from your critical response to an editorial, magazine article, sermon, or letter to the editor. You examine a piece of literature in order to understand it more fully.

Still, you may not enjoy writing about literature because of the fears and limitations you may bring to this kind of study. Many students regard literary interpretation as intellectual mumbo-jumbo in which teachers and students tear poems or novels apart to find hidden meanings and complicated symbols. You may also think that writing about literature requires a more specialized language than you possess. In short, instead of making literature more powerful and exciting for you, literary analysis only seems to make it remote and lifeless. If you feel this way, consider these simple things:

1. A story, poem, or play is someone's words. The words are waiting for you—an audience. You *can* understand them if you give them the time and attention they deserve.

2. Curiosity may be a better guide to literary analysis than a handful of poorly understood critical terms and concepts. Learn to trust your instincts about literary works and be willing to ask questions and to pursue the answers. Don't assume that the answers will be obscure or esoteric. If you trust your curiosity, you can begin to find your way into a poem, novel, short story, or drama.

3. Literature is interesting. Begin your analysis with a puzzling line, a peculiar phrase, an unexpected incident and use it as a focal point for your essay. Unless your instructor has specifically called for a particular kind of discussion, you should feel no obligation to talk about everything or even most things in a poem, play, or

32.4

Lit

story. Narrow your argument to a statement about the literary work that you can prove with evidence drawn either from the text of the work or from your research. A fine point well developed will make a much better paper than a string of generalities about the entire work.

4. Literature involves more than an outpouring of feelings. Literary analyses do sometimes become exercises in self-expression; this is not necessarily inappropriate. But in most academic papers, your instructor will expect you to avoid using the literary work as an excuse for talking about similar experiences you have enjoyed or suffered.

Starting Your Literary Analysis

You may want to start your literary analysis by considering one or more of the following questions that can be raised about a literary work:

1. **Genre.** Does the *kind* of writing that you are studying give the author a perspective that he or she wouldn't have otherwise? Does it create limitations for the author, or does it offer special advantages? What can a writer do in a poem that can't be done in a short story? What can be done in a play that can't be done in a poem?

2. **Speaker.** Who is telling the story? Who controls what we learn from the literary work? Who is speaking in the poem? Is the author speaking, or is it someone else? What difference does it make? Why does the author choose to tell the story, present the poem, or show the drama in that particular way? What distance is there between the author and us, or between the author and the speaker? Whose version of events are we reading?

3. **Character.** How do we learn about the characters? If a poem is at issue and no characters appear except the speaker, how do we learn about him or her? Are the characters revealed by their words, by their actions, by both? What difference does it make? Are they identifiable as individuals, or do they seem to be representative types?

4. **Setting.** What is the setting? Is it localized and shown in specific detail? If it isn't, why isn't it? What kind of environment do the characters live in? What effect does it have on them?

5. **Style and tone.** How does the author speak to us? What does the author reveal about himself by the way he speaks? If characters speak, do they have distinguishable styles? What do they reveal about themselves? What will the vocabulary tell us about the speaker or speakers? Does the style of the sentences tell anything about the speaker or about the work? What images and figures of speech occur? How do they determine the tone of the work?

6. **Structure and rhythm.** Why is the work arranged as it is? What part of the structure gets primary attention? What part seems to get the least attention? When does the author slow down the pace of the work? When is the pace speeded up?

The answer to just one of these questions will usually furnish the material for a short literary paper.

Kinds of Literary Study

Sometimes you may be expected to do a longer examination of a literary work, one which includes materials gathered from a survey of reference and scholarly sources. The following classification of types of literary study may give you some idea of the range of work done in this area. The classification is based largely on a list of areas for literary research compiled by B. Bernard Cohen in his *Writing About Literature.*

Textual Analysis. One kind of literary criticism is devoted to a close examination of the text itself—preparation and publication, revisions, errors or misprintings, various editions, and so forth. Part of the meaning of Book III of *Gulliver's Travels* was clarified, for example, with the discovery—some 175 years after initial publication—of a short passage that had been printed in the first edition but had been deleted thereafter. It is unlikely that you will do highly specialized textual research for the papers you are assigned in undergraduate courses, but you can often find a subject in existing textual problems.

Relationships Among the Author's Works. It is sometimes useful to examine the work at hand by considering it in the light of the author's other works. For example, it may be possible to understand the manner of *Gulliver's Travels* better by considering it along with "A Modest Proposal" and some of Swift's other satires.

Relevance to Biography. Some papers on literary subjects can profitably examine the particular circumstances in the author's life that helped give shape to the work. Why, for example, might it be important that Shakespeare wrote *Hamlet* several years after the death of his only son, Hamnet?

Study of the Creative Process. If primary sources such as letters and diaries are available, it is possible to study a given work for what it reveals about the creative process. What for example, is revealed about Lord Byron in the many letters he wrote, some published in their original form only in this century?

Relation of the Work to Literary Theory. It is also possible to develop fruitful explorations of a work by examining it in the light of theories about art and literature current when the work was written. How, for example, were the novels of Émile Zola shaped by his concept of the "scientific novelist"?

Impact of the Times on the Work. Sometimes it is interesting to approach a work as an artifact, that is, as a record and a reflection of the ideas and events of its own time. For example, how does Puritan poetry in America reflect the social and religious traditions of colonial times?

32.4

Lit

Relationship of the Work to Literary Tradition. A work of literature can be studied in terms of the literary habits, assumptions, and techniques the author has inherited from other writers. You might examine *Gulliver's Travels*, for example, to see how Swift adopted, rejected, or refined the techniques of satire that were already in use.

Relationship of the Work to a Particular Subject Area. Sometimes you can find a worthwhile subject for a paper by looking at a literary work for what it reveals about a particular idea or field of interest. You could, for example, increase your understanding of James Joyce's *Ulysses* and write something of interest about it by focusing on what it says about Irish politics or religion.

Reception of the Work. You can often learn a great deal about a work by discovering how it was received in its own day or at any later time. Some great works were virtually ignored when first published, or were the cause of great scandal or public outrage.

Some Tips on Writing the Literary Analysis

Most literary papers require you to support some limited assertion about a literary work. Consequently, you need to be sure to begin with a carefully focused thesis or hypothesis:

> The character of Billy Budd in Melville's novel deliberately resembles both Adam and Christ.

> The comic moments in Shakespeare's *Macbeth* make the protagonist's crimes seem more, not less, horrible.

Then you must provide the evidence to support your assertion, quoting selectively from the text of the works being analyzed or citing other evidence or authorities. In writing your paper you may want to follow these tips and conventions:

1. Don't paraphrase the literary work extensively or do a plot summary unless that is the actual assignment. Many students think they are analyzing a literary work when they are merely retelling the story. Assume that your teacher knows the work you are discussing reasonably well—unless you have chosen an obscure piece, in which case you might want to supply a complete text if that is convenient.
2. Don't assume that all literary works can be reduced to a simple generalization, maxim, or moral. Most are too complex to be dealt with in such a simplistic way. Moreover, a literary text is read in different ways by different readers. There is not likely to be a single *right way* to talk about a piece of literature.
3. Pay attention to the meaning of the literary terms you employ. Don't use the word *story* to describe fiction and nonfiction alike. Be sure you know what is meant by terms such as *tragedy, comedy, sonnet, satire, persona,* and *soliloquy* if you choose to employ them.
4. Describe the events in a literary work in the present tense: "To all the requests made of him, Bartleby *replies* 'I would prefer not to'''; "Ogden Nash's four-line poem

'The Turtle' *praises* that creature's ability to procreate despite the complications imposed by its shell"; "Romeo *loves* Juliet even though she *is* a Capulet."

5. Be sure to introduce quoted material with an explanatory phrase. Don't just insert passages of a literary piece into your paper without identifying either where the selection is from or what it contributes to your analysis.

6. Be sure to underline the titles of longer works and put other titles of literary works between quotation marks. (See pp. 248–49 for more details about these conventions.)

7. Whenever it is helpful, include between parentheses the date a literary work was published and the author's dates. Do this only once, early in the paper:

John Milton (1608–74), the author of "Lycidas" (1638) and *Paradise Lost* (1667), was also an important figure in the government of Oliver Cromwell.

The paper on pp. 624–627 is an example of a short literary analysis. The student examines a single aspect of a familiar play, *Romeo and Juliet,* relying on evidence solely from within the play to prove a thesis stated in the first sentence of the essay. Notice that the analysis does not attempt to account for every action in *Romeo and Juliet,* nor does it suggest a moral, even though it explores a moral theme in the play. Notice, too, how easily and naturally the quoted passages from the tragedy are incorporated into the writer's own sentences to serve as evidence for various assertions. The quotations seem like part of the analysis.

32.4

Lit

Helpful Reference Works

When writing about literature, you may find the following reference books useful:

General references and indexes

Altick, Richard D. and Andrew Wright. *Selective Bibliography for the Study of English and American Literature.* 6th ed. New York: Macmillan, 1978.

Hart, James D., ed. *The Oxford Companion to American Literature.* 5th ed. New York: Oxford University Press, 1983.

Harvey, Paul and Dorothy Eagle, eds. *The Oxford Companion to English Literature.* 4th ed. New York: Oxford University Press, 1967.

Harvey, Paul. *The Oxford Companion to Classical Literature.* Oxford: Clarendon, 1980.

Holman, C. Hugh. *A Handbook to Literature.* 4th ed. New York: Bobbs-Merrill, 1980.

Magill, Frank N., ed. *Masterplots.* 12 vols. Englewood Cliffs, N.J.: Salem Press, 1976.

MLA International Bibliography of Books and Articles on the Modern Languages and Literatures. New York: Modern Language Association.

Moulton, Charles Wells. *Moulton's Library of Literary Criticism of English and American Authors Through the Beginning of the 20th Century.* 4 vols. New York: F. Ungar, [1966].

Schweik, Robert C. and Dieter Riesner. *Reference Sources in English and American Literature: An Annotated Bibliography.* New York: Norton, 1977.

Spiller, Robert E. *Literary History of the United States: Bibliography.* New York: Macmillan, 1974.

Trent, W.P. *Cambridge History of American Literature.* New York: Macmillan, 1943.

Ward, A.W. and A.R. Weller, eds. *The Cambridge History of English Literature.* New York: Macmillan, 1933.

Watson, George, ed. *New Cambridge Bibliography of English Literature.* 5 vols. Cambridge: Cambridge University Press, 1976.

Novel

Adelman, Irving and Rita Dworkin. *The Contemporary Novel: A Checklist of Critical Literature on the British and American Novel Since 1945.* Metuchen, N.J.: Scarecrow Press, 1972.

Bell, Inglis F. and Donald Baird. *The English Novel, 1578–1956.* Denver: A. Swallow, [1959].

Gerstenberger, Donna and George Hendrick, *The American Novel: A Checklist of Twentieth Century Criticism.* 2 vols. Denver: A. Swallow, [1961–70].

Sample Literary Essay

This short literary analysis was one student's response to an assignment in a Shakespeare course which asked for a short (500 words) analysis of a single pattern of imagery in the tragedy Romeo and Juliet.

Because the paper is short, the essay opens quickly with a paragraph that is almost an abstract of the essay that follows. The play, its approximate date of composition, its author, and the image pattern to be studied are all identified in the first sentence. That same sentence also makes the assertion that the rest of the essay will have to prove: Shakespeare uses gold to contrast Verona's greedy concept of love to Romeo and Juliet's more noble passion. Although the student might have researched the substantial literature on Romeo and Juliet available in any library and read articles on Shakespeare's use of imagery, the only evidence and authority cited in the analysis is the text of the play itself. Each assertion is supported by carefully selected passages from the play.

The paper does not have any notes, nor does it indicate what edition of Shake- speare the student used—a potential problem since various editions of Shakespeare do not always agree on line numbers. But each quotation is identified with an indication of act, scene, and line: (I.iii.88–94). Also acceptable is a form that does away with Roman numerals: 1.3.88–94.

Most of the quotations are skillfully woven into the text so that the sentences move without interruption or hesitation. In one sentence, the writer identifies the referent of a pronoun in square brackets:

In this way, Juliet may "share all that he [Paris] doth possess."

More important than the way the quotations are handled is the support they give to the student's ideas. In the third paragraph, for example, the assertion that Romeo and Juliet's love blossoms and multiplies is enhanced by two passages in which Juliet celebrates the boundlessness of her love. In the fourth paragraph, the crucial connec- tion between gold and death is made by Romeo's declaration that gold is worse than the poison he is buying for himself. The best piece of evidence for the student's argument appears, appropriately, in the last paragraph where the families of Romeo and Juliet attempt to honor their dead children by raising golden statues in their honor. The essay succeeds if its readers are convinced that erecting the statues is an ironic comment on Verona's commercial concept of love.

32.4

Lit

C. Chapman

Good as Gold

In <u>Romeo and Juliet</u> (1595-96), William Shakespeare
uses gold and other images of wealth and bounty to
contrast the city of Verona's mercantile concept of love
with the more bountiful love of Romeo and young Juliet.
The two lovers share an infinite love in a finite world
and, consequently, die misunderstood. They are mourned
inappropriately when, at the end of the play, their
grieving parents attempt to memorialize their deaths with
golden statues--the very image of the greed which, in
part, destroys them.

Lady Capulet typifies Verona's concept of love when
she describes Paris, the young man she favors as Juliet's
husband, as a "book of love," lacking only a golden cover
to complete "the golden story" (I.iii.88-94). Lady
Capulet implies that her daughter should be that golden
cover, a wife to embrace Paris just as a cover enfolds a
book. In this way, Juliet may "share all that he [Paris]
doth possess." Yet before Romeo and Juliet meet, they too
are content to follow the traditional concept of love
endorsed by Lady Capulet. Juliet says to her mother, for
example, "no more deep will I endart mine eye than your
consent gives strength to make me fly" (I.iii.98-99). She
accepts a love neatly bound within the golden cover.

32.4

Lit

Once they meet, however, Romeo and Juliet experience a love that blossoms and multiplies beyond calculation. Juliet declares to Romeo that "my love is as boundless as the sea, my love as deep; the more I give to thee, the more I have, for both are infinite" (II.ii.133-135). This connection between generosity and love distinguishes the traditional world's love from Romeo and Juliet's experience. To know infinite love, one must be as willing to give as to receive love. As Juliet says to Romeo and Friar Laurence, "they are but beggars that can count their worth" (II.vi.32). Her love and Romeo's cannot be counted, cannot be expressed in any but hyperbolic language.

Verona, torn by disputes between the Montagues and the Capulets, cannot understand an infinite, selfless passion. Nor can the young lovers survive in a world that understands only hatred and calculating eye-for-an-eye ethics. Romeo, forced to flee for his life, has learned this lesson well. As he purchases his means of suicide before returning to Verona and Juliet's tomb, he gives the apothecary a gold coin in exchange for a deadly potion, noting that the gold is "worse poison to men's souls" (V.ii.80) than what he is buying. Romeo understands Verona's concept of love as a similar poison because it stifles the natural feelings of passion and love he and Juliet have shared for so short a time.

Even after the death of their heirs, the Montague and Capulet families remain ignorant of Romeo and Juliet's

32.4
Lit

difference from them. The two families attempt to set a monetary value on the infinite love of their children by purchasing garish monuments:

> <u>Montague</u>. . . . I will raise her statue in pure gold,
>
> That whiles Verona by that name is known,
>
> There shall no figure at such rate be set
>
> As that of true and faithful Juliet.
>
> <u>Capulet</u>. As rich shall Romeo's by his lady's lie,
>
> Poor sacrifices of our enmity!
>
> (V.iii.298-304)

The same poison, gold, which symbolizes their tragedy now stands inadequately for their love.

Short story

Cook, Dorothy E. and Isabel S. Monro. *Short Story Index.* New York: H.W. Wilson, 1953 [with supplements].

Walker, Warren S., ed. *Twentieth-Century Short Story Explication.* 3rd ed. Hamden, Conn.: Shoe String Press, 1977.

Drama

Adelman, Irving and R. Dworkin. *Modern Drama: A Checklist of Critical Literature on Twentieth Century Plays.* Metuchen, N.J.: Scarecrow Press, 1967.

Coleman, Arthur and Gary R. Tyler. *Drama Criticism.* Denver: A. Swallow, 1966.

Hartnoll, Phyllis, ed. *The Oxford Companion to the Theatre.* 3rd ed. London: Oxford University Press, 1967.

Palmer, Helen H. *European Drama Criticism, 1900–1975.* Hamden, Conn.: Shoe String Press, 1968.

Palmer, Helen H. and Anne Jane Dyson. *American Drama Criticism.* Hamden, Conn.: Shoe String Press, 1967.

Poetry

Dyson, A.E., ed. *English Poetry: Select Bibliographic Guides.* London: Oxford University Press, 1971.

Kuntz, Joseph M. *Poetry Explication.* Rev. Ed. Denver: A. Swallow, 1962.

Smith, William J., ed. *Granger's Index to Poetry.* 6th ed. New York: Columbia University Press, 1973; 7th ed. (indexes 1970–82). New York: Columbia University Press, 1982.

32.4

Lit

Journals

American Literature

College English

ELH

English Language Notes

English Studies

Journal of Black Studies

Journal of English and Germanic Philology

Modern Drama

Modern Language Quarterly

Modern Philology
PMLA
Review of English Studies
Shakespeare Quarterly
Studies in Philology
Texas Studies in Language and Literature

32.5 Avoiding Plagiarism and Collusion

Plagiarism

Most writers know that copying another's work word for word without giving the author credit is considered plagiarism. But they often assume that this practice is frowned on only when long passages are involved—whole pages or paragraphs. Consequently, they feel free to copy phrases and sentences without using quotation marks or acknowledgments. In fact, *any uncredited use* of another's information or ideas is plagiarism whether the wording is changed or not. Here are some of the circumstances in which you might be accused of plagiarism—and how to avoid them.

1. You commit plagiarism **if you fail to acknowledge the sources of any information in your paper which is not either common knowledge or personal knowledge.** You can regard common knowledge as the basic information within a field: what any knowledgeable person would be expected to know. Common knowledge also includes historical dates and facts and many ordinary observations. Even if you used a reference book to recall the dates of George Washington's presidency, for example, you would *not* have to acknowledge your source since presidential terms fall into the realm of common knowledge. If, however, you borrowed ideas from material that analyzed or interpreted the Washington presidency, you would be expected to cite your source. You can acknowledge a source through footnotes, attribution lines ("As George Orwell puts it in *1984* . . ."), or other forms of documentation approved by your instructor or used within your field.

32.5
Plag

2. You commit plagiarism **if you fail to acknowledge a direct quotation by using either quotation marks or (for longer passages) indention.** Without the quotation marks or indention, a passage copied *directly* from a source might be considered plagiarized even if it were followed by an in-text citation, footnote, or endnote. The note admits that you have used a source, but it does not indicate that you have borrowed someone else's *exact* words. If you repeat the language of a source, word for word, you must use quotation marks or block indention:

```
As E. B. White observes, "This was the American family at

play, escaping the city heat. . . ."
```

```
As E. B. White observes:

    This was the American family at play, escaping the

    city heat, wondering whether the newcomers in the

    camp. . . .
```

3. You commit plagiarism **if you improperly paraphrase the original words of your source.** Some students think that they are paraphrasing and can avoid a charge of plagiarism by changing a few words in each sentence they copy, or by rearranging the shape of phrases or the order of sentences in a paragraph. This is not true. An *honest* paraphrase is one in which you present the ideas from a source in your own words *and* give proper credit to the source for those ideas. Knowing how to paraphrase properly is an essential skill. The following examples demonstrate the difference between legitimate paraphrase and plagiarism of source material:

Original Source (from Alexis de Tocqueville, *Democracy in America*, 1, 248–49): No political form has hitherto been discovered that is equally favorable to the prosperity and the development of all the classes into which society is divided. These classes continue to form, as it were, so many distinct communities in the same nation; and experience has shown that it is not less dangerous to place the fate of these classes exclusively in the hands of any one of them than it is to make one people the arbiter of the destiny of another. When the rich alone govern, the interest of the poor is always endangered; and when the poor make the laws, that of the rich incurs very serious risks. The advantage of democracy does not consist, therefore, as has sometimes been asserted, in favoring the prosperity of all, but simply in contributing to the well-being of the greatest number.

Student Version A: Hitherto no one has found a political form that favors equally the prosperity and the development of all the different classes of society. Experience has shown that it is just as dangerous to place the fate of these classes in the hands of one class as to let one nation dictate the destiny of another. Government by the rich endangers the poor; and the poor make laws that often harm the interests of the rich. Therefore, the advantage of democracy does not consist in raising general prosperity, but simply in adding to the well-being of the majority.

Plagiarism. By omitting any reference to De Tocqueville, the writer implies that these ideas are his or her own. In organization the paragraph follows the source very closely—same order of ideas, same number and structure of sentences. Many of the words and phrases are lifted bodily from the source without quotation marks to indicate that they are not the writer's. In other cases, word order has been simply rearranged and synonyms substituted (*found* for *discovered*, *nation* for *one people*, *adding* for *contributing*, *majority* for *greatest number*).

Version B: De Tocqueville says that no form of government in history has been uniformly beneficial to all classes of society. He maintains that both the rich and the poor, when in control of the government, pass laws favorable to their class and repressive toward the other. According to him, the virtue of a democracy is that it benefits the majority, not that it benefits the whole (248–49).

Paraphrase. The writer admits, both in the text and in a citation, that the ideas in the paragraph are De Tocqueville's. He states them in his or her own words and does not slavishly follow the source. Quotation marks are unnecessary, since none of the phrases are De Tocqueville's.

Original Source (from Lionel Trilling, "F. Scott Fitzgerald," *The Liberal Imagination*, p. 42): Thus, *The Great Gatsby* has its interest as a record of contemporary manners, but this might only have served to date it, did not Fitzgerald take the given moment of history as something more than a mere circumstance, did he not, in the manner of the great French novelists of the nineteenth century, seize the given moment as a moral fact. . . . For Gatsby, divided between power and dream, comes inevitably to stand for America itself.

Version A: Of course the one thing that makes *The Great Gatsby* interesting is its picture of the life of the twenties, but if it were only this it would by now be out of date. Instead, like the great French novelists, Fitzgerald made the particular moment a moral symbol. Gatsby, the main character, divided between power and dream, represents the American dilemma.

Plagiarism. This version does not reproduce the source as closely as Version A of the De Tocqueville passage; it more subtly plagiarizes the original. Again, the writer gives no indication that the ideas expressed are not his or her own. The wording, except for "divided between power and dream," is largely original. The comparison between Fitzgerald and the great French novelists is not original and implies a critical breadth suspiciously beyond the range of most undergraduate writers.

Version B: As Lionel Trilling points out, *The Great Gatsby* is much more than a record of the manners of the twenties. In miniature, Gatsby represents America, "divided between power and dream" (42).

Paraphrase. The writer credits Trilling as the originator of the ideas he presents. He also puts quotation marks around the one phrase he uses verbatim.

4. You commit plagiarism **if you borrow the ideas, examples, or structure of a source without acknowledging it.** Even if the language of your piece is substantially original, you may be plagiarizing if you systematically borrow the examples or organization used by your source. A student who, for example, reports on a major news event by using exactly the same ideas in the same order

as they appear in an article he or she has read in *Time* or *Newsweek* might be accused of plagiarism. Create your own design for an essay and use more than a single source for your ideas.

5. You commit plagiarism **if you take, buy, or receive a paper written by someone else and present it as your own.**

Collusion

Collusion is related to plagiarism. It is usually defined as collaboration with someone else in producing work you claim to be entirely your own. Obviously, you should not allow anyone else to write your papers. But a more sensitive issue here is how much may you allow another person to revise or review your written work. Policies may vary from school to school, but a solid rule to follow is that you should not allow someone else to edit your papers without your instructor's knowledge or permission. In recent years, many students have resorted to private editing and tutoring services to help them with their writing assignments and other academic work. Yet while it may be proper for such services and tutors to counsel students in a general way, it is probably scholastically dishonest for them to modify written work in any substantive fashion. The same restriction holds for any outside help you may receive from a roommate, a friend, or even a parent. This doesn't mean you shouldn't seek the opinions of readers other than your instructors. In fact, such outside reviews of your written work can be very helpful. It does mean that any changes, deletions, rearrangements, or corrections in your essays should be your own work.

> 32.5
>
> Plag

Many schools and writing programs offer their students the assistance of a writing lab or various kinds of peer tutoring arrangements. If you need help with your writing, you should consider using those legitimate services your school offers you.

33

WRITING

AND RESEARCH

This chapter is about an assignment almost universal in writing courses and in many other undergraduate classes: the term paper, library paper, reference paper, or research paper. Whatever it is called, the familiar term paper differs from other writing assignments chiefly in its greater length and its heavier reliance on outside sources and materials. And, of course, it requires *research*.

On the other hand, writing the research paper requires the same attention to audience, topic, organization, and style that all writing requires. In the following sections, you will find a description of the types of research common in the academic and professional worlds, a discussion of the parts of typical research articles, a strategy for library research, a step-by-step plan for preparing a long research report, and a sample library paper.

33.1 Types of Research

Research arises out of a compulsion to answer a question or solve a problem, not out of the need to write a paper; the paper reports the research findings. While you are in school, you may be prodded into research by course requirements that include term papers, but you should not think of research solely in terms of these assignments—which have their own value in increasing what you know about a field or training you to assess and organize information. Nor should you believe that your opportunities for researching a subject are limited only to lengthy, formal assignments. Research should inform much that you write.

What constitutes *research?* Just about any repeatable technique that you can explain and document and which contributes to answering the questions you have raised, supports or refutes the hypotheses you have advanced, or helps interpret or evaluate the problems you are examining. Among the types of research you may encounter in school and in the professions are the following:

1. **Library Research.** This is the kind of research usually taught in writing courses. It involves finding printed information in the library by using appropriate bibliographic and reference tools to locate books, articles, reports, surveys, and so on. The latter sections of this chapter deal extensively with many of the techniques of library research.

2. **Experimental and Empirical Research.** This is the research we think of as "scientific" even though it is not always rigidly methodical nor limited to the traditional scientific disciplines. Experimental research attempts to prove or disprove *hypotheses* by using procedures to limit or precisely control the factors being tested in order to produce significant and repeatable results. Experimental and empirical research usually involves measurements of some kind. The findings are reported through lab reports or other professional articles.

3. **Observation.** Research based on observation can be rigidly scientific or much more informal, depending on what is being studied. Psychologists might observe and report on the behavior of a select group of patients, or teachers might recall their experiences with students in certain courses. Observation may involve the examination of large numbers of people or of political, cultural, or social phenomena (presidential campaigns, clothing fads, buying trends), or it may entail precise descriptions of single events. The limits of the observation must be accurately defined, however.

4. **Case Study.** A case study is a particular form of observation involving a detailed, sometimes prolonged, look at the behavior of an individual or individuals over a

period of time. A sociologist may initiate case studies to explore the impact of a particular social or educational policy on individual families. A medical doctor might examine the effectiveness or the side effects of a new treatment by watching several patients. A writing researcher might trace the progress of several students through their high school and college careers. Case studies require careful observations, detailed narrations and descriptions, appropriate records (sometimes involving video and audio equipment), and unbiased explanations and assessments of the behaviors observed.

5. **Surveys.** Research surveys, such as The Gallup Report used as an example in Chapter 31 (see p. 599), are a kind of quantified observation. They usually involve asking questions to sample the opinion of the public at large or some more specific group (women, Protestants, Mexican-Americans, nonvoters). To be reliable, surveys have to be conducted within certain constraints: questions posed must be phrased to avoid bias; the population studied must be sufficiently large to be representative; the individuals questioned must compose a reasonable cross-section of the population they are supposed to represent; the individuals must be chosen randomly. Polling is an influential kind of research, useful for revealing what people know, believe, and feel.

6. **Interviews.** Interviews can be an important type of research in many disciplines. A case study may actually consist of a series of interviews in which a researcher asks a battery of questions, records the responses, and then evaluates them. Interviews, however, are often far less structured, their value stemming in part from what subjects reveal on their own. Interviews are valuable in the kinds of studies or investigations for which measurement and calculation are not possible or for which the human response is a significant part of the historical record: in an artist's recollection of how a given work was created; in a disaster victim's report of the event; in a diplomat's assessment of the personality of a world leader.

7. **Testing, Trial and Error, Application.** Researchers sometimes do not discover how well an idea, theory, or prod-

uct works until they try it out or test it. Testing often involves experimentation, validation studies, training of testers, and other formal procedures of test design and scoring. It may also be much less formal (but not less complex) when tests involve relatively uncontrolled "real world" trials. Economic theories and concepts, for example, can often be tested only after being translated (usually imperfectly) into policy and legislation; they then must operate in a complex environment under the influence of many variables and imponderables. Whether a "tight money" policy or "trickle-down theory" works is far from easy to test. But the very number of factors that real-world testing brings to bear upon an idea or product can improve concepts developed within relatively closed systems or "ivory towers."

This list of kinds of research is not exhaustive. Nor is it meant to suggest that you will actually be involved in these sorts of investigations in school or on the job. What you do need to know is that there are such kinds of research and that you may be responsible for recognizing and reporting about them accurately.

33.2 The Components of Research Reports

Each discipline has its own expectations and conventions when it comes to reporting the results of research. In school, it has been traditional to think of a term paper as consisting of the following elements:

1. a carefully phrased, often argumentative, thesis statement;
2. a formal outline preceding the paper, listing the major points and supporting evidence;
3. the essay itself, featuring an introductory paragraph, a lengthy section of development, and a concluding paragraph;
4. the supporting documentation, including notes listing each cited source and a bibliography.

33.2

Res

These points are discussed at length in 33.4.

Professional research reports and scholarly articles often include other features and components you should be aware of. Not all these parts are appropriate in every kind of essay, yet you may find good uses for some of them in your own academic work.

1. **Title.** The titles of research reports are informative. Good titles contain key words that indicate their subject and how the reports should be indexed in bibliographies or computer indexes. In general, clear titles are better than clever ones, specific ones better than general. Here are some sample titles from research journals:

   Dropping Out of High School: The Influence of Race, Sex, and Family Background

   Size of Place, Residential Preferences and the Life Cycle: How People Come to Like Where They Live

   Donne's *Holy Sonnets:* The Theology of Conversion

2. **Abstract.** An abstract is a concise summary of the research article, explaining its thesis or hypothesis, its basic procedures, its results, and the conclusions drawn from them. See page 606 for a fuller discussion of abstracts.

3. **Review of Literature.** Authors of research reports or essays commonly survey, summarize, evaluate, and critique important published research materials having a bearing on their own hypothesis, argument, or research findings. This review usually occurs in an early paragraph or footnote. Such a review sets the context for a research essay, enabling a reader to trace the background of an idea or controversy or to understand how new work confirms, extends, or contradicts earlier findings. The review of literature may also indicate gaps in the reading or background of the researcher—the absence of titles or works that should have been acknowledged or referred to before new research was undertaken. A thorough review can also serve as a useful annotated bibliography.

4. **The Hypothesis.** A *hypothesis* is an assumption to be tested; it usually grows out of observations. An investigator notes the regular occurrence of a phenomena, or suspects a particular influence, or predicts an event on the basis of a theory. The hypothesis is a formal, testable statement based upon the observation or theory; it is in

need of confirmation, reconfirmation, or refutation. Research based on a hypothesis attempts to provide the evidence to do that. In contrast, the *thesis* of a paper is ordinarily a statement a writer works to support; a hypothesis is a statement that is still in question.

5. **Method.** Many reports include a detailed explanation of the methods and procedures used in the research. Such an explanation might include a statement of the hypotheses tested; what factors or variables were controlled; how the samples of a surveyed population were selected; what techniques were used to assure reliability; what statistical techniques were used; what training research workers had; and so on. The procedural section in a report serves two main purposes. First, it gives readers the information they need to assess the quality, thoroughness, accuracy, and validity of research, for any conclusions drawn from an experiment are only as good as the methods that produced them. And, second, it provides professional readers with the methodology they need to repeat the experiment, if necessary, to confirm or refute the conclusion.

6. **Results.** A presentation of results typically follows an explanation of methodology. The results may be listed or reported in a variety of ways, depending on the research being done. In this section, the results are usually stated without extensive comment or interpretation.

7. **Charts, Tables, and Graphs.** Charts, graphs, tables, figures, and other illustrative devices are often employed to explain results, although they may appear wherever they are useful in a text. Charts and tables help organize information and make it accessible to readers.

8. **Discussion.** A formal section of discussion may follow a presentation of results. Here the results are interpreted and analyzed. The researchers may draw connections between their results and previous work, assess their successes and failures, or attempt to account for unexpected findings. This is the point in the study where researchers place their work in context.

9. **Conclusions.** The conclusions follow from the discussion. While the discussion may be speculative and prob-

ing, the conclusions are likely to be more qualified, explaining exactly the importance and the limitations of the study. The conclusion may indicate the need for future research to confirm, extend, or re-examine what has been newly reported.

10. **Bibliography.** A full list of works cited is a valuable part of any report, supplementing the review of literature. Like the review, a bibliography assists readers in finding out more about a subject.

11. **Appendixes.** Sometimes reports need to furnish information not directly connected to the main part of the discussion or too lengthy to incorporate conveniently and readably into the text. Such material may be placed in appendixes at the end of the report to aid readers wanting fuller explanations of a concept or procedure, or a more detailed report of results.

Sample Research Report

The following sample research report, substantially abbreviated, contains many of the features and divisions discussed in the preceding section.

Dropping Out of High School: Title
The Influence of Race, Sex,
and Family Background

RUSSELL W. RUMBERGER

Stanford University

RUSSELL W. RUMBERGER

Stanford University

Author/
Academic
affiliation

33.2
Res

This paper examines the extent of the high school dropout problem in Abstract
*1979 and investigates both the stated reasons students leave school
and some of the underlying factors influencing their decision. Particular attention is focused on differences by sex, race, and family background. Data for this reasearch come from a new, national sample of
youth who were 14 to 21 years of age in 1979. A multivariate model
is developed to estimate the effects of family background and other
factors on the decision to drop out of school. Several results emerge
from the study: The reasons students cite for leaving school vary
widely, with women more likely to leave because of pregnancy or
marriage and men more likely to leave to go to work; family background strongly influences the propensity to drop out of school and
accounts for virtually all the racial differences in dropout rates; various other factors, including ability and aspirations, also influence
this decision.*

While various problems have besieged high schools over the years, one problem has remained since their inception—getting students to finish. Many people believe that the incidence of dropping out has diminished over the years to a point where it is no longer a severe problem. Yet recent evidence suggests the contrary. The problem of dropping out, which historically was largely confined to minority and disadvantaged youth, appears to be increasing, especially among white, middle-class youth. This paper briefly reviews recent evidence on the magnitude of this problem and then investigates its causes—both the stated reasons students leave school and some of the underlying factors, particularly the role of race, sex, and family background. Introduction and Review of Literature (using APA documentation style)

Participation in high school has continued to increase throughout this century. To illustrate, the proportion of 14- to 17-year-olds enrolled in high school increased from 11 percent in 1900 to 94 percent in 1978 (Grant & Eiden, 1980, p. 44). But recent evidence from several states indicates that this trend may be reversing. Enrollment data for Ohio show that the number of dropouts has increased 15 percent from the 1975–76 school year to the 1978–79 school year (Kaeser, 1980, p. 5). In California the attrition rate between the ninth and twelfth grades increased from 12 percent in 1967 to 22 percent in 1976 (Camp, 1980, p. 11). National census data confirm these trends: The percentage of high school dropouts among white males, 16 to 17 years of age, increased from 6.3 percent in October 1970 to 9.6 percent in October 1978 (Grant & Eiden, 1980, p. 66). Among white females there was a smaller increase, while for black males and females the proportion of high school dropouts decreased during this period. . . .

Despite the usefulness of these studies in identifying a wide variety of factors that influence dropout behavior, few have examined how these factors operate on different race and sex groups. Some studies have contrasted males and females, while ignoring racial differences (e.g., Combs & Cooley, 1968). Others have focused on particular race or sex groups, but excluded others (e.g., Hill, 1979; Shaw, 1982). Still others have simply used a series of control variables to identify members of different race and sex groups (e.g., Howell & Frese, 1982; Masters, 1969). None of the studies reviewed has

33.2

Res

_____
An earlier version of this paper, "Why Kids Drop Out of High School," Credits was presented at the annual meeting of the American Educational Research Association, Los Angeles, April 13–17, 1981. The research was sponsored by the U.S. Departments of Education and Labor. Researchers undertaking such projects under Government sponsorship are encouraged to express their own judgements. Interpretations or viewpoints stated in this document do not necessarily represent the official position or policy of the U.S. Government. Tim Brown and Julie Zavakos provided expert research assistance for this project, Henry Levin, the staff of the Center for Human Resource Research, and two anonymous reviewers provided helpful comments on earlier drafts of this paper.

examined the influence of various factors on dropping out for separate race and sex groups. In particular, the factors influencing dropout behavior among Hispanics has not been studied previously, even though this group has the highest dropout rate. This study attempts to correct this deficiency by examining the influence of family background and several other factors on the propensity to drop out among several race and sex groups.

Focus of
the study

METHODS AND DATA

Models

Modeling the determinants of dropout behavior is complicated by two facts. First, it is difficult to determine strict causality from all the various factors. Causality can be more easily inferred for family background and other individual traits, such as race and sex, because these characteristics are fixed or determined well before the act of dropping out. But inferring causality from other characteristics, expecially those occurring around the same time as the act of dropping out, is much more problematic. For example, poor performance in school may not necessarily "cause" an individual to drop out of school; rather, for other reasons, that student may display a tendency to drop out and perform poorly as a consequence. Other activities that have been related to dropping out, particularly getting married and becoming pregnant, may all be jointly determined by other factors, not by each other.

Full discussion of
procedure,
including
discussion
of data
and statistical
techniques.

The second difficulty in modeling dropout behavior concerns determining the magnitude of the various factors. Some of the factors that influence dropping out are themselves influenced by other factors. . . .

Data and Samples

Data for this study come from the National Longitudinal Survey (NLS) of Youth Labor Market Experience (Center for Human Resource Research, 1980). The survey consists of a series of annual interviews of a national sample of approximately 12,700 young men and women between the ages of 14 and 21, with an overrepresentation of blacks, Hispanics, and poor whites. The data include a variety of information on the respondents' background characteristics, attitudes, aspirations, educational and labor market experiences, and personal characteristics. This study is based on data from the first survey, conducted in the first half of 1979. . . .

33.2

Res

Statistical Techniques

The dependent variable in both models represents the likelihood (probability) of dropping out of high school. When the dependent variable is dichotomous, ordinary least squares (OLS) regression techniques are inappropriate because the error terms are heteroskedastic and only a nonlinear specification assures that the predicted probabilities fall between zero and one (Theil, 1971). Consequently, probit techniques were employed in the present study. . . . The discussion below focuses on those independent variables that exhibit significant effects on the probability of dropping out.

RESULTS

Model I

The first model included several measures of family background and indicators of current geographic residence. Actual and predicted values for the probability of dropping out based on the first model, with partial derivatives for some of the independent variables, appear in Table III. The partial derivatives estimate the effect on the probability of dropping out of a one-unit change in a particular independent variable, holding all other variables constant.

Report of results, summarized in tables.

TABLE III
Actual and Predicted Probabilities of Dropping Out of High School and Partial Derivatives of Selected Background and Control Variables, by Race and Sex

Characteristic	Female			Male		
	Black	Hispanic	White	Black	Hispanic	White
Actual Probability	20.0	30.8	16.0	25.9	29.3	18.5
Advantaged Background						
Predicted probability	13.4	16.1	10.4	10.4	14.8	12.7
Partial derivatives						
Mother's earnings	−1.1	−1.4	−1.0*	−1.1	2.8	−1.4**
Mother's education	−2.8***	−.6	−1.7***	−1.4**	−.6	−2.3
Father's earnings	.0	−.8	−.4*	−.2	−.3	−.0
Father's education	.1	−.6	−.1	−1.2**	−1.3**	−2.1***
Number of siblings	.5	.9	1.7***	.0	.5	1.5***
Cultural index	−7.1***	−5.6***	−5.6***	−2.7**	−3.1*	−4.6***
Resided outside U.S.*	−13.4	12.1*	−7.3*	−3.9	25.4***	−8.8*
South*	−8.6**	−6.8	−1.9	−5.7*	−11.8**	1.9
Unemployment rate	.0	.0	.8**	−1.6**	−2.6**	.1
Disadvantaged Background						
Predicted probability	29.1	42.9	37.2	22.8	43.5	39.1
Partial derivatives						
Mother's earnings	−1.7	−2.3	−2.1*	−1.9	4.7	−2.6**
Mother's education	−4.5***	−.9	−3.6***	−2.3**	−.9	−4.1
Number of siblings	.8	1.4	3.6***	−.1	.9	2.8***
Cultural index	−11.3***	−9.0***	−11.6***	−4.5**	−5.3*	−8.5***
Resided outside U.S.*	−29.1	16.3*	−19.7*	−6.9	30.1***	−20.8*
South	−15.7**	−12.5	−4.4	−10.5*	−27.6**	−3.3
Unemployment rate	.0	−.3	1.8**	−2.6**	−4.4**	−.1

33.2

Res

In general, the results support previous findings that show family background to be a powerful predictor of dropout behavior. The results also support the notion that these effects vary among race and sex groups. Perhaps the most revealing finding emerges from the actual and simulated probabilities: While the actual probabilities of dropping out vary widely among the six groups, particularly between white and minority youths, in most cases the predicted probabilities are quite similar. The simulations thus reveal that minorities with the same background characteristics as whites are just as likely or even less likely to drop out of high school as whites.

Model 2

The second model assesses the effects of a series of intervening variables on the probability of dropping out after controlling for the effects of family background and other exogenous factors. Because some of these endogenous factors were actually measured after the decision to drop out of school, inferring causality from these variables is inappropriate. But the estimates do identify some of the other factors associated with dropout behavior. Actual and predicted values for the probability of dropping out based on the second model, together with partial derivatives for some of the independent variables, appear in Table IV. . . .

TABLE IV

Actual and Predicted Probabilities of Dropping Out of High School and Partial Derivatives of Selected Intervening Variables, by Race and Sex

Characteristic	Female			Male		
	Black	Hispanic	White	Black	Hispanic	White
Actual Probability	20.0	30.8	16.0	25.9	29.3	18.5
Advantaged Background						
Predicted probability	.3	1.1	.5	7.0	5.6	1.0
Partial derivatives						
Educational aspirations	−.3***	−.7***	−.4***	−1.8***	−2.8***	−.8***
Friend's aspirations	−.1**	−.3**	−.1**	−.8*	−.6	−.3***
Aspires to prof. occ.*	−.1	.0	.1	−3.9***	−3.2*	−.5*
Rotter	.1	−.3	.1*	.7*	.2	.2***
KWW	−.1**	−.3*	−.3***	−.1	−1.3***	−.1**
Married early*	1.9***	2.7*	.8**	1.5	−1.1	.5
Married later*	.4	1.2	.7**	−5.6*	14.5**	2.4***
Child early*	4.0***	8.4***	4.0***	4.7	1.3	.9
Child later*	6.8***	4.0**	3.9***	7.9*	7.4	1.3
Disadvantaged Background						
Predicted probability	17.5	44.2	26.5	35.8	63.2	46.0
Partial derivatives						
Educational aspirations	−8.5***	−9.9***	−8.2***	−4.9***	−9.5***	−11.7***
Friend's aspirations	−2.4**	−4.5**	−2.4**	−2.3*	−1.9	−4.5***
Aspires to prof. occ.*	−1.4	.4	3.0	−13.2***	−15.1*	−8.1*
Rotter	1.5	1.7	1.3*	1.9*	.6	2.6***
KWW	−2.5**	−3.8*	−5.6***	−.2	−4.5***	−2.0**
Married early*	26.9***	20.2*	12.5**	4.2	−3.9	6.4
Married later*	11.0	11.9	11.8**	−22.0*	23.0**	20.1***
Child early*	38.9***	35.7***	33.7***	11.2	4.0	10.4
Child later*	48.3***	25.3**	33.2***	17.3*	15.7	13.6

33.2

Res

DISCUSSION AND CONCLUSIONS

Previous research studies have identified various factors that cause or at least predict the likelihood of dropping out of high school. They range from environmental factors, such as family background and geographic residence, to psychological factors, such as ability and aspirations, to behavioral factors such as early marriage and childbirth. The purpose of this study was to study how these factors, particularly family background, operate differently for members of various race and sex groups.

The findings from earlier research were used to construct two models of dropout behavior. The first model contained a variety of family background measures and some geographic variables. The second model contained, in addition, a variety of intervening factors, both behavioral and psychological, that might influence dropout behavior, but that might also be influenced by family background.

As with all previous studies of dropout behavior, the results obtained from these models have certain limitations. First, it is difficult or inappropriate to infer causality from the various factors, especially from the intervening variables. Because many of the psychological indicators were measured after the student dropped out, it is difficult to know whether any particular indicator contributed to a student's decision to leave school or whether the decision to leave school led to a change in that indicator. Second, while the models reveal associations between the independent variables and the probability of dropping out, they do not reveal the underlying mechanisms that may actually have caused the action. Some of the factors studied, such as attitudes or related behaviors of marriage and childbirth, might really be symptoms, not causes, of dropout behavior. In general, it is much easier to predict dropout behavior from various factors than to identify what really motivates a student to leave school. Third, there are some potentially influential factors that must be excluded from the analysis due to data limitations. In the present study, school factors, such as achievement, were unavailable from the data and thus were excluded.

Despite these limitations, the analysis yielded some revealing results. As earlier studies have shown, family background is a powerful predictor of dropout behavior. Students from a lower social class background are much more likely to leave school prematurely than students from higher social origins. Several explanations might account for this observation, but none can be proven to the exclusion of the others. Higher

The findings of the study are discussed

Discussion of three important limits on the conclusions

33.2

Res

Actual conclusions

educated parents might simply serve as better role models, influencing their children's aspirations for more schooling. Better educated parents may also spend more time with their children, increasing their academic ability. Because higher income families live in wealthier communities with better financed schools, their children are more likely to have more supportive and rewarding educational experiences. In contrast, children from poorer families may feel much more compelled to work and supplement their family's income, as many Hispanic dropouts have indicated (Table II).

. . . .

These findings suggest that the problem of dropping out is by no means a simple one that can be treated with simple solutions. As the array of significant influences reveals, the problem is complex. It requires multiple solutions. The significant influence of family background suggests that the tendency to drop out begins early in a student's life. Attempts to combat the problem should therefore be initiated at an early age as well. Compensatory education programs, designed to overcome initial disadvantages associated with poor social origins, should be strengthened, although they may not completely equalize educational opportunity (Lewin, 1977). Other interventions, such as better counseling inside and outside the schools, might also help overcome the initial disadvantages stemming from lower social class background. These remedies need to be targeted particularly to minority youth, who are much more likely to drop out.

A discussion of the implications of the study, connecting it with other research

The present findings also suggest that attempts to combat the dropout problem should be linked to attempts to combat related problems—early marriage and childbirth. Problems with teenage pregnancy are particularly severe. Schools have generally been unsuccessful in helping young women to finish high school once they become pregnant (Zellman, 1981). More concerted efforts are required.

33.2

Res

The increasing incidence of dropping out among white youth may stem from other factors and thus require still other solutions. In fact, the many problems confronting youth today—unemployment, drugs, venereal disease, teenage pregnancy, as well as dropping out—may be related phenomena. Overcoming them may require more drastic action (Carnegie Council, 1979).

REFERENCES

List of works cited in the report

Alwin, D. F., & Hauser, R. M. The decomposition of effects in path analysis. *American Sociological Review*, 1975, *40*, 37–47.

BACHMAN, J. G., GREEN, S., & WIRTANEN, I. D. *Dropping out: Problem or symptom? Youth in transition* (Vol. III). Ann Arbor: Institute for Social Research, University of Michigan, 1971.

BLINDER, A. S. Wage discrimination: Reduced form and structural estimates. *Journal of Human Resources*, 1973, *8*, 436–455.

BORUS, M. E., CROWLEY, J. E., RUMBERGER, R. W., SANTOS, R., & SHAPIRO, D. *Findings of the national longitudinal survey of young Americans, 1979.* Youth Knowledge Development Report 2.7. Washington, D.C.: U.S. Government Printing Office, 1980.

CAMP, C. *School dropouts.* Sacramento: Assembly Office of Research, California Legislature, 1980.

Carnegie Council on Policy Studies in Higher Education. *Giving youth a better chance.* San Francisco: Jossey-Bass, 1979.

Center for Human Resource Research. *The national longitudinal surveys handbook.* Columbus: Center for Human Resource Research, Ohio State University, 1980.

COMBS, J., & COOLEY, W. W. Dropouts: In high school and after high school. *American Educational Research Journal*, 1968, *5*, 343–363.

DENTLER, R. A., & WARSHAVER, M. E. *Big city dropouts and illiterates.* New York: Praeger, 1968.

[Twenty-five additional sources are listed]

APPENDIX TABLE A1
Glossary

Mother's earnings	= race-specific mean earnings (in thousands of dollars in 1975 of civilian workers 18 years old and older within major occupation groups (U.S. Bureau of the Census, 1977), based on the mother's occupation when the respondent was 14 years old if the respondent's mother was in the household when the respondent was 14 years old
	= 0 otherwise
Mother not in household	= 1 if the respondent's mother was not in the household when the respondent was 14 years old
	= 0 otherwise
Mother not working	= 1 if the respondent's mother was present and not working when the respondent was 14 years old
	= 0 otherwise
Mother's education unknown	= 1 if the respondent's mother was present and her educational attainment unknown
	= 0 otherwise
Mother's education	= years of regular schooling completed by the respondent's mother if the respondent's mother was in the household when the respondent was 14 years old
	= 0 otherwise

33.2

Res

33.3 Strategies and Tools for Research

You should begin any research study by establishing an efficient and flexible research strategy appropriate to your topic. You do not want to run blindly to the library stacks or card catalogue and flip laboriously (but aimlessly) through dozens of volumes or hundreds of cards on the vague expectation that you will eventually locate the materials you need. Instead, you require an efficient route through the most up-to-date and specific bibliographies, indexes, and abstracts you can find on your subject. You want to exploit all significant resources, both within and outside of your library. And you want data and information that is accurate and authoritative.

You can begin by considering the purpose and audience of your research. If you are doing a library-oriented term paper for an introductory course in a discipline, the assignment is partly designed to hone your general research skills and introduce you to various indexes and reference tools. Therefore, you may not want to employ all the devices this section discusses, though you need not exclude using them either. On the other hand, if you are pursuing a topic that is developing rapidly within your field, the avenues to information sketched in this section will be feeders to other, even more particular channels of information. You will discover that each discipline and profession has its own sophisticated structure of research; its tools may include catalogues, registers, indexes, abstracts, guides, statute books, journals, lists of professional organizations and services, data bases, style manuals, handbooks, dictionaries, directories, encyclopedias, yearbooks, texts, annual reports, action guides, statistical sources, standards, and atlases. Mastering the reference and information tools within a discipline is the key to productive and significant research habits. There's no reason to redo, retrace, or recatalogue work that has already been done thoroughly and accurately. You want to get on to new things, sorting keenly through masses of information to find what you want with a minimum of labor.

Following are eight research strategies you can employ in appropriate combinations whenever you face a research problem. Briefly, they are these:

1. Locate experts;
2. Locate sources;

3. Find the best bibliographies;
4. Use the most appropriate indexes;
5. Look for abstracts;
6. Investigate computer data bases;
7. Examine appropriate reference works;
8. Use the card catalogue effectively.

Locate Experts

When you are dealing with a fairly sophisticated problem and you can talk with experts in your area of concern—as is common at most academic institutions and in many professional organizations and businesses—you will save time and energy by asking intelligent questions of them. Obviously, you don't want to bother an expert when you are seeking out basic information you can track down quickly on your own. But when you are exploring more significant or intriguing questions or following up on existing research, it makes sense to talk with teachers, professionals, or colleagues who can direct you immediately to pertinent books, articles, or other materials, especially bibliographies. Such inquiries should never be frivolous, but don't overlook opportunities to seek information at a source, especially as you are moving along in your discipline and beginning to have your work taken seriously. You may have to consult an expert when information you need has not yet found its way into journals, abstracts, or indexes because of the inevitable lags between discovery and publication. Remember, though, that any expert is fallible and a professional opinion often reflects the controversies, politics, biases, and in-fighting within a discipline. Whenever possible, listen to opposing opinions.

Locate Sources

When you are researching a topic of current interest, you can write for information from the professional groups, lobbies, agencies, or institutions that have a stake in it. Even for most term papers assigned in a semester or quarter, there is time (if you start promptly) to ask detailed questions and to gather firsthand information from the very persons or institutions you plan to discuss. A paper on a topic as familiar as gun control, for example, can be lively and interesting if you work from information supplied to you directly by the National Rifle Association on one side of the controversy and the various

33.3

Res

anti-gun lobbies on the other. If you are dealing with problems related to social, political, and governmental agencies, you can visit appropriate offices or call for data and information. The federal government publishes an enormous amount of information on topics of public interest. To find out what is available, consult the *Monthly Catalog of United States Government Publications* available in many library reference rooms or the *Index to U.S. Government Periodicals.*

Also potentially valuable is Gale Research Company's *Encyclopedia of Associations,* published annually. Included in these volumes are the addresses, purposes, and memberships of business, government, scientific, religious, fraternal, athletic, and many other organizations. To tap into the latest books, pamphlets, journals, and documents on social, economic, and governmental issues, you can use the *Public Affairs Information Service* (PAIS), a subject index available in most libraries. The information in both the *Encyclopedia of Associations* and PAIS may be accessible to you through computer data banks. These resources are valuable because they are current. They enable you to explore subjects too recent to be treated in the more traditional bibliographies and indexes.

Find the Best Bibliographies

Bibliographies are lists of books, articles, and other materials on a given subject arranged in various ways (usually alphabetically, topically, or chronologically). They may be massive, general, and unselective, such as the *MLA International Bibliography of Books and Articles on the Modern Languages and Literatures,* or much more limited and specific, with descriptive and evaluative comments called annotations. These more selective bibliographies are often appended to books or articles. Although the comprehensive bibliographies are invaluable collections of information, you'll find that up-to-date lists dealing specifically with your subject are easier to work with and more efficient. If you can locate an existing, current bibliography on your topic, preferably an annotated one, you will save yourself time you might otherwise have to spend tracing material through card catalogues and indexes and then evaluating it yourself. To locate a bibliography, use *Bibliography Index* or, a less current work, Theodore Besterman's *A World Bibliography of Bibliographies.* Or ask an expert to recommend a work. Be alert for books or journal articles on your subject that contain bibliographies or reviews of literature. And, of course, you will find important standard bibliographies in every major field. Here are just a few:

Afro-American Studies—*Black Bibliography*

Anthropology—*Ethnographic Bibliography of North America*

Architecture—*American Architecture and Art: A Guide to Information Sources*

Art—*Guide to the Literature of Art History*

Astronomy—*Astronomy and Astrophysics: A Bibliographic Guide*

Business—*Business Information Sources*

Chemistry—*Chemical Abstracts*

Classics—*Greek and Roman Authors: A Checklist of Criticism*

Geology—*Publications of the Geological Survey, 1879–1961*

Health Sciences—*Health Sciences and Services: A Guide to Information Sources*

History—*Bibliographies in American History*

Linguistics—*Quarterly Checklist of Linguistics*

Literature—*MLA International Bibliography*

Marketing—*American Marketing Association Bibliography Series*

Performing Arts—*American Drama from Its Beginnings to the Present*

Philosophy—*A Bibliography of Philosophical Bibliographies*

Psychology—*Harvard List of Books in Psychology*

Social Work—*Social Work Education: A Bibliography*

Sociology—*International Bibliography of Sociology*

To locate a book not listed in your library's card catalogue, you may need to consult one of the *trade bibliographies.* The most important are:

Books in Print. A listing by author and by title of books included in *Publishers' Trade List Annual,* which lists—by publisher—all books currently in print.

Cumulative Book Index. Gives complete publication data on all books published in the English language, listing them by author and by title. Published monthly, with cumulative volumes issued periodically.

Paperbound Books in Print. Especially useful since some important books are available *only* in paperback. Published monthly, with cumulative volumes issued three times a year.

Subject Guide to Books in Print. An invaluable index to the titles listed in *Books in Print.*

Finally, you may be able to create a bibliography tailored to your specific needs by searching an appropriate computer data base. (See the discussion of computer data bases on page 658.)

Use the Most Appropriate Indexes

A good deal of essential material, particularly on current topics, is available only in periodicals, which range from popular magazines and newspapers to technical journals and learned publications. This material is catalogued in various guides and indexes, some of them published monthly, others annually. To write an authoritative and up-to-date paper, you will often have to make use of periodicals and indexes. Most libraries keep a catalogue, called a *serials list,* of the periodicals they receive. The list may also indicate where the periodicals are indexed. Check with your librarian.

Readers' Guide
The most familiar of periodical guides is the *Readers' Guide to Periodical Literature,* which indexes the articles in more than 120 magazines of general interest. It is published monthly in paperbound volumes which are afterwards gathered in large

33.3
Res

cumulative volumes covering a year or more.

The entries in the *Readers' Guide* are listed alphabetically both by subject and by author. The abbreviations used in the listings—for the titles of periodicals, the month of publication, and various facts about the article itself—are explained on the first page of each volume. On pages 654–55 are reproductions and explanations of four main entries from a monthly issue.

Other Periodical Indexes
In locating sources for a research paper you may find it useful to refer to one of the specialized periodical indexes listed below. Most of them appear annually; the year after the title

shows when publication began. As with bibliographies in the previous section, the indexes listed below are only a few of the many available in various disciplines.

General indexes
Bibliographic Index: A Cumulative Bibliography of Bibliographies (1938)

Biography Index: A Cumulative Index to Biographic Material in Books and Magazines (1946/47)

Catholic Periodical Index: A Guide to Catholic Magazines (1930)

Humanities Index (1974)

Magazine Index (1976)

Poole's Index to Periodical Literature (1802–81)

Public Affairs Information Service (1915)

Social Sciences and Humanities Index (1907–74)

Social Sciences Index (1974)

United States Government Publications Monthly Catalog (1895)

Special indexes

Microlist (1977). Published ten times a year, an author/title and subject listing of new micropublications (microfilm, microfiche). Includes books, periodicals, newspapers, government documents, and microform collections.

The New York Times Index. Monthly index to articles appearing in *The New York Times,* with annual volumes. Since it gives the dates of events, speeches, and important documents, this index is helpful for finding articles of general interest in local papers, as well.

Ulrich's International Periodical Directory. Classifies American and foreign periodicals by subject area and tells which periodical index covers them.

Vertical File Index: A Subject and Title Index to Selected Pamphlet Material. Describes each pamphlet listed, tells how to purchase it, and lists the price.

Indexes in various disciplines
Afro-American Studies—*Index to Periodical Articles by and about Negroes* (1950)

Anthropology—*Anthropological Index* (1968)

Architecture—*The Architectural Index* (1950)

33.3
Res

Review

SAMPLE ENTRIES FROM THE READERS' GUIDE

1 **Venus (Planet)**
   See also
   Space flight to Venus
   Geology
   The basalts of Venus [study by Y. A. Surkov] *Sci Am*
   249:58-9 Ag '83
   Venera 13 and Venera 14: sedimentary rocks on Venus?
   C. P. Florensky and others. bibl f il *Science* 221:57-9
   Jl 1 '83
   Phases
   Mistress of the heavens. J. A. Hynek. il *Sci Dig* 91:48
   Je '83
   Surface
   Venus: global surface radio emissivity [Pioneer radar
   mapper] P. G. Ford and G. H. Pettengill. bibl f il
   Science 220:1379-81 Je 24 '83
   Venus: identification of banded terrain in the mountains
   of Ishtar Terra. D. B. Campbell and others. bibl f
   il map *Science* 221:644-7 Ag 12 '83

2 **Ver Standig, Helen**
   about
   Better than the real thing. D. Di Gregorio. il *Work
   Woman* 8:58 Ag '83
   Veratridine
   Ionizing radiation decreases veratridine-stimulated uptake
   of sodium in rat brain synaptosomes. H. N. Wixon
   and W. A. Hunt. bibl f il *Science* 220:1073-4 Je 3
   '83
   Verbo Church *See* Pentecostal churches—Guatemala

3 **Vercelloni, Isa**
   Not built in a day; tr. by Elaine Greene. il *House Gard*
   155:106-19+ S '83

4 **Verdi, Giuseppe, 1813-1901**
   about
   Don Carlo [opera] Reviews
       High Fidel il 33:MA19-MA21 Jl '83. G. Movshon
   La forza del destino [opera] Reviews
       N Y 16:81 O 10 '83. P. G. Davis
   Rigoletto [opera] Reviews
       High Fidel il 33:MA39 Jl '83. E. Greenfield
   La traviata [opera] Reviews
       High Fidel il 33:MA15-MA18 Ag '83. C. L. Osborne
       Natl Rev 35:1089-90+ S 2 '83. J. Simon
   Verdi victorious. C. Rosen. bibl f il *N Y Rev Books*
   30:33-4+ O 27 '83

■ Explanation

Entry 1 is a **subject entry** on the planet Venus. The list of titles on Venus is subdivided into specific topics: geology, phases, surface. There is also a cross reference to space flight.

Entry 2 is also a **subject entry** about Helen Ver Standig by D. Di Gregorio. The article appears in *Working Woman*, August 1983, on page 58.

Entry 3 is an **author entry.** Notice that Isa Vercelloni's article has been translated by Elaine Greene. It appears in *House & Garden* magazine on pages 106–19 of the September 1983 issue and is continued elsewhere in that issue.

Entry 4 is a **subject entry** listing reviews of operas composed by Verdi and an article about him by C. Rosen that includes a bibliography.

Art—*Art Index* (1929)

Astronomy—*Bibliographic Star Index, 1960–72*

Business—*Business Index* (1979)

Civil Engineering—*Engineering Index* (1884)

Classics—*Essay and General Literature Index* (1934)

Education—*Current Index to Journals in Education* (1969)
Resources in Education (1966)

Environment—*The Environment Index* (1971)

Finance—*F & S Index of Corporations and Industries* (1960)
Index. The Wall Street Journal (1957)

Geology—*Bibliography and Index of Geology* (1933)

Health Sciences—*Completed Research in Health, Physical Education and Recreation, Including International Sources* (1959)
Index Medicus (1960)

History—*America: History and Life* (1964)

Literature—*Essay and General Literature Index* (1900)
An Index to Criticisms of British and American Poetry (1973)

Performing Arts—*Dramatic Index* (1909–49)

Philosophy—*The Philosopher's Index* (1969)

Psychology—*Index of Psychoanalytic Writings* (1956–73)

Social Sciences—*Social Sciences Index* (1974)

Too many students regard *Readers' Guide* as the only periodical index they need to use in their research. The preceding list indicates how many other valuable tools can be found in the reference room of your library.

33.3

Res

Citation Indexes

A special research tool few students are familiar with is the citation index. Such indexes, issued periodically, permit you to trace the influence a given work has had *after* it has been published because these volumes indicate where in subsequently published journals the work is cited again. Thus you can study what is said about a given author or watch ideas develop from one research article to another over a period of time. The citation indexes allow for searches by subject as well as by author and item; they often include the addresses of cited researchers. The major citation indexes are the *Science Citation Index* (1961), the *Social Sciences Citation Index* (1972), and the *Acts and Humanities Index* (1976).

Look for Abstracts

In some disciplines, you can find valuable, up-to-date summaries of the research appearing in major journals. These volumes of abstracts, issued periodically, serve as surveys of research, presenting the latest work and findings. They can save you time by telling you whether a full article treats a subject you are interested in or contains information you need for your research. When your library does not carry the particular journal from which an abstract is drawn, you can usually send for a copy of the journal by using interlibrary loan.

Here are some of the important collections of abstracts in various disciplines:

Anthropology—*Abstracts in Anthropology* (1970)

Architecture—*Building Industry Technology* (1977)

Art—*ARTbibliographies Modern* (1969)

Astronomy—*Astronomy and Astrophysics Abstracts* (1969)

Chemistry—*Chemical Abstracts* (1907)

Civil Engineering—*Meteorological and Geoastrophysical Abstracts* (1950)

Electrical Engineering—*Computer and Control Abstracts* (1967)

Environment—*Environment Abstracts* (1971)

Geology—*Geo Abstracts* (1972)

Health Sciences—*Abstracts of Health Care Management Studies* (1978)

Linguistics—*LLBA: Language and Language Behavior Abstracts* (1967)

Metallurgy—*Metals Abstracts* (1968)

Personnel Management—*Personnel Management Abstracts* (1955)

Petroleum Engineering—*Energy Research Abstracts* (1976)

Physics—*Physics Abstracts* (1898)

Psychology—*Psychological Abstracts* (1927)

Sociology—*Sociological Abstracts* (1952)

Urban Planning—*Urban Affairs Abstracts* (1971)

33.3

Res

Also useful for some projects is *Dissertation Abstracts International* (1938), listing doctoral dissertations from approximately 375 universities in the United States and Canada.

Investigate Computer Data Bases

In many libraries you can research periodical literature and other material by using a computer terminal with access to a variety of data bases. A *data base* is, in effect, an indexed collection of references within a given field made available to libraries through a computer system. Even small libraries can have the capability of tapping in to huge files of information. The actual searching of a data base (for which a fee may be charged) is usually done by trained personnel familiar with given systems manuals and reference tools.

Most libraries have access to selected *data banks*, such as Bibliographic Retrieval Service (BRS) or Lockheed Information Systems (LIS), which are services that provide entrance to the more numerous data bases. In using a computerized search system, you'll need to ask the supervising librarian what data base is most appropriate to your research and whether your library is serviced by a data bank that provides access to that base. You can often do simple author or title searches on your own by following the instructions provided at a terminal. Subject searches are more complicated; you will usually have to discuss your subject with a librarian who will do the investigation. Using key words called *descriptors,* under which information on your topic within a base is indexed, the librarian can usually generate a list of titles from a large number of periodicals, providing you with an instant, highly specialized bibliography. Such searches are not perfect. Your print-out of references may include articles of little value to your research since the data bases are often quite unselective in what they index. But a knowledgeable operator experienced in working a data base can usually help you find what you need.

Data bases are valuable for finding information generated in the last fifteen years or so, but many do not index earlier materials. If your subject requires resources that predate the earliest entries in your data base, you will have to supplement your computer research with citations gained through the familiar printed indexes. Many of the data bases are, in fact, based on printed indexes such as the *National Union Catalog* or the *Congressional Information Service.* Remember that the terminal in the library will provide you only with the citations, not with the articles themselves. Some data bases (such as ERIC) will, for a fee, send you microform copies of materials listed in their files.

Ask your librarian for a list of the data bases available in your library or consult the various directories and source-books (frequently updated) that describe these systems. Sheehy's well-known *Guide to Reference Books* now includes a section on data bases in its supplements. Among the hundreds of available data bases are the following:

Comprehensive Dissertation Index (CDI)

The Information Bank (*The New York Times* Information Services)

Machine Readable Cataloging (MARC). *Lists all books catalogued in English by the Library of Congress since 1968.*

Philosopher's Index Data Base

American Statistics Index (ASI)

Congressional Information Service (CIS)

Current Index to Journals in Education (CIJE)

F & S Index of Corporations and Industries

Educational Services Research Center (ERIC)

Historical Abstracts (HA)

Computerized Engineering Index (COMPENDEX)

Index to Scientific Reviews (ISR)

Scientific Citation Index (SCI)

Smithsonian Science Information Exchange (SSIE)

Examine Appropriate Reference Books

In each field there are many reference books useful for exploring or researching a topic. In general, you should be aware of the various encyclopedias available to provide you with overviews of various subjects (see pp. 670–71), with materials printed in microfilm or microfiche (see *Microlist: An International Record of New Micropublications*), and with guides to reference material such as these:

33.3
Res

Sheehy, Eugene P. *Guide to Reference Books,* 9th ed., supplements. A standard work useful for its comprehensiveness and annotations. It is the updated version of a work still often referred to by the last name of its original author, Constance M. Winchell.

Bell, Marion V., and Eleanor A. Swidan. *Reference Books: A Brief Guide.*

SUBJECT & DATABASE	SECTION/PAGE
TRADEMARKSCAN	C16
Current Affairs	
CNI	D3
MAGAZINE INDEX	D9
NATIONAL NEWSPAPER INDEX	D10
NEWSEARCH	D11
NEWSPAPER INDEX	D11
PAIS INTERNATIONAL	D12
SOCIAL SCISEARCH	D14
UPI NEWS	D15
WORLD AFFAIRS REPORT	D16
Dissertations	
COMPREHENSIVE	A3, B3,
DISSERTATION INDEX	C4, D4
Drug Abuse	
DRUG INFO/ALCOHOL USE-ABUSE	D4
MEDLINE	B6
MEDOC	B7
MENTAL HEALTH ABSTRACTS	D9
PSYCINFO	D13
Drugs (See Pharmacy and Pharmaceuticals)	
Encyclopedic Information	
ACADEMIC AMERICAN ENCYCLOPEDIA	D1
Energy	
DOE ENERGY	A3, C5
ELECTRIC POWER DATABASE	A4
ELECTRIC POWER INDUSTRY	A4
ENERGY BIBLIOGRAPHY	A4
ENERGYLINE	A5, B3, C8, D6
ENERGYNET	A5
ENVIRONMENTAL BIBLIOGRAPHY	A5
NTIS	A9, B7, C12, D12
TULSA	A12
Engineering	
BHRA FLUID ENGINEERING	A1
COMPENDEX	A3
CONFERENCE PAPERS INDEX	A3
EI ENGINEERING MEETINGS	A3
INSPEC	B5
ISMEC	A8
SCISEARCH	B7
Food	
FOODS ADLIBRA	C9
FSTA	A6
Foreign Trade	
FOREIGN TRADERS INDEX	C9
TRADE OPPORTUNITIES	C16
U.S. EXPORTS	C16
Foundations	
FOUNDATION DIRECTORY	A6, B4, C9, D7
FOUNDATION GRANTS INDEX	A6, B4, C10, D7
GRANTS	A6, B5, C10, D8
NATIONAL FOUNDATIONS	A9, B7, C12, D10
Geological Sciences	
CONFERENCE PAPERS INDEX	A3
GEOARCHIVE	B4
GEOREF	B5
ISI/GEOSCITECH	B6
METEOROLOGICAL AND GEOASTROPHYSICAL ABSTRACTS	B7
OCEANIC ABSTRACTS	A9
TULSA	A12

COMPUTER-BASED
INFORMATION SERVICES

Databases Available for Computer Searching

Index

WHAT IS CIS?
　　The General Libraries Computer-Based Information
　　Services (CIS) provides online searching of more than
　　150 databases to produce a tailor-made bibliography
　　on your research topic. Databases are available on a
　　wide range of subjects. These databases are listed
　　in four separate sections: A. Applied Science and
　　Technology, B. Science, C. Business and Economics,
　　and D. Social Sciences and Humanities with
　　information about the files available in your area.

HOW IS A SEARCH REQUESTED?
　　Online searching is done by librarians skilled in
　　computer searching techniques for the files in their
　　subject areas. Contact a librarian who searches
　　databases in your area of research; office and
　　telephone numbers for an appointment are listed in
　　sections A-D. The searcher will discuss your topic
　　with you, develop a search strategy, and run the
　　search.

WHAT ARE THE ADVANTAGES OF DOING A SEARCH ONLINE?
　　Although most of the databases are computerized
　　versions of indexes available in the General
　　Libraries, online searching is quick, thorough,
　　current and convenient. Terms can be coordinated for
　　precise retrieval of relevant material and several
　　files can be searched at one time.

WHAT DOES A SEARCH COST?
　　Charges vary depending upon the file searched, the
　　amount of computer time used, and the number of
　　citations retrieved. The charge for a typical search
　　is $15.00 (see sample costs in sections A-D).

HOW DO YOU PAY FOR A SEARCH?
　　An individual may pay by personal check or funds may
　　be IDT'd from a grant or other University account.
　　Persons paying by personal check must pay when they
　　pick up their bibliography. Results of searches paid
　　by IDT may be mailed at the user's request and risk.
　　Bibliographies printed offline usually arrive about
　　five working days after the search was run.

WHO CAN USE THIS SERVICE?
　　This service is available only to UT-Austin students,
　　faculty, and staff.

The General Libraries
The University of Texas at Austin

33.3

Res

33.3
Res

THE UNIVERSITY OF TEXAS AT AUSTIN
THE GENERAL LIBRARIES

COMPUTER-BASED INFORMATION SERVICES
DATABASES AVAILABLE FOR COMPUTER SEARCHING

D. SOCIAL SCIENCES AND HUMANITIES

DATABASE	SUBJECT AND SOURCE	YEARS OF COVERAGE	CONTACT LIBRARIAN(S)	ONLINE COMPUTER COST PER HOUR	OFFLINE PRINT COST PER FULL CITATION	EXAMPLES OF SEARCH COST FOR 10 MINUTES SEARCH*
ABLEDATA	Provides listings of commercially available products and technical aids for persons with disabilities. The database contains references to rehabilitation products for personal care, home management, vocational/educational management, seating, mobility, transportation, communication, recreation, sensory disability, ambulation, orthotics, prosthetics, and therapy; from the National Rehabilitation Information Center. (B)	Current	Elizabeth Airth or Phillip White, Reference, PCL 2.200, Tele: 471-5944; Nancy Elder, Science Library, MAI 220, Tele: 471-1475.	$31.00	$.25	$19.13
ACADEMIC AMERICAN ENCYCLOPEDIA	Full text database covering the complete 9,000,000 word, 29,000 entry encyclopedia, and spanning a multitude of topics within the humanities, sciences, social sciences, technology, geography, the arts, sports, and contemporary life; from Grolier, Inc. (B)	Current	Goldia Hester or Jerry Breeze, Reference, PCL 2.200, Tele: 471-5944.	$36.00	$.35	$24.98

*WITH 50 CITATION PRINTOUT; INCLUDES COMMUNICATION CHARGES

Murphey, Robert W. *How and Where to Look It Up.*

The Reader's Adviser: A Layman's Guide to Literature.

Shores, Louis. *Basic Reference Sources: An Introduction to Materials and Methods.*

Walford, Arthur J., ed. *Guide to Reference Material.*

Listed below are some specific reference tools that may be useful to you when you are seeking news sources, book reviews, biographical information, and statistics.

News sources

New York Times Index (1960)

Newsbank (1970). Indexes approximately 100 major newspapers, according to subjects, organizations, and individuals in the news.

Facts on File (1961). A weekly news digest with an index.

CQ Weekly Report (1960). Reports on congressional activity.

Editorial Research Reports (1964). Provides discussions of current events and controversies. Indexed by subject; includes bibliographies.

Book reviews

Book Review Digest (1905). Locates and briefly summarizes reviews of books.

Book Review Index (1965). Locates reviews, but does not summarize them. More comprehensive in coverage than *Book Review Digest.*

Index to Book Reviews in the Humanities (1961). Lists reviews of books in art, drama, literature, music, philosophy, and so on.

Biographical information

Current Biography. Provides information on prominent people since 1940.

Dictionary of National Biography. Provides thorough biographical information on prominent British subjects. Does not cover current figures. Includes supplements.

Dictionary of American Biography. The American version of the above work. Includes supplements.

33.3
Res

Who's Who in America. Lists figures of current importance.

Who's Who. Lists facts about living British subjects.

Notable American Women

Dictionary of Scientific Biography

Who's Who in Architecture, from 1400 to the Present

Contemporary Authors

World Authors, 1950–1970

European Authors, 1000–1900

American Authors, 1600–1900

Biography Index. Lists articles and biographical citations for figures in all fields, times, and places.

Statistics

National Basic Intelligence Factbook. Useful facts and figures about all nations. Published by the CIA.

UN Statistical Yearbook

The Statesman's Yearbook

Statistical Abstract of the United States

Gallup Poll: Public Opinion 1935–1971

Survey of Current Business

Dow Jones Irwin Business Almanac

World Almanac and Book of Facts

Information Please Almanac

33.3

Res

In other, more specific areas (literature, psychology, finance, for example), the number of good reference books is almost staggering—far too many to list here in a useful way. Almost every subject area has dictionaries, encyclopedias, handbooks, and guides. When you are researching a topic, spend some time in the reference room of your library. Begin with a guide to research books (such as Sheehy's *Guide to Reference Books),* checking to see whether some reference tool will provide you with the citations or information you need. Be sure to locate the latest edition of the reference work. And read the front matter carefully so that you understand how to use the volume and what are the limits of its coverage. You can waste time using trial and error to figure out what the entries mean or how the work is organized.

Use the Card Catalogue Effectively

The card catalogue is an alphabetical card index of the items in the library. The cards, filed in drawers or trays, are located in the main reading room or other central spot. Most card catalogues, in addition to listing all books in the library, give the titles of periodicals (and indicate what copies the library has), encyclopedias, government publications, and other works. Some libraries now have "card catalogues" on computers, but the information provided is the same.

Almost all books are listed alphabetically in three places in the card catalogue of most libraries: by author, by subject, and by title. The cards issued by the Library of Congress, like those reproduced on page 666, are almost universally used for cataloging. The subject listings of the Library of Congress are also widely adopted. To find information on a given topic, you might first consult the Directory of Library of Congress Subject Classifications (often described simply as the Subject List) to see what term is used in the card catalogue to describe your subject. The subject listings, you'll discover, are sometimes eccentric. Be sure to become familiar with the subject list volume before searching the card catalogue.

You can also save yourself many hours of thumbing through books not relevant to your subject by learning to interpret and evaluate the information given in the card catalogue itself. The subject card includes the following information (keyed to the numbers on the subject card):

1. **Subject.** The subject heading on the catalogue card tells in general what the book is about. Here the general subject is dogs. Also listed on the card (in item 7) are the other subject headings under which the book is catalogued.

2. **Call number.** The call number in the upper left-hand corner tells where the book is located in the library. In many libraries, borrowers obtain books by filling out a slip with the call number, author, title, and the borrower's name and address. If you have access to the stacks, the call number will enable you to locate the book you are looking for.

3. **Author's name.** If you are already familiar with the subject you are investigating, the author's name may tell you whether the book is likely to be authoritative. No-

33.3

Res

Subject Card

```
          1  DOGS
    SF
  2 431       Pearsall, Milo D.  3
    P42      4  Scent: training to track, search and rescue
    1982        / Milo D. Pearsall and Hugo Verbruggen. --
    UGL         Loveland, CO : Alpine Publications, 1982.
             5   xiv, 225 p. : ill. ; 24 cm.

             6   Bibliography: p. 217-221.
                 Includes index.

             7   1. Dogs.  2. Smell.  I. Verbruggen, Hugo.
                 II. Title.
```

Author Card

```
    SF
    431      Pearsall, Milo D.
    P42         Scent: training to track, search and rescue
    1982        / Milo D. Pearsall and Hugo Verbruggen. --
    UGL         Loveland, CO : Alpine Publications, 1982.
                xiv, 225 p. : ill. ; 24 cm.

                Bibliography: p. 217-221.
                Includes index.

                1. Dogs.  2. Smell.  I. Verbruggen, Hugo.
                II. Title.
```

Title Card

33.3

Res

```
                Scent: training to track, search and rescue.
    SF
    431      Pearsall, Milo D.
    P42         Scent: training to track, search and rescue
    1982        / Milo D. Pearsall and Hugo Verbruggen. --
    UGL         Loveland, CO : Alpine Publications, 1982.
                xiv, 225 p. : ill. ; 24 cm.

                Bibliography: p. 217-221.
                Includes index.

                1. Dogs.  2. Smell.  I. Verbruggen, Hugo.
                II. Title.
```

tice that this book has two authors, Milo Pearsall and Hugo Verbruggen.

4. **Title and facts of publication.** The date of publication is sometimes an important clue to the usefulness of a book. This book is reasonably up to date.

5. **Number of pages, illustrations, height.** The number of pages in the book suggests how extensive its coverage is. This book is rather short—225 pages of text. Notice, however, that it contains illustrations that may be useful. (The indication of height—24 cm.—is for librarians.)

6. **Special information.** The catalogue card indicates that the book contains a bibliography that might prove helpful in directing you to other sources. None of the books listed, however, would be later than 1982, the year in which this particular book was published. The book also contains an index.

7. **Other subject headings.** The list of other subject headings under which the book is catalogued may give you ideas of other subject areas to look under for more material on your topic, as well as provide a further clue to the contents of the book listed.

See page 674–75 for the information you will need to copy from the card catalogue in preparing your own bibliography cards.

Some libraries have replaced traditional card catalogues with a file of microfiche transparencies, which can be used with simple machines that enlarge the material and display it on a screen. Microfiche entries will usually not give you as much information as a library catalogue card, but you can still usually expect to find sources listed in three different ways: by author, by title, and by subject.

33.4
Res

33.4 Preparing the Research Paper

The traditional research or term paper has much in common with other writing assignments, but in addition it can provide:

1. Practice in exploring the possibilities of a subject and limiting it so that it can be treated adequately in a paper longer than those you will customarily write; research papers may often range from 1500 to 4000 words.

2. An introduction to the resources of the library and training in the most efficient ways of locating information.

3. Practice in using source material intelligently—choosing between what is useful and what is not, evaluating the ideas of others, organizing and interpreting the information.

4. Acquaintance with documentation and manuscript form typically expected in academic work and in reports and papers prepared for publication.

5. An opportunity to learn something new about a subject and to gain specialized, thorough knowledge of it.

Because the research paper is longer and more complex than most other compositions you may be asked to write, we discuss it here in successive steps:

1. choosing a topic;
2. locating appropriate source materials;
3. preparing the working bibliography;
4. evaluating your material;
5. taking useful notes;
6. planning the paper;
7. writing the first draft;
8. documenting the paper;
9. assembling the completed paper.

33.4
Res

The actual task of preparing a research paper, however, can seldom be divided into such neat categories. The steps overlap and certain operations must be repeated as work progresses. For example, as you get into your reading and research you may decide that your topic needs to be modified; and as you write your paper you may discover gaps in your information that must be filled in by further research. The best advice, perhaps, is to start on the assignment early and to take particular care in choosing and defining your topic so that both your research and your writing will have a clear focus.

Step 1: Choosing a Topic

Ideally, you would never have to begin a research paper by finding a topic; instead you would spend your time refining an interest you already have—narrowing your subject to a workable size or formulating a hypothesis to test. But research papers are often responses to particular course requirements. In some classes, the subject field may be limited by the general assignment (perhaps to various aspects of the United Nations, or to the history of a specific geographic area; but often the choice of a subject will be left up to you.

In either instance, you should be reasonably certain that the specific topic you select will be one that you will like to learn about, to think about, and then to write about. Since a research paper may take as much as five or six weeks to prepare, it can easily become a chore—and be largely a waste of time—unless you feel that what you are doing is of some interest and importance. The suggestions in 20.1, Techniques for Generating Ideas, are as relevant to the research paper as they are to other kinds of writing.

Choosing a Subject Area

Before making a definite decision on your topic, consider your various interests in and out of school. These general subjects may suggest particular topics that you might want to investigate:

1. A subject related to one of the courses that you are now taking or that you intend to take.
2. A subject related to your reading interests (biography, history, science fiction, detective stories) or one related to your favorite hobby or sport (music, clothing design, mountain climbing, baseball).
3. A subject about which you now have an opinion but little actual information.
4. A subject that has aroused your curiosity but that you have never had time or opportunity to investigate.

Limiting the Topic

As soon as you know what general subject area you would like to concentrate on, think about finding a specific topic within that area that can be treated adequately and profitably in a paper of the assigned length. Keep these considerations in mind when you are narrowing your topic:

33.4

Res

Length of the Research Paper. An undergraduate research paper is not expected to be the last word on a topic, but it must be more than a disconnected listing of commonplace facts or a superficial summary of a complex topic. Limit your topic enough so that your treatment of it can be reasonably thorough. The danger of selecting a topic that is too narrow is smaller than the danger of choosing one that is too broad.

Availability of Source Material. Before you begin to read and take notes, find out whether the more important books and periodicals that you will need are available in your college library. Since many sources are usually required for a research paper, you should be certain that enough material is available before you begin your research.

Complexity of the Source Material. For some subjects (chemical structures of synthetic rubber, for example), the available material may be too technical for a general reader to understand—and perhaps too complicated for you to interpret without a good deal of study. You will probably be better off, even in a technical area, with a topic of current general interest. But be sure you know what audience your instructor expects you to address. In some cases, especially in upper-division courses, you may be expected to write a more technical or sophisticated paper. Here are some steps to take to help you determine your approach to your topic:

1. **Do some preliminary reading.** Spend a few hours reading background material in one or more general or special encyclopedias, in some magazine articles, and perhaps in newspaper articles, if your subject is of current interest and likely to be covered by the daily press. This background reading can give you the quick overview of a topic you need to determine, first, whether you want to develop it at all; second, what its divisions or controversies are; and third, how you can develop it using the resources available to you. Among the general and specialized encyclopedias you might want to examine are the following:

   General encyclopedias
   Collier's Encyclopedia
   Encyclopedia Americana
   The New Columbia Encyclopedia

The Encyclopaedia Britannica. Some of the older editions of this work are also worth examining.

Specialized encyclopedias

McGraw-Hill Encyclopedia of Science and Technology
Encyclopedia of Social Work
International Encyclopedia of the Social Sciences
Encyclopaedia Judaica
International Encyclopedia of Film
Encyclopedia of World Art
Encyclopedia of Pop, Rock, and Soul
Cassell's Encyclopedia of World Literature
Encyclopedia of Computer Science and Technology
Encyclopedia of Philosophy

2. **Check reference sources.** Look through the library card catalogue and the guides to periodical literature to see how the general subject you have chosen may be broken down into smaller units. A broad subject like *aviation* might first be limited to *commercial aviation*, then to the *functions of the Civil Aeronautics Board (CAB)*, then still further to *recent safety measures enacted by the CAB.*

3. **Define your idea as precisely as possible.** Even though you probably still will be unable to make a final statement of the central or controlling idea of your paper, your preliminary reading should have given you a reasonably accurate idea of the focus of your paper. This will help give direction to your research, so that you won't later have to discard much material as useless.

Step 2: Locating Appropriate Source Materials

33.4
Res

The previous section (33.3 Strategies and Tools of Research) provides you with the information you need to explore a topic. Choose those methods of research that fit your subject, the assignment, and the resources of your library and college. Be sure to give yourself ample time to collect the information you need, to schedule interviews when necessary, to write for information, and to compile data.

Step 3: Preparing the Working Bibliography

A working bibliography is a list of the books, magazine articles, and other published works that you intend to consult when gathering material for your research paper. The number of references you should collect will depend on the nature of the assignment, but it is always best to begin with more than you will probably need. If your working bibliography includes only a bare minimum of sources, you will probably have to take time later to find more: a book you want from the library may already be out on loan; one article on your list may prove to be too technical; another may merely repeat material you have already collected.

Some instructors may recommend a special system for maintaining a working bibliography and for taking notes. The system recommended below is widely used, and it is convenient.

Each entry in your working bibliography should be written on a separate card, either a 3-by-5 inch or 4-by-6 inch. With only one reference on each, cards can be rearranged quickly for alphabetizing; new ones can be inserted in the proper places and useless ones discarded. You may want to use 3-by-5 cards for the working bibliography and 4-by-6 cards for taking notes, since the larger cards will obviously hold more data and will also be readily distinguishable from your bibliography cards.

Bibliography cards for different types of references are illustrated on pages 674–75. Each card should include all the facts you will need to identify the reference and obtain it from the library. It should also have all the information you will need in preparing the final bibliography. The punctuation suggested here for individual entries is a standard form for bibliographies (see page 691).

33.4

Res

1. **Author's name,** with the last name first, followed by a period. If the book is edited, use the editor's name, followed by a comma, followed by *ed.* If the article or pamphlet is unsigned, write the title first on the card.

2. **Title of the book,** underlined and followed by a period, or title of the article, in quotation marks and followed by a period.

3. **Facts of publication**
   a) **For a book:** the city of publication, followed by a colon; the name of the publisher, followed by a comma; and the date, followed by a period.

b) **For a magazine article:** the name of the magazine, underlined and followed by a comma; the date of the issue, followed by a comma; and the pages covered in the article, without *p.* or *pp.,* followed by a period.

c) **For a journal article:** the name of the journal, underlined (but *not* followed by a comma); the volume number in Arabic numerals; the date in parentheses, followed by a colon; the page numbers, without *p.* or *pp.,* followed by a period.

d) **For a newspaper article:** the name of the newspaper, underlined and followed by a comma; the date, followed by a comma; the section number, followed by a comma; the page on which the story appeared, followed by a comma; the column number, followed by a period.

4. **Library call number,** or the location of a reference work in the library. This information, placed in the upper left-hand corner, should be written just as it appears in the card catalogue, so that you can relocate the reference if the need arises. See also page 701, The Bibliography.

5. **Index number,** a number or code that you assign to the work, should be placed in the upper right-hand corner of the card. This same number should be used on any note cards you make that refer to this source.

Step 4: Evaluating Your Material

Since writing a research paper is in part an exercise in critical judgment, it is important that you learn to evaluate the sources you use. Try to find and use the most informative books and the most authoritative material available to you.

Facts to Consider in Evaluating

Writers engaged in writing their first research papers on unfamiliar subjects are not expected to know offhand that a work by author A is wholly worthless or that author B is considered the foremost authority on the subject. They can, however, arrive at a fairly accurate estimate of their sources by considering these facts:

1. **Date of publication.** If your subject is one for which recent facts are important, see that the sources are up to

SAMPLE BIBLIOGRAPHY CARDS

301.451
L 616 Lerner, Gerda, ed. *Black
Women in White America: A
Documentary History.*

New York: Random House
Pantheon Books, 1972

1

Ref Room
Shelf 1

Fr. [aser], A. [ntonia]
"Mary, Queen of Scots."
Encyclopaedia Britannica
Chicago: Encyclopaedia Britannica, Inc.,
1982. 11:564-65.

2

975.005
Am 3
J. 21

Stegner, Wallace. "Owen
Wister: Creator of the Cowboy
Myth." *American West,*
January/February 1984, 48-52.

3

The difference between a magazine and a journal is usually apparent from their content and format. Magazines generally have a wide public appeal and are published weekly or monthly, with dates corresponding to the issue. Each issue begins with page 1. Journals are usually of more limited appeal (for example, _Journal of Physics_), they are often published less frequently than magazines (many are published quarterly), and the date does not always correspond to the actual date of issue ("Autumn" could be issued between September and November). Therefore the volume and issue numbers are more important, especially since pagination is often continuous throughout an entire volume (volume 1, number 2, might begin on page 223, for example).

Periodical
Desk   4

   Lunsford, Andrea and Lisa S. Ede.
   "Classical Rhetoric, Modern Rhetoric,
   and Contemporary Discourse Studies."
   Written Communication 1(1984):78-100.

Periodical   5
Desk
   "U.S., Soviets Trade Charges
   on Psychiatry Abuse."
   Los Angeles Times, February
   25, 1984, p. 14, col. 1.

date. The most recent edition of a book or an encyclopedia will generally be more useful and authoritative
than an earlier one.

2. **Authority.** Look for books or articles that have made an
   impact in the field you are examining or have been at
   the center of discussion or controversy. Rather than only
   read *about* important studies, read the studies themselves. Don't rely on secondary sources alone when you
   have access to primary materials. And never limit your
   information to what you can find in encyclopedias.

3. **Completeness.** With magazine articles, it is better to
   read the original article as it was printed in full instead
   of a condensation or reprint of it. Similarly, books are
   often more thorough than articles, although you will
   want to be sure that the book's author is reputable.
   Check the bibliographies in the books you look at for
   sources that are referred to often.

4. **Facts and opinions.** Distinguish carefully between an
   author's facts and opinions. Label the opinions "So-and-
   so thinks that. . . ." In general, pay more attention to
   facts (unless your paper is about various opinions), since
   you will need facts to support your own opinions.

5. **Objectivity of the source.** A book or an article based in
   large part upon an author's opinions or biases—particularly when the subject is controversial—should not be
   used as your sole authority on the matter. Read material
   that is diverse before reaching a conclusion.

33.4
Res

When you are in doubt about the reliability of a source, a
librarian, your instructor, or an expert in the field may be able
to give you advice. Reviews in the more specialized journals
evaluate books in their own fields. *Book Review Digest* may
also prove helpful.

Step 5: Take Useful Notes

Accurate and full notes are essential for writing a good reference paper. You can save time when taking notes if you approach the problem efficiently. Don't try to take down everything you read; instead, spend a little time looking over the

book, the article, or the pamphlet to see if it contains the information you want. If you have given enough thought to formulating and narrowing your topic, you will have a pretty clear idea of what you are looking for.

When examining a book, look first at the index and the table of contents to see in what sections your subject is treated. See also if there are any tables, graphs, bibliographies, or further references that might be useful. Skim each chapter to find out what it covers. Then go over it again carefully, taking the notes you will need.

Notes should be taken on either 3-by-5 inch or 4-by-6 inch cards so that you can later arrange the material according to the plan of your paper. It is usually a waste of effort to try to take notes in numbered outline form since you probably won't know the final plan of your paper until you have finished your research. What is important is to make each note card accurate, clearly written, and clearly labeled. Each note card should contain these essential parts, as illustrated by the sample cards shown on page 681:

1. The **heading** at the top of the card, showing what material it contains.

2. The **index number** to identify the source and page number, accurately noted.

3. The **content,** facts or opinions (summarized in your own words or directly quoted) accurately recorded.

Notes that cannot be readily interpreted a week or a month after they have been written are obviously of little use; so too are incomplete or carelessly written notes. You can avoid a good deal of tedious, unnecessary work, including rereading and rechecking, by following these simple rules:

1. Use *one side* of each card only. Your material will then be easier to classify and arrange, and you won't run the risk of overlooking a statement on the back of a card.

2. Include only *one major point* or a few closely related facts from the same source on a single card. If the information is too extensive to write on one side of a card, use two or three cards and number them in sequence.

AN ORIGINAL SOURCE
AND SAMPLE NOTES

The two note cards reproduced below show how material from a source might be recorded. The first card carries quick notes on the highlights of the selection, useful for a paper on dating fossils. The second note card records an actual quotation, perhaps for an essay on desert ecology. Note that both cards include the page number of the selection, a short author/title reference, and an index number keyed to the bibliography card.

```
QH                                          4
88
G46/3   George, Uwe.  In the Deserts of
        This Earth.  Trans. Richard and
        Clara Winston.  New York: Harcourt
        Brace Jovanovich, 1977.
```

Passage from Uwe George's *In the Deserts of This Earth*, page 39:

Our present chronological techniques make it possible to determine, directly or indirectly, the real age of many rocks and fossils. The ancient dream of natural scientists, especially of geologists and paleontologists, has been fulfilled: when they dig up a saurian, they can now say how many millions of years ago the animal walked the earth. When they find a fossil in coal, they can tell when that particular seam was laid down.

In 1650, Archbishop James Usher reckoned that the creation of the world had taken place at the stroke of nine o'clock on Sunday morning, October 23, in the year 4004 B.C. The scientists of the nineteenth century, a good deal more realistic, estimated the age of the earth, on the basis of the fossil record, as about 100 million years. Modern researchers have assigned an age of more than 4 billion years to some samples of rock.

For the scientist who knows how to read them, the strata of the earth's crust and the fossils locked within them represent an inexhaustible potential source of information. In deserts, the forces of weathering have exposed hundreds of layers, among them deep-lying and very ancient ones that date back to the early days of the earth's evolution. Normally, such strata lie many thousands of feet beneath the surface. Thus the desert affords special opportunities for learning about the evolution of our planet. But before we can understand the earth's past and future we must take up the question of how this planet, its atmosphere, and the life upon it came into being in the first place.

■ **Notes Taken for a Paper on Methods of Dating Fossils**

For such a paper, quick notes on various efforts at dating might be sufficient:

Dating at various times

George
In the Deserts ...

present methods - can determine real age of rock and fossils
1650 - Archbishop Usher dated creation - 9 a.m., - Sunday, Oct. 23, 4004 B.C.
19th century - earth about 100 million years old now - more than 4 billion years

■ **Notes Taken for a Paper on Desert Ecology**

For such a paper, an actual quotation might be useful:

Deserts, as a source of information

George
In the Deserts ...

p. 39 "In deserts, the forces of weathering have exposed hundreds of layers, among them deep-lying and very ancient ones that date back to the early days of the earth's evolution ... Thus the desert affords special opportunities for learning about the evolution of our planet."

3. Get all the information *accurately* the first time you consult a source so that you won't have to make extra trips to the library. Be sure to note the page numbers of all passages you intend to quote or refer to in your essay.

4. Put all *direct quotations* in quotation marks. This includes all statements, single sentences, and phrases that you copy word for word from any source. If you omit a word or words in a direct quotation use ellipsis marks (. . .) to indicate the omission (14.2). If you are paraphrasing the source, state the idea in your own language. (See 32.5, Avoiding Plagiarism and Collusion.)

5. Write your notes *in ink* (penciled notes may become blurred with frequent handling) so that you won't have to recopy them. When you use abbreviations, be sure that you will know later on what they mean.

It isn't necessary to write out all your notes in complete sentences; practical shortcuts such as the omission of *a, the, was,* and other such words are good for summarizing material. If the method you use for taking notes in lecture courses or on your textbooks has proved successful, use it also for your reference paper.

Many students now use copying machines as a substitute for taking notes, relying on pages of copied material for their information rather than on their own syntheses of what they have read. Copies provide you with accurate texts of passages you intend to quote directly and save you a great deal of time in acquiring bibliographic entries. But you can easily copy too much material, or lose track of important passages, unless you take the time to annotate and underscore key parts of your reproduced reading. Be sure also to keep track of where your copies come from, perhaps keeping all pages from a given article in a single folder or coding copied material with a number that corresponds with a full bibliography card. If you aren't careful, you can wind up with a table full of confusing and unidentified photocopies.

33.4

Res

Review

SAMPLE NOTE CARDS

Direct quote

> Origins of Parliament   Maurois   1
>
> <u>Hist. of Eng.</u>, 146
>
> "The convoking of the different 'Estates'
> of a Kingdom (Military, priestly, and
> plebian), in order to obtain their
> consent to taxation, was not peculiar
> to England in the fourteenth century."

Summarized material

> Incidence of neurosis   2
> among the poor
>
> Harrington
> <u>Other Amer.</u>, 119
>
> Though there is a myth that the
> richer you are the more neurotic
> you are likely to be, the truth is
> just the opposite: poor people
> suffer from mental illness more often
> than people in any other social class.

Statistical data

> Enrollment in institutions   <u>Stat. Abstract</u>
> of higher education   (1000's) 1979   136

	<u>1950</u>	<u>1960</u>	<u>1970</u>	<u>1975</u>	<u>1977</u>
Total	2659	3216	7136	9023	9589
Public	1355	1832	5112	6838	7275
Private	1304	1384	2024	2185	2314

Step 6: Planning the Paper

The central or controlling purpose of a research paper will be clear in your mind long before you finish investigating all your resources. You should know whether you are trying to prove a hypothesis, or reconcile opposing views, or explain an event or situation. But as you do your research, your attitude toward your subject may change or evidence may point in a direction you hadn't anticipated. Gradually your topic or conclusions will come into focus and you can think about stating a main point or writing a thesis sentence. The shape of your essay will begin to be defined. (Review Chapter 21, Developing and Arranging Material.)

One method of shaping your research paper is to first read through all your notes to refresh your memory and determine a tentative order for your material. Then you can arrange the notes in piles, grouping together all the notes on a particular aspect of your subject. The headings at the top of each card will be useful in helping you sort and arrange your material. At this stage you should note any gaps in your research that will have to be filled in with further reading or other investigation before you start your first draft.

Consider several options for arranging material; don't settle automatically on the first approach that comes to mind, unless your report is following a structure that is conventional for reporting research within your field. If any of the notes you have taken do not seem relevant to the essay you are planning, put them aside for the time being, but do not discard them immediately. Remember, though, that almost anyone engaged in research finds that a good deal of carefully recorded material has to be discarded.

Making a Preliminary Outline

When you have arranged your note cards to your satisfaction, state the central idea of your paper in a thesis sentence (not in two or more sentences nor in the form of a question). Then make a rough outline showing the order in which you intend to present your material. Each point in the outline should contribute in some way to the development of your central idea or thesis. Often your instructor will want to see your working outline before you go much further with the work. To crystallize your plan and to make it possible for your instructor to examine it and make suggestions, you should follow standard outline form. At this stage a topic outline is generally sufficient; if necessary, you can later expand the entries into complete sentences. (See 22, Using Outlines, for a discussion of outlining and outline form.)

Step 7: Writing the First Draft

The first draft of your research paper should be written just as you would write the draft of any other important assignment (as discussed in 23, Drafting, Revising, and Editing). But be sure to keep track of your documentation as you write, listing your preliminary notes on pages separate from your text.

If a passage seems to need more facts or further documentation, don't interrupt your writing to do the necessary additional research. Put a question mark or some other notation in the margin, continue with your writing, and look up the material after you have finished the first draft.

Most research papers are written in a rather formal, impersonal style. Usually there's no need to refer to yourself at all, but if you do, the reference should be brief. (It's also better to say "I" than to use "the writer" or some other third-person references.)

Step 8: Documenting the Paper

Any paper that refers to the research of others or is based on outside sources should acknowledge each and every borrowing from which an idea or statement is taken. Footnotes, endnotes, and other citations in a paper can be handled in a variety of ways. In the past, it was conventional to rely almost exclusively on footnotes or endnotes of some kind, especially in the humanities; in the sciences, documentation was simpler, with short references in the text of a paper amplified by a full bibliography. Now the direction, even in English and the humanities, is toward simpler, less intrusive, yet no less thorough systems of notes. The method of documentation recommended by most instructors in English and the humanities is described on pages 691–701 and illustrated in the student paper beginning on page 715. Alternative forms for notes are described on page 709.

Any description of notes makes their use seem much harder than it really is. If you have taken good notes with the exact sources clearly recorded, you will find that documenting a paper is relatively simple.

Where Documentation Is Needed

When drawing on the work of another writer or researcher, you owe him or her the courtesy of giving credit where credit is due. You also owe your readers the courtesy of providing the sources of your information so that they can judge them for themselves and find additional information, if more is desired. Failure to document borrowed information is at best carelessness; at worst, it is plagiarism, which means offering material written by someone else as your own work (see page 629). Documentation is essential in two situations:

1. **After direct quotations.** Each statement taken word for word from a printed source should have a citation identifying its source. The only exceptions to this rule are well-known expressions, such as familiar Biblical quotations ("Blessed are the poor"), famous lines from literature ("Something is rotten in the state of Denmark"), and proverbs ("A bird in the hand is worth two in the bush").

2. **After all important statements of fact or opinion taken from written sources and expressed in your own words.** Facts include figures, dates, scientific data, and descriptions of events and situations about which you have no firsthand knowledge, such as what happened at a session of the United Nations, how coffee is cultivated in Brazil, or the role of Madagascar in World War II. Opinions and interpretations that are not actually your own would include statements such as one writer's reasons for the popularity of football in the United States or an opinion on foreign policy from a newspaper editorial.

In some publications, notes are also used for comments or additional information that the writer does not wish to include in the text. In undergraduate research papers, however, this practice should be kept to a minimum; if a statement is worth making, it usually belongs in the text.

Documentation is *not* needed for statements that would pass without question. These include obvious facts ("Certain chemicals cannot be used in the preservation of foods in the

United States"), matters of common knowledge ("Hiroshima was devastated by an atomic bomb in August 1945"), general statements, and expressions of the writer's own opinion ("The medical and biological sciences have made enormous progress in the last twenty years").

If you have a full page in your draft without any references, you should probably check it again to see if any documentation is needed. A great many citations on a single page may indicate that some of the material could better be combined or rephrased to eliminate unnecessary references.

The following sections discuss some things to consider in integrating documented material into the text of your paper.

Exercise 33.A

Indicate which of the following selections or statements would require a source acknowledgment of some kind if the material were incorporated into a research paper. Explain your decision.

1. We quickly discovered that to be or not to be was not the question.
2. Eisenhower was Supreme Allied Commander on that June day in 1944 when Fortress Europe was assaulted by British, American, and other Allied troops at Normandy.
3. Only three of the more than 200 students polled by *The Daily Collegian* could name the president of the student government.
4. "Lee embodied the noblest elements of this aristocratic ideal. Through him, the landed nobility justified itself."
5. The best-known components of the atom are the neutron, the proton, and the electron, but there are many other subatomic particles.
6. The senator pointed out that while our rights to life, liberty, and the pursuit of happiness had been secured only after vigorous debate, struggle, and war, media-grabbing interest groups today proclaim rights to everything from day-care centers to pet insurance, with little sense of what natural rights really are. ■

Using Direct Quotations

In incorporating material from sources into your research paper, you will often have to decide whether to quote directly or to restate the material in your own words. In general, direct quotations are preferable only in these situations:

1. **Important statements of information, opinion, or policy.** Whenever the *exact* wording of a statement is crucial in its interpretation, it should be quoted in full:

   President Kennedy told Khrushchev that Russia could not expect to spread Communism abroad without opposition: "What your government believes is its own business; what it does in the world is the world's business."

2. **Interpretations of literary works.** When a statement or opinion in your paper is based on a passage in a poem, essay, short story, novel, or play, quote from the passage so that the reader can see the basis for your interpretation:

   The closing passages of *Moby Dick* also suggest that the whale represents some omnipotent force hostile to man. Ishmael says that Moby Dick rushed at the ship with a "predestinating head," and that "retribution, swift vengeance, external malice were in his aspect . . . in spite of all mortal man could do."

33.4

Res

When you are writing a paper that requires frequent references to a literary work, however, you need to note the edition of the text you are using only once, the first time you use a quotation. Thereafter, you may identify quotations by giving (immediately after the quotation, in parentheses) the page numbers for fiction; the line numbers for poetry; the act and scene for drama (followed by the line numbers if the play is in verse):

Man, who once stood at the center of the universe, confident that he was the end of Creation and could claim kinship with the angels, is now—to use the playwright's favorite figure—shrouded in a "mist" that isolates him from God and shuts off all his questioning about the problems of ultimate order. As Webster has Bosola say of the Cardinal in *The Duchess of Malfi,*

Thou, which stood'st like a huge pyramid
Begun upon a large and ample base,
Shalt end in a little point, a kind of nothing.
(V.v.76–78)

3. **Distinctive phrasing.** If your source states some idea or
opinion in a particularly forceful or original way that
would be weakened by paraphrasing, quote the exact
words:

> Russell does not believe that our age lacks great ideas be-
> cause religion has declined: "We are suffering not from the
> decay of theological beliefs but from the loss of solitude."

Avoid the temptation, however, of quoting too often and at
too great a length simply because you believe the authors you
are reading write better than you do. Save direct quotation
for significant passages.

Integrating Quotations with Your Text

A quotation should be smoothly integrated into the text of
your paper. Even when its source is given in an endnote, it
should be preceded by some brief introductory remark like
"one leading educator recently said that . . ."; "as Edmund
Wilson points out. . . . "When you use a system of documentation that relies on references to a list of works cited, the
citation can be integrated into a skillful introductory phrase.
For example, if the list of references for a paper on medieval
education included a full entry for Frederick Copleston's *A
History of Philosophy,* then a quotation from the book in the
text of the paper would need to include only Copleston's
name and a page number in parentheses:

> According to Copleston, "the general practice in the univer-
> sity of the thirteenth century was to lecture or listen to lec-
> tures on certain texts" (243).

When you use a direct quotation, be sure that it is in
grammatical agreement with the prose that introduces or contains it. Don't hesitate to rewrite the introduction to a quotation or to modify the quotation itself to improve the flow of a
passage:

Clumsy   There are a number of ways to classify trans-
                            lations of the Bible. According to Stanley N.
                            Grundy, "But linguists today generally speak

33.4

Res

of translations as having either literal or dynamic equivalence" (175).

Revised Although there are a number of ways to classify translations of the Bible, Stanley B. Grundy observes that "linguists today generally speak of translations as having either literal or dynamic equivalence" (175).

Remember that you cannot alter the phrasing of a direct quote, but you can decide where you will begin a quotation and where you will end it. You can also use ellipses to indicate omissions from a selection and brackets to identify letters, words, or phrases you may have added to a passage to enhance clarity:

> Jefferson's Declaration of Independence includes a list of accusations: "He [George III, King of Great Britain] has refused Assent to Laws. . . . He has forbidden. . . . He has refused. . . . He has dissolved. . . . He has endeavoured to prevent. . . . He has obstructed. . . ."

In modifying a quoted passage to improve its readability, be sure you do not change its meaning or distort what its author was attempting to say. The best way to learn about integrating quotations in your own work is to observe how professional writers use quotations. (See Chapter 14 for a full discussion of quotation marks and ellipses, and 13.3 for an explanation of brackets.)

33.4
Res

Exercise 33.B

Practice introducing quotations by selecting several paragraphs from an expository essay and summarizing them by using some direct quotations. Vary the way you introduce the quotations.

Example
Some people say the business about the jolly fat person is a myth, that all of us chubbies are neurotic, sick, sad

people. I disagree. Fat people may not be chortling all day long, but they're a hell of a lot *nicer* than the wizened and shriveled. Thin people turn surly, mean, and hard at a young age because they never learn the value of a hot-fudge sundae for easing tension. Thin people don't like gooey soft things because they themselves are neither gooey nor soft. They are crunchy and dull, like carrots. They go straight to the heart of the matter while fat people let things stay all blurry and hazy and vague, the way things actually are. Thin people want to face the truth. Fat people know there is no truth. One of my thin friends is always staring at complex, unsolvable problems and say-ing, "The key thing is. . . ." Fat people never say that. They know there isn't any such thing as the key thing about anything.—Suzanne Britt Jordan, "That Lean and Hungry Look"

Summary with direct quotations
Challenging the idea that fat people are neurotic, Suzanne Britt Jordan argues that plump people are "a hell of a lot *nicer* than the wizened and shriveled." She is tough on thin people, describing them as "surly, mean, and hard" indi-viduals who are "crunchy and dull, like carrots." Perhaps her most interesting suggestion is that fat people are more complex than thin ones: "Thin people want to face the truth. Fat people know there is no truth." ■

Paraphrasing
Although a research paper relies heavily on the writings of others, it should not consist simply of a long string of word-for-word quotations from sources. Like any other paper, it should represent your own characteristic style. Except in the situations described in the preceding section, information from a source should ordinarily be *paraphrased*—restated or summarized in your own words. Otherwise your paper will have a jumbled, patchwork effect that may distract or confuse the reader. Compare the two following passages for effective-ness:

33.4

Res

Too many direct quotations

Authorities disagree about the exact causes of the war. Professor Emily Miller says that "The evidence suggests an alliance between the labor groups and manufacturers prompted the parliament to take unnecessarily harsh measures to protect the trade in manufactured goods" (124). Professor David Alaine suggests another cause: "The fact is that the armaments lobby felt that they had to flex their muscles and make some profits to boot. They talked the prime minister into a little South American venture that swiftly turned into hostilities and factory orders" (14). But J. J. Jamesien interprets events differently: "The two countries disagreed in every way over every issue. There was as much enmity between the general populations as there was between ambassadors, diplomats, and ministers. The only remarkable thing about the war is that it didn't happen sooner" (407).

Effective paraphrase

Authorities disagree about the exact causes of the war. Professor Miller attributes the conflict to an alliance between labor and manufacturers to defend their mutual interests (124) while Professor Alaine traces the cause to armament manufacturers also eager to guarantee their own profits (14). But J. J. Jamesien believes that mutual dislike between the two countries made war inevitable: "The only remarkable thing about the war is that it didn't happen sooner" (407).

The best way to write a smooth paraphrase is to absorb the content of the source passage and then, without looking at it, to write its information down in your own words. When you have finished, you should check it for accuracy and for any unconscious borrowing of phrases and sentences. Remember that even though the words are your own, the information or ideas are not; you will still have to acknowledge the source.

Avoiding Plagiarism

In borrowing any material, you want to be careful to avoid charges of *plagiarism*. Any uncredited use of another's information, ideas, or words is plagiarism. You must be certain to acknowledge in some way any use you make of material that is not your own or not common knowledge. You must be particularly careful about proper documentation when you are paraphrasing. For a detailed discussion of plagiarism and additional material on paraphrasing, see pages 629–33, Avoiding Plagiarism and Collusion.

Endnotes

This handbook follows the Modern Language Association (MLA) documentation style as revised in the *MLA Handbook for Writers of Research Papers*, 2nd ed. (1984). The revised form brings MLA documentation closer in line with forms used in other disciplines, simplifies some punctuation, and relies more heavily on parenthetical references, reducing the total number of endnotes or footnotes likely to appear in a paper. The changes in punctuation are indicated in the sample endnotes and bibliography entries. Carefully study the following explanation of how to make in-text citations; the practice, you will find, is simple and efficient.

Basically, sources in a paper are documented not through traditional endnotes or footnotes, but through short in-text citations keyed to an alphabetical list of *Works Cited*. The citations in the paper itself consist of no more than an author's last name and a relevant page number, both within parentheses: (Shorenstein 36). The list of *Works Cited* provides the full bibliographic information that formerly would have appeared in a first footnote:

```
Shorenstein, Stuart A.  "Pulling the Plug on

    Instructional T.V."  Change   Nov. 1978:

    36-39.
```

Other references to Shorenstein's article in the remainder of the paper would be handled in the same way. If a given author contributes two or more sources to your paper, you obviously cannot cite a particular source by last name alone. In such a case, your in-text note would also include a shortened version of the title: (Shorenstein, *Plug*, 36).

A key point to remember in using this method of documentation is to avoid cluttering the text with unneeded names, numbers, and parentheses. The MLA report puts it simply: "We recommend . . . that writers give only the amount of information needed to identify a work." You can even eliminate the parenthetical reference completely or reduce it to a simple page reference by mentioning the author or work in the text of your essay:

```
Shorenstein indicates that there has been a

phenomenal growth in noncommercial educational

broadcasting (36).
```

This simple reference is enough to tell a reader that the information in the sentence can be traced to page 36 of the article by Shorenstein cited in complete bibliographic detail in a list at the end of the paper. (See the comparison chart on pp. 694–95 and the sample research paper for fuller examples of how to use in-text parenthetical documentation.)

You can, of course, continue to use traditional "content" endnotes or footnotes as you need them to discuss matters worthy of your readers' attention but not sufficiently important to include directly in the text. You could also use a footnote to document a source whenever a parenthetical citation might be intrusive or—for some reason—unduly complicated. But the bulk of your documentation can be handled parenthetically. When you do use the older form of citation, the footnote or endnote number is placed *at the end of the quotation or statement* for which the source is being given; it is never placed before the borrowed material. The number is raised slightly above the line and is placed outside the end punctuation of the statement to which it refers: ". . . nearly 400,000 in 1953."[13] Endnote numbers are generally consecutive throughout the paper in Arabic numerals beginning with 1.

33.4

Res

The notes themselves should appear at the end of the paper on a separate page entitled *Notes.* (Some instructors may prefer footnotes.) Indent the first line of each note and begin with its number, raised, followed by a space before the first word of the note. Double space within and between notes. You may number the first page of notes and you must number any subsequent pages. See the endnotes of the sample paper on page 733.

Sample Endnotes

Most of the following notes could be handled in parenthetical references in the text. However, the following forms are those you would use should you have reason to provide full documentary footnotes or endnotes. The notes given here would be those used for a *first reference*. Subsequent references to the same work can be made parenthetically in the text or through simpler endnotes. For subsequent references that follow immediately after the original note, you need provide only page or line references in parentheses in the text. For references to the same work that do not immediately follow the original reference, you need provide only the author's last name (if not more than one work by the same author is being cited), and the page number:

[12] Gellhorn 150.

If the author contributes more than one source to your paper, a short title is added to the subsequent reference to avoid confusion:

[12] Gellhorn, American Rights 150.

If you use an author's name in the text of your essay, you do not have to repeat it in the note that documents the passage.

Since documentary notes of the kind that follow have been employed in English and the humanities for so long, it is worth stressing that in-text parenthetical references combined with a list of *Works Cited* can substantially replace the need for these particular forms.

Books

One author:

[1] Walter Gellhorn, American Rights: The Constitution in Action (New York: Macmillan, 1960) 178.

Two or three authors:

[2] Giles W. Gray and Claude M. Wise, The Bases of Speech, 3rd ed. (New York: Harper, 1959) 322.

Review

Comparison: Old MLA Form/New MLA Form

The following paragraph uses the traditional form of documentation with endnotes keyed to the text by endnote numbers:

Steaming out of Southampton, the Titanic nearly collided with an American liner, the New York. This near-disaster was taken as a bad omen by some passengers, but most regarded it as a minor incident.[6] The Atlantic was notably calm as the Titanic finished boarding passengers and set sail across the ocean.[7] Life aboard ship was pleasant and relaxing. First-class passengers, some of whom paid more than $4000 for their passage, had their own dining hall and cafe. Even the immigrants in third class enjoyed food and accomodations better than they were accustomed to at home.[8]

Notes

[6] Geoffrey Marcus, The Maiden Voyage (New York: Viking Press, 1969), 44.

[7] Walter Lord, A Night to Remember (New York: Bantam Books, 1976), 55.

[8] Wyn Craig Wade, The Titanic, End of a Dream (New York: Rawson, Wade Publishers, 1979), 18.

Here is the same paragraph using MLA form with parenthetical in-text citations keyed to an alphabetical list of *Works Cited* at the end of the paper:

Steaming out of Southampton, the Titanic nearly collided with an American liner, the New York. This near-disaster was taken as a bad omen by some passengers, but most regarded it as a minor incident (Marcus 44). The Atlantic was notably calm as the Titanic finished boarding passengers and set sail across the ocean (Lord 55). Life aboard ship was pleasant and relaxing. Wade reports that first-class passengers, some of whom paid more than $4000 for their passage, had their own dining hall and cafe. Even the immigrants in third class enjoyed food and accomodations better than they were accustomed to at home (18).

Works Cited

Lord, Walter. A Night to Remember. New York:
    Bantam Books, 1976.
Marcus, Geoffrey. The Maiden Voyage. New York:
    Viking Press, 1969.
Wade, Wyn Craig. The Titanic, End of a Dream.
    New York: Rawson, Wade Publishers, 1979.

More than three authors:

³ Walter Blair and others, <u>The Literature of
the United States</u>. 3rd ed. (Glenview, IL: Scott,
Foresman, 1966) 1:80.

[The Latin abbreviation *et al.* may be used instead of *and others.*] [A state reference is given here after Glenview because many readers would not know that city is in Illinois. No such reference would be needed for Chicago, New York, Houston, and other well-known cities. Similarly, the name of a state or nation might be given to clarify possible misunderstandings: Cambridge, England; Cambridge, MA.]

An edited book:

⁴ <u>Letters of Noah Webster</u>, ed. Harry R.
Warfel (New York: Library Publishers, 1954) 352.

[If the editor's name is more relevant to the citation than the author's, put that name at the beginning of the footnote: Harry R. Warfel, ed., *Letters of Noah Webster.*]

An article in an edited book of selections written by various authors:

⁵ Harry Levin, "Literature as an
Institution," <u>Literary Opinion in America</u>, ed.
Morton Dauwen Zabel (New York: Harper, 1951)
658-69.

A translated book:

⁶ Paul Valery, <u>Monsieur Teste</u>, trans. Jackson
Matthews (New York: Knopf, 1947) 47.

A book for which no author is given:

⁷ The Chicago Manual of Style, 13th ed.

(Chicago: U of Chicago P, 1982) 27.

A multi-volume work, all volumes published in the same year:

⁸ Walter Blair, and others, The Literature of

the United States, 3rd ed., 3 vols. (Glenview, IL:

Scott, Foresman, 1966) 1:80.

[Note that if the note includes a volume number, the abbreviation *p.* or *pp.* is omitted.]

A multi-volume work, the volumes published in different years:

⁹ Harold Child, "Jane Austen," The Cambridge

History of English Literature, ed. A. W. Ward and

A. R. Waller, 15 vols. (London: Cambridge UP,

1907–1927) 12:231–33.

[The volume number here precedes the facts of publication.]

A book that is part of a series:

¹⁰ David Fowler, Piers the Plowman, U of

Washington Publications in Lang. and Lit. 16

(Seattle: U of Washington P, 1961) 23.

Magazine, Journal, and Newspaper Articles

Endnotes for magazine and newspaper articles are handled in much the same way. The volume number is used in noting an article from a scholarly journal. The complete date is used for newspapers and weekly or monthly magazines.

Signed article in a magazine:

[11] Reed Whittemore, "The Newspeak Generation," Harper's Feb. 1977: 20.

Unsigned article in a magazine:

[12] "How to Save Energy," Newsweek 18 April 1977: 72.

Article in a scholarly journal:

[13] Stewart Justman, "Mass Communication and Tautology," College English 38 (1977): 635.

[The month is omitted for journals paged continuously throughout the volume.]

Signed article in a newspaper:

[14] Edward Cowan, "Mapping Out a National Energy Policy," New York Times 10 April 1977, sec. 3: 1.

[The edition of the newspaper is sometimes given. Locate newspaper articles by column, if possible. Unsigned articles are handled in the same way as those in magazines.]

33.4

Res

Subsequent references to articles in periodicals may be shortened in the same way as those for books (see p. 693).

Other Sources

These sample entries will help you arrive at a form for various other source material you may use.

Encyclopedia articles:

[15] Donald Culross Peattie, "Trees of North America," Encyclopedia Americana, 1973 ed.

[If the article is unsigned, begin with the title.]

Biblical citations:

> [16] Matt. 6:26-30.

[The abbreviation is suitable in notes, but not in the text. Often the identification is given in parentheses immediately following the quotation, rather than in an endnote, and very familiar quotations, such as "Thou shalt not steal," are not noted.]

Material at second hand:

> [17] Ronald Bryden, "Pseudo-Event," New Statesman, 4 Oct. 1963, 460, in The Deputy Reader: Studies in Moral Responsibility, ed. D. B. Schmidt and E. R. Schmidt (Glenview, IL: Scott, Foresman, 1965) 78.

[Both the original source and the source from which the material was taken are given.]

Bulletins and pamphlets:

> [18] U.S. Department of Labor, Occupational Outlook Handbook, 1974-75 Edition, Bulletin 1985 (Washington, D.C.: GPO, 1974) 40.

Unpublished dissertations and theses:

> [19] Wallace Joseph Smith, "The Fur Trade in Colonial Pennsylvania," diss., U of Washington, 1950, 19.

[Titles of unpublished works are enclosed in quotation marks.]

Interview:

> [20] John X. Sawyer, Mayor, Santa Fe, New Mexico, personal interview, 1 April 1980.

Movie:

[21] Franco Zeffirelli, dir., *Romeo* *and* *Juliet*,

with Leonard Whiting and Olivia Hussey, BHE Verona

Productions, 1968.

Television program:

[22] *CBS* *Evening* *News*, writ. and narr. Dan

Rather, 22 Nov. 1983.

[You may include the names of the director and producer when that information is important.]

Abbreviations in Endnotes

Standard abbreviations such as those for states (*Menasha, WI; Norwood, MA*) are commonly used in notes (but *New York* rather than *NY* in reference to the city). The following abbreviations may also be used to save space. Follow the recommendation of your instructor about whether to underline those from Latin.

anon.	*anonymous*
ca. or *c. (circa)*	about a given date (*ca.* 1490)
ch., chs.	chapter, chapters
col., cols.	column, columns
diss.	dissertation
ed.	edited by or edition (2nd ed.)
et al. *(et alii)*	and others (used with four or more authors); you may also simply write "and others"
e.g. *(exempli gratia)*	for example (preceded and followed by a comma)
i.e. *(id est)*	that is (preceded and followed by a comma)
l., ll.	line, lines (in typewritten copy it is better to write these out, to avoid confusion with the figures 1 and 11)
MS., MSS.	manuscript, manuscripts
n.d.	no date of publication given
n.p.	no place of publication given
p., pp.	page, pages (the word *page* is never written out in footnotes)
rev.	revised edition or revised by

sic   thus (placed in brackets after an error in
                       quoted material to show that you are
                       aware of the error; seldom used by
                       contemporary writers)
trans. or tr.   translated by
vol., vols.   volume, volumes

"*Ibid.*," "op. cit.," and "loc. cit." are rarely used anymore. It
is clearer and simpler, in most cases, to use a shortened reference to author and title (as illustrated on p. 693).

The Bibliography: *Works Cited* and *Works*
Consulted
The finished research paper concludes with a reference list of
the sources used in the paper. If the list includes only those
books, articles, and other sources that have been documented
in the endnotes, the bibliography is titled *Works Cited*. If the
list also includes references that you have explored in depth
but have not cited directly, the bibliography is titled *Works*
Consulted. Your instructor will tell you which form you should
use.

Your bibliography cards (p. 674-75) should contain all the
information you need to compile the final bibliography. The
form for a bibliography differs somewhat from endnote form:

Endnote entry:

¹ Walter Gellhorn, <u>American Rights: The</u>

<u>Constitution in Action</u> (New York: Macmillan,

1980) 128.

Bibliography entry:

Gellhorn, Walter. <u>American Rights: The</u>

   <u>Constitution in Action</u>. New York: Mac-

   millan, 1980.

Consult these general guidelines and the examples that
follow for an acceptable bibliography form:

1. List all entries in alphabetical order, by the author's *last*
    name, or, if the author is unknown, by the first signifi-
    cant word of the title (disregard *A* or *The*). When two or

33.4

Res

more works by the same author are listed, use a line of seven dashes, followed by a period, instead of the author's name for all but the first work.

2. Do not give the page numbers for books, but do list the inclusive pages for articles in periodicals and newspapers.

3. Do not separate the list according to kinds of publications. Since the bibliography for most student papers is short, all sources should appear in the same list.

4. Do not number the entries.

Double space within and between entries. Punctuation varies in different bibliographic styles, mainly in the use of commas, colons, and parentheses. The form shown in the examples illustrates one widely used style, but be sure to note carefully any different practices your instructor may want you to follow.

Sample Bibliographic Entries

Books

One author:

```
Coleman, James C. Abnormal Psychology and Modern

     Life. 7th ed. Glenview, IL: Scott,

     Foresman, 1984.
```

Two or three authors:

```
Gray, Giles W., and Claude M. Wise. The Bases of

     Speech. 3rd ed. New York: Harper & Row,

     1959.
```

[Notice that only the first author's name is listed last name first.]

More than three authors:

```
Blair, Walter, et al. The Literature of the

     United States. 3rd ed. 3 vols.

     Glenview, IL: Scott, Foresman, 1969.
```

Two books by the same author:

Rush, Myron. How Communist States Changes Their

    Rulers. Ithaca, N.Y.: Cornell Univ. Press,

    1974.

--------. Political Succession in the U.S.S.R.

    New York: Columbia Univ. Press, 1965.

[These may be arranged alphabetically by title or chronologically by date of publication.]

An edited book, especially one of another writer's work:

Shakespeare, William. The Complete Works of

    Shakespeare. Ed. Hardin Craig and David

    Bevington. Rev. ed. Glenview, IL: Scott,

    Foresman, 1973.

An edited collection, date of publication unknown:

Reed, William L. and Eric Smith, eds. Treasury of

    Vocal Music. 6 vols. Boston: Branden Press,

    n.d.

A translation:

Pasternak, Boris. My Sister, Life. Trans. Olga

    A. Carlisle. New York: Harcourt, 1976.

An encyclopedia article:

Peattie, Donald Culross. "Trees of North America."

    Encyclopedia Americana. 1973 ed.

Reprint:

Dexter, Walter. The London of Dickens. 1923.

    Philadelphia: Richard West, 1973.

33.4
Res

Volumes, a work of several volumes:

Macaulay, Thomas Babington. The History of

England from the Accession of James II. 3

vols. London: Dent, 1906.

Volumes, one of several volumes:

Baldwin, T. W. William Shakespere's Small Latine

& Lesse Greeke. 3 vols. Urbana, IL: U of

Illinois P, 1944. Vol. 2.

Dissertation, published:

Garton, Joseph W. The Film Acting of John

Barrymore. Diss. New York U, 1977. New York:

Arno Press, 1980.

Dissertation, unpublished:

Smith, Wallace Joseph. "The Fur Trade in Colonial

Pennsylvania." Diss. U of Washington, 1950.

Series, numbered:

Barnum, Priscilla Heath, ed. Dives and Pauper.

Early English Text Society. Publications,

no. 27·5. London: Oxford UP, 1976.

Series, unnumbered:

Harley, Sharon and Rosalyn Terborg-Penn. The

Afro-American Woman: Struggles and Images.

Series in American Studies. Port Washington,

NY: National University Publications, 1978.

Periodicals

Signed article in a magazine:

Whittemore, Reed. "The Newspeak Generation."

Harper's Feb. 1977: 17-21.

Unsigned article in a magazine:

"How to Save Energy." Newsweek 18 April 1977:

70-80.

Article in a scholarly journal:

Tinder, Glenn. "Community: The Tragic Ideal."

The Yale Review 65(1976):550-64.

Article in a collection:

Ong, Walter J., S.J. "Hopkins' Sprung Rhythm and

the Life of English Poetry." Immortal

Diamond: Studies in Gerard Manley Hopkins.

Ed. Norman Weyard, S.J. London: Sheed &

Ward, 1949. 93-174.

Article reprinted in a collection or casebook:

Altick, Richard D. "Symphonic Imagery in Richard

II." PMLA 62(1947):339-65; rpt. in Richard

II: A Casebook. Ed. Nicholas Brooke.

London: Macmillan, 1973. 101-130.

Daily newspaper article:

Gowan, Edward. "Mapping Out a National Energy

Policy." New York Times 10 April 1977, sec.

3:1.

33.4

Res

Other Sources

Art work:

Remington, Frederic. <u>Mountain Man</u>. Archer M.

    Huntington Art Gallery, The University of

    Texas at Austin.

Bulletin:

Sherald, James L. <u>Dutch Elm Disease and Its</u>

    <u>Management</u>. Ecological Services Bulletin

    No. 6. Washington, D.C.: GPO, 1982.

Computer data:

"Statistics on Freshman English Enrollment."

    Diskette 103. Austin, TX: The University of

    Texas Department of English, 1985.

"MacWrite." Word-processing program for

    Macintosh. Cupertino, CA: Apple Computer

    Co., 1984.

Data base sources:

"Alexander Hamilton." <u>Academic American Encyclopedia</u>.

    1981 ed. Columbus: Compuserve, 1983. Record

    No. 1816.

Interview:

Iacocca, Lee. Personal interview. 1 March 1984.

Letter:

Thackeray, William Makepeace. Letter to Kate Perry.

    25 March 1854. <u>The Letters and Private</u>

Papers of William Makepeace Thackeray.

Cambridge: Harvard UP, 1946. Vol. 4.

Rosner, Mary. Letter to the author. 18 June 1983.

Microfiche or microfilm:

Frank, Werner L. "Micro Software: From Author to

User." Computerworld 30 Aug. 1982: 37-38.

(Microfilm.)

Monograph:

McCarty, Kiernan. A Spanish Frontier in the

Enlightened Age: Franciscan Beginnings

in Sonora and Arizona, 1767-1770. Mono-

graph Series 13. Washington, D.C.: Academy

of American Franciscan History, 1981.

Movie:

Zeffirelli, Franco, dir. Romeo and Juliet. With

Leonard Whiting and Olivia Hussey. BHE

Verona Productions, 1968.

Musical composition:

Mahler, Gustav. Symphonie No. 1. Kalmus

Miniature Orchestra Scores 290. New

York: Kalmus [19--].

Pamphlet:

United States. Dept. of Transportation. Fight

the Hidden Tax. TD 8.2:T19.

Public address:

Carter, Jimmy. "Farewell Address." From the

White House. Washington, D.C., 14 Jan. 1981.

Chaseman, Joel. "The Media Revolution in America:
Television News." Address presented at Town
Hall of California. 27 Jan. 1981; rpt.
Vital Speeches of the Day, 1 April 1981: 374-
78.

Public document:

United States. Environmental Protection Agency.
Summary of the 1985 Budget. Washington: GPO,
1984.

U.S. President. "Report on the Office of the
Secretary of Defense." President's Private
Sector Survey on Cost Control. Pr. 40.8:
C82/Se 2. Washington: GPO, 1983.

Recording on record or tape:

"The Wanderer." Beowulf, Caedmon's Hymn and
Other Old English Poems. Read in Old English
by J. B. Bessinger, Jr. Caedmon, TC 1161.

33.4

Res

Culture Club. "Karma Chameleon." Colour By
Numbers. Virgin Records, Ltd. QET 39107,
1983.

Table or illustration:

Manchester, Alden C. and Richard A. King. "Table
6--Distribution of Grocery Store Sales."
U.S. Food Expenditures, 1954-78. U.S. Dept.

of Agriculture. Agricultural Economic Report

No. 431.

Television program:

CBS Evening News. Writ. and narr. Dan Rather.

9 March 1984.

Videotape:

The Electronic Rainbow: An Introduction to

Television. Videotape. Basic Films, 1977.

Alternative Forms for Notes

Research papers in the natural and social sciences often use systems of reference different from the system generally used in the humanities. The references have the same purpose—to give the author, title, and facts of publication of articles and books used, to acknowledge the source of materials, and to make it possible for a reader to go directly to a source for further information. The details of form vary considerably among the different scientific and technical fields and often among the books and journals within a field. If you are writing a paper for a course in the sciences, you will need to follow the system specified by your instructor or the form of a particular journal or style manual. Whatever system you follow, do not shift from one to another in your paper: consistency is essential in the use of notes.

33.4

Res

APA Style

One of the familiar documentation styles is that of the American Psychological Association (APA). Like the new MLA form, APA uses short, in-text parenthetical notes supplemented by an alphabetically arranged *reference list* of works cited in the research essay. But whereas the textual references under MLA form give author/page citations, APA form usually gives author/date:

    MLA   (Miller 259)
    APA   (Miller, 1973)

It is possible, of course, for an author to publish more than one piece in a given year and for a research essay to include references to several of these works. In such circumstances, lowercase letters are employed after the date to distinguish among the citations:

> (Miller, 1973a)
> (Miller, 1973b)
> (Miller, 1973c)

The letters would also appear in the reference list, coded to the appropriate entry.

A variant of APA form that circumvents this problem attaches numbers to the works in the reference list; the citations in the text, then, are made to this code number, not to an author or date.

In the text:

> While campaigning for the presidency in 1948, Harry Truman stopped to visit some children at a Dallas orphanage to give them "something they'd remember all their lives," a visit from the President (6, p. 259).

In the reference list:

> 6. Merle Miller. *Plain speaking, an oral biography of Harry S Truman.* New York: G. P. Putnam's Sons, 1973.

As with MLA textual citations, those under APA format can be integrated with the text to enhance readability:

33.4

Res

> Truman visited orphans in Dallas during the 1948 presidential campaign (Miller, 1973).
>
> Miller (1973) asked Truman to describe his visit to an orphanage in Dallas during the 1948 presidential campaign.

The reference list used under APA format resembles that used for MLA documentation. Both lists are alphabetical and include information on author, title, place/publisher/date, volume number, and so on. But there are differences. An APA reference list includes only works cited in the paper; an MLA bibliography can be designated as *Works Consulted* to include entries used in preparing the paper but not actually cited in it. APA uses an author's surname and initials in the reference list; MLA permits use of the full first name:

APA   Miller, M.

MLA   Miller, Merle

APA capitalizes only the very first word in titles; MLA capitalizes all major words:

APA   *Plain speaking, an oral biography of Harry S Truman*

MLA   *Plain Speaking, an Oral Biography of Harry S Truman*

The complete guide to APA style is the *Publication Manual of the American Psychological Association* (1983). The research report on pages 640–47 uses APA style.

Step 9: Assembling the Completed Paper

In preparing the final copy of your research paper, refer to the suggestions given in 23.4, Manuscript Form. You will also find it useful to study the sample student paper on pages 714–37. Proofread your final copy before turning it in. A well-researched paper can be seriously marred by careless errors and inconsistencies.

Final Order of Contents

The research paper, usually secured by a paper clip and in a manila folder, should contain all the parts in the order your instructor has assigned. Typically, the completed paper has the following units. Make sure that you include any other material (such as your first outline or first draft) that your instructor asks for.

1. **First page.** The title, author's name, instructor's name, course number, date, and so forth should appear on the first page of the paper, unless your instructor gives you different instructions. See the sample paper which follows.

Review
New MLA Form

If you are familiar with the form of documentation previously used by MLA, you may find this summary of the major documentation changes helpful.

1. In-text parenthetical documentation keyed to an alphabetical list of *Works Cited* replaces most documentary footnote references.
2. Arabic numerals replace most uses of Roman numerals in documentation. Roman numerals are retained only for identifying pages so numbered (i–iv), for references to plays and other works that have been traditionally divided with Roman numerals (*Macbeth* I.ii), and in conventional usages (Richard III, Henry Ford II). Volume numbers, formerly given in Roman numerals, are given in Arabic: vol. 2.
3. Whenever it is possible to do so without confusing a reader, the abbreviations for page and pages (*p.* and *pp.*) are eliminated. Numbers at the end of a citation without any other identification are assumed to be page numbers: Gellhorn 128.
4. The abbreviations l. and ll. are avoided since they tend to be mistaken for numerals. Instead *line* and *lines* are used.
5. Lower case is used consistently for terms such as *ed.*, *trans.*, *vol.*, and *col.*, when they appear in documentation.
6. For journal entries,
   - the comma is eliminated after the name of the journal;
   - a colon is used instead of a comma after the date.

Old form for footnote or endnote

2 Stewart Justman, "Mass Communication and

Tautology," College English, 38 (1977), 635.

New form for footnote or endnote

2 Stewart Justman, "Mass Communication and

Tautology," College English 38 (1977): 635.

7. Colons are used to separate volume numbers from page numbers: 2:345–46. [Indicates pp. 345–46 in volume 2.]

2. **Outline.** Some instructors will expect you to turn in your final outline (topic or sentence outline) and the thesis statement. The revised outline should correspond to the organization of the final paper. The outline of the paper and any other front matter (excluding a separate title page) are numbered using lower-case Roman numerals.

3. **Text of the paper.** The text is the final copy of the paper, complete with charts and diagrams, wherever needed. The numbering of the text usually begins on the second page, with Arabic numerals at the top right-hand corner.

4. **Endnotes.** Any endnotes should follow the last page of text, starting on a separate page entitled _Notes._

5. **Works cited.** The list of works cited or consulted should follow the last page of endnotes, if any, or the last page of text, starting on a separate page.

1
The Disadvantages of Thermal Energy

by

Michael Gragg

English 306

2
Ms. Mary Mathis

3
November 28, 1984

33.4

Res

1 The title page should include the title of your paper, your name, the course name (and section number if required), your instructor's name, and the date of submission. Do not capitalize every word in your title and do not put it between quotation marks:

    Wrong THE DISADVANTAGES OF THERMAL ENERGY
    Wrong "The Disadvantages of Thermal Energy"

Titles may, however, include words or phrases that do appear between quotations or are underlined:

    Correct Deciphering Joyce's <u>Ulysses</u>
    Correct "Five Yards and a Cloud of Dust": The Career of Woody Hayes

2 Identify your instructor by an appropriate title. When you are uncertain about academic rank, use Mr. or Ms.:

    Ms. Mary Mathis
    Dr. Kate Frost
    Mr. Bradley Knopf
    Professor Farmer

3 All items on a separate title page should be centered. Some teachers may ask you to forego the title page for a first page that includes all the identifying material. In such a case, your name, course, instructor's name, and date appear aligned in the upper right-hand corner. The title of your essay is centered about a third of the way down the sheet.

```
                                        Michael Gragg

                                        English 306

                                        Ms. Mathis

                                        November 28, 1984


              The Disadvantages of Thermal Energy


         Exploiting geothermal resources is nothing new.  The

     Greeks and Romans of classical times used hot springs for

     therapeutic and recreational purposes;
```

33.4

Res

This form is common for shorter essays.

4   Outline

Thesis: The full potential of geothermal energy in the
        United States will not be realized until
        technological, ecological, and financial problems
        are resolved.

   I. Introduction
      A. Explanation of geothermal energy
      B. Potential advantages of exploiting geothermal
          resources
  II. Technological hindrances to geothermal development
      A. Mineral deposits and corrosion problems
      B. Changes in hydrological conditions
      C. Drilling problems
 III. Environmental difficulties posed by geothermal
      development
      A. Noise and air pollution
      B. Disruption of thermal reservoirs
  IV. Financial risks of geothermal development
   V. Conclusion

33.4

Res

4 When your instructor requires you to include an outline of your essay, place it after the title page. Be sure to follow a consistent format for the outline itself, as explained in detail in 22.2, Standard Outline Form.

Michael Gragg uses a topic outline here, indicating that his paper on thermal energy will have three major parts. Notice that each entry in his outline (except for the thesis itself) is a phrase; hence, there are no punctuation marks at the end of the lines. The main heads and subheads are carefully aligned.

This outline runs only one page, so it is not numbered. If it ran longer, Michael could have numbered subsequent pages in small Roman numerals (ii, iii, iv) in the upper right-hand corners. But the first page would still be unnumbered.

33.4

Res

5   The Disadvantages of Geothermal Energy

         Exploiting geothermal resources is nothing new. The

    Greeks and Romans of classical times used hot springs for

    therapeutic and recreational purposes; the Japanese and

    other Eastern peoples have known the medical properties of

    thermal pools for hundreds of years (Bowen 24). Turks and

    Icelanders have learned how to employ geothermal sources

    for bathing and space heating. Even today a tribe in New

6   Zealand cooks fish and potatoes in bubbling pools

    (Armstead 16). Robert Bowen, a geologist and expert on

    geothermal energy, notes that boric acid was drawn from

    steam jets as early as the 1700's in Tuscany where the

    first successful generation of thermal power was also

    achieved (24). Today, as fossil fuels grow scarcer and

    nuclear power is beset by controversy, geothermal energy

    seems like one source of power that the United States

    might want to rely on in the future. Yet the full

    potential of geothermal energy will not be realized until

    remaining technological, ecological, and financial hurdles

    are overcome.

         Geothermal energy is produced when heat generated

    deep inside the earth, possibly by radioactivity or

    continental drift (Armstead 15), flows from the center of

    the earth to its surface in the form of water and steam

    (Russell 857). Weaknesses in the crust of the earth allow

    the energy to rise to the surface in the form of hot

    springs, fumaroles, steam vents, and geysers (Armstead

33.4

Res

5 Repeat your title, exactly as it appears on the title page, on the first page of the research paper about two inches from the top of the sheet. Be sure it is centered and only the initial and major words are capitalized. Your text itself begins four lines below the title. The entire essay (including indented quotations and notes) is double-spaced. Paragraphs are indented five spaces.

You should <u>not</u> number your first page. Subsequent pages are numbered in the upper right-hand corner in arabic numbers. The numbers should <u>not</u> be followed by a period.

Michael Gragg wrote his essay on the disadvantages of thermal energy as part of a regular library assignment in a college writing course. His instructor asked for a well-researched essay using a variety of library and research materials. He was urged to choose a topic from a list provided by his instructor. The list included such general subjects as gun control, venereal disease, Utopias, laughter, white-collar crime, child abuse, homosexuality, organ transplants, vampires, and juvenile delinquency. He rejected all of these to explore one that seemed more relevant to his major in engineering: geothermal resources. The topic list he worked from listed these questions as possible avenues for exploration: "What is geothermal energy? Is it a feasible alternative to fossil fuels? How is it to be produced? How expensive is it? What are its limitations? Advantages? What is the government doing to stimulate research in geothermal energy?"

Michael saw the need to narrow the subject. His initial research and his early drafts focused on the advantages and limitations of geothermal energy. But even that subject proved to be too large. As you can see, the final version is narrower still, presenting only the limitations of energy from the earth.

Michael's introduction shows that he was thinking about his audience for the paper: his teacher and his classmates. He realizes that they are likely to know little about geothermal energy. Before he can explain what its limitations are, he has to explain what it is.

6 The first page includes five citations. The first reference to Bowen and the subsequent reference to Armstead show the basic form for parenthetical references: (Bowen 24); (Armstead 16). Then Bowen himself is mentioned in the text of the essay so that the citation at the end of the sentence in which he appears need include only a page number: (24).

33.4

Res

The first three paragraphs introduce Michael's readers to the subject of thermal energy. In this section he summarizes what he has learned about his topic, helping to orient readers to his more limited concern. The expertise he has gained from reading widely now is an advantage to him as he selects the details he thinks are most important in explaining geothermal energy to a "general" audience.

His opening paragraph focused on an interesting historical fact about this "new" source of energy: it isn't so new. With his readers' curiosity aroused, he hones in immediately on what he intends to develop as his main point: ". . . the full potential of geothermal energy will not be realized until remaining technological, ecological, and financial hurdles are overcome." The sentence indicates the nature and order of his subtopics: technological hurdles, ecological hurdles, and financial hurdles. His readers now have a clear idea of how his essay will unfold. They know what to expect.

But some of his readers still might not know exactly what geothermal resources are. Again, Michael shows that he is thinking about his audience when he pauses here in the second paragraph to define his subject and explain where thermal energy comes from.

2

7   15).[1] Such geothermal manifestations tend to occur in
what are called thermal regions, areas where the
temperature gradient of the earth is up to a hundred times
the normal. Many of these thermal areas are within
earthquake belts, but not necessarily near volcanoes

8   (Geothermal "Resources" 1355). In the United States,
there are over a thousand geothermally significant areas
in the West (Denton1). As Bowen reports, "known
geothermal resources on public domain in the western

9   U.S.A. have been estimated to be almost 1.5 million acres"

10   (emphasis added) (38).

These thermal resources are a local, relatively
inexpensive, and versatile energy alternative for the
United States. The McGraw-Hill Encyclopedia of Science &
Technology estimates that geothermal areas in the United
States may hold the equivalent of 430×10^9 barrels of oil
(230). Moreover, geothermal energy is renewable and
relatively stable in price after a plant has been
constructed; if properly managed, the supply of energy is
secure, and it is available in many energy-poor locations

11   (Tillman 599.) John W. Hook, a consulting geologist in

Salem, Oregon, points out one great advantage thermal
plants have over both nuclear and fossil fuel energy
facilities: "Geothermal energy is something that could be
brought on in small increments of power. You can bring
those plants on-line as they're needed" (Chen 189).
Geothermal resources can be used to do more than generate
electricity. In both the U.S.S.R. and Iceland, thermal
areas are exploited for heating and for raising vegetables

7 This portion of the essay is heavily documented. It includes one of only two "content notes" in the essay, signalled by the raised superscript number after the sentence: "... and geysers (Armstead 15).[1]" If you check the notes at the end of the essay, you will find that Michael takes this opportunity to define a word, <u>fumarole</u>, that many of his readers would have found unfamiliar. He defines the term in the notes because he does not want to disrupt his paragraph with the explanation. The note may be unnecessary since his readers could have consulted a dictionary and there are other terms in the essay he does not bother to define (<u>temperature gradient</u>, for example). But it does demonstrate the difference between <u>content</u> notes, which explain, clarify, or discuss an issue related to the text, and <u>documentary</u> notes, which indicate the source of information or quotations. You should use content notes sparingly in an undergraduate essay.

8 The remaining citations on page 2 are parenthetical documentary citations.

9 Also on this page is the first direct quote. It appears at the end of the first paragraph after a short introductory phrase, "As Bowen reports." The quoted passage is short enough (four typed lines or fewer) not to be indented.

10 To emphasize the vastness of America's geothermal resources, Michael underlines the phrase "almost 1.5 million acres." Since the underscoring does not appear in the original quotation, he must include the notation "emphasis added" in parentheses after the phrase. If the underscoring had occurred in the middle of a quotation, "emphasis added" would appear between square brackets, as in this example:

> Give me a dozen healthy infants, well-formed, <u>and my own specified world to bring them up in</u> [emphasis added] and I'll guarantee to take any one at random and train him to become any type of specialist I might select. . . .–John Broadus Watson, <u>Behaviorism</u>

Michael finds a passage in the <u>McGraw-Hill Encyclopedia of Science and Technology</u> he suspects may be important enough to copy completely onto a note card. In writing his essay, however, he uses only one fact from the passage.

It might have been tempting to plunge right in to a discussion of the disadvantages of thermal energy, but Michael asks himself a strategically important question: Why should his readers be concerned with geothermal energy at all? He realizes that his discussion of limitations will make sense to general readers only if they see some reason for working to overcome the problems that prevent widescale exploitation of this energy source. So he writes a single paragraph, full of particular examples, that explains what the potential of geothermal energy in the United States is. The paragraph completes his introduction by making his readers understand the importance of his subject.

11 Whenever you can, you should identify the credentials of an authority you cite, as is done on this page with John W. Hook: "a consulting geologist in Salem, Oregon."

33.4

Res

3

and flowers in greenhouses where the outside climate is
harsh (Armstead 16). Heating homes with geothermal energy
can cut costs dramatically and the necessary equipment
depreciates slowly and lasts a generation (Bowen 133).
Geothermal energy also has many promising commercial
applications, including, as Christopher Armstead suggests,
the desalination of salt water (17). Heat from the earth

12   is used to produce paper in New Zealand and borax in
Italy.[2] The potential of geothermal energy, then, is
quite great.

But the growth of geothermal energy has been slowed
by technical difficulties, environmental concerns, and the
scarcity of "risk capital" needed to spur development
(Lenard 75).

The major technical problems involve mineral
deposits, corrosion of equipment, and changes in the
hydrological condition of thermal sites (Muffler and Ellis
230). Boiling geothermal fluids tend to leave mineral
deposits in wells, flumes, and pipelines. Silica deposits
have caused problems in wells at the Salton Sea field in
California, and calcium carbonate scale has limited energy
production in fields in Turkey and the Philippines. Where

33.4

Res   there is a high concentration of acid in the thermal
waters, corrosion of equipment becomes a major problem.
Drilling in such fields causes most metals to corrode
quickly. The presence of hydrogen sulfide or its
oxidation products in the thermal zone can cause the rapid
degradation of many ordinary building materials, including
concrete, plastics, and paints (231).

12 The second content note appears on this page after the reference to borax. The note explains what borax is and how thermal energy might be used to extract it from other minerals. Again, this is information that would have interrupted the flow of the text, so the facts are moved to the note page.

Michael turns now to the main issues in his research essay, the limitations on geothermal energy. He uses a single-sentence paragraph to signal his shift; in it, he identifies the three technical problems he intends to discuss in subsequent paragraphs. Single-sentence paragraphs are relatively rare in research essays, but they can be—as in this case—useful transitions.

As indicated in his outline and in the preceding transitional paragraph, Michael now begins his discussion of the major technological hindrances to geothermal development. He again divides his topic into parts so that his reader knows he will be discussing mineral deposits, corrosion, and hydrological change. Each problem receives a full paragraph of development.

In another note from Armstead's study, Michael inserts a bracket within a direct quotation to draw together some related ideas. He also takes the opportunity at the bottom of the card to define a word he is not familiar with.

Applications   4

"It [Geo. Energy] is also being used for heat-intensive industries – for example, for paper-making in New Zealand and for the recovery and processing of diatomite in New Zealand."
[Air conditioning is being successfully performed in N.Z. by geothermal means.] ...
and borax is still being produced geothermally

Applications   continued

at Landerello in Italy, in continuation of a process established in the 18th century."

– diatomite: a powder used as filler, filtering agent, absorbent, clarifier, or insulator in industry.

p. 17

The final paragraph on this page is one of the few in Michael's research essay that lacks particular details or examples. He discusses what can happen when a thermal site is exploited, but his material would be more interesting and perhaps clearer with an illustration or particular instance.

4

Extensive production from geothermal wells can cause significant changes in the conditions of the thermal sites. The chemical balance of the waters may be changed

13 by lowered water temperatures and altered gas

concentrations that result when steam and hot water are removed in quantity. The release of pressure in the resevoir may cause cool water from outside the thermal field to seep in and change the fluid capacities of the site so significantly that energy production is no longer possible. Furthermore, thermal activity may diminish in intensity if hot waters are withdrawn in large quantities. In most cases, though, good management and proper respect for the geology and hydrology of a site can preserve the integrity of a thermal resource (231).

Drilling to a thermal source, however, can be a problem in itself. Only relatively few wells and springs have worked their way near enough to the surface for man to exploit, but locating wells may be as difficult as getting to them. In some places, such as the Baca field in New Mexico, the rock that must be drilled is hard and riddled with faults and fractures, causing extensive wear on the drills. Drill poles can corrode, get stuck, or twist off in the hole. The drill hole casing can also wear out and the drill hole collapse. Drilling fluids can disappear into unmapped permeable rock formations (Kerr 668).

Yet even where a site is available and within the reach of drilling capability, environmental concerns may

14 hinder development. Paul Kruger and Carel Otte state in

the

33.4
Res

13 In proofreading the essay, Michael notices that he has omitted a word. He inserts the missing <u>the</u> in the margin and places a caret where the word belongs. Corrections of this kind are appropriate, but if you have to make more than one or two on a page, consider retyping the entire sheet.

   In the second paragraph, Michael makes the transition to the last technological problem he intends to discuss.

   Readers might have benefited here from a more complete discussion of drilling practices.

   With the discussion of technological problems complete, Michael now turns to his second major point: environmental concerns that limit geothermal energy.

14 The citation here includes the full names of the authors and the title of their book worked into the text itself.

5

Geothermal Energy: Resources, Production, and Stimulation

that a major concern of ecological groups is the
modification of terrain around the drilling sites caused
by the building of roads, wells, pipelines, and plants
(200). The impact of development is most evident during
the several years it may take to construct a thermal
plant. Traffic to and from the site may add noise and air
pollution to areas previously unscarred by these
contemporary blights. Animal migratory paths may be
disrupted as well as natural habitats. The Sierra Club
has paid special attention to these problems of geothermal
development (Chen 189).

Drilling itself causes noise and air pollution on a
significant scale, as does the operation of a thermal
plant. Drilling can entail noise in the 120 decibel
range, while the release of steam during testing and
production at a plant can also be noisy (Muffler and Ellis
231). An article in National Parks magazine reports that
this steam may also emit hydrogen sulfide--a component in
acid rain ("Geothermal sprawl" 42). A rain forest in
Hawaii is currently threatened by pollution from a plant
to be built near a volcanic site.

And there are other problems. The withdrawal of
steam and water from the earth raises the question of
wastewater disposal, the threat of land subsidence, and
the possibility that geysers and natural springs may
disappear. A geothermal plant produces thousands of
gallons of wastewater; it can usually be disposed of
harmlessly by pumping it into permeable zones deep inside

33.4

Res

15

On the following note card, Michael copies a passage from Kruger and Otte, but again only paraphrases his source in the essay. He decides that the information is important but he can put it into his own words. A direct quotation would serve little purpose here.

Environmental Impact   6

"The wells, pipelines, and power plants of the producing geothermal field, such as that at The Geysers, modify the existing terrain. This aspect of geothermal development is one of the main objectives voiced by environmental groups."

✓

p. 200

Michael includes more details and particular examples in his section on environmental risks than he did in his paragraphs on technological problems. Note especially the long paragraph that begins with the transitional phrase and topic sentence: "And there are other problems." Here Michael lists a variety of geothermal difficulties along with some particular examples that support his assertions. Notice, too, in how many of his paragraphs Michael draws together information from several different sources to support his ideas. He does not rely too heavily on any single reference work, nor does he vacantly paraphrase his sources.

33.4

Res

15 A spelling error here is detected in proofreading and corrected.

6

the earth. Sometimes, however, no permeable zones are
available. The alternative is to discharge this waste
into streams or other bodies of water. But pumping this
hot, mineral-rich wastewater into rivers or lakes can
alter the biology of an environment, killing off animal
life and vegetation (Power Gen. Alter. 72). The depletion
of reservoirs can cause localized land subsidence, which
is what happened in the San Joaquin Valley of California
after a great deal of groundwater was withdrawn (Chen
189). The drop may be as much as several meters (Muffler
and Ellis 231). And geysers, bubbling springs, and other
surface manifestations of thermal activity may disappear
when such resources are exploited for their potential
energy. The construction of the Wairakei geothermal area
totally destroyed Geyser Valley in New Zealand, and
exploration dried up geysers and springs at Beowawa
Geysers in Nevada ("Geothermal Leasing" 20). Like nuclear
and fossil fuel plants, geothermal energy sites demand
tradeoffs with our natural environment, some of which we
may come to regret.

Finally, there is the matter of cost. At first
glance, geothermal energy seems significantly cheaper than
other commercially available forms. According to Kruger
and Otte, the cost of building a geothermal facility in
the late 1970's ran approximately $150 to $170 per
kilowatt of generating capacity for a steam system and
$210 to $250 per kilowatt for a hot-water plant. Nuclear
plants cost $400 to $600 per kilowatt and fossil fuel
plants between $300 to $400--both significantly higher

16

33.4
Res

16 The citation here uses a shortened version of the full title of the pamphlet, <u>Power Generation Alternatives</u>. This piece, like several other sources used in the research paper, has an unnamed author.

Michael's note card for <u>Power Generation Alternatives</u> contains a technical term (<u>condensate</u>) which he avoids in his essay itself. He may have thought that most of his readers would not be familiar with the word. He phrases his sentence without it.

> *Disadvantages: Condensate hazard*   *17*
>
>   *Steam condensate disposal, because being mineral rich, can cause severe water pollution problems.*
>
>   ✓
>   *p. 72*

Michael's transition to his final major point is explicit. Here's his note card for the bottom half of the page.

> *Costs*   *6*
>
> *In the late '70's cost of construction of geothermal plants are about $150-170 per kw of generation capacity in plants like The Geysers. Hot water geothermal generating systems — about $210-$230. In contrast nuclear units cost $400 to $600 per kw installed, and coal-fired, fossil-fuel plants w/ pollution control equipment run $300 to 400 per kw.*

7

(62). But Armstead points out a significant factor that
may alter this cost advantage when he reports that

17   . . . not all geothermal fields are necessarily
            amenable to economic exploitation, and in order to
            determine whether a field can be profitably put to
            use it is necessary to expend fairly formidable sums
            in carrying out production. If the results are
            positive, these exploration costs have been well
            justified, but if negative, they will have been
            largely wasted except in the interests of pure
            science (17).

So it is that geothermal development requires a
substantial amount of "risk capital" without which
exploration of these resources becomes impossible. Some
legislative approaches have been taken to encourage
production. Bills for tax credits for geothermal energy

18 have been introduced by Don Fuqua of Florida (U.S.
Congressional Record, 6 March 1983 H 94) and Manuel Lujan
of New Mexico (U.S. Congressional Record, 3 March 1983 H
877). Yet geothermal development is likely to be slow
during periods when the price of oil, coal, and other more
traditional fuels is relatively low and stable.

33.4

Res

        Still, geothermal resources retain their remarkable
potential despite a host of problems. There will come a
time when the United States will appreciate the value of
heating homes or generating electricity from energy
arising from deep within the earth. When the technology
is perfected and the economy prepared to absorb the costs,
geothermal energy will be available to help America tackle
its energy problems.

17 This is the only quotation in the paper that is lengthy enough to require indention. The passage begins with an ellipsis mark to indicate material in the sentence that Michael has decided to exclude. Notice also the placement of the page number at the end of the quotation.

Indent a block quotatiòn ten characters from the margin, triple-spacing to separate it from the text, both above and below. The quoted material itself is double-spaced.

The material on financial risks is somewhat less detailed and interesting than the preceding section on environmental concerns. A revised version of this research paper might put the more detailed and emphatic section last.

18 These parenthetical references to the Congressional Record disrupt the flow of the paper because they are relatively long and close together. The reference might be more smoothly integrated with a revision:

The U.S. Congressional Record shows that bills for

geothermal tax credits have been introduced by

Don Fuqua of Florida (6 March 1983 H 94) and

Manuel Lujan of New Mexico (3 March 1983 H 877).

Michael's conclusion is simple, almost hurried. He does, however, refer back to the potential of geothermal energy to end in a way that reinforces the positive aspects he noted in the introduction. The paper thus seems thorough and balanced in its presentation of the topic.

33.4

Res

19   Notes

[1] A <u>fumarole</u> is an opening in the crust of the earth,
usually near a volcano. fumaroles may emit gases such as
hydrogen sulfide and carbon dioxide, or they may produce
steam.

[2] Borax, a chemical compound useful as a water
softening agent and as a cleansing agent, is highly
soluble in hot water, and therefore extractible using
geothermal methods.

33.4

Res

19 If your paper includes any content notes, you can list them immediately after the body of your essay on a sheet entitled <u>Notes.</u> That title should be centered on the page. The notes themselves begin four spaces below.

Content notes are indented and numbered to correspond to the notes in the text. Both in the text and on the note page, the numbers are raised a half space above the line of type:

In the text

. . . and borax in Italy.[2]

In the notes

[2] Borax, a chemical . . .

In the text, the number follows the punctuation without any spacing. On the note page, skip one space after the number before beginning the actual note.

The notes are indented five characters and double-spaced.

20   Works Cited

21   Armstead, Christopher H., ed. Geothermal Energy: Review of
            Research and Development. Paris: Unesco Press, 1973.

22   Bowen, Robert. Geothermal Resources. London: Applied
            Science, 1979.

23   Chen, Allan. "Geothermal Powerhouse." Science News 19
            March 1983, 186-87, 189.

24   Denton, Jesse C., ed. Geothermal Energy. Washington
            D.C.: GPO, 1972.

25   "Geothermal Leasing: The Day Old Faithful Goes Dry?"
            National Parks & Conservation Magazine September
            1979, 20, 22. (Microfilm.)

26   "Geothermal Resources." Van Nostrand's Scientific
            Encyclopedia. 1983 ed.

27   "Geothermal Sprawl to Border Hawaii Volcanoes Park."
            National Parks January/February 1983: 42.

28   Kerr, Richard A. "Extracting Geothermal Energy Can Be
            Hard." Science 12 Nov. 1982: 668-69.
            (Microfilm.)

29   Muffler, L. J. Patrick and A. J. Ellis. "Geothermal
            Power." McGraw Hill Encyclopedia of Science &
            Technology. 1982 ed.

30   Kruger, Paul and Carel Otte. Geothermal Energy: Resources,
            Production, and Stimulation. Stanford: Stanford
            University Press, 1973.

31   Lenard, Lane. "Energy from Earth's Furnace." Science
            Digest July 1982, 70-75.

33.4

Res

20 The parenthetical references in the text refer a reader back to this list for complete bibliographical information, including full titles, dates of publication, and so forth. When the page contains only works actually cited in the body of the paper—as in the case of Michael Gragg's essay—then the reference list is entitled <u>Works Cited.</u> When the list also included books, articles, and other materials read in preparing the research project but not mentioned or used in writing the paper, then the page is entitled <u>Works Consulted.</u> In either case, the heading is centered and the list of references begins four spaces below.

The works are listed alphabetically with the second and all subsequent lines in an entry indented five spaces.

21 Edited book

22 Book with a single author

23 Article in a magazine, weekly or biweekly

24 Bulletin

25 Unsigned article in a monthly magazine; seen on microfilm

26 Unsigned article in an encyclopedia

27 Unsigned article in a bimonthly magazine

28 Article in a magazine with continuous pagination; seen on microfilm

29 Signed article in an encyclopedia; two authors

30 Book with two authors

31 Article in a monthly magazine

33.4

Res

10

32   Power Generation Alternatives. Seattle: Department

          of Lighting, 1972.

33   R[ussell], C[harles] R. "Energy Sources." Encyclopaedia

          Britannica: Macropaedia. 1978 ed.

34   Tillman, J. E. "Eastern Geothermal Resources: Should We

          Pursue Them?" Science 7 Nov. 1980: 595-600.

35   U.S. Cong. Rec. 6 Jan. 1983, H 94.

      -------. March 1983, H 877.

32 Pamphlet; no author listed

33 Initialed article in an encyclopedia (the full names of contributors to the <u>Encyclopae</u>-<u>dia</u> <u>Britannica</u> can be located in the introductory volume)

34 Article in a magazine with continuous pagination

35 Entries from the <u>Congressional Record</u>

GLOSSARY OF GRAMMATICAL, RHETORICAL, AND LITERARY TERMS

absolute modifier. A participle or infinitive phrase that modifies a clause or sentence as a whole. An absolute need not modify a specific word in the main clause:

> **All things considered,** the play was a success.
> **To summarize,** we disliked the plan for three reasons.

An absolute phrase with a subject is called a *nominative absolute:*

> **Her eyes stinging,** she clutched for the towel.

acronyms. Abbreviations pronounced as words: UNESCO, radar, laser, NATO, Amvets.

active voice. See *voice.*

adjective. A word that modifies or relates to a noun or noun equivalent: the *lucky* dog; the car is *fast.*

adjective clause. A clause that modifies a noun or pronoun. Adjective clauses are most frequently introduced by *who, which,* and *that:*

> Many books **that are commercially successful** do not qualify as serious literature.

adverb. A word that modifies a verb, an adjective, or another adverb:

> He walked **quickly.** [modifies verb *walked*]
> It was **extremely** cold. [modifies adjective *cold*]
> She spoke **absolutely** perfectly. [modifies adverb *perfectly*]

Adverbs may also modify complete sentences or clauses:

> **Obviously,** he hadn't read *Coriolanus.*

adverb clause. A subordinate clause that modifies a verb, adjective, adverb, or main clause:

> **When the war broke out,** he fled to Toronto. [modifies verb *fled*]
> She managed the business better **than her husband had.** [modifies adverb *better*]

adverbial. A word or phrase that functions as an adverb.

agreement (pronoun and antecedent). A pronoun agrees in number (singular or plural) with the noun to which it refers, its antecedent:

> The **boy** washed **his** car.   The **girls** washed **their** car.

agreement (subject and verb). A subject agrees in number (singular or plural) with its verb. In English, a singular subject in third person ordinarily adds -*s* to the base form of a verb in present tense:

> I swim.
> They swim.
> He swim**s**.

allusion. A reference to a specific person, event, or place generally from history, religion, mythology, sports, popular culture, or literature.

analogy. An examination or exploration of an unfamiliar object or idea by reference to a more familiar one:

> It is easier to understand the structure of atoms if you think of them as **planetary systems with many orbiting bodies.**

antagonist. In a work of fiction, a character who opposes the main character. In *Hamlet,* for example, Claudius is the hero's antagonist.

antecedent. The word to which a pronoun refers. In the sentence below, *boys* is the antecedent of the pronoun *they, car* the antecedent of *it:*

> The **boys** claimed that **they** had not stolen the **car; it** just disappeared.

anticipating subject. See *expletive.*

anticlimax. In a work of fiction, events occurring after the climax which are less impressive or which seem to contradict or diminish the main action.

antonym. A word having a meaning directly opposite to another word. *Hot* is an antonym for *cold, antagonist* an antonym for *protagonist.*

appositive. A noun or noun equivalent placed beside another noun to supplement or complement its meaning. It has the same grammatical function as the noun to which it relates:

> Your lawyer, **Mr. Bible,** is widely respected.
> The action takes place in Cleveland, **the largest city on Lake Erie.**

article. The words *a, an,* and *the* used before nouns. *A* and *an* are *indefinite* articles: *a* book, *an* alternative. *The* is a *definite* article: *the* book, *the* alternative.

audience. In rhetoric, the person or persons to whom a piece is addressed.

auxiliary verb. A verb used in a verb phrase to show tense, voice, and so on: *am* going; *had* gone; *will* go; *should have been* gone.

bibliography. An alphabetical list of the sources consulted in compiling a research or investigative paper. There are two special types of bibliographies: *selective* and *annotated.* A *selective bibliography* lists the most important or best works on a given subject; an *annotated bibliography* lists the works on a subject and comments on them.

cardinal and ordinal numbers. Cardinal numbers show amount *(one, six, ten);* ordinal numbers indicate sequence or order *(first, sixth, tenth).*

caret. A symbol (∧) indicating that something is to be inserted into a phrase or sentence:

> The ∧ program was inefficient.

case. A noun or pronoun form indicating the word's relationship or function within a sentence. The cases are *nominative* (indicating a subject function), *possessive* (indicating a relationship of ownership or possession), and *objective* (indicating that the word is functioning as the object of a verb, verbal, or preposition).

clause. A group of words with a subject and a predicate. Clauses make up sentences. Within sentences, they are either *independent* or *dependent.* Independent clauses can stand alone as complete sentences:

> **We tried hard** but **we failed.** [two independent clauses]

Dependent clauses (often called *subordinate clauses*) are used like nouns, like adjectives, or like adverbs. They are tied to main clauses and cannot stand alone:

He confessed **that he erased the file.**
After you plant the seeds, water regularly.

cliché. An expression made trite through repetition:

down, but not out   up the creek without a paddle

comma splice (also called comma fault). Two or more independent clauses joined only by a comma:

Many companies are hiring communication experts, they want to improve efficiency.

Comma splices can be corrected by adding a coordinating conjunction, using a semicolon rather than a comma, or revising the sentence structure:

Many companies are hiring communication experts; they want to improve efficiency.
Many companies are hiring communication experts to improve their efficiency.

comparative and superlative. Adjectives and adverbs express degree in three forms: positive degree, comparative degree, and superlative degree.

Positive	Comparative	Superlative
red	redder	reddest
slow	slower	slowest
seriously	more seriously	most seriously

complement. A noun or an adjective in the predicate which follows a linking verb. Unlike an object, a complement is related to the subject rather than to the verb:

Mary is a skilled **physician.** [predicate noun]
The soprano sounded **hoarse.** [predicate adjective]

A noun used as a complement is called a *predicate noun;* an adjective used as a complement is called a *predicate adjective.*

complete predicate. The verb and whatever words are related to it, such as objects, complements, and modifiers:

Hurried students **make obvious mistakes.**
What was evident **was the candidate's popularity.**

complete subject. The simple subject and any words that modify it:

> **Hurried students** make obvious mistakes.
> **What was evident** was the candidate's popularity.

complex sentence. A sentence with one main clause and one or more subordinate clauses:

> As far as Dorothy could determine, [subordinate clause], the administrative position would remain vacant [main clause] until a suitable candidate applied [subordinate clause].

compound-complex sentence. A sentence with two or more main clauses and one or more subordinate clauses:

> After Alan returned from New Zealand [subordinate clause], he apologized for forgetting to take slides and movies [first main clause], but everyone was thankful that he hadn't [second main clause] because he was a lousy photographer [second subordinate clause].

compound sentence. A sentence containing two or more main clauses and no subordinate clauses:

> David requested additional space for the writing lab [first main clause], but his request was turned down [second main clause].

conjunction (coordinating). Words that link terms of equivalent grammatical rank or independent clauses:

> Steve **and** Ludmilla bought a Toyota **and** a Honda.
> Either fix the printer **or** recommend someone who can.

conjunction (subordinating). A word that relates a dependent clause to an independent one. There are many subordinating conjunctions, including *because, although, since, after, if,* and *when.*

> Lester smiled **because** his article had been published.
> **While** Rome burned, Nero fiddled.

conjunctive adverb. An adverb that serves to connect clauses in a compound sentence. Conjunctive adverbs include *also, consequently, however, moreover,* and *nevertheless.* The connective function of these adverbs is weak, and a semicolon should be used before them:

> Maurine turned seventy: **however,** she decided not to retire.

connotation and denotation. A *denotation* is the dictionary meaning of a term. A *connotation* is an association a word has acquired in use. For example, denotatively, a *nightingale* is a nocturnal song bird; connotatively, the word suggests beauty, romance, and love.

coordinating conjunction. See *conjunction (coordinating).*

coordination. In sentences, the linkage of grammatically equivalent phrases and clauses. In paragraphs, the relationship between successive parallel sentences.

> Either **you play to win** or **you don't play at all.** [two independent clauses linked by a correlative expression]
>
> Your team lost for three reasons. **You had no offense. You had no defense. You had no guts.** [three coordinate sentences within a paragraph]

copula. A verb that links its subject to a predicate noun or an adjective:

> She **is** an enginner.
> The days **became** warmer.

Also called a *linking verb.*

correlatives. Pairs of words that function as conjunctions: *either . . . or, neither . . . nor, both . . . and, not only . . . but (also).*

> **Either** the machine will be repaired **or** it will be replaced.
> **Both** Kate **and** Norman drive Volvos.

dangling modifier. A modifier that relates to a word that is only implied in a sentence, not actually stated. In most cases, dangling modifiers must be revised so that the modifier has a specific referent:

Dangling   **To find the information,** the whole pamphlet had to be read.

Revised   To find the information, **I** had to read the whole pamphlet.

demonstrative pronoun. A pronoun that points things out: *this, these, that, those.*

> **These** grapes are tarter than **those.**

denotation. See *connotation and denotation.*

dependent clause. See *clause.*

direct address. A word or phrase, given parenthetically, that names the person or thing being addressed:

> I firmly believe, **fellow citizens,** that justice will prevail.
> It seems, **my overstuffed hound,** that you have had enough Alpo already.

direct object. See *object.*

direct quotation. The words of a speaker presented exactly as spoken. Direct quotations usually appear between quotation marks:

> Clara asked, "Where's the beef?"

double negative. A statement in which a second negative need-lessly repeats the meaning of the first:

> I **don't** know **nothing** about that.

ellipsis. A gap in a sentence, paragraph, or essay indicating material has been omitted. The ellipsis is signaled by three spaced periods called **ellipsis marks:**

> Does this sound harsh? . . . Yes, but I cannot sell my liberty and my power to save their sensibility.

elliptical construction. A sentence construction in which words that are clearly understood are omitted:

> My secretary likes wool better than [she likes] any other fabric.
> Alex is a better draftsman than Audrey [is].

expletive. The words *there* or *it* used in a sentence to lead into or anticipate a subject:

> **It** is a difficult choice.
> **There** are several reasons for our success.

Expletive constructions often cause sentence wordiness. Obscene words or powerful oaths within a sentence are also termed *expletives.*

figures of speech. Expressions of comparison, personification, or association used to intensify statements or to make them more expressive and vivid, usually shifting from the ordinary uses and meanings of words to metaphorical or associational ones. Common figures include *hyperbole, irony, litotes, metaphor,* and *simile.*

finite verb. A verb which can be limited in person, time, or number and which serves as a full verb in sentences and clauses. The *nonfinite verb* forms (participles, infinitives, gerunds) are not limited in person and number and are ordinarily used in phrases:

> I **had gone** before he **arrived.** [finite verbs]
> Before **leaving,** I asked the host **to get** my coat. [nonfinite verbs]

fragment. An incomplete statement—a phrase or a subordinate clause—punctuated as a complete sentence. Some fragments are deliberate and appropriate; others need to be revised into complete sentences:

Fragment   The watch whose movement is broken.
Revised   The movement of the watch is broken.

function words. Words that indicate the relationships or functions of other words in a sentence. Function words include *auxiliary verbs, articles, prepositions,* and *conjunctions.*

fused sentence. See *run-on sentence.*

gender. The classification of pronouns and nouns as feminine, masculine, or neuter: *she, he, it; actor, actress.*

genitive case. See *possessive case.*

gerund. A verb form, typically ending in *-ing* or *-ed,* used as a noun.

Forms:	*Active*	*Passive*
Present	asked	being asked
Past	having asked	having been asked

Gerunds can function as subjects, objects, complements, noun modifiers, and appositives.

> **Having a career** pleased Lydia. [subject]
> We hate **whining.** [object]
> Seeing is **believing.** [complement]
> the **shipping** crate [noun modifier]

homonym. A word that is pronounced exactly like other words but differs in spelling and meaning:

> to, too, two   meat, meet, mete
> their, there, they're   hoarse, horse

hyperbole. An expression that includes deliberate exaggeration for interest and emphasis:

> It was a day to end all days.
> He's the greatest quarterback this side of Saturn.

idiom. An expression in a language that does not follow conventional grammar; or does not seem to make sense, word by word; or does not have the same meaning as the sum of its parts:

> Let's **take in** a movie. [idiomatic verb]
> Mr. Ervin **kicked the bucket.** [not sum of parts]
> I'll have to charge **for** the damage. You will be charged **with** breaking and entering. [idiomatic use of prepositions with a verb]

image. In literary works, an idea or impression vividly created or suggested by language.

imperative mood. The form of a verb that indicates an order or command:

> **Give** me the daggers.
> **Absent** thee from felicity awhile.
> **Drop** dead.

indefinite. An article, pronoun, or adjective that does not specify a particular thing.

> *articles:* **a** house, **an** idiot
> *pronouns:* **nobody, either, several**
> *adjectives:* **some** complaints, **several** items

independent clause. An independent (or main) clause contains a subject and predicate, and is the grammatical core of a sentence:

> S   P
> I laughed.
>
> S   P
> If I were you, I would find a new job.

indicative mood. See *mood.*

indirect address. A report of something spoken that does not include the exact words of a speaker. Sometimes called *indirect discourse.*

> He said that he liked the show. [indirect]
> He said, "I liked the show." [direct]

indirect object. See *object.*

infinitive. The base form of a verb (with or without *to*) or any verb phrase that can be used with *to* to function in a sentence as a noun, an adjective, or an adverb:

> **To be late** is impolite. [infinitive as a subject]
> I have plenty of work **to do.** [infinitive as a modifier]
> He does not like **to express his feelings.** [infinitive as an object]

intensifier. A word that strengthens or adds emphasis to the word or phrase it modifies:

> **very** high and unfamiliar
> **extremely** difficult

intensive pronoun. A pronoun form used to make another word more emphatic:

> Life **itself** is at stake.
> The award was presented by the senator **herself.**

The intensive and *reflexive* forms of pronouns are identical.

interjection. An expression of emotion that either stands alone or is inserted into a sentence without being grammatically related to it: *oh, wow, help, no.*

intransitive verb. A verb that does not take an object: He *sits.*

invention. In rhetoric, the process of discovering what can be said about a subject. Invention can involve various procedures such as asking questions, making lists of important points, brainstorming, and so on.

irregular verb. A verb which does not form its past tense and past participle by adding *-ed* to the base form of the verb. Many of the most common English verbs are irregular.

Base form	Past tense	Past participle
ask [regular]	ask**ed**	ask**ed**
do [irregular]	did	done
drink [irregular]	drank	drunk
see [irregular]	saw	seen

linking verb. See *copula.*

literal language. Language taken in its dictionary or denotative sense. Literally, "He'll propose to her when donkeys fly" means that he will wait until donkeys evolve into airworthy mammals before proposing. Figuratively, the sentence means that he will never propose.

main clause. See *independent clause.*

metaphor. An implied comparison between two unlike things, often used to show some unexpected likeness between the two:

> Life's but a walking shadow . . . .

misplaced modifier. A modifier positioned within a sentence in a way that makes a statement ambiguous, ludicrous, or inaccurate:

> The editors have **almost** written every article in the journal. [*almost* seems to modify *written;* revise to "written almost every article"]

mixed metaphor. A metaphor in which two incompatible images or comparisons are made. Some mixed metaphors are troublesome:

> Our ship of state is tied in knots!

Others are more readily accepted:

> . . . take arms against a sea of troubles.

modal auxiliary. Auxiliary verbs that indicate mood, that is, possibility, necessity, permission, capability, and so on. Some modal auxiliaries are *may, might, shall, must, ought, can.*

modifier. A word, phrase, or clause which explains or relates to another part of a sentence:

> a **red** Ferrari [*red* modifies *Ferrari*]
> **Slowly weaving from twig to twig,** the spider built a web. [phrase modifies *spider*]
> **Everything considered,** this plan seems best. [phrase modifies the entire sentence]

mood. The manner in which a statement is expressed. The *indicative* mood expresses a fact or a statement: I *am* thrifty. The *subjunctive* mood expresses a condition, desire, supposition, or a condition contrary to fact: If I *were* you, I would resign. The *imperative* mood expresses a command: *Bring* the books here.

nominal. A word, phrase, or clause that acts as a noun:

> **She** [pronoun] disliked **cutting the lawn** [gerund].
> **To keep accurate minutes** [infinitive phrase] is the secretary's chief responsibility.

nominative absolute. See *absolute modifier.*

nominative case. The subject form or position of a noun or pronoun within a sentence or clause:

> The **boy** led the campers.
> **Who** broke the ditto machine?
> I am **he.** [*he* is a subject complement; hence the pronoun is in the nominative case]

nonfinite verb. See *finite verb.*

nonrestrictive modifier. A subordinate clause or phrase that does not limit or define the term it modifies. In other words, it does not *restrict* the meaning of the term. If the nonrestrictive modifier is omitted, the meaning of the sentence does not change much.

> Last night's audience, **which included many athletes,** applauded each number enthusiastically.

noun. A word which designates a person, place, thing, quality, action, or idea: *plumber, France, trumpet, anger, flying, honesty.* See Review, page 144.

number. The form a part of speech takes to indicate singularity or plurality.

	Singular	*Plural*
Noun	tree	trees
Pronoun	I	we
Verb	he walks (3rd person)	they walk (3rd person)
Demonstrative adjective	this car	these cars

object. The *direct object* of a verb is a noun or noun equivalent that completes the statement. It answers the question asked by adding "what?" or "whom?" after the verb.

>   S   V   DO
> Careless drivers have accidents. [object is a noun]

The *indirect object* is used with verbs of telling, asking, giving, receiving, and so on. It names the receiver of the message, gift, and so on, answering the question "to whom or what?" or "for whom or what?" It comes before the direct object.

>   IO   DO
> He gave the **heckler** a black eye.
>   IO DO
> She told **me** a fib.

objective case. The object form or position of a noun or pronoun within a sentence or a clause:

> The boy led **the campers.**
> **Whom** did you nominate?
> I like **her.**

ordinal numbers. See *cardinal and ordinal numbers.*

paradox. A statement that seems contradictory, puzzling, or silly, but which proves to be true:

> Each ending contains a new beginning.
> I am innocent of the crimes I have not been accused of.

Gloss

1

parenthetical elements. Items set off within a sentence by commas, dashes, or parentheses. The parenthetical expressions add to the sentences, but are not always essential to them:

> More than half the students are, **if the figures are accurate,** employed in restaurants, bars, or grocery stores.
> The damaged building **(an ugly one, we thought)** was finally removed.

parenthetical documentation. A documentation style which relies on in-text citations of authors and their works rather than on footnotes or end notes.

parody. In literature, a work which closely imitates another work for comic purposes.

participle. A verb form, typically ending in *-ing* or *-ed,* used as a modifier. Participles can serve as modifiers of nouns (a *smiling* candidate, a *drenched* cat), as participial phrases modifying a noun (The plants *getting the most expert treatment* will thrive), or as an absolute phrase modifying the main clause (*Everything considered,* a dictionary seems the most sensible gift).

parts of speech. The categories by which most grammarians classify words as they are used in sentences. The eight parts of speech are *nouns, pronouns, verbs, adjectives, adverbs, prepositions, conjunctions,* and *interjections.* See Review, pages 218–19.

passive voice. See *voice.*

person. Grammatically, a change in the form of a pronoun or noun to indicate one is speaking, spoken to, or spoken about.

First person	I, we
Second person	you
Third person	he, she, it, they

persona. In literature, the character assumed by a speaker or author narrating a work.

personal pronoun. A pronoun that refers to a particular individual, thing, or group of individuals. Personal pronouns have subject, object, and possessive forms: *I, me, mine.* See Review, page 171.

personification. In literature, the attribution of human feelings, behaviors, and form to things (animals, objects, abstract ideas) that are not human:

Time hath a taming hand.—John Henry Newman

phrase. A group of related words connected to a sentence or to one of the elements in it by means of a preposition or a verbal. A phrase has no subject or predicate and cannot stand alone.

He came **from a small town.** [prepositional phrase]
Sentences **containing unrelated ideas** are usually confusing. [verbal phrase]

point of view. In literary and expository writing, the perspective from which a piece is presented to a reader.

possessive case. The form of a noun or pronoun that indicates ownership: *Mara's* notebook, the cover *of the book, mine, his.*

predicate. The verb and whatever words are related to it in a sentence:

> The telephone **rang.**
> George **spent two hours talking with his attorney.**

predicate adjective. See *complement.*

predicate noun. See *complement.*

preposition. A word that functions as a link between nouns, pronouns, or words that act as nouns and the rest of a sentence:

> She came **from** New Orleans.
> We kept the secret **between** us.

prepositional phrase. A preposition, its object, and all modifiers. Prepositional phrases function as modifiers in the majority of English sentences.

> An apartment-dweller **in a large city** can live **in the same place for a year** and never speak **to his next-door neighbor.**

principal parts. The infinitive, past tense, and past participle forms of a verb.

Infinitive	Past tense	Past participle
begin	began	begun
come	came	come
do	did	done
eat	ate	eaten
wash	washed	washed

progressive verb. The form of a verb that indicates continuing action in the present, past, or future:

> I **am cooking.** [present]
> I **was cooking.** [past]
> I **will be cooking.** [future]

pronoun. A word that functions like a noun, but does not specifically name a person, place, thing, or idea. A pronoun is usually used as a substitute for a previously stated noun, called its *antecedent.* See Review, page 171.

protagonist. In a literary work, the hero or main character.

quotation. The report or presentation of the words of a speaker. *Direct quotation* (or *direct discourse*) records a speaker's exact words: The clerk asked *"who will pay for these items?"* *Indirect discourse* records the substance of a speaker's words, but not the exact language: *The clerk asked us who would pay.*

reciprocal pronouns. The pronouns *each other* and *one another.* They relate to action between two or more things.

reflexive pronoun. A pronoun form used to refer back to the subject in an expression where the doer and recipient of an act are the same:

> I had only **myself** to blame.
> He hurt **himself** skiing.

regular verb. A verb that forms its principal parts by adding *-d* or *-ed* to the infinitive form.

Infinitive	Past tense	Past participle
walk	walked	walked
join	joined	joined
arrest	arrested	arrested

relative pronouns. Pronouns such as *who, that, which, whom, whose,* and *of which* that introduce subordinate clauses and are the subjects of them:

> The man **who** knew too much disappeared.
> The battery **that** died was replaced.

restrictive modifier. A modifier essential to the sentence because it limits the meaning. With restrictive modifiers, the relative word is often omitted.

> The only books **[that] Alice read** were novels.
> He is a person **[whom] everyone admires.**

rhetoric. The art of discovering, arranging, and presenting ideas in language appropriate to a given situation.

rhetorical question. A question asked for effect, without expectation of an answer. In most cases, the answers to rhetorical questions are obvious or implied:

> Do we fight, or do we run like shameful cowards?

run-on sentence. Two or more independent clauses joined without appropriate conjunctions or punctuation. Also called a *fused sentence.*

Fused	The day is hot sure could use a drink.
Revised	The day is hot; I sure could use a drink.

satire. A literary work that criticizes or mocks human faults or problems through the use of humor, sarcasm, and wit. Jonathan Swift's *Gulliver's Travels* is a satire.

sentence. The primary constructed unit in edited American English. Sentences are one or more words, punctuated as an individual unit, that say something.

> Nuts!
> Noel Coward wrote *Blythe Spirit* in 1941.

sentence fragment. See *fragment.*

sentence modifier. A word or phrase that modifies the complete sentence rather than a single word or phrase within it:

> **To be honest,** my paper is incomplete.
> **In truth,** we arrived yesterday.

simile. A stated comparison between two unlike things:

> The cut was as jagged and frightening **as an iceberg.**
> **Like spoiled children,** the angry candidates called each other names and pouted.

slang. Informal, usually nonstandard English. Slang expressions are usually inappropriate in edited American English.

slanted words. Language in which the connotative power of words is used to shape a reader's reaction to facts or ideas in an unfair or inappropriate way. Slanting occurs in statements of opinion where a writer assumes that he or she is the only reliable resource.

split infinitive. An infinitive phrase interrupted by an adverb between *to* and the base verb:

> to **ever** see
> to **really** want

Split infinitives that are awkward should be avoided.

squinting modifier. Modifiers confusingly placed so that they could refer to either one of two sentence elements.

Confusing	Your singing *frequently* pleases us.
Revised	Your *frequent* singing pleases us.
	Your singing pleases us *frequently.*

stream of consciousness. In literature, the attempt to represent in language the actual sequence of a character's thoughts.

subject. In a sentence, a noun or noun equivalent (pronoun, noun clause, gerund, infinitive) that names what the statement is about or what the agent of the action designated by the predicate is.

Men work.
To listen is to understand.
Talking is his chief exercise.

subject complement. See *complement.*

subjunctive. See *mood.*

subordinate clause. See *clause.*

subordinating conjunction. A word that relates a subordinate (or dependent) clause to the main clause of a sentence: *because, although, since, after, if, when,* and so on.

subordination. A relationship in which one idea or clause is made dependent on another:

> I worked hard and I produced a first-rate book. [coordinate]
> **Because I worked hard,** I produced a first-rate book. [subordinate]

superlative. The greatest degree among three or more persons, things, or concepts:

> the **most** likely to succeed
> the **greatest** of pianists

Superlative forms also occur in expressions in which no direct comparison is implied: *best* wishes, *deepest* sympathy, *highest* praise.

symbol. In literature, an object or image that represents a larger concept. A lion, for example, may be a symbol of courage.

synonym. A word with a meaning similar to another. *Courage, bravery,* and *valor* are synonyms.

tag question. A conventional question attached to the end of a statement. A tag question consists of a pronoun and an auxiliary verb.

> It is a masterful sculpture, **isn't it?**
> You like opera, **don't you?**

tense. Time as expressed by a verb form. English verbs have five categories of tense: *present, past, future, progressive,* and *perfect.* See Review, pages 116.

tone. The attitude writers express through their language. A piece may be friendly, angry, sarcastic, ironic, and so on.

transitive verb. A verb that takes an object:

> We **broke** the bread.   She **asked** a question.

verb. A word that indicates action, condition, or process: *walk, is, become*. See Reviews, pages 116, 133.

verb phrase. Verbs of more than a single word *(was watching, had been anticipating)* that serve as the predicate of a sentence or a clause.

verbal phrase. A participle, gerund, or infinitive (none of which has a full verb function) plus its object or complement and modifiers. See Review, pages 76.

verbals. Verbals are forms of verbs that act as nouns, adjectives, or adverbs. They are classified as infinitives *(to see)*, participles *(having seen)*, and gerunds *(seeing)*. Verbals cannot serve as predicates to make full sentences; consequently they are described as *nonfinite*. Finite verbs are needed for full sentences.

> the man watching [participle]
> making love, not war [gerund]
> to drive skillfully [infinitive]

See Review, page 76.

vogue words and phrases. Words or expressions that quickly and faddishly become a part of everyday language: *bottom line, interface with, expletive deleted, Where's the beef?*

voice, active and passive. An aspect of transitive verbs indicating whether the action described is done by the subject (active voice) or the object (passive voice). The passive consists of a form of *be* plus the past participle. All other verbs are active.

Active	The general **chose** his aide.
Passive	The aide **was chosen** by the general.
Active	I **will make** the trip.
Passive	The trip **will be made** by me.

word order. The arrangement of words in a sentence. In English, we identify the main sentence elements chiefly by their position in a sentence.

> The **boy** hit the **ball**.
> The **ball** hit the **boy**.

word processing. Writing and editing with the assistance of a computer. The written text first appears on a screen, where it is composed, edited, and (depending on software) checked and formatted. The final text is prepared by a printer connected to the computer.

GLOSSARY
OF USAGE

This glossary lists words and constructions that often cause confusion in writing; it is not, however, a replacement for a good dictionary. Many of these entries are discussed in more detail in the chapter of the *Handbook* in which they occur, for example, *lie, lay* in Chapter 6, Verbs, and *who, whom* in Chapter 8, Pronouns. The index lists the usage entries that appear within the *Handbook*.

a, an. The choice of *a* or *an* depends on the initial sound of the following word rather than the initial letter. Use *a* before words beginning with a consonant sound, *an* before words beginning with a vowel sound: *a* boat, *a* used boat, *a* European country, *an* alligator, *an* F, *an* hour.

able to. A clumsy and unidiomatic expression when used with a passive infinitive: This shirt *can be* [not *is able to be*] washed without shrinkage.

accept, except. *Accept* means "receive" or "approve of"; *except* means "exclude" or "with the exclusion of":

> Everyone has **accepted** the invitation **except** Sam.

adverse, averse. The distinction between these adjectives is subtle. *Averse* is ordinarily used with *to* to indicate that a person or thing dislikes or opposes something else:

> Our secretary was **averse to** typing.
> The students were **averse to** all proposals to increase fees.

Adverse can be used to describe an antagonistic, hostile, or unfavorable thing:

> We were damaged by the **adverse** publicity.
> The officers expected an **adverse** reaction to their proposal.

advice, advise. _Advice_ is a noun meaning "counsel" or "recommendation"; _advise_ is a verb meaning "give advice" or "make a recommendation":

> I **advise** you to follow your instructor's **advice.**

affect, effect. _Affect_ is a verb meaning "influence" or "assume the appearance of"; _effect_ is a noun meaning "result":

> The weather **affected** our tempers.
> The frightened child **affected** a defiant look.
> The **effects** of radiation aren't completely known.

Affect is also a noun, a technical term used in psychology meaning "emotion." _Effect_ is a formal verb meaning "to bring about."

aggravate, irritate. In formal English, _aggravate_ means "make worse" and _irritate_ means "annoy": _aggravate_ the condition; an _irritating_ habit. In general and informal usage, _aggravate_ and _irritate_ both mean "to annoy": his voice _aggravated_ me; the mosquitoes were _irritating._ But since using _aggravate_ to mean "annoy" might irritate some readers, it is useful to maintain the formal distinction.

agree to, agree with. _Agree to_ indicates consent; _agree with_ shows accord: I _agreed to_ sign the petition because I _agreed with_ what it proposed.

ain't. A colloquial contraction meaning "aren't" or "isn't." _Ain't_ is not considered appropriate in most academic and professional writing, although it may appear in narrative or dialogue.

all ready, already. _All ready_ is an adjective phrase meaning that everything or everyone is prepared; _already_ is an adverb meaning "previously":

> Finally the car was loaded and we were **all ready** to leave.
> The train had **already** left when we got to the station.

all right. The only correct spelling. _Alright_ is not acceptable.

all together, altogether. _All together_ is an adjective phrase meaning "in a group"; _altogether_ is an adverb meaning "wholly":

> The sale items were **all together** on one table.
> That's **altogether** another matter.

allude, elude. _Allude_ means "to refer to"; _elude_ means "to escape from."

allude, refer. To _allude_ is to make indirect mention of something; to _refer_ is to state directly:

I knew that his remarks about trees **alluded** to the unfortunate incident at the picnic.

He **referred** to the second paragraph in making his point.

allusion, illusion. An *allusion* is a brief, indirect reference to a person, event, literary work, or the like. An *illusion* is a misleading appearance.

She made a **allusion** to Yeats' "Second Coming."
The little boy's smile created an **illusion** of innocence.

almost, most. *Almost* is an adverb meaning "very nearly"; *most* is an adjective meaning "the greater part of."

He **almost** wrecked the car.
Most drivers try to be careful.

Although in speech *most* is sometimes used to mean *almost*, the two words are not interchangeable.

a lot. Always two words.

among, between. *Among* usually refers to more than two; *between* refers to two only. However, *between* is sometimes used in informal English for more than two. *Between* is always used when the reference is to individual items, even though an "item" might consist of more than one unit:

We had to choose **between coffee and cake** [as one item] **and punch and cookies.**

Do not use *or* between the items: *between him and her.*

amount, number. In general and formal usage, *amount* is used to refer to something as a mass: a large *amount* of black dirt; a certain *amount* of money. *Number* is used to refer to individual items: a large *number* of plants, a *number* of cars.

and etc. The use of *and* with *etc.* is redundant because *etc. (et cetera)* means "and so forth."

and/or. An awkward expression. Avoid it if you can.

and which, but which. The use of *and* or *but* with a relative pronoun *(who, which, that)* in an adjective clause is superfluous and defeats the subordination; only the pronoun should be used:

The sea anemone is a fascinating creature **which** looks more like a plant than an animal.

ante-, anti-. As prefixes, *ante-* means *before* and *anti-* means *against:*

antebellum (before the Civil War)   antifreeze
antediluvian (before the biblical Flood)   antiwar

anxious, eager. _Anxious_ indicates fear, nervousness, or uneasiness; **eager** indicates anticipation:

> I am **anxious** about her physical condition.
> They were **eager** to see New York.

anyone, any one. These words are not interchangeable. _Any one_ refers to one of a certain number of items or people; _anyone_ is a singular, indefinite pronoun and refers only to a person:

> You may choose **any one** of those books to read.
> **Anyone** who pays the entrance fee may enter the race.

Everyone, every one and _someone, some one_ are similar types of words.

anyway, any way, anyways. _Anyway_ means _nevertheless_, and should not be confused with _any way_.

> Even if Liz declines, I'll come **anyway.**
> I'll come **any way** I can.

Anyways is a nonstandard form of _anyway._ Avoid it.

anywheres. _Anywheres_ is a nonstandard form of _anywhere._ Avoid it.

apt, likely, liable. See _likely, liable, apt._

as. When used as a conjunction to introduce adverb clauses, _as_ is often less exact than other adverbs such as _while, when, since,_ or _because:_

> **While** we were eating, we talked about the election.
> We stopped to rest under a tree **because** the sun was so hot.

as, like. See _like, as._

at. Don't use _at_ after _where._ It is redundant.

Not	Where are you at?
But	Where are you?

awful, awfully. _Awful_ is an adverb, _awfully_ an adjective. Note the difference:

> Rover smells **awful.** (that is, the dog stinks)
> Rover smells **awfully.** (that is, the dog has a poor sense of smell)

Both words tend to be used in their colloquial senses, meaning "bad" _(awful)_ or "very" _(awfully)._ Strictly used, _awful_ means "inspiring fear or awe."

awhile, a while. *Awhile* is an adverb meaning "for a certain period of time." *A while* is a noun with an article:

> Can you stay **awhile?** [adverb modifying *stay*]
> Can you stay for **a while?** [noun, object of the preposition *for*]

bad, badly. *Bad* is the adjective, *badly* the adverb. Although *bad* is the preferred form following a linking verb (I feel *bad;* the situation looks *bad*), *badly* is sometimes used, especially after *feel* (she feels *badly* about hurting you). Many people object to such uses of *badly*, however, and it's just as well to avoid them in writing. But do use *badly* when it is called for: The day started off *badly* and got worse.

being as. A clumsy expression. Use *because* or *since.*

being that. To introduce a dependent clause of reason or cause, *being that* is an unacceptable substitute for *because, since,* or *for:*

> **Because** I was so tired, I decided not to go to the party.

beside, besides. *Beside* means "at the side of"; *besides* means "in addition to."

> **Besides** attending the concert we lingered **beside** the monument.

between, among. See *among, between.*

bring, take. *Bring* suggests motion toward the writer: *Bring* me my slippers, please. *Take* suggests motion away from the writer: *Take* my slippers to the closet, please.

bunch. Don't use *bunch* to describe groups of people: "a *gathering* of scholars," not "a *bunch* of scholars."

bursted; bust, busted. The principle parts of *to burst* are *burst, burst, burst* (I just *burst* his bubble; The balloon *burst* yesterday; By tomorrow, the dam will have *burst*.) *Bursted* is not acceptable as the past tense. *To bust* is a slang verb.

but that, but what. Even though *but that* and *but what* are used informally in dependent clauses, *that* is preferable in most writing: I don't doubt *that* he'll be there.

but which. See *and which.*

can be, able to be. *Able to be* is an awkward expression when used with a passive infinitive: Canoes are *able to be* carried easily by two people. *Can be* is preferable: Canoes *can be* carried easily by two people.

can, may. In written edited English, _can_ is used to express ability, _may_ to express permission:

> **Can** you dance? **May** I have this dance?

Can is frequently used informally in the sense of permission _(Can I go too?)_, but it's best to avoid this use in writing.

can't hardly. Such common expressions as _can't hardly_ and _couldn't scarcely_ are double negatives, because _hardly_ and _scarcely_ mean "almost not." Use _can hardly_ instead: I _can hardly_ hear you.

can't help but. This is an established idiom, but many writers avoid it, using instead _cannot but_ (formal) or _can't help._

censor, censure. _Censor_ means "repress" or "remove"; _censure_ means "condemn" or "disapprove," often in an official sense:

> Chicago would like to **censor** X-rated movies.
> The senator whose entire family was on the payroll was **censured** by Congress.

center around. Although this is a commonly used expression, it is considered illogical by many. Use _center on_ or _revolve around_ instead.

cite, site. _Cite_ is a verb, most often used in the sense of "quote" or "refer to"; _site_ is a noun meaning "location," or a verb meaning "place in a certain location":

> Dictionaries often **cite** the way a word has been used by different writers.
> We've found the perfect **site** for a picnic.

complement, compliment. _Complement_ is a noun or verb referring to completion or fitting together; _compliment_ is a noun or verb suggesting praise:

> She saw a hat that would be the perfect **complement** for her suit. It also **complemented** her bag.
> Nancy **complimented** Theodore on his prize. He accepted the **compliment** graciously.

conscience, conscious. _Conscience_ is a noun that describes one's moral sensibility; _conscious_ is an adjective meaning "awake" or "aware":

> She had a troubled **conscience.**
> Stephen was **conscious** of a hiss on the tape.

contact. Many people dislike _contact_ in the sense of "get in touch with" (I'll _contact_ you soon); in general or formal edited English a more precise word is ordinarily used: _see, call,_ or _write._

continual, continuous. Although the distinction has largely disappeared, *continual* refers to an action that occurs repeatedly over a period of time, *continuous* to an action that is in uninterrupted flow:

> The **continual** ringing of the phone began to annoy Joe.
> Many old people live with a **continuous** fear of being robbed.

convince, persuade. The distinction between these words is subtle. It helps to remember that *convince* is usually followed by the pronoun *of,* and *persuade* by the pronoun *to.*

> I was **convinced** of his innocence.
> I was **persuaded** to contribute.

could of, would of. These are mistaken expressions based on the spoken contractions *could've* and *would've.* Use *could have* and *would have* in writing.

couple of. *A couple of* is colloquial. Use *several* or *a few.*

credible, creditable, credulous. *Credible* means "capable of being believed" (a lie can be credible); *creditable* means "worthy of being believed" (a lie should not be creditable); *credulous* means "willing to believe on the slimmest evidence."

> The story the defendant told was **credible.** Moreover, she had established herself as a **creditable** person.
> But she faced a tough, hardly **credulous** jury.

criteria, criterion. *Criteria* is the plural form of *criterion:*

> We established several **criteria** for the position. The most important **criterion** was excellence.

data. Although *data* is used in general and informal usage for both the singular and plural, *datum* is used as the singular in formal writing.

detract, distract. *Detract* means "take away from"; *distract* means "to turn aside" or "divert the attention."

> The litter on the ground **detracted** from the beauty of the park.
> The wailing sirens **distracted** us from our conversation.

differ from, differ with. *Differ from* indicates a contrast; *differ with,* a dispute:

> A Rolls **differs from** a Bentley chiefly in its grille.
> I **differ with** you on that point.

different from. This is the general idiom, but *different than* can be used to avoid an awkward sentence:

Life in a small town is **different from** life in a large city.
Living on a farm means a **different** life-style **than** living in a city does.
Living on a farm means a life-style **different from** the life-style in a city.

discreet, discrete. _Discreet_ is an adjective meaning respectful, cautious, and judicious; _discrete_ is an adjective distinguishing something as individual or separate:

She was **discreet** in discussing her husband's baldness.
The crash was due to three **discrete** failures in the hydraulic system.

disinterested, uninterested. Even though both words are commonly used to mean _uninterested,_ a distinction should be maintained. Use _disinterested_ to mean "impartial": _Disinterested_ judges are better than _uninterested_ ones.

done, don't. All varieties of standard English call for _did_ in the past tense in all persons: I, you, he, she, it _did._ The past participle in all persons is _have_ or _had done._ _Don't_ is the contraction for _do not; doesn't_ is the contraction for _does not:_ I, you _don't;_ he, she, it _doesn't._

due to. There is some objection to using _due to_ as a preposition replacing _because of:_

The quarterback fainted **due to** the heat.
The quarterback fainted **because of** the heat.

However, _due to_ is acceptable as a subject complement after a form of the verb _to be:_

His failures were **due to** insolence.
The crash was **due to** metal fatigue.

due to the fact that. A wordy expression that can usually be replaced by _because._

each and every. The expression is redundant. Use _each_ or _every_ alone.

effect, affect. See _affect, effect._

either . . . or. Singular subjects joined by _either . . . or_ or _neither . . . nor_ are generally considered singular, and take a singular verb:

Either the bicycle or the moped is the transportation of the future.

If both subjects are plural, the verb is plural:

Either bicycles or mopeds are the transportation of the future.

eminent, imminent. *Eminent* is an adjective meaning "noteworthy" or "famous": an *eminent* ambassador. *Imminent* is an adjective meaning "about to happen": The storm is *imminent*.

enthuse. While *enthuse* is fairly common in speech, it is generally better to use another form in writing: *be enthusiastic about* or *show enthusiasm*.

equally as. Redundant. Use the one appropriate word: He was *equally* unwilling a month ago; He was *as* unwilling as his brother.

etc. The abbreviation for *et cetera,* "and so forth." Do not use *and etc.*

every one, everyone. See *any one, anyone.*

except, accept. See *accept, except.*

explicit, implicit. *Explicit* is an adjective meaning clearly defined and forthright; *implicit* is an adjective meaning understood or implied, not directly expressed.

the fact that. A wordy expression. Use *that.*

Wordy	She was conscious **of the fact that** he dislike her.
Better	She was conscious **that** he disliked her.

farther, further. In formal English *farther* is used to refer to physical distance: How much *farther* must we walk? *Further* refers to abstract degree: We will study these suggestions *further.* Although the distinction is not as strictly adhered to in general writing, it is better to maintain it.

fewer, less. *Fewer* is used to refer to countable items, *less* to something considered as a mass:

If there are **fewer** people, it means **less** work for the clean-up crew.

flaunt, flout. Although frequently confused, these words are not synonyms: *flaunt* is to make a show of, or display something ostentatiously; *flout* is to disregard or treat with scorn:

Everyone was tired of the way he **flaunted** his inheritance.
Some people always **flout** the traffic laws.

former, latter. Used to refer to the first or last of two items only:

Ivan and Ken approached. The **former** was my strongest supporter, the **latter** my opponent.

If there are more than two items, use *first, last.*

get, got, gotten. Both *got* and *gotten* are acceptable forms of the past participle of *get:*

> He could have **gotten** [or **got**] more for his money.

Many idioms with *get* are standard in all levels of writing: *get up, get away from, get ahead.* But some expressions are considered informal and should be avoided in college writing: *get on one's nerves, get away with murder, gets me* (for "annoy"), *get* in the sense of "hit" or "struck."

good and. *Good and* is not appropriate in most formal writing.

| Colloquial | The bookcases are **good and** solid. |
| Formal | The bookcases are **extremely** solid. |

good, well. *Good* is an adjective: a *good* time; this cake tastes *good.* *Well* is either an adjective, in the sense of one's health, or, more usually, an adverb: The team plays *well* together. Since *good* is an adjective, it shouldn't be used in place of the adverb *well:* The car is running *well* since it was tuned up.

had ought, hadn't ought. These forms are nonstandard. *Had* should be eliminated from each of them: I ought to go; I ought not to go.

half. Both *a half* and *half a* are standard; choice usually depends on sound and idiom: He ate *half a* pie; He ate *a half* serving. *A half a* is redundant.

The number of the verb is determined by the noun accompanying *half:*

> Half the pie **is** gone.   Half the children **are** sick.

hang. People are *hanged,* pictures and other objects are *hung.* The distinction isn't strictly maintained as far as people are concerned, but objects are never hanged.

hardly. Since *hardly* is a negative meaning "almost not," don't use another negative with it. See *can't hardly.*

he or she. Although *he* has traditionally been used as the pronoun when both sexes are meant, more writers are using *he or she (him or her, his or her).* If constant repetition of *he or she* sounds awkward, try rewriting the passage into the plural *(they).*

hisself. Nonstandard for *himself.*

hopefully. Many readers object to *hopefully* when it is used to modify an entire sentence: *Hopefully,* we will arrive in time. It may help to remember that *hopefully* means *with hope*. Compare these sentences:

> We watched **hopefully** as the debris was cleared.
> We **hoped** some survivors would be found. [not *Hopefully,* some survivors would be found.]

illusion, allusion. See *allusion, illusion.*

imminent, eminent. See *eminent, imminent.*

implicit, explicit. See *explicit, implicit.*

imply, infer. *Imply* means "suggest"; *infer* means "assume" or "draw a conclusion" from a suggestion or implication:

> Even though she didn't say anything, her expression **implied** that she thought her friend was acting foolishly.
> We **inferred** from the manager's remarks that we would not be getting raises this year.

in, into. *In* generally refers to a location within, *into* to the action of going toward the location:

> She decided to sit **in** the chair that she had bumped **into** in the dark.

in regards to. A nonstandard version of *in regard to.* Also acceptable are *regarding* or *as regards.*

incredible, incredulous. *Incredible* means "very hard to believe"; *incredulous* means "not believing, skeptical":

> The gymnast showed **incredible** control on the balance beam.
> John was **incredulous** at the story the little green men were telling.

interface with. Electronic equipment may *interface,* but the term should probably be avoided in describing relationships between people.

irregardless. Nonstandard for *regardless.* Since both *ir-* and *-less* are negative affixes, *ir-* is redundant.

irritate, aggravate. See *aggravate, irritate.*

is when, is where. Often incorrectly used to introduce an adverb clause as a definition:

Incorrect	Theater-in-the-round is when the audience surrounds the stage.
Correct	A theater-in-the-round is one in which the audience surrounds the stage.

its, it's. These two words are often carelessly confused. *Its* is the possessive form of the pronoun *it:* everything in *its* place. *It's* is the contraction for _it is_ or _it has: It's_ raining; _It's_ begun. There is no such form as _its'_.

-ize. Be wary of new words coined by adding _-ize_ to a noun or adjective: _prioritize, sensitize._ However, many words ending in _-ize_ are familiar and acceptable: _criticize, categorize, publicize._

kind, sort. _Kind_ and _sort_ are singular when used with _this_ or _that_ and should be used with a singular noun and verb: _this kind_ of book is my favorite, _that sort_ of person annoys me. If the idea is plural, use _these_ and _those: these kinds_ of books are . . . , _those sorts_ of people . . . .

kind of a, sort of a. Although frequently occurring in speech, _kind of a_ is considered informal in writing. Write: We'll never see that _kind of_ day again.

later, latter. _Later,_ a comparative adjective, refers to time: The _later_ the hour, the longer the shadows. _Latter,_ an adjective or a noun, refers to the second of two items named. See also _former, latter._

lay, lie. _Lay_ is a verb meaning "to put or place"; it takes an object: _Lay_ the books on the desk. _Lie_ is a verb meaning "to recline"; it does not take an object: _Lie_ down for a nap. The principal parts of _lay_ are _lay, laid, laid:_ He _laid_ the books on the desk. The principal parts of _lie_ are _lie, lay, lain:_ She _lay_ down for a nap.

learn, teach. The student _learns,_ the instructor _teaches._ Using _learn_ for _teach_ is considered nonstandard.

leave, let. _Leave_ means "depart or abandon"; _let_ means "permit": _Let_ us _leave_ this place. Using _leave_ for _let_ is considered nonstandard.

less, fewer. See _fewer, less._

let's us. Since _let's_ is a contraction for "let us," _let's us_ is redundant.

lie, lay. See _lay, lie._

like, as. To introduce a prepositional phrase of comparison, use _like:_

> He looks **like** his father.
> Some people **like** the Joneses try to keep up with their neighbors.

To introduce a clause of comparison (with a subject and verb), use _as, as if,_ or _as though:_

> It looks **as if** his father is not coming.
> She wanted to be a lawyer **as** her mother had been.

The use of *like* as a conjunction has become more widespread recently, but it is ordinarily better to use the preferred forms *as, as if,* and *as though.*

likely, liable, apt. Both *likely* and *liable* suggest that something will occur, but in formal usage *liable* is restricted to an unpleasant or disastrous occurrence:

> The tornado is **liable** to damage a large part of town.
> The tornado is **likely** to veer away from town.

The use of *apt* to suggest an occurrence is colloquial. Use *apt* only in the sense of aptitude: She is very *apt* at woodworking.

loose, lose. The spelling of these words is sometimes confused. *Loose* is an adjective meaning "not tight" (*loose* sleeves), or a verb meaning "release" (*loosen* the rope). *Lose* is a verb meaning "misplace" (don't *lose* it).

may, can. See *can, may.*

may be, maybe. *May be* is a verb phrase suggesting possibility; *maybe* is an adverb meaning "perhaps":

> He **may be** the next mayor.
> **Maybe** it will rain this afternoon.

media, medium. Remember that *media* is the plural form:

> Television is a popular **medium** of entertainment.
> Newspapers and radio are also potent **media.**

might of. A colloquial form. In writing, use *might have:*

| *Colloquial* | I **might of** helped. |
| *Formal* | I **might have** helped. |

moral, morale. The adjective *moral* means "ethical" (a *moral* code of conduct); the noun *moral* refers to the ethical significance or practical lesson (the *moral* of a story). The noun *morale* means "state of mind": If all the workers do their share, the *morale* of the group will be good.

most, almost. See *almost, most.*

must of. Nonstandard form of *must have.* Avoid it.

myself. A reflexive or intensive pronoun, used to refer back to *I* in the same sentence:

I hurt **myself**. **I, myself,** am the only one to blame.

It is not more formal or proper to substitute _myself_ for _I_.

nohow, nowheres. _Nohow_ is nonstandard for _not at all; nowheres_ is nonstandard for _nowhere_.

not . . . no. Constructions such as "I don't have no money," or "The tickets will not cost you nothing" are called double negatives, because the second negative needlessly repeats the meaning of the first one. They are common in some dialects, but are not appropriate to written forms of edited English.

number, amount. See _amount, number_.

of, have. Do not use _of_ for _have_ in expressions such as _could have_ and _would have_. See _could of_.

of which, whose. _Whose_ is the possessive form of the pronoun _who;_ it's generally used to refer to persons; _of which_ is the possessive form most often used for inanimate objects:

> One of the most interesting colonial Americans was Thomas Jefferson, **whose** ideas still sound very modern.
> It was a huge house, the rooms **of which** were dank and mildewed.

Often, however, _of which_ is awkward; _whose_ is generally used in such cases: ". . . the room _whose_ walls were painted orange."

off of. A colloquial expression that means no more than _off:_ He jumped _off_ the cliff.

O.K., OK, okay. A colloquial form. All three forms are acceptable.

on account of. Wordy. You can usually substitute _because of_.

party. Colloquial in the sense of "person." Use _person:_ Are you the _person_ who wanted to see me?

per. _Per_ is acceptable in technical communications and certain common expressions (miles _per_ hour, _per_ diem), but should be avoided in general writing whenever possible:

| _Awkward_ | As **per** your letter of May 2 . . . . |
| _Revised_ | Regarding your letter of May 2 . . . . |

phenomena. The plural of _phenomenon_, a fact or event. If you use _phenomena_ as the subject of a sentence, be sure to use a plural verb.

piece, peace. Do not confuse the spelling of these homonyms: *piece* means "portion"; *peace* means "absence of hostility."

plenty. As an adverb, *plenty* is colloquial: Use *very, quite,* or a more precise word in your writing: This coffee is *very* hot. In the sense of "more than sufficient," use *plenty of:* We have *plenty of* time.

plus. *Plus* is a preposition meaning "with the addition of"; its use as a conjunction (John *plus* Mary are going.) is disapproved of by many. A phrase using *plus* should not affect the number of the verb:

> The old apartment complex, **plus** the new townhouse section, contains a total of 225 units.

Plus is also used as a noun (The new lights are a *plus* for the city), but many consider such use journalese or jargon.

practicable, practical. The two words are not interchangeable. *Practicable* means "feasible or usable, but not necessarily proved successful." *Practical,* on the other hand, implies success in its application. An electric car may be part of a *practicable* solution to urban pollution problems; putting on the spare tire is the *practical* method of dealing with a flat tire.

precede, proceed. *Precede* means "to go before": *proceed* means "to continue," "to move along."

> The mayor's car **preceded** the governor's in the parade.
> Let's **proceed** with the meeting.

predominate, predominant. *Predominate* is a verb: The captain's will *predominated* throughout the voyage. *Predominant* is an adjective: His *predominant* characteristic is laziness.

principal, principle. *Principal,* both as an adjective and a noun, means "chief": the *principal* of a school, the *principal* reason. A *principle* is a rule of conduct or action: the *principle* governing the operation of a windmill, *principles* for living.

quote. Some readers regard *quote* as a colloquial form of *quotation.* You may want to use *quotation* in your formal writing.

raise, rise. *Raise* is a transitive verb, taking an object, meaning to cause (something) to move up; *rise* is an intransitive verb meaning to go up:

> Every morning when I get up I **raise** the window shade.
> Yeast causes bread dough to **rise.**

real, really. *Real* is an adjective, *really* an adverb, although in speech *real* is often used as an adverb. In writing, though, you should distinguish between the two:

> Their disagreement was **real.**   You did a **really** fine job.

reason is because. A redundant phrase since *because* means "the reason that." The preferred phrase is "the reason is that."

> The **reason** we are late is **that** an accident tied up traffic.

reason why. A wordy expression. *Reason* alone is usually sufficient.

refer, allude. See *allude, refer.*

respectful, respective. *Respectful* is an adjective meaning "considerate of" or "honoring"; *respective* is an adjective meaning "particular" or "in a certain order":

> He is very **respectful** of his instructors.
> Each application was placed in its **respective** file.

shall, will. In current American usage, *will* is generally used with all persons in the verb for the future tense. In formal usage, however, *shall* is used in the first person for the simple future (I *shall* ask), *will* in the second and third persons (she *will* ask). For the emphatic future, the use is reversed: *will* is used in the first person (I *will* win), *shall* in the second and third (they *shall* leave). *Shall* is not a more elegant term than *will*.

should of. A colloquial form. In writing, use *should have:*

| Colloquial | I *should of* helped. |
| Formal | I *should have* helped. |

sic. *Sic* is a Latin word meaning "thus" or "so." It is generally used only in quoted material, inserted in brackets, to indicate that an error was made in the original, not the copy. Its use has declined considerably in current writing.

since, because. Some careful writers use *since* only to refer to time:

> I have been crying **since** the minute you left.

Avoid ambiguous expressions in which *since* can mean either *because* or *ever since:*

> **Since** you departed, I sold the condo.

sit, set. The verb *sit* (as in a chair) is intransitive, not taking an object: *Sit* down. The verb *set,* meaning to put something down, is transitive, and therefore does take an object: *Set* the plants on the balcony.

site, cite. See *cite, site.*

so. Avoid using *so* alone as an intensifier:

> It was **so** cold.   She was **so** sad.

If possible, complete the expression by adding explanatory details:

> It was **so** cold **the well froze.**
> She was **so** sad **that she depressed her whole family.**

some. *Some* used as an adverb (I was *some* tired) is colloquial; edited English would use *somewhat* or a more precise descriptive word. *Some* used as an adjective (That was *some* concert) is informal, and better avoided in writing.

someone, some one. See *anyone, any one.*

sort. See *kind, sort.*

somewheres. Nonstandard for *somewhere.*

stationary, stationery. *Stationary* is an adjective meaning "fixed in position," "immobile." *Stationery* is a noun referring to writing materials. One way to remember the difference is to recall that both *stationery* and *letter* contain *er.*

such. *Such,* like *so,* is a vague intensifier and, consequently, should be avoided in most academic writing:

> It was **such** a tough exam!

If you use *such* as an intensifier, supply explanatory details:

> It was **such** a tough exam **that half the class failed it.**

supposed to, used to. Because in speech the *-d* ending of *supposed* and the *t-* of *to* are not distinguished, the *-d* is sometimes erroneously left off in writing phrases such as *supposed to* and *used to.* Remember that they are regular verbs in the past tense, and thus require the final *-ed.*

| *Incorrect* | You are **suppose to** stand here. |
| *Correct* | You are **supposed to** stand here. |

sure, surely. In conversation the adjective *sure* is often used in place of the adverb *surely.* *Surely* is the only adverb form:

> We **surely** enjoyed the new exhibit at the museum.

sure and, try and. These are colloquial versions of *sure to* and *try to* and should be avoided.

Colloquial	Be **sure and** stop by.
	Try and help out.
Revised	Be **sure to** stop by.
	Try to help out.

suspect, suspicion. *Suspect* is a verb meaning "distrust" or "imagine": The police *suspected* [not *suspicioned*] foul play. *Suspicion* is a noun, and when used for *suspect* it is a localism, inappropriate in writing.

teach, learn. See *learn, teach.*

than, then. Do not confuse the conjunction *than,* usually used in comparisons, with the adverb *then:*

I would rather get up early **than** sleep late.
Then I have more time to do all the things I want to do.

that kind. See *kind, sort.*

their, there, they're. Confusion of these three words is usually a spelling problem. *Their* is the possessive form of *they: their* house, *their* problems. *There* is used most often as an adverb or an anticipating subject: over *there; There* are five horses in the corral. *They're* is the contracted form of they are: *They're* happy; *They're* certain.

themselves, theirselves. *Themselves* is a plural reflexive or intensive pronoun: They hurt *themselves. Theirselves* is not a standard English form.

this here, that there, these here, them there. These are nonstandard forms. Use *this* or *that.*

thusly. Nonstandard. Use *thus.*

till, until. Interchangeable as prepositions or conjunctions: Wait *till* [or *until*] I get there. Notice that *till* is not a shortened form of *until,* and should not be spelled with an apostrophe. The form *'til* is occasionally seen, especially in "poetic" writing. *'Til* without the apostrophe is not acceptable.

to, too. Confusion of these forms in writing is usually the result of carelessness, not confusion. The preposition *to* is far more common than the adverb *too*, which means "also," "besides," "very," or "excessively."

toward, towards. Either form is acceptable, though *toward* seems to be preferred.

try and, try to. Both are accepted idioms: *try and* is common in general English: *Try and* get your work done. *Try to* is the preferred form in formal English: *Try to* get your work done.

TV. In formal writing, you may want to avoid the abbreviation for *television*.

type. *Type* should always be used with *of* or omitted entirely:

Wordy	It was a sports **type** car.
Better	It was a sports car.
	It was a **type of** sports car.

uninterested, disinterested. See *disinterested, uninterested*.

unique. *Unique* ordinarily needs no modifiers. *Most unique* or *very unique* are redundant expressions.

use, utilize. Some readers object to *utilize*, preferring *use:*

How will they **utilize** their oil reserves?
How will they **use** their oil reserves?

used to. See *supposed to*.

used to could. Colloquial for *used to be able to*. Use *used to be able to, was able to,* or *could* in writing: I *used to be able to* swim quite well.

very. *Very* is an intensifier that has lost some of its power because it has been overused. It is often better to replace *very* with a detail or stronger word:

It was **very** cold.
It was -23°F.

wait on. Common in some dialects in the sense of *wait for*, but in writing should be used only in the sense of "serving a customer."

want, want to, want that. In the sense of "ought" or "should," *want* is informal: You *should* [rather than *want to*] review your notes before the test. In statements of desire or intention, *want to* is the standard idiom: I *want to* get all I can from this year's work. In such constructions *want that* and *want for* are not standard.

was, were. _Was_ is the past tense of _be (is)_ in the first and third person singular: I, he, she, it _was_. _Were_ is the past tense for second person singular (you _were_) and first, second, and third person plural: we, you, they _were_. Use of "we was" or "you was" is not standard.

we, I. _We_ (the "editorial we") should not be used when you mean _I: I_ base _my_ conclusions on information _I_ received from several hotel managers.

well, good. See _good, well._

who, whom. Although the distinction betwen _who_ and _whom_ is disappearing in many contexts, this is the general guideline: use _who_ when it is the subject of a verb, even in subordinate clauses; use _whom_ in all object positions (object of the preposition, direct object):

> **Who** is going to the play?
> **Whom** are you taking to the play? [You are taking whom?]
> He is a man **who** never compromises his principles.
> He is a man of **whom** it's been said, "He never compromises his principles."

whose. See _of which, whose._

-wise. Avoid words in which _-wise_ is used as a suffix to mean "with respect to" or "in terms of." Such expressions may be economical, but many readers object to them strongly:

> **Weatherwise,** the day was perfect.
> Sam didn't do well **gradewise.**

Expressions of manner or direction using _-wise_ are common and appropriate: _otherwise, clockwise, lengthwise._

with regards to. Nonstandard for _with regard to._

would of. An error for _would have._ See _could of, would of._

Xmas. Many readers regard _Xmas_ an inappropriate abbreviation.

you all. An informal Southern dialect form for _you,_ either singular or plural.

your, you're. These terms are often confused. _Your_ is a possessive form: _Your_ house. _You're_ is a contraction for _you are: You're_ going to the game, aren't you?

ACKNOWLEDGMENTS

Acknowledgments

Photo Credits

Borglum—Solon H. Borglum, *The Horse Wranglers* or *Bronco Busters,* bronze. The Archer M. Huntington Art Gallery, The University of Texas at Austin, Gift of C. R. Smith, 1972.

Remington—Frederic Remington, *Mountain Man,* sculpture. The General Libraries of The University of Texas at Austin.

Literary Credits

The sources of quotations used for illustrative purposes are indicated in the text. Special acknowledgment is due for permission to reprint the following selections:

American Airlines—From American Airlines advertisement "Introducing American's Rio Vacations." Reprinted by permission.

Austin—From "Four Kinds of Chance" by James Austin in *Saturday Review/ World,* Nov. 2, 1974. Reprinted by permission of the author.

Baker—Russell Baker, "The Plot Against People." *The New York Times,* June 18, 1968. The New York Times Company.

Baxter—Gordon Baxter, "Peterbilt Pickups." *Car & Driver,* November 1981. Ziff-Davis Publishing Co.

Bidwell—Quote from Bennett Bidwell, *Car & Driver,* December 1983. Ziff-Davis Publishing Co.

Catton—From Bruce Catton, "Grant and Lee: A Study in Contrasts" from *The American Story,* Earl Schenck Miers, editor. Copyright © 1956 by Broadcast Music, Inc. Reprinted by permission.

Chapman—Craig Chapman, "Good as Gold."

Chase—Stuart Chase, "Two Cheers for Technology." *The Saturday Review,* February 20, 1971. The Saturday Review.

Chevrolet—From the advertisement "Move into more. New Chevrolet Celebrity." Reprinted by permission of the Chevrolet Motor Division, General Motors Corporation.

Colligan—"The Light Stuff" by Douglas Colligan in *Technology Illustrated,* February/March 1982. Reprinted by permission of the author.

Commager—From "Presidents Then and Now" by Henry Steele Commager. Reprinted with permission from *Modern Maturity.* Copyright © 1980 by the American Association of Retired Persons.

Computer-Based Information Services—From *Computer-Based Information Services,* September 1983, pp. 40A–40C. Reprinted by permission of The General Libraries of The University of Texas at Austin.

Connor—From "Will Spelling Count?" by Jack Connor in *The Chronicle of Higher Education,* June 2, 1980, vol. XX, no. 14. Copyright © 1980 by The Chronicle of Higher Education. Reprinted by permission.

Crane—Stephen Crane, "The Bride Comes to Yellow Sky" in *The American Tradition in Literature*. New York: W. W. Norton & Co., Inc., 1974.

Cummings—From "anyone lived in a pretty how town," copyright 1940 by E. E. Cummings; renewed 1968 by Marion Morehouse Cummings. Reprinted from *Complete Poems 1913–1962* by E. E. Cummings by permission of Harcourt Brace Jovanovich, Inc.

Didion—From "In Bed," *The White Album* by Joan Didion. Copyright © 1979 by Joan Didion. Reprinted by permission of Simon & Schuster, Inc.

Fischer—John Fischer, *Why They Behave Like Russians*. New York: Harper & Row, Publishers, Inc., 1946.

Florman—Samuel C. Florman, *The Existential Pleasures of Engineering*. New York: St. Martin's Press, Inc., 1976.

Fonteyn—Margot Fonteyn, *A Dancer's World*. New York: Alfred A. Knopf, Inc., 1979.

Fortune—From "Riveters" in *Fortune*, October 1930. Copyright 1930, Time Inc. All rights reserved. Reprinted by permission.

Fowler—Booth Fowler and Saul Brenner, "In Defense of Optimism." *The Humanist*, March/April 1982. The Humanist.

The Gallup Report—"Electoral Reform: Both General Public and 'Opinion Leaders' Support Changes in Electoral Process" from *The Gallup Report*, Feb. 1983, Report No. 209. Reprinted by permission of The Gallup Poll.

George—Uwe George, *In the Deserts of This Earth*. Translated from the German by Richard and Clara Winston. New York: Harcourt Brace Jovanovich, Inc., 1977, p. 39.

Glamour—Glamour Editorial. Courtesy *Glamour*, Copyright © 1979 by The Condé Nast Publications Inc.

Gould—Stephen Jay Gould, "Of Bamboos, Cicadas, and the Economy of Adam Smith" in *Ever Since Darwin*. New York: W. W. Norton & Co., Inc., 1977.

Greenberg—From "Electronic gizmos make us stupid" by Daniel S. Greenberg. Copyright © 1981 by Daniel S. Greenberg. Reprinted by permission of the author.

Greene—From "How Unwritten Rules Circumscribe Our Lives" by Bob Greene in the *Chicago Tribune*, June 2, 1982. Reprinted by permission: Tribune Media Services, Inc.

Haley—From "My Furthest-Back Person—'The African' " by Alex Haley, *The New York Times Magazine*, July 16, 1972. Copyright © 1972 by Alex Haley. Reprinted by permission of Paul R. Reynolds, Inc.

Hall—From "Four Kinds of Reading" by Donald Hall in *The New York Times*, January 26, 1969. Copyright © 1969 by The New York Times Company. Reprinted by permission.

Holt—John Holt, "The Right to Control One's Learning" from *Escape from Childhood*. New York: E. P. Dutton, Inc., 1974.

Jackson—From *The Lottery* by Shirley Jackson. Copyright 1948, 1949 by Shirley Jackson. Copyright renewed © 1976, 1977 by Laurence Hyman, Barry Hyman, Mrs. Sarah Webster, and Mrs. Joanne Schnurer. Reprinted by permission of Farrar, Straus & Giroux, Inc. and Brandt & Brandt.

Jacobs—Jane Jacobs, "Cities Need Old Buildings" from *The Death and Life of Great American Cities*. New York: Random House, Inc., 1961.

Jeans—Sir James Jeans, "A View of the Solar System" from *The Stars in Their Courses*. Cambridge University Press, 1954.

Jordan—Suzanne Britt Jordan, "That Lean and Hungry Look." *Newsweek*, October 9, 1978, Newsweek, Inc.

Kennedy—From "Who Killed King Kong?" by X. J. Kennedy in *Dissent*, Spring 1960. Copyright © 1960 by the Dissent Publishing Corporation. Reprinted by permission.

Lamplight Farms—From "Instructions for Enjoying Your Oil Lamp" in *Lamplight Farms, the Homestead Collection*. Reprinted by permission of Lamplight Farms.

Middleton—From "Storm" by Harry Middleton. Reprinted with permission from *Sierra*, the magazine of the Sierra Club, March/April 1982.

Momaday—From the Introduction to *The Way to Rainy Mountain* by N. Scott Momaday. The Introduction was first published in *The Reporter*, January 26, 1967, and was reprinted in *The Way to Rainy Mountain*, copyright 1969. The University of New Mexico Press.

Morrow—From "A World of Exaggeration!" by Lance Morrow in *Time*, December 14, 1981. Copyright © 1981 Time Inc. All rights reserved. Reprinted by permission from *Time*.

Novak—From *Further Reflections on Ethnicity* by Michael Novak, copyright © 1977. Reprinted by permission of the author.

Orwell—George Orwell, "Politics and the English Language" from *Shooting an Elephant and Other Essays*. New York: Harcourt Brace Jovanovich, 1946.

Parker—From "Good Souls" by Dorothy Parker. Copyright 1919 by The Vanity Fair Pub. Co., Inc., renewed 1947 by The Condé Nast Publications, Inc. Reprinted by permission.

Phillips—Introduction to "The Impact of Mass Media Violence on U.S. Homicides" by David P. Phillips, *American Sociological Review*, August 1983, Vol. 48, No. 4, p. 560. Reprinted by permission of The American Sociological Association and the author.

Quinn—From "The Jeaning of America—And the World" by Carin Quinn. Copyright © 1978 by American Heritage Publishing Co., Inc. Reprinted by permission from *American Heritage* (April/May 1978).

Readers' Guide to Periodical Literature—From *Readers' Guide to Periodical Literature*. Copyright © 1983 by The H. W. Wilson Company. Material reproduced by permission of the publisher.

Rowlands—John J. Rowlands, "In Praise of Gadgeteers" from *Spindrift*. New York. W. W. Norton & Co., Inc., 1960.

Rumberger—Rumberger, Russell W., "Dropping Out of High School: The Influence of Race, Sex, and Family Background." *Review of Educational Research*, Summer 1983, pp. 199–214. Copyright © 1982, American Educational Research Association, Washington, D.C. Reprinted by permission.

Safire—From "Sneer Words" by William Safire, *New York Times Magazine*, January 13, 1980. © 1980 by The New York Times Company. Reprinted by permission.

The Sharper Image Telephone Catalog—From page 11 of *The Sharper Image Telephone Catalog*. Reprinted by permission.

Smith—From "The Japanese Model" by Adam Smith. Reprinted with permission from *Esquire* (October 1980). Copyright © 1980 by Esquire Associates.

Southwestern Bell—"How to Complain" from Southwestern Bell Telephone Directory.

Stewart—John D. Stewart, "Vulture Country." *The Atlantic Monthly*, 1959. The Atlantic Monthly Company.

Van Buren—Taken from "The Dear Abby" column. Copyright © 1980 Universal Press Syndicate. Reprinted with permission. All rights reserved.

Warren—"Manufacturers' Sales Representative" by John C. Warren, Small Business Administration, U.S. Government Printing Office, 1980.

White—E. B. White. "Once More to the Lake" from *Essays of E. B. White*. Copyright 1941 by E. B. White. Reprinted by permission of Harper & Row, Publishers, Inc.

Will—From "Psychiatry, law at cross-purposes" by George Will. Copyright © 1983, Washington Post Writers Group. Reprinted with permission.

INDEX

Index

Page references in **boldface** type refer to the most important discussion of a topic.

GRAMMAR AND USAGE

PUNCTUATION AND OTHER CONVENTIONS